C000154652

The Prospects of the two most remarkable
Towns in the North of England For the
Clothing Trade
viz
LEEDS
As it appeares from Holbeck Road.

THE

PUBLICATIONS

OF THE

THORESBY SOCIETY

ESTABLISHED IN THE YEAR
MDCCCLXXXIX

VOLUMES LX and LXI
for 1985 and 1986

East End, West End:

THE FACE OF LEEDS DURING URBANISATION, 1684–1842

by

Maurice Beresford

Emeritus Professor of Economic History
in the University of Leeds
Patron of the Thoresby Society

THE THORESBY SOCIETY
23 CLARENDON ROAD
LEEDS
1988

© The Thoresby Society and Maurice Beresford

ISSN 0082-4232

ISBN 0 900741 23 6

Published by The Thoresby Society
and printed by the University Printing Service
at The University of Leeds

Contents

List of Figures

Page

Cover

J. M. TURNER, 'LEEDS':

WATERCOLOUR AFTER A SKETCHED PANORAMA OF SEPTEMBER 1816

(*Yale Center for British Art, Paul Mellon Collection*)

Extreme left: the newly built Airedale woollen mill (J. and R. Glover), then Park Mill (Bean Ing), with St Paul's, Park Square, behind it. *Centre:* the spire of Holy Trinity, Boar Lane, with the tower of St. John's, Briggate, just behind; the large mill in front of it is Benyon's flax mill in Meadow Lane to the right of which are the kilns of Petty and Howitt's Hunslet Hall pottery; the classical façade behind them is Wesley chapel, Meadow Lane, opened that year.

The parish church lies further back and to the right where the skyline also includes at least five kilns from the Leeds Pottery in Jack Lane. The single chimney on the extreme right is probably that of Larchfield Mill (Pym Nevins).

The artist's viewpoint, which recent clearances have reopened, was from a stone causeway on the west side of the zig-zag road down Beeston Hill to Holbeck; its wall was being repaired and cloth stretched on tenters in the field. The group of houses further down the hill was known as The Folly, and at the foot of the hill was Holbeck workhouse and Holbeck Low Moorside.

List of Tables

Page

List of Appendices

Preface

ON PROVIDENCE: THE GENESIS OF A BOOK

Providence also casting my Lot in Places that merit a particular Description, was another Argument to induce me hereto.
Ralph Thoresby, Preface to DUCATUS LEODIENSIS (1715), p. v.

Watching the clearance of streets and houses around the University during the nineteen-fifties I had witnessed a cycle in the life of the town being completed, the equivalent of 'dust to dust and ashes to ashes' in the human life cycle, as the bulldozers arrived to press the shattered bricks of demolished houses back into the ground. The clay for many of these bricks had been excavated on the spot before house foundations were dug and streets laid out; a 'good bed of clay' within a field was often advertised as one of its virtues when it was being put up for sale as building ground. Now I could see the clay returning to the earth, broken, powdered, and compounded with whatever remains of material culture had been rejected by the marauding scrap-dealers and other raiders who came like vultures before the official grave-diggers.

For a while, before their redevelopment, the razed open spaces took on again the appearance of that open landscape into which the housebuilders had moved a century or more before, and with which I was familiar from eighteenth-century plans. It is that piecemeal transition from an agricultural landscape to a townscape of streets and factories that forms the subject of this book: itself a townscape now largely eroded.

It was fields which sustained the village of Leeds long before 1207 when Maurice Paynel laid out the burgage plots of Briggate alongside the west end of the village street of Kirkgate in the hope of stimulating crafts and trades in a small borough. For five hundred years the borough remained small: Thomas Donald's survey, made between 1768 and 1770 for Thomas Jefferys's county atlas portrayed a town that – despite the passage of forty years and the addition of a thousand houses – was still confined to the same half dozen streets that comprised Leeds in John Cossins's map of 1725, all set as compactly as if Leeds had been some continental walled town. Within these narrow limits were concentrated all the economic, social and administrative activities that were increasingly making Leeds a place of note in the kingdom.

Yet at the very time of Donald's survey a deliberately planned West End extension of the town was beginning: and from 1786 an East End began to be created, albeit in a fit of absence of mind. By the end of the Napoleonic Wars in 1815 the West End had been lost to industry and smoke, and a second West End was visible in the fields of Little Woodhouse, soon to be ceded, however, as the town's better-off inhabitants made a knight's move to the new suburbs of the northern townships; meanwhile in the fields over which they had jumped, working-class housing was extended as terraces, a form that had once been confined to the exclusive Georgian West End.

Part One of this book examines the environment of an undifferentiated and compact town, using as starting points the two *Prospects* of Leeds published in Ralph Thoresby's history of 1715 and the map produced by John Cossins in 1725. Part Two is concerned with the novelty of a residential West End and Part Three with the origins of working-class housing in an East End that was eventually to be perceived as the extreme embodiment of environmental deterioration. The slowness of that perception lay partly in the economic and social sentiments which prevailed in a country where industrialisation was on a novel scale and where even radical and reforming opinions had other priorities than a solution to a mere Sanitary Question.

Yet it was Robert Baker, a severe and well-informed critic of insanitary Leeds, who wrote in 1842: 'although condemned as a town in its entirety at the first glance Leeds may really have only peculiar points of local influence from whence the gross results are derived'.[1]

Particularity of this sort, descending to individual houses and streets, pervaded the research upon which this book is based, and colours its view of events although I have borne in mind a caution which was once administered to me by the late H. J. Dyos, himself a pioneer of urban microtopography:

> In seeking the largely logistical reasons for Leeds' East End Maurice Beresford must be thought to be going perhaps a shade too far in his otherwise masterly exemplification of these things: here, in the 'wholly local problem of the timing, the motives, the strategy of housing development', he contends, 'here, rather than with aggregates are the foundations of historical explanation'.[2]

There are certainly risks in the practice of particularity.

[1] *1842 Report*, p.23.

[2] H. J. Dyos, review of Beresford, *Paley*, in *Urban History Yearbook 1976*, p.5.

In the following report on the years of interrupted research from which this book has emerged I have tried to echo that sentiment of gratitude expressed by Ralph Thoresby 270 years ago in the quotation at the head of this Preface. I have been lucky to be able to exploit the good fortune of living and working in the very midst of my raw materials: on the one hand the diverse units whose totality is the townscape of Leeds, that great open-air museum; and on the other the written documents that elucidate its history. The description of these source materials is intermingled in my narrative, and it may aid those who will seek particularities in the history of other towns: necessary studies since industrialisation and urbanisation were processes which made English provincial towns less and not more alike.

I first ventured into the history of the Leeds townscape when I needed some nineteenth-century examples of visual economic history to display in my inaugural lecture, *Time and Place* (1960), and encountered the suggestive name of Prosperity Street. I taught myself the elements of research in the history of urban streets by tracing that street in directories and, in order to make a comparison with Cavendish Road, where my academic department was then housed, I turned to the property deeds in the University of Leeds bursary which offered hope of illuminating the process by which landowners, developers and builders had turned fields into streets.

Apart from the research for a bread-and-butter centenary celebration, *The Leeds Chambers of Commerce* (1951), I had been previously concerned with matters mainly medieval and early modern, the more readily since research in modern economic history and particularly that of the Leeds area was then being busily pursued by my colleagues Gordon Rimmer and Eric Sigsworth. Rimmer's essays, written about 1957 and published ten years later in Thoresby Society *Miscellanea*, volume 14, were the first to treat seriously several topics that occur in the present volume. Had he not chosen to migrate first to a Caribbean university and then to the Antipodes, it is unlikely that I would ever have ventured into the history of urban Leeds.

However, my appetite had been whetted by the boxes of deeds for the scattered University properties that I had seen in the bursary while investigating Cavendish Road, and in December 1961 I was encouraged by the University bursar, the late Edmund Williamson, to begin an archive search to make a record of the history of the buildings in what was almost every day a larger area of streets being demolished for the Inner Ring Road, the Polytechnic, the General Infirmary and the new buildings of the University itself. William

Blackledge, University photographer, initiated a methodical photographic record (now in the Brotherton Library) and the Vice-Chancellor, then Sir Charles Morris, arranged for Mrs Mary Forster to be appointed as my part-time research assistant for two years. Together, and with the aid at one time of a University Extra-Mural tutorial class, we built up chronological occupancy tables for each street. It was at this stage that research began to extend, thanks to much good will on the part of the Town Clerk and his staff, into the several thousand boxes of property deeds in the vaults of the Civic Hall that had accumulated when so much of the inner city was acquired by the Corporation for its post-war developments; without this gentle introduction to an inexhaustible source I should never have had the courage in later years to extend the enquiry to every plot of land within the in-township.

My historical work on the campus area was intended at that time to be no more than an act of preservation and record, providing intermittent activity in a local archive when it was not possible to be in London or Gascony working on the records of medieval boroughs and bastides. It was many years later that, encouraged by the University information officer, Simeon Underwood, and aided by the University photographer and his staff, I returned to a study of this area and embarked on the contributions to the University *Reporter* which in 1980 became *Walks Round Red Brick*. Its maps and photographs illustrate more fully some themes that are treated more briefly in Chapter Ten of this book.

The widening of research beyond the campus could not have begun seriously until *New Towns of the Middle Ages* was completed in 1965, and its first reflection in print arose from the visit of the British Association's Summer Meeting to Leeds in 1967 and the commitment of Glanville Jones and myself to edit for that occasion the essays which made up *Leeds and Its Region*. Generals have to set an example to the troops, and in a chapter which I christened *Prosperity Street and Others* I began to consider the fate of some western streets, although Richard Wilson in his thesis and in *Gentlemen Merchants* had already begun an exploration of the estate papers of his namesakes who first created and then helped to destroy the first West End.

A serious intention to attempt a book-length study is attested by the successful application to the Social Science Research Council which resulted in a grant to support Richard Peppard as a full-time research assistant. My report on his work, written in 1968, envisaged that the book would be called *A Prospect of Leeds*, and a typed draft of a first chapter is dated 1970. Distractions of one sort and another together with heavy administrative responsibilities within the University, not to speak of a spell in hospital, all conspired to delay progress.

Materials accumulated in greater bulk than I had envisaged, now that the scope of my researches extended to the whole central area – the 'in-township' – and any resultant book would have been of unmanageable length had not I been able in the meantime to shed some related material into independent publications. An essay commissioned by Stanley Chapman for his symposium *The History of Working-class Housing* (1971) was first intended to be called 'Critics and their Targets', an embryo of what are now the final chapters of this book, but the documentary sources were so luxuriant that it ended as a study of one target only, *The Back-to-Back House in Leeds*.

William Hoskins once said that any historian worth his salt who was left free to roam in a local archive for a day could find enough material for at least one article in a learned journal. It was therefore appropriate that I was able in the Hoskins Festschrift, *Rural Change and Urban Growth* (1974) to exhibit, in detail that would have swamped Chapter Seven here, what riches lay in half a dozen deed boxes relating to the affairs of a Leeds soapmaker, Richard Paley, bankrupted in 1803.

It was among those deeds that a single fire insurance policy issued in London by the Sun Company for a group of back-to-back houses known as Goulden's Buildings alerted me to the possibility that the registers of this company and those of the Royal Exchange, which Stanley Chapman had lately penetrated for his studies of textile mills, might provide a means to date, value, and identify the owners of East End properties that were smaller than those in the Wilson West End. Many footnotes and tables in this volume derive from searches in the fire insurance registers up to 1803; and access to manuscript indexes from David Jenkins greatly eased the task when I decided to extend the searches up to 1826.

For the Leeds conference of the Economic History Society at Easter 1975 I prepared an illustrated lecture bringing together the architectural evidence and that from insurance policies and property conveyances: but in August I left for Virginia to take up a year's appointment as Harrison Visiting Professor of History at the College of William and Mary at Williamsburg. There I was tempted by the available documents to divert my attention to research on the economic and social connections between Yorkshire and Virginia in the years before the Declaration of Independence, so that my study of the first century of fire insurance in Leeds – *Prometheus Unbound* – did not appear until 1982. While in Virginia I received an invitation to contribute to Derek Fraser's *History of Modern Leeds*, resulting in

'The Face of Leeds, 1780–1914'. The composition of that chapter did give me some assurance that it was possible to see some broad themes in the history of the townscape, such as the inadvertency of much slumdom, which have eventually found their place in the present volume.

For the academic year 1980–81 I was awarded a Senior Research Fellowship by the Social Science Research Council to enable the writing of the long-delayed book to begin. As soon as I began to write about the West End I realised that my original starting date of *c.* 1760 left me insufficiently informed on the character of the town before the fission of the West End, and I went back to the city archives in order to see what the rate books and the records of the Town Charities (the Pious Uses Committee) could do to fill the gap. Thus a year passed with more swollen files of notes but very little typescript. Then unexpected problems in the University's School of Economic Studies recalled me to its Chairmanship for a third spell in 1981–83, at the end of which I had accumulated enought credits for the University to allow me study leave for 1983–84 and to make a grant for the preparation of line drawings that would eventually be the Figures in the long-delayed book. Instead the first day of the October term of that session found me in hospital, the least welcomed of all the postponements chronicled here.

Convalescence being completed by Christmas, I turned again to composition, and by October, when I returned to full-time Departmental duties for the final year of my University employment, a half-way point in the book had been reached. Twelve months later my secretary's last service was to hand me back her fair copy of Chapter Ten. No longer with a secretary but with a new word processor I then pushed forward to completion and handed the text to the Honorary Editors at a Thoresby Society lecture on 13 February 1986.

Providence had not deserted me, for this renewed enthusiasm and acceleration suggest that Professor Giles must have injected some stimulant in the course of surgery; and in gratitude I borrow a metaphor from a recurring subject of the following pages by ending this Preface with a dedication

To Geoffrey Giles, MD, FRCS
Who extended my lease
29th September 1983

Author's Acknowledgements

I have mentioned some names in the Preface but long-drawn-out tasks, extending from 1960 to 1986, could not have been completed without the help and advice of others. Possibly as a reward for energies diverted from research to committees, the University of Leeds gave successive temporary appointments to Brian Barber and Steven Blake as my research assistants; that very term is now a nostalgic witness to resources of which universities have since been deprived. Many pages of notes from insurance policy registers, Town Clerk's deeds, Leeds Corporation committee minute books and from deeds in the former West Riding Registry date from that period of affluence. More recently a grant from the University's Research Committee in 1983–84 supported the costs of preparing maps and figures.

Any supervisor of University theses, undergraduate and postgraduate, learns much by looking over his student's shoulders: and thus the names Barber, Connell, Fletcher, Grady, Lingard, Morgan, Morris, Peppard, Treen and (Michael) Ward in my footnotes. I was not the supervisor of the MA thesis of David Ward, who now adds distinction and a northern English accent and attitude to the University of Wisconsin and to American academic geography. However it was work which I suggested to him as a project for an undergraduate tutorial, relating the topography of unenclosed fields in Halton to the later suburban streets, that set off his subsequent work on the fields and streets of other Leeds townships (and then of American cities). I was unaware then that it had also planted an interest in pre-urban topography in my own mind at a time when I was wholly concerned with research into rural fields; and it did not become important to me until those weeks at the end of 1959 when the composition of an inaugural lecture became imperative.

Besides those individuals and institutions already named I am grateful to: Mrs Elizabeth Berry, formerly Archivist to the West Yorkshire County Record Office, for facilitating access to the deeds from the West Riding Registry; David Black and Colum Giles of the Royal Commission on Historical Monuments, England, for advice on architectural history; Peter Brears for drawing my attention to the John Russell sketchbooks; Michael Collinson, formerly Leeds City Archivist, for many facilities, especially for access to Park estate and Paley deeds before they had been listed; Mrs Mary Forster, Hon. Librarian of the Thoresby Society, for facilities to copy illustrations; Mrs Maureen Gorman for typing many drafts and revisions of Chapters 1–10 and all the Tables; Mrs Ann Heap, Local History Librarian, Leeds Central Library; David Jenkins of the University of York for access to unpublished lists of Leeds policies in the Sun fire insurance registers; and Miss Tessa Sidey for information on the Russell sketchbooks. Successive Town Clerks and chief officers of Leeds City and Metropolitan Councils and their staff have given me access to the property deeds and minute books of the former Leeds Corporation in the basement of the Civic Hall, and I am also grateful to the staff of the Guildhall Library, London, for the opportunity to browse among fire insurance records.

Finally, I would like to join the Hon. Editors of the Thoresby Society in their thanks to the individuals and institutions whose generous grants have made possible the publication of this volume.

Hon. Editors' Acknowledgements

The publication of this volume has been assisted by grants from the following:

S. H. BURTON CHARITABLE TRUST
MARC FITCH FUND
TWENTY-SEVEN FOUNDATION
UNIVERSITY OF LEEDS
WEST YORKSHIRE ARCHIVES ADVISORY COUNCIL

A grant from LEEDS CIVIC TRUST and a donation by an ANONYMOUS MEMBER OF THE THORESBY SOCIETY made possible the compilation of an exhaustive index, undertaken by Mr G. S. Darlow.

Help with publicity has been provided by LEEDS & HOLBECK BUILDING SOCIETY.

On behalf of the Thoresby Society the Hon. Editors record their thanks for this generous assistance, and also for the guidance and help of Mr Harry Tolson, Manager, and the staff of the University of Leeds Printing Service during the planning and production of the volume.

Abbreviations and Short Titles

(The short titles relate to books and articles frequently cited in footnotes.)

Atkinson	D. H. Atkinson, *Ralph Thoresby the Topographer; His Town and Times* (Leeds, 1885–57).
Beresford, *Back-to-Back House*	M. W. Beresford, 'The Back-to-Back House in Leeds, 1787–1937', in *The History of Working-class Housing: a Symposium*, ed. S. D. Chapman (Newton Abbot, 1971), pp.93–132.
Beresford, *Face of Leeds*	M. W. Beresford, 'The Face of Leeds, 1780–1914', in Fraser, ed. (below), pp.72–112.
Beresford, *Leeds in 1628*	M. W. Beresford, 'Leeds in 1628: a "Ridinge Observation" from the City of London', *Northern History*, X (1975), 135–40.
Beresford, *Paley*	*M. W. Beresford,* 'The Making of a Townscape: Richard Paley in the East End of Leeds, 1771–1803', in *Rural Change and Urban Growth, 1500–1800*, ed. C. W. Chalklin and M. A. Havinden (1974), pp.281–320.
Beresford and Jones, eds.	M. W. Beresford and G. R. J. Jones, eds, *Leeds and Its Region* (Leeds, 1967).
Billam	[attr. F. T. Billam], *A Walk Through Leeds* (Leeds, 1806).
Bonser and Nichols	K. J. Bonser and H. Nichols, *Printed Maps and Plans of Leeds, 1711–1900, (PTh.S,* XLVII, 1960).
Borthwick	University of York, Borthwick Institute of Historical Research.
Chalklin	C. W. Chalklin, *Provincial Towns of Georgian England: a study of the building process, 1740–1820* (1974).
Directory, 1817, etc.	See chronological list in Bibliography §5, p.531, below.
Ducatus	R. Thoresby, *Ducatus Leodiensis: or, The Topography of the Ancient and Populous Town and Parish of Leedes, and Parts Adjacent in the West-Riding of the County of York* (1715).

Fraser, ed.	D. Fraser, ed., *A History of Modern Leeds* (Manchester, 1980).
Grady	K. Grady, 'Profit, Property Interests and Public Spirit: the provision of markets in Leeds, 1822–29', *PTh.S*, LIV (1977), 165–195.
Hall, ed.	*Samuel Buck's Yorkshire Sketchbook*, ed. I. Hall (Wakefield, 1979).
Kirby, *Manor*	*The Manor and Borough of Leeds, 1425–1662: an edition of documents*, ed. Joan W. Kirby (*PTh.S*, LVII, 1983).
LCA	Leeds City Archives, now WYJAS Leeds Office.
LCD	Leeds Corporation Deeds, Civic Hall.
LCH	Leeds Civic Hall.
Le Patourel	*Documents relating to the Manor and Borough of Leeds, 1066–1400*, ed. J. Le Patourel (*PTh.S*, XLV, 1956).
Leeds Guide	[attr. J. Ryley), *The Leeds Guide* (Leeds, 1806).
LI	*The Leeds Intelligencer*.
LM	*The Leeds Mercury*.
LUL	Leeds University Library.
PP	Parliamentary Papers.
PRO	Public Record Office, London.
PTh.S.	*Publications of the Thoresby Society*.
RE	Royal Exchange fire insurance policies, Guildhall Library, London.
Rimmer, *Cottages*	W. G. Rimmer, 'Working Men's Cottages in Leeds, 1770–1840', *PTh.S*, XLVI (1963), 165–99.
Rimmer, *Marshall's*	W. G. Rimmer, *Marshall's of Leeds* (Cambridge, 1960).
Sun CS	Sun Fire Insurance Policies, Country Series, Guildhall Library, London.
Sun OS	Sun Fire Insurance Policies, Original Series, Guildhall Library, London.
ULD	University of Leeds, Bursary property deeds.
Whitaker, *Ducatus*	*Ducatus Leodiensis*, ed. T. D. Whitaker (1816).
Whitaker, *Loidis*	T. D. Whitaker, *The History of Loidis and Elmete* (1816).
Wilson	R. G. Wilson, *Gentlemen Merchants* (Manchester, 1971).
Wright	[attr. G. Wright], *A History of the Town and Parish of Leeds* (Leeds, 1797).

WRRD	West Riding Registry of Deeds (WYJAS, Wakefield).
WYJAS	West Yorkshire Joint Archive Service.
1833 Report	*Report of the Leeds Board of Health* (Leeds, 1833).
1839 Report	'Report upon the Condition of the Town of Leeds and of its Inhabitants, by a Statistical Committee of the Town Council, October 1839', *Journal of the [Royal] Statistical Society*, II (1840), 397–422.
1841 Abstract	*Abstract of the Report of the Statistical Committee for 1838, 1839 and 1840 of the Town Council of the Borough of Leeds* (Leeds, 1841).
1842 Report	'On the State and Condition of the Town of Leeds', *Sanitary Condition of the Labouring Population, Local Reports* (PP 1842, XXVII (Lords)), 348–409.
1845 Report	'Report on the Condition of the Town of Leeds by James Smith Esq. of Deanston', *Second Report of the Royal Commission for Inquiring into the State of Large Towns and Populous Districts* (PP 1845, XVIII, 312–14).

PART ONE

Verie Thicke, and Close Compacted Together

IN 1628 the royal manor of Leeds was in pawn to the Corporation of London and was about to be sold: two property experts were sent from London to survey it, a lawyer and the Master of the Haberdashers' Company. 'Verie thicke, and close compacted together' was their description of the houses of the town. An earlier manorial survey of 1612 provides a more detailed topography and confirms the concentration of houses at the centre.

In English villages the difference in social status and economic position between the villagers and their lord of the manor was marked by residential segregation, expressed in a castle or manor house. Geographical segregation was less common since manor houses tended to be located within a village; and even where a castle was placed in open country it tended to encourage a community, whether village or borough, to develop outside its gate. Not until squires took to building country houses within parks was total segregation possible. The manor house of Leeds never had this isolation: there was a small park within a pale to the immediate north and west but on the east and south there were the manorial water mills and the houses of fullers and dyers. Very different for the Irwins at Temple Newsam with no village since the early sixteenth century or at Harewood House where the only remnant of the original village was an isolated church in the park.

Within medieval towns, especially walled towns, the segregation of rich and poor was more difficult to achieve, and in this respect the compact Leeds of the late seventeenth century was very like a walled town, both in the close residential location of all ranks of society and in the circumscribed ambit of its streets.

A West End of Leeds began in Park Row in 1767 and an East End in 1786: in the earlier eighteenth century, when the town was continuing a growth discernible in the second half of the seventeenth century, the residential location was confined to new houses in the same streets as those of the medieval town.

No street had been built since 1634 when John Harrison had created his New Street (or *New-Kirke-gate*) leading to the newly founded church of St John.

The East and West Ends of Leeds were each a projection of the town, extending outwards into the fields of the countryside and moving continuously if erratically from the original centre and not regarded as suburbs: the latter term was reserved for later and quite detached developments within the fields of surrounding villages such as Hunslet, Holbeck, Headingley and Potternewton.

The novel functions of the East and West Ends are discussed in Part Two: the five Chapters of this Part are concerned with the town in the first half of the eighteenth century when it was far from homogeneous in its occupations, politics, religion or social class, but yet with its workplaces, inns, shops and habitations close compacted together.

I

A Skeleton of Streets

... or, The Topography of the Ancient and Populous Town and Parish of Leedes ...

Sub-title to Ralph Thoresby, DUCATUS LEODIENSIS (1715)

In the beginning was the land. Its forms and folds cannot be ignored even in essays whose subject matter lies in the eighteenth and nineteenth centuries and concerns urbanisation and industrialisation rather than agriculture. An advertiser who was a protagonist of inland waterways declared in the *Leeds Mercury* of 17 March 1783 that 'Leeds will be a Town of Trade and Commerce as long as the River and Coals last', and public speakers with an historical bent frequently declared later that 'Coals and Water made this town'.

The gift of coals was certainly a gift of Nature, as was that of useful building stone, and important consequences arose from its distribution. Coal of inferior quality came to the surface north of the town, and small pits were scratched into the surface of Woodhouse Moor as late as the early seventeenth century. Pits appear on early maps on either side of York Road and there were medieval workings further east at Knowestrop, but the best seams lay deeper and south of the river beneath the fields of Hunslet, Middleton and Beeston: it is from the last of these townships that the geologists have named the local beds of coal. The townships north of the river did not develop industries dependent on coal and remained green enough to attract extensive Victorian suburbs: the deepest holes in the ground in Headingley, Burley, Meanwood, and Chapel Allerton were not in search of coals but the *delfs* or quarries for building stone and roofing slates.

Netlam and Francis Giles' *Plan of the Town of Leeds and Its Environs*, published in London in 1815, was the first large-scale vision of the town centre in an accurate survey (Fig. 1.1).[1] Many

[1] For references to this and all other maps cited in the text by cartographer and date only, see Bibliography, §6, p. 532 below.

Street
St. John's Place
St. John's Church
Templar Street
Bramley Row
Leylands
Bridge Street
Head Row
Lower Head Row
Lady Lane
Union Street
Wood Street
St. George's Street
Jubilee Street
Mill Garth
Sheepscar Beck
Bond Street
Vicarage
Call Lane
Duncan Street
White Cloth Hall
York
St. Peter's
New Burying Gr
Kirkgate
The Calls
Bridge
Simpson
Boat Builders Yard
Bowman Lane

numerals will be found scattered over it – '8' by the parish church, '14.3½' on the surface of Leeds Bridge, and '26.7' by Trinity Church in Boar Lane. 'The Figures in the Streets,' explains the cartouche, 'denote the Elevation of those Places in feet and Inches above the Waste Wear of the Water Works Engine on the East side of the Bridge,' that is, above the surface of the river Aire. The meandering course of the Hol Beck and the small unnamed streams which formed the township boundaries of Holbeck and Hunslet show that the south bank meanders were almost level: the green at the centre of Holbeck village was only 4 feet above the level of Leeds Bridge while Stones End which marked the town's boundary on Hunslet Lane was 2 feet lower than the bridge. On the north bank, however, the gentle rise towards Meanwood and Woodhouse Ridges began at once with '30.5' at the junction of Boar Lane with Briggate, and '87.4' at St John's church, then the virtual northern limit of the built-up streets of the town. From its crossing of Briggate at '59.6' the Headrow, the limit of the medieval town, sloped downwards to the east as far as '7.9' at Lady Bridge on Sheepscar Beck but upwards – as anyone with heavy shopping bags still knows – towards '71.5' at the beginning of Woodhouse Lane and '77.11' at Burley Bar on Butts Hill, the northwestern limit of the old town.

The choice of a point on the river near the waterworks as a base for determining the levels of other parts of Leeds was not accidental, for since 1698 Sorocold's waterworks had been able to supply the town's piped water only by means of an engine placed near the bridge which pumped river water to two reservoirs in the higher part of town, with a gravity feed from there to subscribers' taps and a small number of hydrants for the town's fire engines:[2] a precise knowledge of levels was therefore crucial when new subscribers wished to be joined to the system, and was not irrelevant when discussions about Improvements to the town turned to thoughts of improved surface drainage and public sewers.

[2] F. Williamson and W. B. Crump, 'Sorocold's Waterworks at Leeds, 1694', *PTh.S*, XXXVII (1945), 166–82.

FIG. 1.1 THE FIRST LARGE-SCALE VISION OF LEEDS, 1815

From the plan by Francis and Netlam Giles: the streets of the town centre from St John's church and the Headrow in the north to the bridge at the lower end of Briggate [*centre*]; the numerals indicate the surveyed heights above the level of the river near the bridge. The survey clearly delineates the *backsides* yards behind the main street frontages, and the obstruction of Briggate by the Moot Hall, the Shambles to the north, and the covered market in Cross Parish. In 1815 Bond Street, Duncan Street and Wood Street were recent additions (cf. Fig. 3.2).

Availability of water concerned not only the needs of personal and household cleanliness: the cloth finishing processes which comprised most of the town's textile industry by the mid-eighteenth century were thirsty for water; the town's first Newcomen steam engine was built for the waterworks in 1698 but for nearly another century the powered industrial operations of grinding, crushing, fulling and forging were dependent on natural power, principally water mills but with a few windmills on the higher ground outside the town. Some of the first generation of improved steam engines to be installed in Leeds textile mills were not to turn machinery but to raise water to the reservoir of a water wheel, very necessary when mills such as Nevins's in Hunslet were sited on a shallow stream.

North of the Aire the streams in the valleys were more vigorous. The most powerful, variously named Adel, Meanwood, Sheepscar and Timble Beck, had a 300-foot fall from its source near Adel Dam to its junction with the Aire east of the town. The mills of Timble Beck were only the last of a series which straddled the beck from the village corn mill of Adel to the mills of the Steander, so conveniently placed between the town and the weavers' hamlet at the Bank. It was an Adel corn mill, Scotland Mill, that Marshall took over in 1788 for experiments in the use of water power for spinning linen thread, the first application of power for textile spinning in the Leeds area. When he moved in 1790 to a purpose-built linen mill nearer town he turned to steam power but still needed water for the engines and for washing and dressing the flax, so that a site was chosen in Water Lane on the Hol Beck.[3]

The greatest source of mill power was the Aire itself, harnessed by two great medieval stone weirs, High Dam and Bondman Dam, the latter thrust across the river bed just south of the manor house and still visible beneath the railway station arches. This weir gave a head of water to drive the King's Mills, a series of manorial mills on the several goits cut across the two fields, Upper and Lower Tenters,

[3] Rimmer, *Marshall's*, pp.26–27 and 33–34.

FIG. 1.2 KING'S MILLS AND WATERFRONT, *C.*1700

The west end of the medieval village was focused on the Manor House (cf. Fig. 1.4): next to it the Aire was harnessed for industrial power by a series of dams: the main dam, High Dam, together with Bondman Dam provided a head of water for a complex of corn, fulling and other mills. By the early eighteenth century this was the industrial heart of Leeds, and the outflow from Pitfall Mills was also being used for Sorocold's town waterworks. Dyehouses were concentrated in Swinegate, and on the islands between the river and the mill-races. East of the bridge were the main quay for the Aire and Calder Navigation and the Town Warehouse.

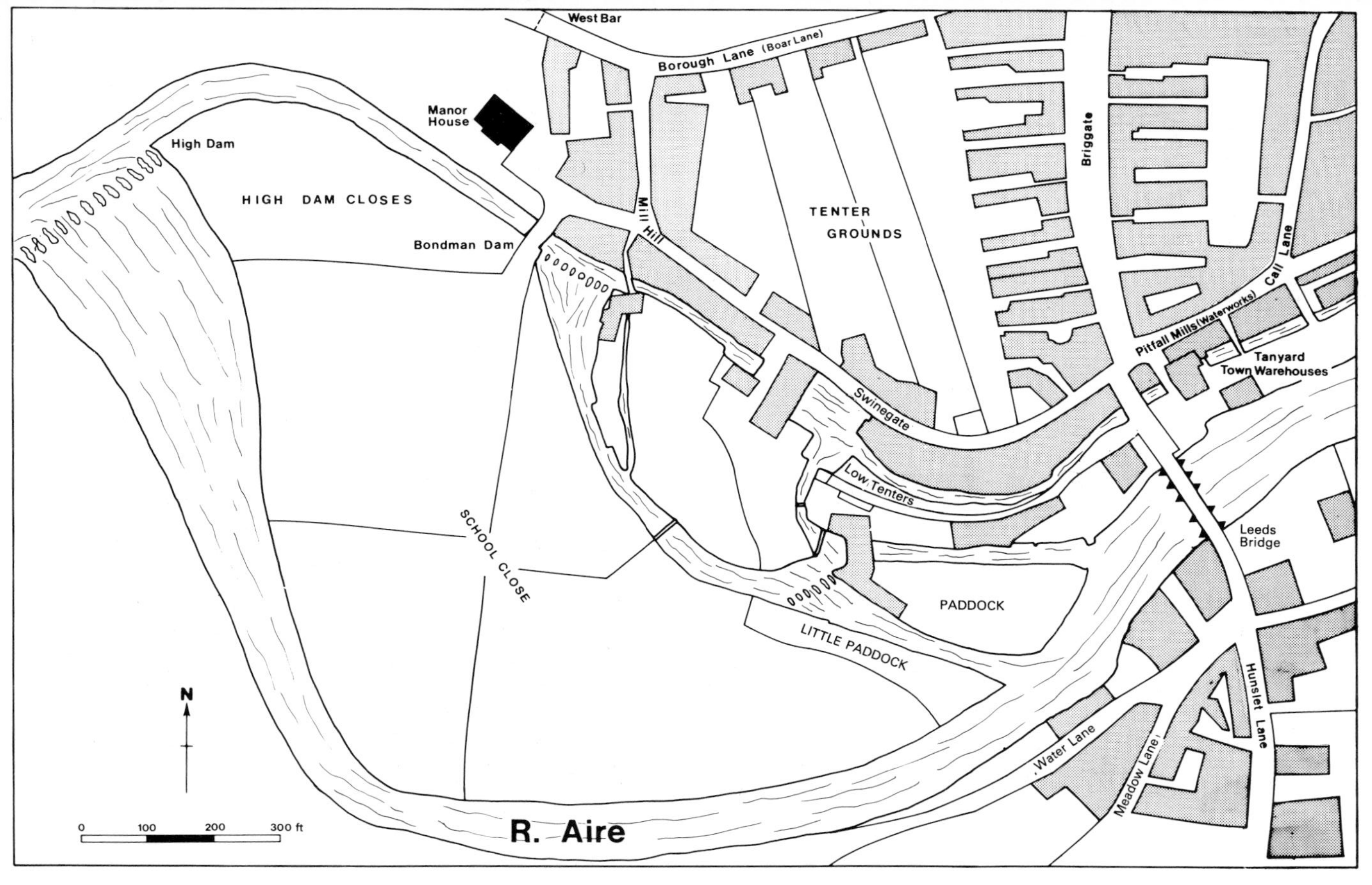
West Bar
Borough Lane (Boar Lane)
Manor House
High Dam
HIGH DAM CLOSES
Bondman Dam
Mill Hill
TENTER GROUNDS
Briggate
Call Lane
Pitfall Mills (Waterworks)
Tanyard
Town Warehouses
Swinegate
Low Tenters
Leeds Bridge
SCHOOL CLOSE
PADDOCK
LITTLE PADDOCK
Hunslet Lane
Water Lane
Meadow Lane
N
0
100
200
300 ft
R. Aire

whose name was indicative of their industrial use (Fig. 1.2). These mills were the monopoly of the lord of the manor or his lessees and we owe the first crude map of Leeds to litigation that was in progress in 1560 to determine whether a mill on Timble Beck (near the present Mill Garth bus and police stations) lay outside the bounds of the manor.[4] Repairs to the dam, goits, wheels and housing of the manorial mill appear in the earliest surviving accounts (1322).[5] Another group of mills using the full power of the Aire, Nether Mills, is probably also medieval although the first documentary reference at present known is from 1636: their weir crossed the Aire at Fearne's Island just below Timble Beck, a site outside the manorial demesne and not therefore appearing either on the plan of 1560 or in the manorial survey of 1612 (Fig. 1.3).

Mill weirs across any river were an asset to industry but an obstacle to water transport, for only the smallest boats could be dragged past them. Leeds was thus a landlocked town, in Robert Unwin's phrase, cut off from seaward traffic not only by the Fearne's Island weir but by that of Thwaite Mill, Hunslet and others further east. It is only after the Aire and Calder Navigation made improvements to the river, by-passing the weirs with canals and locks, that Leeds can be considered a waterside town. The Aire and Calder Navigation Act of 1699 argued in its preamble that the Navigation would ease the pressure on a congested road system, particularly the road going east to Selby and the Ouse, and any natural advantages in the siting and early development of Leeds in its region must be argued in terms of the roads of the Aire valley rather than of its river.

Indeed, any river of size was a potential deterrent to the movement of substantial traffic unless its physical form permitted a crossing by

[4] Ordered by the Duchy of Lancaster court, 16 Nov. 1559: PRO, DL 42/97, f.5; reproduced in E. Wilson, 'A Leeds Law-suit in the 16th Century', *PTh.S*, IX (1899), facing p.1. For a re-drawn version of the crude original (PRO, MPC 109) see Beresford and Jones, eds., p.138 and Fraser, ed., p.9.

[5] Le Patourel, p.12; for the post-medieval topography and assets of the manor see Kirby, *Manor*, pp.xxxix–lxx.

FIG. 1.3 NETHER MILLS AND STEANDER, 1772

The east end of the medieval village, adjoining the parish church and Church Ings, also had its water mills. The Timble (Sheepscar) Beck meandered from Timble Bridge [*top left*] to its confluence with the Aire below Camphor Close [*right*]. It drove a small water mill near the bridge but was mainly used as a source of water for the many dyehouses (D) that lined its banks. The large Nether Mills were powered by the Aire itself, dammed by the great weir at Crown Point which boats were able to bypass through the Navigation lock. The tail-races of the two mills isolated the Steander ('stony-place') and Fearne's Island.

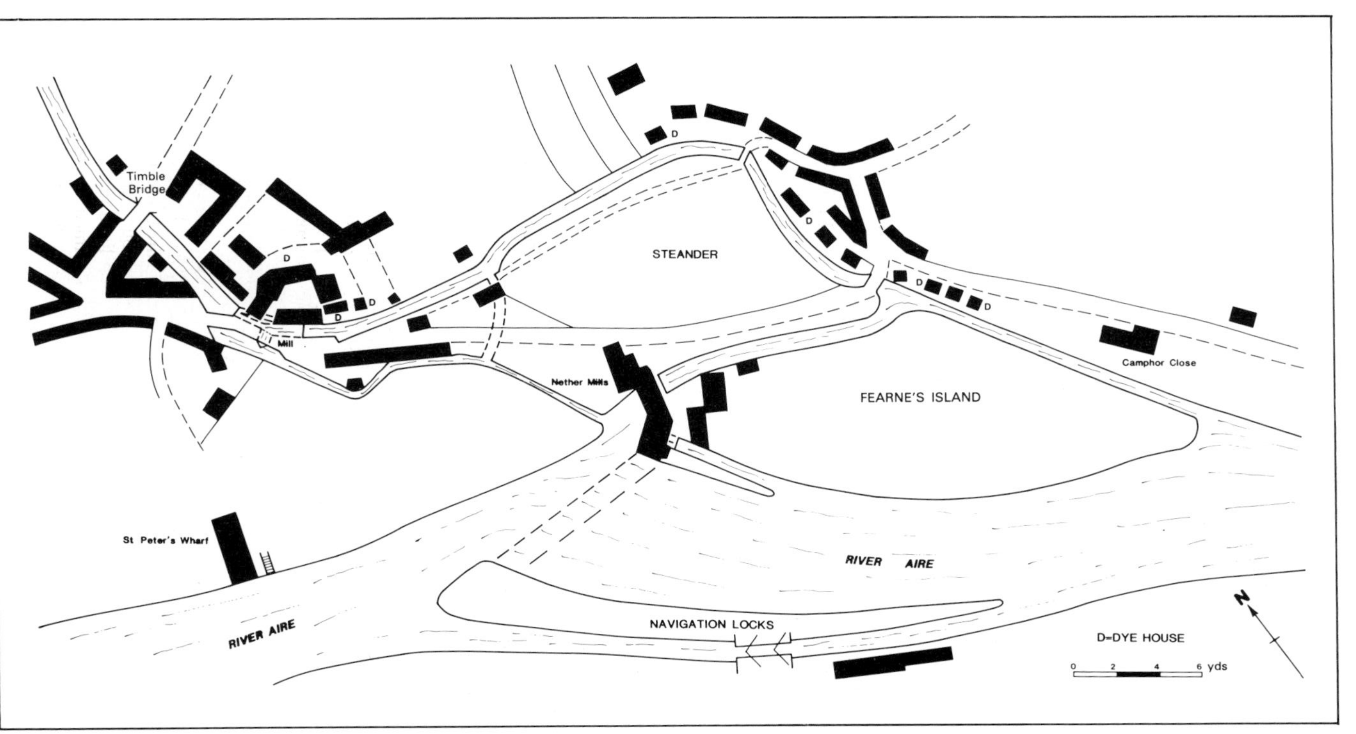
Timble Bridge
D
Mill
STEANDER
Nether Mills
FEARNE'S ISLAND
Camphor Close
St Peter's Wharf
RIVER AIRE
RIVER AIRE
NAVIGATION LOCKS
D=DYE HOUSE
0 2 4 6 yds
N

ford. There was a ford in the shallows below Bondman Weir within sight of the manor house, still significant enough to be shown on the Giles map of 1815; that map has no other ford but an 'Old Ferry' downstream near Hunslet. It is not known whether there was already a ford where the bridge of 1207 was built: and the main tail race from the mills is hardly likely to have been taken so far east (300 yards past the bridge site) if there was traffic from the village to a ford: nor do any of the pre-borough village streets focus on this point; Call Lane and Swinegate keep north of the river, parallel to it. The bridge element in the name of the borough market street, Briggate, and the way in which Briggate curves slightly at the southern end to approach the bridge are witnesses to the importance of the bridge in Maurice Paynel's addition of a borough to the village in 1207.

The topographical significance of Briggate as a compact group of burgage plots set at an angle to the older houses and garths in Kirkgate was first demonstrated by Geoffrey Woledge in 1945.[6] The topography may be more complex than a simple addition, encroaching upon village fields. Since 1945 studies of village morphology have produced many examples of 'polyfocal' villages with more than one original centre, as well as Professor Jones's proto-Celtic villages that have one centre at the church and another by the manor house and mill. Leeds certainly had two centres, with the manor house 700 yards west of the church, and it would now appear that the borough was laid out not at the end of the village but as an intrusion between its two halves (Fig. 1.4).

At the south end of Briggate, as we have just argued, the burgage plots did not extend all the way to the river, and the route from church to manor house by The Calls and Swinegate remained unaltered. Boar Lane enters the west side of Briggate through a gap

[6] G. Woledge, 'The Medieval Borough of Leeds', *PTh.S*, XXXVII (1945), 288–309.

FIG. 1.4 THE INTRUSION OF BOROUGH INTO MANOR, 1207

The original village extended from St Peter's church in the east to the manor house and mills in the west. Kirkgate was its main street. In 1207 burgage plots were laid out in a broad market street, Briggate, leading to a new bridge near the ford; two meandering roads (Call Lane and Swinegate) remained to connect the village to the manor house and mills but Call Lane was now cut off from Boar Lane by the burgage plots which also blocked any westward continuation of Kirkgate that had taken villagers towards the common fields and the town moor at Woodhouse. Subsequently Boar Lane was often called Borough Lane, i.e. the lane leading into the borough from manor house and mills; the borough charter did not exempt the townspeople from the monopoly enjoyed by the lord's mills (Fig. 1.2).

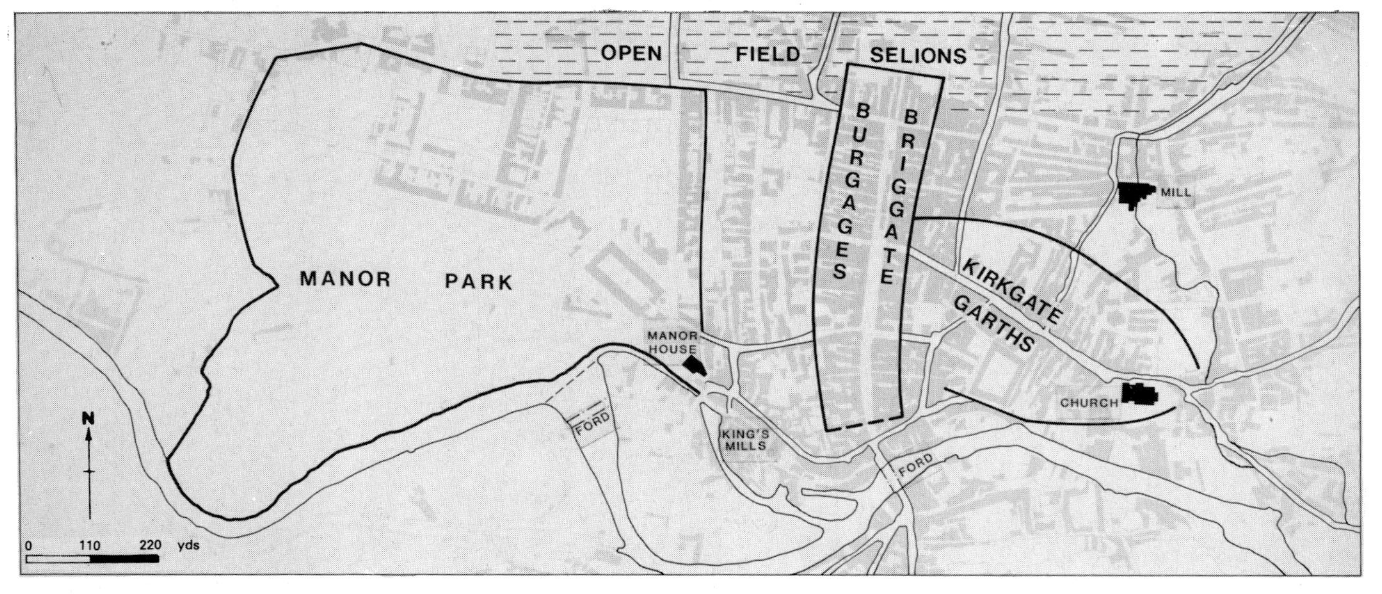
OPEN FIELD SELIONS
BURGAGES
BRIGGATE
KIRKGATE
GARTHS
MILL
CHURCH
MANOR PARK
MANOR HOUSE
KING'S MILLS
FORD
FORD
N
0 110 220 yds

between burgages: an earlier form of its name is Borough Lane, and it may therefore have been a newly-created, direct route from the manor and mills into the borough. A similar gap further up on the east side of Briggate was left for Kirkgate traffic but no corresponding gap faced Kirkgate, and traffic to the north-west had to turn up Briggate and leave by the Upper Headrow. Vicar Lane had no direct access to Call Lane, so that traffic from the north was also funnelled into the borough market place. The importance of this street is emphasised not only by its central position but by its width, some 65 feet, more than three times that of any of the ancient village streets. In 1773 an admiring traveller compared it only to Whitechapel High Street.[7]

Compact as they certainly were, the buildings of late seventeenth-century Leeds were not wholly confined to Briggate and the former village streets in that part of the skeleton whose origins have been examined. Here and there, houses intruded into the fields beyond the limit of the medieval town. The skeleton has limbs, principally in the form of ribbon development along major roads.[8] Those which lay south of the bridge may have been the oldest, accounting for an intrusion of the boundaries of Leeds township into fields which on the face of it would seem to belong actually to Hunslet or Holbeck: for, once the bridge was built, what came to be known as the South Division had distinct advantages. A trio of roads met just south of the bridge, coming from Holbeck, Beeston and Hunslet (and thence from Huddersfield, Halifax, and Wakefield); the cloth market was initially held on the bridge itself, leaving Briggate for the sale of animals and victuals; and a merchant in Water Lane, Meadow Lane or Hunslet Lane was as near the centre of affairs as one north of the river, a position disadvantaged only after 1711 when an indoor trading centre for unfinished cloth was opened in Kirkgate, the first Cloth Hall.

The counting of hearths for taxation began in 1662 and records for the Divisions or 'Parts' of Leeds survive for 1663, 1666 and 1672 in whole or part for the assessments of 1663, 1666 and 1672. The assessments do not exactly match but in all three years a hundred or so houses in the small South Part made up one-tenth of the total. Mill Hill and Boar Lane had twice as many, as did Briggate, although some houses at the north end of Briggate were probably counted with their neighbours in the Headrow to make more than another

[7] British Library, Additional MS.42232, f.32: Forrest's tour.

[8] In 1530 Ward's bequest to the town Highways Charity provided for the repair of roads in five directions; to Kirkstall, Headingley, Beeston, Armley, and Hunslet: LCA, DB 204/2, f.37.9.

TABLE 1.1

Percentage of Households Taxed on more than Five Hearths, by Divisions, 1663–72

Division	Year	Total dwellings	With more than 5 hearths	%
Briggate	1663	223	22	10
	1666	129	13	10
	1672	122	21	17
Mill Hill and Boar Lane	1663	n.a.	–	–
	1666	222	9	4
	1672	178	6	3
High Town or Headrow	1663	172	12	7
	1666	296	15	5
	1672	233	17	7
Kirkgate	1663	113	7	6
	1666	138	8	6
	1672	187	11	6
North	1663	168	6	4
	1666	253	9	4
	1672	257	8	3
East	1663	96	4	4
	1666	n.a.	–	–
	1672	122	4	3
South	1663	77	2	3
	1666	n.a.	–	–
	1672	106	6	6
Urban area	1663	*c.*800	43	5.4
	1666	*c.*860	48	5.6
	1672	*c.*1000	61	6.1

Sources: 1663: PRO, E179/262/9; 1666: E179/210/421; 1672: E179/210/417.

two hundred. Kirkgate had perhaps 150 houses – its three records are not consistent. The largest buildings were in Briggate, including High Town near the Headrow.[9] In 1663, when for the town as a

[9] J. W. Kirby, 'Restoration Leeds and the Aldermen of the Corporation, 1661–1700', *Northern History*, XXII (1986), 130–35.

whole 5 per cent of households were taxed at five hearths or more, Briggate had 10 per cent and High Town, 7 Table 1.1).

The assessments also survive from 1663 and 1672 for that area of Leeds not yet considered, the North and East Parts. There was no Part named from the fourth point of the compass since there were no houses west of the manor house where the manorial part lay (Fig. 1.4), and in later years the area of the former park was consequently reckoned to lie in Mill Hill Division. The East and North Parts had a curious but symmetrical structure, again deriving from an earlier territorial arrangement. In the twelfth and thirteenth centuries the lords of the manor had relied for their villein labour force on those who dwelt in two hamlets, each remote from the town, Woodhouse on the northern boundary and Knowestrop on the east: most of the village of Leeds proper, that is Kirkgate, had been alienated about 1100 by Ralph Paynel's gift to Holy Trinity Priory in York, and attached to the manor of Holbeck. In later years this tangle of jurisdictional boundaries was a fruitful cause of litigious dispute, especially, as with the North Hall sub-manor,[10] over infringements of the mill monopoly.

Before the end of the Middle Ages the inhabitants of the two bond hamlets had free tenure, and the hamlet of Great Woodhouse was substantial, benefiting from encroachments into the extensive area of waste land on the Headingley boundary, with a smaller settlement at Little Woodhouse. The original close link between Leeds and Woodhouse is emphasised by the location of the town's common grazing ground in this quarter, making in truncated form the present public parks of Woodhouse Moor and Woodhouse Ridge. Neither the survey of 1612[11] nor Cossins's map of 1725 suggests that Leeds had spread far up Woodhouse Lane beyond West Bar[12] or up North Street beyond Stones End so that most of the 250 dwellings recorded in the North Part for the Hearth Tax would have been in Woodhouse; a few near Sheepscar mills and a few in Mabgate on Quarry Hill.

Those recorded in the Hearth Tax as in the East Part were also detached from the central streets but less strikingly than Great and Little Woodhouse since Knowestrop had been depopulated, possibly at enclosure and conversion to pasture. The hundred or so dwellings of 1663–72 therefore lay mainly in the hamlet known as

[10] See above, p. 10.

[11] Kirby, *Manor*, pp. 72–154.

[12] The exceptionally large 'Wade Hall' was built between Woodhouse Lane and Wade Lane *c.* 1630–40 on the roadside frontage of Towncliff Close, an enclosed furlong: G. D. Lumb, 'The Old Hall, Wade Lane', *PTh.S*, XXVI (1924), 4.

the Bank, lying on the west slope of Richmond (or Cavalier) Hill and traditionally a community of weavers; there were also a few houses, indicated in the map of 1725 by ill-defined shading on Marsh Lane, the extension of Kirkgate across Timble Bridge towards Pontefract and York.

With these integral but detached parts of Leeds the convenient metaphor of a skeleton begins to break down: unless, that is, it can be some animal skeleton rather than human; some giraffe perhaps, with legs across the river in the South Part, a body in Briggate, a tail in the East Part and in the North a head at the end of a very long neck.

Whatever the metaphor, the inclusion of these once peripheral areas in this Introduction arises not simply because Charles II's tax collectors, like their predecessors, chose to regard them as essentially Leeds but because here lay the fields into which settlement would move in the process of eighteenth-century population growth and industrialisation. But it would not move in all directions at an even pace, and as late as 1847 the surveyors who produced the first Ordnance maps were still delineating fields within half a mile of the parish church to the south, east, and north. Fifty-three such fields were designated as 'building ground' in the tithe commutation award of the same year.[13] The determinants of the direction in which factories and house-building progressed were many and varied, as subsequent Chapters will show, but two topographical factors were of crucial importance, and each of them was inherited from a pre-industrial period. Most obvious is the influence of a network of footpaths, lanes and highways; equally important, though less obvious, is the topography of the fields themselves since the unit of urban extension was in virtually every case the single small field.

The exception, the project of a Park estate, is important enough to merit separate treatment in Chapter Six, but a reiterated theme of the housing and factory developments in other Chapters will be their field-by-field progress. The influence of the size and shape of the existing fields will be dealt with there: their origin can be appropriately considered here.

As Fig. 1.5 shows, the characteristic shape of fields adjoining the town in all quarters (except the manorial park) was long and narrow, four or five times as long as they were broad. The modal size was some 200 yards long and 50 yards wide, giving an area of 2 acres. Such a shape is characteristic of the piecemeal enclosure of open field selions although only a few of the fields have their enclosure documented. The length was that of the selions (strips) in the

[13] Schedule to LCA, RD RT 142.

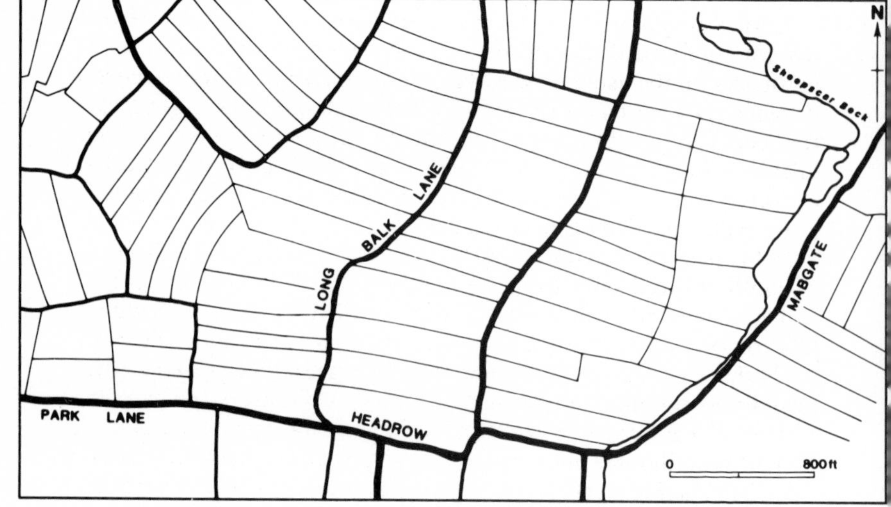

FIG. 1.5 SMALL FIELDS IN THE VICINITY OF LEEDS, *C.* 1700

An important influence on the topography of eighteenth-century Leeds was the predominance of small fields. The area shown here lies north of Park Lane; on the right is the Timble (Sheepscar) Beck. The shape of the many long, narrow fields resulted from the enclosure of blocks of strips (selions) in the former common fields towards the end of the Middle Ages. Access to these for carts and animals was along the headlands (*balks*), here emphasised with a heavy line. These subsequently became public ways (cf. Long *Balk* Lane and the *Head* Row; some became major highways and were turnpiked (Harrogate Road and the Old Bradford Road), but the first length of the Otley turnpike was driven obliquely through the fields (cf. Fig. 9.1). Small fields of this kind formed the basic units for all subsequent property development, whether for villas, terraces or streets.

original *flatts* or *furlongs*, and the width that of the appropriate number of selions to be allocated to a proprietor in lieu of those previously scattered throughout the unenclosed common fields.[14] It was also crucial that Leeds had a large number of small proprietors,[15] typically owning no more than two or three of these fields: this inheritance from the past ensured that land for building would come on to the market fitfully and in small parcels.

[14] For the enclosures, Kirby, *Manor*, pp.xxxix–l.

[15] See below, p.70.

Agricultural practices older than the enclosure also influenced the network of footpaths, lanes and highways which themselves exerted influences on the pace and direction of urbanisation. It was a short-distance network created mainly for the needs of local communication between the villages and the markets in Leeds and between the villages and the selions of their fields (Fig. 1.5). One of these tracks or *balks* giving access to the selions of at least twenty *flatts* formed Long Balk Lane, later Camp Road (Fig. 1.6).

In his plan of the countryside surrounding Leeds (1712) Sutton Nicholls showed only three long-distance highways, those from Halifax, Knaresborough and York.[16] Since the Leeds–Otley–Skipton–Kendal road was one of the first to be turnpiked (1755) it is likely that this too was an ancient thoroughfare although before the turnpike its meandering course took it to Woodhouse Moor by way of Kendal Lane through Little Woodhouse: the direct line of the present Woodhouse Lane significantly cuts across eight of the selion-shaped fields (Fig. 9.1). A field with a frontage on such public roads had distinct advantages in the eyes of any eighteenth-century merchant seeking a site for an out-of-town house (e.g. Figs 3.4, 9.1 and 10.2) for there was access for his carriage and his waggons without any cost of road building, and, as we have seen, ribbon development of this sort had begun in the South Division before 1660.

Thus the pattern of development caught by successive maps of 1772, 1781, 1815, 1821, 1831, 1844 and 1847 was not only of continued ribbon development along thoroughfares and old country lanes but an uneven intrusion into the fields. The piecemeal character of development brought environmental disadvantages which form the subject of Chapters 11 and 12. An editorial in the *Leeds Mercury* of 25 September 1852 criticising such consequences wrote, 'Indeed as to arrangement the whole town might have had an earthquake for an architect.' The true antecedent lay indeed in an earthquake, not a natural disaster but that which had shaken the foundations of age-old agricultural practices and created the enclosed fields of Leeds.

[16] Sutton Nichol(l)s, *Map of 20 miles round Leedes . . .*', published as inset to Thoresby's *Ducatus* in 1715. For the origins of the map see E. Hargrave, 'Some hitherto unpublished letters of Ralph Thoresby', *PTh.S*, XXVI (1924), 388–89 and Atkinson, II, 205–06; Nichol(l)s was the engraver but it was drawn (or perhaps redrawn) by a Mr Shelton.

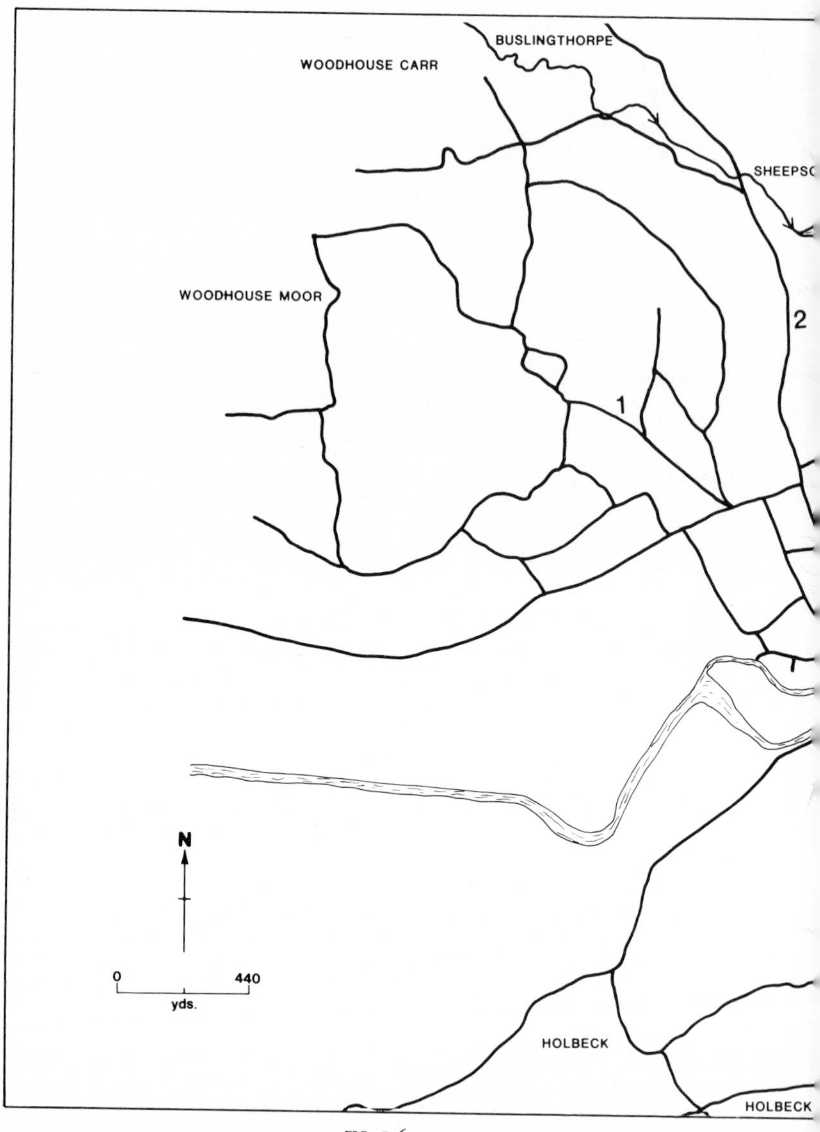

FIG. 1.6

ROADS AND TRACKS AROUND LEEDS, WITH BRANDLING'S RAILROAD, 1758

The network converging on the town's single river-crossing originated in tracks serving the unenclosed arable fields (Fig. 1.5) or giving access for common grazing at the various township moors. Roads to such out-township villages as Holbeck, Hunslet, Burley, Headingley and Chapel Allerton also

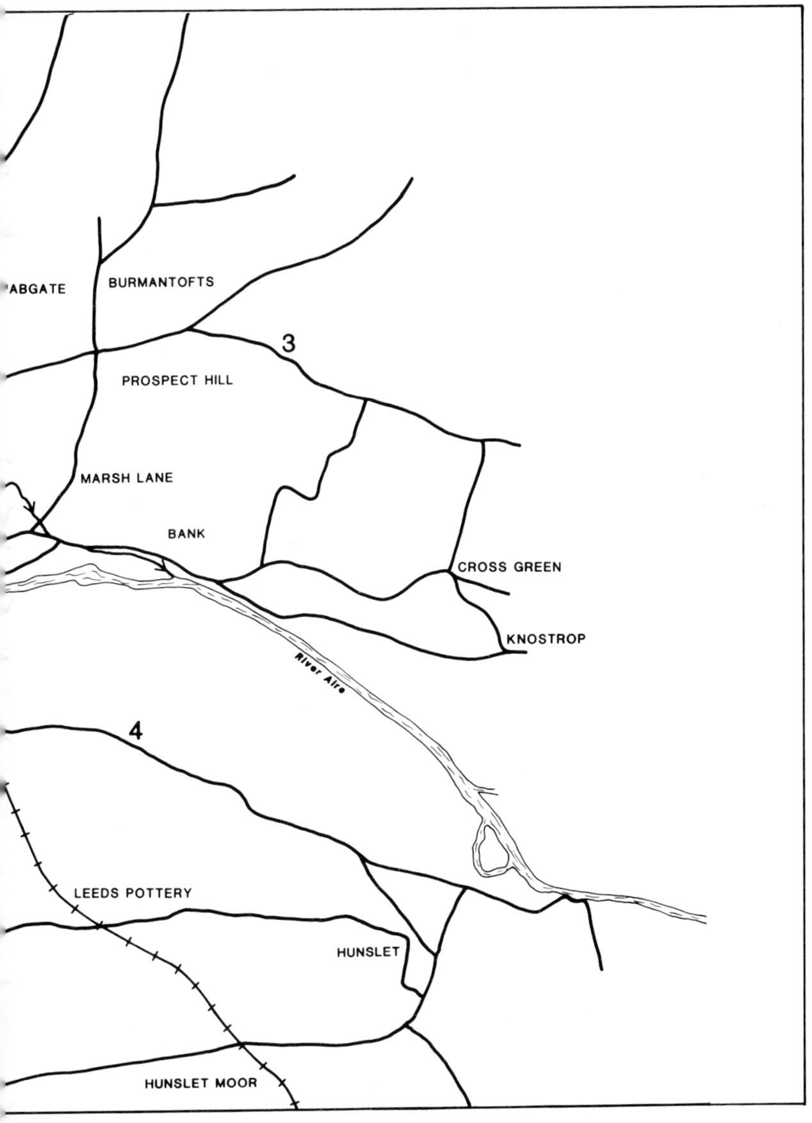

carried long-distance traffic, and by 1758 those to Otley (1), Harewood (for Ripon) (2), York and Selby (3), and Wakefield (4) had become turnpike toll roads. In 1758 an Act of Parliament authorised a private railroad from Middleton colliery past the Leeds Pottery works to its terminus at a staith just south of the bridge.

2
Prospects of Leeds, 1684–1720

... then at the hill-top, taking the rest of the town, and drawing a view of the new Vicarage till noon ... after in my Library; Mr. Buck took a prospect of it.

Diary of Ralph Thoresby, 17 October 1719, cited in D. H. Atkinson, RALPH THORESBY, THE TOPOGRAPHER; HIS TOWN AND TIMES (Leeds, 1887), II, 333.

In 1698 the traveller Celia Fiennes wrote of Leeds: 'It is a large town, severall large streetes cleane and well pitch'd and good houses all built of stone, some have good gardens and steps up to their houses and walls before them; this is esteemed the wealthyest town of its bigness in the [County] ... The streetes are very broad the Market large.'[1] When Defoe visited the town twenty years later he was also impressed with the breadth of Briggate, the market street, and the lively activity therein but he had no comment to make on the appearance of the town other than that it was 'large, wealthy and populous'.[2] These were distinctly more favourable verdicts than that of the surveyors from London in 1628 who had noted houses 'ancient meane and low built'.[3]

Exactly how large, how wealthy and how populous the town was at the end of the seventeenth century cannot be directly determined. Assuming a constant rate of growth between the two years when approximate counts can be made, 1672 and 1740, another 300 dwellings would have been added to the thousand or so recorded at the last Hearth Tax, but some of these were in Woodhouse and the suburbs.[4] The largest villages in the parish, Holbeck and Hunslet, each had no more than 100 or 150 dwellings but the urban claims of

[1] *The Journeys of Celia Fiennes*, ed. C. Morris (1949), pp.219–20.

[2] D. Defoe, *A Tour through England and Wales* (Everyman edn., 2 vols, 1928), II, 204–08.

[3] Corporation of London Records Office, RCE Rental 6.16, f.37; printed in Beresford, *Leeds in 1628*.

[4] For the Hearth Taxes see Table 2.1; unfortunately there was both error and ambiguity in the Leeds entry in the contemporary ecclesiastical census of 1676: *The Compton Census of 1676*, ed. A. Whiteman (1986), pp.563, 567, 577 and 592.

TABLE 2.1

Largest Households in the Hearth Taxes, 1663–72

Number of hearths	Division	Householder	Year
14	Briggate	Hurst	1672*
12	Mill Hill	Busfield	1672*
12	Headrow	Dixon	1672*
11	Briggate	Haddon	1672
11	High Town	Metcalfe	1666†
10	Headrow	Simpson	1663, 1666 and 1672
10	High Town	Lacock	1666
10	High Town	Ibbetson	1666†
10	Mill Hill	Hicks	1672*
10	Kirkgate	Lodge (empty)	1672
10	Briggate	Crowle	1672
9	Briggate	Mann	1672
9	Briggate	Walker	1672*
9	High Town	Potter and Scudmore	1666
9	East	Stable	1663 and 1672
9	East	Pease	1672*
9	South	Hickson	1672
9	North	Rhodes	1666†

* indicates an assessment (with fewer hearths) in 1663 and 1666.
† an assessment in 1663.

Sources: 1663: PRO, E179/262/9; 1666: E179/210/421; 1672: E179/210/417.

Leeds rested not only on its populousness. The 'good' houses which Celia Fiennes noticed were large houses, for the Hearth Tax record enables this size to be assessed. Some of the largest assessments in Table 2.1 were probably inns, the number and size of which are always indication of a town's commercial importance. The fourteen hearths on which Robert Hurst paid tax in 1672 were probably warming a Briggate inn but the twelve hearths of Busfield (Boar Lane) and Dixon (Headrow) were in private houses. The eighteen largest households of the period are listed in Table 2.1. Fourteen of these were in Briggate, Kirkgate, the Headrow or Boar Lane, able to give visitors an instant urban impression.

It was one thing to be sketched by southern travellers between a change of horses but quite another to be the subject of a commissioned portrait. Engraved views of continental towns, usually prospects from a vantage point outside their walls, made up the contents of many seventeenth-century atlases published in Holland, France, and Germany but before 1700 very few English towns had been asked to sit for this kind of portrait. The first *Prospect* of Leeds drawn for publication was made between 1684 and 1689, and two others in 1712 and 1719.

Again, it was one thing for a town to have a few anecdotes retailed as 'history' by visiting journalists but quite another to be made the subject of a scholarly (even pedantic) history published in London. To that, by 1700, only a handful of English towns could aspire, but in 1715 Ralph Thoresby published the first part of a topography and history of Leeds under the rather affected title of *Ducatus Leodiensis*: now that the Marquis of Carmarthen had been made Duke of Leeds, he argued, should not the duke and duchy of York be paralleled by a duke and duchy of Leeds? From the *Ducatus*, and from Thoresby's diary and correspondence, something of the appearance of the town can be reconstructed from the first years of George I's reign when Thoresby's readers extended beyond those local merchants and petty landed gentry whose not always accurate pedigrees filled many of his pages.[5] The work was supported by the learned community of London and the provinces, only a few of whom might be expected to have personal knowledge of Leeds: the printed list of 170 subscribers shows that copies went to both archbishops, six bishops, the Lord Chief Justice, six members of the House of Lords, two ex-ambassadors and ten fellows of Oxford and Cambridge colleges. Like the solitary subscriber from North Carolina, many of these needed some guidance around the town. The *Ducatus* therefore conducted its readers street by street: indeed the full title continued in English . . . *or, The Topography of the Ancient and Populous Town and Parish of Leedes*, and the unattributed quotations in this chapter describe Thoresby's Leeds in his own words.

Since it was an illustrated volume, it was possible to include an engraving of Sutton Nicholls's plan of 1712 showing the countryside for twenty miles around, with three roads converging on Leeds from York, Knaresborough, and Halifax, and a plan of the newly completed waterway, the 'Navigable Course of the River Are [*sic*] from Leedes to the Humber and German Ocean', the latest of

[5] *Ducatus*; the copy in the Leeds Library, donated by Charles Barnard, has manuscript marginal notes on the subsequent ownership and use of buildings, ascribed to 'T. Wilson and Mr. Lucas, masters of the Charity School, and George Bagley'; see also Anon., 'Thoresby's addenda and corrigenda to the *Vicaria Leodiensis*', *PTh.S*, II (1891), 178–79.

'several noble Undertakings, publick and private Edifices promoted for the Honour and Interest of the Town'.

These two plans were on too small a scale for any delineation of the streets of Leeds, and as yet no surveyor or cartographer had given attention to the town, so that as a visual supplement to the perambulation in his text Thoresby's readers were given two engraved *Prospects*. The earlier was the work of his friend William Lodge, drawn between 1684 and 1689, viewing the compact area of the town from a point outside it and looking north-eastwards: 'Leeds as it appears from Holbeck Road' (Front Endpaper) occupied one-third of a folded insert which also introduced readers to prospects of Wakefield, Kirkstall Abbey and Fountains Abbey.

At that date before turnpike road improvement, Water Lane, which followed the side of the Hol Beck from the weavers' village of Holbeck towards Leeds, was a segment of the important trans-Pennine route to Rochdale and Manchester through Halifax although in the *Prospect* there is no bustle of traffic: five men are strolling towards Leeds Bridge where the road crossed the Aire; and two others, with swordsticks, have stopped to chat. The foreground, largely made up of the south bank of the river near its confluence with the Beck, is pastoral, almost bucolic. A young boy fishes with a line while a girl sits and watches; an adult fisherman equipped with rod, line and net is accepting refreshment from a friend's goblet; and on the further bank another fisherman shares a meadow with grazing cows and horses. Yet the title of the engraving declares it a *Prospect* of one of 'the two most remarkable Towns in the North of England For the Clothing Trade'.

On closer inspection the *Prospect* does have evidence that across the meadow lay a town of cloth traders worthy of attention and to be spoken of in the same breath and depicted in the same plate as Wakefield, the county town of the West Riding of Yorkshire. To begin with, there was its size: from his low angle of vision near the river the artist was in no position to offer a bird's eye view of all these houses but he did his best to suggest them jostling each other, roof over roof, with chimneys smoking from hearths warmed by coal from local pits, a sight to delight tax collectors, had hearths still been taxed.

At that time there were few industrial establishments using much coal, and none is depicted in the *Prospect*: apart from the windmills on the heights to the north of the town, its industrial power was man-power, horse-power and water-power. The sluggish Hol Beck drove more than one corn mill in Holbeck, and one of the nine numbered features in the *Prospect* was '7, High Dam' where artistic licence permitted a veritable cataract to pour over the great weir that medieval lords of the manor had built across the Aire to create a permanent head of water for their two groups of manorial mills at the foot of Mill Hill, adjoining the Manor House itself. Corn was milled here for centuries but the wheels were also harnessed to fulling stocks to which clothiers brought their cloths; oil seeds were also crushed here, logwood ground for dye, scythes ground sharp, and tobacco cut and ground for snuff.

In the thirty years between the time of Lodge's *Prospect* and Thoresby's book a primitive steam engine and water-wheel had been installed at the tail end of the mill race to pump drinking water to the waterworks reservoirs in the higher part of town.[6] In general Thoresby's own perambulation paid little attention to the seats of industry and crafts in the town, but, perhaps because as a young man he had lost most of his patrimony in an unsuccessful partnership in a small rape-seed oil mill at Sheepscar,[7] he paused to point out the mill improvements as he stood by the bridge, and then described a new metal workshop south of the bridge where Mr Armitage had a machine that made jacks without filing, cut the teeth of saws, made fowling pieces, and ground and polished razors, scissors and lancets.

Even the largest industrial establishment, the manorial mills, had no more than two storeys. The *Prospect* shows at least nine private houses with three storeys[8] but taller still were the diverse houses of God. St Peter's and St John's churches had gothic towers, and the more recent and modest Unitarian Meeting House on Mill Hill (numbered 6 in the *Prospect*) rose to three storeys with a cupola and small clock tower. Lodge did not distinguish the water mills by a number but next to the Meeting House railings he drew three lines of tenter frames, erected to stretch cloth as it dried after finishing: and sharing the meadow with the fisherman and the grazing beasts were two more lines of fifty-four tenters. No secular public building was named in the *Prospect* but in the background the apex of one steep roof was allowed into vision by exercise of even more artistic licence than the exaggeration of the weir: it was the Moot Hall in Briggate, a wooden building on pillars and soon to be faced in stone, graced with a statue of Queen Anne, and then join the two Anglican churches as the subject of full-page elevations engraved for the *Ducatus*. The final urban element in the *Prospect* was '3 The Brigg Fair': that is, the traditional cloth market located on Leeds Bridge

[6] On 22 July 1694 Thoresby saw lead waterpipes being laid near his house; they were connected to his kitchen on 7 December: Atkinson, I, 338 and 340.

[7] *Ibid.*, I, 320, 337 and 344.

[8] For three-storeyed houses see also Table 3.1, p.39.

itself before its transfer in 1684 to Briggate and later to the Cloth Halls. The four-arched, single carriageway bridge is in the background of the *Prospect* but on careful examination it can be seen that above its parapet the artist has drawn as many pin-point heads gathered for bargaining as his pen would allow, and above them he wrote *Bridge Shotts*, the name for the adjacent hostelries where good value for money was commented upon by Fiennes and Defoe.

Lodge's *Prospect* occupied less than a third of a page: the *Ducatus*'s second *Prospect*, by Francis Place, another friend of the author, was more up to date, and larger, taking up a double page folding outwards. Place also took a more advantageous point than Lodge at which to set up his easel (Fig. 2.1).

Lodge's *Prospect* had been drawn from a southern viewpoint at the confluence of the Aire and the meandering Hol Beck: Place's was from the high ground to the east of the town above the confluence of the Aire with the Timble (or Sheepscar) Beck. This was a stronger beck, rising in Adel with a head capable of driving ten mills before it was harnessed in Leeds itself to turn the wheels of Folkingham's Mill in Mill Garth and then the mills of the Steander. In the Meanwood valley it ran between steep cliffs, and the line of high ground continued east of the town to form Cavalier Hill, a name recalling a Civil War encampment and skirmishes. The hill yielded stone, for the road eastwards which began as Marsh Lane when it crossed the beck at Timble Bridge, continued as Quarry Hill when it began to climb, and later the Leeds-Selby railway line would have to tunnel its way through this obstacle. On the plateau top, just off the York Road, stands a public house that has survived the demolition of Victorian streets to minister to the thirsts of new industrial building.

It is the *Prospect Inn*: from its back door the ground drops almost vertically towards the railway cutting, still giving that uninterrupted view into central Leeds which attracted artists in the past. In Place's *Prospect* one such artist with Cavalier curls, perhaps Place himself, kneels with a sketch board while a mother with baby at her back passes on a walk with her dog. No one else is in sight except for a faun-like male figure kneeling by the artist as if pointing out the town. Perhaps it was intended to be a classical transformation of Thoresby himself, for the latter's diary records a visit from Place in mid-September 1712 and a walk to Cavalier Hill in order to 'make prospects'.[9] On 16 October 1719 Thoresby went again to Cavalier Hill, this time in company with the cartographer Warburton and the artist Samuel Buck, 'to take a new prospect of the Town from

[9] Atkinson, II, 218.

Priestcliff, near Cavalier Hill ... could make little proficiency because of the rain'.[10] Buck's panoramic view, extending across four pages of his sketch book, is preserved in the British Library but was never prepared for publication.[11]

On 25 April 1720, presumably in better weather, Thoresby 'went with Mr Buck and Mr Bland to choose a convenient station upon Cavalier Hill, to take a long prospect of Leeds, designed to be printed', and again on 5 September with his cousin Cookson to see Buck 'give the finishing stroke to the Prospect of Leeds from Cavalier Hill'.[12] He had been helping Buck canvass patrons for subscriptions so that the 'Draughts ... carefully revised and corrected' could be 'Curiously cut on Copper Plates ... by the Hands of the best artists in London'. Thoresby's name appeared among the 166 subscribers in the printed *Proposals for Publishing by Subscription an Accurate and Correct Perspective Draught*, and in January 1722 he personally delivered to the Leeds subscribers the engraved *East Prospect of the Town of Leedes ... from Chaveler* [i.e. Cavalier] *Hill*.[13]

Like the 1719 sketch, the 1720 engraving would be a 'long prospect'; it was to measure 3 ft by 18 in., the view extending across the Aire to the South Division, and on the north side to beyond the last buildings at Town's End. In the engraving prepared for publication in 1720 the foreground is still sylvan (Fig. 2.2). The artist is at work sketching while a friend pats a hesitant dog on the head. The dog's master, with a gun, is holding a conversation with another well-dressed spectator. It is perhaps his greyhound who guards a gun and knapsack. In fields below activity is more vigorous: two men are collecting cloth from thirty-one tenter frames; five men are beating a fleece with rods while a sixth carries away another fleece; a man and a woman approach, weighed down under sacks; horses

[10] *Ibid.*, II, 333.

[11] British Library, Lansdowne MS. 914; published in Hall, ed.

[12] Atkinson, II, 333–34.

[13] *Ibid.*, II, 334–36. The copy in the Thoresby Society's library was described in Bonser and Nichols, p.4, but wrongly ascribed to 1745 perhaps because Buck and his brother, Nathaniel, published from London in that year a *South-East prospect of Leeds in the county of York*. There is another copy in the library of the Society of Antiquaries.

FIG. 2.1 'THE PROSPECT OF LEEDS FROM THE KNOSTROP ROAD', 1715

By Francis Place, reproduced in Thoresby's *Ducatus*. Six major buildings in the town centre were numbered and three others named. The houses in the foreground are on the Bank; below them Fearne's Island, the Nether Mills and the Navigation lock at Crown Point weir (cf. Figs. 1.3 and 2.2).

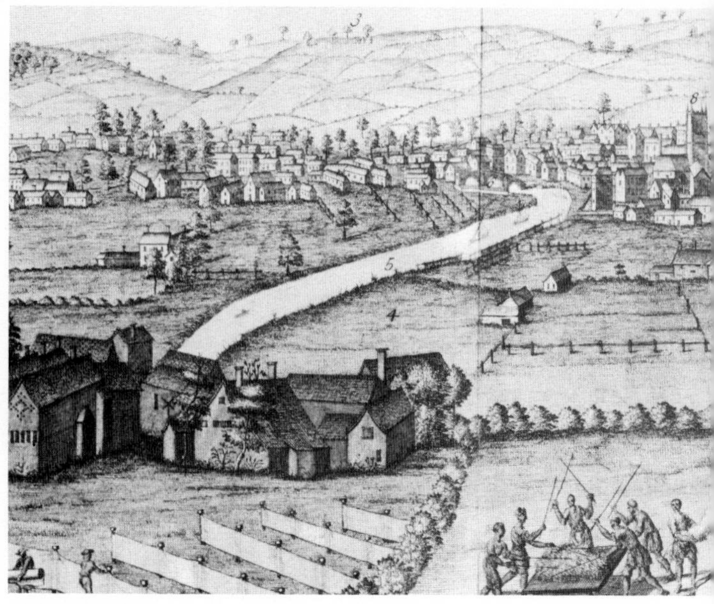

FIG. 2.2 ART AND INDUSTRY IN THE EAST END, 1720

From Samuel Buck's *East Prospect of the Town of Leedes . . . from Chaveler* [i.e. Cavalier] *Hill*, drawn in the company of Ralph Thoresby, as recorded in the latter's diary for 25 April. The artist's head appears bottom centre and behind him workmen are beating fleeces on a table; there are empty tenter frames in the fields beyond. At the foot of the Woodhouse ridge runs the long line of houses in Kirkgate and Vicar Lane: Briggate is hidden from view. Important buildings are numbered: (8) the parish church in Kirkgate; (10) the Atkinson house (cf. Fig. 3.3) adjoining (11) Call Lane chapel and (12) the small White Cloth Hall then just built in Kirkgate; (13) is a side view of the vicarage, then also newly built, at the corner of Kirkgate and vicar Lane. For a continuation northward *see* Fig. 3.5.

graze; several fields have empty tenters. The houses of weavers and the smoking dyehouse chimneys at the Bank are prominent in the left-hand foreground, each building being carefully drawn. Where they can be checked against other sources (as with the Denison house, below) the delineation of roofs, chimneys and windows is precise even in the distant streets, and the quasi-suburbs of Marsh Lane, Quarry Hill and Hunslet Lane are given as much attention as the artist's own dress and the hilltop scrub which surrounds him, even if their precision exposes the hyperbole of Thoresby's claim that 'these very Suburbs called Quarry hill and Mab-gate make a greater Figure than many Towns that are big in the Maps'.

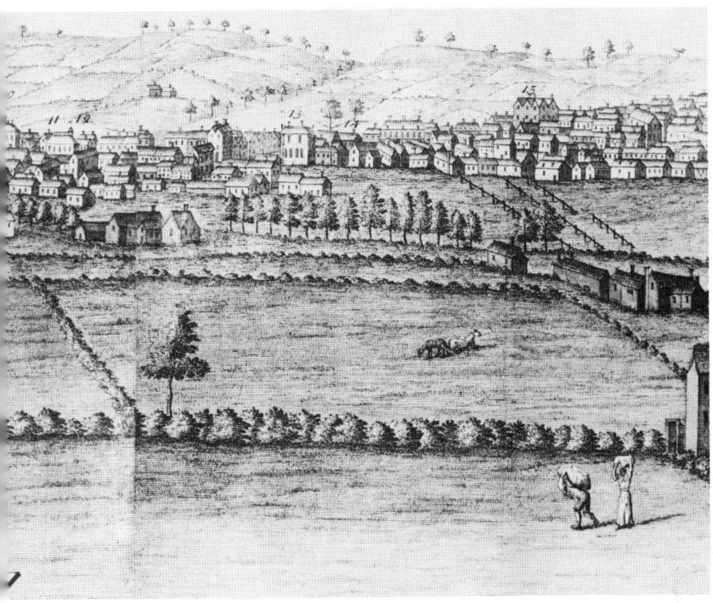

The continuing strength of the tradition of town-centre dwelling is indicated by the location of new building at this period. Progress was so rapid that Thoresby had to modify his text on the eve of publication with an *Addenda* (1714): 'since the preceding Topography was writ several noble Undertakings, publick and private edifices have been promoted for the Honour and Interest of the Town', and then – subduing his civic pride modestly – 'the modern Improvements in Architecture and Convenient Habitations should not excite Vain-Glory'.

The complement of public buildings achieved during Thoresby's lifetime was an indication of perceived urban need and of the wealth available for subscribers to satisfy it.[14] In 1714 Thoresby added his name to a subscription list for a third Anglican church, the eventual Holy Trinity in Boar Lane, needed because the increase in population had left St Peter's, Kirkgate, and St John's, Briggate, overcrowded despite the erection of a new gallery at St Peter's that same year.[15]

[14] In Thoresby's lifetime (born 1658) he had seen the public buildings of the town augmented by the erection of three Dissenters' meeting houses, two privately donated sets of almshouses, a Charity School house in St John's churchyard, and a warehouse for the Navigation.

[15] Atkinson, II, 358–59; the subscription list is LCA, DB 204/2.

The additions to the town's 'private edifices', the 'convenient Habitations' were another evidence of a continual, if slow, growth in numbers: the stock of houses was increasing by about twenty a year in the early eighteenth century, but equally significant was the improvement of existing houses as timber-framed houses were rebuilt or cased with brick.

The observers from London in 1628 had implied that there was considerable room for improvement: 'the houses . . . beinge ancient meane and lowe built; and generallie all of Tymber; though they have stone quarries frequent in the Towne, and about it; only some few of the richer sort of the Inhabitants have theire houses more large and capacious'.[16] The improvement was actually under way in 1628, with Red Hall being built in brick for Alderman Metcalf; Thoresby lived in a house that his grandfather had rebuilt in brick; Call Lane meeting house was of brick and so were the Cloth Hall and Assembly Rooms; St John's vicarage was cased in brick between 1683 and 1686.[17]

No 'private edifice' had been singled out by name or reference number in Lodge's *Prospect* but one of the six numbered buildings in Place's *Prospect* is 'Alderman Atkinson's', drawn in elevation to show its domed roof tower, taller than Call Lane chapel; 'other Turrets in this *Prospect* are the new Cloath Hall, Alderman Cookson's and Mr. Thoresby's'. Such 'turrets' were indeed carefully drawn in the unpublished panorama of Buck's sketchbook, and in the published engraving of 1720 attention was drawn to the private houses of Cookson and Atkinson by the numbers 9 and 10 while Red Hall, not distinguished by either Lodge or Place, was now also assigned a number. Thoresby's house and museum in Kirkgate was no. 14,[18] and Robert Denison's new house and ornamental garden on the northern edge of town (later known as Sheepshanks House

[16] See n.3 above.

[17] Expenditure recorded in accounts printed in G.D.L[umb], 'St John's Church, Leeds', *PTh.S*, XXIV (1919), 385.

[18] Thoresby's house was on the north side of Kirkgate between Briggate and Vicar Lane: it was identified on the first edition of the O.S. 5-foot plan as 'Thoresby's study' and was later numbered both 17 and 18; Gill's Yard (now demolished) must have been the yard with the library that was depicted in the prospect which Buck drew in his sketchbook on 17 October 1719 (Hall edition, p.213 and *Letters addressed to Ralph Thoresby*, ed. W. T. Lancaster, *PTh.S*, XXI (1912), frontispiece). According to a note in the Leeds Library copy of the *Ducatus* (n.5 above) Thoresby's heir sold the Kirkgate property to Matthew Freeman, a barber, and in the rate book of 1740 (LCA, DB 204/3, f.171) Freeman was assessed on the frontage houses there, together with five small buildings in the yard. See also Table 5.5 for another building at the rear.

but unbuilt at the time of Place's *Prospect*) was now delineated with the reference number, 18. In the main text of the *Ducatus*, completed by 1713, Thoresby often paused to compliment such a private house, new or rebuilt.

At the time of Thoresby's death the *Leeds Mercury* had been published each week for seven years. Its columns of 12 September 1725 carried advertisements for the sale of his house, an appeal from his executors for borrowers to return books and manuscripts from his library, and an offer to sell the remaining copies of the *Ducatus* and *Vicaria*. On 6 August 1728 the newspaper adopted a new woodcut for the heading alongside its title, and chose a Prospect, 'A View of Leeds'. The style of the small drawing is crude and the artist unknown.[19] He reverted to the river bank position south of the town that had been used by Lodge but made no attempt to be realistic. Cavalier Hill in the distance is a small mountain and a poorly drawn parish church is dwarfed by the new Holy Trinity. This *View* continued to appear until 5 October 1731.

In 1712, 1719 and 1720 Thoresby had encouraged the artists, Place and Buck, to delineate the splendours of Leeds in *Prospects*, and had accompanied them in their making. At this time the surveyor, John Warburton, was engaged upon a new map of the whole county but its scale would not allow any detailed representation of the streets of Leeds. Thoresby was anxious that Leeds should join the largest English cities in having a town plan drawn on a scale large enough to do justice to its topography. One of his many correspondents on matters historical and theological was Dr Charlett, Master of University College, Oxford who must have expressed support for such a venture; Thoresby wrote to him mournfully on 25 October 1718:

> I showed some of our magistrates what you writ relating to a Survey of the Parish, to shame them for their former neglect, and urge them to rectify it in the designed great new map but they are *semper iidem*. Mr. Warburton may do it at his own expense or not at all. Ours is a great trading town, and a great happiness on that account to all parts of England; but the generality of the inhabitants are so immersed in business of that nature, that they are not solicitous for other matters.[20]

Thoresby received his subscriber's copy of Warburton's Yorkshire map in May 1721[21] but the project for a separate map of Leeds

[19] Reproduced in G. D. Lumb, 'Extracts from the *Leeds Mercury*, 1721–1729', *PTh.S*, XXII (1915), 230. The other headings were a golden fleece and a mounted postman blowing his horn.

[20] Atkinson, II, 315.

[21] *Ibid.*, II, 329–30.

foundered, and for an accurate delineation of the town and of the location of the new houses of the 1720s we have to await the 'New and Exact Plan of the Town of Leedes' by John Cossins, published from London by an engraver with a shop at St Paul's churchyard in 1725, the year of Thoresby's death.

3
Town's End, c. 1725

Mr James Ibbetson of Leedes Merchant is now erecting a Hospital for poor Men near the Chapel in the Call Lane (but repenting of so good a thought lets them for money to tenants.)

The passage in brackets is Ralph Thoresby's manuscript gloss to p. 576 of his own copy of the DUCATUS, now in the Library of the Thoresby Society.

. . . a new erected House nigh Woodhouse Barr . . .

Mortgage (Copley to Roberts), 15 Oct. 1736: LCA, DB 64/2.

JOHN COSSINS'S VIEW OF LEEDS

Thoresby's father had chosen to rebuild the family home in Kirkgate rather than move to some new site on the edge of town. A generation later the same attitude prevailed. In his *New and Exact Plan of the*

FIG. 3.1 HOUSES OF 1725 (*following two pages*)

Four of the elevations of buildings in the margins of Cossins's map (listed in Table 3.1):

(a) 'Mr Robt. Dennison [*sic*] Merc[han]t, Towns end No. 10': a residence with a front garden, built after 1710 and insured in 1718 (cf. Fig. 3.4).

(b) 'Mr Tho. Dennison Merch[ant], Towns end. No. 11': also set back in a garden on the west side of the road nearly opposite 'No. 10'; built after 1720 and later known as Belgrave House.

(c) 'Mr Tho. Lee Merch[an]t. No. 12': on the west side of Lower Briggate, built directly on the street without garden (later, as in Fig. 4.6, three houses, numbered 15–17); nine bays, with indications of a shop front at the left (southern) end; adjoining, a doorway leading backsides by a tunnel entrance to a Yard; fronted with Huddleston stone and the most extensive house in the town, if not so splendid as the Atkinson house (Fig. 3.3); first insured against fire in 1724, then, and for many years, at the highest sum in the town.

(d) 'Mr. Hugh Sleigh, Briggate, No. 1': also directly on the street frontage on the east side of Briggate; three entrances roofed as if for shops and the fourth an elaborately rusticated doorway. Sleigh was an attorney. Late Victorian photographs show the house surviving but without its five urns; the three shop-fronts were then nos 133 (hosier), 135 (jeweller) and 137 (dining rooms) but the elaborate doorway had been replaced by a tunnel entrance to Newsome's Yard.

Mr. Robt. Dennison Merct.
Towns end No. 10
(a)

Mr. Tho. Dennison Merchnt.
Towns end No. 11.
(b)

(c)

(d)

Town of Leedes (*c*.1725) John Cossins delineated a town as compact as that shown in the earlier *Prospects* and, as if to emphasise the loyalty to central siting, decorated the margin of his map with the architectural elevation of fifteen houses, nine of the owners specifically described as 'merchant'. The vicarage and nine other private houses were shown on the map itself. Table 3.1 shows that twenty of these twenty-five houses were in a style indicative of recent building: twenty-one were in the central streets and were therefore the result of rebuilding on old sites in a new fashionable style. The accuracy of Cossins's elevation cannot be tested against surviving buildings, as can houses on his plan of York. They were certainly not conventionalised for, although within the classical tradition, they exhibit variety of size and architectural detail; the realism of one, Robert Denison's at Town's End, can be tested both against Buck's 1720 *Prospect* and late nineteenth-century photographs (Fig. 3.1; cf. Fig. 3.4).[1]

Cossins's was the first Leeds plan to be engraved for sale, and there was no other until 1772 (Fig. 3.2). Like Thoresby's *Ducatus* the work sought prestige and no doubt sales by having a humble dedication. Like Thoresby's also, this was to the mayor and the twelve aldermen, six of whose houses were depicted on the map or in the margins, and to them he added Lord Irwin whose peerage and forty-one-roomed mansion at Temple Newsam gave him a social standing hardly attained by a cloth-town mayor. One townsman, James Ibbetson, did have his armorial bearings drawn in a vacant space on the map alongside those of Lord Irwin and the Corporation, in addition to the depiction of the family house in the margin.

The only public building among the architectural elevations was 'The Town Hall', that is, the Moot Hall in the middle of Upper Briggate which had been rebuilt in 1710–11 with 'Queen Ann Statue in marble' at its front; but the small prison in Kirkgate (1725), the three Anglican churches, the three nonconformist meeting houses, and the Town's Warehouse were shown on the map itself. 'Leedes is a Large Rich and Populous Town . . . and is accounted one of ye best Towns belonging to this County,' proclaimed the loyal cartouche.

[1] The traditional date of 1725, deriving from E. Wilson, 'Two Old Plans of Leeds', *PTh.S*, X (1899), 196–204, was retained here (as the mid-point of the suggested 1721–29 range) although R. M. Allen has since informed me that his copy of Thoresby's *Vicaria*, annotated probably by Thomas Wilson (as in n.5 in Ch.2 above) records the Buck house in Meadow Lane as 'Built 1726'; since this house is depicted on the Cossins plan, it may well have been drawn after 1725.
For authentication of the Denison house see Fig. 3.4; for the Atkinson house Fig. 3.3; for the Lee house Fig. 4.6.

TABLE 3.1

Town Centre: the Twenty-five Houses of Cossins's Map, c.1725

Name on map	Location	Storeys	Bays	Notes*
1. Older style: gables, wings, mullions				
Lawyer [Richard] Wilson	Manor House, Mill Hill	2 + gable	5 + wing	frescoes by Parmentier; demolished, rebuilt 1700
Thomas Calverley	Red Hall, Headrow	3	6	built 1628
Alderman Rooke	Boar Lane, next to Holy Trinity church	2	5 + wing	wide window probably mullioned and transomed; demolished and rebuilt by new owner, 1752
2. New style				
Mr Atkinson†	Call Lane, west side in a croft	3 + domed tower	5	built 1712, insured 1716 'freestone work and dome' (Thoresby, *Ducatus*); painted staircase by Parmentier
Alderman William Cookson (mayor, 1725)	Kirkgate, south side; gardens to river; summer-house	3 + gable	5	first in the town to be insured
Mr Berkenhout‡	Kirkgate	3	11	two houses together, with passage door to garden
Mr Thomas Lee†‡	Briggate, west side, below Boar Lane	3	9	insured 1724; fronted with Huddleston stone
Mr Bischoff‡	Kirkgate, north side opposite Cloth Hall	3	8	porch, and side door for carts
Mr Thomas Denison‡	Town's End, North Street, west side	3	7	segmental pediment over first-floor window: cf. nos. 13 and 14 High Ousegate, York
Mr Dixon‡	Call Lane, east side	3	7	large loading doors on each floor, with hoist; opposite *White Hart* inn
Mr Markham	Hunslet Lane, east side	3	6	asymmetrical

(*continued overleaf*)

TABLE 3.1 (*continued*)

Name on map	Location	Storeys	Bays	Notes*
James Ibbetson Esq.	Kirkgate south side	3	5	porch; pillars and urn
Mr Jacob Busk‡	Meadow Lane	3	5	moulded bands between storeys
Mr Douglas‡§	Austrop Hall, Meadow Lane	3	5	
Mr Robert Denison‡§	Town's End, North Street, east side	3	5	rustication of arched doorway; drawn in Busk's sketchbook, 1719; insured 1718
Vicarage	Vicar Lane and Kirkgate, north side	3	5	built 1717; 48 ft 4 in. wide
St John's Place	St John's church yard	3	5	cased in brick between 1683 and 1686 (*PTh.S.*, XXIV (1919), p.385)
Alderman Brearey	Boar Lane, north side, corner of Cripplegate	3	4	similar to no. 8 Clifton, York
Mr Hugh Sleigh§	Briggate, west side	3	4	asymmetrical with pilasters and rustication; urns on parapet
Mr Thomas Saw[y]er	Boar Lane, to east of Brearey (above)	3	4	ground floor elevated above semi-basement; parapet
Mr Croft Preston‡	Town's End	2	5 + wing	three gabled projections
William Milner Esq.	Simpson's Fold, south of bridge	2	4 + 3 in wing	
Alderman Barstow	Kirkgate, north side with garden and summerhouse	2	?	end view only, with four windows; 'nine rooms' (*LI*, 16 March 1773)
Mr George Green	Bridge	?	?	located on map but not depicted in margin
Mr Nathaniel English	Boar Lane, south side	?	?	located on map but not depicted in margin

* I am indebted to Mr David Black of the Royal Commission on Historical Monuments, York, for advice on architectural details.

† House drawn by John Russell, RA, *c.*1803–04.

‡ Berkenhout, Lee, Bischoff, both Denisons, Dixon, Busk, Douglas and Preston described as 'merchants'.

§ House seen in photographs before demolition.

The scale of Cossins's plan was large enough for any major building to be drawn in elevation in its correct geographical position so long as it stood not on a street frontage but in its own precinct, as did Red Hall, the vicarage in Vicar's Croft and the Presbyterian and Quaker meeting houses; the largest building in the town, the parish church, could be drawn within the area of its graveyard, as could St John's. John Harrison, who built St John's in 1634, had placed it in open ground beyond the north end of Briggate and there was room for Cossins to draw an elevation of the minister's house alongside the church, and Harrison's Free (or Grammar) School to the east of them; while the exceptional width of Briggate allowed the market cross and the Moot Hall to be placed in position although somewhat straitened thereby.

The placing of fifteen houses in the margin was a matter of necessity as well as advertisement: drawn in position, whether in Kirkgate, Briggate or Call Lane, they would have obscured the cartography, so each was given a key number, and eighteen other 'Places in this Map which are not Express'd in Words at Length' appeared in an alphabetical table with letters from *A* to *S* to indicate their position on the map. The only private building in Briggate to be drawn in position was the half-timbered *White Swan* inn, but turned through a right angle so that its facade faced the reader; the *Talbot,* near the Headrow, had to be content with a mere reference letter O. If the merchant houses of Briggate had been given the same treatment the cartographic clarity would have been lost, so that (apart from the Vicarage) the three town-centre houses that could be drawn in position were not on street frontages, but in backside crofts: Atkinson's, Cookson's and Barstow's.

No cartographer before 1815 attempted to show individually every house in town. Cossins indicated the built-up area by cross-shading. This technique, the grey shaded blocks contrasting with the

---

FIG. 3.2 CENTRAL LEEDS, 1725, AFTER COSSINS *(overleaf)*

Features from Cossins's map transposed to a base derived from the Giles plan of 1815. Key: 1: Moot Hall, Briggate; 2: St Peter's church, Kirkgate; 3: St John's church; 4: Holy Trinity church, Boar Lane; 5: Call Lane chapel; 6: Mill Hill chapel; 7: Town's Warehouse; 8: Harrison's Hospital; 9: Red Hall; 10: Vicarage and Vicar's Croft, Vicar Lane; 11: Free School; 12: *(later)* St John's Place; 13: *White Swan*, Briggate; 14: *Talbot Inn*, Briggate; 15: Alderman Atkinson's house, Call Lane; 16: Alderman Cookson's house and garden, Kirkgate; 17: Alderman Brearey's house and croft; 18: Bowling Green, Lands Lane; 19: Manor House, Mill Hill; 20: Alderman Milner's house, Simpson's Fold; 21: Alderman Rooke's house, Boar Lane; 22: Robert Denison's house, Town's End; 23: Thomas Denison's house, Town's End; 24: Workhouse, Lady Lane; 25: White Cloth Hall, Kirkgate.

BURLEY BAR
RIVER
AIR
1
3
4
5
6
7
8
9
12
13
14
15
17
18
19
20
21

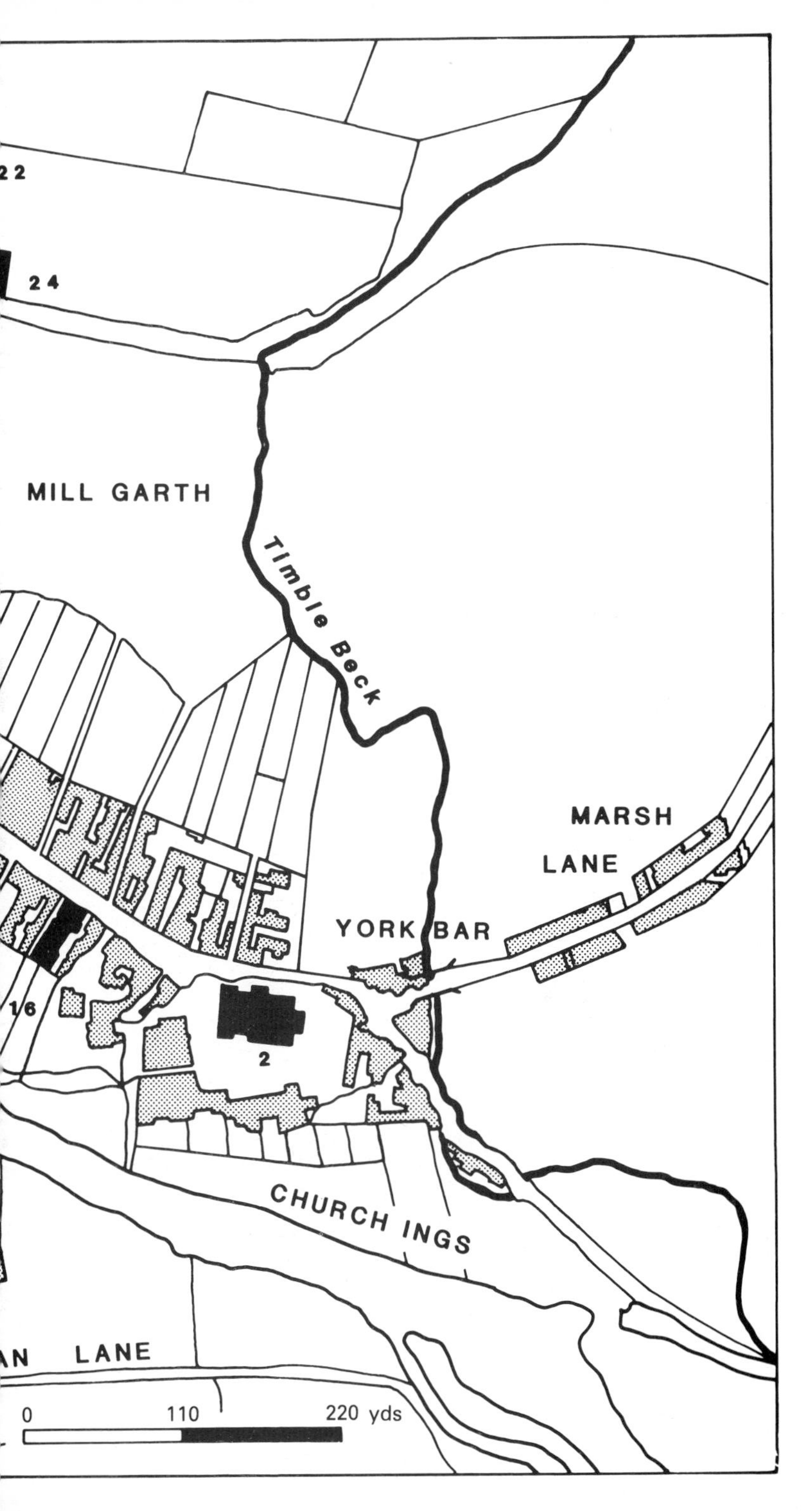

22
24
MILL GARTH
Timble Beck
MARSH
LANE
YORK BAR
16
2
CHURCH INGS
AN LANE
0
110
220 yds

white of the surrounding fields and the little trees in their hedges, emphasises the compact character of the town already displayed in the *Prospects*. The technique also shows what the long-distance *Prospects* could not: the extent of open crofts within the town itself, additional to the house gardens which were included in the shaded areas.

These crofts owed their existence to the distance separating the central streets of the medieval village and borough: if Boar Lane had been placed nearer to Swinegate or Briggate to Call Lane their own backside garths would have been small, and there would have been no such spaces left for later development.

These crofts could be reached from the street only through alleys or entries between houses: four are shown on the north side of Kirkgate and one from the Lower Headrow southwards; one, from Lower Briggate to Call Lane, was named as Currie Entry. In the most compact parts of town some houses had been extended over such alleys, creating tunnel entrances to interior yards rather than to crofts: eleven of these were drawn by Cossins between the west side of Briggate and Lands Lane, and another from Briggate to Kirkgate along the south side of the *White Swan*; on the same side of Briggate he carefully indented the western end of his block shading to show where these alleys entered the crofts.

At only two points in the main street frontages does the line of buildings seem to be broken. At the corner of Kirkgate and Vicar Lane a medieval benefactor had donated a large croft for a vicarage and some surrounding glebe. Cossins drew the elevation of the rebuilt vicarage of 1717 with its orchard and garden behind. Buck's sketch book of 1719 and the plans and elevation drawn for the archbishop of York in 1747 confirm the accuracy of Cossins's elevation.[2] Boar Lane had no broken frontage in 1725 but Thoresby had remarked that it was 'not so close built as the rest of the town', and in 1721 there was certainly an open frontage on the north side, for the trustees of the proposed Trinity church were able to purchase a croft for the church and graveyard (which still interrupt the building line). Similar crofts behind the buildings of Kirkgate, Boar Lane and the Headrow were owned by principal townsmen. If, like Thoresby and Cookson, their crofts adjoined their owner's houses they were used as gardens. In 1687 six crofts behind Kirkgate houses were large enough to be assessed for the hay tithe, that is, they were more than gardens.[3] Many crofts had tenter frames drawn

[2] Hall, ed., p.212; Borthwick, MS.Ter.E., Leeds 1747.

[3] LCD 5258, box 3; G. D. Lumb, 'Lease dated 1687, of the tithe hay in Leeds', *PTh.S*, XXIV (1919), 402–19.

in by Cossins to indicate their industrial use. Alderman Brearey's name appears on a group of crofts immediately behind his Boar Lane house. Adjacent was a bowling green, advertised on 24 April 1727 as 'now in good order'. When Alderman Rooke, also of Boar Lane, purchased it in February 1708 it was described as 'the south end of Hall Flatts, separated by rails and sometime converted to a Bowling Green'; it adjoined a croft called 'the Lands' in 1713, and Lands Lane was shown by Cossins leading to it.[4] These terms, *land* and *flatt*, must have survived from the days when unenclosed open field selions (*lands*) lay within their furlongs (*flatts*), and the Brearey crofts in particular have the characteristic shape of enclosed selions.[5]

The open ground behind the principal street frontages thus had several functions: it was available for recreational private gardens, for vegetable plots and fruit trees, for a little grazing, and for setting up tenter frames handily placed for the merchants' workshops. These uses could alternate with ownership and economic circumstances; but there was always a competing use in the extension of buildings backwards from the original frontage, the *backsydes* where the surveyors of 1628 had found buildings 'lowe and straitened'. The encroachment of building *backsydes* was no novelty and was incomplete in 1725.[6]

Celia Fiennes had seen houses in Leeds with 'good gardens and steps up to their houses and walls before them'. The evidence from Cossins's map is that only four houses in the central area, apart from the vicarage, had gardens and walls – the Manor House itself, the Milner house in Simpson's Fold, Alderman Rooke's in Boar Lane and Mr Atkinson's behind Call Lane (Fig. 3.3). None of these, it will be noted, was in Kirkgate or Briggate and there is no later cartographic evidence to contradict the continuous frontage line assigned to them by Cossins. Photographs survive of Briggate and Kirkgate houses that had certainly been built before 1725, and they

[4] 1708: WRRD, A 360/555; 1713: WRRD, G 96/104.

[5] See above, p.17.

[6] See Chapter 4.

FIG. 3.3 THE ATKINSON HOUSE, 1803–04 (*overleaf*)

Redrawn by John Dixon from no. 7 in John Russell's sketchbook 'I': looking west from Call Lane into Currie Entry with the garden gate to the Post Office, then occupying what had been the largest of the gentlemen's houses in Leeds in Thoresby's time (Fig. 3.2, no. 15), although as early as 30 November 1725 the *Leeds Mercury* was advertising its coach house as 'suitable for a gentleman or as a Packshop for a Merchant'; on the right a corner of the Call Lane Meeting House manse. Atkinson's house was demolished in 1824 for the Central Market (LCD 225).

are unequivocally on a frontage line. Until these streets were paved, drained and levelled there may well have been steps to front doors: when Charles Wesley first preached in Leeds in 1742 he took the vantage point of the pavement outside the barber's shop of Mr Shent in Briggate with his audience below him on the traffic-worn surface of Briggate; 'the threshold of the door was directly over the street'.[7]

Gardens existed in plenty in early eighteenth-century Leeds. At the upper end of New Street, the furthest limit of town, it is not unexpected to find Mrs Frost's house advertised on 2 April 1723 with a garden attached but three weeks later the *Mercury* advertised a house in the Shambles, the most congested part of Briggate, with a 'garden stead', and Samuel Tottie's Briggate property a year earlier (12 January 1722) was a shop, a garden and a summer-house. In Kirkgate the term 'fold' for the backsides area where animals had indeed once been folded was giving place to *garth.*[8] Thoresby's museum, 'a more convenient retirement place in the garden behind the house where I live', can be seen in an unpublished sketch by Buck,[9] and in the garden of his neighbour, Alderman Cookson, sufficient nectarines and peaches were growing in August 1738 to tempt a thief.[10] In 1728 a neighbouring house was sold with 'one of the gardens going to the River Air with a Convenience in that Garden for Bathing in the River, without being exposed to Publick

[7] John Wray, 'Methodism in Leeds' (eleven vols of manuscript notes embodying information from veteran Methodists, 1835–45), Leeds Reference Library, Local History Collection, vol. 1, f. 162, with W. Livesey's print of Shent's shop prior to its demolition in 1787; 'not one half of the shops in Briggate were then occupied other than as private dwellings of a very respectable sort; or as attornies' offices, the whole of which were in Briggate then, as well as several residences of the Aldermen': *Ibid.*, f. 164.

[8] See below p. 84. As late as 1716 a Briggate yard could also be called a fold: WRRD, L44/61. Among many references to Kirkgate garths, crofts and folds are: LCD 1238 (1639), a garth; LCD 1267 (1710), a croft; LCD 300 (1632) and Sun OS 17/32578 (1724), Kay's Fold; 'fold yard' was used as late as 1791: RE 22/125371. A series of plans (Nottingham University Library, Denison MSS H. 20–1) shows how a garth could develop into an urban yard.

[9] Hall, ed., p. 213.

[10] *LM*, 2 August 1738.

FIG. 3.4 WORKPLACE AND HOME:
ROBERT DENISON'S HOUSE, TOWN'S END (*overleaf*)

The five-bay three-storey house (cf. Fig. 3.1) with front garden and railings, later known as Sheepshanks House in North St. Its two-storey extension on the right (south) was probably a counting house; gardens extended behind, down to the Sheepscar Beck, occupying the remainder of the long narrow field purchased for building the house, *c.* 1710; workshops in the garden (Fig. 3.5) developed into finishing shops along the north side of the field and eventually into Hope Mill.

View'. Further west Lockwood's Folly Gardens ran from Call Lane to the river.[11]

All these examples are of gardens at the rear of houses. Front gardens can be identified at two houses but they lay away from the central streets at Town's End.[12] One of these, Robert Denison's house in 1725, survived to appear in several early photographs with a walled and railed front garden, large even though the *Hope Inn* had been built in part of it (Fig. 3.4). This house had an even larger back garden, for it was sighted from Cavalier Hill by Buck, roughly drawn in the sketch book, but given its complete ornamental flower beds and paths in the published *Prospect* of 1720 (Fig. 3.5).

Townsmen already appreciated the open spaces beyond the compact centre. Had not Lodge's *Prospect* showed the river being fished and strollers on the riverside path? Had not both Place and Buck's *Prospects* made the Aire valley a pleasing vista of woods and meadows? And on Cavalier Hill there was a private pleasure ground and 'garden house', a Leeds Vauxhall, where Thoresby, Warburton and Buck took shelter when rain drove them away from the business of taking a *Prospect*.[13]

'Pleasant prospects' was a phrase common in Thoresby's vocabulary as he encountered a good town house in his historical perambulation. A short country walk to one of the three medicinal springs or spaws was popular; in the old park were 'very Pleasant Meadows by the Spring-Garden where a House of Entertainment was, of late Years, erected'; nearby 'the river Aire, along the Banks of which from [Armley] to the Town, is a most delicate Walk; the Water being calm and smooth that it can scarce be discerned to flow'.

[11] *LM*, 12 March 1728 and LCA, DB 197, unlisted survey of 18 Dec. 1754 by Matthew Bentley.

[12] Wray's informants (n.7 above) spoke of railed and walled gardens in front of houses in Briggate, even obstructing traffic near the Moot Hall, but no supporting evidence has been found.

[13] Atkinson, II, 333.

FIG. 3.5 TOWN'S END, 1720 (*overleaf*)

From Samuel Buck's *Prospect* of 1720, to the north of the area shown in Fig. 2.2. Numbers were used as keys: (15) was Red Hall, off the Headrow; (16), St John's church; to the right and below it (17) marks the workhouse and (18) [*top right*] a rear view of Robert Denison's house (Fig. 3.4) with ornamental garden but with small workshops alongside, together with tenter frames. There were others: those top left mark Crackenthorpe Garden (Fig. 7.3). Marsh Lane (19) comprised a straggle of roadside farmhouses with smaller buildings encroaching on their foldyards. The larger industrial building on the hill in the foreground (unnumbered) was probably a dyehouse from which the male and female figures are shown taking cloth.

Another 'House of Entertainment' had been built at 'Pasture Spring upon the little Rill commonly called Holbeck-Beck', the rill which was later to attract Marshall's flax mill. And to the west of Meadow Lane, which did indeed cross meadows on its way to Holbeck Moor, Thoresby noted Austrop Hall, a manor house newly built 'with several pleasant Fields called Hall-Ings'.

IN AND OUT OF TOWN

The immediate countryside may have been attractive for walks and fishing but it would be another forty years before the Dixon estate in Chapel Allerton (centred on Gledhow Hall) and Sir Thomas Denison's Meanwood Hall signalled an awareness of the out-townships as a place of residence. Nor were the hamlets of the in-townships yet utilised for new genteel residences, and the ancient manor houses available for purchase or letting were limited to Knowestrop Hall, North Hall (Burley Road), and the Halls of Great and Little Woodhouse. The wealthiest lawyer in town, Richard Wilson, was building up a miniature country park but it was at the back door of the old manor house of Leeds itself. The known instances of migration to country houses in the proper sense are limited to Denton Hall, Otley, purchased in 1717 by the James Ibbetson whose arms partnered Lord Irwin's on Cossins's map, and Carlton Husthwaite where the Kitchingmans moved about 1725.

The loyalty of the generality of merchants to residences in the central streets was never explicitly stated nor indeed has any contemporary discussion of the issue been noticed before the opening up of the new Park estate in 1767. Perhaps the case was too obvious to be stated.

One factor, operative in most continental and many of the older English boroughs, need not be considered. Although the Caroline borough of 1626 began with high hopes of regulating the whole local cloth trade, those hopes had to be abandoned. There was therefore no restriction of trading to those who dwelt in the burgages of Briggate, and indeed the would-be regulators of 1626 had arranged for the borough to be extended to all ten townships of the ancient parish. Thus the dyers worked unimpeded in Swinegate, the weavers at the Bank and the southern out-townships, while Woodhouse was generally reckoned to be a village of clothiers; and across the bridge in Meadow Lane and Hunslet Lane, outside the medieval borough, there were merchant houses built as substantially as any on a Briggate burgage.

In looking elsewhere for an explanation the character of the newly-built houses in the margins of Cossins's map gives a clue. Their classical architectural facades are deceptive if they are equated with such private houses of the leisured classes as were being then erected in Bath, York and Bloomsbury. Suspicions may indeed be first aroused when Cossins gives Mr Dixon's house in Call Lane a pair of loading doors on each floor and a hoist just below the roof. These Leeds houses were from time to time offered for letting by their owners or put up for sale. From the earliest days of the *Leeds Mercury* (1718) advertisements described these houses, and their fire insurance policies tell the same story: they were at once workplace and home (Fig. 3.4).

Under the same roof or in the adjacent yard was the counting house or office; in the yard was a warehouse for storing goods and housing for the horses and waggons which transported them. Thus Mr Bischoff's house in Kirkgate is shown by Cossins as having not only the usual porch entrance but a wide side-door for carts and waggons, not unlike one leading to a small inn-yard. The Atkinson house was perhaps the grandest on Cossins's map, eulogised by Thoresby for its interior decoration. When advertised in the *Mercury* for letting on 30 November 1725 the ambiguous duality was nicely caught: 'with a Coach House for a Gentleman or Packshop for a Merchant'. The same ambiguity often occurs in the advertisements for garden ground that was declared to be equally suitable for setting up tenter frames. The earliest advertisement for a brand-new house that was both mercantile and domestic is that of 17 September 1727: 'Woodhouse Lane – a Handsome fashionable House with Packing and Dressing Shops or without, a Stable, Garden and Croft', but Robert Denison's new house at Town's End certainly had mercantile outbuildings. Although not shown in Cossins's elevation they can clearly be seen in the Buck *Prospect* of 1720.

The merchant was thus in no different position from a shopkeeper or craftsman: he needed to be near his customers and his market. For cloth, as we have seen, this lay first on the bridge, then in Briggate, and after 1711 at the White Cloth Hall, Kirkgate.

For the growing number of professional men in the town the logic was the same. The vicar of St Peter's lived in a three-storey, five-bay house at the corner of Kirkgate and Vicar Lane; St John's vicarage, another three-storey, five-bay house, lay on the northern edge of town in New Street only because St John's itself had been built by John Harrison in the same field. While it was natural to consult the town's apothecaries in houses with shop-fronts set alongside other retail shops in Briggate or Kirkgate, the services of the doctors and the attorneys could also be obtained at the town centre in a room at their houses or in an office behind.

The number and variety of shops, offices, warehouses and other commercial buildings at this period cannot be determined in the absence of directories, and only a few appear in press advertisements. Other sources must be employed, particularly the registers of premises insured against fire with the Sun company of London, with their descriptions, locations, and the names and occupations of owners and occupiers, firmly establishing the unity of workplace and the home.[14] One family home became a workplace of a rather different kind when Ralph Thoresby retired early from business, bruised by losses, to become an antiquarian collector and author. One of the less antique items in his private museum was described in its published Catalogue as 'A piece of Ceiling of the Hall of this House just under the *Musoeum*, burnt to a perfect Cinder in the Night [in 1689] when the Family were asleep, yet no further damage done, kept as a Memorial of a watchful Providence'.[15]

The first policy to be taken out as an insurance against moments when Providence was less watchful over Leeds houses was in the name of Thoresby's cousin, the merchant William Cookson. It was issued on 5 November 1716. Perhaps it was a coincidence that Cookson, a high Tory and later twice mayor, felt threatened as Guy Fawkes night drew near, with its patriotic bonfires and exultant Whigs, for he had been imprisoned in Newgate as a suspect Jacobite during the 1715 rebellion. In March 1717 Alderman Atkinson insured the town's most highly-valued house. Robert Denison's house appeared in the policy registers a year later, and by the summer of 1719 those of Dixon and Douglas, so that by the time that Cossins drew his map four of the houses depicted on it had Sun policies, and there were thirty-eight other policy-holders in the town (Appendix III.1).

R. G. Wilson has identified thirteen merchant families who 'controlled the town's life' at this time, 'the legends of Leeds: it was their houses visitors noted for their opulence, their fortunes that the newspapers speculated about'.[16] Eight of these oligarchs had taken out fire insurance policies but the number of merchants in Table 3.2 is equalled by that of retailers. From the subscription list to Holy Trinity church in 1721, Wilson calculated that at this time there were just under fifty merchant firms – single or partnerships – and

[14] M. W. Beresford, 'Prometheus Insured: the Sun Fire Agency in Leeds during Urbanization, 1726–1826', *Economic History Review*, n.s., XXXV (1982), 373–89.

[15] Atkinson, I, 267.

[16] Wilson, Ch.2.

TABLE 3.2

Occupations of Holders of Fire Insurance Policies on Houses and Goods, 1716–25

Merchants	14
Retailers	14
Craftsmen	5
Widows and gentlemen	4
Professions	2
Others	3
TOTAL	42

Source: Guildhall Library, London, Sun Insurance Co., Policy Registers, vols. 6–21.

TABLE 3.3

Occupations or Designations of Subscribers to the Charity School, 1705

Occupation	Number of subscribers (percentage in brackets)	Occupation	Number of subscribers (percentage in brackets)
Professions	34 (15)	Craftsmen	27 (12)
Gentlemen and widows	36 (16)	Other	2 (1)
Merchants	51 (23)	Councillors and aldermen*	22 (10)
Retail trade	29 (13)	Non-resident	11 (5)
Wholesale trade	8 (4)		
		TOTAL	220

* Councillors and aldermen were so designated, without occupation being given

Source: LCA, DB 196/1, ff.1–7: Subscribers to a school for the 'Maintainance and Education of Forty Poor Children in the Knowledge and Practice of the Christian Religion as professed and taught in the established Church of England . . .'.

although only a few had yet begun to employ workmen to finish cloth on their own premises, most would have considered a warehouse, counting house and stable as necessary adjuncts to their houses.[17]

An appeal to fund a new Anglican church would hardly attract the support of dissenters. A little earlier, in 1705, the Charity School had appealed for subscriptions and although it was 'the Knowledge and Practice of the Church of England' which was to be taught to the forty children of the poor the subscription list included three Quakers and two dissenting ministers. The record includes the occupation of each subscriber (Table 3.3) except that 'councillor' and 'alderman' were considered a sufficient identification. As with the subscribers to Holy Trinity, merchants made up the largest group by far, and at least half the aldermen were also merchants.[18]

The urban character of Cossins's Leeds is not indicated solely by the number of merchant premises: it was a place where the widows and the spinster daughters of merchants were prepared to stay and live; it had its male annuitants and pensioners; retailers loom as large in Table 3.3 as craftsmen although there would have been many who performed both functions; the professions were represented by attorneys, doctors, apothecaries, schoolmasters and clergy. R. G. Wilson has treated the social composition of the town in detail: here it is only necessary to emphasise that every type of person mentioned in this paragraph would not find it incongruous to carry out his or her working and domestic life under the same roof; that complementary purchases of goods and services could be made within a short distance of home, whether in the open-air markets, the Cloth Hall, the inn-yards, the shops, the offices, or the surgeries. The members of the Corporation had no further to go for their meetings than the Moot Hall in Briggate, the ground floor of which was let for shops or storerooms.[19] In November 1727 the *Mercury* advertised afternoon classes in experimental philosophy in the same Moot Hall; Alderman Lawson's library could be consulted at the Grammar School, then still in the town centre, or Thoresby's at his Kirkgate museum with its overflow stored on the ground floor of a house in Vicar Lane, large enough to be converted after his death into two shops.[20] The new Cloth Hall in Kirkgate, like its larger successor in Call Lane, had the Assembly Rooms as its neighbour with balls,

[17] *Ibid.*, p.17, citing LCA DB 204/3.

[18] LCA, DB 196/1, ff.1–7.

[19] LCA, DB 204/8, f.61.

[20] LCA, DB 197, uncatalogued survey of 19 June 1728; there were also unsold copies of the *Ducatus* and *Vicaria*: *LM*, 7 Dec. 1725.

dancing classes, serious music, card playing and occasional exhibitions. Also close together at the centre were the inns, of which Cossins named only the two largest: multifarious centres of social and commercial activity, the venue for property auctions, cockfighting and travelling players, and the terminus for the increasing number of public coaches.

What set the limits to this compact collection of residences and workplaces? The significant name 'Town's End' was placed by Cossins alongside the northward continuation of Vicar Lane just before it began to traverse the open countryside as New Castle Road, an interesting long-distance ascription in itself. The shaded area on the map denoting continuous building did not come so far: on the west of what was later known as North Street there were only the Grammar School, and then the new house of Thomas Denison;[21] on the east were three of the Leylands closes and the house of Robert Denison. The open nature of the buildings here is also indicated in the Buck *Prospect* of 1720 (Fig. 3.5).

Even when not marked by gates or defences the boundary line of a medieval borough was important for its inhabitants as marking the limit of jurisdiction, privileged tenure and privileged dealing. Privileges of this sort meant little in eighteenth-century Leeds but the traditional limits of the town survived in its four Bars. In larger towns a bar was a substantial gate but the only suggestion in Leeds of a gate is an early eighteenth-century plan showing the East Bar near Timble Bridge as two turrets on either side of the road with an ill-defined double barrier across the road itself;[22] Cossins simply marks a York Barr but Thoresby had noticed a reference in the parish register of 1588 to the burial of a townsman living by a 'Briggstone at Kirkgate End'.[23] West Bar at the end of Boar Lane was not shown by Cossins, nor was North Bar by the workhouse but he did show Burley Barr where the Headrow became Park Lane: tolls were certainly collected here from those coming in to market. Nearby the entrance to Woodhouse Lane was blocked by a swing gate (hence Lidgate as a street name), shown by Cossins as closed. A similar function was performed by Park Stile near the West Bar and Church Stile near the East Bar. If the main purpose of a Bar was toll collection there remained the southern entrance at the bridge. Since

[21] See below, p.59

[22] G. D. Lumb, 'York or East Bar Leeds', *PTh.S*, XXVI (1924), 171.

[23] G. D. Lumb, 'A Thoresby Manuscript', *PTh.S*, II (1891), 158–60.

TABLE 3.4

Distances from Bars to Township Boundaries, 1752

Bar	Boundary	Township	Miles	Furlongs	Yards
Woodhouse	stone	Headingley	1	2	138
North	stone	Potter Newton	0	7	132
Bradford (Burley)	runnel at Grey Stone	Burley	1	1	11
Leeds (Bridge)	Dow bridge*	Hunslet	0	5	127
Leeds (Bridge)	bridge stone†	Holbeck	0	3	0
Marsh Lane (East)	Wyke bridge	Osmondthorpe	1	7	5

* 4 f. 127 yds further to Hunslet.
† 3 f. further to Holbeck Moor.

Source: 'Matthew Bentley's mensuration of the Highways repaired by Leeds', June 1752: LCA, DB 197/1, ff. 540–41.

the cloth market was held on the bridge itself, tolls were collected at its southern end, presumably the 'Leeds Bar' of 1752 (Table 3.4). Further along Hunslet Lane and Meadow Lane were Stones Ends to mark the township boundary.

None of the four Bars was located on the township boundary, so that they were clearly intended to mark some significant inner area. Yet they could not have been markers for the borough limits, for that never extended as far as either East or West Bar and probably not to Burley Bar. West Bar and Burley Bar certainly marked the entrance to the manorial park so perhaps all the Bars were set before the borough was added to the manor.

The origin of the suburb south of Leeds bridge, the South Division, is as mysterious as it is intriguing. Certainly its houses pre-dated the Denison houses at Town's End by at least a generation for their back view, with smoking chimneys, appeared in Lodge's *Prospect*, one house rising to three storeys; and they cluster beyond the bridge in the Buck *Prospects*, although less prominently from their greater distance from the artist's viewpoint. The earliest surviving rate book, of 1713, has substantial properties in the South Division. Although it is not possible to locate more than a few of these precisely they must have lain along either Hunslet Lane or Meadow Lane. Thoresby noted 'the pleasant seats of Magistrates in Hunslet Lane . . . which being the London Road is especially noted by Travellers for the pleasant Gardens and delicate seats of many Gentlemen'.

Travellers from London and the south, where a 'delicate Seat' might imply a country house, would perhaps have hesitated to use the phrase in Hunslet Lane, for early property advertisements and deeds indicate that these Gentlemen had warehouses and workshops alongside or within the premises just like any merchant's house north of the river.[24]

The dimensions of Cossins's map prevented the inclusion of much ground south of the river: his bottom margin ran just south of Bowman Lane, and the direction of 'London Road' (i.e. Hunslet Lane) had to be distorted to fit it in. However, three houses from these frontages are pictured in his margin (Busk, Douglas and Markham) and they are indistinguishable in style and size from houses in Briggate, Kirkgate and Boar Lane. Only the riverside house of William Milner with its orchards and gardens has the appearance and style of a small country house, but while it had fields to the east it looked directly across the river to the waterworks steam engine, and the warehouse and wharves of the Navigation, while to its south and west Cossins's cross-shading indicated the built-up frontages of Hunslet Lane and Meadow Lane.

There was one difference however between the town-centre houses and those of Busk, Markham and Douglas: the former, new as they were, had had to conform at their rebuilding to the existing width of building plots derived from Briggate burgage plots and Kirkgate garths, narrow frontages no more than 20 yards at their widest and no more than 80 yards deep. Those who built in the same style south of the river did so in plots derived from roadside fields, typically of 60 yards width. If they wished, like the builder of Austrop Hall, they could achieve a degree of isolation by setting the building at the further end of the field but the majority clearly valued direct access and their houses fronted the public highway. Later, if they wished, they could add other buildings to complete the frontage across the whole width of the original field, either for their own use or letting. The rate books[25] indicate this type of development of groups of consecutive high-value houses under the same ownership, the first owner-occupied and the others tenanted.

In this sense the houses of the South Division pointed the way to what Cossins showed at Town's End where there were roadside houses, each occupying a separate field whose development can be charted. In 1689 Thomas Denison I, 'merchant adventurer of

[24] e.g. *LM*, 22 Jan. 1722: 'a good House fit for a Master Cloth Worker with conveniences' in Simpson's Fold; LCD 4532 (1743), Smithson's Fold, Meadow Lane.

[25] See Chapter 4.

England' according to the inscription on his grave, bought two fields lying just north of the town; they were known as Green Close and Long Close, each of 1½ acres. Long Close was indeed long, for it extended all along the north side of St John's churchyard to Wade Lane emphasising how John Harrison must have purchased a field of similar size in 1631 when he decided to build the church, vicarage, and almshouses. Immediately south of Harrison's purchase, the block of properties forming the north side of the Headrow also has the same overall dimensions so that the Headrow itself may have been laid out at the head of the borough on one such close.

Thomas Denison left his two closes to his son who built at their east end the house drawn by Cossins both in the margin and in position; the remainder of the hedged closes gave Denison a little of the isolation of a country villa – certainly compared with his previous house in Kirkgate. On the opposite side of New Castle Road the house of Robert Denison was also built in a 1½-acre close.[26] The two Denisons had chosen to have houses that were not part of a street frontage, a terrace or a square; out of town and yet not remote but – it must be emphasised – a fashion not to be followed by others for another fifty years.

A mild form of dissent to have so few proselytes! The 'Handsome fashionable House' in Woodhouse Lane advertised on 12 September 1727 was followed by a 'new, brick, four storey' house of 30 April 1728 but even by 1770 Jefferys's map shows no more than six houses in Woodhouse Lane, and the same number outside the North Bar and Burley Bar.

Dissent in a more usual sense was to be found outside the orthodox limits of town in 1725. Cossins shows only one nonconformist meeting house in the town centre, Call Lane Meeting House (1691). The Presbyterian (later Unitarian) Meeting (House) of 1674 was built just outside the West Bar on land ceded by the owner of the manor house; the Quaker Meeting and Burying Place were shown in a field between Water Lane and the river, on cheap land affording safety from vandalism, to which the unpopularity of the Quakers gave rise. The Methodists in turn were to suffer from the attention of mobs when meeting in the homes of retailers and craftsmen; a move to the Bank brought similar unpleasant attentions from their neighbours and finally an isolated site was purchased at Boggart Close on the slope of Quarry Hill,[27] a field destined to have an important place in the history of house-building in Leeds.[28]

[26] LCD 2284 (ii); WRRD, L 259/345 and 334/439–40.
[27] Wray, as in n.7 above, II, f.123.
[28] See Chapter 7.

Harrison's Grammar School of 1624 and St John's church of 1631, as we have seen, were built in fields that then lay outside the town's end; Harrison also built his hospital, that is almshouses, adjacent to the church. The almshouses of the Jenkinson foundation (1643) were at Park Stile where Boar Lane came to the edge of the manorial park on Mill Hill; Iveson's (*c.* 1695) were in Lady Lane near the workhouse (1623) and Potter's (1736) were outside the North Bar in Wade Lane in a close purchased from Thoresby's son. These sitings cannot however be ascribed to some aversion to the poor as neighbours since the Denisons were happy to build new houses in fields adjacent to the workhouse and Iveson's almshouses, and there were older almshouses intermingled with ordinary houses in Vicar Lane, Call Lane and Kirkgate. Like the later Infirmary (and for that matter the Town Hall, the railway stations or the Yorkshire College in their day) they were simply occupying the nearest available land to the edge of town, neither shunning the town nor being shunned by it.

Of the houses of the poor, at the opposite end of the social spectrum from the merchant houses portrayed on Cossins's map, very little is known. Their presence is attested by the exemptions which the collectors of the Hearth Taxes had allowed to those who were in receipt of poor relief but there must have been very many without separate dwellings, living in tenemented houses. The numbers resident in the town workhouse are known for a slightly later period[29] but nothing of those assisted by out-relief that was financed by the poor rate, by the rents of lands donated to the town charities, and by the various collection plates at Sunday services.

In compensation, as it were, the administration of poor relief produced a series of documents, the poor rate books, where the assessments of property were sufficiently detailed to widen the study of early eighteenth-century buildings beyond those dignified enough to merit Cossins's notice.

To take the rate book which survives from the year after the publication of the Cossins map: fifteen of the houses on the face of the map or delineated in its margins can be identified.[30] The largest rates in town were paid by the Ibbetson house in Kirkgate and the Lee house in Briggate (each at 22*s.* 6*d.*); they were closely followed by Jacob Busk's Meadow Lane house (20*s.* 6*d.*) and Alderman Atkinson's finely decorated and domed house behind Call Lane which had been singled out for particular praise by Thoresby (20*s.*). With the lower assessments the collectors moved among the

[29] 1739–48 in LCA, DB 3, f. 213; 1754–55 in endpapers of LCA, LORB 94 and 110.
[30] LCA, LORB 9: 10 Aug. 1726.

otherwise anonymous houses which peopled the cross-shaded built-up areas of Cossins's plan, concluding with payments of single shillings and of sixpences. These lesser properties did not figure among the early fire insurance policies and they were rarely distinguished separately in the newspaper property advertisements: with the rate books they come into their own.[31]

[31] A manuscript notebook donated to the Thoresby Society by Job Hanson (and now MS. Box V.10) contains 775 names, alphabetically arranged within streets, and has the title 'Leeds Directory of 1725'. The donor, a cashier, was living at 1, Laurel Terrace, Armley in 1925, but his name does not appear in the Leeds Directory of 1927. The source of Hanson's material is mysterious: there were certainly no printed directories at so early a date, either local or national, on which he could have drawn. If it is a compilation from scattered sources it is no easier to deduce what these could have been. The rate books of that date do not give street locations against the names; the 775 names are too numerous to derive from one year's contribution to the West Riding Registry of Deeds: they are not the names of christenings, baptisms and burials for 1725 drawn from the parish registers; the most likely but intriguing explanation is that Hanson possessed or had access to a contemporary manuscript that is now lost.

There is not space to print the names here but the geographical distribution of their addresses is shown below. It is a distribution which is in accord with the later evidence from the private census (Table 5.3), and where (as for New Street) there is other evidence to confirm the number of houses, confidence in the authenticity of Hanson's source is strengthened:

Location of Names in Hanson's 'Directory', 1725

Town Centre		*Fringe, south of river*	
Briggate	137 (18%)	Meadow Lane	81 (10%)
Kirkgate	127 (16%)	Hunslet Lane	21 (3%)
Headrow	61 (8%)		
Boar Lane	23 (3%)		
Vicar Lane	33 (4%)		
'Tenters and Swinegate'	32 (4%)		
Mill Hill	41 (5%)		
Fringe, north of river		*Fringe, east of town*	
New Street	5 (1%)	Mabgate	34 (4%)
Lydgate	6 (1%)	Marsh Lane	49 (6%)
Woodhouse Bar	6 (1%)	Quarry Hill	40 (5%)
Town's End	21 (3%)	Bank	51 (6%)
Park Lane	7 (1%)		
		TOTAL	775

4
An Interior View, 1740–41

. . . all and every the Occupiers of Land, Houses, Tithes and over visible Estates real and personal, of all and every the Inhabitants.

Heading to Poor Rate Book, 1741
(LCA, LORB 10, f.1).

In Cossins's map of 1725 the superior dignity of certain private houses had been signified by their appearance in the cartouche, adjoining a key letter: an 'I' for 'Lawyer Wilson, house and garden'. From 1741 onwards and in the absence of a large-scale street plan until 1815, superior houses can be located by their higher assessments in surviving poor rate books for whose entries, with patience, a geographical order can be reconstructed: thus the Manor House, still the Wilson family home, appears among the assessments in the section of the town poor rate book for 1741 that is headed 'Mill Hill Division', rated at £21. In the previous year the rate assessments had been copied into a notebook and rearranged geographically by the schoolmaster, Thomas Wilson; hence the two dates that appear in the title to this Chapter for the 'Interior View' of large and small properties that a collation of the two sources makes possible.

SOURCES

The town's poor rate books were kept in a room at the workhouse where its trustees met and where the assessments could be scrutinised by any ratepayer contemplating an appeal. In 1844 they passed into the custody of the Board of Guardians and in 1929 to the Public Assistance Committee. In 1949 the surviving books were given to the local history collection at the Leeds Central Library (Table 4.1). The losses are severe: the volume for December 1741 is numbered '86', although it now has only nine predecessors, the earliest being for May 1713; 127 books once covered the years between 1742 and 1805 of which only twenty-six survive, the last being for May 1805. One volume of highway rate assessments from 1765 has crept into the collection, usefully bridging the gap between

TABLE 4.1

Number of Rate Books Surviving, 1713–1805

Year	Number	Year	Number
1713	2	1748	1 complete, 1 partial
1714	2	1750	1
1716	2	1751	1
1717	2	1752	2
1726	1	1754	1
1741	1	1765	1
1742	3	1774	2
1743	4	1790	1
1744	2	1795	1
1745	2	1800	1
1746	2	1805	1
1747	1		

Sources: LCA, LORB 1–37; LCA, TN/M 14/12 (1748, Kirkgate and Mill Hill). All are for the poor rate except 1765 which is for a highway rate.

May 1754 and May 1774. The poor rate books were used for levying the Constable's rate and the highway rate between 1745 and 1748 and probably in other years; no separate assessment books for the Improvement Act rates are known. The Bridge Act rate in 1750 was certainly based on the poor rate assessments.

According to its heading each book contained the assessments made on land and buildings within the in-township 'for and towards the necessary reliefe of ye Lame impotent Old Blind and poor people not able to worke, and for putting out Apprentices'. Thus a rate book forms a virtual directory of the town. Assessments were revised two or three times a year, taking note of changes in ownership and occupancy, and noting when a house was 'vacant'.

Each entry names the owner and the occupier; the gross annual rent of land and buildings had to be given in separate columns, since land paid at a higher rate per £ than buildings; and further columns proceed to a net rent, allowing for expenses and repairs. The sums due, dependent on the rates levied per £ on the particular occasion (Appendix IV.1), are entered in the final column.

The location of particular houses is not immediately apparent in the rate books which have separate sections for each of the eight ancient 'Parts' or 'Divisions', but only those for High Town and Kirkgate from Call Lane have occasional rubrics separating Briggate from the Headrow, and no indication is given of house numbering which probably did not then exist; nor is one side of Briggate distinguished from the other.

In the earliest surviving books there appears to be no systematic order of entries, but from 1741 onwards a comparison of successive books shows that properties occupied the same position each year, their order being disturbed only to insert a building erected since the previous assessment. The 'estimate of all the estates' which Thomas Wilson entered into his commonplace book in 1740 has its entries in the same order as the December 1741 rate book, but with street names entered helpfully as rubrics.[1]

There was a considerable tenacity of ownership from generation to generation. Table 4.2 shows that of twenty-two groups of properties comprising some 100 inns, shops and houses on the west side of Lower Briggate only six changed their proprietor's name between 1740 and 1774. Changes of tenancy were more frequent, and the proportion of tenanted houses was high:[2] at least thirteen of the owners in Table 4.2 did not live in Lower Briggate. Changes of ownership and tenancy gave rise to evidences extraneous to the rate books which enable properties to be more closely located within their streets. Notices of houses for sale or to let increasingly became the staple of advertisements columns in the *Mercury* (and after 1754 in the *Leeds Intelligencer*). Such advertisements were often prodigal of space in describing a property, and its location was usually given. The sales and leases of property gave employment to conveyancing attorneys (solicitors) and thereby produced documents which may still survive to be consulted in archives or private custody.

A Registry of Deeds was established for the West Riding at Wakefield in 1704 and it became increasingly common for conveyances to be enrolled there, where they still remain.[3] Even properties that did not change hands were liable to be mortgaged and thus have their particulars entered in the volumes of enrolments at Wakefield. Admittances to the copyhold properties of Leeds manor and the

[1] LCA, LORB 10; LCA, DB 204/3 contains notes made by Thomas Wilson from a 1740 rate book, now lost.

[2] See below, p.88

[3] The registers are now in the custody of the West Yorkshire Joint Archive Service, in the former Registry building in Newstead Road, Wakefield (Bibliography, §1, below, p.524). The earliest registration of a deed for a Leeds property is February 1704: WRRD, A20/34.

TABLE 4.2

Continuity of Ownership, High Town Middle Division, 1740–74

Owner 1740	Owner 1752	Owner 1754	Owner 1765	Owner 1774
Moore	*	Bagnall	*	*
Pinckney	*	Cottam	*	*
Leyland	*	*	*	†
Smeaton	*	*	*	†
Hey	*	*	*	†
Walker	*	*	*	†
Atkinson	*	*	*	†
Jackson	*	*	*	†
Topham	*	*	*	†
Harrison	*	*	*	†
?	?	Wells	?	?
Lambert	*	*	*	†
Cloudesley	*	*	*	†
Penrose	*	Sechwell	*	*
Barker	*	*	*	†
Sleigh	*	*	Atkinson	?
Pease	*	*	Taylor	?
Denison	*	*	*	†
Denison & Pease	*	*	*	†
Wolrich	*	*	*	†
Kenion	*	*	*	†
?	?	Armistead	*	Dalley

Italic denotes owner-occupied.
* unchanged ownership since previous rate book.
† unchanged ownership since 1740.

Sources: LCA, DB 240/3; LORB 29, 31, 31A and 32.

Kirkgate manor were recorded in court rolls and court books but the majority of Leeds properties were freehold.[4]

Plans of properties were rarely attached to deeds before the late eighteenth century but the very absence of a plan made it the more

[4] The Leeds manor court book (1790–1854) with transcripts of wills and land transfers form parcel 5 of LCD 5258; see also LCA, DB 149 for surveys of the copyholds. For the Kirkgate cum Holbeck manor see LCA, DB 147.

necessary for the documents to include full topographical descriptions and measurements, and to name the owners of adjacent properties, especially since houses did not then have numbers. When it is known from deeds that property *B* had *A* on one side and *C* on the other it is not difficult to search for a sequence of entries, *A B C*, in the rate book and so begin to establish the geography of a street.

When the internal order of the rate books was revealed in this way it was soon apparent that the assessors were moving down one side of a street and then the other, and the solution of the problems in the long streets of Kirkgate and Briggate was expedited by finding that a Middle Division had come into existence covering the central part of Briggate and the western end of Kirkgate, and therefore confining the Briggate entries in High Town Division to the northern end of that street, and the Mill Hill Division entries to the extreme southern end. At a late stage in the research, confidence in this method of identifying properties was strengthened by the discovery of a document among unsorted solicitors' papers which was probably drawn up while the series of rate books was complete, perhaps in 1835 when a municipal rate had to be levied for the first time: in it all Briggate property owners are named and located Yard by Yard, with the names of early eighteenth-century ratepayers added.[5]

Another aid to deciphering the geography of the rate assessments is the survival from 1680 onwards of rentals for the blocks of urban property owned by the town's various charities, together with minute books (from 1685) of the Committee for Pious Uses which administered these endowments.[6] In 1728, when the original 199-year leases of the land left to the highways repair charity were about to expire, the Committee had a survey and revaluation made, issuing new leases at twice the old rents;[7] in 1754 a further survey was made, covering all the Charity lands;[8] and in 1792–94 a third survey was supplemented by an atlas of plans.[9] Thus when a Pious Uses property occurs in the columns of a rate book the exact position reached in the assessors' procession can be determined, and the surveys enable the structure of these properties to be determined (Table 4.3). The Tables in this chapter and the frontage profiles in Figures 4.3 and 4.4 rest on the exploitation of one or more of the sources described above.

[5] LCA, DB 149/32.
[6] LCA, DB 197/1–2.
[7] LCA, DB 197 unlisted survey of June 1728.
[8] LCA, DB 197 unlisted survey of 18 Dec. 1754 by Matthew Bentley.
[9] LCA, DB 204/8.

TABLE 4.3

Fifteen Call Lane Frontage Houses, 1728 and 1754

Tenant (1728)	Frontage length	Rooms on frontage	Number of storeys
Lodge and Wilkinson	60′9″	3	2 + cellar
Lodge and Wilkinson	30′9″	1	1
Mrs Greaves	40′3″	2	2 + cellar
Oates	68′5″	4	2 + cellar
Teal	22′6″	[two cottages]	
Towers	22′6″	2	2
Oates	14′6″	1	1
Denison	[not stated]	10	2 + garret + cellar
Oates	46′4″	3	2 + garret + cellar
Whalley	24′4″	2	2 + cellar
Mrs Wilkinson	58′2″	4	2 + garret + cellar
Robinson	12′6″	[cottage]	
Lambertson	22′10″	1	2 + cellar
Denison	61′4″	5	2
Mrs Waybran	28′0″	2	1

Sources: LCA, DB 204/3, ff.175–77 and LORB 10, ff.65–67; survey of Grammar School estate by Matthew Bentley, May 1754: LCA, DB 197, unsorted; the whole frontage, from south to north, was stated to be 193 yards so that the large Denison house was probably set back in Assembly Court; cf. a survey of June 1728, *ibid.* and large-scale plan of 1793, DB 204/8.

One particular example of identification outside the central streets may be given in conclusion; Christopher Thompson was assessed in the Little Woodhouse section of the North West Division in 1740 for land worth £26 a year but for nothing on buildings; this was explained by a marginal note, ‘a new house empty’. In the *Mercury* for 27 January 1741 Thompson’s ‘new-built House’ was advertised for letting together with 8 or 18 acres of land, whichever a tenant wanted. Particulars of this house and the surrounding 20 acres of Bannister Closes appear in a mortgage enrolled at Wakefield in 1745, and among the papers for Little Woodhouse Hall which survived in a solicitor's office is a sketch of the elevation of 'Mr Thompson's house', *c.*1740 (Fig. 4.1); Bannister Closes reappear in deeds and sale plans whenever the estate came on the market until they were finally submerged under the villas of Clarendon Road.[10]

LAND

In the *Prospects* and on Cossins's map there were three kinds of open ground within the township: an outer ring of fields; the surviving crofts in the town centre, hemmed in by streets; and the gardens (garths) at the rear of almost every street-frontage house. The garths were not separately rated from their buildings so that in the two Middle Divisions the 'land' columns of the rate books are empty. Kirkgate Division did have crofts between the street and the river, a third of them in one ownership, but the rates paid for them made up no more than 1 per cent of the 'land' rates of the in-township. At the other extreme the rates on fields in the extensive North East Division contributed one-third to this total (Table 4.4).

In the very much smaller South Division there were enough inroads upon fields for the rents from land to be reckoned only one-fifth of those from buildings. In Mill Hill Division, where fields came as far as the end of Boar Lane, the town centre buildings on the mill islands and in Swinegate and Briggate were so valuable that 'land' assessments totalled only one-sixteenth of those buildings; the mills and the Navigation, whose warehouse and wharf lay within this Division, paid nearly as much as all the other buildings put together. In the North East Division the 'land' assessments loomed larger and just exceeded the yield from buildings; in the East and North West the rents from land were almost as large as in the North East and considerably exceeded those from buildings. Here if anywhere was rural Leeds,[11] and here was the reservoir of agricultural land upon which subsequent building development would have to draw (Fig. 4.2).

[10] 1741: LCA, LORB 10, f.79; 1745: WRRD, SS 579/781; sketch plan: LCA, DB 5; for later developments see Chapter 10.

[11] The acreage of a landholding was not recorded in the rate books, and has to be sought in scattered sources: an advertisement in *LM*, 27 Sept. 1768, for example, reveals that the Iveson estate (the largest in 1741, Table 4.5) then comprised 112 acres.

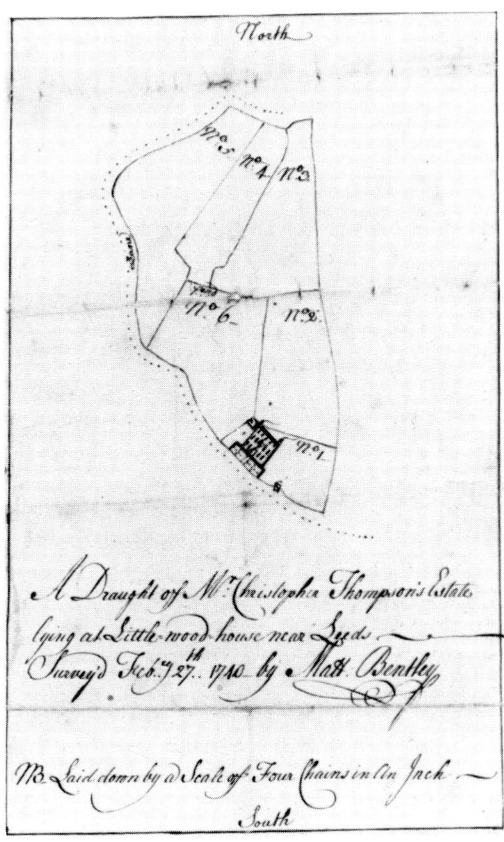

FIG. 4.1 RURAL LEEDS, 1740: THE MANOR HOUSE AT LITTLE WOODHOUSE

'A Draught of Mr Christopher Thompson's Estate, lying at Little-woodhouse near Leeds', by Matthew Bentley; the five-bay, three-storey mansion, then freshly built on the site of an older manor house in no. 1 of the six Bannister Closes. The 'lane' is Kendal Lane and the house, enlarged, still stands.

TABLE 4.4

Relative Rateable Values of Buildings and Land, by Divisions, 1741

	Total assessment £	Buildings £	Land £	Land as percentage of total
Town centre				
High Town	2241	2222	19	1
High Town Middle	748	748	–	–
Kirkgate Middle	737	737	–	–
Kirkgate	1780	1744	36	2
Periphery				
South	1569	1293	276	18
East	1845	805*	1040	55
North East	2318	1123	1195	52
North West	1528	552	976	64
Mill Hill	3097	2929†	168	5
TOTAL	15,863	12,153	3710	23

* Includes water mills (£230).
† Includes Navigation (£500) and water mills (£660).

Source: LCA, LORB 10.

Table 4.5 ranks the twenty largest individual assessments on land, and not surprisingly all but two of these properties lay in the rural Divisions. Only two of the larger estates in Table 4.5 lay near the town, those of Wilson (the Park estate, Chapter 6) and Pawson (the North Hall estate, Chapter 5). The Iveson and Torr properties were attached to working farms but those of Milner, Spencer and Bannister had no farm buildings and were each let to a number of different tenants. In the three rural Divisions seventy-seven properties consisted of land only.

It has already been shown that the fields immediately adjoining the town were small: they were also in dispersed ownership. Of the 107 separate holdings in the peripheral Divisions (Appendix IV.2) fifty-one were rented at £10 a year or less, and seventy-five at £20 or less. Of these, fifty-six lay in the two northern Divisions, where the

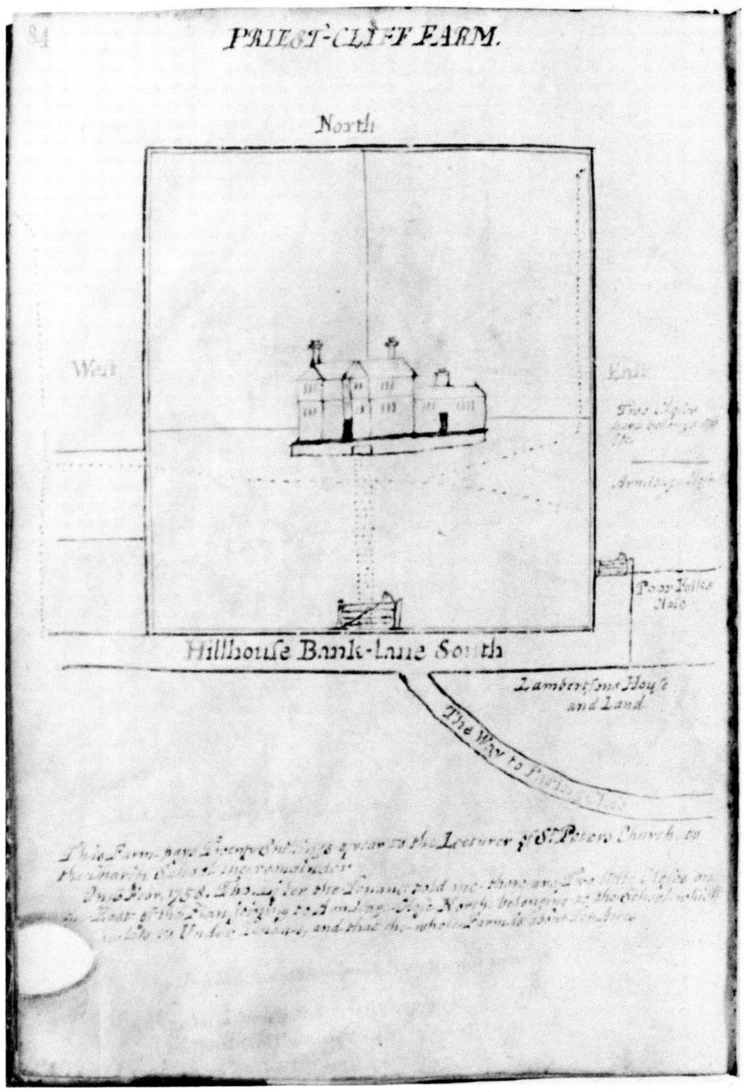

FIG. 4.2 RURAL LEEDS, *c.* 1759: PRIESTCLIFF FARM IN THE EAST DIVISION

Priestcliff Farm lay on Ellerby Lane at the centre of a ten-acre holding which formed part of the endowment of the Town Charities (Pious Uses) Committee. The fields remained unbuilt until after 1847 when the house, possibly rebuilt, was known as Ellerby Lodge.

TABLE 4.5

Landownership: Highest Rated Proprietors, 1741

Division	Name		Value
East	Mrs Iveson (Black Bank)		150†
North West	Ord		149†
North East East	Pawson*	98 42	140†
East	Baynes		130†
Mill Hill	Wilson*		122†
East	Sir W. Milner		119
North West	Spencer		118
North East	Torr		116†
North West North East	Bannister*	64† 40	104
North West	St John's church		94
North East	Watkinson		83†
North West	Denison		79†
North East	Atkinson		70†
South	Bever		65†
North East	Ibbetson*		64†
North East	Fearn		54†
East	Sharp		53†
South Kirkgate	Arthington	41 12	53
North East	Sir W. Rooke		49
North East	Ald. Scott		45

* Settled estate acts for this estate later.
† House property attached to this land not included here.

Source: LCA, LORB 10.

assessed properties were characteristically made up of a low-value building and one of these low-valued pieces of land, the petty estate of a working clothier. By the end of the eighteenth century traditionalists were mourning the passing of the clothiers, driven away to Pennine villages, according to the conventional wisdom, by rising rents as Leeds urbanised.[12]

[12] 'Since my remembrance there were many hundred Clothiers in the township of Leeds; and I believe there are but five now, and the reason is they are driven out by high rents': evidence of John Hebblethwaite, merchant, *Reports from the Select Committee . . . [on] the State of the Woollen Manufacture*, PP 1806, III, p.158.

The rate books do not specify the acreage of properties, so that differences between land values cannot be determined on a field-by-field basis yet the fact that the land in Mill Hill yielded fewer rents in total than the very much smaller area in the South Division confirms the expectation of a rising gradient of rents as the town centre was approached. The rate books are also uninformative on land use: the fields in the foreground of the *Prospects* seem to be under grass, but there was grass and grass. Hay was an important enough crop for tithe disputes to flourish, since horses were the draught animals of private carriages and commercial vehicles, and the town needed its fresh milk from cow keepers and their dairies. Horses and cows apart, grazing ground was more likely to be used by butchers and drovers.

Some fields were given over to market gardens but the most common addition to the landscape of the *Prospects* was the tenter frame, essential for the drying of cloth after it had been through the finishing processes, and valuable enough to form separate items of assessment in the earlier rate books. From these it can be seen that, if the rateable values were realistic, an owner who erected a couple of dozen tenter frames in his field was adding as much to its value as the erection of a pair of cottages in one corner of it, and this would have been important in the calculation of the gain from converting fields to building ground; and a likely delaying factor.

With the extensive agricultural land within the in-township, there were still parts to the north and west where, as in the countryside proper, a man's property might consist of land alone: the North West Division had thirty-one such proprietors in 1741, the North East twenty-seven, and the East fifteen. More common was the landowner who was also rated on buildings, ranging already in 1741 from single cottages to accumulations of tenanted buildings. Richard Wilson, living in the Manor House on Mill Hill, was the owner of extensive field land to the west:[13] this was rated at £122; the manor of North Hall to the east of the town, then owned by Henry Pawson, had land rated at £140 but also comprised buildings rated at £65 in all; Wilson also had buildings, rated at £94, made up of six cottage properties rated at £2 or under and nine houses rated respectively at £21, £19, £10, £9, £7, £6, £5, £4 and £4. Pawson was rated on seventeen cottages and on seven houses with values ranging from £4 to £10. Even in the town-centre Divisions of Table 4.4, where rate books had a predominance of blank spaces in the 'Land'

[13] See Chapter 6.

columns, there are encountered names of house proprietors that occur again in the rural Divisions as proprietors of land.

BUILDINGS

Eighteenth-century economists sensed a unique element in that part of the capital stock which took the form of land, for it could not be increased in area, nor in value except with difficulty, whereas the stock, equipment and buildings of merchants and manufacturers was seen to be augmented on every hand. The rate assessors of Leeds would have concurred.

From rate book to rate book the contribution of land to the total rateable value was being diminished as field after field was taken over for building ground: but every new building, whether cottage, house, warehouse or manufactory, left its mark by an additional entry in the next rate book; and any enlargement of premises likewise called for an upward revision of the previous valuation.

In 1740 the rate book enumerated 1582 separate buildings. The most densely occupied part of the town centre was at the junction of Kirkgate and Briggate, the Middle Division: with twenty-six properties to the acre it was thirteen times more densely occupied than the South Division; one-third of all the central buildings were located in the neighbouring Kirkgate Division.

For sheer size, although they did not contribute to the rates, the dominant buildings of 1740 were not domestic houses but the three Anglican churches, for no secular public building was yet as large; the Moot Hall was small by the standard of English provincial towns and the White Cloth Hall in Kirkgate occupied no wider a frontage than the neighbouring houses of that street.

The highest rated premises were not private residences: while the Manor House was rated at £21 per annum the nearby group of water mills (Fig. 1.2) was rated at £612 and the Nether Mills (Fig. 1.3) at £150. No house was rated at more than £40 but the rooms rented to traders at and alongside the Moot Hall were rated at £42. One of the two £40 assessments was for the *Old George* inn in Lower Briggate, and the other may also have been for an inn. The largest assessments that can be assigned with confidence to private residences lay in the £20 to £30 range (Appendix IV.3).

Nor, as yet, were the largest houses to be found outside the central streets: none of the twelve owner-occupied houses with the highest assessments lay far from the bridge; and only three of the most highly assessed tenanted houses were located in the outer Divisions, and they were farms rather than country houses. A similar distribution between Divisions is found in an additional class of assessment recorded between 1741 and 1754: at the end of the rate books for these years is a list of 'inhabitants assessed on personalty', defined as 'visible Estates real and personal'. In 1741 345 of the richer inhabitants paid these additional rates (Appendix IV.4). They were more likely to be encountered at the town centre but with the South Division again displaying more of an affinity with Briggate and the Headrow than with the rural Divisions. The personalty assessments do not seem to have become conventionalised, for the sums varied from year to year, and they were not in any fixed ratio to the value of a man's assessment on land or buildings.[14]

At another extreme from the high assessments of certain aldermen under all four categories (land, buildings, tenters and personalty) were assessments on buildings with annual rents as low as 15*s*. or £1 per annum, that is from 3*d*. to 5*d*. per week. (The averages for the East, North East, and North West Divisions were £2, £3 and £3 12*s*. respectively while those for High Town and the South Divisions exceeded £6.) In the town as a whole just over half the assessments were for buildings under £2 but Table 4.6 shows that the cottages of the East, North East and the rural part of Mill Hill Division raised the proportion there to between 60 and 70 per cent; only the larger houses of domestic clothiers which were interspersed with the cottages of Great Woodhouse kept the proportion in the North West Division as low as 48 per cent.

In the central area these low-value properties were most common in The Calls, Call Lane and Kirkgate where they lay backsides of frontage houses. Briggate and Kirkgate, although adjacent, were dissimilar. Although Kirkgate, as Cossins's map showed, was not spurned as a home by some of the best families in town, and contained the Assembly Rooms and a Cloth Hall, its average frontage house assessments were lower. Its backsides yard housing, even though less congested at that time than in Briggate, also attracted lower assessments. These were equal to or often lower than those of the many clothiers' cottages that had encroached on the Moor in Woodhouse or of the less numerous farm labourers' cottages of the North East and North West Divisions.

[14] According to Wilson, p.21, 'stock' here was 'an assessment on income'.

TABLE 4.6

Proportion of Properties Rated under £2, Town Centre and Periphery, 1740–41

	Number of properties rated under £2	Total number of properties	Percentage of properties rated under £2
Town centre			
Briggate, west side	52	147	35
Briggate, east side	47	145	32
Kirkgate	194	305	64
Calls and Call Lane	79	105	76
Lower Briggate	18	53	34
Vicar Lane	14	29	48
Headrow	73	145	50
Periphery			
South	100	211	48
East	192	290	65
North East	253	362	70
North West	74	154	48
Mill Hill*	157	254	62
TOTAL	1253	2200	57

* excluding Lower Briggate (above).

Sources: LCA, DB 204/3 collated with LORB 10.

These cottage-like assessments at the town centre will recur when the nature of backsides town-centre housing is examined in a later section. Meanwhile the structure of the rate books, with their differentiation of owners' names from those of occupants, permits further examination of the character of the town centre, particularly of the distribution of owner-occupied and tenanted properties. We begin with landlords.

LANDLORDS

A town with so many tenanted houses has to have its landlords. Leeds had landlords but not a landed lord. There were Georgian towns with most of their buildings in the hands of some great landowner, sometimes residing nearby but more commonly an absentee. Leeds was not one of these: no peer was to be found in its rate book; the interest of the earls of Cardigan was confined to the out-townships while the Harewood and Temple Newsam estates lay wholly outside the borough.

There were Georgian towns where the Corporation was a substantial property owner, often with interests in the town's commons: in Leeds the Corporation held not a single property. The truncated commons at Woodhouse were administered by the nine proprietors who held shares in the lordship of the manor, and the area was being steadily diminished by the encroachment of copyhold cottagers.[15] The Corporation met in a Moot Hall where it was only a tenant of the Charity trustees, and it was they who were the town's largest landlord with sixty-five houses or cottages on their rent roll. The Free (Grammar) School's rental included £110 from forty-three small houses and cottages in the town centre as well as from property in the country; the highways charity repaired bridges and maintained pavements and causeways from an annual income of £140 from a dozen properties in the Upper Headrow.[16]

No single landlord had this number of properties in the town (Table 4.7): in the central streets only James Pinckney and John Heald had more than twenty buildings, and in the rural Divisions only Alderman Jeremiah Barstow, Thomas Pease and Henry Pawson. The last-named was exceptional in having as a base for expansion the demesnes of the North Hall. Richard Wilson accumulated small properties near the Manor House on Mill Hill, but was more concerned with expanding his estate into agricultural land westwards.[17] Pinckney, Heald and Pease held no land and were typical of those who were using backside property for development. The capacity for such a development was limited by the area backside of a frontage although, as the next Chapter shows, no yard was completely infilled by 1740.

The purchase of a second frontage and yard would give an opportunity for further development. Alderman Barstow was rated in 1742 for five houses and twenty cottages in the South Division, the houses and three of the cottages having been 'purchased from

[15] LCA, DB 149 has surveys of licensed encroachments on the Moor and the manorial wastes.

[16] See n.6 above.

[17] See Chapter 6.

TABLE 4.7

Multiple Ownership: Ten or more Properties, 1740–41

Division	Owner	Number of buildings owned	Rateable values		
			Over £10	£2– £10	Under £2, cottages
Town centre					
High Town	Tildesley	17	1	10	6
	Preston	14	0	5	9
High Town Middle (Briggate)	Pinckney	25	3	5	17
Kirkgate	Heald	22	0	2	20
	Atkinson	15	2	3	10
	Wrigglesworth	14	0	0	14
	Ald. Cookson	13	5	2	6
	Flower	11	1	1	9
	Wilkinson and Priestley	11	0	2	9
Periphery					
South	Barstow	25	0	5	20
	Harlington	13	0	2	11
	Wilks	13	1	6	6
	Prince	11	0	0	11
	Mann	11	0	0	11
	Huntington	11	0	0	11
East	Wynne	15	1	1	13
	Parker	11	0	2	9
	Cookson	11	0	2	9
North East	Pawson*	24	0	7	17
	Bradford	17	0	0	17
	Shann	13	0	0	13
	Frankland	11	0	4	7
North West	Pease	24	1	5	18
	John Denison*	15	0	1	14
Mill Hill	Atkinson	19	0	1	18
	Wilson*	18	2	10	6
	Parkinson	18	0	0	13
	Sechwell	18	1	1	11
	Ald. Rooke*	11	5	4	2
	Robinson	11	1	1	8

* also substantial land.

Sources: LCA, DB 204/3 collated with LCA, LORB 10.

Douglas', but the market in whole urban plots seems to have been limited, and even by 1774 no single individual had acquired two or three adjacent main street frontages. Indeed there were few examples in 1740 of more than one frontage in the same hands: there were two Cookson houses (valued at £28 and £24) in different parts of Kirkgate, and a Dodgson pair in Briggate valued at £27 and £21; Samuel Ibbetson had the family house on the north side of Kirkgate, on which properties named The Square were to be developed later, and a second property on the south side.

The only continuous lengths of frontage under the same ownership were the Charity estates in the Upper Headrow, Vicar Lane and Call Lane, but these had not been agglomerated by piecemeal purchase: the original endowments had been streetside crofts with little or no building; the Headrow estate was a 1½-acre croft with only three cottages when Thomas Wade donated it in 1530, and the Call Lane site was an empty close of 2 acres with 193 yards frontage in 1585; Appendix V.3 shows the development by 1754. The Vicar Lane frontage (Appendix V.2) extended for 60 yards with two almshouses nearly adjoining.[18]

Table 4.7 lists the thirty ratepayers who had accumulated more than ten buildings by 1741. All possessed cottage property, but Sir William Rooke was exceptional in having so few. It was also uncommon to have nothing but cottage property: only seven were landlords of cottagers alone. For the township as a whole Table 4.8 shows that it was in the rural Divisions that such landlords were to be found, especially the North West.

There were clearly two bases of development for an ambitious landlord: one, for men like Pinckney and Heald, was in the yards of central streets; the other, for men like Pawson and Wynne, lay in the opportunities at the small industrial hamlets at Sheepscar mills and the Bank. Most fortunate were those who could take advantage of both situations by having substantial farm land as well as a frontage house in a main street with an empty fold or garth backsides.

Only one in seven of all these proprietors of urban cottages was a one-cottage man, the legendary urban peasant. He was invisible in Kirkgate, and hardly visible anywhere else in the town centre. Again, it was at Great Woodhouse, Sheepscar and the Bank that he had to be sought: but although there was no room for him yet at the edge of town he would eventually appear in the East End fifty years later as the owner of a pair of back-to-back houses.

[18] See Table 4.13 and surveys cited in nn.7–9 above.

TABLE 4.8

Number of Proprietors of Cottage Property, by Divisions, 1740–41

	Number of landlords			
	with some cottage property	with more than one cottage	with only one cottage property	with nothing but cottage property
High Town	54	53 (98%)	1 (2%)	2 (4%)
Kirkgate	70	70 (100%)	0 (–)	16 (23%)
Mill Hill	57	50 (88%)	7 (12%)	28 (49%)
South	24	22 (92%)	2 (8%)	7 (29%)
East	66	48 (73%)	18 (27%)	36 (55%)
North East	61	50 (82%)	11 (18%)	36 (59%)
North West	44	30 (68%)	14 (32%)	32 (73%)

Sources: LCA, DB 204/3 collated with LORB 10.

URBAN COTTAGES

Any page of the rate books for the central streets included properties as lowly rated as any of the rural cottages: in Kirkgate and The Calls the proportion exceeded two-thirds, very little different from that in the East and North East; and in Briggate they made up about one-third. The term used for these low-rated town-centre properties was one brought from the countryside, where one- and two-roomed houses were the general rule: it was 'cottage', and the term will be used in succeeding pages for all urban properties with rentals of £2 per annum or less.[19] The terms 'cottage' and 'front house' were used in the 1741 rate book, and were already widely employed in deeds, property advertisements and estate rentals. Matthew Bailey headed his survey of the Charity estates in May 1754: 'an exact Account of the Houses and Cottages'. Most of these cottages appeared in 'the Yards and Backsides belonging to each House': Josiah Oates's 'house' (Table 4.3) on the Call Lane frontage was of two storeys, a 'low room' and 'a chamber above' but in the yard was a one-storey, one-room 'cottage' and a second 'cottage' also of one storey, with

[19] The significance of the term was first demonstrated in Rimmer, *Cottages*.

two rooms; nearby a two-roomed but one-storey building on the street front occupied by Mrs Waybran was also termed a 'cottage'. Another neighbour lived in a house with 'four cottages adjoining backsides'; another frontage 'cottage' did not have its rooms specified but its small size is indicated by its short length of frontage, 12 ft 6 in. A cottage, therefore, was usually a one- or two-roomed house of one or two storeys.

The corresponding assessments for Call Lane in the rate book for May 1754 express the frontage and backside contrast by descending from entries for £18 and £15 to those of less than £2; and the same equation of low values with backside cottages and higher values with frontage houses can be demonstrated from the Charity estates in Vicar Lane, the Upper Headrow and Briggate.

No other contemporary property has left us rentals, but the same pattern of assessments can be found throughout the central streets in earlier rate books. In 1741 a succession of nine proprietors who can be located on the west side of Briggate below the Headrow had the following assessments [in £]:

A: *14*, 9, 3, 3, 3, 2, 2, 2	B: 3, 3	C: *16*, 8
D: *26*, 11, 11, 8, 8, 3, 2	E: *24*	F: *35*, 5
G: 6	H: *25*	
I: *35*, 14, 14, 5, 5, 4, 3, 3, 2, 2		

If these nine had been assessments of rural property it would look as though substantial farms jostled with yeomen's houses and labourers' cottages along a village street but in central Leeds the entries are too numerous for each of the nine to claim a street frontage. This part of Briggate was in fact where Cossins explicitly drew entrances to court yards behind the frontages, and nearly all the larger values italicised above can be identified from other sources as frontage houses: *A* was George Green, grocer, and until the making of the Victorian arcades a tunnel led from Briggate into a yard known as Green's Court; the assessment *D* can be identified with the owner of the *Rose and Crown*, and *F* with the *Talbot Inn*.

The smaller sums must represent buildings located *backsides*, in the phrase of the 1628 survey where a contrast with the more substantial frontage houses was actually made: '. . . only some fewe of the richer sort of the Inhabitants have theire houses more large and capacious: yett all lowe and straightened [i.e. straitened] on theire backsides'. It might seem wrong to assign values as low as £9 and £6 to a frontage, were it not that early nineteenth-century drawings and later photographs do show a succession of Briggate frontages ranging from four storeys to one, including small timber-framed houses which would not have been out of place in a village street. The skyline of this variegated frontage is shown diagramatically in Fig. 4.3 where the height of the rectangles is proportional to the rateable values, and the degree of backside infill achieved in 1740 is shown by the proliferation of low-rise rectangles in Fig. 4.4.

Some frontage properties had not commenced backside infill by 1740 or had progressed no further than one or two houses; it will also be noticed that while nearly all the infills included some cottage property, and some infills consisted wholly of it, it was possible to have subsidiary houses with greater rateable values, described in advertisements as 'substantial houses in the yard'. When these survived long enough to appear in photographs of courts and yards they can be seen next to the frontage property with the smaller properties further down the yard from the street, just as the inns, frequent occupiers of such building plots, had their larger rooms at the front, then the smaller rooms, and then some outbuildings at the end of the yard. The name 'Old Infirmary Yard' in Kirkgate preserved the memory of the period when the Infirmary had been housed in such a complex.

There can be no doubt that these units of development in Briggate had originated as burgage plots in 1207 although the decay of the medieval borough as a lively institution had taken the word 'burgage' from common speech and it was not incorporated in the post-medieval names for any of these units. 'Yard' and 'court' (an abbreviation of courtyard) were the usual terms, linked either to the name of a frontage proprietor or of an inn; 'burgage' was sometimes employed in the formal language of a conveyance or a will.

The street entrance to a yard lay through a tunnel under the frontage house; perhaps all yards once had exits at their further end, as into Lands Lane, but there is no sign of a back lane serving the burgages on the eastern side of Briggate nor those on the west of Lower Briggate. A few of these throughways have survived as public footpaths, particularly where there have been inns.

To preserve access to the infill it was necessary for any building within it to be set back against the edge of the plot, leaving the central space open; the width of the plots was great enough to make it possible, when demand pressed, to have a line of houses on both the

FIG. 4.3 BRIGGATE WEST SIDE, FROM HEADROW SOUTHWARDS: RATEABLE VALUES, 1740–41, FRONTAGE AND BACKSIDES PROPERTIES

The height of each rectangle is proportional to the rateable value of each property [*see* scale, *top left*]: behind the more valuable frontages many properties of lesser value had already accumulated on the former burgage plots in *backsides* yards.

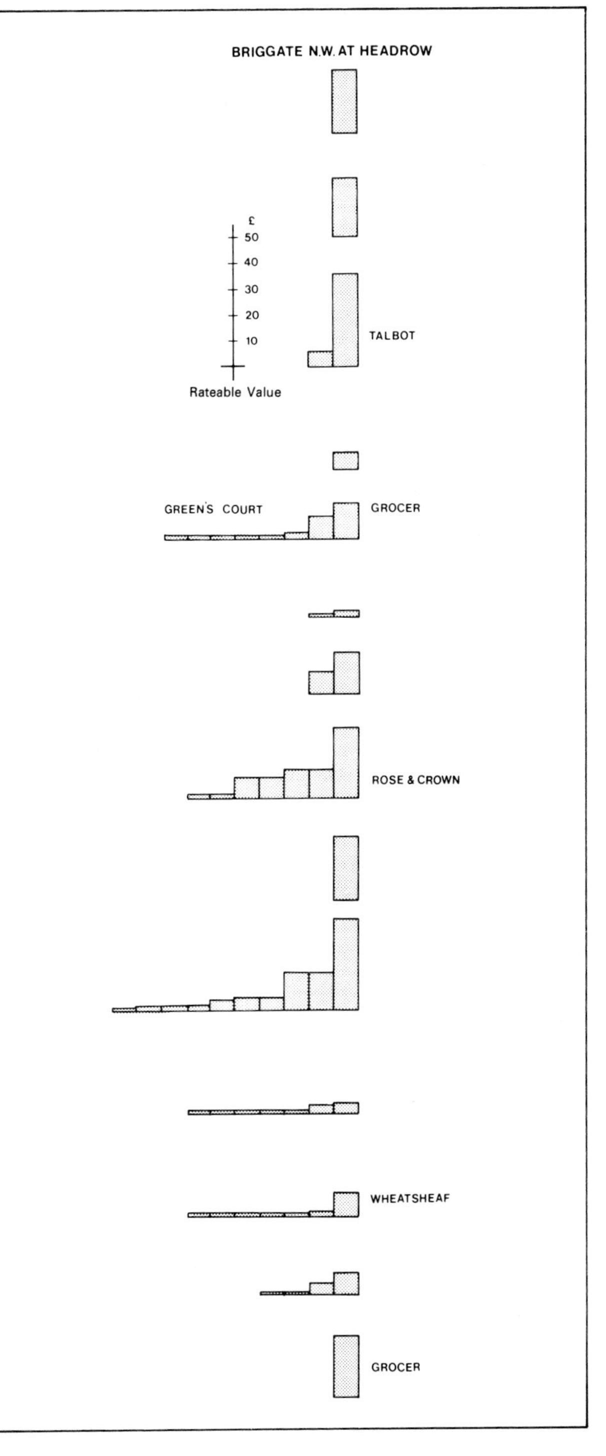

BRIGGATE N.W. AT HEADROW
£
50
40
30
20
10
Rateable Value
TALBOT
GREEN'S COURT
GROCER
ROSE & CROWN
WHEATSHEAF
GROCER

north and south sides, and still leave room for access (Fig. 4.5). When a frontage property was divided by inheritance or sale the two rows of infill houses could pass into different ownership: thus the conveyance of one half of Pinckney's Yard in 1716 comprised 'the north side of the House and the north side of the Fold'.[20]

Before infill began, and often until it was near completion, the backside buildings included some that were domestic to the frontage householder: his stable, his warehouse, his kitchen, his coal house and his 'necessary house' over a cesspit, all usually approached over the open yard; and if the necessary house was approached from inside it could still protrude even when the yard was a public way as in Pepper Alley, Vicar Lane.[21] The domestic equipment of the Fold is illustrated by the conveyance of a house in Call Lane with 'that Backyard or ffold on the South Side of the Messuage, two Coalheaps, one Necessary House or Privity [*sic*], one Middenstead or Dunghill'.[22] Like the privies in the later back-to-back yards, the necessary houses were often shared. The provision of 'six new boghouses or privies in the backsydes' for yard houses in the Lower Headrow facing the Corn Market (1743) was exceptionally generous.[23]

The term 'fold' for Pinckney's Yard in 1716 is as interesting an intrusion into Briggate as the term 'cottage'. Like 'cottage' both must have come by analogy from the streets of the former village. In Kirkgate and The Calls the backside gardens (garths) are called *folds* in many sixteenth- and seventeenth-century deeds, recalling an older use of the ground for winter folding of the villagers' animals. The garth later known as Prince's Yard was Pickersgill Fold when acquired by George Prince, and its neighbour was Kay['s] Fold.

[20] WRRD, L44/61.
[21] Survey of Pepper Alley and adjoining part of Vicar Lane by Matthew Bentley (*c.*1754): LCA, DB 197.
[22] WRRD, BP 693/894.
[23] WRRD, TT 70/104.

FIG. 4.4 BRIGGATE IN THE RATE BOOK, 1740:
RATEABLE VALUES AND OWNER-OCCUPATION OF FRONTAGE PROPERTIES

The diagram shows the highly rated properties on the frontages of former burgage plots along the town's principal street: the length of each rectangle is proportional to the rateable value [*see* scale, *bottom right*]: for values in the yards backsides, *see* Fig. 4.3. Owner-occupied properties [*solid black*] were in a minority. Where known, the use of premises is shown. For clarity the Moot Hall has been included here as an east-side frontage, although it was actually in mid-street.

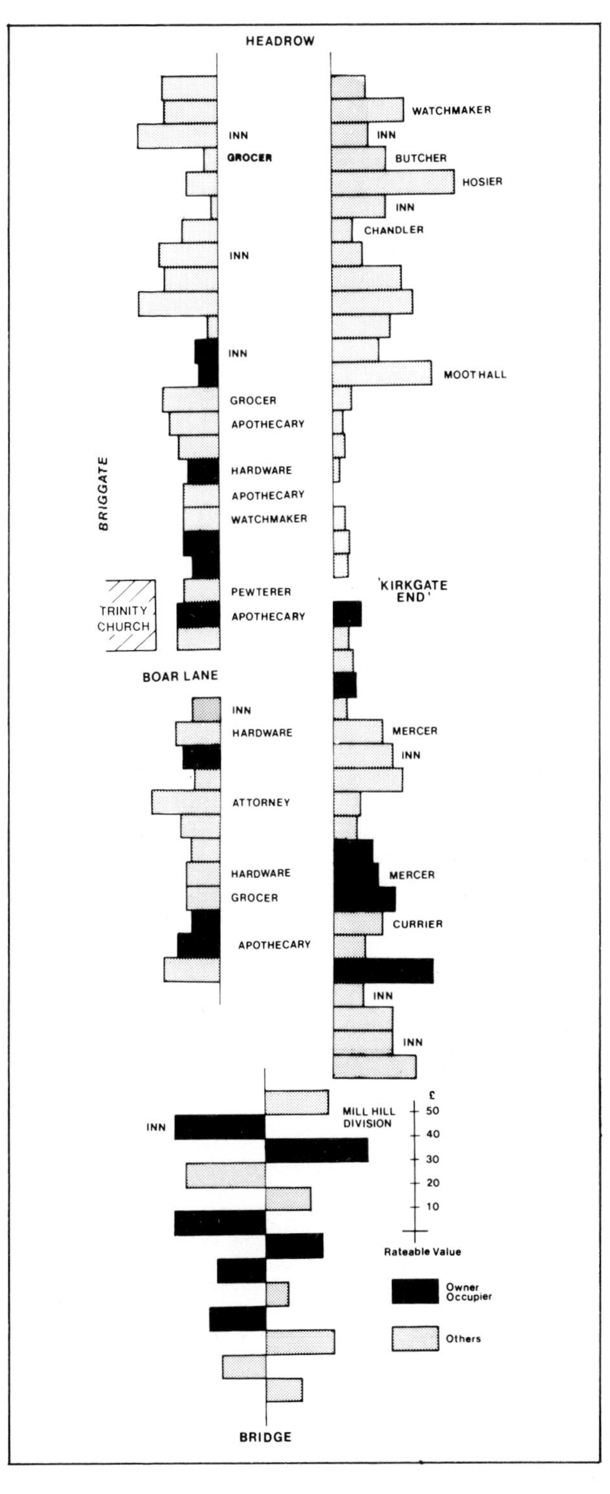
HEADROW
INN
GROCER
INN
INN
GROCER
APOTHECARY
HARDWARE
APOTHECARY
WATCHMAKER
PEWTERER
APOTHECARY
WATCHMAKER
INN
BUTCHER
HOSIER
INN
CHANDLER
MOOTHALL
BRIGGATE
TRINITY CHURCH
'KIRKGATE END'
BOAR LANE
INN
HARDWARE
ATTORNEY
HARDWARE
GROCER
APOTHECARY
MERCER
INN
MERCER
CURRIER
INN
INN
MILL HILL DIVISION
INN
£
50
40
30
20
10
Rateable Value
Owner Occupier
Others
BRIDGE

Along Marsh Lane the pressure on the frontage was less than in Kirkgate, and some of the farms were set back from the street. Yet they too were surrounded by a fold whose semi-circular shape played host to cottage infill although preventing the strict regimentation of a yard. The actual name 'fold' survived for the infilled yards on the east side of Mabgate until their recent demolition, and the name occurs frequently in the villages of the out-townships.

It is difficult enough to discover the occupations of frontage owners once one has left the higher ranks of Leeds society noticed in the *Ducatus* or treated in *Gentlemen Merchants*, but when it comes to the backside tenantry, apart from those in the Charity estate rentals, they are simply names against assessments. The difference between the value of their assessment and the remainder is large enough however for them to be categorised without doubt as in the lowest income brackets: whatever their occupation, the social class of someone paying £2 a year or less in rent cannot be confounded with that of someone in frontage houses paying, as in the examples above, between £15 and £35.

The contrast, it must be emphasised, was one between the value of a frontage house and those lying backside to it. In some towns this might have been the same thing as a contrast between the value of a house occupied by a landlord and those of his tenants: but not in Leeds, for the majority of frontage houses were themselves tenanted, and occasionally a landlord could be found living backsides while he drew rents from a frontage property. Thus Alderman Atkinson lived backside in a house in Briggate worth £26 per annum while the frontage house was let for £46 per annum, the third most valuable in the whole town.

OWNER-OCCUPIERS AND TENANTS

Although owners sometimes contracted to pay rates on behalf of their tenants, the administration of the poor rate called for the actual occupants of each property to be identified by name: for an

---

FIG. 4.5 BACKSIDES DEVELOPMENT IN TURK'S HEAD YARD, BRIGGATE

Drawn by R. Stuart Fell, January, 1973: an elevation of the yard looking southward. The largest building in the Yard, which led backsides from Briggate [*left*] through to Trinity Street [*right*], was the *Turk's Head* itself and its brewhouse; the south side also had four two- and three three-storey cottages, shown here; the backs of these buildings, along the former dividing line of two burgage plots, formed a blind wall to the north side of the next yard, Upton's. The north side of Turk's Head Yard was rebuilt as shops when Old Bond Street (later renamed Commercial Street) was laid out in 1806.

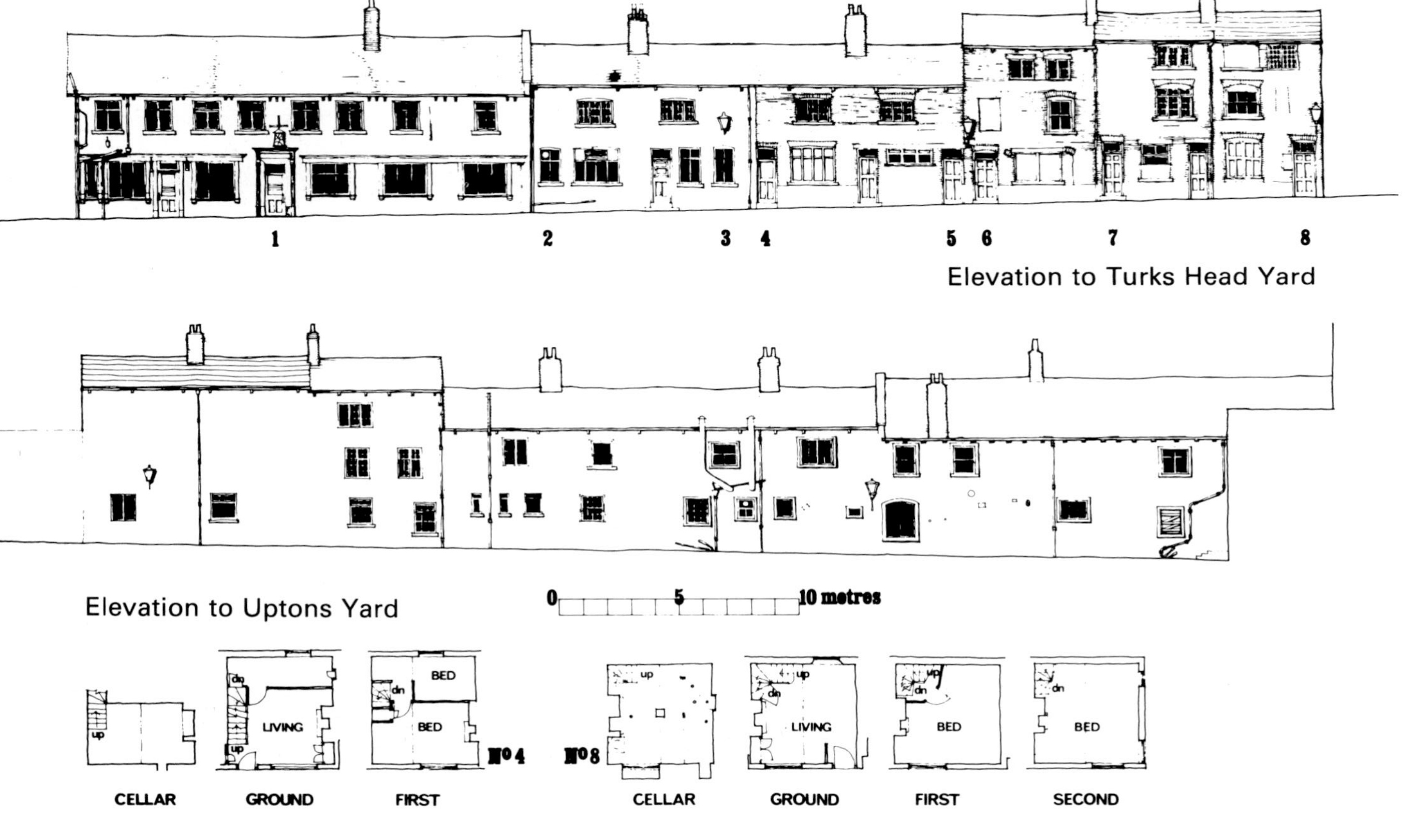
1
2
3
4
5
6
7
8
Elevation to Turks Head Yard
Elevation to Uptons Yard
0
5
10 metres
up
dn
LIVING
BED
Nº4
Nº8
CELLAR
GROUND
FIRST
SECOND

TABLE 4.9

Owner-occupied Properties, by Divisions, 1740–41

Division	All buildings	Number of owner-occupied buildings		Percentage of owner-occupied buildings	
		all	cottage property	all	cottage property
High Town	353	8	0	2	–
High Town Middle	105	7	0	7	–
Kirkgate Middle	78	5	0	6	–
Kirkgate	341	37	4	11	1
South	211	19	4	9	2
East	280	11	3	4	1
North East	362	15	7	4	2
North West	154	20	7	13	5
Mill Hill	307	24	4	8	1
TOTAL	2191	146	29	7	1

Sources: LCA, DB 204/3 collated with LORB 10; in 1742 (LORB 11) there were 145 owner-occupied buildings; in 1752 (LORB 29), 154.

owner-occupier the entry in the 'occupant' column was 'self', and thus all owner-occupiers can be distinguished from tenants, the basis of the Tables which follow.

Table 4.9 shows the preponderance of tenanted properties: only 7 per cent of all buildings were owner-occupied, although the small freeholder clothiers of Woodhouse in the North West raised the proportion in the North West to 13 per cent. As might be expected, very few cottage properties were owner-occupied: none in Briggate, only four in Kirkgate; and twenty-five in the five outer Divisions.

In modern times a tenant is a transient or someone who has not been able to afford to engage in house purchase with the aid of a building society: in Georgian Leeds it was very different. When Thoresby began his tour of large town houses in the *Ducatus* he immediately encountered tenants: Sandford Arthington's 'pleasant seat' occupied by Jasper Blithman; Sir William Lowther's Boar Lane house occupied by Alderman Rooke; and his neighbour, John Skinner, the tenant of Robert Shaw, The additional payment on personalty may be taken to indicate superior wealth: in the Middle Division in 1743 the highest of the thirty-three payments on personalty was Isaac Hancock's (3*s*.) but he did not own the substantial house where he lived;[24] nor did Thomas Walker who paid 2*s*. 6*d*. in personalty; nor did fifteen others from this group.

In the rate books even the owners of large houses will be found living as tenants elsewhere in town: Alderman Timothy Cookson, owner of the seventh largest house in town, had let his house in Briggate to Mr Daniel and was himself tenant of a rather smaller house in Kirkgate owned by his kinsman and neighbour, William Cookson. The six houses in town which were rated more highly than Timothy Cookson's, that is from £42 to £75, were all tenanted: the highest rateable value of an owner-occupied house was £40 (Table 4.10). Tenancies of the larger properties were rarely for more than a year, often only for a quarter. At the expiral of the lease there was a choice of residence, and names frequently reappear at different addresses.

NEIGHBOURS

Social segregation was so characteristic both of the first West End of squares and terraces and of the second West End of villas that its absence before 1768 is important to demonstrate. The profiles

[24] LCA, LORB 10, f.25: his landlord was Richard Hey.

FIG. 4.6 A MIXTURE OF BUILDINGS: LOWER BRIGGATE, WEST SIDE, *c*.1800
(*overleaf*)

'Briggate opposite the Royal Hotel', redrawn by John Dixon from no. 96 in John Russell's sketchbook 'H' (1795–1801): looking across to a large nine-bay building on the west side of the street, the fronts made into three shops and later numbered [*left to right*] as 15, 16 and 17. The whole building was shown by Cossins in 1725 (Fig. 3.1) as Thomas Lee's house; it was owned by Richard Lee in 1800 but he then resided in a detached villa in Woodhouse Lane, St James's Lodge (Fig. 10.1); after Lee's bankruptcy in 1809 the Briggate properties were sold.

A note by the artist's son identifies no. 15 as 'Mr Wormald's shop where [I] was apprenticed'; Bryan Wormald was a woollen draper and between nos 15 and 16 a plain low doorway led backsides through what the sale plan of 1809 called a 'Covered Passage opening into Briggate . . . forever to be left open for the use of the several Owners and Occupiers' within Wormald's Yard. On the left a glimpse of a two-storey house (no. 14); the house on the right of Lee's (no. 18) has quoins and bay windows with steps up to its door and was occupied by a bootmaker; only part of no. 19 appears in the drawing: it is separated from no. 18, which is under the same roof (but without quoins), by the ornamental doorway of a passage leading backsides to the *White Cross Inn* yard.

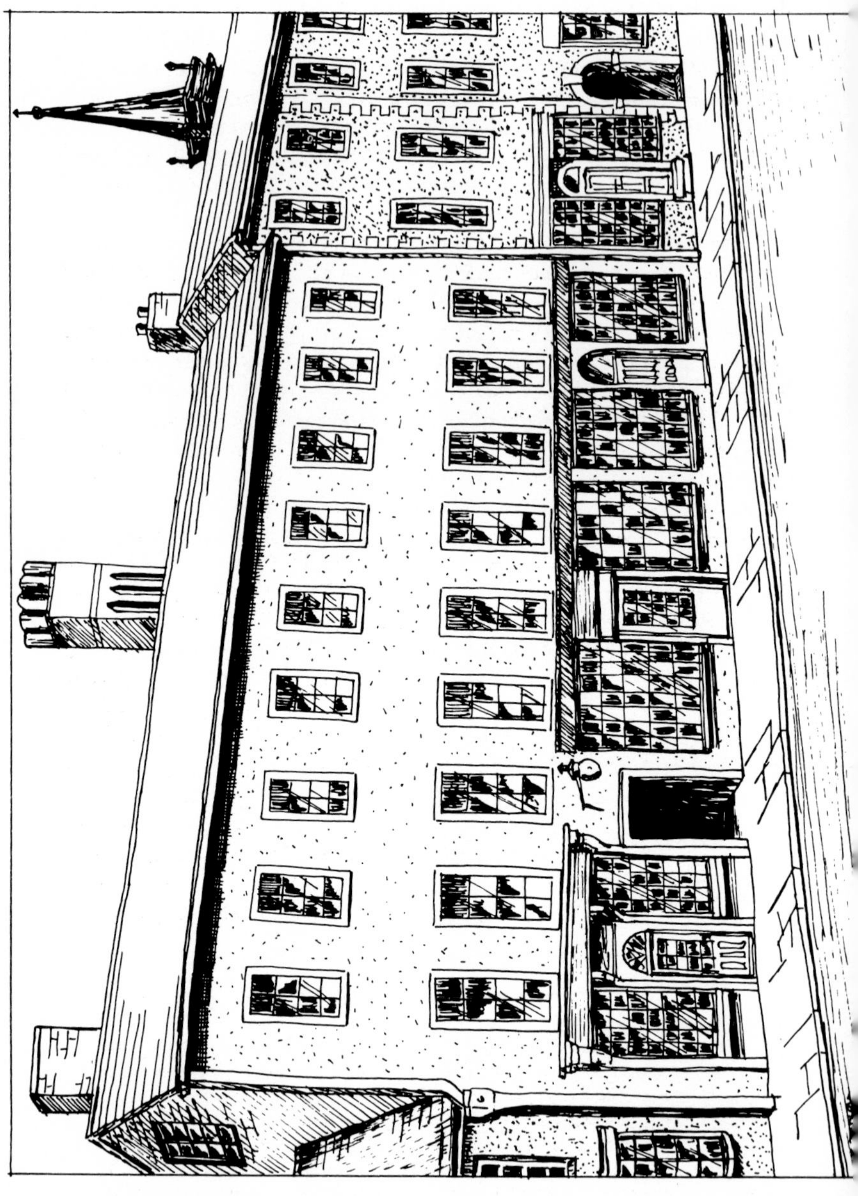

derived from rateable values have already shown a very uneven skyline on the main street frontages, corresponding to the mixture of styles and sizes which still prevailed in the third quarter of the nineteenth century (Figs. 4.6 and 4.7). There was no unbroken succession of high-value properties of similar size such as was to be achieved in Park Row and Park Place, and the few groups of two or three successive high-value properties which can be found usually included at least one inn.

Already by 1740 many frontagers had two or three neighbours backsides but the backsides profile, particularly in Briggate, could have as jagged a skyline as the frontages (Fig. 4.4) for it was exceptional to find nothing but low-rated property, as values in the last column of Table 4.10 demonstrate. There were only two such backsides in Vicar Lane, one in Lower Briggate, and one in Call Lane. Monotonous yards of this kind would accumulate in the Kirkgate folds later but in the mid-eighteenth century the typical crowded Kirkgate yard was that behind the Ibbetson mansion on the north side of Kirkgate between Vicar Lane and Briggate which contained seven middle-value houses and only one cottage, an agglomeration that was sometimes called 'The Square'. Similarly the premises in a Kirkgate fold that formed the first home for the Infirmary must have been larger than cottages.[25]

Away from the town centre the absence of coherent streets in the hamlets of the rural Divisions makes it impossible to reconstruct their topography from the ordering of entries in the rate books. Successive entries in the North West Division can be placed in Great Woodhouse, for example, by reference to the names of owners of large detached houses on the same page, but it is impossible to match any of them to the scatter of cottages which encroached on to the Moor and Carr. With this qualification in mind, two-thirds of the fifty-three owner-occupiers in the three rural Divisions had tenants as immediate neighbours in the columns of the rate books, although

[25] WRRD, EP 31/46.

FIG. 4.7 A MIXTURE OF ARCHITECTURAL PERIODS: LOWER BRIGGATE, *c.*1860 (*overleaf*)

Drawn by John Dixon from an early photograph: the two-bay, two-storey house with garret windows on the right (no. 30) was probably timber-framed; next to it and separated by a low entrance to Trant's Yard is an older low range of three, also timber (nos 27, 28 and 29); next, the square-headed entrance to Golden Fleece Yard (backsides); and then two late eighteenth-century houses (nos 25 and 26); no. 30 was demolished for the widening of Boar Lane in 1869. In the background the rear of houses on the south side of Boar Lane and the tower of Holy Trinity.

B. W. SHARP. PRINTER. 26
ARRACLOUGH
25

TABLE 4.10

Backside Neighbours of Owner-occupied Properties Rated over £20, 1740–41

Division	Owner	Value £	Number of adjoining (backside) properties owned	Values of adjoining (backside) properties owned, £
Mill Hill	Croft (Old George Inn)	40	2	26, 8
Mill Hill	Tho. Oates	40	none	–
High Town	J. Atkinson (Shambles)	30	none	–
Kirkgate Middle	Pawson (Bull and Mouth, Briggate)	30	2	22, 20
South	Madam Milner	28	1	4
South	Ald. Wm. Cookson	28	11	24, 12, 11, 11, 5, 4, + 5 cottages
South	Busk (Meadow Lane)	26	2	cottages
South	Kitchingman	26	3	10, 9, 8
Kirkgate Middle	Atkinson (Briggate)	26	4	46, 13, 12 + cottage
Kirkgate	Ibbetson	25	8	14, 14, 14, 14, 10, 7, 6 + cottage
Kirkgate	Smithson	25	none	–
Mill Hill	Lee (Briggate)	25	7	14, 11, 10, 10, 9, 9 + cottage
South	Ald. Fenton	24	4	11, 7, 5 + cottage
Mill Hill	Mayor Snowden	24	1	16
North West	Ald. Robert Denison	23	5	8, 5 + 3 cottages
High Town	Micklethwaite	23	2	7, 2
North East	Tho. Denison	23	2	10, 7
North East	Nat. Denison	22	2	?
Mill Hill	Recorder Wilson (Manor House)	21	14	15, 10, 9, 7, 6, 5, 4, 4 + 6 cottages

Sources: LCA, DB 204/3 collated with LCA, LORB 10; excluded Moot Hall (£42).

in a hamlet setting this would have been not unlike that contiguity of manor house, farmhouses and cottages which was then accepted as normal in so many English villages.

Even among the highest valued properties there was little immunity from neighbours. Splendid isolation was enjoyed by only

TABLE 4.11

Backside Neighbours of all other Owner-occupied Properties, by Divisions, 1740–41

Division	Total number of owners	No. without own tenants adjacent	No. with own tenants adjoining backsides		
			with 1–5 tenants	with 6–10 tenants	over 10 tenants
Town centre					
High Town	10	7	2	0	1
Kirkgate	25	4	17	2	2
Periphery					
South	18	2	14	2	0
East	19	6	11	2	0
North East	17	7	9	1	0
North West	14	9	4	0	1
Mill Hill	23	9	12	1	1
TOTAL (for the town, including Table 4.10, above)	146	48 (33%)	81 (53%)	10 (6%)	7 (5%)

Source: LCA, DB 204/3 collated with LCA, LORB 10.

three of the nineteen owner-occupiers in Table 4.10 and the two house-owners who were most spaciously endowed with surrounding crofts (Recorder Wilson and Alderman Cookson) had utilised these surrounds for an array of residential and workshop buildings, including cottages. There were thirty-six other owner-occupiers in the town centre with less valuable properties than those in Table 4.10, and Table 4.11 shows that these had certainly been less subject to development, although unevenly since 84 per cent of the Kirkgate owner-occupiers had tenantry backsides, whereas in High Town Division it was only 30 per cent, the average proportion for the whole town.

Like a squire in a village, an owner-occupier in Briggate or Kirkgate might feel that the absence of privacy implied by having close neighbours backsides had its compensation in the knowledge that they contributed to his rent roll. Tenants in frontage houses, a

TABLE 4.12

Backside Neighbours of Highest Rated Tenanted Properties, by Divisions, 1740–41

Division	No. of properties rated £25 and over	With no backside property	Houses only backside	Houses and cottages backside	Cottages only backside
Town centre					
High Town	8	5	1	2	–
High Town Middle	1	1	–	–	–
Kirkgate Middle	6	2	1	3	–
Kirkgate	2	–	–	1	1
Periphery					
South	3	2	1	–	–
East	1	–	–	–	1
North East	–	–	–	–	–
North West	2	1	–	–	1
Mill Hill	6	2	3	1	–
TOTAL	29	13 (43%)	6 (20%)	7 (23%)	3 (10%)

Source: LCA, DB 204/3 collated with LCA, LORB 10; 'highest-rated' is £20 per annum and over.

more numerous class than owner-occupiers, had no such consolation for lack of privacy but the circumstantial evidence is that privacy was not highly valued.

An indication of the psychological distance that separated housing in mid-eighteenth-century Leeds from the later detached villas in Little Woodhouse and Headingley, and how little weight was once placed on the privacy of isolation, will appear from a comparison of Tables 4.10 and 4.11 with 4.12. Not only were the larger owner-occupied frontages more likely to have backsides development than the smaller, but it also appears that backsides development was more likely where the owner was himself resident in the frontage house than when there was an absentee landlord who had the frontage also let to a tenant: nearly half the twenty-nine tenanted frontages of houses with a similar high rateable assessment to those in Table 4.10 had no development behind them; of the fifteen with some development, seven were by houses only, one by cottages, and seven by a mixture of houses and cottages.

It would not always be so: the rate book eleven years later shows eight more owner-occupied houses, but the proportion without neighbouring tenantry had fallen from a third to a quarter, and the colonisation during the interval had been by groups rather than by single houses, with twenty more properties having between six and ten backsides tenants than twelve years earlier.

All this gave to Briggate (and to parts of Kirkgate and the Upper Headrow) in the mid-eighteenth century something like the aristocratic and royal *hôtels* of Paris and such French provincial towns as Dijon, entered past a *concièrge* into a courtyard which served both the seigneur's household on the lower floors and his tenants on the upper floors. On the continent the architectural structure of a many-storeyed house and the four wings around its courtyard made for a vertical arrangement of different social classes on successive floors: in Leeds, on the other hand, with houses of only two or three storeys available on the frontage, the assembly of landlord and tenant was spread backsides, and in lieu of the great gateways of the *hôtels* Leeds had its narrow footway tunnels (some of which still survive), leading through to the backsides yards.

Here in this compact centre, for another quarter-century after 1740, there would have to be accommodated any increases in population as well as the merchants' demand for more workshops and the carriers' for more warehouses: additionally the domestic crafts and the retail trades would have to be accommodated backsides. Another Chapter, concerned with that quarter-century, must intervene before the period when a separate West End and East End came into being.

5
Improvement Within, 1741–67

And ruddy roofs and chimney tops appear
Of busy Leeds, up-wafting to the clouds
The incence of thanksgiving; all is joy;
And trade and business guide the living scene.
John Dyer, THE FLEECE (1757)

Alderman Sir Wm. Rooke's Estate in Boar-Lane was purchased by Richard Wilson Esq. who sold it again to Mr John Dixon, Merchant, whose only son John Dixon Esq. in 1750 pulled down the old House and rebuilt it very handsomely, the stone front being from Huddleston Quarry.
T. D. Whitaker, DUCATUS (1816), p.5

THE GOOD AND BAD YEARS

The far horizon of this Chapter is the initiation of Park Row and the first West End in September 1767, and its theme the paradox that while some aspects of Improvement, whether private or public, were wholly beneficial, giving Leeds more of the accoutrements of a decent provincial town, others increased the pressure on resources of space and drove compactness so far in the direction of congestion that the better-off took refuge in emigration from the central streets.

The West End lay wholly on the land of one proprietor, Richard Wilson, whose estate records happen to have survived almost intact, yet unfortunately including no prospectus, no exposition of the project and none of those claims for the advantages of out-of-town living which were used by later and smaller developers. Later developers also made extensive use of the advertisement columns of the *Mercury* and *Intelligencer* but the Park estate building plots were not advertised, and its houses do not appear there until 29 September 1772 when a first occupant was seeking a tenant or a purchaser for the remainder of his lease. Perhaps, as the Corporation's chief law officer, Richard Wilson felt sufficiently in touch with the limited number of families who were able to afford property of this kind.

The positive advantages of the Park estate and the Wilsons' strategy of development will be discussed in the next Chapter. Here, in the absence of explicit contemporary statements, we must set out what evidence there is for a deteriorating urban environment with only one explicit contemporary statement to cite: the traveller who observed, in the year when Park Row was commenced, that the town was 'large and populous but also dirty, ill-built and badly paved'.[1] Dirt takes us to smoke, domestic rubbish, horse dung, and sewage; 'ill-built' to the further proliferation of cottage property backsides; and 'badly paved' to the first of what were later to be categorised as Improvement Acts, the Lighting and Paving Act of 1755.

Since urban congestion was so closely connected with general economic growth as well as with population growth, it would be helpful to have a chronology of growth to determine whether the years immediately before 1768 were particularly distinctive, but the only annual measure of economic growth locally is that provided by returns made to county Quarter Sessions of the numbers of broad and narrow cloths brought to the fulling mills of the West Riding.[2]

There were certainly lean and fat years for the production of those types of cloth covered by these statistics. Although the volume of broad cloth doubled between 1730 and 1747 it then stagnated for five years before entering a decade of contraction and depression. There was a slow improvement after 1761 and then a very rapid recovery in 1766 and 1767 which took output well past any previous peak and lasted until 1773.

Fluctuations in the economy of the Leeds region were first explored by R. G. Wilson through the medium of the yield of transport tolls.[3] His chronology matches the new evidence from the fire insurance agency.[4] In Leeds the year 1768 was the best year for

[1] Comments by the third Viscount Grimston, 15 September 1768: Historical Manuscripts Commission, *Report on the Mss of the Earl of Verulam* (1906), p.239.

[2] Broad and narrow cloth milled in the West Riding: original returns annually in Quarter Sessions papers, WYJAS; conveniently tabulated in B. R. Mitchell and Phyllis Deane, *Abstract of British Historical Statistics* (Cambridge, 1962), p.189 from *Report of the Select Committee on the Woollen Manufacture* (PP 1806, III, p.25; with reminder from H. Heaton, *The Yorkshire Woollen and Worsted Industries* (Oxford, 1920), pp.414–16, that the increase after 1765 'is partly explained by more stringent inspection': if there was more stringency, then the poor performance of the figures in the years 1768–71 is the more striking.

[3] R. G. Wilson, 'Transport dues as Indices of Economic Growth, 1775–1820', *Economic History Review*, 2nd ser., XIX (1966), 110–23.

[4] M. W. Beresford, 'Prometheus Insured: the Sun Fire Insurance Agency in Leeds during Urbanization, 1726–1826', *Ibid.*, 2nd ser., XXXV (1983), 373–89, based on the records of the company in the Guildhall Library, London, especially policy registers (Old Series, MS. 11936; County (or Country) Series, MS. 11937) and

new premiums that the fire insurance agency had known, and for the whole of the period 1737 to 1820 the annual values of the local fire insurance business, if set alongside the yield of the Navigation tolls and the output of broadcloth, yield significant correlations.[5]

It is tempting to associate the return of fat years in 1767 and 1768 with a trade revival giving an ability to afford new house building at a level of costs as high as that represented by a West End house in Park Row.

The expenditure on West End houses was particularly significant in relation to the general prosperity of the merchant community who were its principal patrons, for it was an expenditure undertaken within quite a short period not by one or two, but by a considerable number of people; and it was probably unprecedented since the rather scattered evidence for its antecedent equivalent – the rebuilding of town-centre frontage houses between 1725 and 1768 – suggests that such rebuilding had been sporadic and the houses less expensive than those in the West End.

The general relation of building to the economic climate in provincial towns was discussed by C. W. Chalklin: 'building was at a low ebb in several major towns in the final war years at the beginning of the 1760s [the Seven Years War ended in 1763] . . . the amount of town building in the 1760s and the 1770s reflected the unprecedented scale of urban population growth'.[6]

It is important to recall that the fifteen lean years for broadcloth had not been uneventful in the town: the first two Improvement Acts (below) were obtained in 1755 and 1760. Two cloth halls and three nonconformist chapels were erected between 1751 and 1758, and the gallery added to Holy Trinity church in 1755 was necessitated by 'the great Increase in Inhabitants within the town'.[7]

calculations from the fortnightly acknowledgement of premiums received from the provincial agents in the Committee Minute Books (MS. 11935). See also Id., 'Fire Insurance Records as a Source for Urban History', *Urban History Yearbook 1976*, pp.7–14.

[5] Calculations from Sun Insurance Co. Committee Books, Guildhall Library, London (MS. 11935) (*Sun*), set alongside the yield of the Navigation tolls (from Wilson, n.3 above) (*Nav*), and the broadcloth output (from n.2 above) (*Clo*):

Nav/Clo: 0.892
Nav/Sun: 0.844
Sun/Clo: 0.878

(I am grateful to Mr David Harkess for making these correlations from data which I supplied.)

[6] Chalklin, p.263.

[7] Petition of 23 April 1751, granted March 1755: Borthwick, MS. Fac.1755, 1. A gallery was added to St John's in 1764, presumably for the same reason: Borthwick, MS. Fac.Bk. 1/372.

Thus even if the years before 1768 saw no massive expenditure on new houses for the town's merchants there was no lack of building of other sorts, in particular an increment of smaller backsides properties. This, as the numbers of townspeople increased, was certainly an Improvement even though the confined location of new housing was bringing its own problems.

There were many connections which could have been observed between local economic growth and the congestion of central Leeds. One of them is suggested in the preamble to the Leeds Bridge Act of 1760 which authorised a new rate of £1500 to meet half the cost of rebuilding and widening the town's only bridge. It was carrying 'the public Turnpike Road from London to Edinburgh by way of Derby, Sheffield, Wakefield, and Boroughbridge' but damaged by the volume of this traffic, 'the great Number of Waggons, Carts and Wheel Carriages almost continually passing'. The state of the bridge was thus 'greatly prejudicial to the Inhabitants, Trade and Commerce of the said Town'.[8]

Preambles to Acts of Parliament, especially local Acts, must be allowed a degree of rhetoric, and few travellers from London to Edinburgh would have come through Leeds, whatever the state of the bridge, when a more direct line was available by the Great North Road. It was multi-directional traffic ending its journey in Leeds, more than Anglo-Scottish traffic, which created a problem for the bridge and central streets. Since there was no river and canal development west of Leeds before 1770 (and then not beyond Gargrave) the increased volume of goods entering and leaving by river could only increase pressure on the important roads which focused on the Leeds warehouses and wharfeside. Between 1740 and 1750 toll turnpikes set up by authority of local Acts of Parliament were created in the directions of Selby, Otley and Elland as well as those two mentioned in the Bridge Act.[9]

In 1758 transport of a different sort was initiated by an Act confirming wayleaves for a waggon way from Middleton colliery down to a staithe at a terminus between Meadow Lane and Hunslet Lane, just south of Leeds bridge.[10] In exchange for Corporation support for their Bill the colliery owners guaranteed to supply at the staithe 23,000 tons a year at a fixed price; and for a slightly higher but

[8] *33 Geo. II cap. 54*.

[9] Fig. 38 in R. G. Unwin, 'Leeds becomes a Transport Centre', in Fraser, ed., pp. 113–41. For considerable annual expenditure on local roads from the Highways Charity see LCA, DB 197/1.

[10] *31 Geo.II cap. 22*, confirming agreements made in Jan. and March 1758, for which see also WRRD, B3 79/14.

still fixed price to deliver coals to the customer's door, be he private householder or industrialist. The Act assured Leeds of 23,000 tons a year at the waggon way terminus: for the first year from which sales data survive 29,000 tons were delivered there; and in the next five years the deliveries increased to some 31,000 tons. Since fewer than one in ten householders lived south of the bridge, everyone else's coal had to be carted over it and through the central streets whereas previously coals both from Middleton and its north-bank rivals had been brought by water and landed on the town side of the bridge.

The first local Act in the category later to be called 'Improvement' was the Lighting and Paving Act of 1755.[11] Since, like the Bridge Act, it had to authorise the levy of an additional rate, a case had to be made in the preamble, and here again the town appears as busy and congested: 'a Place of great trade and large extent consisting of many Streets, narrow Lanes and Alleys, inhabited by a great number of Tradesmen, Manufacturers, Artificers, and others, who in the prosecution and carrying on of their respective Trades and Manufactures are obliged to pass and repass through the same as well as in the night as in the daytime'. The lighting of the streets and the improvement of its pavements would therefore benefit 'not only the security and preservation of the Persons and Properties of the Inhabitants of the said Town but . . . strangers and persons resorting to the several markets kept within the said Town'.

As with the Bridge and later Improvement Acts the execution of this Act was entrusted not to the Corporation but to a large group of elected Commissioners, elected by ratepayers meeting annually in St Peter's vestry. Although the poor rate assessments were to be followed, the Lamp Rate was to be raised only on property within the Bars, whose owners the lamps might most be expected to benefit, and even within the Bars cottage property assessed at less than £3 was exempt. The rates went to purchase and maintain lamps and to pay a Lamp Keeper. The clauses of the Act dealing with paving did not authorise paving at the cost of the rate fund: they were regulatory, making it an offence not to pave in front of one's house. The regulatory clauses extended, in fact, beyond pavements since £5 fines could now be levied on those who failed each Saturday afternoon to sweep their refuse into heaps awaiting collection by the scavengers; and 10*s*. on those who threw on to the street 'Soil, Ashes, Rubbish, Dust, Dirt, Dung and Filth'. Butchers were

[11] *28 Geo.II cap. 41*. 'It is with great pleasure we hear a sum sufficient to support the lamp in Cross Parish and New Street for the ensuing winter is already raised within that district: And that subscriptions are on foot for procuring an Act of Parliament this next session to enlighten the whole town with lamps': *LI*, 29 Oct. 1754.

prohibited from slaughtering sheep, lambs, cattle and swine in the open street except in that part of Briggate which lay to the east of the Moot Hall as far as the Cross, known as the Shambles. Street parking of carriages was also forbidden.

No powers to purchase property for street widening rested with the Corporation and, except for widening the bridge approaches, none were given to the commissioners by the Acts of 1755 and 1760. The width of Briggate was quite exceptional: at its narrowest Kirkgate was only 20½ feet wide, the Headrow (until the 1930s) was eight yards at its widest, while Boar Lane, Swinegate and Vicar Lane were of no more than lane width. A further element in the congestion of central streets – not at all unwelcome in moderation – was their use as open-air markets. The sale of cloth at the traditional place on the bridge had proved too voluminous for the comfort of traffic even fifty years before when the market was transferred to Lower Briggate; after 1711 the greater merchants dealt with their customers in Kirkgate Cloth Hall. In 1756 a second Cloth Hall for white cloth was erected in Meadow Lane, but hardly reducing traffic over the bridge since the majority of merchants would have had to take cloth from the market to their premises north of the river. Briggate had a notorious obstacle in the Moot Hall and the adjoining butcher's shops, the Shambles. This had been noticed by the London aldermen in 1628: 'the Court or Moote House (as they terme it), and from thence upwards are the shambles with a narrow streete on both sides, much annoyinge the whole Towne, yett for theire Convenienciе; and wante of roome, not to be avoided, or placed elsewhere'.[12] There were proposals to demolish it in 1765 but it took another sixty years and an Improvement Act to remove the problem.[13] In 1758 a substantial Mixed Cloth Hall was opened on the edge of town at Quebec, opposite the Unitarian chapel and just within the Park estate. Yet there was at that time no road westwards or northwards from Quebec so that all the business at the Mixed Cloth Hall increased the flow down either Boar Lane or Swinegate, whatever its ultimate destination. Traffic for the south and south-west would then have to cross the crowded bridge while that for other directions – including the west via the old Bradford road – had to pass up Briggate. A project for an enlarged White Cloth Hall in Call Lane was discussed intermittently from 1757 but not achieved until 1775. Despite its exceptional width even the broadest part of Briggate

[12] Corporation of London Record Office, RCE Rental 6.16, f.37; printed in Beresford, *Leeds in 1628*.

[13] *LI*, 9 Oct. 1765.

suffered from the steep ascent from the central gutter to the pavement on the east, confining carriages to the western half.

Besides traffic to the open-air and covered markets, the central streets carried traffic to and from other buildings of importance to the textile industry: the water mills and the warehouses. The main concentration of mills had a tortuous approach, whether from Boar Lane or Swinegate, and the lesser mills by Crown Point had to be approached via Kirkgate and Timble Bridge. The main warehouse, that of the Navigation, had no avenue of approach except alleys leading from The Calls; the small number of private and carriers' warehouses were, on the evidence of insurance fire policies, located in yards backsides and sometimes in the yards of inns. At the time of Wesley's first visit, recalled one old Methodist, 'There were waggon warehouses connected wtih the King's Arms and the Bull and Mouth inn, the waggons starting from which places were loaded in that part of the street, and a great portion of it in the immediate vicinity of these hotels was covered with empty hogsheads or casks'.[14]

Apart from the concentration of fulling at the water mills the craft processes of cloth finishing, located in or behind the merchants' houses, would have scattered traffic rather than concentrated it: with one exception, dyeing. Nothing has been written about this important Leeds industry, largely through absence of records from the small and long-defunct establishments which it comprised. Cloth bought in the white at the Halls had to be taken to the dyehouses, and these (although not power-using) were clustered like the mills on streams and goits within two *cordons insanitaires*, one south of Swinegate and the other down the length of Timble Beck from Sheepscar bridge to the Aire. Dyehouses emitted smoke, as the more explicit *Prospects* showed, in addition to noxious vapours and effluent. It is not surprising that they were surrounded by cottage property rather than residences. John Dyer's poem on the woollen industry, published in 1757, made the best of the smoke as 'the incence of thanksgiving'.[15]

No sector of the textile industry was yet affected by the steam engine: the engines in Leeds were still to be found, using low horse power, within those limited sectors which Thoresby had observed, so that – even taking dyehouses into account – any increase in smoke dirt probably came more from domestic hearths than from industrial

[14] John Wray, 'Methodism in Leeds' (1835–45), Leeds Central Library, Local History Collection, vol. 1, f. 170.

[15] John Dyer, *The Fleece* (1757), as in epigraph to this Chapter.

TABLE 5.1

Recorded and Estimated Population of Leeds In-township, 1740–1801

Year	Numbers recorded or estimated (e)		
	Persons	Families	Houses, including empty
1740	10,638e	2551e	2364
1754	15,221	3624	3413
1771	16,259e	3899	3613e
1772	15,052e	3610e	3345
1775	17,121	4096	3839e
1781	*c.*20,000	4796e	4444e
1797	30,110e	7169e	6691
1797(a)	19,400e	*c.*7000	6533e
1801	30,669	7122	6882

Year	Annual average rate of growth, houses
1740–71	1.7%
1771–75	1.6%
1775–81	2.6%
1781–93	4.2%
1793–1801	3.6%

Note: Basis of estimates: The 1775 ratio of persons per family (4.17) for 1740–81 and the census ratio of 4.2 for 1793–97; a ratio of 4.46 persons per house throughout.

The 1772 figures seem out of line with those for 1771 and 1775; since the latter two derived from field surveys they should be preferred.

Sources: 1740: LCA, DB 204/3; 1754: LCA, LOP.B 31; Joseph Priestley to Richard Price, 3 October 1771, cited by F. Beckwith, *PTh.S*, XLI (1948), 127; 1772: *PTh.S*, XXIV, 34; 1775: British Library, Add.MS.33770 and Bardsley Powell MSS, Aldburgh Hall, Masham, copy in LCA; 1781: John Tuke, *A Map of the Parish or Borough of Leeds* (1781), cartouche; 1797: Griffith Wright, *A History of the Town and Parish of Leeds* (1797), 46; 1797(a): Sir Frederick Eden, *The State of the Poor* (1797), 847; 1801: *Abstracts of the Answers and Returns Made pursuant . . . to an Act for taking an Account of the Population* (1801), 449–50.

establishments. Competition between collieries cheapened local coal and thereby increased its use, but new-built houses were also multiplying the number of chimneys. The argument has come back again to houses.

TABLE 5.2

Estimated Number of Houses, 1775, on Different Assumptions

Division	1775	
	at 4.46 persons per house*	at 1.03 families per house*
High Town	759	762
Kirkgate	779	837
Mill Hill	314	312
South	409	409
East	570	638
North East	539	528
North West	467	491
TOTAL	3839	3976

* The ratios of 4.46 persons per house and 1.03 families per house are those for the in-township in the census of 1801.

Source: British Library, Add. MS.33770.

HOUSES

The progress of house building cannot be measured on an annual basis since the rate book series is defective and there was nothing resembling a census before the detailed private count of March 1775, carried out by twenty-two enumerators. At that time there was considerable local curiosity among *savants* about the pace of population increase and its source: in 1771 Joseph Priestley communicated to his friend Dr Richard Price a count recently made of families in Leeds which totalled 3899; a count was also made from the now-lost rate book of May 1772 and recorded in the notebook of a merchant with a passion for collecting statistics. Its total (Table 5.1) was probably an underestimate but the loss of all rate books between 1754 and 1774 makes an independent check now impossible.[16]

The 1775 census, which went into details of marital status, sex and age, counted 4096 families, according well with Priestley's figures, but it did not count houses. It must be expected that some houses sheltered more than one family but there is no means of knowing what proportion before the census of 1801 when 6882 houses were

[16] See sources to Table 5.1.

occupied by 7122 families, a ratio of 1:1.03. In the 1801 census there were 4.46 persons per house in inner Leeds, and the slightly different results of applying these ratios to the 1775 data are shown in Table 5.2. We may say however that the in-township had about 3900 houses in 1775 compared with 2364 in 1740, an increase of 65 per cent or 1.9 per cent per annum (Table 5.4).

It would be expected that the Divisions experienced different rates of growth over this long period. The nineteen enumerators who shared the house-by-house rounds in the enquiry of 1775 sometimes crossed the boundaries of Divisions in presenting their figures but the final column of Table 5.3 attempts to rearrange their data. The

TABLE 5.3

The Census of Leeds, 1775

Census divisions			Equivalent rating divisions	
Numerators' Divisions as numbered*	Families	Persons	Families	Persons
1 Briggate, east side	97	460	(High Town)	
2 Briggate, west side	157	722		
6 Shambles, Lands Lane and Cross Parish	277	1211		
7 Headrow, New Street and Burley Bar	254	994	755	3387
10 Kirkgate	596	2387	(Kirkgate)	
9 Call Lane, Vicar Lane and Calls	266	1089	862	3476
3 Boar Lane, Mill Hill and Swinegate	237	1039	(Mill Hill)	
5 Upper and Lower Tenters	84	360	321	1399
11 Meadow Lane, Quaker Lane and Water Hall	248	1078	(South)	
12 Hunslet Lane, Bowman Lane & Simpson's Fold	173	746	421	1824
13 Bank and Far Bank	366	1411	(East)	
14 Marsh Lane and Black Bank	250	963		
17 Cross Green, Knowestrop and Osmondthorpe	41	171	657	2545

TABLE 5.3 (*continued*)

Census divisions			Equivalent rating divisions	
Numerators' Divisions as numbered*	Families	Persons	Families	Persons
19 Sheepscar, Buslingthorp, Lorry Bank and N. side of Sheepscar Beck	58	228	(North East)	
15 Quarry Hill, Mabgate and Burmantofts	362	1486		
8 North Town End, Leylands and Millgarth	124	692	544	2406
4 Park Row, Park Lane & Little Woodhouse	96	477	(North West)	
16 Lydgate, Wade Lane & Woodhouse Lane	140	477		
18 Woodhouse, Woodhouse Carr and Nether Green	270	1130	506	2084
TOTAL	4096	17,121		

* The street names were used in the document to identify its 19 Divisions which were numbered and assigned to different enumerators. The Divisions have been re-arranged here to match as far as possible the rating Divisions (in parentheses) but Park Row, here part of Division 4, was rated in Mill Hill, and Middle Division cannot be differentiated.

Source: British Library, Add.MS.33770, ff.57–58.

rate of increase in the North West was exceptional at three times the average even when an allowance is made for the inclusion of Park Row and Park Lane. The North East was unexceptional and Town's End was still very much town's end, as Jefferys's plan of 1768–70 confirms; and since Park Row had been counted elsewhere no impact of the early Park estate development shows in the almost stationary numbers for Mill Hill. Within the areas of the central streets High Town and South had a very different experience from Kirkgate which, already the largest Division in 1740, had the second lowest rate of growth of all the Divisions. Was this because of saturation? Hardly, since with a vision denied to the men of 1775, we know that room was going to be found for another 239 houses in that Division by 1801, and 179 more between 1801 and 1821 when saturation was reached. High Town and South, on the other hand, had about the same rate of growth as each other, twice the average. High Town was nearer saturation. There were many advertisements similar to one for 'a very improvable Freehold Estate' of eight houses behind the *King's Arms* and the *Red Bear* (11 March 1777) and a comparison of the High Town rate books between 1740 and 1754 suggests that development took the form of further infill to yards with existing cottages rather than colonising new territory by occupying crofts. A quarter of owner-occupiers in 1754 still had no neighbours backsides. High Town absorbed 183 houses between 1775 and 1801 but no more thereafter. The South, as the empty fields on the 1815 map show, was able to take another 566 houses between 1801 and 1821.

There is an important difference between, on the one hand, the increases in High Town and the comparable rates for the South and East Divisions and, on the other, the exceptional rate for the North West. High Town, as we already know, found its additional space backsides, but the others, especially the East and North West, had room and plenty to spare, either at clusters near the edge of town or at the hamlets themselves. Put another way, the extra 350 houses in High Town had doubled the density per square yard in the limited area behind the frontages, and the extra 150 in Kirkgate increased the density by 24 per cent. For those whose yards were not developed there was still a view like that over 'a pleasant Garden' from 'three large Bow Windows facing towards Chappell-Town and Gledhow' but for others the vistas were closing in.

What we do not know is whether these increases, if felt intolerable, came about at a steady rate or were concentrated in the years just before the flight to the West End began. Nor do population studies help: Professor Yasumoto has shown that the natural increase by excess of baptisms over burials made a contribution only in the years 1748 to 1755 so far as the in-township was concerned; but on the same evidence the out-township villages had a continuous natural increase which must have had an effect on the busyness of the town as their market centre. The unknown and crucial figure is the number of immigrants from outside the town.[17]

If the rateable value of the town is any indication of growth, it had been rising steadily at 1.3 per cent per annum between 1741 and 1754 but when a figure is next available, in 1765, the intervening period

[17] M. Yasumoto, 'Urbanization and Population in an English Town: Leeds during the Industrial Revolution', *Keio Economic Studies* (Tokyo, Japan), X (1973), 61–94.

TABLE 5.4

New Houses Built, by Divisions, 1740–75

Division	Stock in 1740	Stock in 1775	Estimated increase	Percentage increase	
				Overall	Annual average
High Town	353	759–762	c.350	100	2.9
Kirkgate	617	779–837	c.150	24	0.7
Mill Hill	387	420*	c.130*	8	0.2
South	211	409	c.200	100	2.9
East	280	570–638	c.320	114	3.3
North East	362	528–539	c.170	47	1.3
North West	154	467–491	c.330	214	6.1
TOTAL	2364	3839–3976	c.1500	64	1.8

* The 1775 figure for Mill Hill (312–14) is so much smaller than the 420 at the 1772 count from the rate books (elsewhere an underestimate) that about 100 Mill Hill houses must have been included in High Town or Kirkgate. In the absence of other information, 50 have been deducted from each Division and assigned here to Mill Hill.

Sources: 1740: LCA, DB 204/3; 1775.

had shown an average of only 0.3 per cent in what had been lean years for trade, with war cutting off transatlantic markets for cloth; an average annual increase of 1.3 per cent was achieved again in the period 1765–74.[18]

If attention is concentrated on the number of properties assessed for rating this crude measure of growth again shows a poorer performance after 1754. Between 1741 and 1754 there were 863 additional entries in the rate books, an average annual rate of 2.6 per cent: between 1754 and 1765 this rate was halved, and was not exceeded until 1800–05 (Table 5.4).

The development of individual properties over this period can be followed in successive rate books. Thus the stagnation after 1754 suggested above was certainly noticed in Kirkgate where, in the rate books for the Middle Division, there were no additional entries between 1744 and 1765 but ten between 1765 and 1774. Development was sometimes indicated simply by an assessment rising in

[18] Calculated from LCA, LORB 10–37.

value as a property was improved or extended; but sometimes by additional entries as new buildings were added.

The watchmaker, James Pinckney, encountered in Chapter 4 as an early example of an owner of multiple properties, died in 1751 leaving his estate to the Charity School. Since 1726 the rents for its mixture of houses and cottages had remained unchanged at £93 a year, and for probate in 1752 they were valued at £100 a year. The trustees of the charity then sold the properties to Pinckney's executor, the apothecary Michael Cottam, and when Cottam's assessment was made in 1754 the rent roll from the twenty-five entries 'Cottam, late Pinckney' totalled £125.[19]

There were several types of rent roll increase. There might be negotiated increases affecting only some of a group of properties, as in the ten houses acquired in June 1747 by Thomas Armistead. The largest of these, a frontage house on Briggate ('T' in Appendix V.1), Armistead at first occupied himself and was rated as an owner-occupier at £16 a year until 1754; but in the rate books of 1765 and 1774 this frontage house was tenanted at £24 a year. A second house remained empty for five years but then a tenant was found who paid £13 10*s*. a year, raised to £14 in 1765 and £18 in 1774. A third was also empty until 1752 when a tenant began to pay £12, raised to £17 in 1774. The smaller properties were less difficult to let, and their rents in total increased from £23 10*s*. in 1747 and 1748 to £78 in 1754 and £84 in 1765.

Emptiness was always a risk for a landlord: the most valuable house in town brought its owner £75 a year in rent from 1741 to 1748 but was empty in 1749 and again in 1750 until it was divided and let to two tenants at the end of the year. It was again empty in 1754.

Increases of rent recorded in the rate books were usually individual and sporadic but general increases could occur when a group of leases expired together: after long leases had expired in 1752 the rents from the extensive Charity estate on the corner of Woodhouse Lane and the Headrow were increased from £16 to £27. A more common change to find in successive entries is a mixture of rent increases and additional rents for properties erected since the last assessment: thus Harper, after whom Harper's Yard was named, added £40 to his income between 1752 and 1764: £22 from increased rents on three of the houses but £16 from three new houses backsides.

The Harrison Charity property was always clearly distinguished in the rate books: in 1750 the trustees owned four houses and four smaller properties built on the west side of what Harrison had named

[19] LCA, DB 196/1, f.127.

TABLE 5.5

Development of Rateable Values: Frontage Properties in Briggate (Kirkgate Middle Division), 1741–74

	A	B	C	D	E	F	G	H	I	J	K	L	M	N	O
1741	76	53	72	18	35	46	18	100	29	28	67	48	67	26	36
1742	85	53	91	18	35	46	18	100	29	28	67	48	67	26	36
1744	84	53	91	18	35	?	?	83	29†	28†	67	48	67	26	36
1745	84	53	91	18	35	66	26	83	29	28	67	48	67	26	36
1747	84	53	109	18	35	62	26	102	29	32	67	48	67	26	36
1750	84	53	106	18	35	62	26	106	29	32*	67	48	58	26	36
1751	95	53	112	19	35	66	26	77	19†	47	68	46	70	26	37
1752	95	53*	112	19	35	66	26	77	19	50	68	46	70	26	37
1754	95	94	112	19	38	66	26	74	19	50	68	46	70	26	37
1765	95	88	136*	32	35	66	26	113	32*	40	54*	91	90*	26	30
1774	95	88	200	?	32	88	26	160*	38	40	46	?	90	26	31

* Denotes a change of ownership.
† Indicates a transfer within same family, after a death.

Source: LCA, LORB 10–32.

New Street, yielding an income for the charity of £53 per annum. By 1751 the rent roll was £67, and only £5 of the increase was due to higher rents: four cottages had been built backsides, and a fifth was added by 1754.

Development behind an older frontage, on the east side of Briggate near the Headrow, can be traced by following the name Eamonson through the rate books from 1741 to 1765. A single house stood on the frontage up to 1750, when it was valued at £57; this was divided into two (with some loss of value) from 1751 but two cottages added backsides nearly redressed the balance; the rent level of 1750 was exceeded by 1754 when three more cottages had been added, and reached £135 by 1765 when three more cottages and four substantial houses had been built in the yard.

The progress of town-centre frontage values in the same period is illustrated further by assessments for twenty consecutive frontage properties in Briggate (High Town Middle Division), set out in Appendix V.1 and for a further fifteen Briggate frontages from Kirkgate Middle Division in Table 5.5. The former increased its annual value from £319 to £431 (35 per cent) and the latter from £719 to £1083 (51 per cent).

Surviving surveys, a full series of rentals, and finally the plans drawn in 1793 for the components of the Town Charity (or Pious Uses) estate enable its development to be charted more fully than properties known only from the rate books. Appendix V.2 sets out the changes on the Free School estate in Vicar Lane between 1728 and 1793 while Appendix V.3 shows another aspect of change and improvement of rentals at the town centre between 1754 and 1793 through the conversion of four frontage houses (on what is now the site of Lewis's department store) into shops.

The charity estates were unique in possessing a run of adjacent frontage properties so that it was not yet possible for any private town-centre landowner to engineer any comprehensive development such as that which in the 1820s would produce the Bazaar and New Shambles or towards the end of the nineteenth century the various Briggate shopping arcades.

Outside the town centre a scattered landownership similarly inhibited any large-scale initiation of streets; and where, exceptionally, as with the Ibbetson and Pawson estates, there were groups of adjacent fields under a single owner, the abortive result of schemes which were promoted there in 1755 and 1765 was discouraging.

James Ibbetson, whose coat of arms had decorated Cossins's map, died in 1739. The ancestral house was in Kirkgate: nine years before his death Ibbetson purchased 'a very large Yard or Backside containing near half an Acre of Ground situate in the centre of the town and capable of very great Improvements': in the conveyance it was described as a former Fold but now the yard of the *Cock Inn*, with the former cockpit behind it. Houses and wool warehouses were erected here, presumably of some pretensions since they were described in the family settlement as 'a street called The Square'. At Town's End, next to the Denison house, Ibbetson also owned two closes, the Leylands (of 2½ acres) and Fountain or Tenter Close (of 4 acres). All this property was inherited by James's son, Henry, who further improved The Square by connecting it up to the town water main; he also purchased a house next to his father's and demolished it to build a connecting house at a total cost of £1800, increasing the rateable value of the enlarged house by £35.[20]

All these facts are recited in the preamble to a private Act of Parliament obtained by Henry, now ex-mayor and a baronet, in 1755. The object of the Act was to free his inheritance from the entail in the family settlement which had prevented him selling any part of

[20] There is a full account of property in Leeds in the entail: LCA, DB 27 (6 June 1767); see also LCA, FW 206 (1719) and WRRD, BM 669/848.

it or granting long leases. It was not Sir Henry's intention to dispose of his Kirkgate house which he needed for his own residence since his father had left Denton Hall to his elder brother. His interest lay further north at Town's End where, as the Act declared, 'Leylands and Fountain Close are so situated that there is now fair Prospect and Opportunity, by granting Building-Leases, to make a great Improvement of the same'.[21]

Prospect perhaps, but not, in the event, Opportunity. The Leylands were notorious in the early twentieth century as a ghetto of poor housing and this has led some historians to regard them as an early out-of-town development. This is incorrect, as the empty fields on plans of 1781 and 1815 demonstrate. Ibbetson found no takers for the land released from entail by the Act, and the expense was in vain.

It is highly unlikely that he had it in mind to create streets of cottage property. The merchant Bernard Bischoff, once an emigré of Basle, had just cemented his respectability by building a third house opposite the Leylands to match the two large Denison houses, and it would be to customers of this sort that the project of 1755 looked. Its failure probably lay in its unlucky timing, for in 1756 the Seven Years War began, and the output of broadcloth that year was the lowest for twenty-five years; but the Act was also unattractively framed in permitting not freehold sales but ninety-nine-year leases. Apart from the manorial copyholders Leeds was a town of freeholders not of ground landlords and leaseholders and, as the next Chapter will show, the Wilsons who successfully initiated the West End as a leasehold estate were eventually forced to enfranchise the leaseholders and sell the remaining land as freehold.

In 1765, three years before the first house was built in the West End, a second disentailing Act for a Leeds estate was approved by Parliament, also with the intention of releasing land for sale.[22] The lady named in the Ann Wilson Settled Estates Act was a daughter of William Wilson, the merchant son of the Recorder, Richard Wilson I. Ann's maternal grandfather was the wealthy merchant Henry Pawson who had left his property, including the manor of North Hall, to Ann's mother, now widowed. It was her mother's marriage settlement from which it was now necessary to break free if any of the settled lands were to be put on sale with a safe title.

The North Hall estate was larger and more compact than that of the Ibbetsons. It comprised six closes and covered 45 acres but hope

[21] *28 Geo.II cap.10.*

[22] *5 Geo.III cap.25*; WRRD, CO 294/423.

was to be deferred here for almost as long as at the Leylands. While this project came at a better time for cloth merchants than in 1755, its site was much less attractive than Town's End, and might be reckoned positively unattractive. The six closes were centred on Lady Bridge where the demolished manor house had stood at the foot of Quarry Hill. The ground was low-lying and bisected by a beck which came already polluted from the oil-mill, tannery and dyehouses of Sheepscar and formed the open sewer for east Leeds; while here again the Act envisaged leaseholds limited to twenty-one years. When we next encounter the names of these closes it will be in the title deeds of back-to-back houses in the first years of East End streets.

THE EVIDENCE FROM FIRE INSURANCE[23]

In the period between 1754 and 1774, with no poor and only one highway rate book surviving, a less complete but in some ways more informative view of buildings in Leeds can be obtained from the registers of fire insurance policies which were taken out with the Sun and Royal Exchange companies. The London-based Sun company established a part-time agency in Leeds in 1737 and maintained a virtual monopoly here until 1784 when the Royal Exchange opened an office; a local fire company was founded in March 1777 but closed down in 1782, with the Sun taking over its policies and as a public relations exercise buying its rival's fire engine and presenting it to the town.[24]

There was no Great Fire of Leeds. The town had no such disastrous visitation of fire as that which struck Blandford in 1731 with the loss of 400 homes or Wareham in 1762 with 133 losses. Brick replaced or encased timber houses, and the smaller properties which made for the greatest congestion were all of brick. A greater risk came from the numerous industrial processes which required the application of heat: in a minor way where the cloth pressers worked, and in a major way where cloth was dyed or where soap and other detergents were boiled. The town also had its brewers, bakers,

[23] For the following paragraphs *see* Beresford as in n.4. A personal name index to Sun and Royal Exchange policies for Leeds between 1727 and 1826 can be consulted on request to the author; Dr D. T. Jenkins has compiled a numerical list identifying the Yorkshire policies issued by the Sun between 1797 and 1840, and a more detailed list of references to textile firms. This material has been used in his *The West Riding Wool Textile Industry, 1770–1835* (Edington, 1975) and 'The Cotton Industry in Yorkshire, 1780–1900', *Textile History*, X (1979), 75–95.

[24] Guildhall Library, London, MS. 11932, vol. 12, 10 Oct. 1782.

TABLE 5.6

Premiums from Sun Fire Insurance Agency in Leeds, 1740–69

Years	Annual average	Highest in decade
1740–49	33	40 (1749)
1750–59	84	122 (1759)
1760–69	269	392 (1768)

Note: Insured values cannot be deduced from premiums remitted since differential risks were reflected in different premium rates per £ value. Nor can total insured values be determined since fire and fire-fighting has destroyed or damaged some of the policy registers for this period.

Sources: London, Guildhall Library, MS.11935; Sun Insurance Co., Committee Minute Books: fortnightly record of remittances.

seed-oil crushers, tallow-makers, distillers, tobacco-millers and smiths, all potentially incendiary; nor were inn- and stable-keepers unaware of accidents which could be kindled by negligent or inflamed customers.

The earliest insurances (Appendix III.1) were taken out in London in 1716 but in November 1737 the *Mercury* advertised that 'Mr. John Wilkinson of Leeds being appointed Agent for the Sun Fire Office application may be made to him for new insurances on houses or goods. And on producing the last receipts he is empowered to receive yearly payments on the insurances already made.' An agent in Leeds at that time had less potential business than the fashionable spa of Scarborough or the county town at York: in the first twelve months of his agency Wilkinson remitted £21 in premiums to London while his counterpart at York remitted £182 and Scarborough £226. This first Leeds agent was a merchant as was the second, his nephew James, who took over the agency in 1754. His remittance to London was no more than £69 in that year but there was more substantial progress in the next two decades, as set out in Table 5.6. Initially, as might be expected, the agent was concerned with the insurance of existing properties and those of the most value, although there was always a temptation not to declare their full value.

The first client was Henry Penrose who insured on 6 December 1737 'two houses in Briggate fronting the street tenanted by John Aughton, pewterer and Thomas Jackson whitesmith', each valued ('exclusive of outbuildings') at £150. The same day Councillor

George Priestley insured 'his own house fronting the street in the Lower Headrow' for £100, together with a stable, a malthouse 'now converted to tenements', and a second smaller house: £300 in all. Priestley's trade was the grinding of clothworkers' shears.

Since, as we have already found, owner-occupiers like Priestley were exceptional, some policies were taken out by tenants choosing to insure only the contents: in March 1738 James Lister, 'printer at the corner of New St.', insured £100 of household goods, £50 of furniture and £50 of stock in trade but not the house, while on 17 January of the same year John Bilton, currier, insured on £50 of goods and £150 of his stock in trade, but not the house in the Upper Headrow where these were housed. One of these policies taken out in the first year of the agency reached £1000: that of the widow Sarah Whitelock, owner of the oil-crushing mill at Sheepscar. The mill house was valued only at £50 but 'the gutts or other materials of the said Mill' for £700. She had £100 of 'rape ore in stock' and £100 of 'rape oyle in the warehouse'. The warehouse itself was valued at only £50, the first of many instances of a building having only a fraction of the value of its contents. William Cowell's house 'fronting the Market Cross' was insured for £50 but his stock in trade – he was a flax dresser – at three times that sum. James Livesey, merchant, prudently insured 'his goods in a warehouse hired of John Willis, fronting a lane and the river' for £500, and the first policy with a single item as valuable as £1000 was not for a building but for contents: the warehouse stock of Josiah and Samuel Oates, stuff-makers in Mill Hill (January 1749).[25]

Because of developments backsides to frontage houses the pendants of smaller properties were covered by a single policy: Priestley's malthouse, above, is the earliest reference to a single building tenemented but small yard-houses at £15 or £30 soon become noticeable although at first the backsides properties most commonly found in policies are, like the Whitelock premises, workshops and warehouses.

There were also insurances of cottage property away from the yards at the Bank hamlet: in 1760 Abraham Naylor who owned a £100 house in Marsh Lane insured five houses at Hill House Bank 'newbuilt under one roof' for £40 each; in the same year John Rogerson, clothmaker, had just erected '15 tenements under one roof in one range adjoining': both would seem to be descriptions of

[25] These policies were: Penrose, Sun OS 48 75483; Priestley, 48 75484; Lister, 48 76648; Bilton, 48 75895; Whitelock, 50 77785; Cowell, 50 75625; Livesey, 50 76413; and Oates 85 114722.

early terrace rows, and at £20 the Rogerson houses may well have been single-storey. At 10 per cent of their capital value, a good return for the time, these would have had annual rentals represented by the £2 entries in the rate book.[26]

Frontage houses are as easily distinguishable by their higher insured values as they are in the rate books. Their insured values soon exceeded the £100 and £150 of the first decade of the agency: William Satterthwaite's house in Boar Lane 'fronting the street' was the first to reach £200 in 1751 and Ann Cunliff's in Kirkgate followed in 1754. New houses in Bath at that time were being insured for £500–£800. A decade later several attorneys and surgeons were insuring Leeds houses for £500 and £600 each. The first premises to be insured for £800 were at Holbeck Lodge which Martin Brown insured in January 1758, the earliest of an important and revealing series of merchant-manufacturers' policies. His policy was for £4300, a sum exceeded by only two other policies over the next decade (Table 5.7)[27]

The largest of these was in the name of the merchant John Blayds for £7100 in April 1765. Blayds, thrice mayor, insured his own house for £1000 with household goods to the same value;[28] the remaining £5100 was the valuation of two other groups of property in Leeds in addition to one adjoining his own house: in all three were packing and dressing shops, a counting house and workshops.

The second largest policy in 1768 was that of George Green, grocer. He had property scattered over the town. In Briggate his own house, valued at £500, had nine houses backsides and two stables although he may already have been living in a larger house (£600) outside Woodhouse Bar. More valuable than any house in the town was Green's new warehouse by the bridge, valued at £2100 with contents worth £1000. This was 'part unfinished' in December 1761 and replaced a house and warehouse (shown on the Cossins map) which the Improvement Commissioners had acquired from Green and demolished for street widening under the terms of the Bridge Act of 1760: his occupational interest was also expressed in a small cheese warehouse (£100) adjoining.[29]

The importance of warehouse space in a town at a transport interchange is emphasised by the high value of two adjacent riverside warehouses belonging jointly to Peter Birt and Sir James Ibbetson. In 1758 they acquired a half-share on the lease of the tolls on the

[26] Naylor, Sun OS 132 174992; Rogerson, 134 178917.

[27] Satterthwaite, Sun OS 92 124958; Cunliff, 105 140819; Brown, 121 160904.

[28] Blayds, Sun OS 160 218935; and see Fig.9.1.

[29] Sun OS 130 186728.

TABLE 5.7

Largest Insured Values of Buildings on the Eve of the West End, 1758–66

Date	Name	Total insured value, £	Houses, £	Domestic contents, £	Industrial buildings, £	Industrial contents, £	Notes	Insurance Policy number: Sun OS
1765	Blayds, Hunslet Lane & Briggate, gentleman	7100	1000* + 1800 1700	1000	1200 400	–		160 218953. The Hunslet Lane property is located in LCA, DB 179
1760	Green, riverside & Shambles, grocer	5000	2000	–	2100	1000		139 186727–8
1758	Brown, Holbeck Lodge, merchant	4300	800* + 100	–	350	1500	£1000 stock of wool, canvas and bags	121 160904 and 146 199367
1760	Ibbetson & Birt, riverside	4000	–	–	1500	2500	'warehouse' and 'lower warehouse'	131 174301
1765	Lee, Briggate and Boar Lane, merchant	3800	2000*	500	800	500		164 225988 and 148 202034

1759	Barron & Priestley, Mill Hill, stuff-makers	3100	–	–	–	1200	'part timber'	129 169346
1761	Dixon, Briggate, Kirkgate, etc., merchant	3000	3000	–	–		includes *Kings Arms* inn, £1000 (also below)	136 180929
1763	Lodge, Chapeltown, merchant	3000	700*	900	360	1040		146 198839 and 176 247641
1763	Oates, merchant	3000	500*	450	300	1000		148 200571 and 108 302295
1763	Walker, Simpson's Fold, woolstapler	3000	500*	1000	500	1000		149 202748
1765	Markham, Lee & Dawson, Holbeck	3000	300*	300	900	1500		162 222028
1766	Dixon, Gledhow Hall	2600	1600*	–	–	–	'unfinished'	172 240217
1762	Gautier, Lydgate, merchant	2500	400*	–	200	–		145 196043
1763	Molyneux, Town's End, merchant	2100	350*	–	–	–		146 198845 and 162 222751

* Owner-occupied properties

Source: London Guildhall Library, Sun Insurance Co., Policy Registers, Old Series. In 1767 and 1768 no new policies exceeded £2000. For later high-value policies see Tables 10.1 and 10.2(b).

whole Aire and Calder Navigation and in 1760 took out an insurance for the Upper and Lower warehouses, valued at £1500 together with £2500 of contents 'in trust'.[30] Most merchants' premises had their own warehouse in their yard, insured for £50 or £100. In 1765 two specialist 'London carriers' had warehouses insured in Boar Lane, and two 'warehouses called Londonderry' at Mill Hill were insured in the same year for £200 each: their owners had a third warehouse adjoining. Rather later Thomas Bowling insured 'his common carrier's warehouse' in the White Horse Inn Yard with stock three times the value of the building; and also 'stock in his other warehouse in the same Yard wherein the Newcastle and Sheffield carriers' goods are deposited'.[31]

Insurance of property against fire was far from universal but few of the important names in the town are missing from the registers. At one time or another all the best people could have been encountered at the agents' office: all fifty-one of those who paid duty on silver plate between 1757 and 1762 had policies,[32] as had all those who paid carriage tax between 1753 and 1766;[33] while, looking a little ahead, of eighty-five 'persons paying tax on male servants' in 1780, sixty-six (77 per cent) had policies,[34] and 100 of the 168 names in the Leeds section of the *Northern Directory* of 1781 will be found in the policy registers; and at the end of the century the mayor and his deputy, the recorder, all twelve aldermen, and twenty out of twenty-four councillors held policies.

With this coverage almost every policy – and there are about twenty a year surviving – adds something to the history of Leeds in the decades before the factory; each property is located in its street and often more precisely; the place of residence of non-Leeds owners is always given; the renewal of policies brings evidence of additional

[30] Sun OS 131 174301.

[31] Jackson and Fisher, Sun OS 208 302296; Londonderry belonged to Thomas Close of the Drony Laith dyeworks, 207 299871; Bowling, 208 301447.

[32] PRO, T 47/5 (1757–62), with seven Leeds names; these records and the two next cited are a remarkable directory of the upper part of Yorkshire society in the mid-eighteenth century.

[33] PRO, T 47/2 (1754–66), with fifty-one Leeds names.

[34] PRO, T 47/8 (1780), with eighty-six Leeds names; printed by J. J. Cartwright, 'List of Persons in Yorkshire who paid the tax on male servants in 1780', *Yorkshire Archaeological Journal*, XIV (1898), 65–70. Nobody in Leeds could match the fifteen servants at Temple Newsam and the sixteen at Harewood House. The largest number in Leeds was the eight in the household of Thomas Wilson, a London and Wakefield merchant, former farmer of the Navigation tolls, who had just inherited the West End estate of his brother, the Recorder of Leeds: they were presumably all at the Manor House; William Denison at Town's End and John Blayds at Woodhouse Lane each had four resident male servants.

building; and future industrial revolutionaries are encountered in a prehistoric stage. John Marshall's father, Jeremiah, insured £1500 of stock in a linen draper's shop 'nigh the Bridge' in 1760 where he was simply a tenant; in 1796 his son insured his newly-built flax mill at Holbeck for just over £25,000.[35] Evidence from the policies will form an important part of Chapter Ten when the fire risks of newly-built factories with steam engines guaranteed their prompt appearance in the agency books.

For its first forty years the various holders of the Sun Fire Insurance Agency were writing policies in which the addresses of the insured premises, if located in Leeds, were virtually all in the central streets. The registers of policies for the years 1768 to 1770 are much depleted by loss and damage but when continuity is resumed a new group of locations appears. On 5 July 1770 an insurance for £1500 was taken out on 'a new building not quite finished intended for a General Infirmary';[36] by that time the house of Thomas Barstow Jnr was completed on a plot in Park Row next to the manse of Mill Hill chapel and looking across to the Infirmary. With its insurance for £600 (and a further £140 for out-offices and stables),[37] the new houses of the West End begin to take their place in the policy registers alongside those from the traditional sites of the town centre. Leeds had had its New Street since John Harrison laid out his short avenue of approach to the new church of St John: now, after a century and a half, its Improvement Within was to be augmented by Improvement Without, and by an array of new streets in the West End.

[35] Marshall Snr, Sun OS 153 176853; Marshall Jnr, Sun CS 7 663500.
[36] Sun OS 198 286590.
[37] Sun OS 303 461805.

PART TWO

The Dispersal

EVEN if the Improvement Act was doing little to ameliorate the environment in general, a wealthy townsman could make some private improvement for himself by rebuilding the family home in a more commodious style. The grangerised edition of the *Ducatus* in the possession of the Leeds Library has marginal notes which identify eight large houses noticed by Thoresby that had been demolished between 1743 and 1757. The most remarkable was Jeremiah Dixon's purchase in 1743 of Sir William Rooke's house in Boar Lane and its replacement by a house faced in Huddleston limestone that was said to have cost £4500. In 1765 Richard Wilson, the borough Recorder, rebuilt the Manor House at an unknown cost: the rate assessment promptly doubled. John Ismay, the diarist, who visited Leeds in 1767 viewed 'Ye House Gardens and ornamental Canal of R. Wilson Esq. . . . and several neat and superb Buildings for ye Merchants'. Since it is certain that no new streets were created at this time it must have been such renewals and renovations which John Dyer celebrated in his poem *The Fleece* (1757).

There was an alternative way of improving one's condition, although a drastic one: to move away into the countryside, thereby implying some abandonment of a daily supervision of trade and business, subordinating the merchant role to that of a gentleman, and moving from the social life of a market town into that of country squires. Yet in 1763, twenty years after his expensive rebuilding in Boar Lane, the merchant, Jeremiah Dixon, sold that house to his partner, purchased an estate at Gledhow, and engaged the fashionable architect, John Carr, to build a Hall.

From 1767 new residences in the West End provided a compromise between migrating and rebuilding: segregated from the more distasteful aspects of town and yet not too remote from the workplace; homes in a distinctly superior social setting yet accessible to the familiar religious and social institutions of the town.

By the end of the century a town once compact had developed new streets in forms that were recognisably those of a West and an East End. After the event the marked segregation implied by these two Ends might seem to have arisen from a single stimulus, the one perhaps a reaction to the other, the westerners distancing themselves as far as possible from the sight and sound and pollution of an East End where industrial smoke was a new and less attractive 'incence of thanksgiving' than that which Dyer had found in 1757. Yet in fact the first building plot was occupied in the West End twenty years before there was a single East End street in Leeds. Thus if environmental deterioration was an element in the westward migration of the better-off, it must have been the Centre and not the East End which repelled them.

After thirty years the West End streets, laid out within the fields of one proprietor, were not quite completed but an alternative West End was already under way elsewhere. Some part of the blame lay in a failure to exclude factory industry from the West End. In the East End, which was not initiated as a place with factories nor as a slum, there was also an element of failure to apprehend the long-term results of decisions made in the 1790s, although this was more understandable where development was being undertaken not on the land of one individual but of many.

The two Chapters of this Part describe the strategy – and sometimes the fatal absence of strategy – by which these separate developments were initiated on the two opposite flanks of the town, and Part Three will discuss the subsequent corruption of good intentions by unanticipated mischances.

6
The Genteelest Situations

Although some parts of Leeds are very dirty and smokey, the genteelest situations are certainly very pleasant.

Letter of Sarah Fisher to Jane Fisher, 4 June 1801: Ogden and Ferguson papers, New York Genealogical Society, uncatalogued MS.

Park Place is a fine row of elegant houses, new, extremely neat, large and well built. The rooms inside are as elegant as on the outside.

Shorthand diary of John Russell, RA revisiting Leeds, 1801: transcribed in G. C. Williamson, JOHN RUSSELL, R.A. (1894), p.67.

A WEST END FOR LEEDS

The West End of Leeds was initiated in September 1767 by the grant of a building lease for a plot of land on the Wilson estate (Fig. 6.1). By 1797 it comprised Park Row, South Parade, East Parade, Park Place and Park Square (Fig. 6.2). In this area, approximately 33 acres, and along a total building frontage of just under one mile (5181 feet) there had been erected 122 houses, a General Infirmary and an estate church. In relation to the existing stock of houses in 1767, some 3000, this made a trifling addition; similarly it made up only a small proportion of the 3000 new houses built in Leeds between 1767 and 1797: but it was a novel and significant development nevertheless, for its residents enjoyed a lower density of population per acre than anywhere else in town while its house values were among the town's highest. No similar development was attempted at this period anywhere else in Leeds, and it may well have been the first attempt in any northern industrial town to break the traditional acceptance of town-centre residence for all social classes.

In 1757, a decade before the name Park Row first appeared in documents, the poet John Dyer wrote lines in his *Fleece* that have been often taken to refer to Leeds:

Some with even line
New Streets are marking in the neighb'ring fields,
And sacred domes of worship.[1]

Yet if Dyer ever had Leeds in mind it was as prophet rather than chronicler, for the Ibbetson estate development project of 1755 had already come to nothing; and while there was indeed a new building being completed at the west end of Leeds in 1757 it was dedicated not to worship but to commerce, being a Mixed Cloth Hall for the sale of finished cloth. It is unlikely that the Cloth Hall was intended to be the first stage in what became a residential West End for its alignment was not congruous with either Boar Lane or Park Lane and its oblique position eventually presented some awkward problems in the siting of the Park estate streets. Richard Wilson, lawyer and Recorder, was then seventy-nine years old and only four years from his death, and the sale of land to the Hall trustees was probably no more than a public-spirited action to provide a site for a building of great public utility.[2] His eldest son, also a Richard, a lawyer and Recorder,[3] inherited the estate in 1761 but did nothing further for another six years, in the first four of which he was preoccupied with rebuilding the family home on or near the medieval manorial site on

[1] J. Dyer, *The Fleece*, ed. Edward Thomas (1903), p.96; he also wrote of 'th'increasing walls of busy Manchester, Sheffield and Birmingham' (*Ibid.*, p.97) but oddly, in a poem about the Fleece, he named no town from a wool textile area.

[2] WRRD, BS 38/6. Sir James Ibbetson's grant of a building lease for Gomersal Cloth Hall, on the other hand, was intended as the prelude to a general issue of building leases on adjoining Ibbetson land: preamble to *Acts Local and Personal, 16 Geo. III cap.4*.

[3] For the Wilson family see Wilson, pp.198–203. It is useful to distinguish here the various Richard Wilsons: (I) b.1678, d.1761, son of Thomas Wilson (d.1694) and Elizabeth Sykes; (II) b.1710, d.1776, unmarried, son of (I) and Anna Lockwood; (III) b.1752, d.1787, eldest son of bishop Christopher and Ann Gibson; and (IV) Richard (Fountayne) Wilson b.1782, son of (III) and Elizabeth Fountayne. There were also two Christophers: (I) the bishop, b.1715, d.1792, third son of Richard I; and (II) the bishop's third son, b.1763, m. Sophia Pearse.

FIG. 6.1 THE ACCUMULATION OF THE WILSON (PARK) ESTATE IN THE WEST END, 1780

There was a small medieval park west of the manor house (boundary shown here as dotted line), but by the end of the seventeenth century a series of sales to various purchasers had broken it up into small closes; some of the purchasers' names remained attached to the closes in the eighteenth century when successive Wilsons, living in the rebuilt Manor House on Mill Hill [*extreme right*], used the profits of their law practice to reconstitute the estate; by 1780 further purchases extended it westwards almost to the township boundary. (The St Peter's Hall property [*top left*] was disposed of in 1778.)

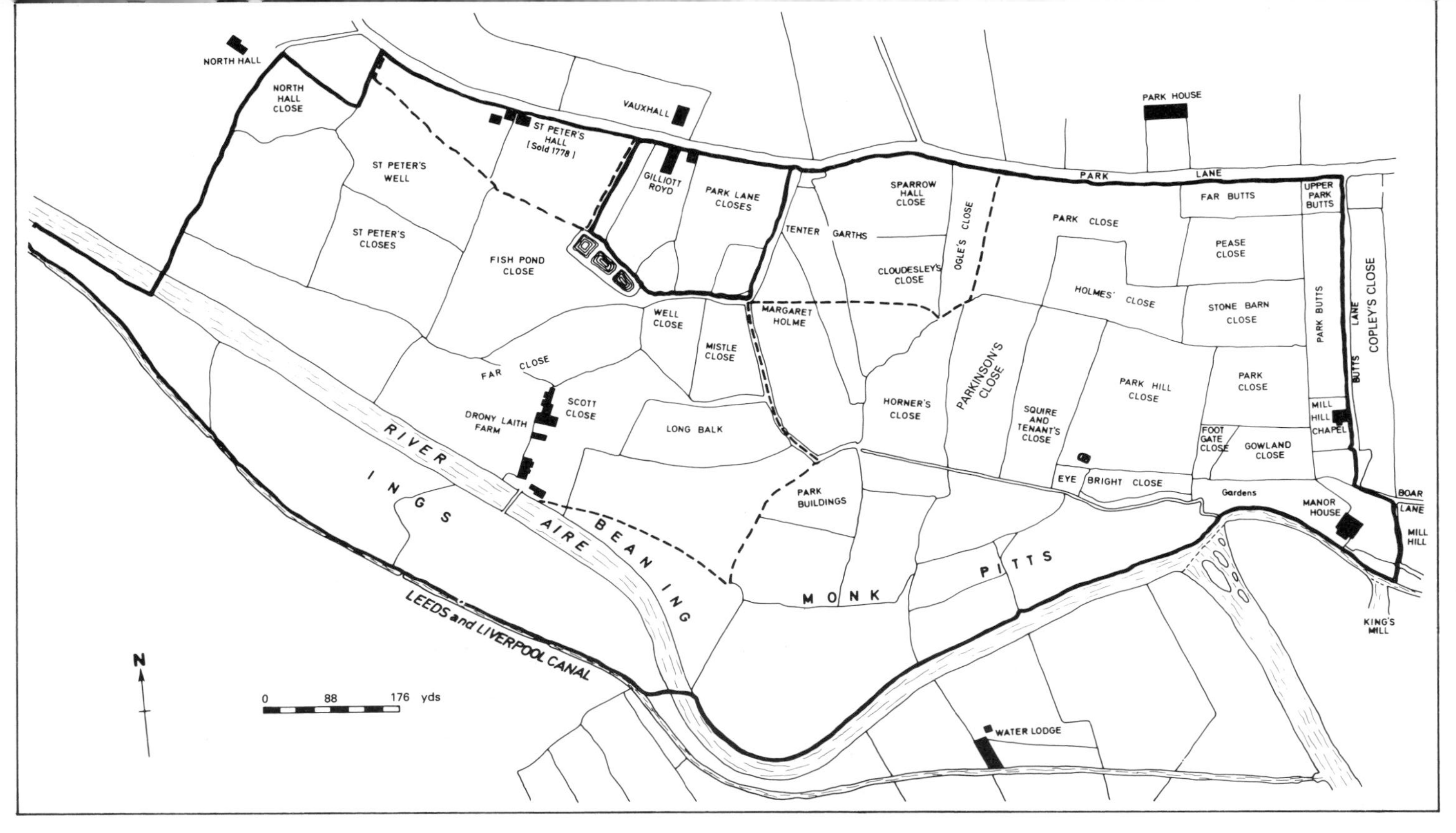
NORTH HALL
NORTH HALL CLOSE
VAUXHALL
ST PETER'S HALL [Sold 1778]
ST PETER'S WELL
ST PETER'S CLOSES
FISH POND CLOSE
GILLIOTT ROYD
PARK LANE CLOSES
PARK HOUSE
PARK LANE
SPARROW HALL CLOSE
TENTER GARTHS
CLOUDESLEY'S CLOSE
OGLE'S CLOSE
PARK CLOSE
FAR BUTTS
UPPER PARK BUTTS
PEASE CLOSE
HOLMES' CLOSE
STONE BARN CLOSE
PARK BUTTS
BUTTS LANE
COPLEY'S CLOSE
MARGARET HOLME
WELL CLOSE
MISTLE CLOSE
FAR CLOSE
SCOTT CLOSE
DRONY LAITH FARM
LONG BALK
HORNER'S CLOSE
PARKINSON'S CLOSE
SQUIRE AND TENANT'S CLOSE
PARK HILL CLOSE
PARK CLOSE
MILL HILL CHAPEL
FOOT GATE CLOSE
GOWLAND CLOSE
EYE BRIGHT CLOSE
Gardens
MANOR HOUSE
BOAR LANE
MILL HILL
KING'S MILL
PARK BUILDINGS
PITTS
MONK
RIVER AIRE
INGS
BEAN ING
LEEDS and LIVERPOOL CANAL
WATER LODGE
N
0
88
176 yds

Mill Hill as a Manor House[4] at an unknown cost but causing its rateable value to rise from £21 to £40.

The Wilsons were too modest to embody either their forenames or surname in their Leeds street names as the Colmores had in Birmingham and the Russells in Bloomsbury but the 'Park' element in three of the names was taken from that part of their property which was known as the Park (or Parks) estate, the character of which will be described in the next section of this Chapter. The street nomenclature carefully avoided 'street' in favour of the more prestigious 'Row', 'Parade', 'Place' and 'Square', terms familiar where Georgian architects had already set an acceptable fashion in Bloomsbury, Bristol and Bath.

Birmingham already had its Colmore Row but, on the evidence of Chalklin's study of the provincial towns, no northern town – not even Liverpool or Manchester – had begun to build its West End when the first houses were being erected in Park Row. The years following the end of the Seven Years War in 1763, as we have already seen, brought the Yorkshire cloth industry out of its long depression. In 1768 the leases of the properties that formed the Grammar School endowment expired: the rent roll had been £150 a year but the trustees were confident enough to ask – and then obtain – £450 a year after the renewals.[5] Subscriptions for the building of an Infirmary costing £4600 were raised without difficulty in 1767–68,[6] and the frequency with which the same years saw building developments initiated elsewhere in England is indicative not of imitation but of a shared general prosperity. Sir Thomas Gooch obtained an Act of Parliament in 1766 enabling him to grant leases for building on the demesnes of the manor of Birmingham. In Manchester Edward

[4] In 1694 Richard Wilson had inherited a 'brick house on Mill Hill': LCA, DB 58/1. In 1628 'The Mannor house of Leedes stoode by the riverside moted rounde about with a dike now almost quite earthed upp': Beresford, *Leeds in 1628*, p.137; also Kirby, p.156. 'Scarborough's Hotel, the King's Arms, at the bottom of Bishopgate Street . . . once the residence of the Right Rev. Christopher Wilson, D.D., late Bishop of Bristol': J. Heaton, *Walks Through Leeds* (Leeds, 1835), pp.6–7.

[5] LCA, LPC 72/4.

[6] S. T. Anning, *The General Infirmary at Leeds* (Leeds, 1963), I, 4–7.

FIG. 6.2 DEVELOPMENT ON THE WILSON (PARK) ESTATE, 1793

From a plan by Jonathan Teal, August 1793. Park Row, South Parade and East Parade surrounded the 'Square' and Park Place was also completed. Park Square had not progressed far beyond its eastern side; a site for St Paul's church is indicated within the square. Sources of industrial smoke, brought by the south-west prevailing wind, were Drony Laith dyeworks (A) and Gott's Bean Ing woollen mill (B). There were also industrial premises on the south side of Park Lane (C) in the former Tenter Garths (Fig. 6.1).

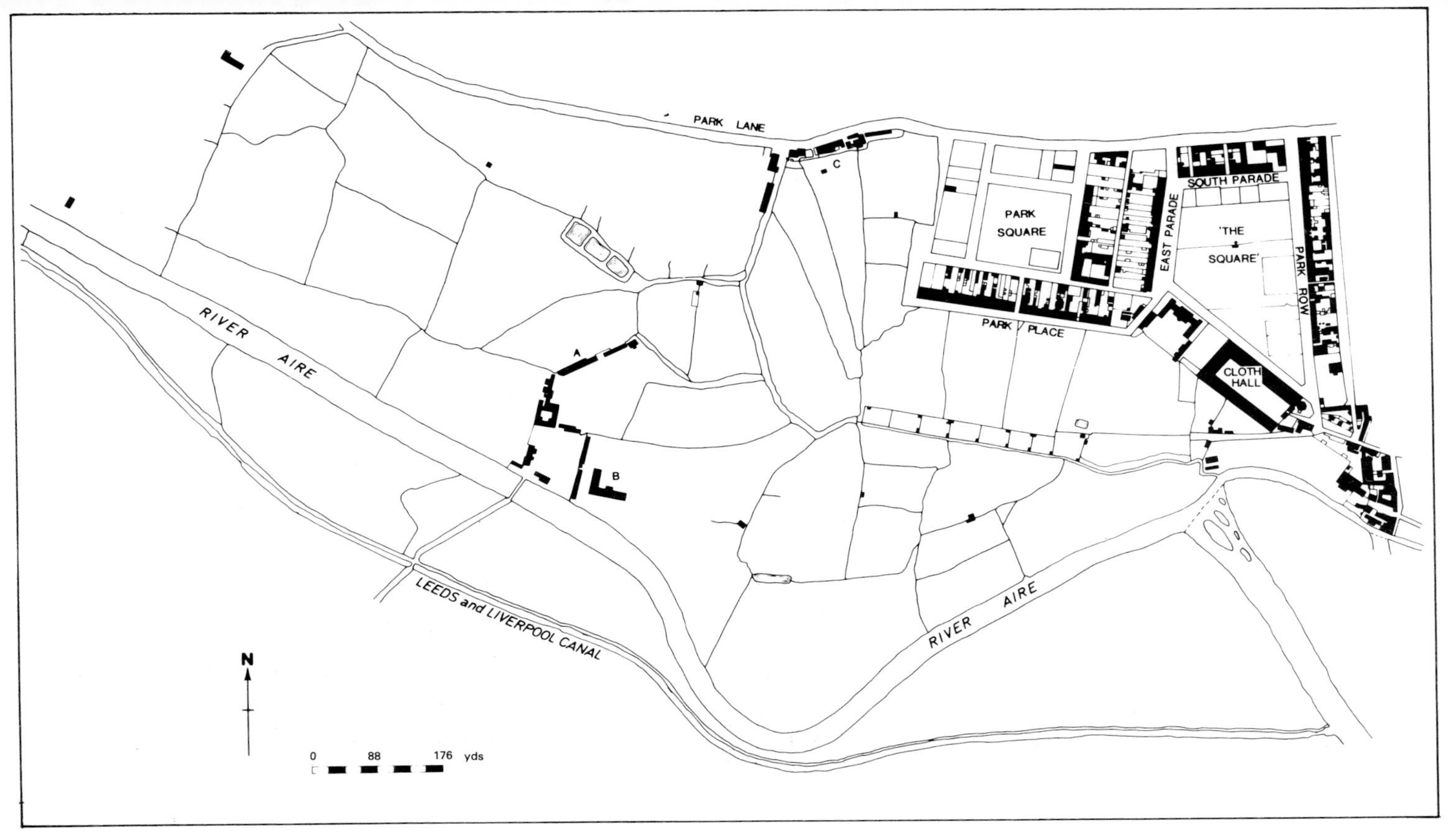

PARK LANE
C
PARK SQUARE
SOUTH PARADE
EAST PARADE
'THE SQUARE'
PARK ROW
PARK PLACE
CLOTH HALL
RIVER AIRE
A
B
LEEDS and LIVERPOOL CANAL
RIVER AIRE
N
0
88
176 yds

Byrom founded St John's church in 1768, the first stage in the development of his estate between Deansgate and the Irwell; and about 1770 Sir Ashton Lever began to convey parcels of land west of Piccadilly. In Liverpool, where much land belonged to the Corporation, there had been intermittent and unschematic development of new streets earlier in the century;[7] nearer to Leeds a small West End was planned at Wakefield in 1775[8] but the most widely discussed project contemporary with the Wilsons' was that for Edinburgh New Town.[9]

The Wilsons' streets were a less ambitious project than that New Town, than the contemporary expansion of Bath beyond its walls or than the new squares of London north of Oxford Street. Yet the Park Row frontage, in its single, plain straight line, measured only a few yards less than the Royal Crescent at Bath, while Park Place was longer than any single street being laid out in Bath, and longer than Colmore Row in Birmingham. In its local context the project was even more remarkable: as Table 6.1 shows, it envisaged new houses along frontages extending for more than 5000 feet at a time when the opposing frontages of Briggate measured together no more than 3400 feet, and the two sides of Kirkgate 2700 feet.

THE PARK ESTATE TO 1767

In whatever town, an extensive and designed array of squares and terraces could be engineered only when enough vacant land was available under one ownership and possessing a clear legal title, unencumbered by restraints on the disposition of building plots such as might reside in entails or marriage settlements. In general, as we have already seen, the land surrounding mid-eighteenth-century Leeds consisted mainly of freehold land; it was abundant, stretching in all directions, and none of it proved to be too steep or too

[7] Chalklin, pp.81–112.

[8] South Parade, Wakefield was the first stage of an extra-burghal suburb but never completed: its date is given variously as *c.*1775 (*The Buildings of England: The West Riding of Yorkshire*, ed. N. Pevsner (2nd edn, Harmondsworth, 1967)), p.534 and 'the early 1790s' (*Wakefield District Heritage*, ed. K. Taylor (Wakefield, 1976), pp.70–1). In Sheffield five houses on what later became the north side of Paradise Square were built in 1736 and completed as a square in 1771 but this development was too near the parish church to qualify as a West End. A grid of streets at Alsop Fields was commenced in 1776: *Sheffield and Its Region*, ed. D. L. Linton (Sheffield, 1956), p.232.

[9] James Craig's 'Plan of the new streets and squares' was accepted by the Council in August 1766 and published the next year: A. J. Youngson, *The Making of Classical Edinburgh* (Edinburgh, 1966), pp.70–74.

TABLE 6.1

Park Estate: Frontages, Plot Areas and Leasehold Rents, 1767–1810

Street and dates of leases	Frontage length in feet	Number of houses	Average frontage per house in feet	Ground rent per foot of frontage, in shillings	Plot depth in feet	Plot area, thousand sq. ft	Notes
Park Row							
Mill Hill chapel and burial ground, 1674	180	–	–	0.23	165	30	Excludes 'The Square' interior ground
Houses, 1767–76	885	23	38	1.0	165	132	
South Parade							
Houses, 1776–80	408	6	68	1.5	160	64	
East Parade							
Houses, 1779–88	599	19	32	1.5	208	125	
Park Place							
Houses, 1788–1800	814	22	37	2.2	205	164	
West Street							
Mixed Cloth Hall, 1757	400	–	–	*	200	8	*Freehold sale, £420
Infirmary, 1768	300	–	–	1.1	200	6	
Park Square							
East-side houses, 1788–94	498	14	36	2.0	63	32	Excludes 'The Square' interior ground
West-side houses, 1791–97	529	22	24	2.0	63	33	Includes 5 houses facing Park Lane and 6 facing St Paul's St
St Paul's church, 1791–93	210	–	–	Free gift	48	10	
North-side houses, 1794–1810	350	–	39	1.9	39	14	
South-side houses, 1797–1802	188	8	24	1.4	48	9	
TOTAL	5361	114	–	–	–	–	

Source: LCA, DB 32, 58 and 239.

waterlogged for building. Its disadvantage was that so much lay in small fields with very dispersed ownership.

There were three exceptions: the Ibbetson, Pawson and Wilson estates. The first named was freed from legal restraints by Act of Parliament in 1755 but did not attract interest: the properties were scattered; no single piece was larger than 6 acres; and this had the workhouse at one corner.[10] The preamble to the Pawson (Ann Wilson) Settled Estate Act of 1767 declared that 'there is now a Fair Prospect and Opportunity, by granting Building Leases, to make a great Improvement': but unrealistically for, although the Pawson fields were more compact than the Ibbetsons', they were placed on either side of Timble Beck near to the dyehouses and the town's oldest burial ground.[11]

The estate which Richard Wilson inherited in 1761 had many advantages: it was made up mainly of contiguous fields and was clear of buildings except for the farms at Drony Laith and St Peter's Hill; it was an untramelled freehold; and it lay west of town immediately adjoining the end of Boar Lane and the Cloth Hall. No description of the estate has survived earlier than a survey made just after Richard's death in 1776 and the succession of his merchant brother, Thomas. There is no map before 1793, in the time of Christopher, the youngest of the Wilson brothers, and heir to Thomas (Fig. 6.2) but it has been possible to reconstruct the earlier topography of the area (Fig. 6.1) thanks to the preservation of title deeds and leases from each component of the estate, still wrapped in bundles corresponding to an original inventory made for the firm of solicitors who managed the family affairs after there ceased to be a Wilson learned in the law.[12]

Christopher Wilson's ownership of the estate was short-lived: he did not inherit until 1789 and died in 1792; in 1789 he was well-established far from Leeds, and never occupied the Manor House where his two elder brothers had lived. He was successively prebendary of Westminster and Finsbury, the latter a life appointment. He married a daughter of a bishop of London and at the age of sixty-eight became bishop of Bristol in 1783. His biographer

[10] *Acts Local and Personal, 28 Geo.II cap. 10* and p.112, above. For what such Acts had to override see B. English and J. Saville, *Strict Settlement* (Hull, 1983).

[11] *Acts Local and Personal, 5 Geo.III cap. 25* and p.113, above; Ann Pawson married William Wilson (1718–64), brother of Richard, Thomas and Christopher Wilson.

[12] LCA, DB 32/15 and 239/1–3: for the scattered Wilson documents in LCA, DB see Bibliography. All statements in the text concerning particular leases, renewals, rents, building costs and mortgages derive from these sources, not all of which are catalogued.

revealed how he had demonstrated the parable of the talents in a remarkable way although it is not clear whether he had been aware of his eldest brother's project in the West End of Leeds.

> The amazing improvement on the prebendal manor of Finsbury is worthy of notice. The history of the church affords but few instances of such an increase in value; and still fewer of its individuals have amassed such an immense fortune from a such slender means – a life interest in fields worth initially only £39 13*s.* 4*d.* a year. It may be said, such opportunities seldom occur; but the merit of the man must not be forgotten, who was equal to the chance. He was an able calculator; and possessed a persevering spirit . . . It appears that he received more than £50,000 clear of all deductions in his lifetime, and he charged this estate in his will with legacies to the amount of £50,000 more.[13]

Building leases on the Leeds Park estate could not bring such opulence: it was one thing to be in a position to cater for the northern overspill of the City of London and find oneself ground landlord of Finsbury Square but quite another to provide for the much smaller number in Leeds who could be tempted into a novel form of living and who were able to meet the building costs. Table 6.3 shows how slowly the total of ground rents climbed.

The 'Park' estate was not a misnomer: most of the Wilson property lay within Mill Hill Division, and in the (highway) rate book for 1765 it can be identified as a large house on Mill Hill, a group of commercial buildings at its rear towards Boar Lane, and 85½ acres of agricultural land to the west; all were leased to tenants except for the Manor House.[14] The demesne estate of the Leeds manor had been broken up after Charles I's sale in 1628: the rights of lordship were equally divided among nine purchasers; the enclosed fields of the demesne found many purchasers but the park, then divided into pasture closes of various sizes, passed into single ownership. The survey of 1628 recorded that there was

> one parcell of ground called the Parkes, which hath beene reputed demeasne, which Conteyne by estimacion about Forty acres or thereaboutes . . . now in the tenure or occupation of Josias Jenkinson . . . for anie mannor house belonging to the Mannor of Leedes wee knowe none . . . we have hard that theire beene in ancyent tyme a mannor house which stood upon the Millne Hill.[15]

Jenkinson eventually sold the Park to Richard Sykes (1627–93), the father-in-law of Thomas Wilson (1680–94). The Wilson inheritance

[13] R. V. Taylor, *The Biographia Leodiensis* (1865), pp. 200–02.
[14] LCA, LORB 31A, f. 55.
[15] Kirby, p. 156.

from Sykes included this manor site, a one-ninth share in the manorial title, and seven closes that were 'part of the reputed Parks';[16] by 1748 (Appendix VI.1) further purchases in and beyond the ancient park doubled the area of the estate, but there were no further augmentations to the rent roll between 1748 and 1775 except from commercial and industrial buildings at Mill Hill; in 1765 these included a warehouse, a dyehouse, the *Black Lion* and several private houses. The only subtraction in this period was the sale of land in Gowland Close for the Cloth Hall (1757).

AN URBAN STRATEGY DEVISED: RICHARD WILSON AND PARK ROW, 1767–76

Even though not a resident in the new streets, having the Manor House for himself, Wilson's interest lay in ensuring that they lacked nothing in gentility: which, in the Leeds context, was the gentility of a community of gentlemen merchants. Some of the desirable qualities were already there in the site: as near to the town centre as any undeveloped site could then be, and adjacent to the largest Cloth Hall; yet not bordering a public highway for (except Park Row) the new streets led only to each other; a slight southerly slope for drainage; with a view of the riverside meadows but raised above any flood line; and minimally subject to smoke from the industrial workshops and dyehouses of Mill Hill and Timble Beck thanks to the direction of the prevailing south-westerly winds.

To these locational advantages the design of the estate would add others. The new streets were wider than any except Briggate and, apart from seclusion, those who took up building leases could expect two advantages not enjoyed at the town centre. A low overall density was to be assured by determining the plot size and each line of houses was to have a quality of privacy unique in Leeds. Unlike the houses in the old streets looking across the roadway to other house windows, their residents would enjoy a double advantage: not only would the *Row* and the two *Parades* be single-sided but they looked into an open space of 6¾ acres left in front of them, sacrificing some 2000 feet of frontage line, equivalent to another Park Row. It was known as 'The Square' even though its shape, due to the presence of the Cloth Hall on its southern flank, was that of a square plus a triangle. It was overbuilt later, so that today the names of the two Parades seem obtuse, with South Parade at the north and East Parade at the west: but the windows in the Parades did once

[16] WRRD, O 541/822.

look in the directions of their names. Since Park Square remains as a public garden of 1½ acres its original design can still be appreciated. The long line of Park Place also had its amenity, now lost: the Giles plan of 1815 shows the gardens which lay opposite each house across the roadway, leading down to an ornamental canal and having uninterrupted views of the riverside meadows.

In 1767 no house in old Leeds had a garden between it and the street, and back gardens were disappearing under bricks and mortar. Ornamental front gardens were not part of any contemporary urban fashion even in Bath and the spas, places less workaday than Leeds. Garden ground for market gardening was available in fields at the fringe, such as Crackenthorpe and McAndrews Gardens to the east of town, and it was possible to rent portions of fields subdivided rather like modern allotments; and cultivated, presumably, by servants. The kitchen garden adjoining the house, once a feature of the garths in Kirkgate and Call Lane, would not reappear until a quite different style of West End residence appeared in the form of the villas described in Chapter Ten.[17] The houses of the Park estate followed the old fashion (which was not abandoned in Bloomsbury or the spas) of abutting houses almost directly to the pavement; with, at the most, a gap to give light and access steps to a basement entrance; over this gap a short flight of stone steps or *paces* climbed to the front door. With no front garden it was the more important that pavements so near the drawing room and dining room windows should not bustle with traffic and that passers-by would be mainly the social equals of the lady of the house. To this the wide streets and the open squares contributed.

The West End streets were based on a rectilinear or grid-iron design with its east-west axis parallel to Park Lane, the northern limit and at that time the only highway leading towards Kirkstall bridge and the upper Aire valley. The name of the surveyor responsible is not known but grid-iron plans – what Dyer had called 'an even line' across the fields – did not require much sophistication. Nothing so elaborate as a Circus or Crescent was envisaged, and the

[17] In one of the older town gardens behind William Cookson's house in Kirkgate it had been possible to grow peaches, pears and nectarines: *LM*, 27 Aug. 1738. 'The first and largest of the New Gardens situate near the Cloth Hall' (*LM*, 20 Feb. 1781) were probably those near Park Place alongside the ornamental canal leading to the Manor House; 'garden grounds' on the Wilson estate were assessed for rates seven years earlier: LCA, LORB 32 (1774), Mill Hill Division.
The first front gardens in Leeds may have been in Carr Place, Claypit Lane in 1807: WRRD, FA 234/300; with 'Twelve Yards in Depth suitable for Gardens': *LM*, 6 April 1807; 'intended a handsome Row': *Ibid.*, 22 June 1807.

first field to be occupied, Park Butts, was virtually a rectangle within which it was only necessary to continue the subdivision initiated a century earlier when ground had been leased for Mill Hill chapel and its burial ground. The line of West Street, the south side of the first square, was predetermined by the long side-wall of the Cloth Hall. Although the Hall was rectilinear, covering some 6500 square yards in the former Gowland Close, its axis had been placed north-west to south-east in order to have an entrance as near as possible to Boar Lane.

There is no record of preliminary negotiations with potential leaseholders but the first lease was signed in September 1767 and a second in the following January. Negotiations were also concluded in August 1768 with the trustees of the General Infirmary to lease building ground which adjoined the Cloth Hall and continued the alignment of its northern side.[18] Richard Wilson's father had been prepared to sell land for the Cloth Hall ten years earlier but now the Infirmary, like all the occupants of the residential streets, was permitted only a sixty-year lease with the obligation to pay an annual ground rent at the same rate, one shilling per foot of street frontage. The change from the father's freehold sale to the son's leaseholds is another indication that the father had not looked beyond a single development.

The Jefferys plan of Leeds, surveyed in 1768–70, shows two or three houses erected in Park Row; there is no other town plan before 1781 by which to chart its progress and, with the Wilsons' 'old ledger' from before 1791 not surviving, the main evidence for the progress of Park Row must come from the leases and renewals preserved in the office of the family attorney, documents crucial to the long-term management of the estate since they established title, specified the dates when the twenty-year options to renew the leases would occur, and recited the covenants which defined the obligations of ground landlord and leaseholders.

Although a bachelor like his brother Thomas, Richard Wilson's technique in exploiting land for building leases was similar to that already used by aristocratic landowners attending to the interests of their children's children rather than those of the immediate moment. By granting building leases for a term of years a landowner ensured himself a fixed income from the ground rents. It was an ideal arrangement for those who did not wish to involve themselves with the capital cost of speculative building or the problems of managing

[18] LCA, DB 32/18. Particulars of this and all the leases cited in the text will be found in Appendices VI.2–VI.6, arranged by streets.

rented houses. The leases of the empty plots were assigned either directly to someone intending to have a house built or to a master craftsman within the building trades acting speculatively who would later seek to sell the house he had built, together with the unexpired part of the ground lease with all its rights and obligations.

The ground landlord's principal obligation was to provide and surface the roadway and pavement in front of each lot. The natural slope southwards would have facilitated surface drainage although nothing was said of this in the covenants. There were no town sewers at that time; no interior lavatories are mentioned in descriptions of the houses, and sanitation must have been by outside privies at the rear over ashpits. Small backyard buildings of this size can be seen in the large-scale plans. Some yards had their own wells and pumps but the whole estate was well below the level of the town waterworks reservoir, to which residents could be connected by pipes, and gravity would have provided a good head for tap water. There was as yet no gas; and since the provision of the Lamp Act did not operate outside the Bars the obligation to light fell on each householder, probably achieved by lamps on iron brackets above the street steps of each house.

For the owner of any extensive estate there was also the hope of profiting indirectly from the house building towards which they had had to contribute nothing. As buildings multiplied the surrounding fields would become more attractive as building ground, and higher ground rents obtained. A low ground rent, fixed for a term of years, also tempted the leaseholder to build over as much of his plot as possible – to the ultimate advantage of the ground landlord – since the rent was determined solely by the frontage length of the plot, initially one shilling per foot per year.[19] If the lease ran to expiry then all the buildings reverted to the ground landlord: or, as happened in the end to the Park Row properties, an earlier bargain could be struck and the tenure converted to freehold on payment of a sum for enfranchisement; meanwhile, at intervals, lump sum payments ('fines') could be obtained from tenants wishing to renew their leases.[20]

[19] A site in Park Row with warehouses already erected was advertised with the incentive 'no more ground rent when houses are erected': *LM*, 19 March 1776.

[20] From 1800 to 1803, when the ground rents totalled £400 a year, the average revenue from renewal of leases was £72: First Schedule to *Acts Local and Personal, 43 Geo.III cap. 30*; see also Appendices IX.1 and IX.2 below. The strategy of building leases is fully explained in Chalklin, Ch.4; for such a strategy in action elsewhere see D. J. Olsen, *Town Planning in London* (New Haven, 1964), Chs 3 and 6; Survey of London, *The Grosvenor Estate in Mayfair, Part 1* (1977), Ch.III and Appendix 1.

With the long frontage of Park Row at his disposal Wilson was able to offer leaseholders a width of plot to suit their individual needs, always maintaining a minimum width. In Briggate a burgage plot 50 feet wide would carry two houses, and in Kirkgate a typical house had an 18-foot frontage: that of the first Park Row plot, leased to Thomas Barstow on 15 September 1767, had an untypically large width of 57 feet (Appendix VI.2), a frontage not to be exceeded until large houses were built as centrepieces to the east and north sides of Park Square in 1790 and 1793.[21] This was not the end plot of the Row; that adjoined Mill Hill chapel, and early in 1768 the chapel trustees took a lease of it as a site for a manse. Their new minister, Dr Joseph Priestley, had just arrived in Leeds and had to take lodgings while the manse was being built: thereby giving Leeds a place in the history of chemistry, for it was then that his proximity to a brewery made him aware of the effluent gases and curious to analyse them.[22]

Alone of the houses in the Row, the manse was set well back from the pavement in the manner of the chapel itself.[23] The others when completed formed a facade 800 feet long, broken only by a narrow passage between nos 6 and 7: the gap where Commercial Street entered in 1823 was achieved only by demolishing no. 7. With such an all-but-continuous frontage there would need to be a back entrance but this was no problem since Butts Lane was a public way. In early insurance policies the school room of Mr Hodgson's Academy at no. 12 was located 'over a stable in the Back Lane', and in 1784 Dunderdale's insurance policy for no. 19 included his 'Back Lane warehouse'.[24] The line of the former Back Street is now followed by Basinghall Street.

Built over so many years and for different clients the houses within the frontage were probably as varied as those surviving in Park Place or Park Square. Of their height the Ordnance Survey plan tells us nothing, but the dimensions shown in Table 6.1 would allow for simple two-bay door-and-window houses at nos 16–17 and 21, three- and four-bay houses on most of the other plots, and five bays at Barstow and Thompson's houses, nos 2 and 30. There was probably no more than one servant's bedroom. In the census enumeration for 1801 the average number of residents in Park Row

[21] LCA, DB 239.

[22] J. Priestley, *Experiments and Observations* (2 vols, 1775), II, 269. Priestley left Leeds in May 1773 just before the minister's house was complete: W. L. Schroeder, *Mill Hill Chapel* (Leeds, 1924).

[23] An engraving showing the chapel and manse forms the frontispiece to J. Priestley, *The Leeds Infirmary: a Sermon* (Leeds, 1768; repr. 1910).

[24] Hodgson: Sun OS 351 541141; Dunderdale: 262 398634 and 264 398634.

was only just over five: this can be compared with the large households of ten or more in South Parade.[25] (Hodgson's Academy at no. 12, with thirty-nine females resident, and Sigston's next door with eleven, have been excluded from this count.)

If building took place close to the date of each new lease then it travelled from both ends of the row towards the centre where a large 150-foot plot remained vacant until 1776 when it was taken by the merchant Richard Markham to build four houses, one for his own residence and three to rent, forming nos 11–14. Nos 15–18 had also been developed as a resident- and-tenant quartet five years earlier by another merchant, Thomas Armistead. We can suppose, from examples elsewhere on the estate, that such multiple ownership made for unity of architectural style within each quartet.

Architects and builders, often the same persons at this period, cannot be identified for all the houses on the Wilson estate but when Armistead took his lease the four houses had already been erected by Thomas Adamson, 'carpenter' and the same Adamson certainly built nos 19–22. He advertised no. 22 as 'new built' in September 1772, nine months after taking up the lease of the plot. This house and no. 21 were taken by Henry Ibbetson, woolstapler, whose widow owned them both in 1808. He also took a lease of no. 7 (not built by Adamson) in the same year. All eight houses built by Adamson appear in the rate books of 1774.

Adamson did not himself reside in Park Row among the merchants for whom he built houses but he would have been a master carpenter rather than the mere tradesman that the term 'carpenter' implies today, and the same was true of William Smith, 'bricklayer', who leased a plot large enough for a pair of houses in 1772 and another in 1773, and a plot for another pair in 1775. Another master carpenter, William Hargrave, was the first owner of no. 5 which he probably built himself and he will be encountered later in Park Row and Park Square both as a speculative builder and as a house landlord. Smith also built there but Adamson's name does not reappear. He may have overstretched himself financially by a commitment to develop such a long frontage in Park Row for in November 1775 he sub-let 115 feet of the 150-foot frontage to a partnership of a London and a Leeds merchant while mortgaging his own interest in the remainder.[26]

A rough estimate of the capital value added to the land when Park Row was completed in 1776 would be £15,000 (Table 6.2); the

[25] LCA, LPC 104, Mill Hill Divison.
[26] LCA, DB 32/27.

TABLE 6.2

Park Estate: Construction Costs of Buildings, 1767–1813

	£	
Mixed Cloth Hall, 1757–58	5,300	
Infirmary, 1768–71	4,599	(and new wings, 1782 and 1786 *c.*£700)
Park Row, 1767–76	15,000	(23 houses)
South Parade, 1776–80	6,000	(6 houses)
East Parade, 1779–87	8,600	(19 houses)
Park Place, 1788–1800	18,000	(23 houses)
Park Square, 1788–1810	37,000	(16 houses)
Drony Laith Dyeworks	1,000	
Bean Ing Cloth Mill	9,400	
St Paul's church, 1791–94	10,000	
Court House and Prison, 1811–13	10,000	
TOTAL	124,899	

Sources: Cloth Hall, Infirmary and St Paul's church, K. Grady, 'The Provision of Public Buildings in the West Riding of Yorkshire, *c.*1600–1840' (unpublished PhD thesis, University of Leeds, 1980), Gazetteer; other items estimated from values in leases, sales and insurances at dates as close as possible to their construction. The values for Bean Ing Mill and the Drony Laith dyeworks are insured values, without contents.

immediate gain to the estate was the accumulation of ground rents (Table 6.3) which had then reached £62 a year. Yet this was a small sum in comparison with the income from the rest of the estate, to say nothing of £9000 invested in turnpikes, canals and the Navigation. Just before his death Richard Wilson was negotiating the purchase of Drony Laith farm, with its 44 acres of fields to the west of the Park estate, at a price of £5000:[27] in brick-and-mortar terms that was about the cost of building the Cloth Hall (£5300) or the five largest residences in Park Row. The overseers of the poor also rejoiced in what builders, whether speculatively or on contract, had achieved: for between the rate books of 1765 and 1774 the assessed value of buildings on Wilson land in Mill Hill Division had more than doubled.

[27] LCA, DB 32/7.

TABLE 6.3

*Park Estate: Accumulation of Ground Rents from Leaseholds, 1767–99**

Year	Park Row, shillings	South Parade, shillings	Park Place, shillings	East Parade, shillings	Park Square, shillings	Annual total of new rents, shillings	Rent roll, nearest £
	New rents of the year						
1767	53	–	–	–	–	53	3
1768	87	–	–	–	–	87	7
1769	90	–	–	–	–	90	12
1770	–	–	–	–	–	–	12
1771	314	–	–	–	–	314	27
1772	222	–	–	–	–	222	38
1773	40	–	–	–	–	40	40
1774	–	–	–	–	–	–	40
1775	84	–	–	–	–	84	45
1776	–	330	–	–	–	330	62
1777	–	118	–	–	–	118	67
1778	–	90	586	–	–	676	101
1779	–	–	–	180	–	180	110
1780	–	68	–	–	–	68	113
1781	–	–	–	–	–	–	113
1782	–	–	–	–	–	–	113
1783	–	–	–	–	–	–	113
1784	–	–	–	54	–	54	116
1785	–	–	194	230	–	424	137
1786	–	–	147	209	–	356	155
1787	–	–	–	320	–	320	172
1788	–	–	462	98	–	560	199
1789	–	–	100	–	89	189	208
1790	–	–	107	–	643	750	246
1791	–	–	54	–	210	264	259
1792	–	–	–	–	–	–	259
1793	–	–	–	–	430	430	280
1794	–	–	104	–	310	414	301
1795	–	–	–	–	–	–	301
1796	–	–	–	–	193	193	312
1797	–	–	–	–	555	555	339
1798	–	–	–	–	–	–	339
1799	–	–	–	–	96	96	343
TOTAL	890	606	1754	1091	2526	6867	£4982

* Table excludes rents from Infirmary site, leased 24 Aug. 1768 for £16 10*s.* per annum (LCA, DB 32/18) and some improved rents at Mill Hill on the old fringe of the Park (DB 24/11 and 60).

Sources: Leases: LCA, DB 32/19 and 58/33; ledger, 1791–1829: DB 32/7.

BEYOND EAST PARADE: DEVELOPMENTS BY THOMAS WILSON, 1776–89

The London merchant Thomas Wilson was already sixty-three when he succeeded his lawyer brother in July 1776. A survey of the estate later that year[28] shows Thomas residing in the Manor House, and he seems to have been actively interested in the affairs of the estate. In London at one time he had advanced money to assist his younger brother in his land speculation. In February 1777 he concluded his late brother's negotiations for the purchase of the Drony Laith freehold and purchased an additional close that July. Three years later the estate was consolidated on its southern side by the purchase of the three Monkpitts closes at the riverside (Appendix VI.1). All these additions were far from the boundary of the projected streets and could not have been bought for immediate building ground; nor at that time could anyone have envisaged that in 1792 foundations would be laid in part of Drony Laith's fields for the world's first woollen mill.

The next increments in ground rents from the Park estate came from the large houses in South Parade, the westward extension of Park Row (Table 6.3). It was not commenced at a propitious time for a town of cloth exporters, with an American war in progress, but all six houses were completed by 1780. Five of these, all built by William Smith, were occupied by merchants; the partners in the firm of Lloyd and Cattaneo were neighbours at no. 2 and no. 3, of which the builder was William Smith (Appendix VI.3).[29]

All these six frontages exceeded 60 feet, allowing for houses as large as would be found anywhere in Leeds at the time. They had high insured values, from £1000 to £1700, and rateable values of £18 and £20. The former was the same as that of the largest house in Park Row, and the latter as Ikin's house and warehouses on the double frontage at the corner of Park Row and Park Lane. No. 3, with its 100-foot frontage, had a ground-floor study as well as the usual three main living rooms and kitchens; there were seven bedrooms 'exclusive of the Servants' Rooms in the roof', the 'Base [i.e. basement] Floor used for a Servants Hall, Brewhouse, and Wash-house' with stabling for four horses, a saddle house and two granaries. At the rear were 'two small Houses and Warehouses for Wool, Cloth and Stuffs; Press shops, Dressing shops and other Conveniences'. Part of the square opposite had been walled for an

[28] LCA, DB 32/1; the lost first volume of the ledger (DB 32/7) may have been begun at this time.

[29] LCD 6048.

orchard. For these desirable frontages with their southern aspect 1*s.* 6*d.* per foot of frontage had been obtained. The merchants needed access to their back premises so that a wide space was left for a centre 20-foot private road passing through to Park Lane.[30]

After the leasing of all the South Parade plots there was an interval of three years before East Parade began; the later years of the American war were not good ones for the cloth trade. The first to be built was no. 16 at the north end next to South Parade.[31] This house, the only one in the Parade to be shown on Tuke's map of 1781, stood on a plot leased in December 1779 and was insured against fire in July 1780.[32] In general East Parade was composed of modest houses, certainly much smaller than South Parade (Appendix VI.4). Because of the ground already occupied by the Infirmary the frontage was 200 feet shorter than Park Row, which it faced across the Square. In this position plots were favoured by doctors and surgeons, and no. 1 eventually became the first premises of the Leeds School of Medicine. It was found possible to obtain as much per foot of frontage as in South Parade, and with no existing road at the rear to constrict plot size more than 200 feet could be allotted for their depth, compared with 165 feet in Park Row and 160 in South Parade. Unlike South Parade, the facade of houses was completely unbroken, and access to their rear was provided by the narrow Park Cross Street running from Park Lane to the continuation of West Street; in due course this would also give backside access to houses on the east side of Park Square.

The southern half of the Parade (1785–87) was certainly the work of John Kendall 'cabinet maker', probably the 'John Kendall joiner' who was later to build Kendall's Row, an early line of back-to-backs (1793) in the South Division.[33] Between 1784 and 1787 William Smith, the master bricklayer already encountered at work in Park Row, was building nos 8–15; no. 16 was leased as early as 1779 and although its builder is not recorded it may well have been Smith.

[30] Insured values:
no. 2 (Bischoff, 1790: Sun OS 366 569216) £1000
no. 4 (Cattaneo, 1782: Sun OS 303 461807) £1300
no. 5 (Armitage, 1794: Sun CS 8 636170) £1700
nos 6–7 (Markland, 1802: Sun CS 49 739169) £1225

In their warehouse behind nos. 4 and 5 the firm of Lloyd and Cattaneo had goods insured for £6000 in 1782 (Sun OS 303 461806). The Lloyd and Cattaneo houses, with the entrance to their yard between, are clearly depicted in the background of R. D. Chantrell's watercolour, 'The Philosophical Hall, Leeds, 1821' (Leeds City Museum).

[31] LCD 6048.

[32] Sun OS 285 431614.

[33] Illustrated in Fraser, ed., fig. 19.

Although not completed so quickly as East Parade, Park Place was launched in 1785 almost at the same time, and its plot depths were virtually the same (Appendix VI.5). A continuation of West Street into what is now St Paul's Street gave back access to Park Place and (later) to the south side of Park Square. The Park Place ground rents were the highest obtained on the estate at a uniform 2*s*. 2½*d*. per foot of frontage. The architectural style of the long terrace, balanced on either side of a short central opening, need not be described since most of the twenty-three original houses remain. Neither Smith nor Kendall has been traced at work there, and since nos 8 to 22 can definitely be assigned to William Hargrave he may have built the remainder, for which there is no documentary evidence. The frontage widths assigned to the earliest houses at the eastern end were appropriate to houses with four bays but smaller houses followed. Even so, insured values of £1000 and over are found at nos 7, 12, 18 and 20; the house with the highest rateable value was no. 7 at £23.[34]

By the year of his death in 1789 Thomas Wilson had seen a doubling of the yield from ground rents, and there had been some improvements also at Mill Hill. It was during this period that the future industrialist, John Marshall, left school to help his father equip a new warehouse for linen that had just been erected on land leased from Wilson.[35] The industrial and commercial building so near the Manor House may signify that Thomas Wilson had ceased to occupy the family house but the rate book of 1790 does show the premises, 'late Wilson', as owner-occupied.[36] There was little chance that his successor, the third brother, would leave his bishop's palace to reside here.

AN ABSENTEE DEVELOPER, 1789–92: CHRISTOPHER WILSON, BISHOP OF BRISTOL

When Thomas Wilson died in 1789, Park Place was only one house away from completion and two plots in the centre of the east side of Park Square had already been leased (Appendix VI.6). The year 1790 was a remarkably successful one, resulting in new ground rents of £32, the largest of any annual increment enjoyed by the estate,

[34] Insured values:
no. 7 (Dunderdale, 1800: Sun CS 33 703832) £1450
no. 18 (Cotton, 1789: Sun OS 364 562787) £1000
no. 20 (Plowes, 1803: Sun CS 53 746483) £1150

[35] Rimmer, *Marshall's*, pp. 13–14.

[36] LCA, LORB 34, f. 30.

and by March only two of the fourteen plots on the east side of the square remained unleased. The price obtained, 2*s*. per foot of frontage, was only slightly less than in Park Place and when the large corner plot at the north-west corner was taken up in January 1791 all must have looked set fair for a rapid completion. An additional cachet was given in November when the Revd Miles Atkinson, the owner of no. 9, agreed to provide the funds for St Paul's church[37] on land donated by the bishop,[38] but in the event no other lease was taken during the remainder of 1791 nor in 1792, the year of the bishop's death. In August the executors of the estate commissioned a survey which showed no houses beyond the church on the south side, and none on the north and west sides.[39] The nature of the bishop's will had certainly thrown into doubt the validity of leases subsequently granted but there may have been a general absence of business confidence even before the outbreak of war with France in 1793. Writing of that year in his study of speculative building in other provincial towns, Chalklin concluded: 'In London, Bath and Bristol, the collapse was immediate.'[40]

All the identifiable developments in Park Square were certainly undertaken by speculative builders. The name of William Lawrance, who described himself comprehensively as 'carpenter, joiner and architect', first appears in the lease for no. 10 which was built on the widest frontage in the square but he also built the smaller pair nos 11–12 and perhaps 13–14 also. Hargrave moved on from his work in Park Place to nos 4–7 and perhaps 1–3. There is only one insurance policy for this period, that taken out in 1790 by Hargrave, probably for no. 6, valued at £500;[41] this had a £15 rateable value, as had all the larger houses between nos 5 and 9; no. 10, the largest, was assessed at £20.

Despite the loss of the original south side, enough survives of the other facades for the quality of the square to be appreciated from the vantage point of its central lawns and flower beds. The large no. 8 on the east side and the corresponding nos 40 and 41 on the north side are in the ornate gabled style favoured for the centrepieces of Park Place and the large houses of South Parade, set off by their

[37] See below, p. 156

[38] *LI*, 4 Oct. 1791; first service, 13 April 1794; first burial (Thomas Close, once of Drony Laith), 13 Jan. 1796: 'Burials at St Paul's Church', *PTh.S*, XV (1905), 56.

[39] LCA, DB 32/3B.

[40] Chalklin, p. 281.

[41] Sun OS 374 578936; the importance of the backside warehouse in Park Square is indicated by the £2000 for which David Rimington, brandy merchant, insured his contents in the same year: Sun OS 369 572073.

square-roofed and plainer neighbours on either side. There are good bay and staircase windows surviving at the rear of many premises but visible only after effort.

A STRATEGY IN ABEYANCE, 1792–1809

Neither Christopher Wilson's principal heir, his infant grand-nephew, nor his second son, Christopher, to whom a life interest in the Leeds estate was bequeathed, were likely to return to occupy the family home on Mill Hill. The grand-nephew had his deceased father's house, Rudding Hall at Follifoot. He was not unwilling to take to completion an agreement which his father had made with Wormald and Gott in 1791 for the sale of 11 acres of land adjoining the site of their Bean Ing woollen mill[42] but doubts had arisen whether Christopher, as life tenant only, could prejudice the rights of the eventual heir by such an irrevocable sale. The consent of the court of Chancery was obtained in June 1793 and buttressed the next year by a private Act of Parliament authorising this sale and confirming the renewal of building leases for Park Row and South Parade that were coming up for renewal now that the first twenty of their sixty years had passed.[43] The lessee had this right of renewal on payment of one year's ground rent, and it was prudent for him to extend the sixty-year term to eighty and to take advantage of a continued contract for a ground rent immune from increases in the inflation that was then beginning.

The surviving large-scale plan of August 1793 (Fig. 6.2) probably accompanied a valuation, now lost, which took stock of the estate's potential for further development. It shows that no houses had yet been built on the south side of Park Square, and gaps remained on the northern and western frontages. When new leasing began again on the west side of Park Square in 1795 it proved still possible to obtain 2*s*. per foot of frontage for the new ground rents but on the north side, where Hargrave was then building nos 43, 44 and 45, the rate dropped to 1*s*. 10*d*. and when Lawrance took all the remaining south side in 1797 for a row of seven houses he paid only 1*s*. 5*d*.

Two other builder architects are named in leases of this last period of development in the square: John Cordingley, 'carpenter', built nos 26–27 and also no. 42 on the north side and Thomas Johnson

[42] *The Leeds Woollen Industry, 1780–1820*, ed. W. B. Crump (*PTh.S*, XXXII (1931)), 256; RE 25 134905 and 26 133485, Jan. and March 1793.

[43] *Acts.Local and Personal, 34 Geo.III cap. 32.*

'architect' built nos 39–40 on the same side. Cordingley sold no. 42 to his client for £2500 and when Hargrave's no. 8 next changed hands in 1800 it fetched £1240. The insurance policies confirm that offices and press shops were still thought appropriate for backyards here, and it has already been pointed out that no. 10 had (and has) an archway on its frontage wide enough to admit waggons to workshops and warehouses at the rear.

With the original streets still incomplete and the French war beginning it cannot have seemed the right moment to plan further, beyond assenting to the construction of a new turnpike road to Kirkstall bridge and Bradford commencing at the south-western end of Park Square and thence across the undeveloped Wilson fields until it reached the township boundary. The new thoroughfare would be useful for traffic generated at Gott's Mill and would increase the potential value of the building ground alongside it but the residents of The Square and Park Square cannot have been pleased to see and hear the Leeds–Bradford traffic, which had previously gone along the old road from Park Lane via Burley, roll past their doors.

Worse was to come: in an estate survey made in April 1806 the central open ground in Park Square was sketched in as divided into four lots to make a 'new street' although a second plan of February 1809 reveals the project abandoned but only after the central plots had been 'sold to the Inhabitants' to preserve their (and now our) amenity.

The more extensive square in front of Park Row was less fortunate. It had already lost any pretentions to be a recreational or ornamental open space when residents of South Parade had been allowed to wall the land in front of their houses as garden ground and 'the residue used as tenter ground'. The whole area was offered for sale and in 1805 found speculative purchasers in the partners, William Thompson and John Lee who paid £15,560 for the 32,760 square yards (10*s.* 6*d.* per square yard).

The outright sale of this area, as opposed to a leasehold, was made possible by a second Wilson Estate Act obtained in 1803.[44]

THE REWARDS OF STRATEGY

The social and economic distinctions which welded like with like and determined the acceptable boundaries of groups and classes were imported to the Park estate, not created by it. They depended, as R. G. Wilson has shown, on occupational identity, particularly that

[44] Preamble to *Acts Local and Personal, 43 Geo.III cap. 30.*

of merchant; by loyalty to and attendance at Church or meeting house; and by extensive intermarriage.[45] Residential segregation on a new estate was both a bold declaration that social boundaries existed and a powerful way of reinforcing them although the Park estate never comprised all the top rank of Leeds society. Some had too recently rebuilt their Boar Lane or Briggate properties.[46] There is no difficulty in establishing the social exclusiveness of the residents, whether by the recurrence of the names of leading families in the directories or by the occupations named in the leases – lawyers, clergy, surgeons, and merchants. In 1792 three of the seven houses of South Parade were occupied by merchants who had been mayors of the town; the fourth by a prominent attorney and the fifth by Martha Busk whose merchant husband had just died leaving upwards of £15,000.[47] In 1792–93 fifteen gentlewomen, spinsters or widows were paying ground rents as householders, and the directories reveal more who were living in rented houses on the estate.

Another indicator of the type of resident attracted to the Park estate is the high value of domestic contents that were insured against fire. In three successive policies registered on 11 July 1782 Thomas Barstow of no. 2 Park Row insured £350 in household goods, £100 in clothes and £40 in gold and silver plate; Henry Cattaneo insured his new house in South Parade for £1250 with domestic contents of £550; while Thomas Markland, who had just purchased a house which was described in the *Intelligencer* as 'elegantly fitted up', insured £400 in household goods, £200 in clothes, £200 in books and £100 in plate. Whether anyone was refused as socially unacceptable we cannot know from the type of documents available.[48] Certainly the Wilsons, although by this time Anglican and Tory, did not exclude dissenters and Whigs, for the end house in Park Row had Dr Joseph Priestley as its first occupant and, of the twenty-four trustees from the Mill Hill meeting house who signed the lease for that building plot, four were later to take up leases.

In any event, social ambition would have to be matched by a long purse in order to be a resident on the Park estate. All, according to the Wilson Estate Act of 1794, were 'large and valuable dwellings'.[49] Quite apart from any minimum standards embodied in the initial agreements the plot widths, which in a terrace or a row had to be completely filled, determined the minimum size of houses. The

45 Wilson, Chs. 2, 4, 7, and 8.
46 See above, p. 112
47 Wilson, p. 242.
48 Barstow: Sun OS 268 461805; Cattaneo: 268 461807; Markland: 268 461804.
49 *Acts Local and Personal, 34 Geo. III cap. 32*, preamble.

average in Park Row was 38 feet, and in South Parade 68 feet (Table 6.1). Large houses implied high maintenance costs including the employment of resident domestic servants. The surviving household census returns for 1801 do not differentiate servants but it is unlikely that the fourteen persons in Bolland's house at no. 41 Park Square, built five years earlier, were all members of his family.[50]

There is no comprehensive source of information on the prices paid to builders for these houses since the leases were concerned only with ground rents; occasionally a lease recalls that the leaseholder has purchased a house from a previous leaseholder who was the builder. It is known therefore that the speculative builder and master bricklayer, William Smith, who erected nos 7–10 Park Row, sold no. 7 to Henry Ibbetson for £700, no. 8 for £900 and no. 9 for £676, sums confirmed in the first instance by an insured value in 1771 of £700, 'unfinished'. William Hargrave, master carpenter, who built at least fourteen of the houses in Park Place speculatively, sold no. 15 for £1000 and no. 16 for £1400. No. 8, in the centre of the east side of Park Square was insured for £900 in 1799 and sold for £1240 a year later, and the more ornamented no. 42 on the north side was sold in 1799 by its builder, the master carpenter John Cordingley, for £1500. Six years after Thomas Adamson, master carpenter, had built no. 19 Park Row he sold it to the linen merchant, David Dunderdale. Its new owner had a policy for £950; the end house, no. 23, was insured for £600.[51] Five insurances in excess of £1000 survive for houses in Park Place. Policies are known for five of the seven houses in South Parade, none for less than £1000. East Parade houses were more modest, typical sale values being £500 but with one insurance of £900 and another of £750. Few policies are known for Park Square, possibly because by the time that it was under way (1788–97) the Sun company was losing its near-monopoly, and the policy registers of its competitors have not survived to inform building historians.

Rateable values also indicate the superior quality of West End houses. When the overseers of the poor made their assessment for May 1790 Park Row was complete. Each house assessment included in a single sum its domestic and commercial buildings: the highest (no. 14) was for £22; there was one at £20, one at £16, two at £15, one at £14, two at £12 and three at £10. Later streets on the Park estate had some houses with larger rateable values than these: 18 Park Place and 14 Park Square at £24, with 1 and 4 Park Place at £23.

50 LCA, LPC 104, Mill Hill Division.

51 Ibbetson: Sun OS 268 404709; no.8 Park Square: CS 26 686922; Dunderdale: OS 262 392792 with £2000 worth of goods in rear warehouse insured in 264 398634; no.23 Park Row: OS 377 583977.

These assessments were based on the annual rentals, which cannot easily be turned into capital values but some prices paid for new houses can be recovered from leases, particularly where a lease was being transferred from a builder to a buyer who then reimbursed the builder for the cost of the house. In general, however, the bulky Wilson archive is not very informative about house prices. The Wilson interest was that of ground landlord, so that when a house changed hands the Wilsons' attorney would draw up a new ground lease but would not be concerned with the conveyances that recorded the change of ownership of the house. These would be drawn up by the vendor's and purchasers' lawyers, and retained in their offices after being taken to Wakefield for registration. The registered deeds are now freely available for study but, from considerations of privacy, an enrolment at the West Riding Registry, although a verbatim recital of a conveyance, was permitted to exclude the sum paid.

The West End houses can be more usefully placed in context by comparing their rateable values with properties elsewhere in town that were occupied by gentlemen merchants. Even in 1774 there were only a few premises not in the West End where assessments matched those just cited, although the Wilsons' own Mansion House was rated at £44, a sum equalled only by the Ibbetson house in the Square in Kirkgate then tenanted by Samuel Buck, who would succeed Richard Wilson as Recorder in 1776. The houses that matched the most valuable on the Park estate were a small group of detached roadside houses on the fringe of town: in Woodhouse Lane the detached house of Samuel Elam (Portland House) was assessed at £25, and Joseph Elam's Claremont (Little Woodhouse) at the same sum; the Jowitt house on Hunslet Lane paid the same. John Blayds's Claypit House on Woodhouse Lane (Fig. 9.1) was assessed at £24, the Dalley Manor House at Great Woodhouse near the moor (Fig. 10.2) at £23 and the older Denison house at Town's End (Fig. 3.4) at £22.

As we have already seen, owner-occupiers in central Leeds were harder to find than landlords with tenants, even at the highest social levels. In the new, quality building on the Wilson estate it might be expected that there would be a larger proportion of owner-occupiers. Yet only half the houses in Park Row in 1774 were owner-occupied; others were owned by Park estate residents who had leased more than one plot and thus had neighbours who were their tenants. Particularly in the early years, builders were landlords for a number of years, perhaps by design, perhaps while they waited for a buyer. The master carpenter, William Hargrave, lived in his own

TABLE 6.4

Park Estate: Tenants and Owner-occupiers, 1790

Rateable values £	Number of owner-occupiers	Number of tenants
30	1	–
20–29	8	2
10–19	36	12
6–9	6	2
TOTAL	51 (76%)	16 (24%)

Source: LCA, LORB 34.

house at no. 5 Park Row from 1771; between 1785 and 1794 he was building fifteen houses in Park Place, six of which he still owned in 1796. In that year he had an even larger rent roll from houses in Park Square that he had probably built. Table 6.4 shows that by 1790 there were sixty-seven completed houses on the estate, and a quarter of these were occupied by tenants.

With so sound a security there were no problems in obtaining a mortgage once a house was built and, like the conveyances, a mortgage would be duly registered at Wakefield. The eighteenth-century attorney in Yorkshire, as Michael Miles has shown,[52] was active as a middleman raising loans from one set of clients for other clients who were in need. As Recorder and attorney, with one brother a bishop and another a prosperous London merchant, Richard Wilson had all the right social and professional contacts for acting as a broker in loans. None of the Wilson brothers, judging from their ledger, seems to have invested their own money in Park estate house mortgages but they were not averse to advancing money directly and indirectly to the builder-developers. When a new ledger book was opened in 1791 William Hargrave had a loan of £1500 at 5 per cent which was still outstanding in 1806, and Thomas Lawrance, architect and builder, was paying interest at the same rate on a loan of £1300 in 1794 and for the next fourteen years.[53]

Indirectly the Wilsons assisted by postponing the initiation of leases until a lessee had completed his building. After Bishop

[52] M. Miles, 'Eminent Practitioners' in *Lawyers, Courts and Industrial Society*, ed. G. R. Rubin and D. Sugarman (1984), pp.470–503.

[53] LCA, DB 32/26.

Wilson's death the Estate Act of 1794 recalled that: 'it was agreed with several Persons for granting to them Building Leases . . . several of the Persons have actually erected and are erecting large and valuable Dwelling Houses, and other Buildings, upon the Premises agreed to be demised to them in confidence that such Leases will be granted to them.'[54] Speculative builders could also be allowed a deferment of a lease until a purchaser had been found. In December 1771 Richard Wilson leased to Thomas Adamson, another master carpenter, a plot of land in Park Row. At an unspecified earlier date there had been an agreement between them for such a lease but in the interval Adamson had built four houses (nos 15–18) and these were now sold. The lease was, therefore, executed in the name of their purchaser, Thomas Armistead, who then occupied one of the four, renting two of them to gentlewomen and the other to the Revd Miles Atkinson, then an assistant cleric (lecturer) at the parish church.

Finally, the estate assisted the builders in the most practical way. On any building ground it was usual to take clay uncovered in the excavation for foundations and cellars, if it was suitable, and convert it to bricks nearby. There must have been a particularly good bed of clay beneath the undeveloped fields west of Park Square for the brickmaker Benjamin Wilson, who erected five houses in the plot at the north-west corner of Park Square between 1791 and 1797, paid royalties on clay taken for 960,000 bricks in these years, and was leased a second field from 1798 to 1803 during which time more than a million bricks were made from it.[55] Smoke from brickworks might be thought to have diminished the attraction of residence in Park Square but nostrils seem to have been more tolerant of smoke than they later became. Was it not perhaps that the sight of smoke, whether from dyehouse, brickyard or occupied house chimneys, was more exhilarating than the clear air which denoted idleness, stops of trade and unlet houses? It might be argued that the admission of brickworks smoke dates from a period when Park Square was virtually complete and when Christopher Wilson's heirs were living far from Leeds.[56] Yet twenty years earlier, on the eve of commencing South Parade, Thomas Wilson confirmed his deceased brother's purchase of Drony Laith (Fig. 6.1) where the tenant, William Close, had just converted farm buildings into a dyeworks. That purchase had not been made in order to suppress the smoke, which was not at all unwelcome, considering that as Close's

[54] *Acts Local and Personal, 34 Geo.III cap. 32*, preamble.
[55] LCA, DB 32/7.
[56] See below, p.279

dyehouses flourished his rent increased, amounting in 1801 to £400 per annum, that is as much as the total of all ground rents on the estate (Table 6.3).

Inside the area of the streets there was more care taken. Very specific prohibitions had been from the beginning a standard part of every lease. Indeed, nothing emphasises the novelty of segregated residences as much as these long recitals of 'noisy, noisome or dangerous Trades or callings'. For what were they but a conspexus of economic activities then to be found at the centre not only of Leeds but of any decent-sized English provincial town? Without them there would have been no town, but gentility would now want to keep them at a distance.

The standard restrictive covenant used by the Wilsons had over thirty prohibitions. In the list below they are re-arranged by categories of offensiveness, using the standards of this new gentility of manners: for the dislike of 'dangerous Trades' was not a benevolent concern for the safety of employees in these occupations but an anxiety not to live as neighbour to a building where chemical explosions, noxious effluents or outbreaks of fire might arise; in other words, not to live as the majority of townspeople were living in the central streets.

Processes using heat, with smoke or smells:
dyehouse, dryhouse, common brewhouse, tallow boiling, soap boiling, sugar refining, pot and pipe making, glue making, distillery, blacksmith, whitesmith, pewterer, tinner, baker.

Processes with smells, other than above:
chemist, tanner, flax dresser, skinner, currier.

Buildings attracting crowds:
alehouse, inn, tavern, tippling house, skittle alley, gin shop, bowling green, playhouse, coventicle, public school, private academy, meeting house for any public congregation or religious assembly.[57]

The last prohibition might seem to read strangely in the face of what, late in the development of the estate, could be claimed its crowning feature, St Paul's church (Fig. 6.3). Private Anglican churches for the residents of a new estate were not unknown elsewhere: a church was the first building on the Byroms' Manchester estate; there was another St Paul's in a square on the Colmore estate, Birmingham (1777–79) and the main West End estate at Wakefield was named St John's after the church built there in its square (1791).

[57] The list is compiled from leases in LCA, DB 58/19 and 33 together with LCD 9447.

St Paul's, Leeds, was not therefore a place of 'public congregation' but more akin to the private chapel in the grounds of a great country house or to the railed gardens at the centre of a London square to which only residents had a key. The church had seating for over 1000 but all the pews were reserved and a rent of 16*s*. a year had to be paid. Although the 1801 census found one or two houses in the square with ten and eleven residents, servants included, the average number was six.[58] It would have needed the attendance of every man, woman and child, master, mistress and servant, to have come near to filling the church from the 132 houses on the estate: and it was probably never full after the opening service. As a later incumbent wrote to the archbishop: 'until the character of the church is changed from proprietary to parochial, to the population at large it will continue to be very much the same as if there were no church at all'.[59]

There was in fact no covenant to be broken by its building since the site, taking up about half the southern side of the square, was the free gift of Bishop Christopher Wilson who had inherited the estate in 1789, the year when the square was commenced. The whole cost of the church, £10,000, was met by one donor, the Revd Miles Atkinson, the owner of no. 9. The foundation stone was laid in October 1791 but bishop Wilson died just before the first service in May 1794. He was not buried in the town of his birth but the architects of St Paul's had allowed for residents, if they wished, to have a more seemly burial than was becoming possible in the overcrowded parish graveyards. There could be no open graveyard so near the front windows of the most expensive houses on the estate but the floor of the church was built high enough to permit a subterranean mausoleum where in 1796 the first burial, that of the dyer, Thomas Close from Drony Laith, took place,[60] and in 1811 Atkinson himself was buried here. The dignity of burial in a crypt

[58] LCA, LPC 104, Mill Hill Division.
[59] Borthwick, Faculty papers.
[60] 13 Jan. 1796: G. D. Lumb, 'Burials at St. Paul's Church', *PTh.S*, XV (1905), 56.

FIG. 6.3 ST PAUL'S CHURCH, PARK SQUARE (1793)

Drawn by Thomas Taylor for Whitaker's *Loidis and Elmete* (1816). The church was built for the residents of the Park estate on a site within Park Square given by Christopher Wilson, bishop of Bristol, and at the expense of the first minister, Miles Atkinson. Consecrated in September 1793; all pews were private and burial vaults were available below: fifty years later the minister, the Revd J. A. Beaumont reported that few proprietors were resident, 'very much the same thing as if there were no church at all'. It was demolished in 1905, the site now the Water Board offices.

had once been reserved for princes and bishops: on the Park estate it was now sufficient to be a bishop's tenant.

There was much less uniformity of architectural detail within the Park estate than is visible within similar developments in Bath and Bloomsbury.[61] Demolition makes this impossible to demonstrate in Park Row and South Parade but a glance at Park Place, superficially the most uniform of the streets, immediately shows differences in horizontal ornamentation extending to major frontage features in the various doorways: all of course within the prevailing limits of classical taste. Even nos 6 and 18, intended to balance each other as the centrepieces of the two halves of the Place, turn out to be no twins: no. 18, built ten years after no. 6, has striking pilasters affixed to its facade. No. 8 on the east side of Park Square formed a similar centrepiece (1788) and it was matched in 1793 by another triangular-gabled house, no. 42, at the centre of the north side, an effect then confused by the building of no. 43 in 1796 in a similar style and with the same *oeil de boeuf* window in the gable but, having a frontage narrower than no. 42 by 14 feet, mustering only five bays rather than six.

Another witness to the lack of an imposed uniformity is the variety of frontage widths; these are apparent from the large-scale Ordnance Survey plans but are given precision by the dimensions recorded in the leases[62] and set out in Table 6.1. No. 2 Park Row, the first on the estate to be leased, was 57 feet wide but no succeeding lease in that street was for so wide a frontage; Dr Priestley's house at no. 1 was 42 feet wide, no. 23 was built to a 45-foot frontage, and no. 17 was only 21 feet wide. The only sequence of identical widths in Park Row was to be found in nos 11–14, all built for the same owner to a 37½-foot module which arose from equal sub-divisions within a 150-foot frontage for which he had taken a single lease. Park Place, the other long frontage, shows similar inequalities with signs that two modules were used: a narrow one of from 25 to 32 feet and a broad module of from 41 to 50 feet. The absence of uniformity may have been reinforced by the chronology of building: in no street did the building progress steadily from one end to the other. In Park Place no. 4 was the first plot to be leased, nos 1–3 not being taken up for another three years, while seven years then elapsed before nos 8 and 9 were leased, and it was sixteen years after its commencement before all the gaps on the frontage were filled.

[61] For the architecture see D. Linstrum, *Historic Architecture of Leeds* (Newcastle upon Tyne, 1965) and *West Yorkshire Architects and Architecture* (1978).
[62] LCA, DB 239, unlisted.

Yet the most striking difference between house and house was found not in the appearance of their frontages, but in what lay backsides. Within each street the depth of the plot was identical but the degree and character of the infill behind the frontage house was very varied, and behind the classical facade were things not to be encountered behind the Circuses, Crescents and Squares of southern England. There one might certainly find mews and the occasional workshop of a saddler or a coach-repairer: but nothing like the warehouses and cloth-finishing workshops here in the West End of Leeds.

These were initial features and not afterthoughts. By March 1776 Arthur Ikin, cloth merchant, had erected 140 feet of workshops along the Park Lane side of the northernmost plot in Park Row, and on 19 March he advertised the remaining ground in the *Mercury* with the incentive that 'there will be no more ground rent when houses are erected'. Table 6.5 shows that at least twelve other plots in Park Row carried buildings appropriate to the calling of a merchant in addition to the stables and 'Necessary Houses' (privies) found behind every residence. No. 19 had a small house in the yard, rated at little more than a cottage (£4), but the back buildings were rarely residential, usually workshops, warehouses and counting houses. There were packing shops where the cloth was prepared for its travels and although there was no machinery at work in their hotpress shops nos 5, 7 and 13 were approaching the forbidden limits of the restrictive covenants.

That is, gentility and commerce were demonstrably still compatible. It was acceptable for attorneys to see their clients in an office at their home, for the addresses of insurance agents and bankers to be the same as their residence, and for the surgeon William Hey to see his patients in the plain two-bay surgery which he built alongside his more ornate five-bay house in Albion Place (Fig. 6.4). Why should a merchant's house not have buildings ancillary to his calling? For the workpeople and customers the Park estate houses were generally provided with access by a back lane but pre-existing development on Park Lane made it necessary to leave a space at the centre of South Parade in order to gain rear access.

No. 10 Park Square rejected any such fig leaf. Its 65-foot frontage allowed for an archway entrance to be left alongside the house: by courtesy of Barclays Bank who have restored this property, the gates of the archway are usually open, and at the rear can be seen the fine windows of the residence, including a high staircase and an immense bow; a few yards further back are the Victorian successors to the workshops which had helped to raise no. 10's assessment in 1790 to

TABLE 6.5

Park Row: Premises behind Houses

House number	Name	Insured values		Description	Rateable values	
		House £	Back premises £		House £	Warehouse £
2	Barstow	600	170	Office, coach house and stable (1782)	18	10
4	Rayner	400 (1778)	–	–	12	13 (1795)
5	Hargrave	–	300	Office, warehouse, hot press shop (1797)	10	10 (1795)
7	Matthewman, woollen merchant	600	600	Warehouse, counting house, dressing & packing shops, hot pressing shop + £2000 in contents (1801)	12	10 (1795)
8	Lister, merchant	400	250	Warehouse and offices + £1000 contents (1788)	10(1774)	
11	Markham	300	250	Stables and schoolroom (1802)	10	5 (1790)
12	Hodgson, schoolmaster	625	700	'Academy in the Back Lane' (1788)	12	10 (1790)
13	Tolson, woollen merchant	500	500	Warehouse, workshop, hot pressing shop, stable (1801)	10	17 (1795)
17	Clayton	300	50	Stable (1801)	9	7 (1805) 'wool warehouse'
19	Dunderdale, mercer and draper	950	300	'Warehouse and house occupied by widow Rogerson in yard' and 3 'necessaries' [i.e. privies].	14	6: warehouse 4: house (1790)
20	Thompson, merchant	750	200	warehouse (1806)	12	5 (1790)
					12	18 (1795)
21	Ibbetson, woolstapler	350 'not finished under one roof'	300	Warehouse, kitchen and house adjoining (1778)	12	4 (+2 for house) (1790)
23	Ikin (Iken), cloth merchant	600	800	Warehouse, counting house, stable + £1600 contents (1801)	20	15 (1800)

Sources: Rate books, 1774–1805: LCA, LORB 154, 185, 195, 206 and 215. Insurance policies: no. 2: Sun OS 303 461805; no. 4: Sun OS 267 401846; no. 5: Sun CS 22 672160; no. 7: Sun CS 41 722542; no. 8: RE 13 102198; no. 11: Sun CS 48 734110; no. 12: Sun OS 351 541141; no. 13: Sun CS 41 726491; no. 17: Sun CS 40 719159; no. 19: Sun OS 262 392792 and 264 398634; no. 20: Sun CS 72 791048; no. 21: Sun OS 268 404709; no. 23: Sun CS 40 719775.

£20. On the north side of no. 5 before demolition outbuildings of 1795 could still be seen together with a tell-tale hole in the floor of a former Necessary House. No. 31, on the opposite side of the square, also has an original workshop, end-on, while nearby the cultural tradition remains but transformed in the only Park Square warehouse that most people in Leeds will now know, The Warehouse nightclub, set at the back of nos 24–25.

Important architectural features can still be observed in Park Place and Park Square (Figs 6.5, 6.6 and 6.7) but even here nos 15–22 were replaced long ago by Thomas Ambler's Moorish-Venetian clothing warehouse, commissioned by John Barran in 1878. St Paul's church, although replaced by the offices of Yorkshire Water, can be studied in contemporary engravings (as in Fig. 6.3), and there are photographs of some houses in South Parade before their demolition earlier this century. There were Victorian intrusions in East Parade which provided an excuse for the planning authority to disregard the fate of the remainder until very recently; the demolition of houses at the east end of Park Place soon after the war was a sad commentary on the civic pride of city Council members and the quality of advice available from their officers. There was some subsequent repentance and the city's publicity now takes proper pride in the conservation and renovation of the remaining parts of Park Place and Park Square, although while attention was being concentrated in Park Square serious losses were permitted from among the older buildings in Lower Briggate.

Of the houses in Park Row, the first street in the West End, there is virtually no visual record: the earliest engravings concentrated on the public buildings near the Cloth Hall and by the time that photography began in Leeds the residences were being acquired in ones, twos and threes to make way for larger buildings. Insurance and banking, once carried out from the houses of agents or partners, now demanded purpose-built offices in a variety of resurrected architectural styles; a Gothic Beckett's Bank by Sir G. G. Scott in

---

FIG. 6.4 INFILL BETWEEN THE CENTRE AND THE WEST END: ALBION STREET (1792) (*overleaf*)

Redrawn by John Dixon from no. 9 in John Russell's sketchbook 'I' (1803–04): a view dominated by an eight-bay house built for the surgeon, William Hey, in 1793: probably the first house in the street and always the largest, insured in 1797 for £1000. Facing south with a walled garden, it was more akin to houses then being built in Park Square than to its smaller street-frontage neighbours in the foreground although no house in the square extended to eight bays. The garden was later sold for the site of the Stock Exchange and a new street, Albion Place, bearing the name of Hey's house which is still standing.

FIG. 6.5 18–20 PARK PLACE (1788–91)
In the foreground the five-bayed no. 20, built for the merchant, John Plowes in 1789; on its right the smaller no. 19, built two years later for the gentleman, J. T. Vincent; then no. 18, also of 1788, each of its five bays pilastered and its triangular pediment marking the centre point of the nine houses in the western half of the Place, all built by William Hargrave, master carpenter, between 1788 and 1794.

1862, a Venetian Renaissance by George Corson in 1869 and a Gothic fantasy by the same architect for the Sun Assurance Company in 1877. The first to fall, however, had been no. 7, demolished when Commercial Street was extended westwards in 1823.

For the character of the house interiors, insured contents apart, we must turn to sale advertisements or tenantry inventories: one of the latter, for 9 Park Row in March 1778, arranged the contents within an 'Eating Room, Drawing Room, Back Parlour, Best Kitchen, Front Passage, Kitchen, Front Bedrooms, Back Bedroom, Cellar and Bedroom over Kitchen'. Nine months earlier another Park Row house was advertised as:

> A Spaceious New-built *House*; with all convenient Offices, and will be ready to enter into at Lady Day 1778. The Kitchens Laundry Pantries

FIG. 6.6 8 PARK SQUARE (1789)
The centrepiece of the eastern side, built in 1789 for William Wilson, gentleman: five bays with area basement and a triangular pediment similar to no. 18 Park Place (Fig. 6.5): without pilasters but with later drainpipes; to either side smaller houses.

Cellars and Servants' Hall are fitted up with Strong Ranges, Copper and Set-Pots, Stoves, Smoak-Jack, Shelves, Stone-Tables, Sinks, Stone Gantles, Binns for Wine etc. The Butler and Housekeeper's Rooms with Tables and cases for China and Glasses, a large Dresser with Drawers and a convenient small-Oven. The Dining and Drawing Rooms elegantly fitted up with Marble Chimney-Pieces, beautifully carved, and the others with all the Lodging-Rooms, finished with genteel Chimney-Pieces, fixed grates and very fashionable Paper. Apply to Mr. Markham.[63]

Mr Markham's name identifies the house as one of the four between nos 11 and 14. His advertisement seems to give rather more attention to Downstairs than Upstairs but when another Markham house was advertised in 1776 it revealed that there were six bedrooms among the Lodging Rooms, all again with 'genteel

[63] *LM*, 24 June 1777.

FIG. 6.7 11 PARK SQUARE (1790)

On the eastern side, built in 1790 by William Lawrance, 'carpenter, builder and architect', responsible for many houses in the square including perhaps no. 8 (Fig. 6.6). No. 11 resembles no. 8 and has a similar doorway but its frontage is narrower and it has a simpler roof line. Many of those who subsequently owned West End villas resided earlier in the larger houses of the square: the engineer Peter Fairbairn lived in this house in 1839, immediately before moving to a new villa in Clarendon Road (Fig. 10.5).

Chimney-Pieces and very fashionable Papers'.[64] In the larger house of William Cookson in South Parade there were eleven bedrooms, according to an advertisement of May 1811.[65] Thomas Bolland's house at 41 Park Square had two front bedrooms, three back bedrooms and two garrets for the servants, and despite conversion to offices some of its friezes and ceilings can still be identified.[66]

[64] *LM*, 1 July 1776.

[65] *LM*, 18 May 1811. The adjoining Lloyd and Cattaneo houses in South Parade are fully described in earlier advertisements: *LI*, 13 Feb. and 19 March 1792; for Mr Busk's, see *LM*, 2 Oct. 1802.

[66] Simpson Curtis and Co.: deed bundle 9447, tenancy agreement, 4 Aug. 1835 (deeds seen by kindness of Mr Blackmore).

Behind East Parade, Park Row and Park Square former outbuildings fulfil a variety of modern purposes. Apart from caretakers, residents have long departed; stoves and smoke-jacks are idle, and instant coffee-making for the offices is the limit of *haute cuisine*. At the time of writing an economic recession has brought its quota of display boards offering vacant office accommodation but entrepreneurial hopes still remained: future economic historians may like to know that in March 1984 a former cellar and kitchen on the east side of Park Square was opened as an expensive restaurant, Downstairs at Upstairs prices. By March 1985 the venture had failed.

THE STERILE YEARS, 1792–1816

Neither Christopher Wilson nor the eventual heir, his young nephew, were likely to return to the family home on Mill Hill. As we have seen, his nephew inherited Rudding Hall, Follifoot, from his father, while Christopher threw up his legal studies on the day he learned of his inheritance and came to live at Oxton Hall near Tadcaster, his interest thereafter lying solely in horse racing, an expensive taste.[67] There were soon indications that the absentee landlord was quite indifferent to the original conception of a West End estate. In 1796 a substantial plot behind nos 32 and 33 Park Square was leased to Phillips, Oates and Co. not for a residence-cum-workplace but for a group of buildings – warehouses, dressing shops and press shops – which were an embryo factory although as yet without steam engines.[68] The Act of 1803 indicated further disinterest in the estate for, in addition to the clauses concerning leases, it permitted the life tenant to overcome the disadvantage of fixed ground rents by selling land freehold in small parcels and enfranchising existing leaseholders. The proceeds had to be held in a trust fund for the next heir but the income was meanwhile all Christopher's.

Perhaps because some members of the Lords might question so rapid an overturn of a lord bishop's will the preamble to the Act was exceptionally long in its justification, and the argument rested wholly on the fact of non-residence at the Manor House which was described in the following terms, a virtual epitaph for the first West End.

> a large House, heretofore called and used as a Mansion-House, but which has for several Years past been let, and together with the

[67] Wilson, p.200.

[68] LCA, DB 32/23 and LCD 3888.

> Out-Buildings and Offices, converted into the Ware-Houses, Store-Houses or Depositaries of Persons carrying on Trade within the said Town; and from the great Increase of Manufacturing Trades of late Years, and particularly from the Erection and Construction of a great Number of Fire [i.e. steam] Engines, and other Erections for carrying on the Manufacture, the said House, heretofore used as a Mansion-House, would be a very unhealthy Place of Residence, and in no Respect eligible for the said Christopher Wilson, who is wholly unconnected with Trade: But such House, and the whole of the said Property within the said parish of Leeds would sell to great Advantage to Persons engaged in the Trade and Manufactures of the Place.[69]

Further evidence of indifference to the original concept can be seen in two projects which followed upon the Act. In the estate survey made in April 1806 the central open ground in Park Square was to be divided into four lots in order to make a 'new street' which was sketched on the plan;[70] a second plan of February 1809 reveals that the plan for a street had been abandoned and the land 'sold to the Inhabitants' to preserve the amenity.[71]

The more extensive square in front of Park Row was less fortunate. It had already lost any pretension to be a recreational open space: the residents of South Parade had been allowed to wall land in front of their houses as garden ground and 'the residue used as tenter ground and a brick garth'. When offered for sale after the 1803 Act it found speculative purchasers in the partners, William Thompson and John Lee. They paid £15,560 for the 32,760 square yards (9*s*. 6*d*. per square yard) in March 1805, but when Lee died two years later no takers had been found for any of the plots.[72]

Wilson had done well to make the sale, for the remainder of his anticipated building ground was no more sought after than the Thompson and Lee plots. The survey of 1806 showed no new building on the estate beyond the limits of 1796, and there was to be virtually no further interest from builders until after the end of the Napoleonic wars.

Another survey and valuation were made in 1816, when the proprietor was advised that the freeholds would raise £68,500 if buyers could be found.[73] The difficulty was that for most of the plots buyers remained hypothetical for another decade.

69 *Acts Local and Personal, 43 Geo.III cap. 30*, preamble.
70 LCA, DB 32/3.
71 LCA, DB 32/3A.
72 Billam, p.23; *LI*, 26 Nov. 1810; LCA, FM 252/293; Oates C1 (plan 1819) and C2–3 (deeds); LCD 2838.
73 LCA, DB 32/6A and B, following the release of lands by *Acts Local and Personal, 56 Geo.III cap. 13*.

Thus by allowing industry to enter the estate on the west, and by their indifference to the surrounds of the Manor House once they had ceased to be resident, the Wilsons had not only retarded the last stages of development in Park Square but destroyed the possibility of extending the first West End into more terraces and squares. Those who bought plots after 1816 accepted and completed the environmental degeneration.[74] When the cholera struck in Leeds in 1832 it found victims both in the East End and in the West where, north of Bean Ing mill, the Park estate was now in a tangle of back-to-back streets, factories and the gas works.

HALF-WAY HOUSES: A POSTSCRIPT TO THE WEST END. ALBION STREET AND COMMERCIAL STREET, 1792 AND 1802

In 1792, the year when no new plots were leased on the Wilson estate, an independent development was successfully launched in two fields nearer town.[75] We have already seen that the space between Boar Lane and the Headrow was occupied by a series of long crofts parallel to Briggate. In February 1792 Thomas Rawlinson, who owned the northern half of one of these closes, made an agreement with Joshua Turner, the owner of the other half: they would create a new street 'completely paved and ready for leading all Kinds of Building Materials'.[76] It was a little longer than Park Row and since it was designed to have buildings on both sides there were new frontages available for 800 yards in all. The plot depths which the close allowed were 50 yards but, unlike the Park estate, Albion Street plots were offered freehold, an indisputable attraction.[77]

The first house to be erected was insured in September of that year,[78] and in July 1793 the surgeon William Hey bought a large parcel on the east of the street on which the architect Thomas Johnson erected the residence then known as Albion Place which now serves as the offices of the Law Society (Fig. 6.4). It was insured comprehensively: £1000 for the 'house and offices under one roof'; £170 for household goods, £30 for musical instruments; £10 for plate; £40 for apparel and books; with stable and coach house for £20.[79].

[74] See below, pp.284 – 86

[75] Pevsner was misled by its western position to assign this street to the earlier Park estate development.

[76] LCA, DB 75/5, 1 Feb. 1792; street 'now making', *LI*, 9 Aug. 1792.

[77] *LI*, 20 Feb. 1797, 1 March 1802, 15 Aug. 1805 and 2 April 1810.

[78] Sun OS 388 604761: Thomas Wroe; two months later the surveyor Jonathan Teal was in possession of three houses: RE 25 135155.

[79] LCA, DB 75/5 and Sun CS 22 672934.

This was not to be a wholly residential street. On 9 July 1792 the *Mercury* had announced the laying of

> the first Stone of the Concert Room in the street now making from Boar-Lane to the Upper head-row (and which we understand to be called Albion Street). On the ground floor will be a Hall for Woollen Manufactures which will accommodate such as are excluded from the Cloth Halls, and afford great convenience to the manufacturers of blankets etc. in the sale of their goods.

This building was completed in April 1793.

Despite its patriotic name the new street clearly welcomed nonconformity and outsiders. The hall underneath the Music Hall became known as the Tom Paine Hall (despite the fact that on Christmas Eve 1792 a zealous congregation of 4000 Anglicans charged from the parish church and burnt Tom Paine in effigy); the Independent Albion chapel was built just behind it (and insured against fire for £600 in April 1793);[80] and the first West End Methodist chapel on the street frontage further north. It was insured in December 1802 for £2500, more than twice the cover for the Old Chapel on Quarry Hill.[81] The New Chapel had a back entrance in the cul-de-sac leading from Park Lane which is now known as Butts Court but then as Turner Street, after one of the street's promoters.

In February 1797 Turner's widow advertised seven houses in the cul-de-sac together with a 330-foot frontage at the bottom of the west side of the street for which she made no modest claim: 'the Situation of this Piece of Ground is remarkably pleasant, open and airy, and is the most eligible Place for building upon in the Town of Leeds'.[82] Griffith Wright's description of Albion Street in 1797 as 'an entire new-built street' was therefore rather optimistic but the development had certainly proved attractive.[83] One 'house and warehouse under one roof' was insured for £1000 and contained £2800 of insured goods.[84] In 1806 the *Leeds Guide* described Albion Street as 'new and well-built . . . perhaps the pleasantest in the town . . . the houses . . . are remarkably well built and are chiefly inhabited by professional gentlemen as no retail shops are allowed to be opened in it'.[85]

[80] Sun CS 22 678182.
[81] Sun CS 52 741551.
[82] *LI*, 20 Feb. 1797.
[83] Wright, p.26.
[84] Sun CS 12 648177: Rider and Clayton, woolstaplers, 29 Oct. 1795; CS 4 625757: 'the New Circulating Library', printed books insured for £130, 29 March 1794.
[85] *Leeds Guide*, p.73.

Further development was encouraged. In 1802, when sales were stagnant on the Wilson estate, a new street was cut to the south of Hey's house giving access to Lands Lane and the rear of the Briggate burgage plots. Its name, Commercial Street, indicated that like Albion Street it had no intention of being purely residential. The proprietors of the Old Circulating (the Leeds) Library erected a purpose-built building on the north side and opposite the Library was the new building for Nicholson and Brown's bank.[86]

The architect Thomas Johnson was involved in the development, for on 15 August 1805 he advertised in the *Mercury* two large building plots, using language similar to Mrs Turner's eight years earlier:

> Those parcels of Ground in an airy, healthful, and pleasant Situation, near the Central Part of Leeds, and convenient for the Market, as a Foot Way is, and a Carriage Way will shortly be, opened from thence to the Top of Briggate, which make those Two Parcels of Ground more eligible for Building upon than any other in the Town of Leeds.

The author of the *Walk Through Leeds* (1806) was equally confident that Commercial Street 'when finished will open into Briggate'[87] and the Giles plan of 1815 shows burgages demolished for this new street which entered Briggate immediately opposite the entrance to Kirkgate. Its name, although taken from the London West End, was plainly commercial: it was to be Bond Street.[88]

[86] *Directory, 1817*, p.184.
[87] Billam, p.30.
[88] *LI*, 9 April 1806.

7
The Sons of Labour and the Middle Ranks: The First East End, 1785–1803

In St Peter's Square the houses are equally remote from Splendour and Meanness, and are occupied by Persons in the Middle Ranks of Society . . . High Street is occupied by the Sons of Labour.

THE LEEDS GUIDE (1806), p.78

St Peter's Square is large but not so elegant [as Park Place] although the houses are new.

Shorthand diary of John Russell, RA, visiting Leeds in 1801: transcribed in G. C. Williamson, JOHN RUSSELL, R.A. (1894), p.67

THE PREHISTORY OF THE EAST END: MABGATE, QUARRY HILL, MARSH LANE AND THE BANK

Tuke's map of Leeds in 1781 caught the West End in progress, recording one house just built in East Parade. To the east of the town his map confirms that no new street had yet been built. Yet the census of 1775 (Table 5.3) had counted 1021 families living east of town and only forty-one of these in the distant hamlets of Cross Green, Knowestrop and Osmondthorpe. On the Bank and Far Bank, reached by a road along the foot of Cavalier Hill, there were 368; along Marsh Lane towards Black Bank and Pontefract Lane there were 250; and along Quarry Hill and Mabgate another 362. Tuke's map shows that most of these families lived in roadside clusters of houses, and since some of these in Mabgate, Marsh Lane and East Street were located by their property deeds in 'folds', they were occupying former farmyards. It is in the nature of farms to be scattered at intervals along a lane and not to present the uniform frontage of an urban street, being often set back from the lane.

It was these spaces, behind and between, into which houses were fitted, called 'cottages' indeed but certainly not built for some swelling local band of agricultural labourers. One such group developed on a Marsh Lane property owned by the Free School and can be seen in detail in a survey and large-scale plan made in 1793;[1] a jagged frontage along Mabgate from York Road to the Green, can also be seen in later maps.[2] As early as 1757 James Whiteley, a stuff-maker, had insured his Mabgate dwelling house and workshop 'under one roof' for £200 and included in the same policy other buildings 'facing' and 'fronting': a warehouse; a workshop; seven houses and six cottages: the houses and cottages were valued only at between £30 and £40 each.[3] There was also piecemeal building along the south side of the York turnpike as it began to climb Quarry Hill. In these ribbon developments, the meaner image of similar accretions of merchants' houses along the Otley, Wakefield and Elland turnpikes,[4] the builder had no need to incur expenditure in making roads. In March 1778, a group of fourteen adjacent cottages on Quarry Hill was advertised and the owner of the land emphasised this advantage in his advertisement: 'the High-Road betwixt Leeds and York is lately repaired in a Manner that will render the Estate very public and eligible'.[5]

These houses presented a curious paradox: by one measure of density there was a family occupying each 25 square yards but the isolation of the lines of buildings gave a much lower overall density. On the Bank Musgrave had forty-three cottages next to 3920 square yards of open ground, and adjoining these Tobias Appleyard, brewer and owner of Hill House with its Bowling Green, had built thirty-four cottages but left an area of 5190 square yards undeveloped.

They had defined no access road; nor did Weavers' Square, the name for an inward-facing group of twenty-seven cottages already in existence in 1787 when Richard Kendall, shoemaker, purchased the close in which they lay: in 1789 he mortgaged seventy-one cottages and was rated for ninety dwellings in 1790, and among the accretions must be counted Kendall's Buildings, a group of thirty-six back-to-back houses, and Pork Alley, a line of ten mean, one-storey one-room houses of which pre-demolition photographs survive. Their low valuation of £10 each for fire insurance is not

[1] Reproduced in Beresford, *Back-to-Back House*, fig.3.1 from LCA, DB 204/8.

[2] Brotherton Library, University of Leeds, Lupton MS. 128; LCD 28.

[3] WRRD, DB 206/258; Sun OS 118 156680.

[4] See below, p.254

[5] *LM*, 31 March 1778.

surprising. Their rateable values, 13*s.* 8*d.*, were among the lowest encountered in the town.[6]

At the foot of Hill House Bank near its junction with the riverside track (later East Street) was Tinsdill's Court, originating in a line of five back-to-back pairs erected by John Tinsdill after a purchase of 1784 but set far enough back from the road to allow another further thirty-nine houses to be packed in by 1815. Half of these were rated at under £1. His Court became known as Blue Bell Fold, and it was here that the cholera began in Leeds in 1832.[7]

These non-street alignments were more fitted for a colony of squatters than for the houses of townsmen, although an advertisement of 1785 for five copyhold houses newly rebuilt at Hill House Bank put the best face it could upon the matter: 'they adjoin one another in a compact manner, and stand in an open and pleasant Situation having an agreeable View of the adjacent Country'.[8] The 'pleasant situation' gave rise to problems when it had to be located more precisely. Needless to say, no compiler of a directory took notice of this level of Leeds society, but houses had to be located for such official purposes as conveyancing and fire insurance. The phrase 'in a field' constantly recurs: Isaiah Baynes insured his house and warehouses in 1787 'in a field at the Bank' along with 'a tenement in the field in the tenure of a labourer'.[9]

Further east it was no different: there was no turnpike and only a track leading to the Bowling Green at Hill House on the level top of Cavalier Hill with its prospect of Leeds below. The track along the riverside had no road or street name: simply 'Bank' until it met Ellerby Lane at 'Far Bank'. The hillside was poor agricultural land, and therefore cheap. As Buck's *Prospect* had shown, the Bank had its weavers' cottages similar to those which had been permitted by the lords of the manor to encroach on the Moor and Carr at Great Woodhouse but, from the mid-century, here and there on the hillside a few larger groups of cottages came into existence, forming lines along the inside edge of closes in order to leave the remainder of the fields free for grazing or tenter frames, and served with no access by a distinguishable road.

In later years the track to Hill House became known as Richmond Road but it had no defined carriage way or pavements even in 1815 when the Giles plan showed it simply as 'Hill House Bank' (Fig. 7.1). The 'fifteen tenements nigh Bank under one roof at £20 each',

[6] Sun CS 74 793666.
[7] The re-naming is explicit in WRRD, FU 245/246.
[8] *LI*, 18 Oct. 1785.
[9] Sun OS 344 527818.

insured by John Rogerson, clothier, in 1760 became known as Well Houses: they were grouped along a hedgeline at right angles to the track.[10] Nearly opposite was Ingram Hall, owned in 1789 by Eli Musgrave, stuff-merchant of Kirkgate. The Hall, which appeared in Buck's *Prospect*, had fallen in the world: in a policy of October 1782 it was valued at £140 but 'occupied by labourers'. Musgrave's father had built, just before 1785, fourteen houses which became known later as Musgrave Fold from the name of a field to the north of the Hall in which they stood. Their rateable value was £2 10*s*. 0*d*. each, that is in the 'cottage' class. By 1789 Eli Musgrave added twenty-seven cottages along the hedgeline of another close to the south of the Hall, that long line of single-room houses which became known as Spitalfields: their insured values ranged from £7 to £14 each and they were rated at less than £1 each.[11]

The South Division, where there was growing employment in merchants' finishing shops, had no Bank up which to expand or Moor on which to encroach; the adjacent Moor was the prerogative of Holbeck and Hunslet although in a field just over the Hunslet boundary there was one early development akin to the hedgeline properties in the East Division: Grey's Walk, a line of '16 tenements under one roof', was set along an old footpath behind Hunslet Lane and insured by the merchant, James Eyre, in 1775 for £15 each, and in 1782 as '18 cottages under one roof in a field' for £11 each. They were clearly in the Pork Alley, Weaver's Square and Spitalfields class, probably of one room.[12]

There were no fold developments along the Harrogate, Otley and Bradford roads to the north and west; the weavers in the northern Divisions had access to building space in Great Woodhouse: but along Mabgate (Fig. 7.2) and the Wakefield and Elland roads (Hunslet Lane and Meadow Lane) the infill behind the frontage houses was continuing as it was in the remaining ground behind the central streets. In 1770 John Northouse, upholsterer of Boar Lane,

[10] Sun OS 134 178917.

[11] Sun OS 304 465548; 365 563517; *LI*, 31 March 1800; LCD 1225.

[12] *LM*, 28 Dec. 1773; Sun OS 302 462468; CS 14 656302.

FIG. 7.1 THE FIRST EAST END, 1815

From the Giles map of 1815: [*top left*] an agglomeration in the farmhouse folds along Marsh Lane (cf. Fig. 3.5); [*centre*] piecemeal development on Hill House Bank, forming Well Houses, Kendall's Row. Pork Alley, Weavers' Square, Muck Lane, Stock's Fold and Spital Fields (cf. Table 7.1); [*centre*] the barrack-like blocks are Paley's two mills (Bank Low and Bank Top) with housing nearby at Well House Place; [*bottom right*] the Hill House Building Club houses at Far Bank forming King Street and Queen Street (Appendix VII.2e).

High Street
St. PETER'S SQUARE
Off Street
Marsh Lane
Sexton Lane
York & London Road
EAST DIVISION
Well Houses
Well House Place
Richmond Hill
Shoulder of Mutton House
Kendell's Row
New Causeway
Bilhouse Bank
Spital Fields
Star & Garter
Wear
Fearn's Island
King Street
Queen Street
Cavalier Hill
Far Bank
Old Ferry
Ellerby
to Knowstrop
NAVIGATION

FIG. 7.2 AN EAST END FOLD BEHIND MABGATE
Two-storey blind-back houses set against the side of Tunstall's Fold behind Tunstall's tobacco-pipe workshop on the north side of Mabgate; developing piecemeal from 1790, hence the breaks in pavement level and the different heights of roof. The surface was still unpaved when this photograph was taken in 1901.

who in 1763 had only two frontage houses in Kirkgate, insured '12 cottages lately erected in the Boot and Shoe Yard in Kirkgate' each consisting of a low room, chamber, pantry, cellar and coalhouse, and all underdrawn (i.e. with a board floor below the roof). These were reckoned to be worth £12 each, and by 1782 five other houses valued at £10 each had been added to the Yard.[13] In their day the Boot and Shoe Yard cottages were to be as notorious as those in Blue Bell Fold.

Although not all can be located so precisely in time and space, developments of this sort help to account for the estimated increase of 600 houses within the in-township between 1775 and 1781, an annual average of 100. Such estimates, which continue with an average of 120 a year in the next twenty years, are not implausible.

[13] *LI*, 3 April 1770; Sun OS 151 203569 and OS 300 459986.

Rimmer counted the houses recorded in the rate books and found an average increase of 200 per year between 1790 and 1795, and fifty per year between 1795 and 1800.[14]

Although the estimates in Table 5.1 offer data for 1775, 1781 and 1797 there is no source for the interval years but there is evidence that there were not smooth annual additions to the number of houses. If indeed 600 houses had been built between 1775 and 1781 it displayed unusual confidence in a period when the cloth trade was disrupted by the American war; Chalklin's study of building in the provincial towns put the recovery from this disruption no earlier than the mid-1780s when 'the recovery in building . . . led to the biggest boom of the century. It was one in which all towns participated . . . The great expansion in industrial output, and of the internal and overseas trade which accompanied it, led to massive migration to industrial towns and major ports, creating an unprecedented demand for housing'.[15]

In Leeds the year 1786 was hardly over before it acquired the reputation of an *annus mirabilis*. 'Such is the increase of the trade and inhabitants of this populous town', declared the *Intelligencer* on 27 March 1787 'that there have been in the last, and will be erected in the present year, near four hundred dwelling houses'. Statements of this sort must have been based on some knowledge of the rate books but since those between 1775 and 1789 have been lost there is now no possibility of checking. This memory of 1786 as an exceptional year was certainly rife seven years later when the boom was beginning to falter and the *Universal British Directory* thought it worth recalling that in Leeds 'the increase of building in the year 1786 was nearly 400 houses'.[16]

The year 1786 was certainly one in which remarkable initiatives, individual and corporate, conjoined. In September master builders were driven to advertise for carpenters and joiners, and again for bricklayers in February 1787, while in April the master joiners who advertised for carpenters promised an advance in wages to match the cost of provisions.[17] Yet even the two most forward of the projects launched in 1786 had progressed no further than eighteen houses 'unfinished' when they were insured in June 1787,[18] and the *Intelligencer*'s four hundred houses must have recorded the ambition of such projects rather than their achievement.

[14] Rimmer, *Cottages*, p.187.
[15] Chalklin, p.274.
[16] *The Universal British Directory* (2nd. edn, 1793), p.533.
[17] *LI*, 12 Sept. 1786 and 16 Jan. 1787.
[18] RE 13 102207 and 102208.

TABLE 7.1

Multiple Ownership of Cottage Property in the East End, 1790–1805

	Owner	Number of houses rated at £1 or under			
		1790	1795	1800	1805
East Division (Hill House Bank & Far Bank)					
	Kendall	53	61	65	65
	Tinsdill	36	28	27	23
	Musgrave	36	18	17	53
	Paley	24	41	45	157
	Appleyard	12*	15	20	30
	Stocks	9†	13	13	12
	Rhodes	1	9	10	12
	Pickering	–	23†	23	23
	Priestley	–	17	16	11
	Walker	–	16	16	12
	Barker	–	10	9	?
	Upton	–	9	11	44
	Rooke	–	–	14	13
	Stirk	–	–	8	14
	Joy	–	–	7	20
	Scott	–	–	–	10
North East Division					
Ebenezer St	Beverley	37	37	37	39
Mabgate	Asquith	29	32	34	34
Quarry Hill	Boynton	19	36	36	37
Quarry Hill	Maude	18	18	to Johnson (below)	
Ebenezer St	Greaves	18	18	18	'sundry cottages'
Mabgate	Rider, N.	17	12	14	17
	Fawcett	16	(to Paley below)		
Mabgate	Rider, D.	14	12	16	13
	Wilson	15	19	to Johnson (below)	
	Mawhood (Baxter)	13	17	17	17
Quarry Hill	Whiteley	13	14	15	16
Quarry Hill	Clarkson	12	18	18	18
Quarry Hill	Garforth	11	11	11	11
Quarry Hill	Randall	9	9	11	10

TABLE 7.1 (*continued*)

	Owner	Number of houses rated at £1 or under			
		1790	1795	1800	1805
	Hudson	8	17	18	20 (Atkinson)
Union St	Eastburn	7	7	14	14
Union St	Brown	6	18	18	18 (Mellon)
	Bradford	6	6	to Johnson (below)	
Skinner Lane	Paley	3	34	25	26
& Marsh Lane	Wood	3	3	12	12
	Holroyd & Blagborough	–	18	18	18
	Watkinson‡	–	14	25	15
	Dunn‡	–	14	25	22
Quarry Hill	Skelton	–	12	13	16
	Upton	–	11	11	11
	Aveyard	–	10	14	14
	Mann‡	–	9	9	9
	Westwood	–	7	13	13
	Woodhead‡	–	6	8	19
Mabgate	Linsley	–	5	9	9
	Scott‡	–	–	14	19
Union St	Ambler	–	–	8	11
	Riley‡	–	–	–	20
	Coward	–	–	–	11
	Johnson (included above 1790–95)	–	–	48	31

* Including 4 cellars at 10*s*. each.
† For insured values see Appendix VII. 1.
‡ Built on parts of McAndrews Garden purchased from Paley.

Source: LCA, LORB 34–37.

A scrutiny of newspaper advertisements for the sale of land, a type as old as the newspapers themselves, also suggests that the concept of a whole field being turned into streets was recent. One such field, the six-acre close known as McAndrews Garden, in Marsh Lane, was taken in 1784 for the most extensive of Richard Paley's developments, adding some 300 houses in the next twenty years:[19] but when Mrs Ann Wilson had advertised it ten years earlier it was solely as pasture ground, and between 1765 and 1784 Wilson trustees had managed to sell only half an acre from the 45 acres that they had ready for disposal after their estate Act.[20] In the South Division John Green had 7 acres on offer since 1773. They lay next to Camp Hall where Water Lane had been diverted across his land, 'paved twenty feet Broad, with Headingley-Moor Stones and a Flagged Causeway four feet broad to be made on the Side thereof' but despite this advantage the eventually notorious streets known collectively as Camp Field were not commenced here before 1807.[21]

Table 7.1 identifies from the rate books of 1790–1805 the forty-eight house-owners with the largest number of small properties in the East End. Together in 1805 they owned just over a thousand properties, a mixture of one-room cottages and two-room back-to-backs. Half of these little bricks-and-mortar empires had been in existence in 1790; five years later, three-quarters; and virtually all by 1800: part of a more widespread retardation of growth which will bring the word 'laggard' into the title of Chapter Eight. How much older than 1790 these agglomerations were, it is not possible to say in the absence of rate books. Multiple properties in the East End do not appear in insurance policies before 1784 (Appendix VII.1), and it is therefore likely that this pattern of ownership had arisen, not from the purchase of existing properties but from the erection of cottages in groups over the five years, 1785–90, before the data in Table 7.1 commence. The Leeds building clubs began their activities in the same years.

CLUB STREETS: THE BUILDING STRATEGY

The sporadic developments in folds and farmyards at Marsh Lane and on the Bank were separated from the town by the Timble Beck and by the closes on either side of Timble Bridge: Mill Garth and Crackenthorpe Garden to the west; McAndrews Garden and the Boggart Closes to the east (Fig. 7.3). Much of this land lay within the Ann Wilson (Pawson) settled estate which had been so unsuccessfully marketed in 1765. Now, within the three years 1787, 1788 and 1789 all this open ground next to town came into the possession of developers some of which were building clubs. A military operation

[19] See pp. 215–20 below.
[20] *Acts Local and Personal, 5 Geo.III cap. 25.*
[21] LCD 5944; *LI*, 12 Dec. 1809.

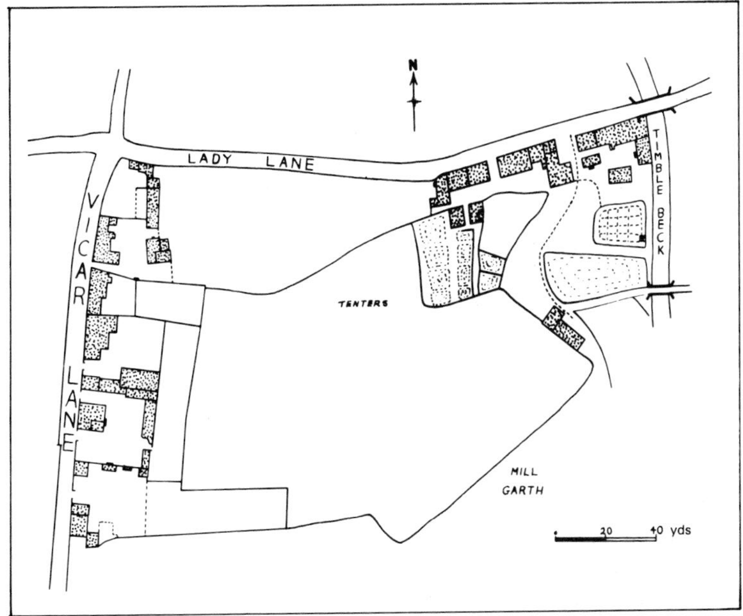

FIG. 7.3 CRACKENTHORPE GARDEN, 1784

From a survey by John Crookes, made when part of a field lying between Vicar Lane and Lady Lane was conveyed to the trustees of the Crackenthorpe Garden Building Society, whose members then built Union Street. The remainder of the field went to private speculators who built Nelson Street, Ebenezer Street and George Street (Figs 7.7 and 7.9). The field took its name from an earlier owner, Abraham Crackenthorpe, a market gardener from Kent, but in 1784 the field was let as tenter ground; tenters were shown here by Buck in 1720 (Fig. 3.5).

could hardly have been better planned although in fact there was no coordination: competition rather, for both clubs and private developers were hoping to sow a very similar crop of buildings in these fields (Tables 7.2 and 7.9).

For convenience this Chapter will first consider the clubs, then the private developers and then the building style, the back-to-back terrace, which both employed. The advertisement for building craftsmen which had appeared in the *Intelligencer* on 12 September 1786 gave an indication that the complete invasion of a whole close was imminent. It was Boggart Close, a six-acre field on the lower slope of Quarry Hill, where a small portion had already been sold by Lord Hawke as the site for a Methodist meeting house and burial

TABLE 7.2

The First Building Clubs in Leeds, 1786–87

Name and location	Date of purchase of site	Area, acres	Purchase price, £	Price per acre, £	Number of lots	Number of members	Total length of street, feet	Frontage width of each lot, feet	Number of houses erected	Average number of houses built on each lot	Cost of land per lot, £
Union Row (Quarry Hill)	July 1786	0.62	120	193	22	18	368	16.7	32	1.45	5.45
Boggart Close, Greater (St Peter's Square)	October 1786	3.83	533	139	30	21	1170	39	61	2.03	17.77
Boggart Close, Lesser (High Street)	October 1786	1.6	267	166	61	44	1002	16.4	152	2.49	4.38
St James Street (Woodhouse Lane)	February 1787	3.19	750	235	85*	37–40	1490	17.3	94	1.10	8.72
Hill House Bank (King Street and Queen Street)	June 1787	1.2	?	?	42	24	819	19.5	106	2.52	?
Crackenthorpe Garden (Union Street)	August 1787	1.43 } 2.5† }	1293	329	52	23	1025	19.5	114‡	2.2	9.05
TOTALS:					292	167/170					

* Excluding one lot immediately 'extinguished' to make an alley.
† Simultaneous sale of 2½ acres non-club developers: 277 dwellings by 1801.
‡ The 1801 census enumeration (LCA, LPC104) includes cellar dwellings in its total of 166.

Sources: WRRD and LCD cited in footnotes to Chapter 7.

ground; on 6 October he sold the remainder of the close, some 5½ acres, for £800. The purchasers were two groups of trustees: one of 'a Club for Building Dwelling Houses on the South Side of the Boggard Closes [*sic*]'; and the other of a similar Club for 'the North Side'.[22]

Friendly societies or clubs with members subscribing towards house-building had been known elsewhere before 1786 but in the autumn of 1786 the vendors of closes to the east of Leeds suddenly began to look to such clubs as potential purchasers.

On 28 November Josiah Wood, hatter and cottage-landlord in the yards between Briggate and Vicar Lane, advertised two closes measuring 1½ acres which lay at Black Bank, so named from the coal pits out on York Road, well east of town. This became 'an agreeable distance' in the advertisement, where the other virtues of the land were said to be that

> it is well watered and commands a beautiful Prospect, contains a good bed of clay, and to any Club or Society of Manufacturers that wish to make a purchase of an eligible Situation for erecting Dwelling Houses will be found to be a very desirable spot.

In the same issue of the *Intelligencer* a 2½-acre close next to Green End House, at the north side of Mabgate, was commended to the attention of 'any Club or Society of Manufacturers that wish to make a Purchase for erecting Dwellings upon'. Indeed, as early as July 1786, but leaving no trace in the newspapers, a small club had actually bought a close for its twenty-two members on the opposite side of Quarry Hill to the fourteen-cottage terrace of 1778. Since the terms 'union' and 'friendly society' were then interchangeable, the club named its terrace 'Union Row' (Fig. 7.4).[23]

In the absence of documents the day-by-day operation of the Leeds building clubs can be only imperfectly known, and it is clear from what evidences do remain that the six clubs of 1786–87 operated variously and had different ambitions and different types of member. Sufficient evidence also exists to arouse suspicions that these Leeds clubs did not operate and could not have been intended to operate according to the simple model of a self-help savings club with the aim of providing houses for occupation by their members. The eventual proportion of owner-occupiers will be seen in Table 7.4 but it is clear that the clubs had also become a mechanism for producing landlords – and not only small landlords at that.

[22] LCD 1774, 2109, 4872 and 8433 for the Greater Club; 767, 1479 and 1794 for the Lesser Club; for both, WRRD, DC 19/15 to 101/116, *passim*.

[23] See pp.477–78 below; above; LCD 1602 and 1188E.

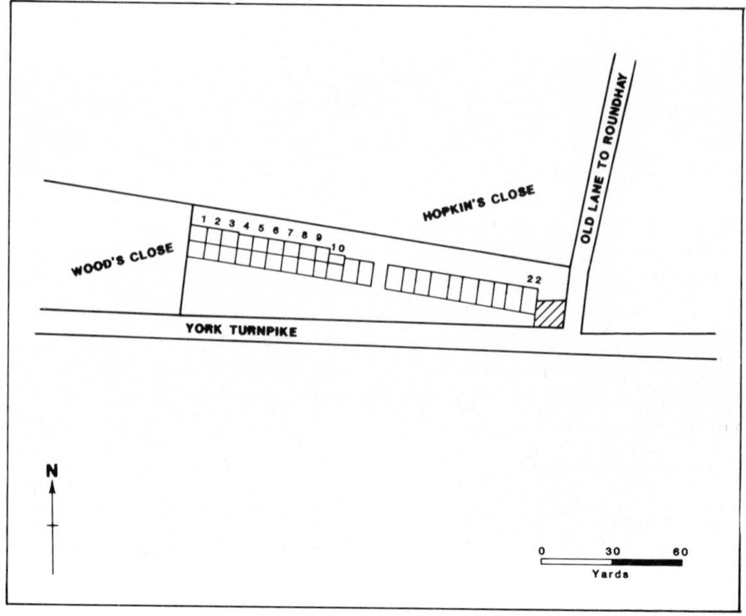

FIG. 7.4 THE FIRST BUILDING CLUB: UNION ROW, 1786
Ten pairs of back-to-backs and twelve one-room cottages on the north side of Quarry Hill, the 'Union' being the association of eighteen members in the town's earliest building club (Appendix VII.2(a)). The slope of the hill prevented back-to-backs being continued for the whole Row.

Nevertheless their method of organising the recruitment of capital for house building did differ from that on the leasehold estate which monopolised the West End developments discussed in the previous Chapter. They were indeed clubs (or 'unions' or 'societies') with identifiable members, and it will be useful to sketch the organisation of a typical terminating building society before noting how the Leeds clubs departed from this model. The chronology of the clubs, lists of members and their occupations, and other factual information will be found in Appendices VII.2(a)–(f).

The historian of the building-society movement, Seymour Price, was able to draw upon several rule books to determine the mode of operation of the terminating societies in the Midlands.[24] No rule book or minute has survived to illumine the day-to-day procedures which founded and sustained the Leeds clubs except for the Alfred

[24] S. J. Price, *Building Societies, Their Origin and History* (1958).

FIG. 7.5 KINGSTON TERRACE: THE FAILURE OF A BUILDING CLUB

The Kingston Terrace Building Club, with fifteen shareholders, was formed in April 1826 to build in Middle (or Watkinson's) Close, a field on the north side of Woodhouse Lane just beyond the turnpike bar. The only club houses built were the three shown here as 'Kingston Place'; in 1831, with four of the shareholders bankrupts and five others dead, it was described as 'an unfortunate and losing Speculation'. The large stone pillars of the entrance gates to the private roadway still survive, and its rough surface has still (in 1988) to be adopted as a public highway.

Place Terminating Building Society founded as one of the many speculative and optimistic ventures of 1825 and ending dramatically with the arrest of its secretary at Liverpool as he was about to embark for America with embezzled funds.[25] The uncompleted Kingston Terrace, opposite the University in Woodhouse Lane, still stands as a memorial to another club of the same year with a dishonest officer (Fig. 7.5).[26] Three others were founded in 1825 with more success but the failures were sufficient to discredit the terminating societies

[25] W. G. Rimmer, 'Alfred Place Terminating Building Society, 1825–43', *PTh.S*, XLVI (1963), 303–30; the most detailed of any study of a pre-permanent society in England.

[26] LCA, ACC 1148, Emsley.

and encourage the new form of organisation embodied in the Leeds Permanent Society of 1848. There had been an earlier flurry of interest in 1816–17[27] but there is no evidence for other building clubs in the thirty-year interval since the six clubs of 1786–87 (Table 7.2).

The history of these six early clubs, five of them in the East End, is known from a handful of newspaper advertisements; from their regular occurrence in the registers of the Sun and Royal Exchange fire insurance companies (Table 7.9) and from original property deeds which have passed to the Corporation when East End streets were purchased for slum clearance and road schemes and St James Street taken for the site of the Polytechnic. It is fortunate, with such small and scattered properties, that these recent developments have brought together documents which were dispersed among the several thousand property-owners concerned. Once the names of trustees were known from such survivals it was possible to go further and trace many of the original conveyances and subsequent mortgages by their enrolment at the West Riding Registry of Deeds in Wakefield.

The composition of the clubs' membership is an essential piece of evidence in the discussion which follows. It cannot be learned from any register of members, for none has survived in Leeds, but since any legal document of the day identified persons by their occupation or status, the title deeds (whether original or enrolled) have enabled this information to be assembled, while something of the procedure of the clubs can be learned from the deeds which recited the initial deed for the sale of land to the trustees and the subsequent partition among members. Among the deeds of several houses in St Peter's Square[28] and Union Street were found printed booklets setting out not only the title to the land but the clubs' articles of association. A

[27] Club Row and Club Court, York Rd., 1812: LCD 4795 with 20 lots; Low Lane (Fountain St), 1817: LCD 8889 with 16 lots; Bedford Street and Place, 1826: Sun CS 165 1070574–5; Kingston Terrace, 1826: *LM*, 10 Oct. 1826.

There were also clubs in Kirkstall and Headingley at this time (ex. inf. C. Treen) as well as Friendly (Benefit) Societies which used property as one form of investment for their funds, e.g. The Commercial Building Society of 1826 'holden at the house of John Ainley, known by the sign of the Crown' had investment property which made them the landlord of Wormald's shop in Briggate (Fig. 4.6): WRRD, JO 359/363; similarly in 1817 the Duke of York Benefit Society at the *Albion Inn* purchased a close at Hill House Bank: LCD 4860/17/10.

After 1832 Leeds also had its Freehold Land Societies, giving their members property qualification for the franchise after 1832; and then the Permanent Society of 1848, initially with 'funds for working class cottages entirely': evidence of Thomas Fatkin, *Royal Commission on the Housing of the Working Classes* (PP, C.4402 of 1885), II, p.371.

[28] LCD 812, deriving from Lot 6, Boggart Close Greater Club.

deed will normally reveal how many members there were in a club and the number of the plot assigned to a particular member. Uniquely one deed parcel for a property in High Street contained a plan of the whole street in 1790 with each member's plot numbered and identified (Fig. 7.6).[29]

Leeds cannot claim to have originated building clubs. They seem to have begun between 1775 and 1778 in Birmingham, then a much larger town than Leeds. In the cotton-weaving towns of Lancashire they were active at the same time as in Leeds; the woollen-weaving town of Elland had a building club for New Street in 1790.[30] The building clubs were a specialist type of provident society, part of the great friendly society movement of the eighteenth century. As Chapman and Bartlett have written: 'The principal difference between the friendly society and the terminating building society was one of choice of benefit. While the friendly society members pooled their savings against the contingencies of sickness, old age, funeral liability or (less often) unemployment, the building club offered planned saving for house purchase'.[31]

The essential elements in the life of a terminating society were set out by Rimmer thus:

> The purpose and rules of the Society were formalised in Articles of Agreement which every shareholder signed. Their aim was to build a number of [uniform] dwelling houses equal to the number of shares . . . When work began on the foundations of a new house, the shareholders would ballot to decide who would eventually own [that house] . . . When finished each house would be let at an annual rent fixed by the trustees. Tenants had to pay their rents twice a year . . . If a member tenanted his own 'future' house and refused to pay rent he forfeited his share and lost his membership. When every shareholder had a house, the Society would pay its debts, convey the property individually to each shareholder and terminate its existence. Until then the property would be held by trustees, and a shareholder could transfer his interest to an outside party. Any shares forfeited owing to a breach of rules were to be sold at public auction.[32]

A comparison which would have been appreciated in a town of mills is that of the overshot waterwheel where water accumulates in a bucket until the crucial moment when its weight begins to move

[29] LCD 435 (Crackenthorpe Garden).

[30] WYJAS, Calderdale Office, Misc. MS. 459/1.

[31] S. D. Chapman and J. N. Bartlett, 'The Contribution of Building Clubs and Freehold Land Societies to Working-class Housing in Birmingham', in *The History of Working-class Housing*, ed. S. D. Chapman (Newton Abbot, 1971), pp.221–46.

[32] Rimmer, 'Alfred Place Terminating Building Society, 1825–43', p.309.

the wheel downwards; the bucket empties and the next is ready to be filled. Right until the last minute, when a club was truly terminating, there would be some member who had paid his subscription from the beginning, watching more fortunate members build their houses and awaiting the moment when his own bucket began to fill. An intermediate position of this sort is caught in Teal's plan of High Street in 1790, four years after the foundation of the club: it shows thirty-one houses built and thirty plots still vacant (Fig. 7.6). Earlier that year rate assessments had been levied on twenty-nine houses, so that two must have been recently completed when Teal made his survey. Similarly the rate book of 1790 fails to account for eighteen of the fifty-two lot-holders in Union Street but in 1795 all but six were assessed, and all fifty-two appear in the rate book for 1800. In St James Street, where the club progressed most haltingly, the vacant lots were numerous enough in 1790 for a rate to be levied on the 'Subscription Club', not as house proprietors but in the 'landowner' category.

Why would someone wishing to own a cottage property need to enter into a 'union' with others in a Subscription Club? It was certainly not because of any economy in scale during the building operation, for club houses were added to the members' plots one by one, and did not have to be uniform in height even though their width was governed by the standard frontages of club plots. Just as in the West End, the club streets for which we have photographs show adjacent houses with differences in height and minor external features (Figs 7.8 and 7.14), and even when builders are found as club members they were not responsible for more than a few houses in each street. The answer to the question lies elsewhere.

The terraces and clusters of cottages on the Bank had been erected for letting to tenants, not speculatively for sale. They tended to remain as undivided blocks: even if they came to be put on the market by executors of wills or assignees in bankruptcy the blocks formed single lots at the auction. Thus, for anyone wishing to become owner of a single small house, the market in older cottages

---

FIG. 7.6 HIGH STREET ST PETER'S, 1790

In 1789 sixty-one building plots were assigned by lot to the members of the Boggart Close Lesser Building Society (Appendix VII.2(c)), and the ground immediately to the south assigned to the members of the Greater Building Society for St Peter's Square (Figs 7.13 and 7.14). This unique plan, drawn by the surveyor, Jonathan Teal, on the back of a conveyance catches the operation of the Terminating Society a year later: the weekly subscriptions of members had accumulated sufficiently for thirty-one members in turn to have received their plots, on each of which a pair of back-to-backs could be built.

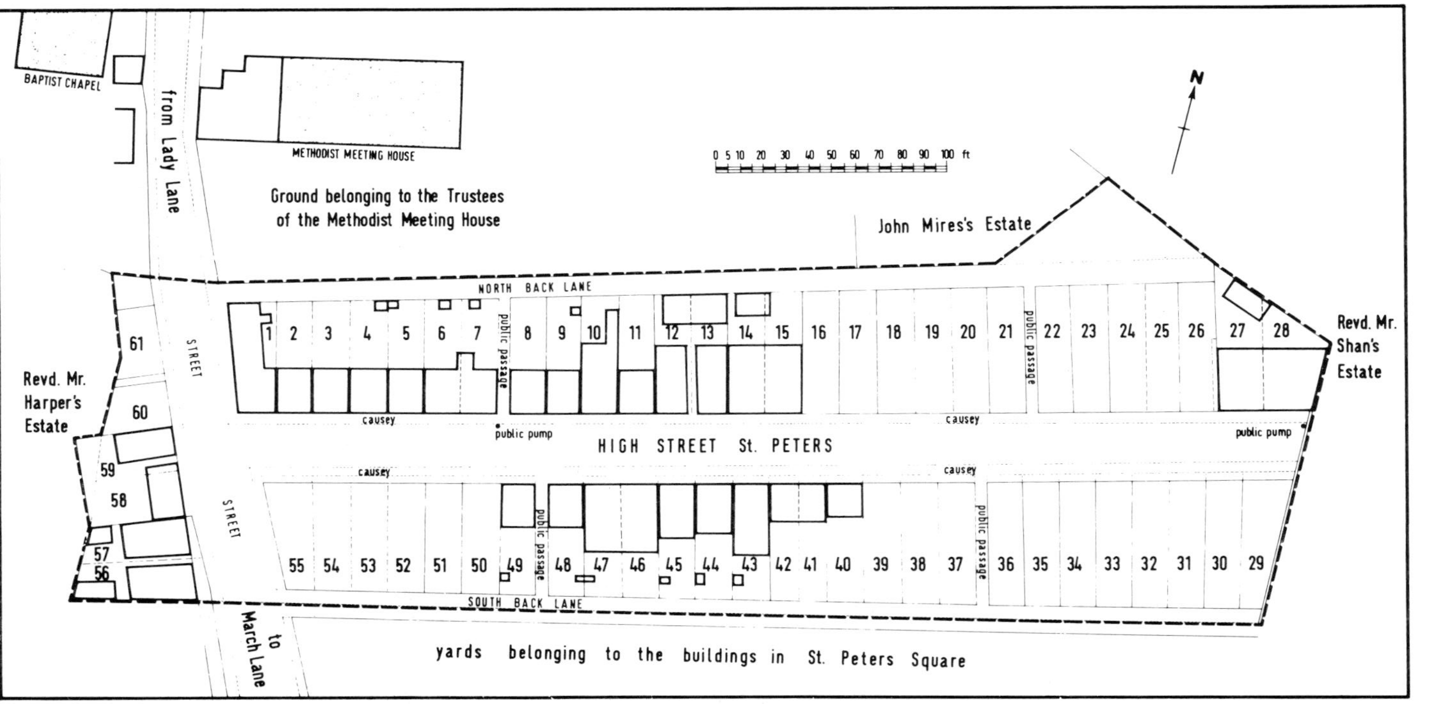
BAPTIST CHAPEL
from Lady Lane
METHODIST MEETING HOUSE
Ground belonging to the Trustees of the Methodist Meeting House
0 5 10 20 30 40 50 60 70 80 90 100 ft
N
John Mires's Estate
Revd. Mr. Shan's Estate
Revd. Mr. Harper's Estate
NORTH BACK LANE
public passage
causey
public pump
HIGH STREET St. PETERS
STREET
SOUTH BACK LANE
to March Lane
yards belonging to the buildings in St. Peters Square

FIG. 7.7 CLUB AND NON-CLUB HOUSES IN NELSON STREET

The houses on the two sides of what came to be called Nelson Street had very different origins. The first sale of land in Crackenthorpe Garden (Fig. 7.3) was in 1785 to the speculative builder, Abraham Croft, who built five pairs of back-to-backs, each centred on a tunnel giving rear access. The southern side of this terrace with the tunnels at intervals can be seen on the right hand side of this photograph, taken for the Council Sanitary Committee in 1901: the two men are probably Council officials.

In 1788 the trustees of a building club purchased an adjoining part of the former Garden, and its members subsequently filled their plots with back-to-backs, comprising Union Street and Union Court (Fig. 7.9): on the left can be seen the rear of houses on the north side of Union Street, also with tunnels at intervals; the brick buildings incorporated in the later pavement were yard privies. By 1791 the four houses nearest the camera, centred on a tunnel, were erected together by a schoolmaster, Joshua Eastburn, who held four shares and drew nos 43–46 in the club ballot.

The space between the two developments was laid out as Nelson Street. Despite their different origin the houses on the two sides of the street have identical size and style: one room on each of two floors. Gratings in the pavement here denote domestic coal or storage cellars: the absence of railings between the pavement and the houses confirms that there were no cellar dwellings (cf. Figs 7.9, 7.11 and 8.3).

was not helpful: even the cottages in the central yards were usually auctioned in groups. Until after 1785 no speculative builder was erecting cottage property for sale to single purchasers, and the land market was not geared to the sale of single plots of land so small as that appropriate for an urban cottage, some 30 square yards (below). The leasehold development on the Wilson estate had shown how single-house plots could be acquired, but for larger houses, and the two landowners who had been attempting leasehold development to the north and east of town had not descended to the offer of small plots.

There were, as we have seen, quite a small number of small fields adjacent to the centre of town other than the larger closes on the Ibbetson and Ann Wilson estates. To take up one of these for speculative subdivision was as yet no certain route to profit. In the typical field, 120 to 200 feet wide and about 600 foot long, there was about 2 acres of ground. The width of minor streets at that time was between 30 and 40 feet (say, 35) and a further 18 feet on either side for cottages would need a ribbon of total width about 53 feet (35 + 18). Within each ribbon, the 600 feet length of a field would accommodate two facing rows of thirty-three cottages if each had the usual 18 feet width.

A developer would need to be certain that, once he had purchased the field and divided it into cottage-sized plots, there would be potential house-owners, and the minimum number needed to absorb a field of the size exampled above was considerable: a 150-foot wide field had room for three complete street-and-cottage ribbons so that 178 purchasers would have to come forward. Arithmetic of this sort must have been at the front of any developer's mind, and – from the total inactivity before February 1785 – the effect was paralytic. Even in 1785, it must be noted, the first developer and builder to appear in Appendix VII.3, Abraham Croft, was able to avoid taking on a whole field: he found Ann Wilson, who had just sliced a portion off the four-acre Crackenthorpe Garden for the site of Brumfitt's Mill Garth carpet factory, willing to make another excision at the northern end of the Garden and sell him enough land for a terrace of sixteen houses, the future Nelson Street (Fig. 7.7).[33]

The subscription element in the building clubs gave access to the land market for persons without the immediate capital to deal with a landowner or developer as Croft had done. On the other hand the cooperative element in a club's organisation allowed its organisers two virtual certainties: that plots would be taken up; and that, so long as members' contractual obligations were fulfilled, their subscriptions would assure a fund for the purchase money. This did

[33] LCD 3359 and 3644.

not have to be immediately available in full if the trustees could arrange a mortgage of the club's land for the meanwhile, and mortgages also seem to have been readily available to club members on the security of a cottage property, once its title was theirs.

The six Leeds building clubs were of different size but within each club the members were assured of an equal quantity of land for their subscriptions. The shape of the land purchased by the trustees was as rectilinear as possible and, with the street placed at the centre, the plots for houses on either side of it had equal depth, so that the number of members was determined by the number of (approximately) 6-yard frontages which could be fitted in each side. Except for the first club, Union Row, all the club houses were arranged to face each other across streets. This itself was a remarkable innovation, commonplace as the street-form is today: the West End had not produced this form, and it can be plausibly argued that no true street had been erected in the town since John Harrison laid out the short length of New Street (alias New Kirke-gate) by St John's church in 1634.

With equal-sized plots there had to be some method of overcoming the inevitable variation in the attractiveness of sites. Except for the road-side Union Row and the self-contained St Peter's Square all the club streets were culs-de-sac ending at a field boundary: at the end of High Street was Wall Flatt, undeveloped until later; and at the end of St James Street was the field known as Sunny Bank, shown as penetrated by Oxford Row in a map of 1831 but in fact not built upon until 1839. The inequality of location was matched to the egality of membership by invoking Chance.[34] Gambling was always useful in the eighteenth century for inducing partnership in a venture, from South Sea companies to tontines and from lotteries for the holders of government stock through to the markets in reversions on leases for lives and other speculations based on the expectations of heirs.

[34] A Preston club first threw dice, and the winner decided which lot he would have to build on: Price, *Building Societies*, p.61.

FIG. 7.8 HIGH STREET ST PETER'S

From an amateur photograph, *c.*1900, looking eastwards up Quarry Hill towards Lemon Street. The street was erected by the members of the Boggart Close Lesser Building Society in 1789 and 1790 (Appendix VII.2(c)). It consisted of back-to-back houses with one room on each of two storeys; backsides were courtyards approached by tunnels: one of these, with the yard name above it, can be seen between the house steps on the left.

From the Teal plan of High Street (Fig. 7.6) and from lot numbers regularly recited in the title deeds of other club houses we know that the frontage plots were numbered serially along one side of a street, continuing back along the other (or, in the case of St Peter's Square, around the square). Every plot in the High Street plan, whether built upon or not in 1790, has the member's name upon it, and these names correspond to those in the eventual conveyances. This confirms that the allocation of positions, favoured and unfavoured, had been already made by lot. Yet the distribution of empty and built plots in 1790 makes it clear that building on the lots had not proceeded smoothly from no. 1 onwards, for although nos 1–15 had been built upon there were vacant plots between 15 and 27, and two other blocks on the south side were also vacant (Fig. 7.6). The order of building on lots cannot have been determined by a second lottery, for no chance would have given wins to fifteen successive numbers; similarly the Hill House Bank club trustees declared when making their conveyance of all the lots in February 1791 that lots 20–23 and 36–40 still remained to be built upon: these nine lots lay in compact blocks on the south side of each street which again cannot be the product of chance;[35] and when St James Street was caught by the rate assessors of 1790 and 1795 in mid-course it is clear that building was in progress (on both sides of the street) from ends to centre; how the club committee satisfied members' aspirations in the order of building cannot be known.

According to the classic rules cited above, a member moved up the queue each time that sufficient subscriptions had accumulated in the treasurer's hands to meet the expense of starting one further house. In Leeds, and certainly in Birmingham, this did not mean waiting until the previous member had completely filled his plot, which was always large enough to take a second house built back-to-back to the first, and usually a third house or cottage in the courtyard behind.[36] The plan of High Street in 1790 shows that only five or six members had built backsides: the allocation of lots for members to build had not been delayed by the fact that twenty-six members had gone no further than a frontage house, even when the eventual intention was the complete occupation of a plot with a back-to-back pair. The gap in time between intention and achievement could be wide. At the commencement of High Street in 1787 William Barwick, whitesmith, had been allocated the plot numbered '4' in respect of his membership.[37] When he sold the plot in November 1792 the deed

[35] WRRD, DF 371/449.
[36] See below, p.203
[37] LCD 1749.

stated that he was conveying to John Pottage, grocer from Snaith, a house which he had built and 'land for another'. When eventually Pottage came to dispose of the property in November 1815 it consisted of a pair of houses back-to-back, Pottage 'having erected the second'.[38]

This piecemeal occupation of plots admirably matched the acceptance of a house form, virtually universal in Leeds, that took up no more than 30 to 36 square yards of land, with a ground-floor room some 5½ yards square, and the possibility of a separate one-room cellar-dwelling below to cater for tenants with incomes too low to afford the rent of an above-ground cottage. The widths of plots in High Street, Union Street, King Street, Queen Street, Union Row and St James Street all lay between 5½ and 6½ yards, the frontage width of the standard back-to-back house in Leeds; and all had the depth to permit development beyond the frontage.

A club member could thus play a dual economic role: facing the street forwards he was an owner-occupier but facing backwards (and sometimes downwards to a cellar) he was a landlord. That is, in miniature, he was akin to the Briggate landlords encountered in Chapter Five who had frontage houses and shops where they themselves lived, and tenanted houses at the backsides.

There were distinct economic advantages to a member in this duality, a practice which continued long after the disappearance of building clubs. In 1885 the Secretary of the Leeds Permanent Building Society, giving evidence to the Royal Commission on the Housing of the Working Classes, described how Leeds artisans would acquire a small plot of land to erect two houses back-to-back, living in the front house and drawing rent from a tenant in the other house to help pay off the mortgage.[39] Just under a century earlier Jonathan Hopkinson had two plots numbered 17 and 18 in St James Street. In December 1789 he insured four small houses 'occupied by self and others', that is, two on each plot.[40] In the rate book of 1790 he was assessed as owner-occupier of one house, as landlord of two others, while the fourth was empty. In 1795 he was an owner-occupier now with three tenants, and the assessment of each house, 35*s*., was typical of the 'cottage' range.

Thus their club membership had not only allowed Hopkinson and his fellows, through their pooled savings, to have access to a land market which they could not have hoped to enter individually: it also

[38] WRRD, DC 75/86.
[39] Fatkin as in n.27 above, pp.371–79.
[40] RE 17 114236.

gave them an opportunity, once a plot was their own, to have a share, via the rents of tenants, in the buoyancy of demand for house-room in a part of town where development had been set off by the club street.

Mortgages of newly built houses were very frequent, as in the West End; thus club membership provided an owner-occupier with a roof over his head, a source of weekly income from his tenants backsides, and access to borrowed money for any profitable investment which came into view. There is as yet no study of the Yorkshire mortgage market in this period, although materials are abundant, not least in the packets of deeds utilised in this chapter. Uniquely, each of the Hill House club's conveyances of 29 March 1791 was to two persons (see Appendix VII.2(e)) and the differences in their occupational status make it likely that one of each pair was a mortgagor and the other a mortgagee.[41]

THE MYTH OF SELF-HELP

Two quotations from Price's history of building societies express the myth admirably: 'they were the creation of ordinary men, artisans and craftsmen who realised the virtue of self-help .... These early societies existed *for one purpose only*: to provide each and every member, *and no one else*, with a house erected by the Society and paid for out of its funds'.[42] Chapman and Bartlett's study of the Birmingham clubs subsequently cast doubt on the participation of the 'ordinary man'. They wrote: 'subscription rates clearly excluded all but those whose incomes consistently allowed a comfortable margin above subsistence .... The aristocracy of labour, many of whom were able to climb the ladder to economic independence during periods of trade expansion, were also expressing their independence by helping one another to become property-owners'.[43]

Their doubts, and more, are confirmed by a close study of the structure of the Leeds building clubs. Unfortunately there is no record of the size of membership subscriptions for any Leeds club but the magnitude can be roughly estimated, and it lay beyond the capacity of even the most skilled employed person: the most skilled

[41] WRRD, DF 372/451 to 395/480 consecutively.

[42] Price, *Building Societies*, pp.9 and 19; my italics.

[43] Chapman and Bartlett, 'The Contribution of Building Clubs', pp.9 and 19; confirmation from a recent wider study will be found in M. H. Yeadall, 'Building Societies in the West Riding of Yorkshire', in *Building the Industrial City*, ed. M. Doughty (Leicester, 1986), pp.57–105.

operatives in Cookson and Fawcett's carpet-making establishment were certified by the major magistrates as earning 18*s.* a week in January 1787 when the wage was just about to be reduced, with the magistrates' approval, to 17*s.* Now the Hill House Bank club, with forty-two uniformly small houses built for its members, was terminated in March 1791. Subscriptions cannot have begun before the summer of 1787 when the trustees purchased Camphor Close. Building cannot have been long delayed since nineteen plots were occupied by February 1788, and twenty-three houses, the whole of King Street, were insured by the club committee in January 1789.[44] By the time of the rate assessment of May 1790 there were at least seventy houses completed on thirty-six plots, perhaps thirty months after building began. At the very least the membership would have been charged with about £6 per plot for the land and £25 for each house (and some were insured for £33). Spread over thirty months, £56 amounted to nearly £2 per month: and if thus quite beyond the means of the minority of the highly-skilled, earning £3. 12*s.* a month,[45] how much more beyond those of the 'ordinary man'?

We have already seen how the Leeds plots were of a size that usually accommodated at least two houses, so that even if a club member lived in one house he could not avoid being landlord of at least one another. It is not the inevitability of landlordism, however, which casts doubt on the clubs being co-operatives of members seeking to live in their own houses.

First doubts arise when members are found owning not only more than one house but more than one plot. Even the smallest club, at Union Row, had four members with two plots each: one of these members, Isaac Fletcher, stuff-weaver, had a house on each plot when the club reached termination in May 1789, and in May 1790 he insured one more.[46]

The full extent of multiple lot ownership is seen in Table 7.3. The 292 lots in the six clubs were owned by 178 members; two-thirds were owners of single lots and just under a quarter owned two lots; six members owned five lots or more in their club, and individuals will be found as members of more than one club. In St Peter's Square the grocer, Robert Randall, had five lots and the nurseryman, Thomas Barnes, four. In High Street the Teal plan placed the name Barnes on four more plots, and the whitesmith William Lindley was also a member of both the Lesser and Greater clubs with three plots

[44] Sun OS 359 353499.

[45] As discussed in Rimmer, *Cottages*, pp. 181–83 and 192–96.

[46] Sun OS 369 570099.

TABLE 7.3

Multiple Lot Ownership in the Leeds Building Clubs

Club	Total number of members	Number of club members with: one lot	two lots	three lots	four lots	five lots	more than five lots	Total number of lots
Union Row	18	14	4	–	–	–	–	22
Boggart Close Greater (St Peter's Square)	21	17	2	–	1	1	–	30
Boggart Close Lesser (High Street)	46	34	10	1	1	–	–	61
St James St	42*	24	7	2	3	2	one of 6 & one of 13	85†
Hill House Bank (King St and Queen St)	30	20	8	2	–	–	–	42
Crackenthorpe Garden (Union St)	23	6	10	3	3	1	–	52
TOTALS	178	115 (65%)	41 (23%)	6 (5%)	8 (5%)	4 (2%)	2 (1%)	292

* Lots 40–42, ownership unknown
† One other lot extinguished to provide an alley

Source: WRRD and LCD cited in footnotes to Chapter 7.

in High Street. In St James Street it was perhaps natural and loyal for the president, the apothecary David Joy, to have five plots, and he at least did reside on one of them; as did the pocket-book manufacturer Richard Kendall who had no fewer than fourteen plots, but Thomas Barnes reappears in the St James club as a committee man and owner of three plots.

The multiple lot owners who did not even reside in the club street made up a class of members who had clearly entered a club solely for the purpose of becoming the owner of tenanted property. Ascertaining a person's residence at this period is not easy unless he was a member of a profession, a shopkeeper, or a substantial craftsman: in which case his name may appear in the directory of 1798. Thus it can be shown that Tobias Appleyard lived in The Calls and not in a club

TABLE 7.4

Building Club Streets: Owner-occupiers and Landlords, 1795

Club	Lots owner-occupied, without tenants alongside	Lots owner-occupied with tenants alongside	Lots wholly tenanted	Lots unbuilt upon	Totals
Union Row	3	–	19	–	22
Boggart Close Greater (St Peter's Square)	5	3	22	–	30
Boggart Close Lesser (High Street)	5	2	27	27	61
St James Street	8	11	48	18	85
Hill House (King and Queen Streets)	4	2	34	2	42
Crackenthorpe Garden (Union Street)	6	10	30	6	52
TOTALS	31 (11%)	28 (9%)	180 (61%)	53 (18%)	292

Source: LCA, LORB 35.

street; that Thomas Barnes lived in none of the streets that his various clubs had built, but in Briggate.

The directories consistently ignored the smaller streets. That of 1798, the fullest of its day, named only two inhabitants from the 152 houses in High Street, and none of those in Union Row, King Street or Queen Street. Were it not for the rate books, with their distinction between owner-occupied and tenanted houses, it would be impossible to know what the members of the Lesser Club intended to do with their houses. With the aid of the rate books there is no doubt (Table 7.4).

When the names of lot-owners from the Teal plan of 1790 are sought in the rate book of that year, early in the club's life, twenty-three of the thirty-two plots with houses upon them were occupied solely by tenants. The record is consistent. When the fifty-two plots of Union Street were completed, thirty-four were occupied solely by tenants; and in the same year when seventy plots in St James Street were built upon, forty-nine were without a resident owner; the larger houses of the members of the Greater club in St Peter's Square were rather more attractive as residences but even here only seven of the thirty plots were built upon by members who resided there. Union Row had only six of its twenty-two plots occupied by resident proprietors in 1790; and by 1795 only three. In 1800, by which time 292 lots were occupied, fifty-one had a club member residing upon them. If there was such a thing as an urban peasant, proprietor of his own brick-and-mortar smallholding, self-help in the form of the Leeds building clubs had singularly failed to produce him.

Even without the rate book evidence the known occupations of certain club members are not compatible with residence in a back-to-back house in a club street: it is unlikely that Joseph Longbotham, innkeeper, kept his inn in one of his little houses in Union Row built on lot 5; or that Lucas Nicholson, attorney and future town clerk, lived in High Street; still less that the carpet manufacturer Thomas Brumfitt, who had just erected a factory with a steam engine on Mill Garth, was resident on his plot in Union Row.

It was universal practice at this time in any legal document to identify a person not by a house number, of which there were very few, but by occupation or status. From such documents it has been possible in Table 7.5 to identify the occupation of all but three of the owners of the 292 lots in the six Leeds clubs. Chapman and Bartlett were obviously right in identifying the Leeds clubs as designed for the aristocracy of labour although there were fewer textile craftsmen 'enjoying the benefits of mechanisation at a previous stage in production [to the factory]' than they imagined.[47] Overall, no more than 15 per cent of club members fell into this category and there were nearly as many from retail shops and the food trades (Table 7.5).

Taken together, 59 per cent of the lots were held by artisan craftsmen. Yet beneath this predominance of artisan craftsmen there was a tendency for different clubs to cater for different interests. In Union Row two-thirds of the lots were held by members in the textile trades but only one-sixth in High Street; a third in Hill House Bank: but none at all in Union Street which was a street where two-thirds of the lots were taken by craftsmen from the building trades, the predominant trade also in High Street. In St James Street the predominant group was made up of non-textile craftsmen, and in

[47] Chapman and Bartlett, 'The Contribution of Building Clubs', p.238.

TABLE 7.5

Building Club Members: Number of Lots held by Occupational Groups

Club	Number of lots	Building trades*	Textiles†	Craftsmen‡	Professional clerical	Propertied	Shopkeepers and food trades	Merchant	Farming, etc.	Number with occupation unknown	Notes
Union Row	22	2	14	–	–	2	3	–	1	–	64% in textiles
Boggart Close Greater (St Peter's Square)	30	6	3	1	1	4	9	2	4	–	30% shopkeepers or food trades
Boggart Close Lesser (High St)	61	22	11	16	5	2	1	–	4	–	36% in building trades
St James St	85	8	2	30	8	5	3	7	19	3	37% of known occupations are craftsmen
Hill House Bank (King St, Queen St)	42	4	13	3	–	1	17	2	2	–	40% shopkeepers and food trades
Crackenthorpe Garden (Union St)	52	35	–	4	4	–	2	4	3	–	67% in building trades
TOTALS	292	77 (26%)	43 (15%)	54 (18%)	18 (6%)	14 (5%)	35 (12%)	15 (5%)	33 (11%)	3 (1%)	

* Joiner, plumber, glazier, mason, carpenter, cabinet-maker.
† Cloth-dresser, presser, dyer, weaver, clothier, packer, carpetmaker, cloth-miller, stuff-weaver.
‡ Tailor, whitesmith, watchmaker, clockmaker, shoemaker, card-maker, roper, stay-maker, miner.

Source: WRRD and LCD cited in footnotes to Chapter 7.

St Peter's Square and Hill House Bank of shopkeepers and food traders.

Since a quarter of all lots were held by building craftsmen it might seem that they had entered, like the Park estate leaseholders who were builders, in order to build and re-sell but they seem to have been smaller men than those whose names appear in the Park estate leases, and they were certainly not erecting club houses in order to re-sell them. Of the Crackenthorpe Garden members, the only builder not to retain his houses through to 1805 (after which rate books cease to survive) was Joseph Dixon who disposed of his four tenanted houses between 1790 and 1795.

Nor were building craftsmen among the large multiple-lot owners: the seventy-seven lots ascribed to this trade in Table 7.5 were owned by forty-two different persons, and only two joined more than one club; as we have seen, they were attracted most to the Crackenthorpe Garden club, occupying nearly half its lots.

Far from being a group 'benefiting from early stages of mechanisation' they came from the least mechanised of all trades: and out of what they earned as joiners, plumbers, glaziers, masons, carpenters and cabinet makers, erecting and fitting out for others the industrial, domestic and public buildings of the town, they were able to subscribe to a savings club (spiced with an element of lottery) by which they could themselves become householders and landlords.

THE BACK-TO-BACKS: HOUSES FOR THE SONS OF LABOUR

In their uniformity (though not in their form) the East End houses erected in High Street, Union Street, Union Row, King Street and Queen Street would not have disgraced the classical ideal expected of a West End: yet their uniformity was imposed not by good taste but by the limited income of their tenants, the consequent low level of rents that could be paid, and thereby the limit to the capital sum which a landlord would lay out for a house.

The form of these houses is not unknown since they survived in use long enough to be recorded in photographs, some from the 1890s and some from the 1930s, usually taken by officers of the Corporation's Sanitary Committee engaged in the preparation of clearance orders for Unhealthy Areas. The progress of individual streets can be followed in the published maps of Giles (1815) and Fowler (1821, 1831, 1844) and the ground plans of individual houses and their surrounding courts and yards are clearly delineated in the sheets of the Ordnance Survey's five-feet-to-the-mile maps surveyed in 1847 and published in 1850.

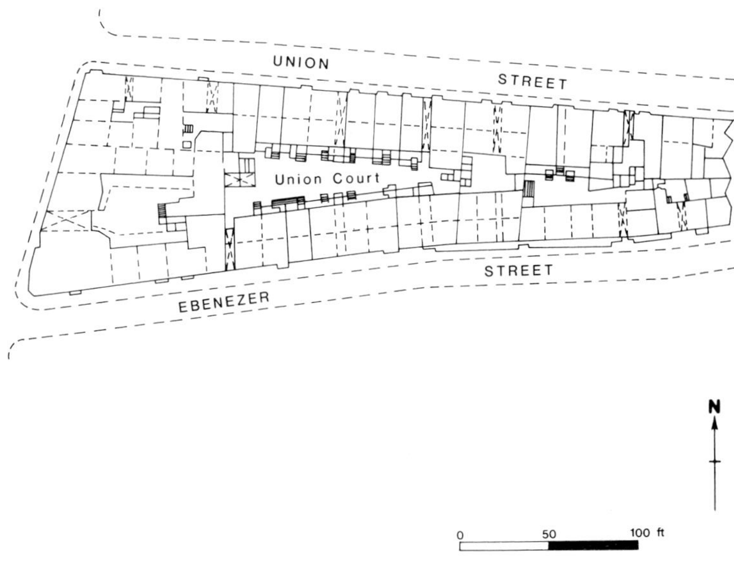

FIG. 7.9 BACK-TO-BACKS, INTERIOR COURTS AND CELLAR DWELLINGS: UNION STREET AND EBENEZER STREET

Union Street was built by the members of the Crackenthorpe Garden Building Club (Fig. 7.3 and Appendix VII.2(f)); simultaneously Ebenezer Street was developed on another part of the same field by private speculators; the intervening ground formed courtyards; the additional steps alongside house doorways indicate entrances to cellar dwellings.

Looking only at the facades of these streets a visitor from southern England might at first see nothing different from a row of village labourers' cottages: brick construction, slate roofs, stone steps to a front door, a ground-floor window with hinged wooden shutters and a bedroom above (Figs. 7.7 and 7.8). Most were of two storeys although outside the club streets photographs reveal three storeys and the occasional one-storey house. Yet at intervals in these streets the facades were broken not by a complete gap between houses but by a narrow tunnel limited to the ground floor, with part of a first-floor room extending over it (Fig. 7.10(a) and (b)). Such tunnels leading to a back garden or rear house-door are not uncommon in the midlands and the south of England, but at the end of these tunnels in Leeds one did not enter a back garden nor did one use it to approach a servants' or tradesmen's entrance at some back door. The door in the yard beyond the tunnel was the entrance to a separate house, usually of one room per floor, a mirror image of the frontage house with which it shared a central party wall. Thus the back-to-back was contrasted with the 'through' house by having only one entrance, and windows restricted to whichever side of the house had the door.

A wide field would permit several parallel terraces of back-to-backs to be built in it, and if there were then any ground left over, a row of 'blind-backs' was built, one room deep on each floor (Fig. 7.9); over such rooms the roof was usually pitched at the conventional angle, giving the appearance of a normal terrace but from the rear it could be seen that the back wall fell from the apex of the roof in a vertical brick cliff.

Larger versions of the back-to-back extended to three storeys, giving three rooms per house (as in photographs of Ebenezer Street) but some three-storey back-to-back pairs (as in Millwright Street) are known from photographs to have been made up of separate dwellings on each floor: access to the one-room dwellings on the first and second storeys was gained from a steeply-inclined staircase in the tunnel leading straight from the street, and (but for the sight of stairs) looking very like a yard tunnel.[48]

There seems to be no reason why some English towns had back-to-backs and others not; but despite the disapproval of sanitary reformers the affection for them persisted longer in Leeds than anywhere else. Between 1886 and 1904 two-thirds of all new houses erected were back-to-back, although a by-law of 1886 had forced a space to be left after every four pairs, in which yard privies were placed. In 1892 a row of four pairs was built, and still stands, in the grounds of Claremont, where the Thoresby Society has its library and meeting room, and in a modified but still back-to-back form they were being built in Harehills forty years later.[49]

Thomas Cubitt declared that he had never built a back-to-back in London and they do not seem to have been a feature of the London industrial districts. Liverpool, Manchester and Bradford once had back-to-backs but fell out of love with them by 1861. Darra Moir's

[48] For a two-storey house of this sort see L. Caffyn, *Workers' Housing in West Yorkshire, 1750–1920* (Royal Commission on Historical Monuments, Suppy. Ser. IX (1986)), pl. 54; not there located but in Millwright Street, Leylands.

[49] Claremont Grove: four pairs of back-to-backs with end yard formerly used for ashpits and privies. For continued back-to-back building: Beresford, *Back-to-Back House*, p. 119, fig. 20 and pl. 7 (Luxor Avenue, Harehills, built 1907–08).

official *Report on Back-to-back Houses* in 1910 was concerned with the whole country but cited examples in a very limited number of towns, all northern. Barry and Smith's earlier study of 1888 reported 'discontinuance' where back-to-backs had once been built in Lancashire, the Potteries, the Black Country and the West Riding.[50]

Such an uneven distribution is hard to explain. The back-to-backs seem to have lingered longest in the wool textile towns but there was no functional role for them in any domestic industrial process; there were many industrial areas with wages as low as Leeds but without a back-to-back in sight; and they do not seem connected to high land values: they were built in Leeds on dear land and on cheap land, and eventually north, south, east and west into every suburb.

It is easier to suggest how the form became accepted so swiftly in Leeds. I have argued elsewhere that a prototype of the working-class cottage, without a back door but with the same floor space of approximately 6 yards by 6, was already prevalent in Leeds even though no street of back-to-backs was built before 1787. It was the inevitable form when cottages began to encroach backsides in yards and folds, particularly in the narrower ones of Kirkgate. These yards had no entrance other than from the frontage (so that the tunnel makes an earlier appearance here also). The length of the yard tempted the insertion of cottage after cottage, as in the Boot and Shoe Yard (Fig. 12.1), replacing such out-buildings as stables, garden sheds and haylofts which already lined the boundary walls. If a central space was to be retained so that the furthest cottage could be reached – there was no exit to a field or back lane – then there was room only to line the two sides of the yard with single-room houses facing inwards.

This style was exactly that of the *blind-back* (above), and every back-to-back terrace was equivalent to two lines of blind-backs set against each other. So this was pre-figured in the yards as infill developed in each. The owners of adjacent yards were building blind-back cottages, so that along each boundary wall of the yard a line of blind-back houses in one ownership was built against another (facing in the opposite direction) in the next yard. Lifted bodily from the yard and set down in a field, houses in this form made a terrace of back-to-back pairs.[51]

50 L. W. Darra Moir, *Report on Back-to-backs*, PP XXXVIII of 1910; F. W. Barry and P. G. Smith, *Joint Report on Back-to-back Housing to the Local Government Board* (1888).

51 L. Caffyn, *Workers' Housing in West Yorkshire*, chs.1–3 with many plans and photographs of back-to-backs locally. A wider survey will be found in S. Muthesius, *The English Terraced House* (Yale, 1982), esp. ch.12.

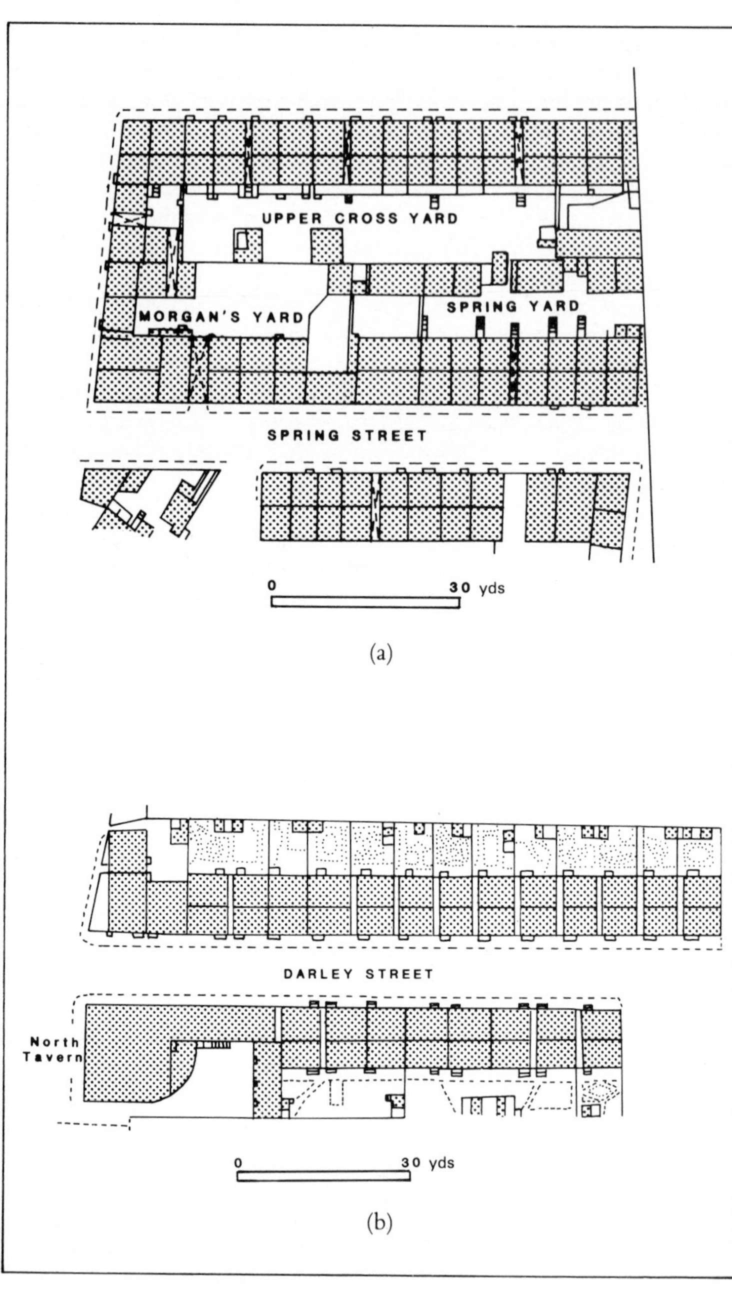

UPPER CROSS YARD
MORGAN'S YARD
SPRING YARD
SPRING STREET
0
30 yds
(a)
DARLEY STREET
North Tavern
0
30 yds
(b)

The long affection of Leeds for back-to-back houses demonstrates that they were not in themselves considered as low quality, inferior housing, whatever the views of later sanitary reformers. Some club members were content to live in them, and exactly the same size and form were chosen by those individual developers and speculative builders who created the remainder of the East End. Furthermore (below) purchasers of larger houses in St Peter's Square and St James Street were not deterred by the immediate proximity of back-to-backs.

There is no record of the interior fittings of the early back-to-backs, and the very few surviving interior photographs are of dilapidated properties on the eve of demolition a hundred and fifty years after their erection. The streets were certainly unsewered, while paving was at the expense of each proprietor, should he care, and small outbuildings which the Ordnance Survey plans show in some yards were probably privies. The streets lay outside the range of the piped supply from the town waterworks. The title deeds of the Union Row houses indicate a well and pump in each yard, and Teal's plan of High Street shows two 'publick pumps'; lot 55 happened to cover the site of a small spring with alleged curative properties (from which Ralph Thoresby drank) and it later became the rather unlikely site of a spa bath-house.[52] This street had footpaths ('causeys') 4 ft 6 in. wide on each side, and the carriageway was 19 ft 9 in. wide, about three-quarters of the width of Park Row and Albion Street. Union Street and the two Hill House Bank club streets were 12 feet wide. St Peter's Street, which formed the western side of St Peter's Square and was also a thoroughfare from York Road to Marsh Lane

[52] M. W. Beresford, '2, 4 and 6 High Street', in *Lantern Slide Leeds*, ed. S. G. Burt (Leeds, n.d. [1984]), cover and frontispiece.

FIG. 7.10 TYPES OF BACK-TO-BACK STREETS

Redrawn from the Ordnance Survey five-foot plan surveyed in 1847. In the Spring Street development (a) the field was long enough to accommodate a frontage for fifteen back-to-backs on one side of Spring Street and eleven on the other; it was broad enough to lay a similar row against the top side of the field without direct access to a street. A few other single houses were inserted within the yards.

In Darley Street (b) a narrower field was developed with an axial street; the houses on the upper side, although back-to-back, have gardens (and a privy) at their rear.

JOSEPH

past the Paley developments (below), was 30 feet wide but had a causeway only where it passed the Square. All the club streets were castigated for the low quality of their paving, drainage, sewerage and water supply in the sanitary enquiries of 1839–42.[53]

Some histories of working-class housing, written from hearsay rather than documents, assert that houses of this type were jerry-built and ramshackle. They did indeed become targets for criticism within fifty years of being erected, but from the point of view of housing improvement their fault lay in the other direction: they did not fall to pieces quickly enough, and their structures withstood storm and tempest until the clearances of the mid-1930s while the environment deteriorated around them. The actual criticisms levied against the back-to-back streets will be examined in Chapter Twelve, and the view will be taken that the deficiencies came not from their architecture nor from any original malevolence but from their unregulated proliferation and their industrial environment.

Fifty years after their first appearance another element in the house-form of these streets began to attract public criticism although not to be regulated by any by-law for a further thirty years: this was the cellar dwelling, a one-roomed habitation lying wholly or mainly below street level and approached by its own external steps from the street.[54] Several photographs look down from street level to the upper part of the house door and to the only window of such a dwelling (Fig. 7.11), and their presence can be deduced when the large-scale Ordnance plans show thin lines along the pavement next to a house which are too long to be protruding steps. In the West End these lines would have indicated iron railings (such as survive in Park Square and Park Place) running along the edge of a subterranean *area*

[53] See Table 13.20 below.

[54] The location of cellar dwellings can be traced from the minutes of the Council's Scavenging and Nuisance (Cellar Dwellings) Sub-committee, 1868–80: Leeds Civic Hall strongroom, shelf 85, dating from the period when cellar dwellings were being inspected and in some cases closed.

FIG. 7.11 CELLAR DWELLINGS UNDER BUILDING CLUB HOUSES IN HIGH STREET

Frontages of the two-storey back-to-back houses on the north side of High Street show that each has a separate cellar dwelling, evidenced by exterior steps with wooden or metal railings to protect pedestrians on the footpath; in 1901, the date of this photograph, a beer house in the ground-floor room of this house was dignified with the name *Pineapple Inn*.

to give light to the windows of a basement with its kitchens and other domestic rooms; these were an integral part of the main house, reached by an interior staircase but there was sometimes a door in the area reached from the street by steps and used as an entrance for servants and tradesmen.

The cellars which lay below the back-to-backs were of a very different sort. They were separate one-room dwellings, unconnected by an interior stair to the ground-floor room above them and reckoned as separate 'houses' by the census-takers of 1801. Nor was a cellar dwelling confined to the frontage half of back-to-backs: at the west end of Union Street it was to backside houses in Union Court that the Ordnance Survey plan gave the conventional sign for steps going downward, and these lay alongside the different sign for the protruding doorsteps leading up to the ground floor of the back-to-back houses. Title deeds for the Court confirm that there were five cellar dwellings here,[55] while title deeds for six houses (that is, three back-to-back pairs) on the north side of Ebenezer Street across the yard of Union Courtyard included three cellar dwellings below, presumably at the back.[56] In Clarkson's Court, on the south side of Ebenezer Street, sixteen messuages owned by William Clarkson had four inhabited cellars below them.[57]

In the rate books of 1790–1805 the cellar dwellings were marked by rateable values below those of a single back-to-back, usually 10*s.* or 12*s.* as against 25*s.* for each half of a back-to-back pair. The rubric 'cellar' sometimes occurs: in the rate book of 1790 Thomas Appleyard, owner of lots 36–38 in Queen Street, was assessed on seven tenanted houses with another 'empty' and against a blank space for the sum due was noted, '4 empty cellars': in the next rate book he paid on eight houses and four cellars. It was certainly an up-down-and-under dwelling of this sort which was the subject of an advertisement in the *Intelligencer* of 20 May 1789 for a house in the

[55] WRRD, DG 72/106, April 1791; DX 4/6, Dec. 1796.

[56] LCD 320 and 363.

[57] Clarkson's Court, named after William Clarkson: LCD 398. Court names often refer back to an original owner: e.g. Stainburn Square and Court 'erected by John Stainburn': LCD 911; Lawrence Yard, St Peter's Square, at the rear of plot 14 in the Greater Club ballot, drawn by William Lawrence, joiner.

The listing of court names in directories (as in *Directory, 1817*, pp. 164–69), and then the large-scale plans (pp. 379–80, below) and the street-name plaques affixed after the 1842 Improvement Act all reduced the chances of re-naming when ownership changed.

same street: 'a well-built Club-House lately owned by William Musgrave being one large Cellar, a House, and a Chamber, each five yards square, and ground to build upon', together with 'Club-Houses of the same dimensions in the possession of Christopher Waggett and Henry Parkinson'.

Musgrave's house in Queen Street, with the 'ground to build upon' was subsequently completed to make a back-to-back pair with a shared party wall. Once joined, these Siamese twins proved difficult for lawyers to separate for conveyancing purposes so that it became virtually impossible for them to be bought and sold except in pairs; dwellings in cellars were even less likely to be parted from superstructures but nevertheless they usually found their way into the descriptive clauses of deeds of title, and were generally proclaimed when properties were advertised in newspapers. It was even possible for a cellar dwelling to be reckoned a 'cottage', as when two houses in Ebenezer Street were conveyed in December 1796 'with two cottages under' whereas at their first purchase in April 1791 the two houses were 'in a new street called Ebenezer Street . . . with the Cellars under the same'.[58]

THE NON-CLUB STREETS IN THE EAST END, 1785–1815

The boundary between the East and the North East Divisions ran along Marsh Lane so that the East End club houses in Union Row, Union Street, High Street and St Peter's Square contributed to the 1454 new houses added to the North East Division between 1772 and 1801 (Table 8.6). The four club streets accounted for about 420 of these (Table 7.2). It is less easy to trace the non-club houses in the Wakefield Registry of Deeds, and with no fresh survey of the town made between Tuke's map of 1781 and the Giles map of 1815 not every new street can be precisely dated; rate books do survive from 1790, 1795, 1800 and 1805 so that (provided its owner or tenant's name is known) a new house of that period can be assigned to a five-year range.

[58] Sun OS 295 446369: illustrated in Beresford, *Face of Leeds*, pl.25, where the house (of one room) at the lowest level, open to the Court, prefigured what came to be termed an *underdwelling*; a line of these, set into a hill slope, formed Line Fold (*Ibid.*, pl.27); houses over the underdwelling, usually conventional two-storey back-to-backs, had access by a wooden gallery.

Table 7.1 shows that, of the landowners with substantial numbers of cottage properties in 1805, many were already established before 1790. The names of Musgrave, Kendall and Tinsdill relate to the dispersed rows scattered over the slopes of Cavalier Hill on the East Division[59] and those of Clarkson and Randall to the houses which lined the York turnpike from Lady Bridge past the junction with Mabgate and to the shapeless courts which had begun to accumulate behind the frontages, such as Skelton's Yard, Globe Yard, Allison's Yard and the yard dignified with the name of Boynton Street. Tunstall's Fold in Mabgate was probably also built by 1790, and Linsley's Fold followed. The folds along Marsh Lane, including those surveyed for the Pious Uses Committee in 1793, were also filling up at this time. All these cottage properties were either back-to-backs or one-room dwellings; there seem to have been no cellar dwellings until the club streets although Johnson's Square on the south of Quarry Hill ingeniously utilised a disused quarry to build three-storey blind-backs, two storeys above ground and one down in the quarry, entered by a tunnel with descending steps.[60]

None of the developments so far mentioned took place along newly laid-out streets. These began to appear almost simultaneously in two areas, each adjacent to club ground. Immediately south of Union Street, and within Crackenthorpe Garden, three streets – Ebenezer, George and Back George – were laid out with access to Vicar Lane. In McAndrews Garden a grid of four streets was laid out with access to Marsh Lane: these were St Peter's Street, Off Street, Brick Street and York Street, part of the extensive projects of Richard Paley.[61]

Both McAndrews Garden and Crackenthorpe Garden had been part of the settled estate of Ann Wilson, and earlier in the century had indeed been used for market gardening, the one by a Scottish and the other by a Kentish man. There had been attempts thirty years before[62] to develop a leasehold estate here on the Park model but in December 1784, after Ann Wilson had left the Leeds area to become Mrs Thomas Norcliffe Dalton of Oxton Hall, her trustees accepted the unlikelihood of any one purchaser taking the whole estate and began to negotiate the sale of the two Gardens in three portions. A plan of Crackenthorpe Garden (Fig. 7.3) was commissioned from

[59] See above, p.173

[60] See note 58 above.

[61] See below, pp.215–20

[62] See above, p.113

the surveyor, John Crookes.[63] The first purchase, two months after the marriage, was by the builder, Abraham Croft, who took enough ground on the northern edge of Crackenthorpe Garden to accommodate twenty-four pairs of back-to-backs in what he was to call Nelson Street;[64] then the carpet manufacturer, Thomas Brumfitt, took ground in the south-east corner on which he intended to build a carpet factory alongside Mill Garth;[65] the last and most interesting purchase, taking up the larger part of the Garden, demonstrates how closely the club and non-club developments were connected without feeling of rivalry and competition.

A conveyance of August 1787 to Samuel Blagborough, Thomas Glover, Christopher Heaps and William Smith – names already known to us as club members – specifically stated that the four were acting in a double capacity: as club trustees for 1.43 acres but private purchasers of the remaining 2½ acres.[66] A small area was bought by the trustees of a proposed Baptist chapel and burial ground which eventually gave the name to Ebenezer Street.[67]

Blagborough and his partner, Alexander Turner, and then Turner's son, George were responsible for developing the larger part of their 2½ acres as building ground. Ebenezer Street was laid out in fifty-five plots of the same size as those of club lots in Union Street and, like them, destined to bear back-to-backs; a photograph of Ebenezer chapel after it had fallen into disuse shows that some of the adjoining houses ran to three storeys.

The next new street to the south, Back George Street, had twenty-one pairs of back-to-backs on its north side while its southern side was formed by the back entrances to the twenty-four pairs of houses on the north side of George Street. The shorter southern side of that street was made up of twenty-four plots large enough for back-to-backs. Census enumeration ledgers have survived from 1801, wherein 175 houses were counted in Ebenezer Street and eighty-six in the two George Streets; Nelson Street then had fifteen houses.[68]

[63] LCA, DB Map 373.

[64] LCD 435, 1864 and 3644.

[65] *LI*, 1 May 1797.

[66] LCD 1842.

[67] For Ebenezer Chapel see D. C. Dews, 'Two Eighteenth-century Baptist Chapels', in Burt, ed., *Lantern Slide Leeds*, pp.20–21. In the West End at St Paul's burials were in vaults beneath the church but here an open burial ground in Ebenezer Street was commenced in 1786: PRO, RG4 3432.

[68] LCA, LPC 104, North East Division: cf. Tables 1–3 and fig. 3 in P. Laxton, 'Liverpool in 1801', *Transactions of the Historic Society for Lancashire and Cheshire*, CXXX (1981), 73–113, a study also made possible by an unusual survival of census data for 1801 from individual households.

Cellar dwellings were found in the back courts of these streets and on some frontages. There were other respects, such as insured and rateable values, as well as street width, house dimensions and architectural appearance, in which these streets matched the adjoining club street; the occupations of owners and tenants are more difficult to determine. Since not all the title deeds can be located it has not been possible to present the occupations of house-owners in the non-club streets in the same way as for Union Street but those which are known do seem like the same mixture of the Middle Ranks and the Sons of Labour, and indeed several were also club members: army captain, farmer, widow, inn-holder, joiner, plasterer, cabinet maker, wheelwright, pawnbroker, stonemason and carpenter.

Their similar house dimensions also gave Ebenezer Street and Union Street virtually identical numbers of persons per house in 1801 with 3.9 and 4.0 respectively, but while Union Street had only nine of its 170 houses occupied by more than one family, among the 176 houses in Ebenezer Street there were twice that number, and there was the same higher proportion in the two George Streets where the number of persons per house rose to 4.4. In all three streets families were small, the average being 3.8 (Table 7.6).

It would seem that Turner and his associates fulfilled very much the same economic role – to their own profit – as the establishment of a building club; that is, to make available to the twenty-three purchasers a plot of land appropriate to their need, but a fraction of the size of a whole close, whereon some could become owner-occupiers and others landlords. Unlike the club lots, there was no certainty that Turner would find takers but in the buoyant conditions following 1785 all the streets in Crackenthorpe Garden were finished at about the same time. As in the clubs, several took multiple plots; and, like some of the club trustees, Turner himself showed his faith in the venture by retaining a plot on which he built houses that he retained as landlord. Croft remained as landlord of the whole of Nelson Street until his death.

Turner and the other purchasers had not obtained their share of the Garden cheaply: £400 an acre was high enough to be thought remarkable by Sir Frederick Eden in 1797.[69] By the end of his sales in December 1796 Turner had disposed of 3.23 acres: the lowest recorded price for one of his plots was 3*s*. a square yard (or £726 an

[69] F. M. Eden, *The State of the Poor* (1797), p.847.

TABLE 7.6

Census Enumeration, 1801: Population of Club and other East End Streets

		Houses*	Families	Population	Persons per house
Club					
Union St		166	179	675	3.9
St Peter's Sq.		61	61	243	4.0
Speculative Building					
George St		86	91	393	4.5
Ebenezer St	(Turner)	175	192	685	3.9
Nelson St	(Croft)	15	15	63	4.2
Duke St }		73	73	296	4.1
Off St }	(Paley)	84	86	347	4.1
York St }		69	75	307	4.5

* Each half of back-to-back counted as a unit; also yard cottages.

Source: LCA, LPC 104: no other streets are differentiated by name in the surviving copies of the enumerators' schedule.

acre) and the highest (at 6*s*.) was £1,452 an acre (Appendix VII.4). His other expenses were small since each purchaser contracted to pave and flag the appropriate length of street and to share in the maintenance of the access road from Vicar Lane, the present Harewood Street. Turner had only to have the ground surveyed and staked out in plots, pay for the newspaper advertisements, and settle his attorney's bill for the legal fees connected with the initial purchase and the draft contracts for sale of the plots.

RICHARD PALEY IN THE EAST END

Turner's developments lay next to a club street and resulted in very similar houses. It was a bold venture whose success depended on there being demand for about 250 houses, the total achieved in his completed streets by 1801, yet in the full knowledge that there would be competition in the provision of small cottage property both from the club streets and from other developers. The most ambitious of these was Richard Paley.[70]

When he came to Leeds from Langcliffe near Settle in 1771 as a young married man he had no other asset besides his wit and his wife's generous bridal portion. In 1775 he set up as a soap-maker in a yard on the west side of the parish churchyard in premises leased from the widow of his cousin, the merchant William Cookson, and in 1779 extended into a partnership with the brewer, Tobias Appleyard. He purchased land out at Knowestrop in 1780, but owned no land in town until, infected with the spirit of 1786, he contracted to purchase one of those closes which had been advertised[71] as suitable for a building club.

It was not his nature to do things by halves. In 1803, when the Malton Bank foreclosed upon one of his mortgages and brought him to bankruptcy, he owned 56 acres of building land. He had erected 275 houses on various parts of this; he had disposed of another 10.7 acres in parcels on which other men could build, and thereby enabled some 200 pairs of back-to-backs to be added to the town's housing stock. Alongside this activity he had become a partner in the Bowling Iron Works and in works in London and Bristol. Earlier than the flax mill of Marshall and the woollen mill of Gott, he erected the town's first two cotton factories; in one of these he installed a pirate steam engine on which James Watt junior was sent from Soho to spy out patent infringements.

His progress is charted in Appendix VII.3. As may be imagined, the name Paley became the most frequently encountered name in the town rate books: at its peak his total assessment on buildings reached £539 at a time when Gott's mill was rated at less than half that sum and the most valuable industrial property in town, the King's Mill complex, at £400.

The rate books demonstrate how Paley became the town's greatest private landlord (Table 7.7). His building undertakings, whether houses, mills or foundries, were designed to add to his rent roll and he did not participate actively in the business of erecting houses for sale: twenty-nine of the forty-nine houses which he built and sold were in two tranches, one in 1796 and the other in 1802, each in order to raise cash, for in the same month he had to resort to large mortgages in order to relieve problems in another part of his business empire.

70 The following paragraphs derive from a more fully documented study: Beresford, *Paley*.

71 See above, p. 183

TABLE 7.7

Land and Buildings belonging to Paley, 1790–1805

Division	Rateable value of land, nearest £				Rateable value of buildings, nearest £				Number of houses			
	1790	1795	1800	1805*	1790	1795	1800	1805*	1790	1795	1800	1805*
Kirkgate	11	9	3	–	18	122	83	56	2	16	25	18
East	56	79	73	27	58	209	270	300	35	57	71	185
North East	20	23	17	14	9	149	183	138	3	10	16	71
Others	–	–	–	–	4	4	4	5	–	–	1	1
TOTALS	87	111	93	41	89	484	540	499	40	83	123	275

* The data from the 1805 rate book relate to the property held by Paley's assignees in bankruptcy.

Source: LCA, LORB 34–37.

His ambition was most clearly shown in his acquisition of land for parcellation, nearly 50 acres in all. The earliest purchases, made at the same time as those in Crackenthorpe Garden and also from the Wilson estate, were of McAndrews Garden, which lay north of Marsh Lane and west of Timble Bridge, and of Forster's Close or Old Garden which faced it on the town side of Timble Beck. In the Old Garden purchase he was joined by the timber merchant Thomas Dade, beginning a new partnership whose strategy was later made plain in a 'note for Counsel' drawn up by the solicitor acting for the administrators of the bankrupt estate in 1807.

> Mr. Paley long previous to his Bankruptcy and Mr. Thomas Dade in his lifetime became Joint Purchasers of Sundry Estates in Leeds which were Conveyed to them as an undivided Moiety to Mr. Paley and his Heirs. Mr. Dade's Moiety was between himself and his partner Mr. Edmund Maude . . . Mr. Paley and Mr. Dade purchased the above Estates with the sole View of parcelling them out in Building lots and from time to time proceeded to sales of sundry parts thereof . . . Mr. Paley has also erected Sundry Buildings upon other parts of the Joint Estate.[72]

There were signs even before 1803 that the demand for housing in Leeds was not running at a rate which could absorb anything like the area of building ground which Paley had accumulated (Tables 7.7

[72] LCA, DB 203, 'Notes for counsel', undated.

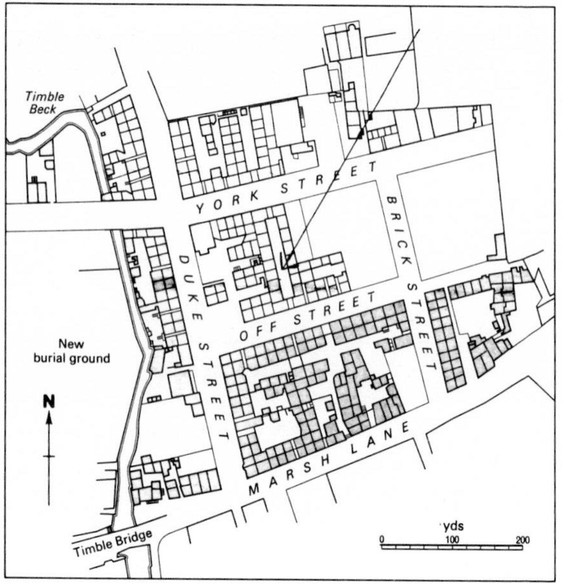

FIG. 7.12 LAGGARD DEVELOPMENT IN McANDREWS GARDEN AFTER 1801

From plans of 1807 and 1809: after his purchase of the field in 1787 Paley began to sell plots of various sizes to developers. The long and narrow plots accommodated off-street yards usually named, like Riley's [*arrow*, *centre*], after their developers. These yards were accessible only through tunnels under street frontage houses. Paley made no sales here after 1801 and was declared bankrupt in 1803; in 1815 the Giles plan shows that no more sales had yet been achieved here.

and 7.8; Appendix VII.3; Fig. 7.12). All Old Garden was sold by 1803 but nearly an acre of it had gone to accommodate the dead rather than the living, as an extension of the crowded parish church burial ground, one of those moves which contributed to the eventual degradation of the environment for the cottage property just built there. In McAndrews Garden there were nearly 300 houses by 1803 but they were at an overall density of 138 to the acre so that nearly a third of the Garden was still empty when a plan was drawn in 1807 to accompany a settlement of the residual claims of Thomas Dade's heirs.[73]

[73] 1807 plan: LCA, DB 233; 1809 plan: DB Map 119.

TABLE 7.8

Paley's Sales of Land and Houses, 1788–1803

Year	Area, acres	Houses
1788	*	–
1789	–	–
1790	½	–
1791	–	–
1792	½	1
1793	3	2
1794	*	–
1795	1¼	–
1796	1½	15
1797	¾	4
1798	*	6
1799	¼	–
1800	1¾	2
1801	¾	5
1802	*	14
1803	–	–
TOTAL	10¼	49

* less than ¼ acre

Source: LCA, DB 233.

In Old Garden the plots which Paley sold as building ground simply followed the edge of the field, leaving a central area which eventually became the burial ground. In McAndrews Garden the problem of access to the interior of what was a much larger field was solved by driving four new streets through it: St Peter's Street to give access to Marsh Lane and York Road, with Duke Street, Brick Street and Off Street penetrating the interior. These were the same 9-foot width as the streets in Crackenthorpe Garden or Boggart Close but set much further apart. Consequently, as well as the back-to-backs on the actual street frontages, there was room for a succession of long courts each rather like a Kirkgate garth, being lined with ten or more blind-back houses.

The names of these, Riley's Court, Mann's Court, etc., commemorate the sub-developers to whom Paley sold the Garden parcels, names that are found as landlords in the rate books of 1800 and 1805.[74] The houses which they built were of the same dimensions and architectural style as the cottage property being erected elsewhere at the same time, and their tenants were probably very little different. The rate books give their names but not their occupations, and the names in the street directories of the day did not descend to their level: but the terms in which the *Leeds Guide* of 1806 described Duke Street are familiar: 'new built, and intended for artisans and small shop keepers'.[75]

HOUSES FOR THE MIDDLE RANKS: ST PETER'S SQUARE AND ST JAMES STREET

Back-to-backs with cellar dwellings below might suit the Sons of Labour but what of the Middle Ranks? Table 7.9 shows the similarity between the houses erected in five of the club streets and the contrast with those in the remaining two, each dignified with the name of a saint. Union Row, Hill House Bank, Crackenthorpe Garden and the Boggart Lesser members all received plots with street frontages measuring between 5½ and 6½ yards. Except in the more constricted space of Union Row, the plots were roomy enough to permit an average of between 2.5 and 3.2 houses per plot. The actual houses differed little in size, and this was recognised by the narrow range within which their rating assessments lay, the average all lying between £1.25 and £1.53. Union Street and High Street included some three-storey houses, and this may account for their position at the higher end of this range, confirmed by rather higher insured values.

Even had the names of the Boggart Greater and Boggart Lesser clubs not already implied some distinction between the character of their intended houses, the difference would be apparent from the statistics in Table 7.9. The larger and more valuable houses in St Peter's Square revealed by the rate books and insurance policies were made possible by lots double the width of those in the other club

[74] LCD 1259 and 1402; DB Map 119; LORB 36 and 37.
[75] *Leeds Guide*, p. 77.

FIG. 7.13 ST PETER'S SQUARE IN THE EAST END
The north side of the square photographed by Alf Mattison, *c.* 1910. It was erected by members of the Boggart Close Greater Building Society in 1789; the oval railed garden in the centre was held in common by the residents. After demolition as an Unhealthy Area the site was occupied by Quarry Hill flats, themselves subsequently demolished. (*See also* Fig. 7.14.)

FURNISH AT BLAND'S

TABLE 7.9

Rateable and Insured Values of Buildings in Club and Adjoining Streets, 1789–1807

	Number of houses identified	Average value £
(A) Rateable Values:		
Club		
Union Row	28	1.25
Queen St	40	1.35
King St	53	1.35
High St	48	1.53
Union St	196	1.53
St James St	83	2.45
St Peter's Sq	35	4.3
(B) Insured Values:		
Club		
King St	31	23
Queen St	9	33
Union Row	6	33
Union St	71	44
High St	13	48
St Peter's Sq	47	115
St James St	25	127
Non-club		
Hill House Bank	133	16
York St	12	17
Ebenezer St	85	30
St Peter's St	50	30

Sources: LCA, LORB 34–37 and policies in Sun and Royal Exchange registers.

FIG. 7.14 CLUB HOUSES IN ST PETER'S SQUARE

A three-storey building (actually two houses) [*right*] formed the centrepiece of the houses forming the north side of a square, erected in 1789 by members assigned to lots 23–30 (Appendix VII.2(b)) of the Boggart Close Greater Building Society, and adjoining the Lesser Society's houses in High Street (Fig. 7.6). Each house had its small railed front garden and there was a communal railed garden in the centre of the Square. Photograph by Alf Mattison, *c.*1910

streets and set around a central railed garden in the manner of Park Square, assigning to each lot 'one thirtieth Part equally to be divided of and in the area of the said Square'.[76] A square of this sort attracted rate assessments averaging £4.3, three times that of houses built for the Lesser club members, and although back-to-backs were later crammed into some of their gardens the original properties in the square were all through houses with an average insured value of £115 (Fig. 7.13).

A surviving photograph of eight houses on the north side of the square (lots 23–30) reveals the character of Middle Rank architecture (Fig. 7.14). Small front gardens, railed from the footpath, occupied the point where, on the Park estate, there would have been area basements, and there was no external entrance to the domestic cellars. A back lane ran behind all the houses, a frontier between the Greater and Lesser clubs, and the access for horse-drawn traffic and tradesmen; there was also room for a stable in each back garden.

On the north-western corner (lot 30) the first three houses were of matching style: two storeys in plain brick, three wide bays with a pair of double-sashed windows on each floor. A Georgian style akin to the West End was given by pillared doorways in the central bays, surmounted by triangular pediments. As in Park Row, a taller house of three bays marked the centre of the row, and it was dignified with a string-course between its first and second floors, although in one way an architectural *trompe d'œil*, since the triangular pediment surmounted not one but a pair of adjoining doors, revealing that behind the single facade were two separate dwellings.

To the east of the central house the builders reverted to two storeys with only single sashed windows. These rather smaller houses were certainly divided vertically: those on lots 23, 25 and 26 had the same pairing of doorways under one pediment as the central house while on lot 24, a four-bay house again, its builder acknowledged the interior division more openly by placing the windows in the central bays and one doorway at each end. The Ordnance Survey plan of 1851 confirms these divisions and shows a similar mixture of styles on the eastern and southern sides of the square, for which no photographs are known. There were no cellar dwellings.

The interiors of two houses on lot 30 were described in an advertisement placed in the *Intelligencer* of 19 July 1788 by the joiner, James Woodhead, who was probably their builder, and the seedsman Thomas Barnes, club member in respect of lots 9, 10, 16 and 30:

[76] LCD 812.

Two New-erected Brick Houses situate on the North Side and at the Entrance to St. Peter's Square, one of which consists of a Kitchen Cellar, Front Room, a Stair-case, Two Front Chambers, and a Garret in the Roof . . . the other has a large Cellar, Two rooms on the first Floor, Two Chambers and a Garret in the Roof . . . there is a Well of Water in the Back Yard and a Pump put down which will serve the whole of this Lot.

Two unfinished houses were also advertised. The garrets are indicated in the photograph by dormer windows inserted in the front roofs which were covered with large slates, probably from Woodhouse.

The sale did not materialise, and Barnes was forced to turn landlord. He was still the owner when he insured them for £150 in December 1789 and November 1790. By this time he was failing to pay the mortgage interest and in December had to sell the houses.[77]

A sale advertisement following a death can be as informative of a house's appearance and contents as one forced by bankruptcy, and the 'valuable and neat' household furniture of the late George Brown is advertised in the *Intelligencer* of 30 December 1805:

All the Valuable and Neat HOUSEHOLD FURNITURE of the late MR. GEORGE BROWN, St. Peter's Square, Leeds, comprising handsome Four-Post Bedsteads, with Chintz and other Hangings and Window Ditto, excellent Feather Beds, Mattresses, Blankets, Quilts, and Counterpanes, a beautiful Mahogany Secretaire and Book Case with Glass Doors, Mahogany Chairs, Dining Card and Tea Tables, (fine Wood) Floor and Bedside Carpets, Pier and Dressing Glasses, Mahogany Book Case, Chests of Drawers, Night Tables and Bason Stands, Bed Rooms and other Chairs, China and Glass, Kitchen Utensils and other Effects.[78]

The character of Houses for the Middle Ranks in the St James Street club can also be approached through the language of advertising. The club's president, the apothecary David Joy, inserted a long advertisement in the *Intelligencer* of 17 February 1789 which seems to have been aimed more at a clientele who were seeking houses in which to reside rather than to be a source of rent.

On an elevated piece of Ground having a gradual descent from top to bottom, the whole Street commanding a Prospect of Six or Eight Miles over the River Air [*sic*] and the Leeds and Liverpool Canal comprehending in its View the villages of Beeston, Churwell,

[77] LCD 1794.

[78] Insured for £1400: Sun CS 40 719154; the highest valued house in St James Street, at £350, was William Walker's, next to Leigh's and on the corner with Woodhouse Lane: Sun CS 221 674144.

> Gildersome, and the Woodland of Farnley; and from the back part of the west side of the Street, part of Great Woodhouse and Little Woodhouse House belonging to John Denison Esq., and Bramley, Wortley and Armley and many other agreeable and extensive Objects too numerous to be related; with Partiality it may be added (though many malicious Aspersions have been advanced to the contrary) that a very good supply of Water will be provided, as there will be one Pump at (nearly) the top of the Street . . . another about the Middle and a Third at the Bottom. Wells can also be dug.
>
> Several Lots of Freehold Ground, each six Yards in Front and from Front to the extreme Rear 22, 23, 24 and 25 yards (up to 30) with Privilege of Bricks which are procured in the Field at a saving of 2*s.* 6*d.*, 3*s.* per 1000; any not desirous of building themselves may be accommodated with a House according to their own Plan.

But, as Barnes had found in St Peter's Square, there was no certainty of sale, and this is shown by the phrase 'to be let or sold' in an advertisement of 7 April 1789 for a three-storey house belonging to John Leigh, whitesmith, who had subscribed to lots 84 and 85 in the St James Street club:

> Pleasantly situated at the Upper End . . . a new-erected Dwelling House, with four Cellars, one a kitchen, two Rooms on the ground floor, three Chambers over, three Rooms in the attic storey, and a Garden adjoining with other conveniences suited for a genteel family. Stove grates are fixed in each room, also spouts on each side of the house for conveying water into a reservoir on the back thereof. There is also a Pump fixed in a good Spring Well, a few yards distant from the House, and from where the occupier of the House has the right to draw water.

Other architectural indications that the fortunes of St James Street were expected to rest on its attraction to the Middle Ranks rather than to the Sons of Labour could be seen in its cellars and its bedrooms. When houses were subsequently advertised for sale the number of bedrooms rose as high as eight; and the cellars were for beer and wine, not for subterranean tenant residence; and the provision for the occupants' water supply was distinctly better than in Union Street and High Street. These were houses which the compilers of street directories would not ignore.

But since the houses faced no square, and the street was no wider than Union Street or High Street there was even from the beginning a touch of inelegance here. Nor is the street flattered later in its life by photographs which happen to come from the lower end of the street, its meaner part, where some of the club lots were not built over until after 1815, and then with back-to-backs. Yet even the larger houses at its upper end abutted directly on to the pavement without railed front gardens, and superiority was achieved by building over more than one lot, by having mainly through houses, and by abstaining from backside infill.

Consideration of St James Street, the contemporary of the East End club streets, has brought us into another quarter of Leeds, neither East End nor West End. The members of the St James club must have derived a certain cachet from their immediate neighbours: the house of John Leigh on lots 84 and 85 was only one step down from Woodhouse Lane, and from its back windows there was a view into the grounds of a newly erected villa, St James Lodge, from which the name of the street probably derived.[79] Club houses on the opposite side of the street overlooked Portland House, then about twenty years old, the home of the Quaker merchant family, the Elams. The Elam house was the most northerly of that line which had crept up Woodhouse Lane to make a Town's End beyond the old Bar, but the more recent St James Lodge must be reckoned a denizen of that second West End of villas in Little Woodhouse, which will be the subject of Chapter Ten.

Thus its setting, its prospectus looking towards gentility, and the long delay before its completion all serve to mark St James Street out from the club streets of the East End: yet the delays, and the eventual capitulation at its southern end to houses for the Sons of Labour give it an affinity with those streets of a laggard and innocent East End which form the subject of the next Chapter.

[79] Insured for £1200: Sun CS 57 756291.

PART THREE

An Earthquake for an Architect

THE streets of the West End – and indeed St Peter's Square in the East End – were conceived as an ordered unity even though different master builders and architects determined the form of individual houses. The designer of the overall scheme for the Park estate, his identity unknown, was truly an architect; and it was the failure to complete the Park estate in an orderly manner, and the absence of any such controlling mind in the streets beyond it that provoked a comment in the *Leeds Mercury* of 1852 equating the West End of Leeds with its East End, each part as disordered as if an earthquake had afflicted it, a second Pompeii or Lisbon.

For nearly a generation after 1767 the Park estate was unchallenged as the most desirable residential location in the town, until in the last decade of the century a second West End began to attract residents to the slopes north of the town, particularly between Woodhouse Lane and Little Woodhouse. Ownership of land was dispersed in this quarter but a piecemeal development, field by field, exactly matched the architectural form which was becoming fashionable among those who were building new houses of the more expensive sort, for a detached villa was now being favoured rather than a house in the terraced Parades and Squares.

'Earthquake architecture' was not an aesthetic criticism of the villas and their architects: the infiltration of individualism into classical architectural styles was slow and inoffensive, and the facades of such villas as Springfield House and Belle Vue would not have been out of place on the north side of Park Square. It was a criticism of the stage of development subsequent to the villas, a second generation development, when this new West End saw individualism dissolve into anarchy, and order into an earthquake landscape; but the interval of time between these generations was briefer than that which had separated the first West End from the second.

In the spring of 1831 the solicitors acting for Newman Cash, a Quaker stuff merchant, owner and occupier of the Little Woodhouse villa, Springfield Lodge, were preparing to have printed an *Abstract of Title* for the fields which had been purchased fifty years earlier when the villa was built. Cash was not contemplating the sale of his villa but of part of its grounds where plots for two long terraces of small houses were being staked out. The adjoining fields belonging to the heirs of Mrs Julia Lyddon would certainly have been developed similarly had not their title been weakened by prolonged litigation; and when a Chancery suit was at last settled in 1853 it was no longer a question of building villas, but of high density housing, continuing the back-to-back terraces that had commenced meanwhile further south with Warwick Place and Warwick Terrace. It was this piecemeal development, partly the infill of villa grounds and partly the occupation of small intervening fields, that deprived the second West End of order, and attracted to it high density housing, continuing the back-to-back terraces that crept northwards from the fallen first West End. Although there was no immediate flight to a third West End it was no coincidence that, whereas the Cowper 'New Leeds' project of 1825 at Chapeltown had foundered in bankruptcy, George Bischoff in 1829 and 1830 was able to begin the sale of one-acre plots at Headingley Hill and thus initiate the first of the remoter suburbs.

No ambitious building club was launched in the East End after 1790, and after Paley's bankruptcy in 1803 his agglomeration of building ground saturated the market and was disposed of only slowly; the characteristic development of adjacent fields was piecemeal and laggard with a multitude of short streets, culs-de-sac and backside courts. In the West End the remaining part of the Park estate was also slow to be developed, and then with a mixture of factories and working-class housing more appropriate to a classic East End.

In 1832 an earthquake of another kind hit Leeds and other industrial cities in the form of the cholera, and its occurrence in the former West End demonstrated the diffusion of high density housing with low sanitary standards that were themselves related to the piecemeal character of development. The report prepared by Robert Baker for the local Board of Health in 1833, and another organised by the Council's Statistical Committee in 1839, publicised the consequences of that development which were given wider circulation by Baker's contribution to Chadwick's Blue Book of 1842. Together these reports were a blow to a nascent civic pride.

The *Epilogue* follows Baker's method of particularisation, and uses a plan of 1842 to illustrate the northward diffusion of an East End in the haphazard creation of Brown's Square behind Skinner Lane, with the highest density of population that could then be achieved. Finally the frontier between East End and West End that had become so blurred is discovered surviving in the unlikely surroundings of the town's first municipal cemetery, also initiated in 1842.

8

An Innocent and Laggard East End

To judge from the style of the houses erected already, it [Templar St, Leylands] *will make a very respectable addition to this town's end.*

THE LEEDS GUIDE (1806), p.81.

I am convinced on mature reflection that Residences and Steam Engines will not do near each other.

Report of Earl Cowper's surveyor on Leeds (1825): Herts. CRO, Cowper MSS, T.4952

This great work [the Leeds–Selby railway station] *has been much less noticed by the public than it deserves, the principal reason for which is that it is situated in the least agreeable extremity of the town.*

LEEDS MERCURY, 2 March 1833.

Just as people may be unfairly haunted by their past, so in History some topics are beset by our knowledge of their future. The East End of Leeds is doubly haunted: by its frequent citation in the classic literature of sanitary reformers in the eighteen-thirties and -forties: and by the photographs of a classic slum that were taken from the eighteen-nineties onwards. In both, the place-name 'Leylands', fields just beyond Town's End in North Street, often figured. Yet at its birth the site for Templar Street was admired, as the quotation at the head of this Chapter shows, and of an adjoining field the same *Guide* wrote: 'new erections in and near Lady Lane are very considerable, and will probably in a few years time diverge into new streets and squares for which there is sufficient room on the north side'.[1] Yet History is about Time as well as Place; and the Sanitary Movement was separated by more than forty years from the initiation of an East End by the building clubs and speculative developers. Thus, taking the risk of exaggeration, the first East End in contrast to its ultimate character may be called 'innocent'; and the long years of transformation justify the term 'laggard'.

[1] *Leeds Guide*, p.79.

AN INNOCENT EAST END

Innocence, like virginity, is perhaps best defined by a series of negative propositions. Certainly, although there were English towns where better residential areas were propelled westwards in repulsion from an East End, Leeds was not one of those. No streets existed east of town when the West End began in 1767: nor would there be any for another twenty years. What were later recognised as the classic ingredients of an East End were then still encompassed within the town centre. There, in the older part of town along Swinegate and the Isle of Cinders was the largest concentration of dyeworks; and close by was the largest assembly of mechanical power in the group of water mills that formed the King's Mills estate (Fig. 1.2). There, on Leeds bridge and between the narrows alongside the Moot Hall and Shambles, was the greatest concentration of foot and vehicular traffic; and there by the riverside on Warehouse Hill was activity by day and night, the resorts of sailors and porters, the centre of low life and dirty toil. Compared with these older central areas the first East End streets might be described in sylvan terms, as contemporaries sometimes did.

As we have seen, the first new streets were surrounded by open ground: and although it was no part of Paley's intention they remained so after his bankruptcy. High Street was not continued eastward until its first houses were thirty years old, and over in Crackenthorpe Garden the north side of the line of houses in Nelson Street marked the effective end of street building within fields on the eastern side of the Harrogate turnpike. Across Lady Lane from Nelson Street the Leylands fields remained largely open ground despite Molyneux having found a purchaser for them in 1791.[2] In the same year, Robert Denison's house was up for sale, with an open aspect very little different from that which it had enjoyed when it had appeared in Buck's *Prospect* at the beginning of the century; and also in the sale were three adjoining closes 'capable of being converted into one or more Rows of elegant Buildings (with Gardens in Front) commanding a beautiful Prospect, or otherwise of forming a handsome Street.'[3] Yet the Giles large-scale map of 1815 is able to confirm how much of the East End lay unbuilt upon thirty years after development had begun.

[2] LCA, DB 39/9 with plan; the absence of continuous building north of the Leylands in 1787 was attested by Richard Bramley's house, Grove Place, being located as 'the Grove in the fields north of the town': Sun OS 346 532507.

[3] *LI*, 7 July 1791.

Although the long-term deficiencies of this piecemeal development were to emerge in later years, few of these appeared while houses were new and fields not contiguously built upon. There may have been, as the *Directory* of 1817 put it, a 'continuity of buildings' between Marsh Lane, Burmantofts, Quarry Hill and Mabgate to 'form a populous district' but it was a continuity of ribbon development of roadside folds.[4] Behind lay the empty spaces which were the despair of Paley's assignees, while on the Bank the streets made little progress towards the older clusters of dispersed properties. Indeed the top of the Bank was still regarded as a place of social resort. In 1797, in the course of his *History* in epistolary form, Griffith Wright surveyed the new East End from a position very near where Buck and Thoresby had gone for their *Prospect*. The whole tone of the description was commendatory: 'there is a house of entertainment with a Convenient Bowling-Green known by the name of Richmond Hill: from this eminence we have a fine view of the Town of Leeds; on the Bank below are [five named] Cotton Factories besides a number of Mills, Dyehouses and various Manufacturers of Machinery on the river from Water Lane to Timble Bridge.'[5]

In March 1796 the engraver Robert Riddell had advertised his *South-West View of the Town of Leeds taken from Beeston Hill*, that is across Hunslet towards the East End, 'forming a beautiful and extensive scene'.[6] Nor, according to an advertisement seven years later, was the view back from the East End towards Hunslet any less regarded:

> To be Lett: A New-built and Most-complete House at Hill-House Bank within one mile of Leeds fit for the immediate reception of any large Merchant's family ... and from nine to ten acres of Meadow Land. The above premises would answer extremely well for a Young Ladies Boarding School, or for an Academy, being in a most healthy and pleasant situation. The air is fine and the prospect beautiful, commanding a view of the River.[7]

Innocence may sometimes be sheer inapprehension of consequences, which is no more than saying that all except prophets (and then only the most percipient) are blessed with ignorance of the future. Nowhere is this better illustrated than in the mixed social character of the development in Boggart Close. Had not the whole of the Close been purchased by the same trustees? were there not

[4] *Directory, 1817*, p.18.
[5] Wright, p.38.
[6] *LI*, 7 March 1796.
[7] *LI*, 15 Oct. 1803.

members happy to join both the Greater and Lesser clubs? did not the back windows on the north side of St Peter's Square look straight over the garden wall into the courts and cellars of the back-to-back houses on the south side of High Street? It did not seem unreasonable in 1786 to design a square for the Middle Ranks in a quarter where no industrial building was to arrive for another thirty years; nor for the Middle Ranks to take up plots immediately adjoining the Sons of Labour when these were the only Sons of Labour in sight.

Nor was enthusiasm for East End squares exhausted by the one built in Boggart Close. In 1806 the *Leeds Guide* anticipated 'new streets and squares' in the Leylands;[8] and ten years earlier Brumfitt had advertised building ground in Crackenthorpe Garden, surplus to his requirements for a carpet factory, as suited for development into a residential square.[9]

Initially, like the West End before it, the East End took over from the central streets a very limited range of functions: almost entirely that of residence. The workshops and warehouses that lay backsides in the West End were integral with the merchants' residences and were also a direct transplantation of forms from the central streets. By virtue of restrictive covenants the West End had no retail shops; there were no open-air markets; there were no public buildings for thirty years until St Paul's church was built in 1797, for the Infirmary, the Cloth Hall and the Court House in Park Row were not designed for the particular use of West End residents, being replacements or appendages to public buildings in the central streets.

In the East End the transfer of function from the town centre was also mainly one of residence although the number of small nonconformist chapels is perhaps significant; they were the only public buildings in that quarter. Although, like many working-class streets, those of the East End eventually had corner shops there is no evidence that lot holders erected buildings designed as shops. Inns

[8] *Leeds Guide*, p.79.
[9] *LI*, 1 May 1796.

FIG. 8.1 BANK TOP MILL: YARD INTERIOR, 1905

Bank Top adjoined Bank Low Mill, having its entrance in Well Street (Fig. 7.1): both mills were steam powered, initially for spinning cotton, and were mortgaged by Richard Paley in 1796. Paley had built them in 1790 within a close on Cavalier Hill purchased the previous year. The first steam engine here was built at Low Moor, Bradford, but James Watt successfully claimed breach of patent, and a 36 h.p. Boulton and Watt engine was installed in 1796. Soon after 1800 cotton spinning was abandoned for silk, and later for flax and wool. When this photograph was taken it was turning wool waste into rag.

and public houses also came later: the *Sir John Falstaff* in St Peter's Square and the *Pineapple* in High Street were converted residences, the latter simply the ground floor of a back-to-back-with-cellar dwelling (Fig. 7.11).

There is no way of knowing whether handicrafts were initially exercised in the houses of the new streets. The fact that a property deed assigns a craft occupation to some house-owner or that directories gave craft occupations against some East End addresses cannot determine whether a craft was exercised there or at a master's workshop elsewhere in town.

Since none of the East End houses were built as merchants' residences it was, initially, much less a place for manufacturing industry than the West End; or than the central streets where Rhodes built a mill at Lady Bridge in 1767, Cookson a carpet factory in Kirkgate before 1787, and Brumfitt another carpet factory by Mill Garth. Lupton erected a cloth-dressing mill at Town's End in 1788, with a beam engine and reservoir, immediately next to the finishing shops in the grounds of the two former Denison residences (Sheepshanks, later Hope Mill; and Bischoff's on Hartley Hill). The only purpose-built industrial buildings among the new streets were the kersey printing shop erected by Paley in 1787 for Liddle and Co. in Sykes Yard, York Street and the foundry which he built in Duke Street for Cawood.[10]

In due course the lost innocence of the East End would be signalled by – amongst other things – its pall of industrial smoke, generated from the factories in its streets or driven across the river from the mills in the south and south-west of town to circle over the slopes of Cavalier Hill and Quarry Hill. Yet the new streets need to be seen in relation to the chronology and geography of the new steam-powered mills and associated industry. Without doubt there were new East End streets before there was East End industry: had the East End continued to spread outward in the way that the new streets began in 1785–86 it would have formed a residential suburb, less industrialised than the West End with its packing shops and hot presses or than the vicinity of the town mills with its dyehouses and the waterwheels harnessed for fulling, scribbling, grinding and shearing.

In 1797 Griffith Wright saw five cotton factories below him as he stood on Cavalier Hill. By that time all had steam engines installed,

[10] The dating of these industrial premises derives from the gazetteer and references in M. F. Ward, 'Industrial Development and Location in Leeds North of the River Aire' (unpublished Ph D thesis, University of Leeds, 1972).

TABLE 8.1

New Industrial Building in the East and North East Divisions, 1764–1814

Name	Owner	Function
1764 Sheepscar Dyeworks	Holroyd	dyeing
1767 Lady Bridge Dyeworks	Rhodes	dyeing
1784 Mill Garth Mill	Scarth	dyeing
by 1787 Kirkgate Mill	Cookson	carpets
1787 Kersey printing shops, York St	Paley for Liddle and Co.	printing
1788 Town's End	Lupton	cloth dressing
1790 Bank Low Mill	Wilkinson, Holdforth and Paley	cotton spinning
1790 Bank Top Mill	Paley	cotton spinning
1791 Old Foundry, Duke St	Paley for Cawood	machine making
1791 Mabgate Mill	Blagborough and Holroyd	cotton spinning
1791 Far Bank Mill	Wright	cotton machinery
1793–98 East Street Mill	Gibson	carpets
1794 Crown Point Mill	Hodgson	corn
1795 Black Dog Mill	Gowland and Clark	cotton spinning and wool scribbling
by 1796 Lady Bridge Mill	Brumfitt	dyeing and carpets
1796 Bank Mill	Markland, Cookson and Fawcett	cotton spinning and wool scribbling
1796 Scott Hall Mill	Burrows	cotton
1797 Mill Garth Street Mill	Bowling and Atkinson	flax
1798 Marsh Lane Mill	Paley	flax
after 1798 Steander Mills	Upton	flax
after 1798 Steander Foundry	Upton	foundry
1800 Mill Street	Paley for Cawood	foundry
1811 Oatland, Meanwood Road	Oates	cloth finishing
1811–15 York Bridge Mill	Gratton	oil and mustard
by 1812 Lady Lane Mill (horse)	Wood	tobacco
1812 Hope Mill, Mabgate	Lawson and Walker	flax
1814 Millgarth Mills	Garsed	flax

Source: M. F. Ward, 'Industrial Development and Location in Leeds North of the River Aire' (unpublished PhD thesis, University of Leeds, 1972).

TABLE 8.2

*Industrial Premises Rated at over £40 per annum, 1790–1805**

Location	Owner	Function	Rateable value, £	Year
King's Mills (water)	Neville	multi-purpose	435	1790
Bean Ing	Wormald & Gott	woollens	217	1795
Nether Mills (water)	Fearne	multi-purpose	200	1795
Sheepscar Mill	Whitelock	mustard and oil	103	1800
Knowestrop (water)	in shares	all purpose	100	1790
Crown Point Mill	Denison & Wilkinson	corn	100	1800
Water Lane Mill	Leeds–Liverpool Canal Co.	canal warehouse	100	1800
Bank Mill	Markland, Cookson & Fawcett	cotton and worsted	90	1800
Little Woodhouse Mill	Oates	rasp	70	1805
Bank Low Mill	Wilkinson, Holdforth & Paley	cotton	70	1805
Dock Street & Warehouse Hill	Aire–Calder Navigation	warehouses	70	1795
Water Lane Mill	Kaye	flax	68	1790
?	James Rhodes	?	63	1805
Mill Garth Mill	Bowling & Hinchliffe	flax	58	1795
Drony Laith	Close	dyeworks	57	1805
Bank Top Mill	Paley	cotton	55	1805
Sheepscar Mill	Holroyd	dyeing	55	1795
Buckram House, Water Lane	Wilson	linen	50	1800
Bowman Lane Mill	Chadwick	dyeing	49	1800
Black Dog Mill	Markland & Gowland	cotton	42	1805
Mabgate Mill	Blagborough & Holroyd	cotton	42	1805

* Marshall's mill lay outside Leeds township in Holbeck.

Sources: LCA, LORB 35–37; M. F. Ward, 'Industrial Development and Location in Leeds North of the River Aire' (unpublished PhD thesis, University of Leeds, 1972).

although Blagborough's in Mabgate began with a waterwheel which was disposed of in the second-hand market when a Boulton and Watt engine was bought.[11] In the far distance Wright saw the two mills that are usually regarded as the pioneers of the new industrial age in Leeds: Gott's woollen mill at Bean Ing and Marshall's flax mill on the Hol Beck near the edge of the South Division; although both were preceded by Mabgate cotton mill and the two Paley cotton mills, Bank Low and Bank Top[12] (Fig. 8.1 and Table 8.1).

Placed in the same close but not adjoining, the two Paley mills came nearest to forming an industrial block but from James Watt's correspondence we know that his son, on the lookout in 1796 for engines in Paley's mills which might be infringing his patent, had to approach the mills across open ground, unconcealed from the garrison look-out;[13] and Paley's bankruptcy helped to preserve the isolation of the two Bank mills for another twenty years. The most highly rated mills of this period are listed in Table 8.2. In 1815 the Giles map (Fig. 7.1) showed open ground around these mills and behind Paley's flax mill in Marsh Lane; Cawood's foundry was then still the only building in Mill Street, the private road from Marsh Lane to the Bank mills. Cotton Street and Silk Street, alongside Bank Low Mill, were mere aspirations.

Photographs of these mills taken before demolition (or in a few cases, their present appearance) are deceptive indications of their original size, for all were later to be extended or totally rebuilt. The ground plans of the original mills can be measured in the Giles survey, the number of storeys is often stated in insurance policies and in sale advertisements, for cotton manufacture did not remain long in these Leeds mills, and others than Paley were forced into bankruptcy or sales. A plan and elevation of one mill remains among the Boulton and Watt papers: it had twenty bays in three storeys, and five more in two.[14] From the same source something is known of the rate of coal consumption since reduction of coal consumption (and hence of smoke) was an important element in Boulton and Watt's campaign for the merits of their engines against others.

[11] *LI*, 13 June 1796.

[12] WRRD, DM 256/263; *LI*, 24 Oct. 1796; D. T. Jenkins, 'The Cotton Industry in Yorkshire, 1780–1900', *Textile History*, X (1979), 75–95.

[13] Birmingham Reference Library, Boulton and Watt MSS: out-letters, 7 Dec. 1795 and 7 Feb. 1796; in-letters, 20 June 1797.

[14] J. Tann, *The Development of the Factory* (1970), pp. 17–19 (Markland, Cookson and Fawcett's mill at the Bank, 1792).

TABLE 8.3

Steam Engines Insured in East End Industrial Buildings, 1793–1803

Date	Location	Owner	Function	Value & horse power	Insurance references
Jan. 1793	Mabgate Mill	Blagborough & Holroyd	cotton	£100 20 h.p. Boulton & Watt	Sun OS 392 610103
June 1793	Lady Bridge Mill	Brumfitt	scribbling	n/a	Sun OS 395 615715 & Sun CS 14 654989
Nov. 1791	Bank Mill	Markland, Cookson & Fawcett	cotton	£1500 30 h.p. Boulton & Watt	RE 21 127048
July 1796	Sheepscar Dyeworks	Holroyd	dyeing	£50	Sun CS 14 656783
Sept. 1796	Black Dog Mill	Gowland & Clark	cotton	n/a 20 h.p. Boulton & Watt	RE 31 152714
Dec. 1796	Bank Low Mill	Wilkinson, Holdforth & Paley	cotton	n/a 36 h.p. ordered but not purchased from Boulton & Watt	Sun CS 37 713824 & RE 32A 154786
Oct. 1799	Mill Garth Mill	Armistead & Spence	flax	£40	RE 32A 179574
May 1801	Crown Point Mill	Sowden & Hodgson	corn	£600	Sun CS 40 717931
Dec. 1803	Steander Mills	Lobley	cotton & wool	£250	Sun CS 57 758053

Most Leeds smoke, domestic and industrial, came from coal from Middleton bought at the staith by the Bridge End terminus of the colliery railway for, as the 1817 *Directory* put it, 'the town is principally supplied with coal from the pits at Middleton'.[15] From data in the colliery's ledgers Rimmer estimated that domestic consumption in Leeds rose from 28,000 tons in 1771 to 53,000 in

[15] *Directory, 1817*, p.40.

TABLE 8.4

Industrial Building in the East and North East Divisions, 1815–33

Name	Owner	Function
1818 Gas Works, York Street	Leeds Gas Company	gas
1820 Low Fold, East Street	Howard	cotton and carpets
1820 Hope Foundry, Mabgate	Lawson and Walker	foundry
1823 Cloth Dressing Mill, Byron and Mill-wright Streets	Walker	flax
1825 Elmwood, Long Balk Lane	Lord and Raburn	cloth finishing
1825–26 York Street Cloth Mill, Stainburn Square	Button	cloth finishing
1825–28 Low Close, Sheepscar	Halliley	cloth finishing
1828 Linen Factory, ex Riding School, York Road	Robinson	linen
1830 Brunswick Brewery, Melbourne Street	Singleton	brewing
1832 Low Fold, Melbourne Street	Jackson	cloth finishing
1833 Sheepscar Tobacco Mill, Sheepscar	Simpson	tobacco

Source: M. F. Ward, 'Industrial Development and Location in Leeds North of the River Aire' (unpublished PhD thesis, University of Leeds, 1972)

1801 while industrial consumption moved from 5,000 to 8,000 tons. Between 1811 and 1814 the annual sales at the staith reached 88,000 tons.[16] All these figures include coal for the older dyehouses, breweries and foundries and it may be significant that the first

[16] W. G. Rimmer, 'Middleton Colliery, near Leeds (1770–1830)', *Yorkshire Bulletin*, VII (1955), 50.

TABLE 8.5

New Industrial Building in South Leeds, 1754–1817

Date	Location	Owner	Function
1754	Camp Hall	Wilson	linen and buckram
1756	Old Brewery, Meadow Lane	Denison, Jacques	brewery
1763	Brewery & Malthouse Hunslet Lane & Crown Point Road	Arthington	brewery
1776–80	Water Lane	Leeds–Liverpool Canal Co.	terminal warehouse
1781	Crown Point Rd	Sykes	malthouse
1785	Mustard Mill	Dibb	mustard
1786	Brewery	Sykes	brewery
by 1788	Bowman Lane Mill	Chadwick	dyeing
1788	Water Hall Mill	Kaye	flax & sacking
1791	Mill 'A'	Marshall	flax
by 1794	Meadow Lane (later Trafalgar Mill site)	Charnock	woollen merchants
1796	Water Lane (later Round Foundry)	Murray	machine making
1796	Water Hall Mill	Armistead	oil & mustard
1796	Borough Mills, Fleece Lane	Smithson, Rayner & Ritchie	woollen merchants
1803–04	Mill Street Mill	Benyon	flax
by 1815	Marshall St Mill	Brown	flax
by 1815	Fleece Lane	Hill	brass foundry
by 1815	Land's Court Mill, Water Lane	Land	flax
by 1816–17	Mill 'B'	Marshall	flax
by 1817	Mill 'C'	Marshall	flax
1817	Whitechapel Tannery (former chapel)	Coultate	tanning

Source: E. J. Connell, 'Industrial Development in South Leeds, 1790–1914' (unpublished PhD thesis, University of Leeds, 1975).

prosecutions against nuisance from smoke were brought not against East End mills but town-centre dyehouses on Mill Hill.[17] The steam engines identified in the East End between 1793 and 1803 are listed in Table 8.3.

Despite the availability of land, eagerly and frequently advertised by others besides Paley's assignees in bankruptcy, the number of East End factories built between 1800 and 1815 was small, and when the 'twenties and 'thirties brought a more lively interest in industrial investment (Table 8.4) the East End was far from having a monopoly of attention, as Table 8.5 shows.

The open ground around so many of the East End factories even as late as Fowler's plan of 1831 demonstrates not only the laggard entry of large industrial premises but also the indifference of mill-owners to providing working-class housing alongside their mills. Paley, perhaps, might have gone further had bankruptcy not halted him, but even he erected houses alongside only one of his mills, Bank Top; no other mill-owner in the East End has been identified as the owner of millside houses, and the name of partners in the town's largest industrial enterprises are rarely found against the multiple entries for cottage property in the rate book of 1805.[18]

What of residential segregation at this period? Certainly the successive creation of a West End and an East End had produced two areas with separate characters, each unlike the traditional intermixture of classes in the centre of town. West of town the Park estate was made up of houses whose size – and hence their rent or purchase price – excluded all but the wealthiest, although from this social group there were some who lingered in Briggate and Boar Lane: for the attorney and the apothecary were not so likely to move as a merchant who might feel cabined and confined and be glad to have space for his workshops in the backsides of a roomier West End.

From the evidence of the building-club membership the first movement to the East End was made up of craftsmen, artisans and retailers who were already established in the town. It is more difficult from the documentary sources to identify the more

[17] Nussey smoke case: *LM*, 27 April 1811.

[18] There was a line of cottages alongside Scotland Mill in the very remote part of Adel Beck. The owners of the Leeds Pottery, remote enough to need an insert on the Giles map, did have eight cottages 'occupied by their servants': Sun OS 208 302865 (1771); Holroyd and Blagborough built eighteen near Mabgate Mill between 1790 and 1795 (LCA, LORB 34–35, North East Division); of the factory owners listed in *Supplementary Report of the Factory Commissioners, Pt. 2* (PP 1834, XX), pp.437–52, Benyon in Holbeck had built 'a few', Brown at Bagby Mill, Woodhouse, eight but solely for overlookers (foremen) and Willans also only for his overlookers. No other instances have been noticed.

numerous band of their tenantry, not all of whom need have come from the town centre. Yet it is surely possible to deduce something from the almost uniform architecture and house-size in the East End, for – like the West End – it had its single architectural style. In the West End was the classical uniformity imposed by a cultivated taste which prescribed conformity in the elements of a terrace and a square. Now in the East End a uniformity of incomes prescribed a house-size, generally the two rooms making up one half of a back-to-back, with its rents related on the one hand to the return on the landlord's investment but on the other to the level that the generality of tenants could afford.

Rents and returns on capital are not well documented before the sanitary enquiries of the 1830s. It was then reported that pairs of back-to-backs had cost £80 each including land and that a return of at least 7 per cent was expected: from those figures an annual rent of £5 12*s.* (2*s.* 2*d.* a week) should have been expected from each house in the pair.[19] The rateable and insured values known from the earlier years of the East End (Table 7.9) suggest rather lower costs and rents than these. Yet even if the first East End landlords were differentiated from their tenants by their possession of capital (and probably a higher income, less interrupted by intermittent unemployment), the difference in social status was not large enough to deter many landlords from living in the front half of a back-to-back while collecting rents from the rear and from the cellar dwelling beneath. Thus, at their own level, the East End streets were repeating the conjunction of landlord and tenant which had always characterised the central streets.

As Table 8.6 shows, the two decades preceding the sanitary enquiries of 1833 and 1842 had seen some 4500 houses added to the East and North East Divisions, and, with complete fields then filled with houses, it was natural and proper in 1842 to measure the density of residential occupation. It was an unpleasant statistic. Yet, although the average house-size and the number of inhabitants occupying each of these twenty-five square yards was very much the same in 1842 as when the houses were first built, the intervening passage of time – more than fifty years in many cases – does make it necessary to see differences.

The most obvious is that houses, like their inhabitants, aged. Yet defects that go with age need not be defects initially. In 1801, of the houses in the North East Division, 70 per cent were less than twenty

[19] Rimmer, *Cottages*, p. 194.

TABLE 8.6

New Houses Built in the East End of Leeds, 1775–1831

Division	1775 Estimated stock	1775–1801 New houses	1775–1801 Annual rate of growth	1801–11 New houses	1801–11 Annual rate of growth	1811–21 New houses	1811–21 Annual rate of growth	1821–31 New houses	1821–31 Annual rate of growth
East	600	614	3.9%	132	1.1%	665	4.9%	995	4.9%
North East	530	1422	10.3%	641	3.3%	1221	4.7%*	1769	4.6%†

* Lower sub-division 4.6%; Upper sub-division 4.8%
† Lower sub-division 4.2%; Upper sub-division 4.9%

Source: 1775: Table 5.3 above; 1801–31: census.

years old; in the East Division the proportion was 60 per cent. And while it is true that the East End houses had a novel and meaner architectural form than either those in the West End or those on the older street frontages in the centre of town, they did resemble both in size and form the yard dwellings that lay backsides of the central streets[20] where the term 'cottage property' had first been coined; and even the densely packed courts of Paley's streets were no more warrens than the Kirkgate yards, with the advantage of having newer roofs, newer walls, newer doors, newer windows and newer chimneys. The East End landlords were not forcing their tenants into some newly invented degradation.

It is sometimes said that the new houses were of poor construction. There is one instance often cited where a house blew down in a storm but it was in fact a post-1815 house and not in the East End. There may have been deficiencies in the provision of amenities within and without but the photographs of the East End streets taken at the end of the nineteenth century show sturdy houses with good windows and shutters: those who lived in these houses on the eve of their demolition in the nineteen-thirties might well have reflected that it would have been better had the structures not been built so long-lasting.

Another difference to be noted between the age of innocence and the later age of criticism arises because a field was not instantly overwhelmed with housing. Thus, so long as a field was incompletely built upon, there is the same ambivalence in measured densities of occupation as we have noticed in the earlier street-less terraces which dotted the sides of the Bank. For single houses (or single terraces) the density was indeed high (Table 8.7): but in terms of the wider aspects, such as access to light and air or the pressure on natural drainage and access to water supply, the open spaces in the unbuilt part of a field – and even more in adjoining fields that were still wholly agricultural – the statistics from half-built areas can be misleading.

[20] See above, p.80 and 208

FIG. 8.2 THE 'NEW LEEDS' OF 1825, LAGGARD IN 1847

As well as the New Leeds of detached villas projected on the Cowper estate in Chapeltown, just north of the in-township boundary, the buoyant year of property speculation, 1825, saw a second 'New Leeds' within the township but on a meaner site, with meaner houses but no less laggard in its progress than the other. As this extract from the sixty-inch Ordnance Survey shows, the streets on the slope between the Sheepscar Beck and Cherry Row were incomplete twenty-two years later. All were back-to-back pairs except for the one-room houses enclosing Mushroom Court and those in Firth Street, set aginst the edge of the field, looking into Barker Square.

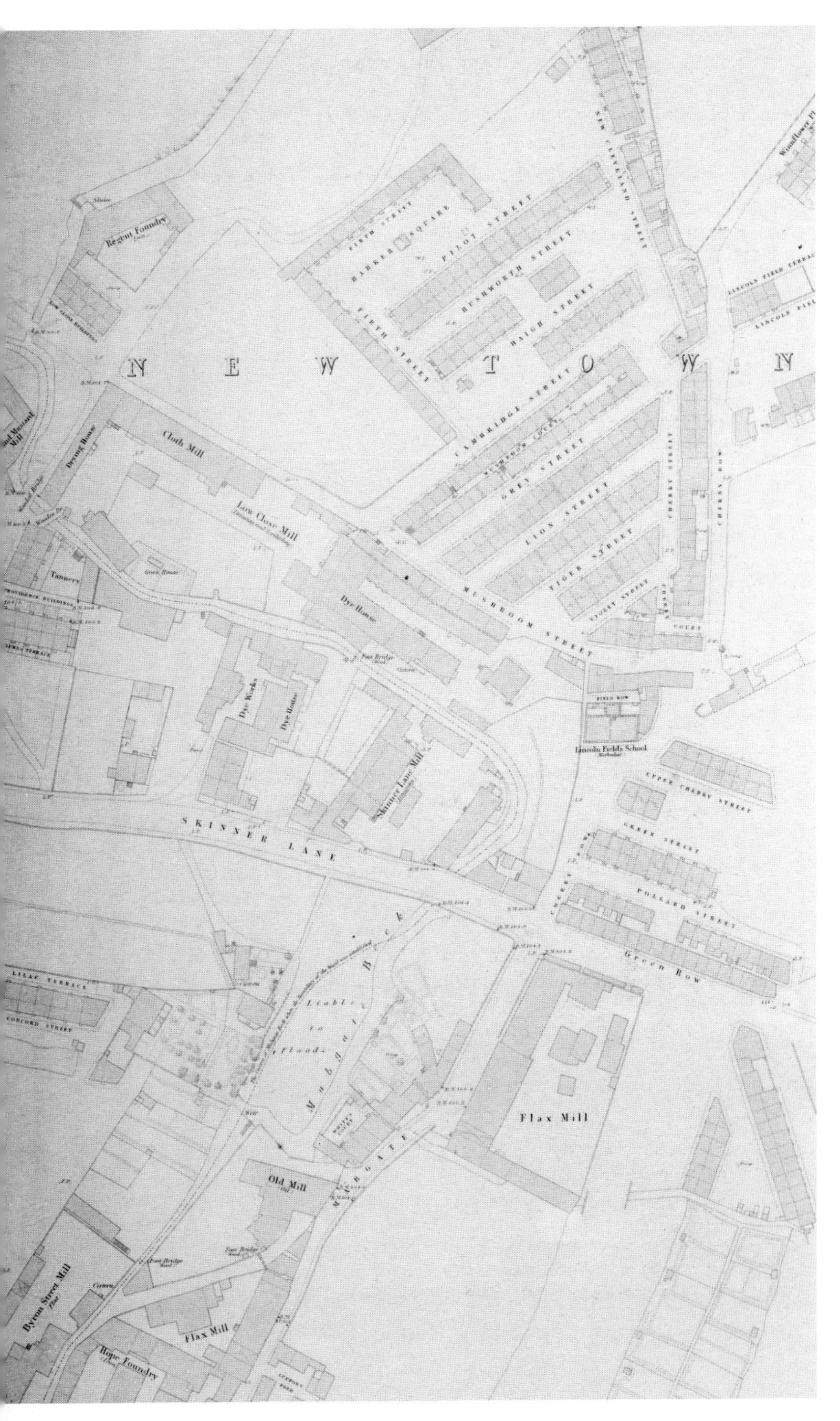

NEW TOWN
Regent Foundry
Firth Street
Barker Square
Pilot Street
Rushworth Street
Haigh Street
Cambridge Street
Grey Street
Lion Street
Tiger Street
Violet Street
Mushroom Street
New Cleveland Street
Cherry Street
Cherry Row
Lincoln Field Terrace
Lincoln Fields School
Cloth Mill
Drying House
Low Close Mill
Tannery
Providence Buildings
Dye House
Dye Works
Foot Bridge
Skinner Lane Mill
Skinner Lane
Field Row
Upper Cherry Street
Green Street
Pollard Street
Green Row
Lilac Terrace
Concord Street
Liable to Floods
Mabgate Beck
Mabgate
Flax Mill
Old Mill
Byron Street Mill
Rope Foundry

TABLE 8.7

Overall Ground-plan Densities of Kirkgate Yards and Back-to-back Streets, 1850

	Number of separate dwellings	Area of houses, street and yards (sq. yds)	Average area per dwelling (sq. yds)
Kirkgate Yards			
Boot and Shoe	44	2,466	56
Royal Oak	50	2,644	53
Back-to-back streets with courtyard housing			
Camp Field (Fig. 8.4)	184	12,500	68
Cross St	82	5,000	61
Duke St (McAndrews Garden)	272	12,500	46
Back-to-back streets without courtyard housing			
Darley St (Fig. 7.10(b))	42	2,220	53
Reuben Ter.	60	3,361	56
Lower and Cross Templar St	56	2,500	45

Source: Ordnance Survey plan, 60 in. = 1 mile, 1850; cf. Fig. 7.10.

To argue that there was no wilful creation of a slum in the East End of Leeds is not to deny that there were strong grounds for disquiet by the end of the eighteen-twenties: the progress of that disquiet forms the subject of our final chapter. Meanwhile, moving from the debit to the credit balance, we should note that the various efforts of building-club members, speculators, and developers in the East End had another achievement to their credit: new housing had kept pace with population. Between 1775 and 1801 the borough population increased by 23,000, half of those in the in-township. Nearly two-thirds of the increase arose from in-migration, younger people more immediately demanding of house-room than the smaller number arising from excess of births over deaths.[21]

The poorer immigrants from the countryside and the country towns would not be likely to take up tenancies in the new streets, still

[21] M. Yasumoto, 'Urbanization and Population in an English Town: Leeds during the Industrial Revolution', *Keio Economic Studies*, X (1973), 47–60.

less to own houses there, although they might well have come to the cellar dwellings. However, a much shorter-distance migration of artisans and shopkeepers from the central streets to the new East End, which the 'place of birth' entries in the census enumeration cannot reveal, would have left some room for newcomers centrally. As will be seen in Table 8.9 the number of persons recorded per inhabited house in the two Divisions of the East End actually fell between 1801 and 1811, and was still below the 1801 level in 1821. The density of occupation in some of the new streets (Table 7.6) was even lower than their Division averages while in the central area the figure had risen in all five Divisions.[22] Of one of these, Kirkgate, the *Leeds Guide* of 1806, which had nothing critical to say of the environment of the new streets, wrote: 'as fashionable people, and with them fashionable tradesmen, have deserted it, the street is fallen into disrepute'.[23]

With hindsight we can be wiser than prophets, and know that in due course the disrepute of the Kirkgate yards would become notorious to a readership much wider than that of the *Leeds Guide*; and worse: that to this notoriety the East End streets, club and non-club, would be conjoined. Yet in 1786 that notoriety was nearly half a century ahead. The slowness of apprehension and the long innocence of the East End were in no small measure the result of its being a laggard East End, slow in growth after its initial burst and slow to receive the invasion of new industrial building.

A LAGGARD EAST END

In 1797, perhaps looking back a little, Sir Frederick Eden published an account of Leeds in which he took heart – being concerned with *The State of the Poor* – from what he had seen or heard about new building in all quarters of the town:

> Of the prosperity of Leeds, the high price of land and water, the many new streets in the town, and the manufactories and villas in the neighbourhood, erected and erecting, are a very convincing proof... Land in the skirts of the town sells for £300 and £400 an acre and there are instances of ground well adapted for building selling for £1000 an acre.[24]

[22] This and all subsequent population and housing data from 1801, 1811, 1821, 1831 and 1841 derive from the printed *Enumeration Abstracts*.

[23] *Leeds Guide*, p.16; nevertheless it remained the Vicarage until 1826: LCD 21 and Borthwick MSS, Reg. 40a, f.135.

[24] F. M. Eden, *The State of the Poor* (1797), pp.847–48.

These sums can indeed be substantiated: Thomas Coupland had paid £2500 for six acres off Park Lane in 1792 and had sold them later in the same year to John Child for £3500.[25] Nearer the East End Matthew Rhodes had bought 5½ acres of the undeveloped Leylands closes in May 1792, and in June he sold 1¾ acres adjoining Lady Lane to Robert Bramley for £2244 (£1280 an acre);[26] in September 1798 three members of the Woodhead family, all joiners, paid Rhodes £900 an acre for an adjoining plot.[27]

Yet Appendix VIII.1 shows how slowly the developers were able to dispose of this land as building plots: a row of fourteen one-room cottages named Bramley's Row[28] was commenced in 1798 and was shown as completed when the Giles' plan was surveyed in 1815. This was exceptional: Bridge Street, Edward Street, Lydia Street and Templar Lane were then only partially built, and of the 659 houses built in the North East Division between 1790 and 1815 only 243 stood in streets which were completed; two-thirds of the houses added to the East Division in the same years stood in uncompleted streets (Appendix VIII.2).

Nor had some other area supplanted the East End Divisions as the site for new working-class cottages. Inevitably there was little or no room at the centre: only seven houses were added to the whole of Mill Hill Division between 1801 and 1811, and thirty-five to Kirkgate; while the number in High Town actually fell. In the small South Division the western frontage of Meadow Lane was already completely lined with houses but gaps remained on the eastern side. In 1815 Hunslet Lane had no new occupation of frontages beyond those shown by Tuke in 1781. Some of the 179 houses built in this Division between 1801 and 1811 were infill backsides of Meadow Lane where two or three narrow access ways to the interior courts were dignified with the name of 'street' or 'row'. Only two developments south of the river bore any resemblance to activity in the East End: at the eastern end of Bowman Lane, the joiner, John Kendall, erected eighteen back-to-backs to make Kendall Row and sold the remainder of the field to James Cooper, cheesemonger, in 1793: Cooper erected sixteen blind-back houses in Cooper's Court.[29] Their example was not followed but from 1806 in Camp Field a close-knit but incomplete development had produced 102

[25] LCD 698 and 15149.
[26] WRRD, DK 149/202.
[27] LCD 1691.
[28] LCD 2082.
[29] LCD 6448 and 8649.

dwellings by 1815, almost all of them in back-to-back rows (Fig. 8.4 and Table 8.7).[30]

The available sources do not permit the exact chronology of each East End street to be followed as fully as those in the Club streets or in Paley's fields but the slower development after 1795 is fully confirmed both by the house-count which Rimmer made in the rate books and by the census counts of 1801 and 1811. Rimmer found a thousand houses added to the in-township between 1790 and 1795 but only two hundred between 1795 and 1800. There was some resumption with the peace of Amiens in 1801 but the renewal of war dislocated commercial life and the impetus was not maintained through all that decade. The census counted 1305 more houses in 1811 than in 1801; no rate book is available after 1805 but Rimmer reckoned that 900 houses had been built between 1800 and 1805, thus leaving less than half that number for the rest of the decade.[31]

The East End certainly bears out such a chronology since Paley, who contributed 114 houses to the East and forty-five to the North East Division after 1800, was bankrupt early in 1803. Even with this massive single contribution in its early years the decade showed an overall rate of growth markedly smaller than the years on either side (Table 8.6). It is also significant that the list of other landlords who paid rates on multiple properties (Table 7.1) which was augmented by sixteen names between 1790 and 1795 gained only two between 1795 and 1800 and three between 1800 and 1805. Likewise the enthusiasm for building clubs had died: the small and ill-documented Union Place (Waterloo Street) was built in York Road between 1809 and 1810 and Club Court begun on the opposite side of York Road in 1812 with Club Yard added to it between 1816 and 1821: ten pairs of back-to-backs in all.[32] Thereafter no club is known in the East End.

The shadow of the bankrupt Paley lay over the land market for twenty years after his bankruptcy, as Table 8.8 shows. Assignees in bankruptcy were appointed in the Spring of 1803 to liquidate his estate and recompense his creditors. They soon disposed of his personal goods, the Knowestrop soap works, and the Marsh Lane foundry but it was difficult to find purchasers for the 56½ acres of field land which he had accumulated, even though most of it lay near to town at Marsh Lane. It mainly consisted of virgin fields which Paley had not begun to develop but the plans drawn for public

[30] LCD 5944; *LI*, 12 June 1809; F. M. Lupton, *Housing Improvement, a Summary of Ten Years' Work in Leeds* (Leeds, 1906), pp.9–10.

[31] Rimmer, *Cottages*, p.187.

[32] LCD 4556; *LI*, 24 February 1804.

TABLE 8.8

Disposal of Paley Estate by Assignees in Bankruptcy, 1803–23

Year	Area, acres
1803	‡
1804	6¾
1805*	½
1806*	½
1807*	8†
1808	2½
1809	–
1810	‡
1811*	3¾
1812	–
1813	–
1814*	1¾
1815*	16¼
1816*	7
1817	–
1818*	2¾
1819	‡
1820	‡
1821	¼
1822	6
1823	1½
TOTAL	56½

* public sale by auction.
† includes settlement of claims by Maude, late partner's heir.
‡ less than ¼ acre.

Source: LCA, DB 233.

auction sales in 1809 and 1810 also show substantial vacant plots in the very base of his initial operations, Forster Close and McAndrews Garden.[33] Public auctions in 1805 and 1806 disposed of no more than half an acre on each occasion (Table 8.8). The impatient creditors twice dismissed the assignees and appointed others. In 1807 Edmund Maude, the heir of Paley's former partner, agreed to accept eight acres in settlement of his claims to land which his father and Paley

[33] LCA, DB Map 119 and DB 233.

had bought jointly and, while this removed some doubts about the assignees' clear title to the other land which they were attempting to sell, the market was not aided by Maude's subsequent attempts to sell this allocation. The sale of 1809 disposed of no land, and in 1810 only one lot, measuring less than a quarter of an acre, found a buyer.

The interrupted chronology of streets in the East End of Leeds is similar to that found elsewhere. Chalklin's study of the pace of building in other commercial and manufacturing towns demonstrates the impact of the economic depression which followed on the heady years of the early 1790s. 'About 600 houses were erected in Manchester township between 1796 and 1801 compared with over 3600 between 1788 and 1796', he wrote.[34] Slacker economic conditions were relayed to the housing market by the increased chance of short time or unemployment for tenants of cottage property; by a diminished inflow from the countryside to seek work; and perhaps by straitened purses for those who were likely to join the town's landlords. In the absence of evidence, micro- or macro-economic, the mechanism must be uncertain. A mayor of Leeds, for example, asked in 1823 to inform the Privy Council of the local reaction to a commercial depression, was convinced that in Hard Times a capitalist was led to invest in houses rather than in industry: 'Owing to the reduced profits of Trade many Individuals Chusing [*sic*] to sink their Capital in Building rather than risking it in Trade. The increase has been principally in Cottages, and by the influx of Labourers and Strangers from the Country'.[35]

Dislocation and disappointment of expectations did not come only from war: indeed, on all previous experience, no reader of Eden in 1797 would have expected the fat years which had begun with the canal mania of 1793–94 not to have been eventually followed by the lean. Accumulating stocks of goods in warehouses would still demonstrate that demand had been wrongly forecast; the coming of peace and resumption of war would still bring their own dislocations; individual errors of judgement would still bring bankruptcy not only to partners in banks but to giants like Paley and Hirst as well as to the retailers and craftsmen whose bankruptcy notices made frequent appearances in the *Intelligencer* and *Mercury*.[36] Good and bad

[34] Chalklin, p.282.

[35] LCA, LO M6, f.281: 18 Feb. 1823.

[36] Paley: Beresford, *Paley*; Hirst's own apologia is his *History of the Woollen Trade . . . Commencing with a memoir of the Author* (Leeds, 1844), p.10: 'when I retired from business in 1824 I began to buy building land on speculation. Some have said it was this which ruined me; but it was the Currency Bill of 1825, for it reduced property more than half in value'.

harvests would still set the economy in contrary directions. An *obiter* of Mr Justice Littledale at the York assizes, reported in the *Mercury* for 18 July 1829, related fluctuations in grain prices to the prosperity of the clothing towns: 'by saying the prices [of wheat] are high this year we may say that they will be low next year and a large proportion of the money spent this year on the purchasing of foreign grain will be applied next year to the purchase of clothing'.

With a high proportion of both old and new property in Leeds intended for letting, the ability of tenants to pay was crucial in obtaining a return from investment, and Hard Times cannot be expected to have encouraged landlords to add to their stock of houses. Tenants with a steady income, large enough not to be crippled by high food prices in bad harvest years, enabled a house to have the commendation 'well tenanted' if their landlord was advertising the house for sale.[37] Of less fortunate tenants a Leeds agent wrote to a Denison who had become a Nottinghamshire squire: 'the tenants are very poor, and when they get in Arrear they go off in the night and Day time, and are not worth distraining upon or following. This is bad property and I should recommend you strongly to part with it'.[38]

Judge Littledale was right: there would be no certainty that one year would be like another even when the Napoleonic wars were over, and in poor years for trade the well-endowed landowner would be prudent to wait. This was the advice given to Earl Cowper in 1819 by the surveyors whom he had commissioned to report to him in distant Hertfordshire on the prospects for developing his land in Woodhouse and Chapeltown. The post-war boom had collapsed; broad and narrow cloth output for that year was down to the levels of 1793 and 1794 respectively; 1820 was little better.

> In order to bring the projected Sale before the Public it will be highly necessary to watch the time when the Manufactures and Trade of the Town of Leeds are in the greatest prosperity, and perhaps at the present time some postponement may be prudent.[39]

Yet it was only a year since the *Intelligencer* had reported:

> Streets and Squares are springing up in all directions . . . while smaller tenements and cottages are increasing to an incredible extent.[40]

[37] Eight new houses in Top Close, continuing High St, were advertised as 'in an open airy situation, well tenanted': *LM*, 5 Jan. 1817.

[38] Nottingham University Library, MS. De/H 27.

[39] Herts. CRO, Cowper MS. T 4950, f. 17.

[40] *LI*, 27 July 1818.

The cycle would continue: no other decade in the nineteenth century saw a rate of housing increase to equal that between the two census counts of 1821 and 1831 (Table 8.6) especially marked in the East, North East and Lower North West Divisions: yet it had its good and its bad years. It was in 1832 that an official survey for Leeds noted 'a very flourishing condition about five or six years ago ... receiving a great increase in population and building. This increase has, since that period, experienced a check: few buildings are now in course of erection ...'.[41] The chronology is confirmed by a similar retrospective comment in the *Mercury* of 28 May 1831: 'In the year 1825 there was a great spirit of speculation in building which produced a glut of houses and ever since there has been an extraordinary number of empty and unoccupied houses'. Fig. 8.2 illustrates the disappointed hopes of Griffith Wright: 'Leeds New Town' projected in 1825 and far from complete in 1844.

THE PROFITABLE PATH

My own first discovery of laggard street development was accidental. I had been intrigued by the confident naming of Prosperity Street through which I often walked on my way from Meanwood valley to the University when the inner circle bus was running erratically. I pursued its name through street directories, from its initiation in 1874–75 to its long-delayed completion in 1901: prosperity had waned and returned through no fewer than three complete cycles of fat and lean years before the street was completed. Nor was Prosperity Street part of some ambitious project in the Paley mould: there were only forty pairs of back-to-backs in it, twenty on each side of the street.[42]

It would be wrong, however, to see the incomplete streets of the East End earlier in the nineteenth century exclusively as the temporary product of a down-turn in a trade cycle which would reverse when better times came; a stutter in the economic system caught at some bad moment such as the outbreak of a continental war or a collapse in the mania for railway construction. Incomplete streets were a feature of any year, good or bad, a fact easily demonstrable when street maps became more frequent and directories virtually annual. Any prudent developer had to have patience.

This was the advice given in September 1816 by Henry Teal, the most frequently employed land surveyor in the town. He looked

[41] *Report on the Borough of Leeds*, PP 1831–32, XL, pp.195–96.

[42] Beresford, *Time and Place* (Leeds, 1960), pp.4–5 and pl.1; hence 'Prosperity Street and Other Streets', in Beresford and Jones, eds., pp.186–99.

TABLE 8.9

Persons per Inhabited House, East End and Central Areas, 1801–21

Divisions	1801	1811	1821
East End			
East	4.43	4.31	4.36
North East	4.49*	4.32	4.47
Central Areas			
Mill Hill	5.2	5.3	5.47
Upper	4.75	4.67	4.91
Middle	4.46	4.85	4.90
Kirkgate	4.59	4.75	4.98
South	4.73	4.73	4.80

* See Table 7.6 for more detailed evidence from the census enumerator's returns of this year.

Source: Census Abstracts.

beyond the post-war boom and was unconcerned to forecast exactly when prosperity would next return: the future he portrayed was confident but long-term: 'if divided into building lots the field will fetch from 4*s*. to 6*s*. per yard square but it would in all probability be 15 or 20 years before all was disposed of... consequently the present worth is only about 1*s*. 10*d*. per yard square or £400 an acre'.[43]

Thus laggard, incomplete streets were much more than the product of particular misfortunes or misjudgments. They were endemic. It seems inescapable that there was an overall glut of building ground. This can be demonstrated by simple arithmetic since with hindsight we know what it was reasonable to expect in the way of demand. For at all moments when houses and heads were counted (Table 8.9) the number of extra dwellings built since the previous count had kept pace with the increased number of families. Seemingly it would have required remarkable rises in working-class incomes or remarkable reductions in the cost of new houses for this equilibrium to have been disturbed.

In these circumstances what relation did the supply of building ground have to the number of houses that needed to be built? what

[43] LCA, DW 906(i).

space would be needed for the 1305 houses erected between 1801 and 1811? for the 3000 in the next decade? and for the 4874 in the next, that fastest-growing of all decades (Table 8.6) which ended with the cholera? The answer cannot be given simply by considering the area needed for the actual houses: the standard house-size, it has already been argued, was taken over from the cottages of the infilled Kirkgate yards[44] and gave a ground-floor plan of some 25 square yards for a back-to-back pair. Yet even the densely packed yards had their yard space, and if houses were to be set out within a field there had to be some general access from a public highway.

The logistics determining the alignment of houses and streets when fields were laid out as building ground were in no way influenced by statute or local by-law: until 1842 neither the unreformed Corporation nor the commissioners executing the Improvement Acts had the power to make building regulations or to regulate the form of streets. The objective, common to both the speculator and the building-club members, was to maximise the use of land. To minimise the space devoted to access was the obverse side of the ambition which led to the back-to-back, in Baker's oft-quoted phrase, 'part of the economy of buildings which are to pay a good percentage'.[45] In those rare instances where a highway frontage was still available for building, every square foot of ground could be made to yield rents, but everywhere else a developer had to consider how he would engineer some means of access even at the price of dead ground which paid no rent. The direct cost of access was of less importance than the indirect, for paving, flagging and drainage could be neglected at will. The indirect cost, unavoidably, was that any access space paid a nil percentage in rents.

How could an East End street be most profitably laid out? It would certainly not be in single terraces per field like those in the more extensive and expensive West End, for a terrace of cottages with one-room ground plans – a size matching what the generality of tenants could afford – had a high ratio of dead ground (Table 8.10). A pair of facing terraces would reduce the proportion of dead ground and an appropriate architectural form was already available as a pattern in the facing rows within the Kirkgate yards.[46] The building clubs, with their lines of back-to-back houses on either side of a street, had shown an even more economical pattern, further reducing the ratio of houses to street area; for there was no need to

[44] See above, p.252

[45] *1842 Report*, pp.4–5.

[46] See above, p.250

TABLE 8.10

Notional Proportion of Dead (Access) Ground in Streets of Different Forms

Type of house	(1) Area needed for dwellings			(2) Area needed for street and yard, etc			Ratio of ground area (col. 2) to dwellings area (col. 1)
	depth (yds)	width (yds)	area (yds^2)	depth (yds)	width (yds)	area (yds^2)	
Single terrace with houses of one-room ground plan (e.g. Union Row)	5	5	25	11	5	55	1:2.2
Terraces of houses face to face across a street, each with one-room ground floor plan (e.g. Kirkgate yards)	10	5	50	11	5	55	1:1.1
Terraces of back-to-back houses face to face across a street (e.g. Union St)	20	5	100	11	5	55	1:0.55

cede further dead ground for access when rear houses could be approached via a tunnel.

Where the shape of the club ground permitted building in courtyards at the rear of back-to-backs it reduced the street:house ratio further, as in parts of High Street and Union Street. Paley had shown how it was possible to exploit the square shape of McAndrews Garden for more elaborate interior courtyards whereby there were more houses backsides than on the street frontages: Riley's Court in Off Street[47] had four frontage houses and fourteen backsides; Scott's Yard and Mann's Yard each had two on their frontage to York Street and twelve backsides. In the irregular spaces backsides of Quarry Hill and Charles Street there were interior courtyards of all shapes, including courtyards reached only through courtyards (such as Waterloo Court) or semi-subterranean courtyards in disused quarries such as Johnson's Square. Phótographs of

[47] See below, p. 263

FIG. 8.3 AN EAST END YARD: YORK YARD

A backside courtyard of 1820 photographed in April 1908. It shows [*left*] the rear of a back-to-back with its other half fronting York Street. Its neighbour was built a little higher to permit a single-room cellar dwelling below, entered beneath the raised steps at the corner. On the right, beneath the cliff-like wall of three blind-back houses, are two more cellar dwellings. Elsewhere in this Yard were one-room houses at ground level, similar to the older cottages lining the Boot and Shoe Yard (Fig. 12.1).

such courts would one day be standard ammunition in the submissions made by medical officers of health to the Council's sanitary committee (Fig. 8.3). The well-known grim photograph of Riley's Court is framed by the archway of the tunnel entrance leading from Off Street at the south end, with the tunnel exit to York Street seen smokily in the distance at the other end of two facing rows of one-roomed cottages.[48] In Camp Field, a remarkable high-density development begun in 1806 within a single field in the South Division near the Marshall and Benyon flax mills (Fig. 8.4), there were 'streets' named as well as 'rows' but they denoted nothing more than prison-yard alleys between the back-to-back terraces packed into the field: the 12,500 square yards of Camp Field and its 184

[48] Beresford, *Back-to-Back House*, pl. 5.

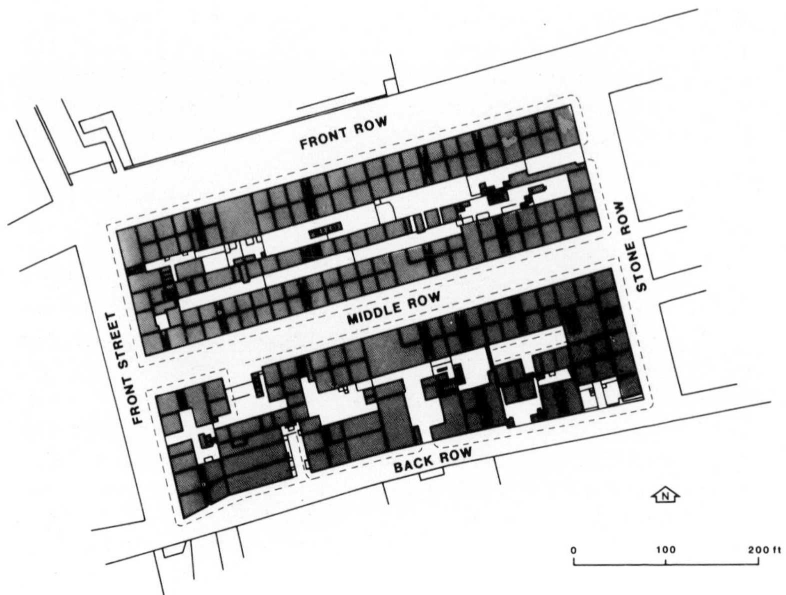

FIG. 8.4 PIECEMEAL DEVELOPMENT: CAMP FIELD, AN ISLAND OF HIGH-DENSITY HOUSING WITH INTERIOR COURTS, (*c.* 1807)

These rows were known collectively as Camp Field. Although convenient for the nearby flax mills of the South Ward they were placed in a field unconnected to any thoroughfare. Their 'improvement', achieved by demolishing the interior lines of houses, under the powers of the Housing of the Working Classes Act, 1890, was one of the earliest clearances undertaken by the city Council.

dwellings made up an island of habitation, the nearest public road being reached by way of 'Long Lane', a three-yard-wide footpath across open ground.[49]

Back courtyards, limited access ways and consequent high overall densities of dwellings per acre were to be found also on the Bank and Quarry Hill where fields were broad and often irregular in shape as the streets accommodated themselves to the hillside slopes. In these fields, many of them once held by Paley, an acre of ground (as in Fig. 7.12) could carry eighty dwellings.

In the North East Division the densities, even in the wholly back-to-back streets, were rather lower, and back courtyards infrequent. Out of town on Long Balk Lane (Camp Road) and Claypit Lane and

[49] Lupton, as in n. 30 above.

along the Otley and Harrogate turnpikes there were roadside closes available as building ground in the 1790s but of a shape which had minimal access to the costless highway frontage, forcing developers to lay out interior streets on the axial line of the long narrow closes (about 200 yards long and from 40 to 60 yards wide). These had resulted from the enclosure of open field furlongs,[50] and it was along the shorter sides of such fields that the existing highways, once balks for farm traffic, ran. Thus when Paley began to develop White Cross Close in 1792 he had room for no more than seven houses on its 40-yard frontage to Sheepscar Lane, the Harrogate turnpike; in order to utilise the 400-yard depth of the remainder of the close he had to lay out a new road, Skinner Lane, down the long southern side. His twin bay-windowed merchants' houses with workshops (1793) are illustrated in Fig. 8.5. In 1796 he began to line the northern edge of the close with blind-back two- and three-storey cottages and made economical access to these through a tunnel beneath one of the houses on the turnpike frontage.[51]

In 1796 these developments north of Skinner Lane were separated from the first penetration of the Leylands closes by eleven other fields of similar size and shape, each to be eventually occupied by axial streets leading eastwards from the turnpike. The pattern was first set by Templar Street begun in 1796. By 1815 seven of the eleven closes carried some street development although ominously all of them, including Templar Street, were still incomplete (Fig. 8.6).

[50] See above, p.17

[51] For this development, Beresford, *Paley*, Figs. 11.2 and 11.3 and pp. 302–05.

FIG. 8.5 A NEW RESIDENCE IN SKINNER LANE WITH INTEGRAL WORKSHOPS (1792)
(following two pages)

(a) Redrawn plan based on that of 1815 by J. Crookes details the right-hand half of a large three-storey semi-detached house built on the north side of Skinner Lane by Richard Paley in 1792 as an investment; he had just laid out this street along the southern edge of White Cross Close to lead from the Harrogate turnpike to the tannery and mills on Sheepscar Beck. Like the larger villas of the period, each of the houses had accompanying warehouses and workshops but here accommodated at the rears under the same roof; in place of the surrounding grounds of a villa each had a side garden: that on the east [*right*] was designated 'building ground' in 1815 but was still vacant in 1838 when the grounds on the west side were taken for Brown's Square (Fig. 14.1(a) and (b)).

Key, showing uses in 1838: A: rowing shop; B: stable; C: gig house; D: privies; E: ash place; F: warehouse; G: wash house.

(b) the two residences and workshops before demolition; redrawn by John Dixon from a photograph, *c.* 1960.

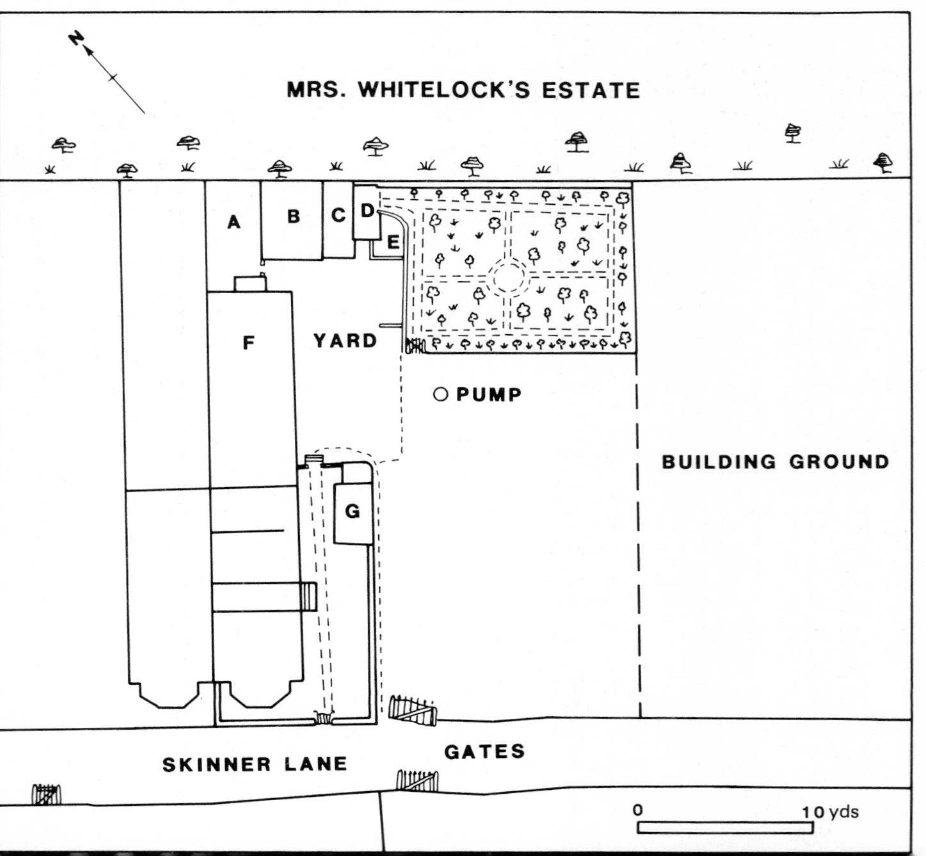

N
MRS. WHITELOCK'S ESTATE
A
B
C
D
E
F
YARD
PUMP
G
BUILDING GROUND
SKINNER LANE
GATES
0
10 yds

(b)

Since the ownership of these small fields was diffuse – a consequence of the partition of the open fields among many small proprietors – the decision to place a field on the market as building ground did not lie with a single landowner or his agent, as it had on the Wilson estate. Each owner had to make his own judgement on the way the wind would blow – would it be '15 or 20 years before all was disposed of'? – and on the yields from traditional uses such as market gardening, tenter ground or grazing ground if he retained the field.

A decision, once made, was a long-term commitment, irreversible once the first pair of houses was erected. But if the wind blew intermittently, the partially developed fields were in limbo between building and other uses, for the cloths on tenter frames and the vegetables in the gardens could hardly remain there in security. The field in which Darley Street (Fig. 7.10(b)) was built was one of five abutting on to the Harrogate turnpike which were market gardens in 1815, shown with paths and internal bedding divisions on the Giles map. The Ordnance Survey plan of 1850, on a larger scale than the map of 1815, was able to show meticulously where gardens, paths and shrubberies were then to be found in the grounds of the villas on the other side of Harrogate Road: but around the incomplete eastern part of Darley Street the map was now a featureless blank.

Yet, with so many developments initiated, was not disappointment inevitable? The argument can be drawn together considering the arithmetic of glut which is apparent as soon as the actual increase in houses built is set against the area of land actually on offer. By this measure Paley had been over optimistic even at the beginning of the East End when houses were not being erected beyond the building-club fields and the 38 acres of ground which he had accumulated in the East and North East Divisions. This would have been enough for 3800 houses at the lowest density of the day (Table 8.7), but had there been no other developers in town, Paley would still have

---

FIG. 8.6 LAGGARD DEVELOPMENT IN THE LEYLANDS, 1815

The extract from the Giles plan covers an area to the north of that in Fig. 1.1. Despite their proximity to Town's End and the new streets of 1788–90 between Lady Lane and Vicar Lane, the fields immediately north were at an early and piecemeal stage in 1815. On the western side of North Street there was an interrupted line on the frontage only, made up of the Lupton and Bischoff detached houses: what looks like an embryo street opposite Hope Street is in fact the Lupton workshops adjoining those of Bischoff.

On the eastern side, the field boundaries dictated that the four streets off Lady Lane and the four off North Street would be culs-de-sac and all were far from completion. Trafalgar Street was at this stage made up of through houses: but Nile, Hope and Templar Streets which had begun in that fashion had already succumbed to back-to-backs.

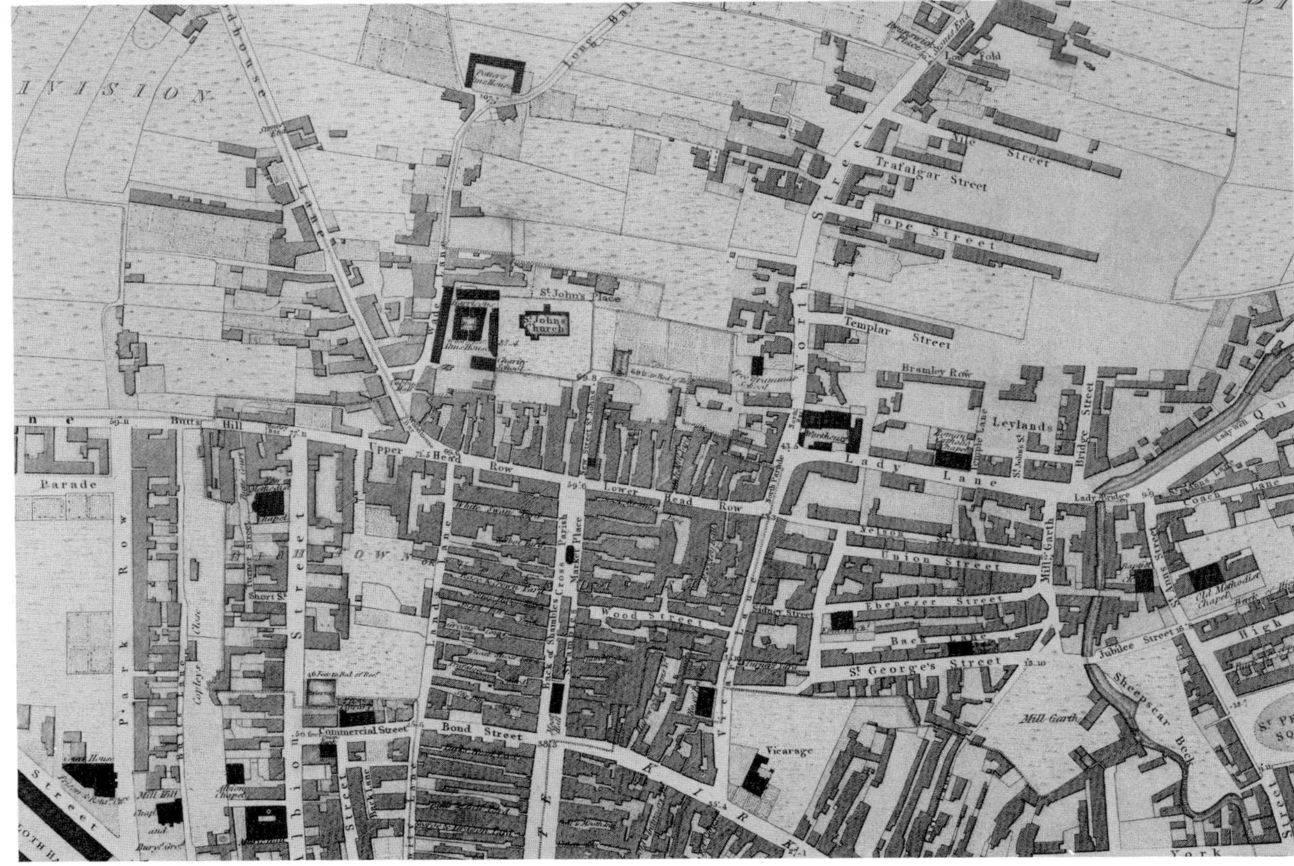

North Street
Trafalgar Street
Hope Street
Templar Street
Bramley Row
Leylands
Bridge Street
St. John's Place
St. Johns Church
Upper Head Row
Lower Head Row
Lady Lane
Nelson Street
Union Street
Ebenezer Street
Back Lane
St. George's Street
Wood Street
Sidney Street
Mill Garth
Lady Bridge
Jubilee Street
Sheepscar Beck
Vicarage
Market Place
Bond Street
Commercial Street
Short St.
Copley's Close
Park Row
Parade
Butts Hill

unsold plots in 1801 since only 2400 houses were erected in the two decades, 1781–1801; and so, had he been alive, in 1811, for only 1305 houses were erected between 1801 and 1811, and some of these were on the fourteen acres of the Leylands closes which had now been put additionally on to the market by Armitage and Rhodes.[52]

Nor were these three the only names to appear in advertisements for building ground, often indifferently for houses or factories even though, as we have seen, there was no large accretion of mills at this time in the East End. An advertiser offered a field of 1¾ acres on York Road in February 1804 as 'convenient for building a Dwelling-House, or erecting a Factory upon, as Water may be procured at moderate depth sufficient for a Steam Engine of any Power'. House-owners and factory-owners alike remained indifferent to the blandishment of the advertiser until, eight years later, the little Club Court Building Society took a quarter acre of it.[53]

The sluggishness of demand constantly dashed sellers' hopes, and if a site was open to contagion from industrial development the very character of demand could change. When Robert Denison advertised territory within the grounds of the family mansion at Town's End in 1791 there were two possibilities suggested for its use, neither of which occurred: 'this Estate is capable of being converted into one or more Rows of elegant Building (with Gardens in Front) commanding a beautiful Prospect; or otherwise of forming a Handsome Street'.[54] The name of the street that eventually occupied this field, Hope Street, was not without its own element of irony for it was not commenced until seventeen years after the advertisement, and it was neither handsome nor furnished with a Prospect, being made up of an equal number of one-room cottages and back-to-back pairs.

In the decade between the censuses of 1811 and 1821 there were 1886 houses built in the East End but absorbing only 23 acres, all (and more) of which the assignees in Paley's bankruptcy would have been only too pleased to supply; but there were others anxious and willing to dispose of land, as the newspaper advertisements show. Some locations were in the East Division but sellers began to appear across the boundary in the North East Division, particularly near Hope Street in the Leylands. Appendix VIII.1 lists thirty-two pre-1815 developments which have been traced in that Division. These were predominantly working-class houses: Brunswick Place and Nile Street were exceptional. By the time of the Giles plan in 1815

[52] LCD 2037, with *Abstract of Title of Matthew Rhodes* (1828).
[53] LCD 4643 and 4795.
[54] *LI*, 19 July 1791.

659 houses had been built, 450 in back-to-back pairs, 169 as one-room cottages and forty as two-room houses, but the laggard spirit prevailed here also, for only one-quarter of the developments, comprising about one-third of the houses, had resulted in completed streets.

By 1815 housing had also spread over the boundary from the North East into the North West Division (Appendix X.1) but there it was less compact than either the East Division agglomeration or the more recent terraces in the Leylands. None of the nine developments in this Division were contiguous. Providence Row, begun in 1793, was described in 1806 as 'standing among green fields with walls and fruit trees in front of each house',[55] and Grove Place (begun 1802–06) and Carr Place (1807) were also isolated among fields rather as the first lines of cottages on the Bank a generation earlier, but of distinctly better quality, as were most of these houses in the North West Division.

The widespread diffusion of the East End had hardly begun: only Reuben Street was made up wholly of back-to-back houses and in Coburg Street they occupied only two of the eighteen plots; the other seven developments were void of back-to-backs. Yet the same laggard spirit was present as in the East End: Providence Row was completed in four years, and all the plots in Reuben Street, begun in 1808, were sold by the end of 1809 but such speed was unusual: no other projects of this period were complete by 1815.

By 1815 in both the North East and North West Divisions there had been a small intrusion of industrial building, as Tables 8.1 and 8.2 show, but there were also new buildings of a different character scattered over the fields, not absent from the North East but more numerous in the North West. On 31 August 1795 the *Intelligencer* advertised a project for fields near Providence Row, then more than half way to completion, but with a different aim: 'Very soon will be offered for sale in Lots all that large Close of Land belonging to the Rev. Mr. Baynes situate on the north side of Woodhouse Lane which from its nearness to the Town, airy and healthy Situation is very eligible for Building upon'.

The advice given to the Baynes family by their surveyor is also on record: 'The eligibility of the Situation is such, being on a gentle declivity to the South and East, as would induce Gentlemen to purchase for building Country Houses'.[56] Yet if there were vacant lots in Park Square, why should Gentlemen be looking elsewhere? It is to the fate of the first West End and to an alternative West End of villas that the next Chapter must address itself.

55 'Mr. J. Nelson, woolstapler built it': *Leeds Guide*, p.82; Wright, p.96; plan of 1793, LCA DB 204/8.

56 LCA, DW 906(i).

9
The Fall of the First West End

St Paul's [i.e. Park] *Square is in so unfinished a state that one can scarce form a judgement of it.*

Shorthand diary of John Russell, RA revisiting Leeds, 1801: transcribed in G. C. Williamson, JOHN RUSSELL, R.A. (1894), p.67

While we are making improvements in some parts, at great expense, nuisances are arriving in others; and nowhere more manifest than at the West End of the town.

LEEDS INTELLIGENCER, *5 Aug 1822.*

Witness: I was once under the catacombs of St Paul's church; that is a place where they bury the dead in small squares . . . and there was one grave which had been filled, with a flag against it, and the moisture had exuded from the body through that flag in all directions, and there were millions of black fleas covering it . . .
Mr. R. Yorke, MP: You speak of St Paul's, Leeds?
Witness: Yes.

Evidence of Robert Baker to the Select Committee on the Health of Towns, Effects of Interment, PP 1842, X, Qq. 2588 and 2590.

The West or Worst End *of a City . . .*

Byron, DON JUAN (1823), canto XI, xlv.

The eventual character of the East End, its innocence lost, could not be ascribed to one individual alone: the building ground accumulated by Paley was slowly dispersed among many proprietors; the other landowners were disposing of small fields in small ventures and with mean ambitions. Thus the crucial but uncoordinated decisions on the location and form of its dwellings were taken by a dozen or more landowners, half a dozen building clubs and hundreds of would-be houseowners: all unregulated by any public authority. Leasehold tenure might have given some overall powers of control but after the Wilson (Pawson) estate's early failure to dispose of its land in leasehold the East End became wholly freehold, and in the back-to-back streets restrictive covenants were unknown.

In the West End, however, where there was only one major landowner, it was difficult for the Wilsons – and particularly the bishop's son, Christopher – to escape responsibility for a similar deterioration in the environment.

Even if the earliest admission of industry to the West End had something of that excusable inapprehension of the future which we have noticed in the placing of the first East End mills, there was soon no concealment of Wilson's indifference to the preservation of a residential West End. The preamble to the Act of 1803 has already been cited with its plea that the Mansion House was 'a very unhealthy Place of Residence and in no Respect eligible for the said Christopher Wilson'; and in 1816 after a valuation had revealed that the Mill Hill part of the estate, not included in the 1803 Act, could fetch £68,500 as freeholds, its sale was authorised by another Act with similar language in its preamble: 'the Residue of the said Estates ... consists of Freehold Grounds, and of Houses and other Buildings, the Occupation of which has of late Years been rendered less eligible in consequence of the Erection of Fire [i.e. steam] Engines and other Buildings, on adjoining or contiguous Grounds, for carrying on of Manufactures'.[1]

There was another echo of the East End in the West: for grand designs, even if embodied in preambles to Acts of Parliament, could still falter and development be laggard when building ground was in generous supply in relation to the demand for it from increased population and manufactories. The fall of the residential West End, anticipated in 1803 and 1816, was not immediate, and it was only in the decade 1821–31 that the old distinction between the two Ends faded. At the end of that decade a great panorama of Leeds was engraved for publication, as wide as either of the Bucks'. Unlike theirs it viewed Leeds from the south, looking northwards to a riverside foreground that was made up continuously from east to west of mill buildings and smoking chimneys (Back Endpaper).[2] In 1832 the cholera, by appearing simultaneously in the back-to-back and courtyard houses of the East and West Ends, would demonstrate that the fall of the West End, delayed more than was anticipated in 1803 and 1816, was now complete.

[1] *Acts Local and Personal, 56 Geo.III cap. 13.*

[2] J. Rhodes, *Western Panoramic View of Leeds* (Leeds, 1832); Bonser and Nichols, no.69.

THE WAY THE WIND BLEW

In 1806 a sentence in Ryley's *Guide* combined an affirmation of a still innocent East End with an apprehension that all was not well in the West. High Street and St Peter's Square, he claimed, were pleasantly free of smoke from manufactures, and what smoke did come in was being brought by the wind from the west, that is from the dyehouse chimneys and those 'fire' or steam engines in the west that Christopher Wilson had cited in 1803 as evidence for a deteriorating environment.[3]

Manufacture had never been excluded from the initial residential development on the Park estate but the workshops, packing shops and warehouses at the rear of the merchants' houses had no steam engines, and the noxious trades and crafts were barred by restrictive covenants in the leases. In the more remote parts of the estate the Wilsons had been tolerant of purely industrial building even while they were still living at the Manor House. Thomas Lodge built workshops and packing shops on the west end of St Peter's Hill at the end of Park Lane in 1772; on other peripheral fields the dressing shops of Child and Cordingley were erected by 1792; and in 1796 a substantial plot behind nos 32 and 33 Park Square was leased to Phillips, Oates and Co. for a group of buildings – warehouses, dressing shops and press shops – which made up an embryo factory even as yet without steam engines. Near what is now the junction of Park Row and Cookridge Street workshops had spread across the Blayds estate (Fig. 9.1). Further west, in Burley Road alongside North Hall, John Beckett, banker and son-in-law of Bishop Wilson, had a horse spinning mill insured in 1796 at the first-class rates for woollen mills and would soon have a steam engine there; Beckett himself had left the family home at North Hall for the more secluded Gledhow Hall, built for him by John Carr.[4]

[3] *Leeds Guide*, p.78.

[4] Lodge: *LI*, 21 April 1772 and *LM*, 13 Aug. 1776; Child: WRRD, DK 194/260; Phillips: LCD 3888 and LCA, DB 32/33. Knubley and Wainwright's mill in Park Lane was converted from horse to steam power in 1800: RE 32A 179636 and 37 172280.

FIG. 9.1 WORKSHOPS ADDED TO A WEST END RESIDENCE: THE BLAYDS ESTATE, WOODHOUSE LANE, 1809

By 1809 the Blayds estate consisted of fields (*cross-lined*) and the buildings in solid black. The industrial part of the merchant's business was carried on in the press and finishing shops which had accumulated around and behind the original family home on the Woodhouse Lane frontage: Gott's master and eventual partner, Wormald, had similarly developed two fields to the south. Blayds moved his residence first to the villa of Claypit House [*top*] and then to Park Lane House [*left*], a mansion which was eventually sold to the Corporation as a site for the Town Hall.

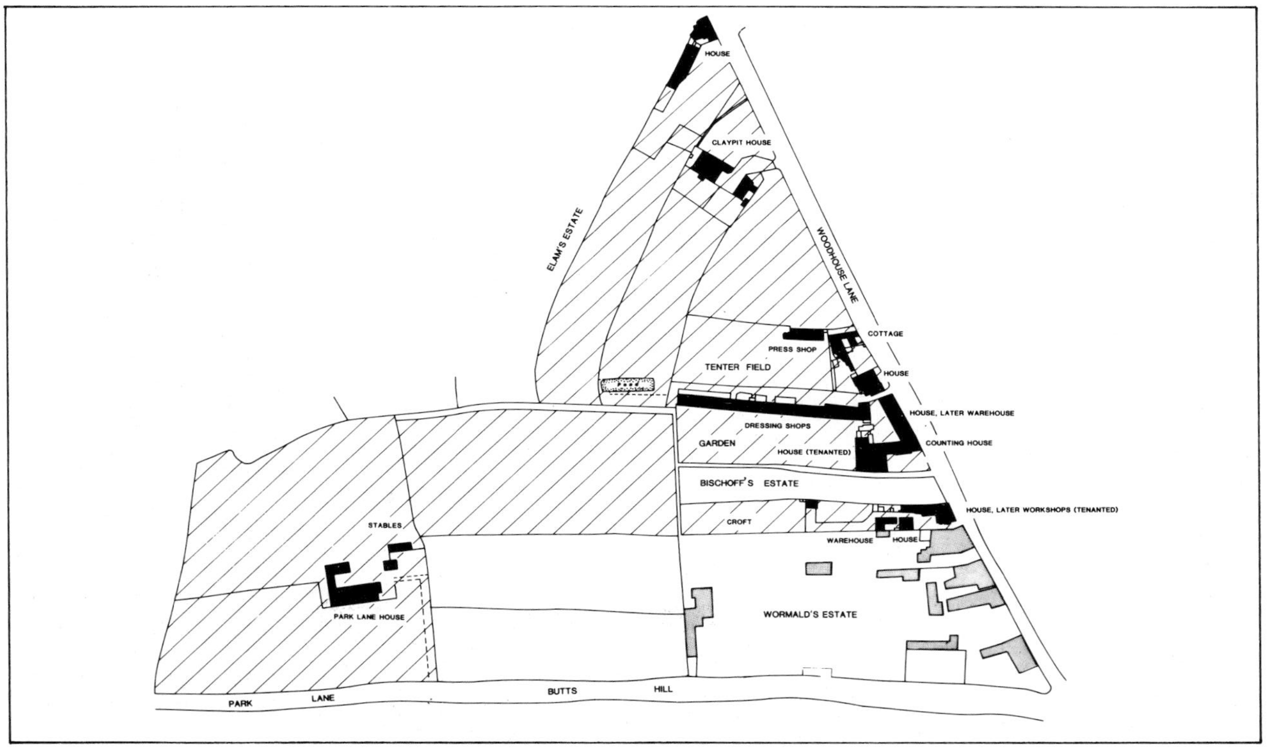
HOUSE
CLAYPIT HOUSE
ELAM'S ESTATE
WOODHOUSE LANE
COTTAGE
PRESS SHOP
TENTER FIELD
HOUSE
HOUSE, LATER WAREHOUSE
DRESSING SHOPS
GARDEN
HOUSE (TENANTED)
COUNTING HOUSE
BISCHOFF'S ESTATE
HOUSE, LATER WORKSHOPS (TENANTED)
CROFT
WAREHOUSE
HOUSE
STABLES
PARK LANE HOUSE
WORMALD'S ESTATE
PARK
LANE
BUTTS
HILL

It is sometimes written or implied that it was a Wilson who opened the door to industry in the West End by a willingness to sell the field named Bean Ing when the partners, Wormald and Gott, were seeking a site for a manufactory more spacious than could be accommodated among the workshops behind Wormald's house near Burley Bar in the Headrow. The conveyance of the site where Bean Ing Mill was built does not seem to survive but it was recited in a deed of 27 December 1820 when the partnership was dissolved: then the estate was said to have been assembled by the purchase of Bean Ing and Horner's Close on 17 March 1792 from Thomas Woodcock; of Scott's Close on 30 December 1795 from the Rt Hon. Frederick Montague; and Monk Pitts and Park House from William Potgeisser on 27 July 1798.[5] Yet if a Wilson did not open the door, a doorstep was certainly provided.

Bean Ing meadow was isolated from any highway and the river could not be used for navigation. Haymakers and cowherds could reach it by tracks but there was nothing suitable for traffic to and from a manufactory until in 1791 Bishop Wilson agreed to an exchange of lands enabling a direct road to be cut northward from the mill gate across Wilson land to the Bradford New Road, a turnpike which was then just about to be built, commencing on the west side of Park Square.[6] Although commonly known later as Bean

[5] LCA, North 1/4, partition deed; the first insurance of the mill 'unfinished' in April 1793 located it 'at Droney [*sic*] Laith': RE 25 133485.
[6] LCA, DB 32/15.

FIG. 9.2 PARK MILL, BEAN ING

The first and largest of the Leeds woollen mills, commenced in 1792 and famous in its day throughout Europe. The Luddites failed to destroy it but now only a length of foundation wall survives after its demolition for the *Yorkshire Post* building.

(a) a view of the ultimate length of the northern range with a bell cupola: before this extension, completed in 1829, the entrance lay down a private road (*see* Fig. 6.2) but the new road to Wellington Bridge (1819) was brought alongside this range where an arched entrance [*centre*] had been built to accommodate the largest waggons. Since Drony Laith had been demolished for the new road this range may have housed the dyeing processes.

(b) the southern facade of an earlier range, with a clock turret, which had once formed the northern limit of the mill as in Figs 9.3 (1806) and 9.5 (1814). The four bays beneath the clock were built in 1793–94 and survived the great fire of 1799; the remainder dates from 1800. The workrooms stretching from end to end on the third and fourth floors, with their large windows, were used for burling (mending) the woven pieces and for the hot presses. The chimney [*left*] is from a later engine house, the first steam engines being at the scribbling and fulling mills on the riverside.

(a)

(b)

Ing the new mill's original name did not hide its West End location and its connection with the Wilson estate: it was Park Mill (Fig. 9.2).

Initially steam engines played a minor role in the clothmaking processes which were gathered together at Park Mill. The finishing processes employed heat and would produce some smoke but its amount was insignificant besides that from Drony Laith. There, rather than at Bean Ing, industry and industrial smoke first entered the West End, and Drony Laith was Wilson property from 1777 when Jeremiah Dixon sold the farm and its fields for £5,500.[7] The sitting tenant, who continued now as Wilson's tenant, had already converted the farmstead to house the looms of piece-workers making coloured cloth.

> On this spot there stood beyond Memory of Man a Manufactory for Worsted Stuffs where also the worsted was dyed for the purpose and this Manufactory about 1767 was converted into a large Dyehouse and occupied by a certain Mr John Close. It was at this time the largest dyeing concern in the neighbourhood of Leeds and there were many Chimnies in it. At that time the works were distant about half a mile from the Town, surrounded by fields.[8]

The landlord did not discourage his tenant's expansions. There were already forty chimneys in 1777 and Close 'enlarged his dyehouse from year to year'. In 1781 twenty waggons a week were bringing 1776 corves of coal to Drony Laith from the Middleton railway staith,[9] and the proximity of these dyehouses probably explains the remote location chosen for their new mill by Wormald and Gott, separated as it was from the Leeds–Liverpool canal by the river Aire (not there navigable) and needing an exchange of lands with Wilson before there could be access to a highway. It was this exchange which probably gave rise to the belief that Bean Ing had been bought from the Wilson estate.

Once Park Mill was built the dyeworks expanded further: a rateable value of £28 in 1790 – already exceptional for a building – more than doubled by 1805; their insured value in 1771 was £900, and in 1795 £8050;[10] by 1801 the Wilsons' annual rent from Close was £400 at a time when the total rent from the residential leaseholds (Table 6.3) was only £334.[11]

Thus from the beginning the residents of Park Square must have been used to a certain swirl of smoke on its way to the East End;

[7] LCA, DB 32/27.

[8] Defendant's brief in Gott smoke case: LCA, DB 116.

[9] LCA, M 9, f.60.

[10] Sun OS 207 299871; RE 30 148066.

[11] LCA, DB 32/7.

and there was also smoke from an adjoining field fronting Park Lane where Benjamin Wilson made over two million bricks between 1793 and 1803;[12] and expectations of a quiet residential precinct were further dashed by the arrival of the Leeds–Bradford turnpike in 1794.

For most of its course within Leeds township the turnpike passed over Wilson land and was as much part of a public invitation to development as the Wellington Bridge turnpike constructed across the fields south of Park Place would be in 1816. The plan of the estate made in 1793 was an aid to the development of such a strategy although action was delayed by the low demand for building ground all over the town.[13] R. F. Wilson came of age in 1803 and was thus able to give assent to sales from the Park estate, as expressed in the Act of 1803, but even now that potential purchasers had a more secure title there was no immediate interest. Hopes were obviously rising in April 1806 when Teal was commissioned to produce another plan covering the whole estate and drawn on the same scale as in 1793 (Fig. 9.3). Useful as an indication of where 'intended streets' would run, the plan is also witness to the stagnation of the previous ten years since apart from the turnpike and the drive to Park Mill the landscape was unchanged.[14] The intentions for the future were proclaimed by fifty-five numbered lots west and south of Park Square, eighteen larger lots of a field each along the Bradford turnpike, and eleven more whole fields along the river bank between Park Mill and the Manor House; all were offered as freeholds, and meanwhile Wilson had been profiting from renewal fines and enfranchisements of the residential leaseholds (Appendices IX.1 and IX.2).

No interior streets for these twenty-nine fields were sketched on the plan, and it was probably hoped that they would find purchasers from among 'those Persons engaged in the Trade and Manufacture of the Place' whom the 1803 Act envisaged needing space for warehouses or workshops. It was for such intended uses that the Fish Pond closes were levelled in the autumn of 1803 by bringing in 145 loads of rubbish.[15]

The proportions of the 'intended new streets' alongside Park Square were generous, and the building plots, although comprising

[12] *Ibid.*

[13] LCA, DB 32/3B.

[14] LCA, DB 32/3: 'divided into Lots as the same is intended to be sold'.

[15] LCA, DB 32/8, Oct. 22 1803. It was the availability of contiguous roadside plots which eventually gave the West End its line of industrial buildings in Wellington St and Kirkstall Rd; the availability of land in the East End spaced the mills more widely among fields already occupied with housing.

smaller areas than a whole field, would have been quite large enough to take houses of traditional West End proportions. There was less certainty that an absentee landlord who had disposed of freeholds would be as watchful in the enforcement of restrictive covenants as a ground landlord with an interest in the quality of property erected on his building lots, but the issue was academic since in the event almost no building ensued. The only houses built here between 1803 and 1806 were in a short terrace south of the Infirmary, Eye Bright Close, certainly quality buildings since one was taken by James Holdforth, the silk manufacturer and Paley's partner in Bank Low cotton mill.[16]

The 1806 plan also admitted a willingness to sacrifice the centre of Park Square as building ground, defeated by the inhabitants' purchase of it for a collective garden.[17] The dissection of the older Square between Park Row and East Parade was also proposed, and the names 'Thompson and Bolland' were written across this part of Teal's plan. Thompson was a resident of Park Row, and Bolland was the Wilsons' family solicitor. Wilson had agreed in March 1805 that he would sell the 6¾ acres at £2300 an acre (9*s.* 6*d.* per sq. yd), a distinct improvement on a trickle of rents from garden ground and tenters. In fact Teal was premature in designating the ownership: Bolland withdrew in 1807 and nothing was done until Thompson completed the purchase alone in 1809,[18] probably stimulated by the news that the Improvement Commissioners were seeking a central site for a court house, magistrates' offices and a small prison under

[16] LCA, DB 32/8 (1804); 'a house belonging to my father in 1803; he refused £2500 for it': James Holdforth's evidence in MS. minutes of the Committee on the Leeds Improvement Bill, 1842 (House of Lords Record Office).

[17] Above, Chapter 6, p. 149

[18] LCD 2838; WRRD, FM 252/293; LCA, Oates C. 1 and 2.

FIG. 9.3 INCOMPLETE DEVELOPMENT OF THE WILSON (PARK) ESTATE, 1806

From a plan of April 1806 (cf. Fig. 6.2, 1793): St Paul's church occupied the south-east corner of the former open area of Park Square (cf. Fig. 6.3) together with a line of houses to its west; the north and west sides of the Square were unfinished. Further encroachment on the centre of the Square was envisaged, with the line of two streets sketched in: these were prevented in 1809 when the inhabitants of the Square purchased the ground for common use.

The large rectangular plots to south and west of the built-up area were in anticipation of further sales, centring on a projected east-west street from the Cloth Hall towards Bean Ing, and a second new street continuing Park Place westward, the eventual 'Bradford New Road'.

The dotted area shows what still remained unsold in 1817; a sale plan was then printed, offering 123 smaller plots but much was still shown as 'building ground' in Fowler's 1833 plan; *see* Fig. 12.2 for development by 1842.

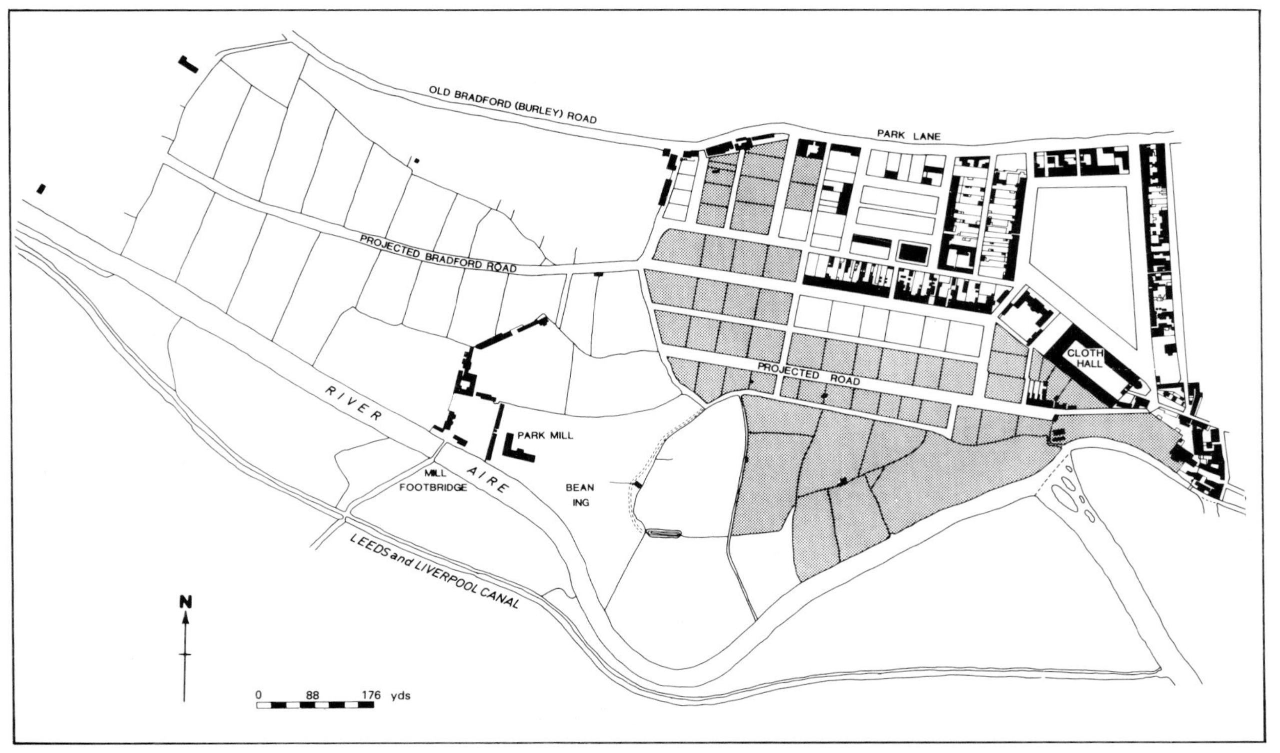
OLD BRADFORD (BURLEY) ROAD
PARK LANE
PROJECTED BRADFORD ROAD
CLOTH HALL
PROJECTED ROAD
RIVER AIRE
PARK MILL
MILL FOOTBRIDGE
BEAN ING
LEEDS and LIVERPOOL CANAL
N
0 88 176 yds

powers given in the Improvement Act of that year.[19] Thompson sold off the south-east corner for this purpose but then encountered the same sluggish demand for residences in this quarter as Wilson himself. At the time of his death in July 1815 Thompson had built only one warehouse and two houses opposite the Infirmary, two others opposite the Cloth Hall with shops, and two others were unfinished:[20] these scattered buildings are those shown on the 1815 Giles plan, and there were no more in 1819 when printed sale plans were prepared with projected streets and building plots of 152 square yards each.[21] Except for a second public building, the Philosophical Hall, nothing more had been built when Fowler surveyed Leeds in 1821 and a fresh prospectus was issued in January 1823 with covenants appropriate to good class houses: 'to be fronted with Stone of Tool'd Ashler or red dressed bricks, and to have all the front Windows checked or recessed back with three storeys and thirty feet in height at least'.[22] Few were actually built, and the vacant spaces in Greek Street, Russell Street and their neighbours became part of the central business district of Victorian Leeds, made up of banks, commercial and public offices (Fig. 9.4).[23]

The progress of development was almost as slow on the remainder of the area comprised in Teal's plan. There had been an auction sale at the *White Horse* on 1 October 1806 at which ten of the fields found purchasers but only five plots were then built upon, all near Park Lane to the west of Park Square.[24] Teal's son, Henry, was commissioned to make an up-to-date plan in 1809 for another public sale.[25] The sales of 1809 produced no new residential development and very little else except for Eye Bright Place, a group of two or three houses. The Giles' plan of 1815 has only three buildings on

[19] *Acts Local and Personal, 49 Geo.III, cap. 122.*
[20] LCD 2838.
[21] LCA, Oates C.3.
[22] LCA, Oates C.2.
[23] South Parade and East Parade also began to lose residents in favour of commercial buildings, some purpose-built, some conversions. The facades of nos.2 and 4 South Parade were illustrated in the *1849 Directory* but as part of an advertisement for an Upholstery and Cabinet Manufactory located there.
[24] LCA, DB 58/33.
[25] LCA, DB 32/3A.

FIG. 9.4 THE FALL OF THE WEST END: THE LOSS OF ITS FIRST SQUARE, 1813
The first encroachment on the open West End 'Square', where trees and bushes were still to be seen on the western [*left*] side of Park Row in this drawing by Joseph Rhodes, was the Court House and Prison, erected in 1811–13 and financed by a rate under the Improvement Act of 1809; the trees on the right fringed the burial ground of Mill Hill chapel.

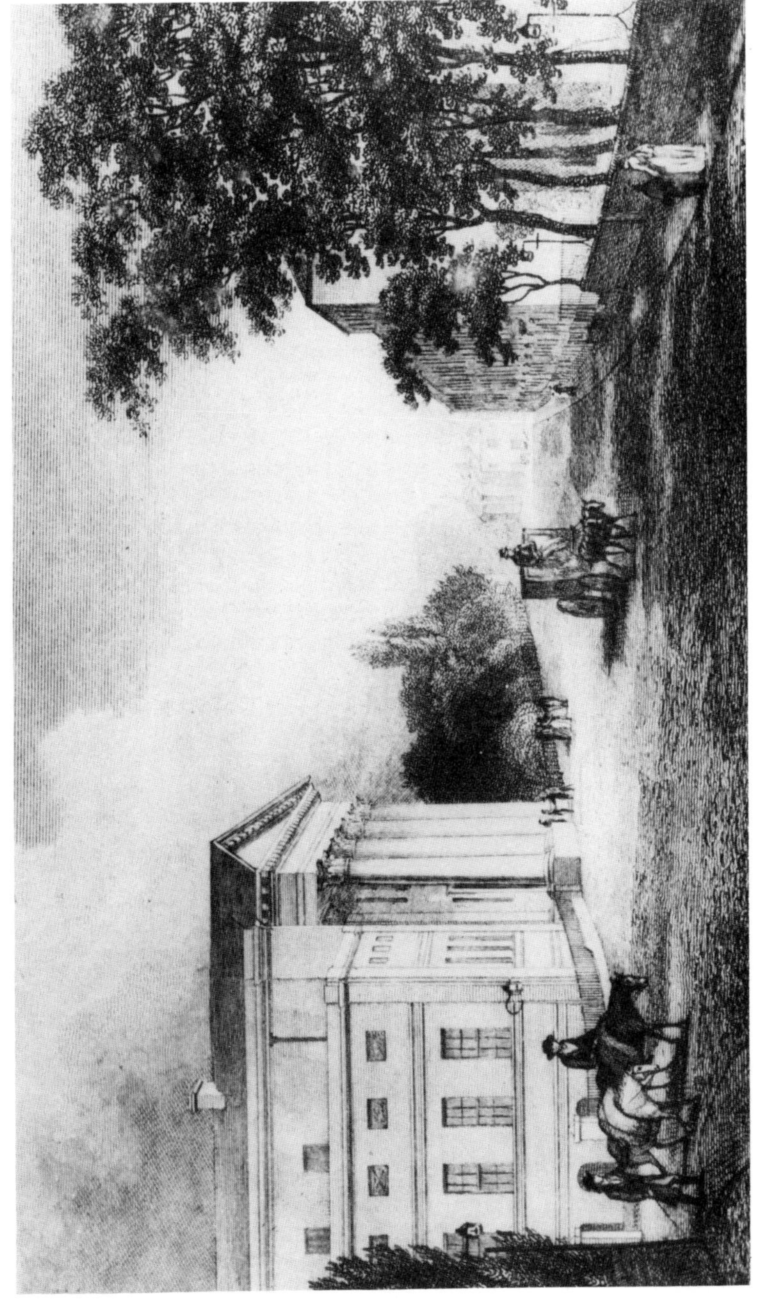

former Wlson land which were not there in 1793, and all three were mills. Two were on the Bradford turnpike (Old Mil and Airedale Mill) and the third was later known as Grove Street or Lisbon Street Mill.[26] In 1807 a steam engine was added at Drony Laith.[27]

Dyehouses were still multiplying faster in the West End than cloth manufactories, especially around the Manor House. In the post-war boom of 1816 Wilson obtained a second private Act to release the Mill Hill properties for sale after showing that he now had country property elsewhere with a rent roll sufficient to meet the obligations of the marriage settlement.[28] In December 1816 Teal was commissioned to produce a large-scale plan and valuation for the Mill Hill properties and a smaller scale plan of all the properties remaining unsold from the earlier sales. The latter was subsequently printed as a sale plan for the public auction in 1817.[29] Teal reckoned that the Mill Hill properties – the *Griffin*, the *Black Lion* and a congested group of warehouses and press shops – had a gross rental of £711 but could raise £11,000 if sold as freeholds.[30] Five of the eight lots were disposed of at the sale and the others privately during 1818, and the expected amounts were paid for them. Leaseholds of the Park estate residences were being converted into freeholds from 1808 (Appendix IX.2): the Acts of 1803 and 1816 seemed to have met their objective.

If the other 115 lots of the sale plan could have found purchasers Wilson would have made £67,413 but there was less interest in this building ground: the Infirmary bought 4000 square yards along King Street at 10*s.* 7*d.* a square yard. Twenty of the lots consisted of the small allotments or gardens which lay in front of each Park Place house and these were purchased individually by the residents for a total of £5500. Joseph Green of Bradford, who was currently developing Greek Street and Russell Street, bought fourteen lots along the north side of Wellington Street; Teal himself bought six lots; and Wormald rounded off the Park Mill estate to the line of Queen Street: but of the 115 lots, sixty-five remained unsold in 1818 and were disposed of slowly, a few remaining in Wilson's hands at his death in 1842.[31]

[26] M. F. Ward, 'Industrial Development and Location in Leeds North of the River Aire, 1775–1914' (unpublished PhD thesis, University of Leeds, 1972), gazetteer appendix.

[27] Sun CS 73 797920; in 1807 the Sun agent called these 'a line of mills out of the town': Guildhall Library MS. 11932, vol. 17, 10 Dec. 1807.

[28] *Acts Local and Personal, 56 Geo. III, cap. 13.*

[29] LCA, DB 32/6A and 6B.

[30] LCA, DB 32/5 and 58/46.

[31] LCA, DB 32/5 and 6.

The influence of the Wilsons on the form of the West End was almost at an end: Teal's sale plan, by its alignment of lots, had determined how wide the streets would be and where they would run; and the new turnpike of 1817, named Wellington Street in the plan, extended Eye Bright Place westward to the new Wellington Bridge beyond Park Mill, providing a central avenue. The 'intended streets' of the plan were as generously laid out as the older part of the Park estate and the plots were large enough to be divided up for traditional West End houses. Whether that would be done or smaller parcels be offered for meaner houses; or whether the buildings should be warehouses or mills: these decisions were now in the hands of intermediate developers like Green; they and not the Wilsons would henceforward determine the character of the West End.

In his *Directory* of 1817 Baines was still prepared to accept that Leeds did still have a distinctive residential West End:

> The buildings to the east of Briggate may properly be termed the 'old Town', those to the west the 'new Town': the latter forming the residence of the more respectable part of the inhabitants, the former that of the lower orders ... The west end is to be preferred as a residence by those who have it in their power to make a selection.[32]

This was a traditional but increasingly optimistic view: those like Green who had land from the Wilson sales of 1817–18 did not find immediate development at all easy: in 1821 Fowler's published plan of the town repeated the line of 'intended streets' as in 1817 but could show few houses built along any of them; beyond the Wellington Street baths there were only three houses in King Street and a few more in Queen Street; further west a few houses for 'middling tradesmen' were going up in Lisbon Street but little more.

Meanwhile the Wormald and Gott estate centred on Park Mills was undergoing changes which brought further building ground on to the market. That estate had reached its greatest extent with the purchase of Drony Laith from Wilson in 1814 for some £10,380.[33] Its components at that time were delineated on a large-scale plan by William Mounsey (Fig. 9.5).[34] Bean Ing meadow was used as tenter ground; the former Park House in the adjoining field, which had been bought from the merchant Pottgeisser in 1798, was now converted to a series of dyehouses; Park Mill had wool warehouses, baths, dyehouses, an engine house, a gasworks, weaving shops,

[32] *Directory, 1817*, pp. 1 and 16.
[33] WRRD, HI 377/400.
[34] LCA, DB 78.

stables, a press shop, counting house, smiths' and millwrights' workshops and a warehouse. At Drony Laith were: a dyehouse, warehouse, engine house, press shop, dwelling house, spinning rooms and weaving shops, a stable and barn, a wet house and dry house, and a further small line of dwellings (Fig. 9.5).

It was the zenith of empire. The Wormald and Gott partnership was dissolved in December 1816, and by 1820 an amicable partition of the estate had been agreed.[35] The southern part of Drony Laith was incorporated in Park Mill where Gott now extended the northern facade to create the long barrack-like block which remained until 1955 when Leeds City Council, not awakened to the significance of industrial archaeology, allowed the world's first woollen mill to be demolished so that the Yorkshire Conservative Newspaper Company could build a new home for the *Yorkshire Post*; of Gott's stonework only the riverside embankment wall survives, and the brick boundary wall on the eastern side may also be original. The northern part of Drony Laith, with the farmstead, was assigned in the partition of 1820 to Henry Wormald: the Wormalds were no longer active in business so that the farmstead and cottages were demolished and their surrounds added to the land on offer in the West End as building ground (Fig. 9.6).

FINISHING STROKES

The years 1821 and 1822 marked a turning point in the development of the West End. Until then the novel element had been the introduction of successive manufactories, but fields had been left as building ground rather than to be developed for housing of a more menial kind. There had been an obvious reluctance to continue good quality residential building even though plots were available in plenty, but in 1821 and 1822 house-builders were again seen at work in the West End after an interval of nearly thirty years. They were

[35] LCA, North 1/4.

FIG. 9.5 THE ISOLATED GOTT INDUSTRIAL COMPLEX AT DRONY LAITH AND BEAN ING (1814)

Drony Laith farm house was adapted as a dyeworks by Thomas Close in 1767 and then extended. It was probably the reason for Wormald and Gott purchasing the neighbouring field, Bean Ing, in 1792 as a site for the first range of their manufactory, Park Mill. A wooden bridge was built across the Aire (and the Leeds–Liverpool canal) for workpeople coming from Holbeck and Armley; the Aire was not navigable to this point, and until the Wellington Bridge turnpike was built past the mill gate in 1818 vehicular traffic left by a drive [*top centre*] cutting across the fields to the Bradford New Road turnpike.

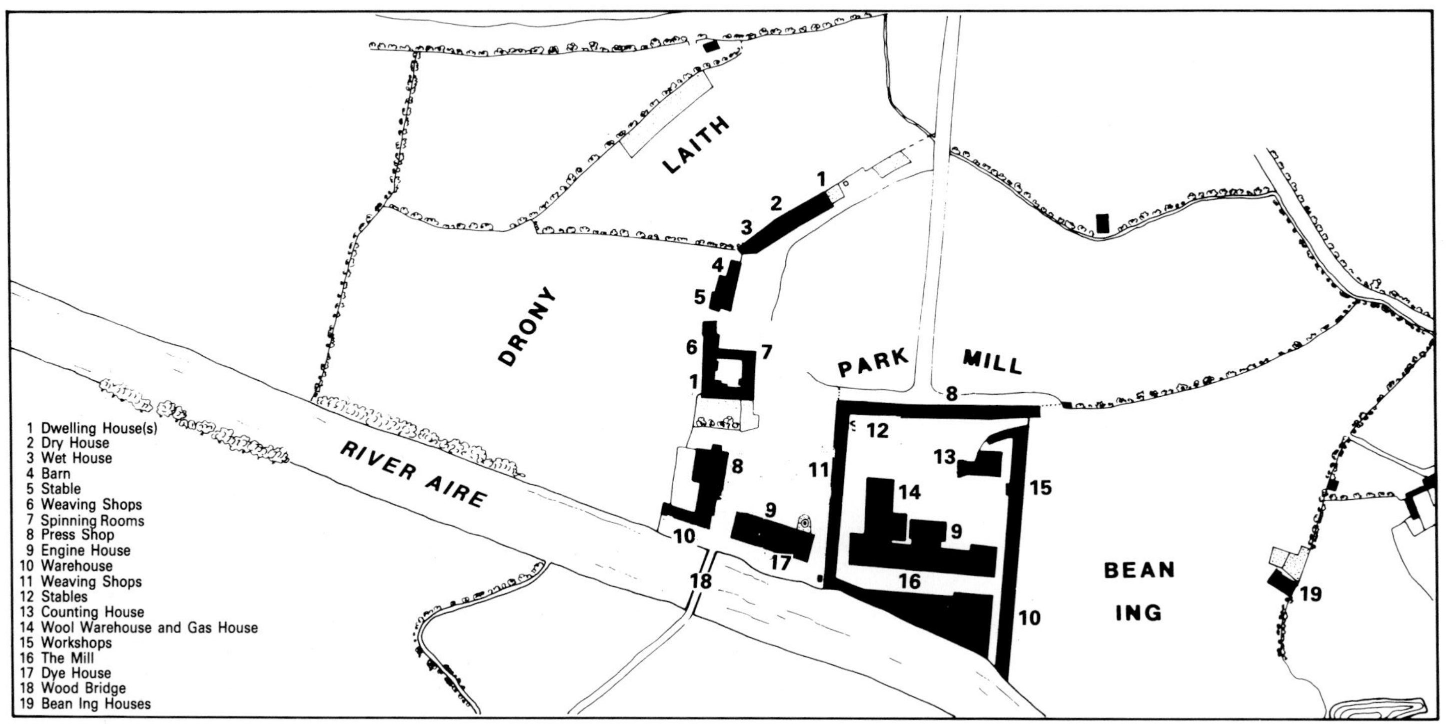

LAITH
DRONY
PARK
MILL
BEAN
ING
RIVER AIRE
1
2
3
4
5
6
7
1
8
9
10
17
18
11
12
13
14
9
16
15
10
8
19
1 Dwelling House(s)
2 Dry House
3 Wet House
4 Barn
5 Stable
6 Weaving Shops
7 Spinning Rooms
8 Press Shop
9 Engine House
10 Warehouse
11 Weaving Shops
12 Stables
13 Counting House
14 Wool Warehouse and Gas House
15 Workshops
16 The Mill
17 Dye House
18 Wood Bridge
19 Bean Ing Houses

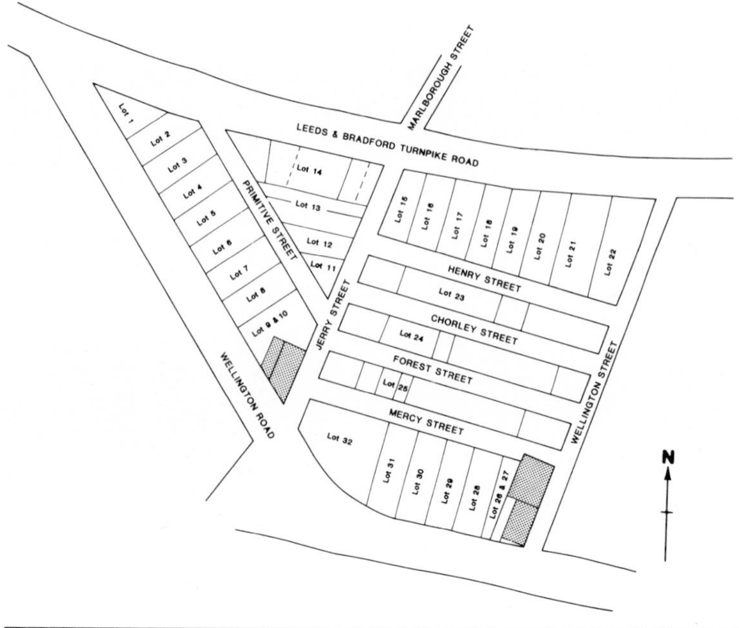

FIG. 9.6 STREET DEVELOPMENT IN THE WEST END ON THE SITE OF DRONY LAITH, 1832

A sale plan of 1832: the former Drony Laith industrial buildings (Fig. 9.5) were demolished for the westward extension of Wellington Street (or Road) in 1818. Building ground was offered in 32 lots; development, not completed until 1844–47, took the form of back-to-back terraces and courts together with St Phillip's church (built on lot 32, donated by the Gotts), a National School (lot 31), Bethesda Methodist chapel (lot 24) — hence Primitive Street — and the extended *Wellington Inn* (lots 9 and 10).

working in a very different architectural style: these new streets of 1821 and 1822 had back-to-back houses and courtyards, and the end of hopes for residential development of the traditional kind was prophesied in a report in the *Intelligencer* of 5 August 1822:

> Within the last three or four years no less than three dry houses have been erected close to the west end of Park Square, hitherto with impunity, which has caused the proprietors of one of them during the past week to commence erecting a steam engine. This, we doubt not, will put the finishing stroke to business in that quarter.

In 1822, encouraged by a recent Act of Parliament, a committee was formed in Leeds to bring pressure on manufacturers with the smokiest chimneys (Table 9.1). Several took remedial measures and

TABLE 9.1

Horse Power in West End Mills, 1824

Owner	Use	Maker of steam engine	Horse power
W. Gott and Sons (Wellington Rd)	woollen cloth manufacture	Boulton and Co., Birmingham	40
Stansfield and Co. (St Peter's Hill, Park Lane)	stuff manufacture	Fenton and Co., Leeds	35
Robert Glover (Airedale Mill, Bradford New Road)	woollen cloth manufacture	Fenton and Co., Leeds	32
Chorley and Uppleby (Park Lane)	woollen cloth manufacture	Fenton and Co., Leeds	20
York and Sheepshanks (Old Mill, Bradford New Road)	woollen cloth manufacture	Fenton and Co., Leeds	18
J. Calvert (Bradford New Road)	dyeing	Stirk and Co., Leeds	10

Note: Additionally, witnesses in the Gott smoke trial of 1824 said that smoke was emitted from the premises of Jonathan Foster (Bradford New Road End) paper manufacturer, and from those of Pickard; the latter does not appear in Directories.

Sources: Gott trial, as in Table 9.2; William Lindley, 'Number of steam engines engaged in the different branches of manufacture in Leeds, March 1824': University of Leeds, Brotherton Library, MS. 18 (provenance unknown; presented by John Marshall's grandson Stephen, 1887; possibly made for the anti-smoke committee at the time of the Gott prosecution. Lindley was a dyer, a former tenant of Wilson at Mill Hill and neighbour of Nussey and Winter, the contestants in the 1811 smoke case).

the attendant publicity cannot have encouraged residential building in the West End.[36] Even greater publicity was given in the spring of 1824 when an information was laid against Gott in respect of Park Mill: 'that you did emit divers noisesome, unwholesome and offensive smells, stenches, smokes and vapours from ten stoves and ten furnaces consuming coal, charcoal and coke'.[37]

[36] Thomas Winter, a merchant occupying the former Manor House, had sued a dyer in 1811 for damages from smoke: Winter *v.* Nussey; York Assizes, *LM*, 27 May 1811.

[37] *LI*, 4 March 1824; 'a matter affecting the health and comfort of a whole population': *Directory, 1822*, 30.

Gott elected for trial before a special jury at the York assizes, attracting national attention.[38] 'Important to manufacturers' was the heading in the *Intelligencer* of 8 April which devoted all four columns of its central page to a verbatim report of a trial 'which excited a very great interest through the country and brought together some of the most eminent engineers in the kingdom'. For the first time in its history the *Intelligencer* furnished its readers with a map, a double-column copy of a plan produced for the jury to indicate Gott's mill and the other dyehouses and mills which occurred in the evidence, with two circles drawn respectively 'a quarter- and a half-mile from Mr Gott's highest chimney', taking in Park Square, Park Row and East Parade.

There was no doubt, from the witnesses called, that there was a massive drift of smoke whenever a fire was stoked at Bean Ing. One single furnace was said to consume in a day as much as a private house in a year. A crocodile from a girls' academy had to flee with soiled dresses; traffic on the turnpike passed through blackness; clothes could not be hung out to dry; fruit and vegetables were tainted; dairymen had to wash blackened cows before milking; shrubberies dropped soot on to ladies' dresses as they walked in their gardens.

Gott had prepared a defence which included a claim that he was employing the best technical measures to repress smoke that were available but the judge stopped the trial and directed the jury to find for Gott after a succession of witnesses had supported the other part of the defence: that the complainants had been well aware of the smoke when they came to build on the Park estate, whether before 1792 from Drony Laith or after 1792 from Park Mill, thus depriving them of any claim for damages by nuisance.

The *Intelligencer*'s account can be supplemented by unused witnesses' statements which were gathered by Gott's solicitor for the instruction of counsel. These papers include statements designed to show that the value of building ground had not fallen as a result of its smokiness, and data were gathered which provide a very useful view of the progress of West End housing since the census of 1821 and Fowler's plan of the same year. Over five hundred 'second-class' dwellings had been built within a half-mile radius of Bean Ing, and since none appeared on Fowler's plan they must all have been

[38] The following paragraphs are based on the voluminous material gathered by Gott's solicitor for the information of defending counsel, now LCA, DB 116; the papers in Brotherton Library, University of Leeds, Gott MSS, Box VII; and the full report of the trial in *LI*, 8 May 1824.

TABLE 9.2

Buildings Erected within a Half Mile of Bean Ing, 1793–1824

	Completed by Feb. 1824	Unfinished in Feb. 1824
Good dwelling houses	105	1
Second-class dwelling houses	512	16
Mills	6	1
Dyehouses	3	2
Chimneys in mills and dyehouses	31	–
Chapels	1	–

Source: LCA, DB 116: R. *v*. Gott, York Lent Assizes, 1824.

recently built (Table 9.2). The witnesses left the meaning of 'second-class' in no doubt: 'a description of houses built as cheap as possible for labouring people. Two or three of them were blown down during this winter . . . No houses of a better description than cottages have been built between Mr Gott's mill and the Infirmary'. The depressed years after the collapse of the post-war boom had brought 'a general reduction in rents from the depression of Trade' but now in 1824 it was very different; Mrs Briggs, whose husband was 'the first to build in Lisbon Street', said, 'no sooner is a Row staked out than applications are made for them, and before the Shells are filled they are actually enjoyed . . . There is an entire change of the class of inhabitants from middling tradesmen to labouring mechanics. There is now a new steam engine in this very street'.

There would be certainly no shortage of demand for working-class housing. The manufactories which had come to the West End before 1821 had to draw their workers either from central and eastern Leeds or from Holbeck and Armley across the river. Gott had built no housing for his workers but he did provide a wooden footbridge across the Aire to Green Lane and the canal lock so that Armley and Holbeck could be reached without going down into Leeds to the only bridge which the town had before Wellington Bridge. Immigration and natural increase doubled the population of the Lower North West Division – this area – between 1821 and 1831.

Nor was Lisbon Street the only place where new steam engines were to be seen. By the time that the boom of 1825–26 was over the four factories in the West End had increased to twelve, and to Park

Street in 1825 came the Oil Gas Works Company, a rival to that in the East End which derived its gas from coal and coke, but no less noxious. The *Leeds Directory* of 1834 no longer assigned the West End to the 'more respectable part of the Inhabitants':

> Streets of cottages open from the great Western road: a vast population pours forth at specific periods of the day to their vocation of industry and toil; and although the avenue to the town by the Wellington Road is commodious, open and airy, the other which conducts the traveller to St. Paul's Church and Park Square is now one of the meanest, the most irregular and the most unpleasant in the whole circumference of Leeds.[39]

This writer was in fact sacrificing truth in order to make a contrast between the housing along the old and new turnpikes. The south side of Wellington Street was indeed still 'open and airy' between the Cloth Hall and Park Mill, and the Wormald fields at Drony Laith had as yet no purchasers, but 'streets of cottages' could have been seen to the east of them from Park Square through Lisbon Street to Wellington Lane (Appendix IX.3). In the burst of prosperity in the mid-thirties the blank spaces were being filled in. Between 1823 and 1834 the West End added thirteen factories at a time when the East End gained only eight, and by the time of the first Ordnance Survey in 1847 the south side of Kirkstall Road had become a chain of mills, tanneries and foundries with short back-to-back streets facing them, while on the south side of Wellington Street the open space east of Park Mill, once Bean Ing meadow, was designated for the terminus and goods yards of the Leeds and Thirsk railway. 'Are not the cottages at the west end of the town contiguous to the mills and factories?', asked a member of the Commons Select Committee on the Improvement of Boroughs Bills in 1842. The witness was Edwin Eddison, the town clerk, and his reply was succinct: 'They are'.[40] A more discursive but informative dialogue took place when James Holdforth, silk manufacturer, appeared before the Lords Committee on the Leeds Improvement Bill of 1842. (Holdforth's father had been the first occupant of Eye Bright Place but then had been one of the earliest emigrants from the West End, appearing at Burley in the 1817 street directory.)

> Q. Does it happen to be within your knowledge in consequence of this prevalence of smoke property is greatly deteriorated in value?
>
> A. I think so – property within the action of the smoke is certainly greatly deteriorated in value.

[39] *Directory, 1834*, i, p. 171.

[40] PP 1842, X, Q.880.

Q. Have you any instance within your own knowledge you can speak of?
A. Yes – a very unfortunate one – with abundance of Mill property, I have been obliged to build a Mill in a District free from smoke – I cannot carry on some of my finer processes of work in the Town of Leeds more especially in my own Mills, or in the locality of my own Mills where I have a great deal of building property.

Q. Is there a house which you know to have been a good deal depreciated?
A. There is a house in which I once lived at the West End of the Town – a house belonging to my father in 1803; my father refused £2500 for it – I should be very glad now to take if I wanted to sell the place and should not be able to get half the money for it; and that in consequence of the smoke coming to it – it being now surrounded by smoke, and formerly a pure clear situation.

Q. Particularly the smoke of these Dyers?
A. From Dyehouses as well as from steam engines that property is affected.

Q. Whereabouts is that?
A. It is at the west end of the town not far from the Infirmary; formerly there was no road to my house but now there is a road and the Neighbourhood is filled with Steam Engines and Dyehouses – the Garden which in my recollection was very productive will now grow nothing – I do not think it will grow a blade of grass.

Q. What was the name of it formerly?
A. It was called *Eyebright place*, it took its name from a peculiar spring of water just below the Hill – fine cold water – people came and washed their Eyes and faces. It is called *Eyebright*.[41]

Those who in 1842 supported legislation to control smoke pollution, argued, like Baines at the time when the first measures of this kind were proposed, that laws were necessary to protect the health of the labouring class who were too poor to take the only other means available for avoiding smoke: to live somewhere else. In 1845 two prominent Leeds citizens gave evidence to another Commons Select Committee, that on Smoke Prevention. The mayor, Darnton Lupton, was one who had managed to avoid smoke by migration: 'Three miles out where I live we have no smoke . . . it is on high ground. House property value is much lessened in Leeds by the smoke – yes, very much indeed; almost 25 to 30% because everyone does as I did a few years ago. I went out, I could not bear it any longer; and *everyone who can* is going out of town'.[42] John

[41] Evidence as in n. 16 above.

[42] PP 1845, XIII, pp. 560–62. My italics.

Atkinson, the town's leading solicitor and agent for Christopher Wilson's heir, R. F. Wilson, also gave evidence to the same end:

> Park Place and Park Square which used to be the residences of the best families in Leeds, have been gradually desecrated for several years past in consequence of the increasing smoke.
>
> There the houses are too large for persons of moderate means to live in, and are too smokey for those who could live in them. They are in the best part of Leeds, and the parties are driven out of town; they live a mile or two out of town now, and as they have the means of omnibuses they can do it. They used to live near their businesses.[43]

THE FLIGHT INTO EGYPT

The West End had had its age of innocence, longer than that in East End, but it was now clearly fallen. Given the direction of the prevailing winds the eastern part of an industrial town could hardly avoid an eventual deterioration. As Mr Justice Bayley observed in the Gott smoke trial, 'it was not to be expected that in a particular place such as Leeds where it was necessary to carry on manufactures that a man could enjoy the same purity of air as was to be found elsewhere'.[44]

Initially the failure to extend the Park estate streets owed more to a general disinclination to build than to a distaste for the presence of Park Mill and the chimneys at Drony Laith. Then between 1809 and 1822 all was indecision: no commitment to streets of any kind: but some further mill building fatally condoned (Table 9.3). The *Intelligencer* was correct in seeing a significance in that finishing stroke of August 1822 when a dyehouse near Park Square installed a steam engine. There was another finishing stroke which attracted less attention in the newspapers: for on plots which had been part of the Wilson estate developers were again prepared to build, but for 'labouring mechanics'. Property in Park Square and Park Place was under the same double seige as that in St Peter's Square: from the drift of smoke and from the contiguity of the Sons of Labour.

There were three main symptoms of a fallen West End. The first was seen when those able to afford high quality new building – immigrants or migrants from the town centre – failed to continue the squares and terraces of the Park estate: characteristic of the years between 1793 and 1822, it gave rise to the abortive streets of 'building ground' sketched in on Fowler's town plan of 1821 and to

[43] *Ibid.*, p.576.
[44] *LI*, 8 May 1824.

TABLE 9.3

Industrial Building in the West End, 1815–1833

Date	Name	Owner	Function
1811	Chorley Lane Mill	Chorley and Uppleby	cloth-finishing
1819–25	Oxford Mills, Oxford Terrace	Hardisty	cloth-finishing
1821	Grove Street Mill	?	cloth-dressing
by 1822	Airedale Mills, Kirkstall Road	Glover	cloth-finishing
1822–24	Old Mill, West Street	?	machine making
by 1823	Airedale Dyeworks, Kirkstall Road	Calvert	dyeing
1824	Aire Street Mills	Shann	cloth-finishing
	Brunswick Mills	Binns	cloth-dressing
	Gas Works, New Park Street	Oil Gas Co.	gas
1824–29	Perseverance Foundry, Kirkstall Road	Whitham	foundry
1825	Wellington Bridge Mill	Bruce, Dorrington and Walker	cloth-finishing
	Pickard's Mill, Kirkstall Road	Pickard	dyeing
	Spring Garden Dyeworks, I	George	dyeing
1826	Perseverance Mill, Kirkstall Road	Sheepshanks	cloth-finishing
1827	Schofield's Dyeworks, Kirkstall Road	Schofield and Reffitt	dyeing
1828	Spring Garden Dyeworks, II	Wood and Horsfall	dyeing
	Wellington Foundry	Fairbairn	foundry
	Joppa Tannery	Rhodes and Nickols	leather
1829	Grace Street Mill	Eyres	cloth-finishing
by 1833	Dean Street Mill	Greenwood	machine making

Note: Table excludes finishing shops integral with residences at Belle Vue, Denison Hall, North Hall, St Peter's Hill, Claremont, Little Woodhouse Hall, Belmont, Mount Pleasant, Sunny Bank, Woodhouse Lodge, Springfield House, Claypit House, Portland House, Bagby House, St James Lodge, Hirst's dressing shops, Cankerwell Lane, 1803–19.

The first building not related to residence was Park Lane dressing shops (1796–1801) for Phillips, Oates where there was a steam engine by 1824.

Source: M. F. Ward, 'Industrial Development and Location in Leeds North of the River Aire' (unpublished Ph D thesis, University of Leeds, 1972).

the loneliness of the family house of Edward Baines, proprietor of the *Mercury*: Baines took a building plot in King Street, next to the Infirmary, about 1817 but remained the only resident in the street for nearly twenty years.

The second symptom was the availability of an alternative West End to the north and north west of town: this, commencing a little before 1793, forms the subject of the next Chapter: by 1815 it comprised over forty detached villas, an incomplete square, two or three incomplete terraces and the remnants of the building-club street at St James. A third symptom, which the Select Committee dialogues have already introduced, was an actual flight from the West End by those whose parents and grandparents had been Park estate leaseholders. This final section of Chapter Nine examines the evidence for that type of disaffection, for it might be thought that a capture of potential recruits for an alternative West End would undermine old loyalties and be paralleled by a general migration of those already settled in the first West End.

Individual instances are certainly thrown up whenever successive directories are compared: Edward Markland was in South Parade in 1793 and 1803 but at Brunswick Place in 1817; George Matthewman in Park Row in 1803 but at Carlton Lodge, Woodhouse Lane in 1817; Ikin and Co. still had premises at the north end of Park Row in 1817 but the residence of Thomas Ikin was 'Headingley' and that of John Gawthorp, once in Park Square, was now 'Chapeltown' (Table 9.4).

It is easier to demonstrate single instances of the West End falling from favour as a residence than to establish a complete chronology and identify the periods when departure was most rapid. Were there annual rate books, one might determine a 'normal' mobility and the period when the West End became exceptionally restless but the five-year gap between rate books in 1780–1805 and then their complete destruction prevent any quantification of changes in property ownership and tenantry on a yearly basis. Street directories, necessarily confined to identifying residents and not owners, appeared at too wide an interval for the establishment of normal annual rates and the identification of years of critical decision.

All discussion of residential migration in Leeds must be seen against a long tradition of internal mobility even when choice had been confined to a smaller group of town-centre streets.[45] Within the Park estate the practice continued, especially among widows, spinsters and annuitants, many of whom were tenants rather than

[45] See above, p.64

head-leaseholders. Even though their publication is intermittent the few late eighteenth-century street directories and the charitable subscription lists published in the *Mercury* and *Intelligencer* show many changes of address within the estate. For this reason the tabulation of Park estate residence in Tables 9.5(a) and (b) treats residence as continuous so long as it remained within one of the five streets.[46]

It must not be hastily concluded that the disappearance of a name from successive directories is a positive proof of outward migration. Of the fifty-six names in Table 9.5(a) which appear in the 1817 Directory but not in that of 1822, only seventeen can be traced to other parts of the borough; thirty-six simply disappear. Between 1798 and 1817 when the names of thirty-one residents on the Park estate disappeared from the street directories only nine can be traced elsewhere in the borough; between 1817 and 1822 there were fifty-six residents lost but only twenty names traced elsewhere.

Edward Baines once observed, in regard to the owners' names which appeared on the stalls in the cloth halls, that remarkably few remained unchanged over the period of the Napoleonic wars, encompassing as it did not only a series of commercial crises but important structural changes in the organisation of the textile industries. This was the period spanned by the first of the comparisons made in Tables 9.5 (a) and (b), and Baines's observation could well be applied to the Park estate; and death might also be expected to have taken an exceptional toll since it was in the nature of a new and expensive estate that its residents would already be middle-aged when they came to it and elderly in the early years of the nineteenth century. To have half the residents of 1798 still appearing in the directory of 1817 was in the circumstances no sign of restless disaffection. It was less encouraging that in the next five years fourteen residents would leave Park Row, nine East Parade, seven Park Place, while Park Square lost twenty-three. That these were the crucial and exceptional years of disaffection is indicated by the directory of 1830 showing only two refugees coming west from the centre since 1822, even though there had been extensive building in 1824–25 in every alternative part of the borough. The next period of active house construction was in 1833–35 when the first streets (as opposed to rows and terraces) appeared in Little Woodhouse and when medium-sized housing began in Headingley. The flight had begun. No family that was resident at South Parade in 1817 can be

[46] The following pages are based on successive printed directories identified by years: for which see Bibliography §5, p. 531 below.

TABLE 9.4

Identified Migration from the First West End, 1798–1830

Name	West End address	New address		
		Northern Divisions of in-townships	Out-township	Elsewhere
1798–1817				
Atkinson	Park Square	Sheepscar		
Bischoff	Park Place	Claypit House, Woodhouse Lane		
Gawthorp	Park Square		Chapeltown	
Ikin	Park Row		Headingley	
Matthewman	Park Row	Carlton Lodge, Woodhouse Lane		
Markland	South Parade	Brunswick Place		
Scaley	Park Row	Sheepscar		
Temple	Park Row			Post Office, town centre
1817–1822				
Benyon	Park Place		Headingley	
Barwick	Park Square	Blenheim Terrace		
Birchall	Park Square		Burley Grove	
Eagland	Park Row	Coronation Street		
Hardisty	Park Square	Little London		
Hives	Park Square		Chapel Allerton	
Kendall	Park Row	St James Street		
Knubley	Park Place	widow to Portland Street		
Motley	East Parade		Osmondthorpe	
Nevins	Park Square		Larchfield, Hunslet	
Pearson	South Parade	Brunswick Terrace		
Ridsdale	East Parade	Woodhouse Grove		
G. Smith	Park Square	Little Woodhouse		
Stansfield	Park Square		Burley	
Thackray	Park Square		Kirkstall	
Ward	Park Square		Leathley Lodge, Hunslet	
Wilkinson	Park Square	North Street		

TABLE 9.4 (*continued*)

Name	West End address	New address		
		Northern Divisions of in-townships	Out-township	Elsewhere
1822–1830				
Humble	South Parade	Blenheim Terrace		
Lapage	Park Place	Mount Preston		
Rawson	Park Square	Hanover Square		
Stott	Park Square	Blenheim Square		
Walsh	Park Row	Little London		
J. Gott	Park Square		Wyther	
S. J. Birchall	Park Square	Springfield House		

Source: Leeds directories, 1793–1820.

traced there in 1842, and of the ninety-three names from the whole estate in 1817 only fifteen appear there in 1842.

A similar chronology can be seen in collective biography: in 1798 one-third of the thirty-six members of the unreformed Corporation, a self-perpetuating Anglican-Tory oligarchy, lived in the West End; but in 1817 there were not twelve but seven Corporation members at Park estate addresses (Table 9.6). Yet the number did not fall in the next thirteen years and the same impression as from Table 9.5 is given: a second exodus postponed until the eighteen-thirties. In 1830 of the nineteen elected members of the Improvement Commission seven were living in the West End but in 1842, when the mayor, Darnton Lupton, went to London from his home at Potternewton to deliver his dictum to a Parliamentary committee that 'all who could were leaving town', an examination of the sixteen aldermen's addresses shows only one in the West End and ten, like the mayor, in out-townships. No alderman lived nearer the town centre than Joshua Bower at Hopewell House in Woodhouse Lane and his neighbour, Joseph Bateson at 1 Hillary Place.

Yet alongside those whom death, bankruptcy, marriage or an aspiring taste removed from the Park estate there were some remarkable examples of loyalty as the last line in Table 9.5(a) has shown: ten families resident on the estate in 1842 had been there since at least 1798, and two of the ten did not disappear from directories until 1849. Appendix IX.4 results from an examination of the whole succession of residence in one street, and its repeated letter

TABLE 9.5(a)

Continuity of Residence, Park Estate, 1798–1842

	Number of residents located					
	Park Row	South Parade	East Parade	Park Place	Park Square	All
1798 Directory	19	7	7	18	10	61
Still resident, 1817 Directory	8 (40%)	4 (57%)	3 (43%)	12 (66%)	3 (30%)	30 (50%)
New names, 1817 Directory	14	1	9	9	30	63
All names, 1817 Directory	22	5	12	21	33	93
Still resident, 1830 Directory	7 (33%)	2 (40%)	3 (25%)	14 (66%)	9 (27%)	35 (38%)
Still resident, 1842 Directory	2 (9%)	– –	2 (16%)	7 (33%)	4 (12%)	15 (16%)
Resident, 1798–1830	1	–	2	5	2	10

TABLE 9.5(b)

Continuous Residence, Park Estate, 1798–1830

Park Row	no. 18, Dibb
East Parade	no. 2, Armitage
	no. 14, Grace
Park Place	no. 12, Gatliff*
	no. 15, Kershaw*
	no. 20, Blackburn
	no. 21, Walker
	no. 22, Rhodes
Park Square	no. 1, Rawson
	no. 18, Walker

* To 1849

Sources: Directories, 1798, 1817, 1830 and 1842.

TABLE 9.6

Distribution of Residences of Corporation Members, 1798, 1817 and 1830

	Old town centre	New West End	Meadow Lane, Hunslet Lane	NE and NW Divisions	East End	Outside
12 Aldermen						
1798	2	4	2	3	–	1
1817	2	2	2	3	–	3
1830	2	1	2	2	1	4
24 Councillors						
1798	7	8	5	2	1	1
1817	4	5	3	6	2	4
1830	5	6	1	8	–	4

Source: Directories.

'S' emphasises the continued appearance of the same family name against the numbered houses of Park Place.

Park Place was unique among its neighbours in having its houses numbered, but it was not ease of identification which made it seem suitable for a detailed study of migration.[47] It was the worst situated of the Park streets and seemingly the most likely to show migration. Its restricted plots allowed little room for outbuildings, so that there was little of that inertia induced by the presence of workshops which might maintain loyalty to family houses in Park Row and Park Square. Of all the streets it was the worst placed for the impact of industrialisation. It was a terrace and not an inward-facing square, and the residents looked to the outside world rather than to each other. Beyond their front garden plots was the building ground of King Street, Queen Street and Wellington Street. Like all building ground these fields were being slowly stripped of their clay and the bricks burned on the spot. 'Many Brick Kilns are made in front of Park Place', ran one heading in the brief which Gott's solicitor made

[47] 'principally inhabited by affluent merchants and gentlemen who have retired from business', *Leeds Guide*, p.67: whence came their striking absence of backside warehouses and the presence of gardens facing the houses across the Place (later over-built).

for the smoke trial in 1824, and at the trial a brickmaker's son, John Spencer, testified that his father had once employed him to sleep as a security guard in the half-finished houses of Park Place: 'almost lost in smoke . . . people did not trouble their heads about smoke at that day . . . but there have been so many Gentlemen's houses built within the last twenty years that people talk about it more than they did'.[48] Park Place was the nearest to Park Mill and had known Drony Laith smoke from the very beginning. It was therefore vulnerable to the type of falling property values which Atkinson described in 1845: houses too large to be occupied by the less fastidious 'persons of moderate means', but it was then too far from the centre to be compensated by entering that new category of use from which Albion Street, Park Row and the two Parades were beginning to benefit – as offices for the professions and the banks.[49]

Yet a loyalty to established ways was nowhere more strongly expressed than at nos 20, 21 and 22 Park Place, situated at its smokiest end where the widow Blackburn and three of the town's leading entrepreneurs were happy to remain resident for over forty years. It might be argued, but implausibly, that these four were imprisoned in Park Row because they could not afford any capital loss if they sold a house declining in value in order to purchase another out of town. On the contrary there is plain evidence of a positive enthusiasm for living in Park Place by some who could certainly have lived elsewhere. In the Directory of 1830 the occupant of no. 6 was the Revd Richard Fawcett, for the archbishop had given permission for the old vicarage in Kirkgate to be sold to provide a site for the new off-street market, and the proceeds were used to purchase a house elsewhere to be a vicarage: the choice fell on no. 6 Park Place, and six years later the minister of the new Christ Church in Meadow Lane made his home not in Meadow Lane but at no. 13 Park Place.

In the subsequent developments from 1830 to 1880, when house after house in Park Row, South Parade and the streets of the 'Square' infill between them were demolished to make room for banks

[48] LCA, DB 116.

[49] The bank of Farrar, Williamson and Co. took over a residence in Albion St in 1825 (*LM*, 1 Jan. 1825); by 1836 eight other banks were located nearby. The southern end of Park Row was chosen for the new Commercial Buildings in 1824 (*LI*, 18 Nov. 1824); no. 2 Park Row was converted soon after into a set of offices and named Benson's Buildings after Jarvis Benson, its last domestic owner-occupier. The first offices were let to an accountant, a barrister, an architect, a land agent, four solicitors, two commission agents, a law stationer, and the Leeds Stamp office. (I owe this information to Mr S. J. Lingard.)

and insurance offices, East Parade formed a watershed. The house facades of East Parade, Park Place and Park Square remained virtually intact until after 1950: they did not retain their residential character that long but their site seems to have lain too far west of what was then the central business district to attract new multi-storey offices. Their former dining rooms, drawing rooms and bedrooms were capable of being adapted to the legal and medical professions' modest needs for space, even in some cases maintaining until the twentieth century that association of workplace and home that would have been familiar to the first inhabitants of those streets.

Yet on the eastern side of the watershed the Park Row, Albion Street and South Parade entries in successive census enumerations were becoming shorter and shorter. A census-taker had a different approach from the compiler of a street directory: the census was concerned with overnight residents only, and no one had to be counted twice. Thus the daytime occupants, from bank manager to the humblest bank clerk, were enumerated where they slept, whether in Far Headingley mansion or in Hunslet terrace: if there were residents to record in Park Row they were the handful of caretakers.

DENISON HALL

The most spectacular of the flights from the West End of Leeds, after all, came before a single brick had been laid at Park Mill and from a house that lay not in the first West End but in what was to become the heart of the second, and in circumstances so unique that the event is typical of the history of neither.

In 1785 John Wilkinson, then aged twenty-seven, inherited the substantial fortune of his uncle, the Leeds merchant, Robert Denison, with whose firm he had served his apprenticeship. The Denison house and surrounding workshops were at the north end of the town (Fig. 3.4) but the nephew was already living in the countryside east of Leeds at Potterton Lodge. His uncle's intention, as expressed in his will, was that John should not benefit from the legacy if he withdrew from business, and it was probably to satisfy the trustees that nine closes near Little Woodhouse Hall were purchased in June 1786.[50] On 27 June the *Intelligencer* carried an advertisement for 'three or four score stonemasons to assist in

[50] Purchase of ground from John Elam (of Claremont): WRRD, CG 21/27 and CS 634/928; sale to Wormald: WRRD, EZ 176/264 and FE 20/27; RE 11 95834 and 26 132267.

building the Hall of John Denison Esquire', Wilkinson having paid the pious homage not unusual in some circumstances and changed his surname.

The new Hall in its semi-parkland setting looking down to Park Lane did not follow the plain brick Georgian style of its neighbours, Claremont and Little Woodhouse Hall (Fig. 10.6). It took 101 days to build, and the masons erected 13,680 cubic yards of stone into an edifice three storeys high at the four-bay centre and two at the three-bay wings, 104 feet in overall length. Its initial rateable value of £70 confirms what the eye can still admire, that this was the largest private house in central Leeds, and quite fit, with its balustrades, pediments and urns, to stand in some country parkland; and indeed its first name was 'Woodhouse Park'.

> A New and Elegant Stone-built Mansion House, called Woodhouse House, consisting of a Drawing Room, Dining Room, Billiard Room, Library, Breakfast Room, Servants Hall, Kitchen, Housekeepers Room, and Butler's Pantry, on the Ground Floor; a Gallery sixty feet by twenty, six Lodging Rooms, with convenient Dressing Rooms upon the first Floor; and nine Bed Chambers in three Attic Storeys, with two double Coach-Houses with Servants Rooms therein, Stabling for fourteen Horses, Brew House, Wash House, and other convenient Out-offices belonging thereto; and six Acres of rich Meadow or Pasture Land, in Front of the House, partly surrounded with a Plantation of Forest Trees, Evergreens, and Flowering Shrubs, in great Perfection.[51]

Yet the house was still intended as a residence for a gentleman who was also a merchant for, as its insurance policies and the later large-scale Ordnance Survey plan show, it had a line of outbuildings along Kendal Lane (where their walls still survive) which were workshops backsides in the very fashion of merchants' houses in Park Row and South Parade.

Denison married in 1787 but his wife may never have seen Little Woodhouse for, despite the terms of his uncle's will, Denison rapidly turned from merchanting to the life of a gentleman *solus* and, as his obituary in the *Intelligencer* of 15 May 1820 claimed, probably never took up residence in the house that still bears his name. At Ossington, four miles from Tuxford, he had a genuine country house, built in 1727 and therefore already surrounded by a maturing parkland from which the village had been conveniently removed, leaving the parish church alongside the Hall to serve as the family

[51] *LI*, 18 Jan. 1791.

mausoleum.[52] It is there and not in Leeds parish church that Nollekens's funerary statue of Denison must be sought although the reliefs on its base, a ship with wool bales, and a sheep, do refer back to the Leeds origin of his fortune.

Denison, his daily life divorced from business, could afford to move to the Nottinghamshire countryside. A total rejection of Leeds in this fashion was rare: until 1817 there was only one recorded case of migration from the West End to an out-township (Table 9.4). The colonisation of Headingley Hill, the first of the village suburbs in Leeds, did not begin until 1829. In his 1816 edition of Thoresby's *Ducatus* T. D. Whitaker wrote of 'country villas' to which a 'dread of smoke' had driven their proprietors but their 'countryside' lay no further than the fields of Little Woodhouse and Sheepscar that lay undeveloped behind the frontages of the Otley and Harrogate turnpikes.

The role of these villas, available from the mid-seventeen-nineties as an alternative to the first West End, was not to lure residents from the first West End. Only four villa names appear in the thirty-five identified migrations from the Park estate, and in none of these cases was the migrant either the builder or the first occupant of a villa (Table 9.4). Judging from the names of the villas' first occupants (Table 10.1) the second West End was colonised directly from houses in the old town centre rather than by a knight's move via the first West End. Those who did leave the Park estate at that time went typically to the newer terraces and squares that were beginning to be built in the North West and North East Divisions, rather than to the detached villas. These villas, terraces and squares form the subject of the next Chapter.

[52] N. Pevsner, *The Buildings of England: Nottinghamshire* (Harmondsworth, 1951), pl. 49(b) for the statue of William Denison, elder brother of Robert, John Wilkinson's benefactor; and the dust jacket of Wilson, *Gentlemen Merchants* for the portrait of Robert Denison with Ossington in the background.

10

A More Extensive and Agreeable Prospect: the Rise and Fall of a Second West End

The premises are situate on a Declivity, commanding a more extensive and agreeable Prospect than the greater Part of the new erections about Leeds.

Advertisement for house in St James St, LEEDS INTELLIGENCER, 8 March 1791.

Little Woodhouse . . . of late years has been made choice of some of the wealthy inhabitants of Leeds for building their country houses.

Griffith Wright [attr.], A HISTORY OF THE TOWN AND PARISH OF LEEDS (1797), p.34.

A neat modern villa, brick and slate, detached offices, stabling etc. in complete repair, and a cotton spinning and Packing House built by the tenant.

Survey of Woodhouse Lodge, Woodhouse Lane (1808): Herts. CRO., Cowper MSS, 4949, f.48.

The chaos between Springfield Place and St James Street is quite as grievous as that about Marsh Lane. No quarter of the town exhibits worse arrangement of streets, a worse principle in the interior construction of houses, or a greater feebleness of build than this area . . . which is almost entirely new.

LEEDS INTELLIGENCER, 25 September 1852.

'IN A FIELD'

In 1786, about the same time as the first insurances of East End cottages, the Sun Company issued a policy for the merchant, Frederick Oates, in respect of a house which at £900 matched those on the Park estate in value but which was very different in location and style. It was later known as Belmont but in the policy register it had both anonymity and a vague address: 'On Frederick Oates' Mansion House in a Field at Little Woodhouse, £700; on his Household Goods and Wearing Apparel therein, £400; Plate therein £50; Stables and Laundry, £100; Four cottages at the Top of the Field,

£100: total £1350'.[1] The imprecision was excusable: the four cottages backed on to the country lane which, as Cankerwell Lane and Kendal Lane, meandered towards Woodhouse Moor through the hamlet of Little Woodhouse but the residence itself was set midfield on the slope of the hill between the hamlet and Park Lane, its front rooms looking down over the half-completed Park estate towards the river.[2]

In his account of Leeds in 1797 Griffith Wright commented on the 'country houses' which merchants were building at Little Woodhouse,[3] and Table 10.1 shows that by the end of the century there were some forty-five detached houses of this sort, making up an alternative or second West End. The proprietors were virtually all merchants, including fourteen names from among the town's seventy-two largest dealers as measured by the list which Thomas Hill drew up in 1782.[4]

In 1816 the Revd T. D. Whitaker published his *Loidis and Elmete*, an extended history of the area treated by Thoresby a century before, and drawing heavily on that work. From time to time Whitaker paused to make comparisons between the Leeds of Thoresby's day and his own. 'Could Thoresby return to survey the environs of his native town, no change would perhaps more attract his notice than the numbers of commodious and cheerful villas which dread of smoke and desire of comfort have drawn around it . . . a rood of land about a country house is a little landscape'.[5]

'Villa' was not actually used in the name of any of these houses, 'Lodge', 'Hall' and even 'Cottage' being favoured together with imported prestigious names such as Claremont, Belle Vue and Vauxhall. The first use of 'villa' which has been noted is in 1808 when Earl Cowper's surveyors described Woodhouse Lodge, then some twenty years old, 'as a neat modern villa, brick and slate, with detached offices, stabling, etc.'.[6] However, Whitaker's use of the word legitimises its employment here for all those detached houses of various sizes and styles which were spread in an arc around the northern slopes of the in-township from Little Woodhouse across to

[1] Sun OS 330 521500.

[2] The house was 'surrounded by a plantation of 12 years growth with gardens and choice fruit trees': *LI*, 13 Aug. 1810; the bow-windowed dining room measured 18 ft by 29 ft, the drawing room 18 ft by 23 ft, the breakfast room 15 ft by 17 ft; there were five first-floor bedrooms and six in garrets: LCD 10354.

[3] Wright, *History*, p.34.

[4] G. D. Lumb, 'Extracts from an old Leeds Merchant's Memorandum Book', *PTh.S*, XXIV (1919), 37.

[5] Whitaker, *Ducatus*, p.87.

[6] Herts. CRO, Cowper MS. T 4949; plan of 1819: 4967.

TABLE 10.1

Chronology of Forty-Five Detached Houses and Villas Built outside Town Centre before 1815

Date,	Name and location, with Division*		Owner	Rateable value, £				Insured value, £	References
				1790	1795	1800	1805		
1701	Drony Laith	NW	Dixon, dyer	28	33	40	57		LCD 20969
c. 1740	Little Woodhouse Hall	NW	Thompson, gentleman	12	14	15	15		
by 1765	Claremont, Little Woodhouse	NW	Elam, merchant	19	36	52	54	1000 (1782)	Sun OS 357 549557
by 1765	Vauxhall, Park Lane	NW	Strother, merchant	9 part empty	28	20	9 part empty		LCD 10990
by 1771	Great Woodhouse Hall	NW	Dalley, gentleman	10	10	10	10	600 (1786)	Sun OS 339 521500
by 1774	North Hall, Burley Rd	NW	Beckett, gentleman	18	18	25	?		
by 1774	Portland House, Woodhouse Lane	NW	Elam, merchant	23	30	38	20	700 (1778)	Sun OS 269 404618; *LM*, 29 July 1777
1778	Claypit House, Woodhouse Lane	NW	Blayds, merchant	52	52	57	68	300 (1785)	Sun OS 326 502551; LCD 2603
by 1781	Mount Pleasant, Little Woodhouse	NW	Rhodes, merchant	–	–	–	–	4200 contents only (1800)	ULH, deeds, no. 2. CS30 698726
rebuilt 1783	Springfield Lodge, Little Woodhouse	NW	Sutton, gentleman	–	–	–	–		ULD 273; *LM*, 18 March 1783
1785	Park House, Park Lane	NW	Calverley, gentleman	15	15	15	18	700 (1785)	Sun OS 328 503477
1786	Belmont, Little Woodhouse	NW	Oates, merchant	30	30	30	32	900 (1786)	Sun OS 339 521500: 'in a field'.
1786	Denison Hall	NW	Denison, merchant	70	empty	41	part empty	3100 (1785)	RE 11 95834
by 1787	St Peter's Hall, Park Lane	NW	Buck, gentleman	17	17	25	28	contents only (1787); 500 (1788)	Sun OS 346 532507 Sun OS 351 525419
1787	Grove House, Claypit Lane	NE	R. R. Bramley, merchant	15	15	18	19		
1788	Campfield House, Long Balk Lane	NE	Rhodes, merchant	21	20	58	23	660, unfinished (1788)	Sun OS 357 549569

TABLE 10.1 (*continued*)

Date,	Name and location, with Division*		Owner	Rateable value, £				Insured value, £	References
				1790	1795	1800	1805		
by 1789	Woodhouse Lodge, Woodhouse Lane	NW	Earl Cowper, peer	–	11	11	17	500 (1798)	Sun CS 18 663907
by 1789	Woodhouse Grove, Woodhouse Lane	NW	Shepley, gentleman	–	–	–	–	800 (1789)	Sun OS 364 561514
1789	Claypit Hill House, Claypit Lane	NW	Hardwick woollen draper	13	13	13	13	contents only (1789); 430 (1795)	Sun OS 365 563803; LCD 16301
1790	Ridge [Hillary] House, Woodhouse Lane	NW	Hebblethwaite merchant	–	28	28	56	400, unfinished (1790); 600 (1791)	Sun OS 370 573802; Sun OS 376 581433; ULD 196
by 1790	Fountaine 'Terrace [*sic*], Sheepscar Lane	NE	Blagborough, merchant	14	14	10	10		WRRD, DO 248/323; LCD 110
by 1790	Bagby House, Woodhouse Ridge	NW	Ord	35	35	35	19	400 (1793)	Sun OS 392 611604
by 1790	Sheepscar Grove	NE	Whitelock, dyer	53 with mill	53	103	55	house, 500 (1790)	RE 20 119329
by 1790	Not located, Park Lane	NW	Lodge	15	15	15	15	680 (1793)	Sun CS 2 620327
by 1790	Carlton Lodge, Woodhouse Lane	NW	Clayton, merchant	11	21	22	20		
by 1790	Carr House, Little London	NW	Wilson, merchant	10	10	10	10		
1791–92	Belle Vue, Burley Road	NW	Wainhouse, merchant	–	21	21	25		Sun CS 2 620636
1792	Not named, Skinner Lane	NE	Paley, soap manufacturer	–	28 (pair)	28	28	800, pair (1792)	Sun OS 391 608640
1792	Lovell House, Sheepscar Lane	NE	Lupton, merchant	–	9	10	41	300, unfinished (1792)	Sun OS 388 605086
1792	Sheepscar [Cottage] House	NE	Cadman, tobacco manufacturer	–	12	12	18	460 (1792)	Sun OS 388 605086; LCD 2948
1793	Campfield Lodge			–	–	–	–		
1790–95	Carlton Hill, Woodhouse Lane	NW	Shann, cloth dresser	–	11	11	11		

(*continued overleaf*)

TABLE 10.1 (*continued*)

Date,	Name and location, with Division*		Owner	Rateable value, £				Insured value, £	References
				1790	1795	1800	1805		
1790–95	Carlton House, Woodhouse Lane	NW	Bramley, merchant	–	13	13	13	600 (1803)	Sun CS 55 753764
c.1795	Springfield House, Little Woodhouse	NW	Livesey, merchant	–	22	22	22	2000 (1805)	Sun CS 70 784204
1791–95	St James Lodge, Woodhouse Lane	NW	Appleby, merchant	–	–	?	33	3400 (1801)	Sun CS 40 719154
1792–95	[No Name], Long Balk Lane	NE	Turner, merchant	–	17	41	43		WRRD, GX 419/546; LCD 16276
1796	Beech Grove, Woodhouse Lane	NW	Murgitroyd, merchant	–	–	13	18	800, unfinished (1796)	Sun CS 14 654911; ULD 4
1797	Wintoun House, Sheepscar Lane	NE	Darnton tobacco manufacturer	–	–	22	22		
1795–1800	Long Balk (Elmwood) House, Long Balk Lane	NW	Lapage, drysalter	–	–	17	17		LCD 22840
1795–1800	Park Lane	NW	Spence, merchant	–	–	13	38		
1799	Beech Grove House, Woodhouse Lane	NW	Rhodes, merchant	–	–	–	39	1300 (1804)	Sun CS 63 771349; ULD 2
by 1800	Grafton House, Sheepscar Lane	NE	Fountaine, merchant	–	–	15	18		
1802	Hill Top [Ridge House], Woodhouse Lane	NW	Grainger, merchant	–	–	–	28		WRRD, FF 126/179 'newly erected', 1804; ULD 192
1803	Claypit House, Claypit Lane	NW	Briggs, merchant	–	–	–	24		LCD 16301
by 1814	Yeadon House, Woodhouse Lane	NW	Shepherd, merchant	–	–	–	–		LCD 8445

* The following houses at or near Woodhouse Bar are excluded: Jowitt's house, Wade Lane (1778); Turner's, Wade Lane (by 1790); Miss Blayds's, Woodhouse Lane (by 1790); Wormald's, Woodhouse Bar (by 1790); Howarth's, Wade Lane (1792–95). The South Division is also excluded: it had large detached houses, some dating from the early eighteenth century and with large rateable values (e.g. Smithson, Meadow Lane £77 in 1790) suggesting workshops. Chadwick's Lodge (£11 in 1790) still survives near Crown Point Bridge. It was built between 1800 and 1803 (Joshua Tetley & Co., Archive, MS.115).

Sheepscar, although, as Table 10.1 shows, the erection of this type of house was actually coming to an end while Whitaker was writing, to be supplemented and succeeded by the terraces and streets which form the subject of the second section of this Chapter.

A 'dread of smoke' is familiar from the previous Chapter. On the extreme south-west of Little Woodhouse the villa at St Peter's Well on Burley Road was advertised in 1811 as 'being on the West Side [it] is seldom or ever incommoded by smoke.'[7] Of Woodhouse Lane, which ran through the middle of this desirable territory, the *Leeds Guide* of 1806 wrote: 'From the elevated situation . . . and the fine prospect it affords of Airedale combined with its freedom from smoke of manufactories it has become a favourite place for building on, especially genteel detached houses'.[8] Fields on the east side of Woodhouse Lane near its junction with Blackman Lane were advertised in the *Intelligencer* of 7 September 1795 as 'Capital Building Land. That large close . . . which from its nearness to the Town, its airy and healthful situation, is very eligible for Building upon. It commands most beautiful picturesque and extensive Prospects to the South, South-East and South-West'. Thus a villa owner, though so near to town, could not only feel that his immediate surroundings were still country-like but that he was incorporated in the whole Yorkshire countryside through the view of woods and fields across the Aire.

The hamlet of Little Woodhouse had its own manor house, rebuilt as a residence for Christopher Thompson on a new site in 1740, and subsequently enlarged.[9] When it was advertised for sale in the *Intelligencer* of 18 January 1791 readers were told that it stood 'upon a delightful Eminence, and commands a most extensive and beautiful Prospect which cannot be interrupted by any Buildings or Plantations' – hardly true since Belmont had been built in the next field to the east after negotiating a right of access to share the private carriage way up from Park Lane to the manor house.[10] Yet almost half the forty houses which can be placed in the villa category were built before any smoke was emitted from Park Mill, so that if there was indeed a 'dread' before 1792 it could only have been inspired by dyehouse smoke from Drony Laith.

It has been shown in the last Chapter that the villas were not peopled by refugees from the first West End but by an independent migration from the town centre, Meadow Lane and Hunslet Lane;

[7] *LI*, 13 May 1811.
[8] *Leeds Guide*, p.116.
[9] WRRD, E 22/20; LCA, DB 204/3, f.219; DB 5/2 and 5/18.
[10] LCA, DB 6, unsorted.

TABLE 10.2(a)

Rateable Values of Park Estate Houses compared with Villas, 1800

	under £10	11–15	16–20	21–25	26–30	31–35	36–40	over 40
Park Estate								
62 houses	0	37	19	5	–	–	–	1
	–	(61%)	(31%)	(8%)	–	–	–	(1%)
39 villas	4	10	4	7	3	2	2	7
	(10%)	(25%)	(10%)	(17%)	(8%)	(5%)	(5%)	(17%)

Source: LCA, LORB 36.

TABLE 10.2(b)

Insured Values of Seventeen Villas, 1778–1805

£1–500	£501–1000	£1001–2000	£2001–3000	over £3000
3	8	3	1	2
(18%)	(48%)	(18%)	(6%)	(12%)

Sources: Sun Insurance Co. and Royal Exchange policies; *see also* Table 10.1 above.

FIG. 10.1 THE VILLAS OF THE SECOND WEST END IN LITTLE WOODHOUSE, 1800

In 1800 almost every field was occupied by a detached villa and its grounds; the untouched group of fields in the centre were Wade Preston's Brogden Closes where his heiress and neice, Julia Silly (Mrs Lyddon) was later to embark on a troubled development of villas (Preston House and Virginia (Cottage (now Lyddon Hall)) and terraces (Lyddon Terrace and Beech Grove Terrace (*see* Fig. 10.10)).

Key: A: Great Woodhouse Hall (*see* Fig. 10.2); B: Ridge House; C: Bagby Lodge; D: Woodhouse Lodge; E: Beech Grove House; F: Beech Grove (*see* Fig. 10.3); G: Hillary House; H: Denison Hall (*see* Fig. 10.6); I: Claremont; J: Little Woodhouse Hall; K: Springfield House; L: Belle Mount (Belmont); M: Springfield Lodge; N: Mount Pleasant; O: St James Lodge; P: Portland House.

In 1988 (E), (H), (I), (J) and (K) were still standing, together with Belle Vue to the south-west of Denison Hall.

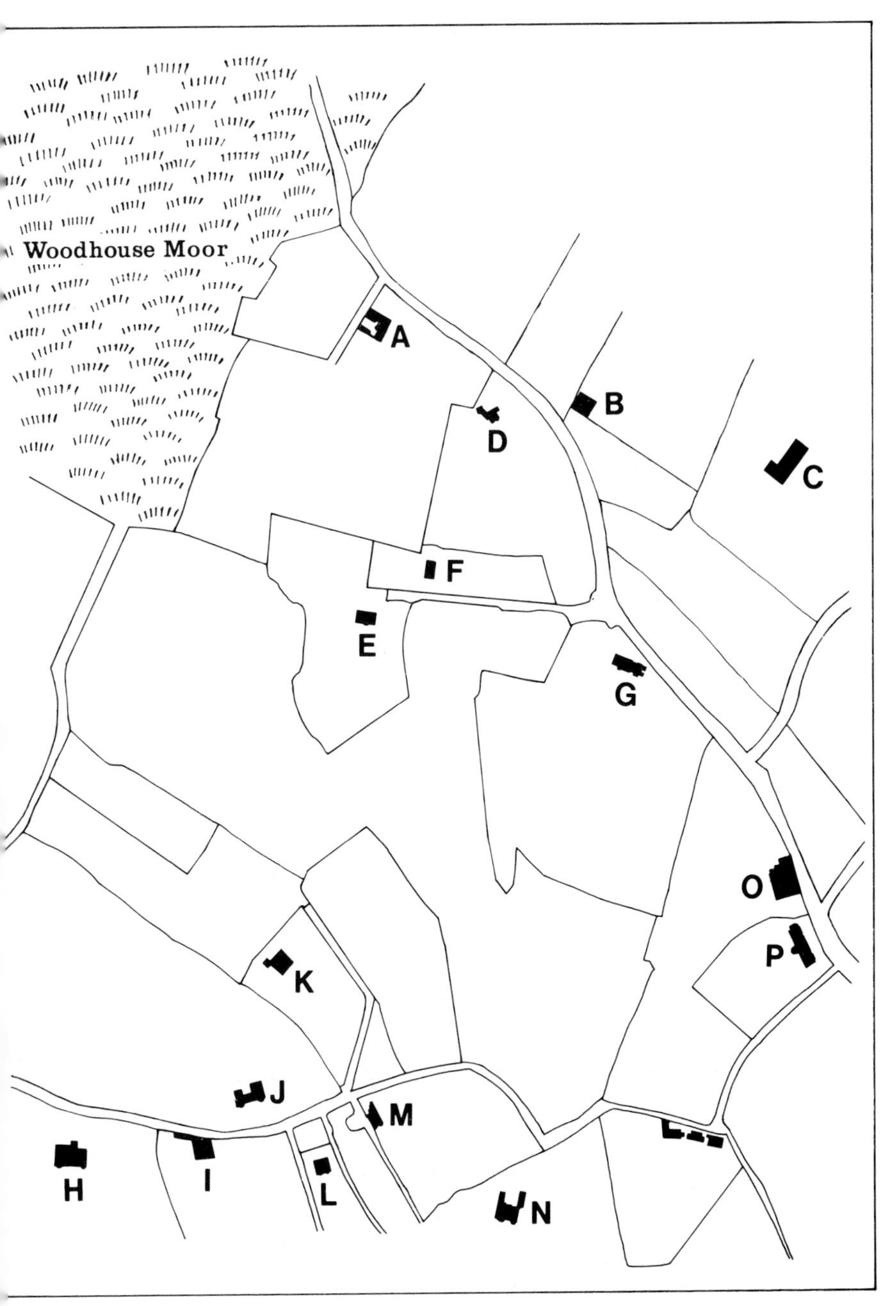
Woodhouse Moor
A
B
C
D
E
F
G
H
I
J
K
L
M
N
O
P

and their chronology is very similar to that of the Park estate, beginning in the late seventeen-sixties and continuing only to the late seventeen-nineties.

The villas, Denison Hall excepted, did not have the dimensions of true country houses but they were certainly larger and had more outbuildings than could be accommodated on a West End building plot. Their comparative cost is difficult to establish in the absence of building accounts, and when they changed hands the conveyances usually recorded a single sum for house and land together, but the contrast with the Park estate can be seen in their greater insured and rateable values in Table 10.2(a) and (b). An ambition to be a villa owner certainly needed to be matched by a longer purse than that of a leaseholder building on the Park estate, for there were also the costs incurred by the ambition to have a 'rood of land' as surrounds to the villa. Nor was Whitaker's poetic rood exactly that of the surveyor's quarter-acre: the smallest fields available for purchase as villa sites measured four or five roods, and if a country residence was to be made by converting one of the farmsteads in what Whitaker called 'the skirts of Leeds' an even larger area of land was involved (Fig. 10.1).

The agricultural land of the northern Divisions necessarily had its farmhouses, and there were one or two manor houses. Both Great and Little Woodhouse had their Halls with attributes fitting them for merchant residences or for conversion: they were large enough to house a family, with servants and spare rooms for guests, and they possessed what was increasingly being seen as an element in any 'desire of comfort', that is not only a healthy site with a good view, but isolation from an immediate neighbour. The back windows of

---

FIG. 10.2 FROM MANOR HOUSE TO VILLA: GREAT WOODHOUSE HALL, 1799

Redrawn by John Dixon from no. 97 in John Russell's Sketch Book 'H' (1795–1801). The house was not named by the artist other than as 'Mr Sawyer's', but was located as 'the last house on the left at the top of the hill' in no. 40 of the same sketch book which is a closer view of the main piers of the double gates with cornices and urns, looking across a road (Woodhouse Lane) over fields towards Buslingthorpe windmill. Russell's diary for 1801 records that Mr Sawyer 'took me to see . . . the Sunday Schools on Woodhouse Moor'.

Just short of the Moor, on the south side of Woodhouse Lane, was Great Woodhouse Hall, built *c.*1720 by Thomas Pease and inherited by his granddaughter, Elizabeth Taylor, who married Colonel St George Dalley in 1771 (ULD 218). A large house with an identical plan and double gates is shown on the five-foot OS plan, and the identification confirmed by the rate book of 1800 when Mrs Dalley's tenants were 'Sayer [i.e. Sawyer] and Co.': in size and general appearance the Hall closely resembled Little Woodhouse Hall. It was subsequently extended and tenemented but demolished in 1958 for the University's Mechanical Engineering building.

Great Woodhouse Hall (Fig. 10.2) looked over an area large enough to become the later Leeds General Cemetery, now re-christened St George's Fields.[11] Little Woodhouse Hall was built almost alongside Kendal Lane, the slender focus of that hamlet, but there were seventeen acres of field land behind it extending northwards over what are now Clarendon Road and Hyde Terrace.[12] From Drony Laith was farmed all the western half of the Park estate, and further west the fields to the boundary with Burley were farmed from North Hall which by 1774 was regarded as a suitable residence for John Beckett, 'gentleman'; Sheepscar Grove may also have been a farmhouse before an industrial complex developed in the mid-eighteenth century around the water mill.

Claremont, just across Kendal Lane from Little Woodhouse Hall, may have originated as an older house serving the western half of an estate divided into two when Little Woodhouse Hall was rebuilt (Fig. 4.1). When John Elam was offering to lease it in September 1778 it had 'about 15 acres of Grass Land, lying before the House, which commands an extensive Prospect, beautifully interspersed with Villages, Woods, Gentlemen's Seats etc., etc., and through which run in View the River Air [*sic*] and the Leeds and Liverpool Canal'. A stop press addition suggests that Elam suspected that fifteen acres, even with the view, might be more than prospective customers would fancy: 'The following addition to the Advertisement of Mr. Elam's House at Little-Woodhouse, inserted in the first page, came too late to be added in its proper place, viz., "That the Premises will be sold for £4000 or let for £160 per Ann. and a more or less quantity of Land will be let with the house, if required"'.[13]

There was extensive agricultural land in Burmantofts and in the East Division with its farmhouses on York Road and Pontefract Lane (Fig. 4.2) which might have made gentlemen's houses had they been more salubriously positioned: no villas were attempted east of town. In the South Division there was an old manor house at Austrop Hall but its twelve acres of farmland had been overwhelmed with industry by the end of the eighteenth century and the

[11] Plan of the estate, 1796: LCA, DB Map 389; photograph of interior before demolition: LCLLH, C.LIE. Woodhouse, nos. 1–4; the full estate covered thirteen acres.

[12] Plan, 1732: LCA, DB 5/18; Jeremiah Harrison Estate Act, 1794: *Acts Local and Personal, 34 Geo.III cap. 14*; the estate covered fifteen acres.

[13] *LI*, 15 Sept. 1778; for an account of the house see B. and D. Payne, *Claremont* (Leeds, 1980).

TABLE 10.3

Rateable Values of Land adjoining Detached Houses, 1800

	Rateable value		Area, where known, in acres
	Land £ s.	Buildings £ s.	
Drony Laith	34 18	40	–
Little Woodhouse Hall	26 15	15	17¼
Denison Hall	22 10	82	13
Elmwood House	17 5	17	10
Carlton House	14 15	13	–
Claremont	12 7	16 10	–
Ridge House	12	15	9¼
Great Woodhouse Hall	11 3	15	–
Carr House	11 10	12 10	–
Bagby Lodge	11	40	–
Claypit House	9 14	10	–
Springfield House	7 13	15	–
Belmont	7 3	15	5
Woodhouse Lodge	7 0	11	5¼
Grafton House	6 10	15	–
Belle Vue	5	12 10	3½
Lovell House	5	10	–
St James Lodge	4	20	–
Sheepscar Cottage	4	12	–
Sheepshanks House	4	30	–
Grove House	3 10	20	–
Wintoun House	3 10	15	–
Beech Grove House	3 4	12 10	2
Campfield House	1 15	20	–
Vauxhall House	1 10	8	–
Turner, Long Balk Lane	1	16	–
Park House	1	10	–
Paley, Skinner Lane	nil	28 (pair)	–

Source: LCA, LORB 36.

Hall turned into tenements.[14] Water Hall, with 24 acres,[15] and the 'capital messuage' in Simpson's Fold, with 2¼ acres,[16] probably originated as small manor houses, and from the late seventeenth century there were roadside houses along Meadow Lane and Hunslet Lane, fit for residence by some of the more important merchants a century later but not augmented by further building of villas in what, in any case, was a constricted area.

The rate books do not record the area of land surrounding each house but since buildings and land paid different sums per pound of annual value it was necessary to enter the two values in separate columns: thus the single field in which Vauxhall House had been built was rated at £3 in 1774 and the house at £14; while in the same year Drony Laith was rated at £26 and its field at £145; North Hall at £28 and its fields at £107; Claremont at £25 and its fields at £25. Table 10.3 shows the position after the invasion by villas was almost complete. The value of the Drony Laith industrial buildings had increased and the area of its fields been diminished by sales so that the 'land' and 'buildings' assessments were now almost equal; the Claremont estate had also been diminished but some of its former fields contributed to the 'land' assessments at Denison Hall and Belmont.

The smaller land values in Table 10.3 belong to the true villas, not farms and manor houses but purpose built. These, whether along the Harrogate turnpike (Sheepscar Lane) or the Otley turnpike (Woodhouse Lane) were erected in single fields purchased for the occasion, and as has been shown[17] there were many fields of some two or three acres abutting on both turnpikes (Fig. 1.6). Two such fields at Town's End had been taken for the Denison houses at the beginning of the century.

No further progress was made along Sheepscar Lane until about 1788 but the frontage of Wade Lane outside the north bar was first occupied by houses during the seventeenth century.[18] One of these must have been the 'Handsome fashionable House, with Packing and Dressing Shops, a Stable, Garden and Croft in Woodhouse Lane' advertised in the *Mercury* of 12 September 1727. Later the new straight line of the turnpike in 1754 would cut diagonally across the

[14] LCD 4598. The Hall was probably that shown by Cossins in 1725 as Douglas's: E. Wilson, 'Two Old Plans of Leeds', *PTh.S*, IX (1899), 200.

[15] *LM*, 10 March 1728; 25 Jan. 1731; 12 Aug. 1788.

[16] LCD 18089.

[17] See above, p. 19

[18] For the large house here, known as 'Wade Hall' see G. D. Lumb, 'The Old Hall', *PTh.S*, XXVI (1924), 17.

fields, giving convenient small areas to accommodate frontage houses and backsides workshops.

The turnpike's toll gate was set further out of town beyond Blackman Lane (Fig. 10.10), encouraging residential and commercial development between the new and old bars: in Tuke's map of 1781 half a dozen houses cluster near the old bar although no record of their character survives; the transition to roadside villas is shown in two properties on the west side of the Lane which were separated from each other and from town by intervening closes of grazing or tenter ground. Portland House, so named by the Quaker export merchants, the Elams, was already erected when the rate assessment of 1774 was made and the Blayds' family house with the more mundane name of Claypit House was first recorded in 1778. The 'little landscape' of the Elam house occupied one whole close but Blayds acquired several contiguous closes (Fig. 9.1); near to the town bar was a smaller and older roadside house which seems to have served as a residence for various spinsters and widows of the Blayds family after Claypit House was built.[19] After the older Elam moved to Roundhay and his brother to Claremont the Woodhouse Lane property was advertised as

> to be Lett to the Best Bidder . . . for a term not exceeding 17 years . . . a good and commodious Dwelling-house, pleasantly situated by the Road Side, leading from Leeds to Woodhouse wherein Mr. Samuel Elam deceased lately dwelt . . . also at the Back a close of Land, containing about 2 acres, and a neat Garden planted with divers Sorts of choice Fruit Trees, with a Hot-House and Fish-Pond therein.[20]

We have already seen in Chapter Seven that a field north of Portland House was taken by a building club with ambitions a flight above those in the East End, advertised in February 1789 as:

> Leeds Building Club, St. James Street, Woodhouse Lane. To be lett, Several convenient new-built dwelling houses of different descriptions, fit to accommodate either small or large genteel families . . . in a

[19] LCA, DB 179.

[20] *LM*, 15 Sept. 1778; RE 8 90478 (1784); Sun OS 357 549557 (1788).

FIG. 10.3 A VILLA OF THE SECOND WEST END: BEECH GROVE (1796–1884)
(*following two pages*)

(a) a view from the east by the manufacturing chemist and amateur artist John Bilbrough, 5 June 1884, with the note: 'they began to pull it down June 12th in the afternoon'.

(b) the demolition in progress 'as it appeared on June 19th 1884': a southern view from John Bilbrough's sketch book. The demolition allowed the Yorkshire College to extend its buildings westwards towards Woodhouse Lane. (Bilbrough's 'Beech Grove House' should be Beech Grove; Beech Grove House still stands in the grounds of the University Union.)

Beech Grove House — Mr Lawson's (front view)
John Bilbrough June 5th 1884

(a)

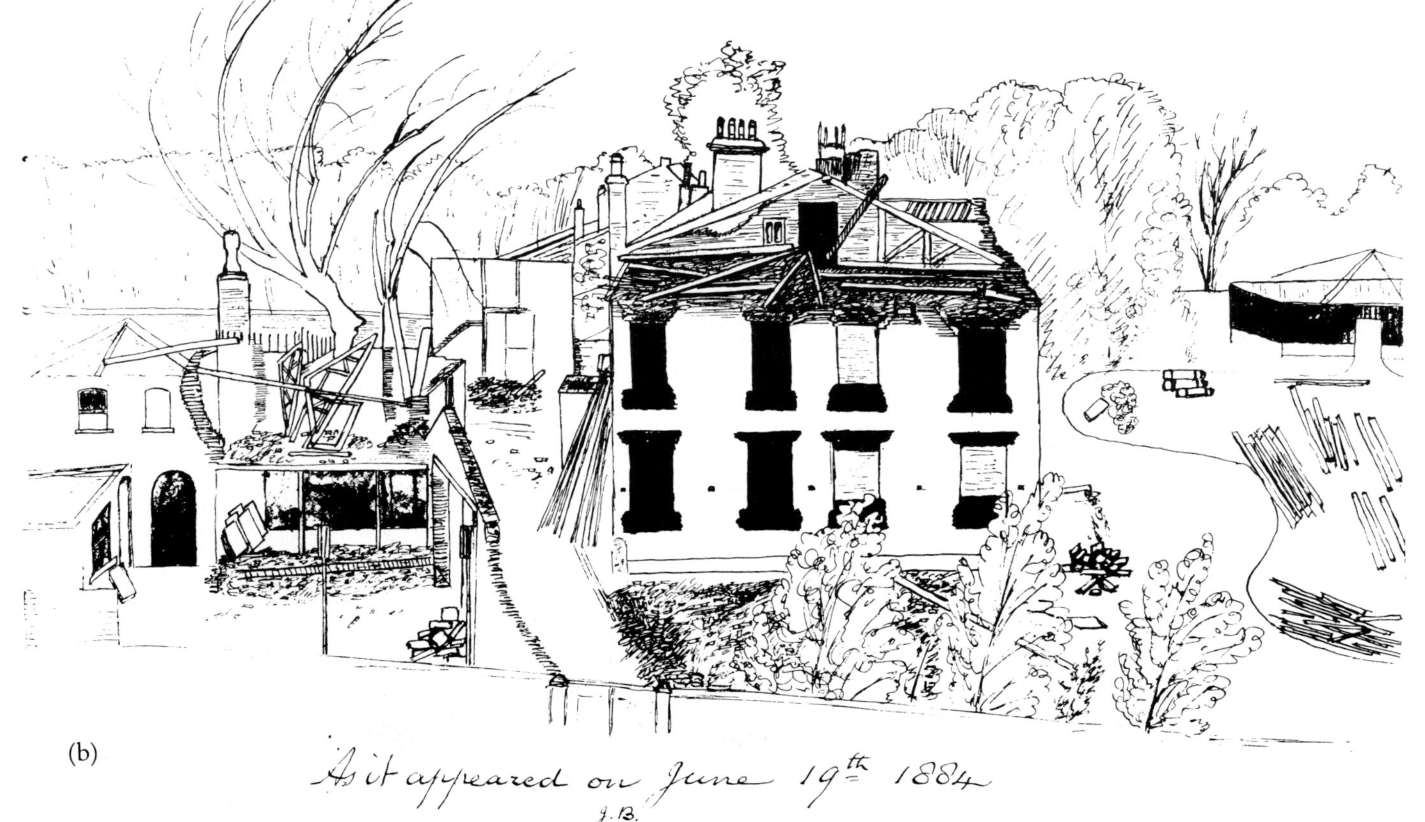
As it appeared on June 19th 1884
J.B.

(b)

pure and salubrious air, free from the noxious vapours and putrid exhalations which the greater part of the town of Leeds and the new-erected buildings therein are subject to.[21]

In the 1798 *Leeds Directory* six merchants had addresses at Woodhouse Bar but thirty-two in Woodhouse Lane. Between 1791 and 1795 St James Lodge was erected in the field immediately north of the incomplete St James Street,[22] and the line of villas continued on the western side of Woodhouse Lane past Ridge (Hillary) House (1790)[23] to Beech Grove (1796) (Fig. 10.3(a) and (b)), Beech Grove House (1799),[24] and Woodhouse Grove (1789)[25] with its carriage way crossing the field to enter the Lane on the town side of the toll bar. The surrounds of Beech Grove House were described in 1805, when the house was six years old, as 'Pleasure Grounds agreeably laid out, Plantations, Gardens, Peach House and Stoves, well stocked with choice Fruit; also a Coach House and Stabling for Five Horses, and about Two Acres of Garden contigous'.[26]

The north–south axes of most of the Little Woodhouse closes made it possible for the villas to have a southern aspect from their back windows, looking down the hill slopes; the Sheepscar Lane villas, where the closes ran east–west, had to be placed sideways on to the road if they were to have the best aspect but this did enable their front rather than their back rooms to have the most desirable aspect; the eastern aspect was less pleasing, with the dyehouses of Sheepscar Beck and the tanneries of Skinner Lane only a quarter mile away. This group of villas also knew something of that inapprehension of possible consequences already noticed in the East End[27] for some of the villa owners who also had land on the east side of the Lane were willing to sell it to be laid out in smaller building plots for the Leylands streets.

The solitude of the villa, so very different from the tight architectural grouping within Park Place and the even tighter inward-looking life of the two West End squares, had to be reconciled with access. There was stabling for five horses at Claremont, for eight at St James Lodge and six carriage houses with stabling for eighteen horses at Little Woodhouse Hall: these horses

21 *LI*, 2 Feb. 1789.

22 LCD 12170; *LM*, 22 Feb. 1791.

23 *LM*, 10 April 1802.

24 Beech Grove: LCA, DB 43/2; ULD 4 and 38; Sun CS 14 654911 (May 1796), 'unfinished'. Beech Grove House: ULD 3.

25 ULD 4.

26 *LI*, 1 April 1805. In 1806 the *Leeds Guide* (p.83) wrote of Woodhouse Lane: 'a favourite place for building on, especially genteel detached houses'.

27 See above, p.253

and carriages needed access to a public highway while the finishing, packing and press shops together with the warehouses that lay behind the villas all presupposed access.

For the roadside villas of Woodhouse Lane and Sheepscar Lane their front gardens of lawn and shrubbery would have a single or looped carriage drive. The scale of the five-foot Ordnance Survey plan, surveyed in 1847, is large enough to show all these little landscapes of the late eighteenth century still intact: at the rear of the villa the two-acre closes gave room for gardens in which fruit trees seem to have been favoured as useful decoration. Claremont had a hot-air greenhouse 22 yards long; Little Woodhouse Hall had a 'hot wall' 80 yards long, presumably the present perimeter wall to the north.

Any villa occupying fields that did not abut upon a highway needed to find access over adjacent fields in the same ownership or otherwise to negotiate a right of way. At the very last stage of villa building in this area, Mrs Lyddon's development on the Brogden Closes necessitated traffic from the isolated Preston Lodge coming north across the closes and into Beech Grove Terrace before it could reach Woodhouse Lane.[28] When she acquired more land to the west for Virginia Cottage, the never-completed Lyddon Terrace, and the abortive Mount Preston she had to devise a network of projected streets to serve them, just as Paley and Wilson had had to do in the past (Fig. 10.10).

Of the villas in Little Woodhouse only Vauxhall House in Park Lane and St Peter's Hill in Burley Road had access to a major thoroughfare.[29] The very steep rise of the valley side on the north of Burley Road prevented any access to the fields on the St John's estate west of Belle Vue which remained the westernmost house until Westfield Road was developed for ordinary street housing in the eighteen-sixties. Belle Vue had to have a long curving drive to surmount the cliff, and it is perhaps significant that Michael Wainhouse's workshops and warehouse[30] were placed, not near the house itself, but at the Park Lane entrance to the drive.[31]

[28] Plan of 1739: ULD 6. For the Lyddon estate development see pp. 355–58 below.

[29] LCD 84337; some of the grounds of Vauxhall House, Park Lane were taken *c.* 1826 for Hanover Place and the remainder in 1847 for Hanover Square chapel, the ground floor of which survives in 1987 as a ruin; see below, p. 355, n. 106.

[30] LCD 3027 with plan of mill; description in WRRD, RS 138/121.

[31] Sun CS 2 620326. The declivity is now marked by the level access from Hanover Square to the roof of the car park which has replaced Little Woodhouse Mill. Wainhouse's villa, Belle Vue, has been restored but is invisible from below in Burley Road.

Little Woodhouse Hall, Claremont, Belmont, and Denison Hall were built alongside the two narrow lanes, Cankerwell and Kendal, which reached the hamlet of Little Woodhouse in a meandering course which served before the turnpike was constructed in 1754 as the way from Leeds to the Moor and Otley. As the length of Kendal Lane behind Claremont still shows, these were narrow lanes hardly suited to waggons and carriages. In turn the new houses acquired direct carriage ways down the hill to Park Lane. From Little Woodhouse Hall, rebuilt on its new site about 1740, a quarter-mile long drive, five yards wide, was laid out in 1742 making a direct line to Park Lane: despite interruption by the Inner Ring Road and the hospital buildings a length of this road with its stone setts survives as Chorley Lane between Belmont Grove and Clarendon Road. When Frederick Oates built Belmont in 1786 an additional agreement was made, reciting that of 1742, to give

> full and free liberty for Frederick Oates to pass and repass at all times and on all occasions both on foot and on horseback or with horses, carts and carriages into and over a certain way lying on the east side of the premises of John Elam at Little Woodhouse to the closes lately purchased by Frederick Oates and his brother Joseph Oates.[32]

Similarly Springfield Lodge is shown in the Giles plan of 1815 with its own drive to Leighton Lane, while Mount Pleasant had another running along a line as straight as any surveyor's ruler directly into Park Lane.

Sheepscar Lane, Long Balk Lane and Claypit Lane – all ancient access ways to the common fields – were so placed as to give natural access to any field immediately north of the town that would be taken over for a villa, but on the ridge to the east of Woodhouse Lane beyond the toll bar it was necessary to make arrangements for access to the interior. Thus when fields between Carlton Lodge and Woodhouse Lane were being offered for sale in June 1796 the carriage way across them was retained: 'A Close of Ground, called the Upper New Close, adjoining Woodhouse Lane, containing One Acre Three Roods and Twelve Perches, or thereabouts . . . With this Lot will be sold the Carriage Road leading up to the Dwelling House occupied by Mr Clayton, subject to Mr Clayton's Right of passing with Carriages thereon'.[33]

The costs of acquiring such solitude were not trivial. The villa itself cost as much, if not more, than a Park estate house and the grounds might cost at least as much as the house. The westernmost

[32] Wayleave, 15 July 1786 in LCA, DB 6, unsorted.
[33] *LM*, 25 June 1796.

of the Little Woodhouse villas was Belle Vue, to build which Michael Wainhouse acquired 3½ acres in February 1792 at £390 an acre;[34] in Woodhouse Lane near the turnpike bar the two acres for Beech Grove and its ground were purchased in April 1796 for £300 an acre;[35] nearby in October 1788 John Hebblethwaite had paid £2000 (£216 an acre) for closes extending over 9¼ acres, and in 1795 he added three more acres to extend the ground of his newly-built Ridge (later Hillary) House.[36] When Thomas Coupland contracted in 1793 to buy the Little Woodhouse Hall estate he was ready to pay £300 an acre, and on his bankruptcy in 1821 the house was valued at £3100 and the land surrounding it at £6595 (£388 an acre).[37]

The commodiousness, the cheerfulness and the comfort which Whitaker attributed to the villas had been expensively achieved, and such care was essentially that of an owner-occupier. 'Intended for his own use, unfinished' was the description of Ridge House when John Hebblethwaite first insured it in 1790.[38] Hebblethwaite retained his residence there for fifty years.[39] The first West End had a greater proportion of owner-occupiers than the old town, and in the rate books the villas of the second West End appear almost all as owner-occupied, with 'self' in the 'occupier' columns.

Once installed, a family was not easily dislodged, except by bankruptcy. Coupland lost Little Woodhouse Hall to his creditors in 1821 and Nicholson lost Claremont when the bank in which he was partner collapsed in 1818. There were lengths of occupancy which exceeded those already noted (Table 9.5) for some houses in Park Place. Much depended on the needs of the familial structure: a long-living head of household would have an eldest son who could establish his own residence elsewhere within his father's lifetime, and thus be unlikely to take over his father's house at death; if there were younger sons, a widow, or unmarried daughters, on the other hand, a second generation might be happy to retain occupation.[40]

Beech Grove House had effectively only two families as owners between its erection in 1799 for Abraham Rhodes and its sale to the

[34] LCA, DB 209/7.

[35] ULD 4.

[36] ULD 191.

[37] 1793: LCA, DB 5/3; bankruptcy valuation: PRO, B3/3975/3417/954.

[38] Sun OS 370 573802.

[39] *LM*, 4 Nov. 1793; 'Mr. Hebblethwaite's elegant stone house near the toll house': *Leeds Guide* (1806), p. 139; 'I lived in the house near the Toll Bar for 42 years': affidavit of 1 Oct. 1833: ULD 296.

[40] For a general statement of the importance of generational differences in Leeds see R. J. Morris, 'The Middle Class and the Property Cycle during the Industrial Revolution', in *Wealth and Stability*, ed. T. C. Smout (1979), pp.91–112.

University in 1925 by the heiress of that John Ogden Marsh who bought the house from Rhodes in 1840: she, together with her elder sister, came to the house with their father in 1840 as a girl of three and died there in 1925. The beneficiaries of her will were scattered over England and were glad to accede to her wish that the University be given first refusal.[41] Between 1896 and 1925 the Yorkshire College (subsequently the University of Leeds) had accumulated property around Beech Grove House from its original base in the grounds of the other villa, Beech Grove (1796) which came on the market in 1877 when the engineer John Lawson reached retiring age and no longer needed to go down daily to his Mabgate works. The College's first buildings were erected in the garden of Beech Grove, leaving the villa for other uses until the ground was needed for the Dyeing Department[42] in 1884: Fig. 10.3(a) is a drawing of 'Mr. Lawson's House' from John Bilbrough's sketch book (1884), just before the demolition.[43]

The architectural form of the villas can be seen now only in Little Woodhouse although a number of them survived in the North East Division until after 1945 and are recorded in photographs. Of the earliest period Little Woodhouse Hall and Claremont are not badly obscured by Victorian additions and alterations; of the period 1785–1800 Belle Vue (1791–92) has been carefully restored and preserved in a setting of modern houses; Springfield House (*c.*1795) has been skilfully welded into architecture fit for laboratories and workshops; Beech Grove House (1799) is intact within the grounds of the University Union; and Denison Hall (1786) stands proudly overlooking Hanover Square.[44]

No villa, as far as is known, was erected by a speculative builder: the capital outlay was too large and the customer demand too specific. Yet even though each villa was *sui generis* the canons of good taste gave them a classical conformity in architectural style, setting them apart from the proliferations of fancy which were to mark the next generation of villas in Victorian Headingley, Chapel Allerton and Potternewton. Photographs of Belle Vue, Claremont and Springfield House survive to point this conformity.

The two largest detached houses, Little Woodhouse Hall and Denison Hall, were exceptional in drifting early into being tenanted. Their size placed them in an awkward corner of the property market

[41] ULD 3.

[42] M. W. Beresford, 'Red Brick and Portland Stone', in P. H. J. H. Gosden and A. J. Taylor, eds, *Studies in the History of a University* (Leeds, 1975), pp. 133–80.

[43] Sketch books: LCA, Town deposit.

[44] See above, p. 303

especially in the less happy years between 1803 and 1815. In 1806 the *Leeds Guide* noted that Woodhouse House (that is, Denison Hall) was in no-man's land. 'It has remained untenanted for several years: it is too large for a man of moderate fortune and too near the town to be relished by the country gentlemen'.[45] A tenant was eventually found in Sir Richard Johnstone, Bart., who remained there until Denison sold the house in 1806. Johnstone was so firmly established that in 1816 Whitaker made the mistake of attributing the actual erection of the Hall to him:

> Since our Author's [i.e. Thoresby's] time the healthy and pleasant situation of this Hamlet of Little Woodhouse has occasioned the Erection of many Villas in a Style of Elegance to which he was a Stranger. All these, however, indeed every other Residence in the Parish, are eclipsed by an House erected by the late Sir Richard Johnston [*sic*].[46]

A large house could be divided into two for tenanting: the manufacturers Gott and Jowitt each occupied half of Denison Hall through the 1830s and 1840s, and Little Woodhouse Hall was divided for two tenants by 1794. Even though after its purchase by John Atkinson in 1821 there was only a single owner, the front and back gardens of the Hall both bore the scars of previous division in the form of partition walls, one of which still straddles the present-day Dental Hospital's supplementary car-park. In English law the joint ownership of property, whether between business partners such as Wormald and Gott or between members of the same family, was an acceptable concept, but, as with flats earlier in the present century, the practitioners of conveyancing did not take easily to the idea of a once-unitary house being divided for sale to two different parties, and no example has yet come to light of a villa being divided for two purchasers.

Thus the larger houses tended to pass early and undivided into institutional ownership. Claremont was a nursing home before it became the headquarters of the Yorkshire Archaeological Society, the Thoresby Society and the Leeds Civic Trust. Little Woodhouse Hall was purchased by the city from the surgeon, William Hey, for the Judges' Lodging in 1864, and later it housed the former Teacher Training Department of the College of Art before a period of dereliction from which it has emerged, restored and gleaming, to be a medical residence for the Leeds Hospital Authority. At Beech Grove House will be found part of the University's School of

[45] *Leeds Guide*, p.84.
[46] Whitaker, *Ducatus*, p.93, n.

Education, and Belle Vue has been restored as a private students' residence within a redeveloped housing estate on Westfield Road. Springfield House in turn was restored in 1983 as the centrepiece of a home for High Technology. Mrs Lyddon's Preston Lodge is also within the University campus, housing (in 1988) the Department of Virology, and Virginia Cottage is now the warden's house within the hall of residence which bears Mrs Lyddon's name, its residents no doubt grateful that she did not remain Miss Silly all her life.

What even these surviving buildings cannot show, however, is a full range of original outbuildings, for only fragments survive: part of the north-west wing of Claremont at the end of Claremont Avenue; outbuildings to the north-west of Denison Hall, together with much of its boundary wall to Kendal Lane and to the former Claremont gardens; a boundary wall and gates from Little Woodhouse Hall, and part of the Park Lane frontage wall to Vauxhall House.

Thus they misleadingly appear to be solely residences whereas all, from Denison Hall down to the smallest, were designed to combine home and their finishing shops in the continuing tradition of Leeds merchants before they aspired to be gentlemen. These workshops, warehouses and counting houses appear alongside the villas in the fire insurance registers and are sometimes specified in the rate books; sale advertisments would always specify such an asset. They can also be recognised on the large-scale maps as separate buildings within the villa precincts, often lining one side of the close in which the villas had been built. Thus the catalogue for the sale of the bankrupt Richard Lee's St James Lodge on 28 September 1809 offered as Lot 1:

	a.	r.	p.
A CAPITAL MESSUAGE, situate in Woodhouse Lane, with Stabling for Eight Horses, Coach House, Saddle House, Brew House, Laundry, and other Attached and Detached Offices, a spacious Court or Area planted with Trees and Shrubs, forming a convenient and ornamental Approach and Carriage Road to the House and containing .	0	1	28
PLANTATIONS, PLEASURE GROUND and PADDOCK, contiguous to the House, containing	5	1	9
FREEHOLD PART of the GARDEN, containing	0	0	21
COMPTING HOUSE, WAREHOUSE, CROPPING CHAMBERS, ROW-SHOPS, DRAWING CHAMBERS, WOOL WAREHOUSE, with SPACIOUS ROOMS for many other Mercantile Purposes, near to, but all Detached and separated from the House, and which may either be occupied with it or let off, as best may suit the convenience of a Purchaser. In the			

> Occupation of Messrs. Richard Lee and Thomas Lee, and containing together with the Road to the Garden, and the Freehold Part of the Tenter Ground 0 2 7
>
> A Small but Convenient DWELLING HOUSE in the Plantation, suited for the Residence of a confidential Servant and his Family, in the Occupation of John Beckwith 7 1 25
>
> The preceding Property forms together the most complete eligible and valuable Situation in the Town or Neighbourhood of LEEDS, for the Residence of a Merchant of large Family and of extensive Business. The Buildings are all nearly New and in complete Repair, and admit of being occupied either altogether by a Merchant who is desirous of having the whole of his Business carried on, from the Warehousing and Preparation of the Raw Material, to the complete Finishing and Packing of his Goods, under his own Eye; or by letting off the Warehouses, Mill and Shops, which are at present quite Detached, the House, Offices and Grounds about it, will form a Residence extremely convenient, and suitable for a large genteel Family, either in or out of Business, who are desirous of living near the Town of Leeds.[47]

A year earlier Earl Cowper's 'neat modern villa', Woodhouse Lodge, had 'a cotton spinning and packing House built by the tenant';[48] another villa had

> An extensive DOUBLE WAREHOUSE, containing Two Counting Houses, Packing Shops, Press Shops, with every other Convenience for carrying on an extensive Business, with about Two Acres of Land lying contiguous, and about Thirty Yards of Tenters, and an excellent and never failing Spring of Water (alone worth a Thousand Pounds), adjoining the Warehouse.[49]

At Hill Top (later Ridge House) in 1813:

> Adjoining the same is a large strong-built Warehouse, 19 yards long and 13 yards deep, four stories high; and near to this but separated from it, is another large Building 11 yards long and 9 yards deep, three stories high, used as a Dressing shop and Press house, capable of containing a great number of workmen.[50]

The sale notice of Springfield House in May 1799 was more explicit about the industrial importance of a private water supply:

[47] *Sale Particulars of the Estate of Richard Lee, 28–9 September 1809*: Thoresby Society Library; the sale must have been unsuccessful since the Mansion House was next advertised for sale by private contract: *LI*, 15 Jan. 1810.

[48] Herts. CRO, Cowper MS.T 4949.

[49] *LI*, 19 Nov. 1804.

[50] *LM*, 6 March 1813.

> A large well-built Warehouse, 27 yards by 12 properly divided, for Dressing, Packing-Shops etc ... By the lower Field is a Spring of Water that has never failed when all the Springs in the Neighbourhood have been dry, and the water is conveyed through the Dressing-Shops and is of the first consequence to any Merchant who wishes to dye his own Grain Colours, as it gives a superior softness in the finishing of Cloth.[51]

The conjunction of home and commerce was well demonstrated at Claremont. Firstly the house itself in the language of an advertisement by Lucas Nicholson in the *Intelligencer* for 19 July 1813:

> A Capital and Spacious Mansion House, well suited for the Accommodation of a Large and genteel Family, most delightfully situated at Little Woodhouse, within a few Minutes Walk of the Centre of the Town of Leeds, consisting of a Dining Room, Twenty Seven Feet by Eighteen; Drawing Room, Twenty one Feet by Eighteen, with a Marble Hearth, Chimney Piece, Register Stove etc; Breakfast Room, Twenty two Feet by Sixteen; Sexagon Library, Nineteen Feet, with Stone Safe and convenient Closets; Store Room, Eighteen feet by Twelve, completely fitted up with Closets, Drawers, Shelves and Hot Hearth Stove; Butler's Pantry, with useful Drawers and Closets, excellent Kitchen and back Kitchen with a complete Patent steam Kitchen, Oven, Grate and every other useful Fixture; Brewhouse with Set-Pots, Copper, Lead Cooler and a Pump, supplied from a never failing Spring of pure and soft Water which is also conveyed into a reservoir by Pipes into the Brewing vessels and Set Pots, and also into the Store Room and Butler's Pantry; Seven good Lodging Rooms, with Dressing Rooms to each, and Four Servants Rooms; a double Coach House, Stabling for Five Horses, and Cowhouse, Hothouse, Greenhouse and spacious Garden with an excellent South Wall about Eighty Yards long, partly filled and clothed with choice Fruit Trees; also a Paddock in Front of the House containing about Five Acres rich Meadow land surrounded with a Plantation in which various Fruit Trees are interspersed.

These domestic quarters are now transformed to house the libraries and meeting room of the Yorkshire Archaeological Society and the Thoresby Society, while the cellars – curiously not mentioned in the advertisement – have been fitted out as an archive repository where, among other things, Thoresby's own annotated copy of the *Ducatus* is stored for safety. The 'rich Meadow land' has now been taken for the houses of Woodhouse Square and the later Claremont streets but even in 1813 the southward view from the dining and drawing room windows ended in industrial premises, as Nicholson's own insurance policy of 27 November 1800 reveals: his

[51] *LM*, 17 May 1799.

house was then insured for £850, the contents for £540 and the outbuildings for another £450 but along the Park Lane frontage of the Paddock was a range of industrial premises occupied by Messrs Knubley and Wainwright:

> Packing Shop and Press Shop with the Workhouse and Chambers over, used for Spinning Woollen yarn and Weaving cloth by the Hand only: £600.
> Scouring Room, Ware Room and Drying House for Woollen Goods with the Chambers over the same used for Weaving Cloth by the Hand only: £200.
> Fulling and Scribbling Mill near: £600.
> Steam Engine House near: £100.
> Two Stables, Rowing Room and Brushing Room and the Chambers over used for shearing cloth: £300.[52]

Any garden ground of a 'little landscape' was always under threat from the prosperity and expansion of a merchant business that needed more and more workshop and warehouse accommodation: the extent of encroachment on to the 'cheerfulness' of the 'little landscape' of Claypit House into the garden and then into contiguous closes of the Blayds establishment can be seen in the plan of 1809 (Fig. 9.1).

Up to 1945 no villas had been demolished except Mount Pleasant, taken for the site of the present Leeds General Infirmary when the hospital was moved from the town centre to its present site in 1860, and Beech Grove, demolished in 1884 when the Yorkshire College's Dyeing Department was built. After 1945 the topography of the former villa territory was radically changed, producing not only the demolition of many villas, including all those from Sheepscar Lane, but the massive demolition of streets, rows and terraces. In Little Woodhouse the city council, while stopping short of calling the area a slum, took powers of compulsory purchase which enabled the area to be partitioned like some latter-day Poland for the benefit of the two campuses of the University and the Polytechnic, the Infirmary, the Medical School and the Inner Ring Road. This author assisted at a midnight wake promoted by the last tenant of Belmont on 7 March 1978, the eve of an eviction order,[53] with the contractors' bulldozers pawing the ground outside, the building being sacrificed so that

[52] RE 40 179636; it is not clear whether the firm's insurance of a warehouse for £500 a year earlier (RE 36 169535) was for one of these premises.

[53] Leeds County Court, Yorks. Regional Health Authority *v*. H. W. Hunter: order of 11 Jan. 1978; pre-demolition photographs of this Listed Building are in Royal Commission on Historical Monuments, England (National Monuments Record), 11/1814 (1976) and 14/192 (1977).

ambulances at the Clarendon Wing of the Leeds General Infirmary could have a clear turning circle. In Great Woodhouse and Sheepscar the cleared area was taken mainly for high-rise flats and then for neo-terrace housing although Sheepscar itself disappeared under a vast highway interchange. In its midst, sole survivor of its period and the repository for records of many early periods, is the Leeds office of the West Yorkshire Joint Archive Service, formerly the Sheepscar Branch Library.

THE SQUARES

The town centre of Leeds, like most English towns, had no open ornamental square, and the market-place which elsewhere often became a town's principal open space, had been subordinated in Leeds to the rival claims of traffic, culminating in the demolition of the Moot Hall and the transfer of the open-air market to the Vicar's Croft in 1826.[54] For public assemblies the yard of the Cloth Hall was the usual venue, with processions and demonstrations using the rather remote location of Woodhouse Moor, the traditional site of the town's annual fairs. Victoria Square, so small that few citizens today could locate it, did not appear until 1858 and City Square not until the end of the nineteenth century.[55]

Two residential squares were the centrepieces of the first West End and the form made a brief appearance in the East End at St Peter's Square but no square was created in the second West End until after villa building had come to a halt. Although projects for squares appeared alongside those for rows and terraces in the seventeen-nineties only three – Queen, Blenheim and Hanover – appear on Fowler's map of 1831. The regal and ducal names speak of their ambitions but all three had delayed starts followed by periods of stagnation; a fourth, Woodhouse Square, was several times promoted but had only a single house by 1831 and was not named by Fowler.

Queen Square was first projected in 1803 by the Bischoff brothers, John and George, who had owned Claypit House and adjoining closes since 1787. (This was not the same Claypit House as the Blayds' in Woodhouse Lane.) Advertisements in the *Mercury* of 29 January and 19 March 1803 announced that

> Land is to be divided and sold off in such Lots as will afford Convenience for Houses of various descriptions, with warehouse room if wanted.

[54] Grady, *Markets*, p.167.

[55] G. Black, 'Colonel Harding and City Square', *PTh.S*, LIV (1977), 106–08.

> Building Ground in an airy pleasant Situation will be sold in Lots to build good Dwelling-Houses upon with room for out-offices or warehouses behind, and Gardens in front 12 yards deep.

Nothing came of this offer, and by 13 March 1806 the *Intelligencer* announced the commencement of a different project in the same close.

> Two Houses for sale now in the shell state in Queen Square built upon the best Principle in an open Situation and well supplied with Water

but by 1815 only the western side and three houses on the northern side had been built. The eastern side was completed after the war, the northern side abandoned half completed, and the south side never commenced. In 1822 the proprietors of nineteen of the twenty-five houses then in existence purchased the centre of the square and covenanted 'to keep it open and to lay out, beautify and ornament the same and to plant the same with trees and shrubs'.[56] The houses of the square are small and betoken a modest ambition; they would not be out of place in a terrace, and their architectural style is plain, similar to those at the north-east corner of Park Square (Fig. 10.4).

Once John Denison had left Denison Hall (Fig. 10.6) for Ossington, his house was embarrassingly large for purchasers or tenants,[57] and its extensive grounds on a south-facing slope might seem the classical situation in which to engineer a great square especially since in the grounds north of Woodhouse Hall, less favourably placed, a project of 1791 had anticipated no fewer than three squares: 'The Estate would form three very capital Squares and is most eligibly situated and circumstanced for Building Ground'.[58] Yet when Denison Hall was sold to Harry Wormald in 1806 he retained his 'little landscape' intact,[59] and the Giles plan of 1815 shows it inviolate and completely surrounded by plantations.

On 18 May 1818 the *Intelligencer* named two squares among its congratulatory list of civic improvements: 'Streets and Squares are springing up in all directions: Hanover and Brunswick Squares, Coburg Place, Wellington Road, King and Queen Street, and Brunswick Place are amongst the more ornamental and better order of buildings'. Nothing came of a Brunswick Square but hopes of a Hanover Square in front of Denison Hall were to rise and fall more than once in the next thirty years.

56 LCD 3398.

57 'Too large for a man of modest fortune and too near the town to be relished by the country gentlemen': *Leeds Guide*, p.84.

58 *LI*, 18 Jan. 1791.

59 WRRD, FE 546 766.

FIG. 10.4 QUEEN SQUARE, BEHIND WOODHOUSE LANE
The square was projected in 1803 'for houses of various descriptions, with warehouse room if wanted', and designed as three terraces around a communal central garden and the fourth (south) side open to Claypit Lane; two large houses with warehouses were commenced on the north side in 1806. Between 1810 and 1815 the nine houses forming the west side (seen here from the north) were completed but made up of smaller residences only. Between 1815 and 1822 thirteen small houses filled the east side and three larger houses were added to the north side, leaving it still incomplete. In 1822 the house-owners purchased the centre of the square for a perpetual garden.

Meanwhile Little Woodhouse Hall and Claremont had also changed hands again. The Hall's new proprietor from 1793, the distiller, Thomas Coupland,[60] did nothing immediately to promote any of the three squares of 1791 but an advertisement in the *Mercury* of 27 April 1805 did indicate a revival of hope for utilising the Hall fields, this time for a single square.

> Several closes of land delightfully situated in Little Woodhouse in Leeds which are intended to form an elegant square, according to a plan which may be seen at the office of Mr Coupland. The proprietor will

[60] LCA, DB 5/3.

engage that there shall never be any buildings erected within [i.e. within the centre of] the square. The land contains a valuable bed of clay and is well supplied with excellent water.

No square was ever to be built in these fields which eventually were taken for Clarendon Road and Hyde Terrace but the name 'Woodhouse' was adopted for a second series of projects; this time in the grounds of the neighbouring house, Claremont, purchased from Denison by the banker, Lucas Nicholson, in 1793 but again on the market following Nicholson's bankruptcy in 1812.[61] The estate was divided: the southern half, adjoining Park Lane was sold in 1818 to Francis Chorley, partner in Chorley and Uppleby, and it became the site of the Chorley mills:[62] the remainder, some 5½ acres with the house, was bought by John Hill of Ripon in 1817 and in 1824 he entered into partnership with Joseph Green of Bradford and a builder, Samuel Green. Joseph Green, who was also involved in speculative development in the Park Row 'Square', contracted to buy the estate from Hill but seems to have been in immediate financial difficulties and was unable to complete the transaction.[63] In the *Intelligencer* advertisement of 14 July 1825 the purchase was wrongly stated to be completed:

Woodhouse Square: The improvements of the West End of the Town are now likely to proceed with vigour. The spacious area at Woodhouse lately occupied by John Hill, Esq., is purchased by Mr. Green who is now setting it out as a beautiful square intended to be called Woodhouse-Square; it is to consist of handsome and genteel houses. When completed this project will form a great acquisition to the uniformity and elegance of that part of the town.

This was in the news columns. No advertisement was inserted until 18 August when the house was advertised for sale together with the grounds lying in front of it.

The estate is well supplied with Water, well Roaded, and contains with the Site of the Buildings near an Acre of Ground, exclusive of a spacious open Area in Front, about to be laid out, and for ever used as Pleasure Grounds by the Owners and Occupiers of a beautifully designed Place, to be called Woodhouse Square, and of which the above Mansion is to form the upper Part.

The quality of the square was partly to be determined by the prohibitions within the restrictive covenants which were printed with the proprietor's Abstract of Title.

[61] WRRD, DN 351/463; FW 579/596.
[62] LCA, DB 5/2.
[63] WRRD, GR 456/454.

> No worse elevation shall be erected thereon than that specified or drawn on the margin of this conveyance. There shall not be erected: a dyehouse, a dryhouse, a glasshouse, a brewhouse, a slaughterhouse, a melting tallow house, a house for boiling soap, for candle making, for baking, for refining sugar, for making pots, for tobacco pipes, for burning blood, for making glue, as a public alehouse, inn, tavern, tippling house, bowling green, cockpit, skittle alley, ginshop, retailing of spirits, distilling, a playhouse, a conventicle, a meeting house, a Public School, an Academy, a blacksmith, a whitesmith, a pewterer, a tinner, a flaxdresser, a tanner, a skinner, a currier, a hatmaker or a chemist.[64]

The building boom of 1825 collapsed without any purchaser taking up a lot in the 'beautifully designed Place' and in August 1828, pursued by creditors, Hill divested himself of the estate:[65] a thousand square yards from the eastern end of the garden were sold to John Atkinson, who had acquired Little Woodhouse Hall after Coupland and Co.'s bankruptcy in 1822.[66] This part of the garden faced the Hall across Kendal Lane and its purchase gave Atkinson a guarantee of an uninterrupted view from his front windows.[67] The grounds to the south of the house, and Claremont itself, were sold to the surgeon Thomas Chorley who then came into residence.[68]

A plan of 1828 shows that Hill's projected square was nearly twice as large as the eventual Woodhouse Square, occupying almost all the grounds of Claremont and being long enough to accommodate an oval garden at its centre.[69] The plan shows no houses erected although Hill had sold one plot at the south-eastern corner, next to Chorley Lane where in 1828 or 1829 Samuel Green built two houses. One, which eventually became no. 1 Woodhouse Square, faced north and the second eastward into Chorley Lane. The latter was demolished during the revision of the plan for the square in 1838[70] in order to give a carriage way to the rear of the houses on the south side of the square but the former survived until the recent clearances for the city's inner ring road.[71]

Thus the oldest surviving houses in the square are later than these first hesitant beginnings: they are now amalgamated into the premises of Swarthmore Educational Centre, an institution which

[64] LCA, DB 5/14.
[65] LCA, DB 5/8.
[66] WRRD, HN 663/654.
[67] LCA, DB 5/8.
[68] LCA, DB 5/1, with plan of 1818; and 5/2.
[69] LCA, DB 5/1, plan of 2 Aug. 1828.
[70] See below, p.338.
[71] LCD 1574.

subtly and happily combines many of the activities proscribed in 1825, being at times a playhouse, a conventicle, a meeting house, a Public School and an academy; and while its students may not learn how to burn blood they certainly make pots.

Francis Chorley seems to have had no designs to further the square, and the initiatives passed to the owners of the Hall. Just before his death in December 1833 John Atkinson had a new plan of the estate made, perhaps buoyed by optimistic accounts of developments elsewhere in the town, but by the time that his affairs were settled and his sons, co-heirs, in firm possession, the boom had passed.[72] Yet their hopes persisted, and on 25 May 1836 Woodhouse Square returned to the advertisement columns of the *Mercury*.

> Eleven thousand square yards of building Ground in the most eligible Part of the immediate Neighbourhood of Leeds; well adapted for genteel Residences, having the advantage of the Town with Country Air, and intended to form a Square, to be called Woodhouse Square. The North Side is occupied by the Mansion of Francis Chorley Esquire. The Houses on the East and West Side will have ornamental gardens in front; and the Interior (which will be given by the Vendors) will be laid out in Pleasure Grounds, with spacious Roads and Gravel Walks.

A month later the news columns of the *Mercury* announced that a site had been offered 'in Woodhouse Square', perhaps on the analogy with St Paul's in Park Square, for a proposed church to be named St George's, although in the event a site on Christopher Beckett's Mount Pleasant estate was chosen.[73]

The Atkinson brothers were obviously aware that a new access road was essential if the square was to attract purchasers for its building lots, and on 7 December 1837 they made a formal agreement to develop their inheritance which was 'of considerable value but could be much increased in value for Building purposes if a better access could be gained for it by an improved road'. The architect John Black had already been commissioned in January 1836 to draw up a plan for an access road which would start in what is now Oxford Place, cross the Beckett fields in front of Mount Pleasant and enter Kendal Lane over the grounds of Springfield Lodge, east of Belmont, and a concordat with these parties was recited in the Atkinsons' agreement.[74]

[72] LCA, DB 5 fully documents these projects; proposed plans of March 1835, Aug. 1836 and 1838 (undated) are DB Map 701A–C respectively; Map 701A precedes the concept of a through Clarendon Road.

[73] *LM*, 25 June 1836.

[74] LCA, DB 5/10; DB Map 701B is the earliest to show a through road on the line of the future Clarendon Road.

The surveyor S. D. Martin was now employed to buy out the owner of the house blocking the rear of no. 1, built in 1828, and to treat with the owner of Claremont who did not at first take kindly to the suggestion of a sale but in January 1839, after some bad-tempered exchanges through the intermediary, he agreed to relinquish ownership of the estate on condition that he could remain as tenant in Claremont under a seven-year lease.[75] Martin's valuation of the house at £3350 in May 1838 was 'on the supposition that the Square be open forthwith on the original [i.e. the 1828] plan. The building of the Square will bring the Public within 17 yards of the Dining Room Window'.[76] It is significant in view of this comment and the actual purchase price of £4000 that the square of 1839 was much reduced in area from that of 1828, occupying only the southern half of the grounds of Claremont which then remained intact until Claremont Avenue and Claremont Villas were built there in 1897; as a result the central garden had to be reduced from an oval to a circle and the north side was left open for a vista from Claremont, similar to that from Denison Hall in Hanover Square.[77]

The printed plan of 1839 shows that the proposals of 1837 for an access road were abandoned since the St John's church trustees had agreed to sell land to widen the northern end of Kendal Lane near the Moor which was to form the first part of a new road, Clarendon Road, coming down through the Little Woodhouse estate and passing between Claremont and the Hall to form the eastern side of a square before turning eastward to St George's church and Great George Street. It was to have a lodge and a gate at the Moor end to ensure its privacy. An agreement was also made to give access from Woodhouse Square to Hanover Square via a short new road, Denison Street. A second new road, Hyde Terrace, was laid out behind Clarendon Road.[78]

[75] LCA, DB 5/21.
[76] LCA, DB 5/4 and 39.
[77] See below, p. 344 and Fig. 10.6.
[78] LCA, DB 5/22–4; DB Map 701C.

FIG. 10.5 QUEEN VICTORIA IN THE SECOND WEST END: WOODSLEY HOUSE (1840) This detached villa was built in 1840 for Peter Fairbairn, partner in the Wellington Foundry, engineer and machine-maker, whose previous home was at 11 Park Square (Fig. 6.7). Greek columns disguised a plain brick front with little privacy from the road (a); they reappeared in the entrance hall and stairs (b), more spacious than anything in the first West End. The rooms at the rear had more privacy, with a commanding view westwards, improved in 1859 by the division of Kendal Lane into what is now Victoria Street. Fairbairn had been mayor when Victoria and Albert came to open the Town Hall in 1858 and stayed overnight in this villa. It has now been renamed Fairbairn House.

(a)

(b)

Neither Clarendon Road nor Woodhouse Square proved as attractive as the Atkinsons had hoped. At the north end of Clarendon Road Woodsley House was built in 1840 as an impressive home for the engineer, Peter Fairbairn (Fig. 10.5) but by the time that the Queen and Prince Albert came to stay at the house in 1858 only five other building plots had been taken up for villas. Progress within the square was hardly more encouraging: by 1858 there was one house on the west side, none on the east, and ten on the incomplete south side.

The largest of these, at the south-west corner was built in 1840 and is now known as Waverley House. Its five-bay, three-storey frontage under a single pediment conceals an interior division for the two families, both Atkinsons, who were the first owners. The house is attributed to the architect John Clark who had supervised alterations at the Hall after John Atkinson's death and had designed St George's church (1838); a similar duple house was designed by Clark to occupy the first two plots (now nos 30 and 2) in Hyde Terrace (1840), and Woodsley House (above) is also attributed to him.[79] The first development on the south side of Woodhouse Square did not take place until 1844 when no. 2, a two-storey brick house with prominent quoins, was built for the dancing master, Richard Willis. In 1845 R. W. Moore, the architect, bought the three next plots on which he erected the three matching houses, nos 3, 4 and 5. In 1846 Moore married the owner of no. 3 and resided in the square until his death in 1891.[80] Although their deeds have not been inspected it is likely that he was also responsible for the design of the large double-fronted house (nos 6 and 7) which forms the centre-piece of the row, and for nos 8, 9 and 10 which so clearly aim to match the other trio.

These five cannot have been built earlier than 1853. When the Atkinsons mounted an auction sale of sixty-three lots in 1847 there was general indifference: in the square the only plot taken up was no. 9 for which 8*s.* per sq. yd. was offered; the end plot was withdrawn after only 5*s.* 6*d.* had been bid; no bidder was found for any other plot.[81] Thus there was vacant ground in this century for a primary

[79] LCA, DB 5/38 and 64; Clark's plans and elevations, dated May 1839, are with DB Map 701. One scheme for the west side of the Square envisaged two detached and three large semi-detached houses; another, five semi-detached and one detached; the present Waverley House is a variant of the semi plan. In July plans for Hyde Terrace were prepared, suggesting thirteen semi-detached houses, each similar to the pair that now form nos 30 and 32.

[80] Deeds of Swarthmore Educational Centre, seen by kindness of Warden.

[81] LCA, DB 5/10.

school to occupy the remainder of the western side and for a brush manufactory to complete the southern side.

The garden in the square remained with the Little Woodhouse Hall estate, the house-owners contracting to pay an annual rent for its use: 'the proprietors of each Lot are to contribute rateably with the proprietors of the other Lots to the expense of keeping the Pleasure Ground in order and of making the Walks and all future Improvements therein'.[82] The five-foot Ordnance Survey plan, surveyed in 1847, shows that the grounds had indeed been laid out in walks with trees, although rather less elaborately than in Joshua Major's Square.[83] In 1855, when the Hall was sold to the Corporation the trustees of the town Highway Charity purchased the interior of the square for an open space, leasing it in 1906 to the Parks Committee who now maintain it.[84]

Hanover Square, named as a project in 1818, had a very similar sporadic development extending into the 1890s. The first signs that a square might be developed in the grounds of Denison Hall occur in 1824 after the estate was purchased by George Rawson, a partner in a firm of stuff merchants. An *Abstract* of his title was printed to be distributed to interested parties: 'the Title of Mr. George Rawson to an Estate situate at Little-Woodhouse, in Leeds in the county of York, now laid out in Building-Lots, and called Hanover Square and Hanover Street'.[85] In the same year a plan of the intended square and plots was drawn up by Henry Teal, the surveyor, and Joshua Major, 'landscape gardener'. Like Woodhouse Square, it was to be three-sided, leaving an open vista northwards to Denison Hall[86] (Fig. 10.6). On the east and west sides, nearest to the Hall, a pair of double-sized plots was intended but only the eastern plot was taken up by the time of Fowler's map of Leeds in 1826 'with the Latest Improvements': on it was built a large three-storey, six-bay brick house which served until recently as the YWCA hostel (no. 10A). Five more houses of this size would have filled the eastern arm but by 1827 when John Teal drew a 'Plan of an estate at Little Woodhouse as divided into Lots for Sale' no others had been built.[87] On 31 July

[82] LCD 1574.

[83] See below, p.342.

[84] LCD 207. These pages have been typed in Claremont Avenue in a house built in 1898 within the grounds of Claremont, and the much-delayed square has been a useful exercise ground for author and dog in the intervals of composition which itself has not been free from delays.

[85] LCD 15355.

[86] Joshua Major, 'landscape artist', also prepared a plan for the General Cemetery grounds: LCA, DB Map 671.

[87] LCA, DB 5/1.

FIG. 10.6 VILLA GARDEN INTO SQUARE:
DENISON HALL (1786) AND HANOVER SQUARE

The Hall, the largest building of its day in Leeds, was built for John Denison in 1786, an ornate residence but with workshops at the rear on Kendal Lane in the style traditional for Leeds gentlemen merchants, as witnessed by the surviving building with two chimneys [*left*]. Denison soon deserted Leeds for a country seat in Nottinghamshire. The house proved difficult to sell or let — 'too large for a man of moderate fortune and too near the town to be relished by the country gentlemen' (1806): it was at one time divided into two but is now a community home. A project to turn its grounds into an elegant Hanover Square was mooted in 1818 and 1824; one large house was built in 1814, five more between 1828 and 1834, but no more until 1870 when smaller houses began to be built; the square was not completed until 1897. The central space is now a public garden.

1828 the *Intelligencer* carried a notice from Joshua Major of a revised plan for the disposition of lots.

> Hanover Square – J. Major announces to his Friends and the Public a Change in the Plan by which it is intended that Houses shall be erected in this delightful Situation. It having been intimated that the former Elevation was too Expensive, a more simple Plan for Single Houses has been adopted, upon which it is proposed that the Whole shall be uniformly completed, and which may be seen at J. M.'s Office, No. 24, Bank-Street; or at the East Lodge, entering to the Square. J. M. takes

this Opportunity of requesting his Friends to visit and examine this most eligible Building Ground, which, notwithstanding its convenient Proximity to the Town, enjoys from its great Elevation, and the well known Prevalence of Westerly Winds, a happy Freedom from the Nuisance of a Smoky Atmosphere. The Pleasure Ground, (an Area of Four Acres, tastefully laid out in Flower Beds, Grass Plats, and Plantations of well grown Shrubs, and noble Forest Trees) is the common Property of all the Householders; and presents Advantages which few Squares in the Kingdom can equal.

The Lots he is commissioned to Sell, will be disposed of on the most reasonable Terms.

Rawson did not himself live in the Hall where John Gott, son of Benjamin, was resident as tenant but he appears with his son, George, junior, in the *Directory* of 1834 living in two of the four houses which had been built at the southern end of the west side of the square. These, and another – sometimes called Hanover House – at the east end of the southern side were all that had been achieved between 1828 and 1834 although Hanover Street was also commenced at this time. Rawson then took in two partners for the venture, John Clapham of Woodhouse Lodge and his son, John Pele Clapham.[88] Twenty-one lots were sold, twelve to the former on the western side and nine to the son on the eastern. J. P. Clapham was himself the first occupant of Hanover House (*c.* 1831) but he sold it to George Smith, the banker, when he moved up to a larger house (now no. 10A), sometime before 1834. He also commissioned the architect Pritchett of York to design a terrace to occupy his side of the square but the boom of 1833–34 passed, leaving the square no further advanced.[89] In 1836 Teal devised another plan with thirty-eight lots but these proved no more attractive[90] and another plan was drawn up in 1840 in connection with the agreement which Rawson and the Claphams made with Atkinson's heirs[91] to link Woodhouse and Hanover Squares by means of the new Denison Street.[92]

That agreement also drew up a list of restrictions upon building in the square: no bricks were to be made in the square from its clay; no offensive businesses were to be carried out; houses could be of two or three storeys but the sides of the square had to end with groups of identical height; no house was to be of less rateable value than £45; all house fronts were to be of red dressed stock bricks and their roofs covered with Welsh or Westmorland slate, and all windows

[88] LCD 8438 and 9442.
[89] Ex. inf. Mrs D. Payne.
[90] LCA, DB 42.
[91] See above, p. 338.
[92] Bonser and Nichols no. 87.

recessed; there was to be a flagged pavement of six feet, and an area of six more feet left between houses and pavement; windows could not be opened in the walls of the two end houses facing the Hall where William Gott and John Jowitt were now tenants.

The plan of 1840 confirms that no building had taken place in Hanover Square since 1834: the future proved to be no brighter.[93] The restrictive covenants protected the square against an enemy within who might seek to erect smaller and inferior houses but it was unable to protect it against enemies without, the creep of industrialisation and back-to-back houses on the southern side of Burley Road. Not a single house was built on the south side of the square until 1870 and it took six years to complete that side; building on the east side lasted from 1870 to 1897, and that on the west side from 1881 to 1893: and no grand house was built next to the Hall on that side to match no. 27 on the east side, as had been intended in 1824.

It can only be assumed that somewhere along the line of Kendal Lane a frontier was developing, perhaps merely one of fashion, generating a distaste for living on the southern side of the Lane or a feeling that urban Leeds intruded on the southern side of the frontier whether by smokiness or proximity of mills. It can hardly have helped that Chorley's mill was next to Woodhouse Square and St Peter's Mill to Hanover Square.

To the east of Woodhouse Lane in the North West Division there was only one other square successfully promoted after Queen Square,[94] that is Blenheim Square, although the *Intelligencer* of 14 July 1825 had announced that three fields on Woodhouse Lane near the Moor were to be taken for a square. The location of this abortive project is unknown but it is unlikely to have been Blenheim Square which was first announced in 1822 and designed as a pair of facing terraces, each of fifteen substantial houses set in a single field between Blackman Lane and Bagby Lodge, the carriage drive from which passed through the square.[95]

The conveyances of the building plots included covenants to preserve a uniformity of architectural style and the mutual enjoyment of the oval garden which was to be laid out between the two terraces. Uniformity was achieved and the garden has now been rescued from long dereliction. The houses of the one terrace that was built lack the Georgian flourishes which were still acceptable in the neighbouring Blenheim Terrace (Woodhouse Lane, 1825–39) but

93 LCD 144551.
94 See above, p.332.
95 LCD 8933: 'Finsbury alias Blenheim Square'.

they were designed for a good class of occupant. In the census of 1841 eight of the fifteen heads of household were of independent means; there were also two solicitors and two dissenting ministers.

Development had not been rapid: by the time of Fowler's 1831 plan a projected 'Finsbury Square' was shown, but only in outline. Eight houses were built between 1831 and 1834 and the northern side was complete by 1839. In the name 'Finsbury' the developers may have invoked the London square of the same name where Bishop Wilson had been so successful: but in vain, for in 1847 the Ordnance Survey found no southern side to the square; and later in the century a row of mean houses was built against the front garden wall of the Lodge, so that (as in Hanover and Woodhouse Squares) incongruous juxtapositions of architectural style are witness to frustrated hopes and delayed development.

Although the North East Division did not lack villas it was not favoured with squares. The villas fitted well into the sloping ground above the Sheepscar valley but squares needed level ground and that was uncomfortably near the Beck. On the ridge at the boundary with the North West Division there had been talk of a Brunswick Square in 1818 but nothing came of it, and it would not have been easy to fit a square into the characteristic long, narrow fields there. Elmwood Square in Claypit Lane was announced in 1825 as a development within the grounds of Elmwood House (Fig. 10.7), a villa built between 1795 and 1800, but it also proved abortive.[96] When the widowed Mrs Lupton attempted to recover the family fortunes in 1830 by creating Merrion Street alongside the cloth factory at Town End her plan allowed for a small square in the next field which was to have a prestigious London name, Belgrave Square: 'to be laid out as an Ornamental Pleasure Ground, and for ever kept open for the joint use of the Residents in the [Belgrave] Place; and the expense borne by the Purchasers of the several Lots, in proportion to the length of their respective Frontages'.[97]

Although plots in Merrion Street were taken up from 1832 those in the square remained vacant until the scheme was abandoned and the land sold in 1836 for Belgrave chapel, while across the township boundary in Chapeltown at Earl Cowper's 'New Leeds' of 1825 there were intended to be squares as centrepieces for the 'elegant and

[96] *LM*, 4 Aug. 1825.
[97] Brotherton Library, University of Leeds, Lupton MSS, Box 127; LCD 3298; plan of 1830: LCA, DB Map 365, reproduced in Beresford, *Face of Leeds*, Fig. 13.

FIG. 10.7 THE WEST END BEYOND WOODHOUSE: ELMWOOD HOUSE (1795–1800) This villa, originally named Long Balk House after the lane (Fig. 1.5) in which it stood, was built between 1795 and 1800 for the drysalter (i.e., druggist), Samuel Lapage of Boar Lane. It was one of several from that period (*see* Table 10.1) when out-of-town sites were being sought upon the rising ground to the north of town, as yet untouched by factory smoke nor yet faced by the terraces in the Leylands (*see* Fig. 8.6). In 1825 Elmwood Square was projected in its grounds but a steam-powered woollen mill had just been built there and the fields soon became terraces, engulfing but not destroying the villa. In the early 1950s, when this photograph was taken, it was occupied by a club for Polish immigrants.

appropriate Designs for Villas and Fancy Cottages', but villas and squares alike foundered in the promoters' bankruptcy.[98]

Although the difficulties which plagued the promoters of squares coincided with the first developments of an alternative kind in the suburbs of Headingley and Potternewton,[99] the fate of the squares does not denote a total rejection of Little Woodhouse and Sheepscar for respectable building since residences of a size and quality equal to

[98] *LM*, 30 July 1825; LCD 10505(ii); plan of 1828, centred on a 'Clavering Square' in Beresford, *Face of Leeds*, Fig. 33.

[99] C. Treen, 'The Process of Suburban Development in North Leeds, 1870–1914', in *The Rise of Suburbia*, ed. F. M. L. Thompson (Leicester, 1982), pp. 158–209.

those projected in Woodhouse and Hanover Squares were now being erected in rows and terraces. The plots on Clarendon Road in particular were large enough to accommodate detached architect-designed houses. Woodsley House was a true roadside villa fit for any West End, Grecian and red-brick in its facade. Where else but Woodsley House did the Queen and her consort sleep in 1858 when she came to open Leeds Town Hall?

TERRACES, STREETS AND ROWS AMONG THE VILLAS

Table 10.1 has shown that there was still enough open ground in the North East Division to attract seven villas between 1790 and 1800, three of them (Campfield House in Long Balk Lane; Grove House in Claypit Lane; and Wintoun House, Sheepscar) with rateable values of £20 or over. A purchase of one of the long, narrow two-acre fields, such as were beginning to prove so accommodating for back-to-back terraces, would offer enough ground for one villa and its appropriate surrounds, although houses in terraces or rows were more frequent in this area. Appendix VIII.1 lists the thirty-two rows, terraces or streets which had entered this Division before 1815, and although some of these – such as Brunswick Place – were intended to be genteel there was an ominous number of back-to-backs, a few of them in fields not far from the southernmost villas such as Campfield House and Grafton House. After 1815 (Table 10.4) the penetration of streets and rows was more pronounced although, since two-thirds of the houses in 1815 were in streets not then completed, there was no immediate invasion of new streets here. Of the forty-nine streets commenced between 1815 and 1831 most derived from the building boom of the mid-twenties, and the collapse of that boom helps to explain why the unfinished street had not been eliminated as a characteristic feature of the Leeds townscape. Over a half of the 1158 houses erected here between 1815 and 1831 stood in unfinished streets.

The North West was the Division where villas had begun, yet the owner of Carlton Lodge, on the east side of Woodhouse Lane, was clearly hesitant in 1796 when he advertised nearby closes as 'very convenient either for private gentlemen or for merchants or Manufacturers to build upon; and if not disposed off [*sic*] on or before the said Fifth of July, the owner intends afterwards to advertise them to be sold in small Lots'.[100]

Those particular closes were still unsold thirty years later but by

[100] *LM*, 25 June 1796.

TABLE 10.4

Streets and Terraces Commenced in the North East Division, 1815–31

Name	Commencing date	State of development, 1831			
		Complete		Incomplete	
		Houses	Back-to-back houses, pairs	Houses	Back-to-back houses, pairs
Acorn St	1821–26	–	–	–	11
Anchor St	1826–30	–	12	–	–
Anglesea St	1826–30	–	–	1	8
Apple St	1826–30	–	11	–	–
Bean St	1821–26	–	–	–	10
Bell St	1821–26	–	–	–	25
Bread St	1821–26	–	12	–	–
Brewery St	1821–26	–	23	–	–
Brunswick St	1825	–	–	22	–
Byron St	1821–26	–	–	17	–
Cambridge St	1825	–	–	–	26
Cannon St	1821–26	–	–	–	16
Cherry St	1826–30	–	–	–	8
Cloth St	1826–30	8	–	–	–
Concord St	1821–26	–	31	–	–
Darley St	1826–30	–	–	3	4
Edgar St	1826–30	–	–	–	6
Elmwood Grove	1826–30	–	–	14	–
Elmwood Ter.	1826–30	–	–	14	4
Fitzwilliam St *see* Lemon St					
Gower St	1821–26	–	23	–	–
Grey St	1825	–	–	19	20
Imperial St	1821–26	–	–	–	6
Lion St	1825	–	15	–	–
Livery St	1821–26	–	7	–	–
Mason St	1826–30	–	–	2	14
Millwright St	1820	29*	–	–	–
Moscow St	1826	–	12	–	–
Mulberry St	1826–30	–	12	–	–

TABLE 10.4 (*continued*)

Name	Commencing date	State of development, 1831			
		Complete		Incomplete	
		Houses	Back-to-back houses, pairs	Houses	Back-to-back houses, pairs
Myrtle St	1821–26	–	–	–	–
New Cleveland St	1826–30	–	11	–	–
Noble St	1826–30	–	–	–	9
Pea St	1821	–	12	–	–
Pendulum St	1826–30	–	–	–	3
Pink St	1821–26	–	8	–	4
Plane Sq.	1825	–	–	–	–
Plato St	1826–30	–	–	–	5
Prince St *see* Millwright St					
Regent St	1821	23*	–	–	–
Rose St	1821–26	–	8	–	–
Rushworth St	1825	–	–	–	26
Saint St	1826	17	–	–	–
Sun St	1826–30	–	13	–	–
Tiger St	1825	–	–	–	7
Time St	1826–30	–	9	–	–
Tulip St	1821–26	–	–	–	4
Vandyke St	1821–26	–	–	–	32
Wheat St	1821–26	–	–	–	5
Whitehall St	1821–26	–	–	1	7
Windsor St	1826–30	–	7	–	8
TOTALS		77	452	93	536
TOTAL OF HOUSES			1158		

* probably single-room houses.

Sources: Dates from directories, maps, and deeds; Charles Fowler, *Plan of the Town of Leeds* . . . (1831); size of houses from Ordnance Survey, *Five-foot Plan* . . . (1850).

TABLE 10.5

Streets and Terraces Commenced in the Second West End, 1815–31

Name	Commencing date	State of development, 1831			
		Complete		Incomplete	
		Houses	Back-to-back houses	Houses	Back-to-back houses, pairs
Bedford Pl	1825	–	–	31	–
Beech Grove Ter. (formerly Preston Pl.)	1825	–	–	3	–
Blenheim Sq.	1822	–	–	8	–
Blenheim Ter.	1826	–	–	6	–
Blundell Pl.	1825	5	–	–	–
Carnaby St	by 1831	–	–	2	–
Hanover Pl.	1825	8	–	–	–
Hanover Sq.	1824	–	–	5	–
Hanover St	1826	–	–	7	–
Lyddon Ter.	1826	–	–	2	–
Oxford Row	1822	–	–	13	3
Portland Cres. (formerly Place)	c.1826	–	–	2	–
Portland St	c.1826	–	–	1	19
Rockingham St	1826–30	–	–	8	–
Springfield Pl.	1831	–	–	6	–
TOTALS		13	–	94	22
TOTAL OF HOUSES			151		

Sources: Dates from directories, maps, and deeds; Charles Fowler, *Plan of the Town of Leeds* . . . (1831); size of houses from Ordnance Survey, *Five-foot Plan* . . . (1850).

1815 there were closes in the North West Division which had been disposed of in smaller lots than were needed for villas and developed as rows or terraces (Fig. 10.8 and Appendix X.1) but only nine in all compared with the thirty-two in the North East, and of these only Reuben Street (1808) was made up wholly of back-to-backs. The subsequent ventures initiated between 1815 and 1831 are listed in Table 10.5. These showed no greater haste to completion than those

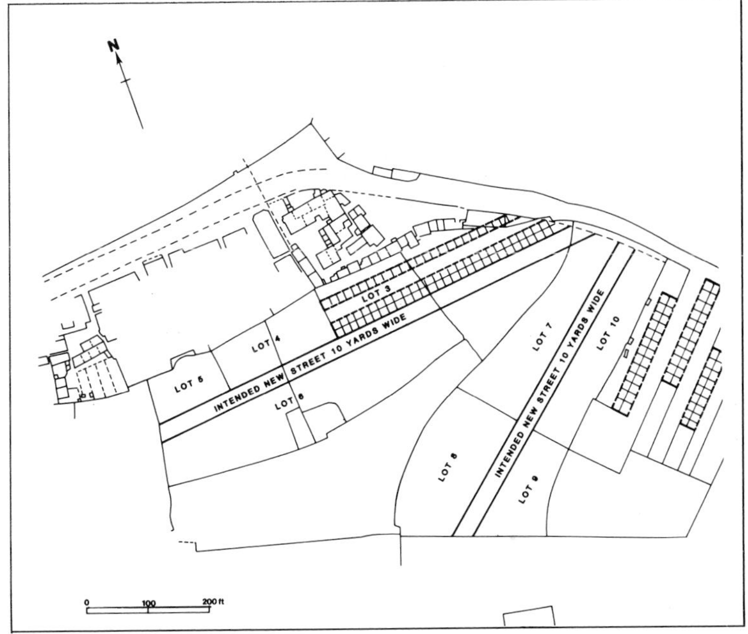

FIG. 10.8 BACK-TO-BACK TERRACES IN GREAT WOODHOUSE, ACCOMMODATED IN LONG NARROW FIELDS, 1837

[*Right*]: three incomplete terraces ('Little Huddersfield'), begun *c.*1831; [*centre*]: two fields subdivided and on offer as Lots 3–10 with sketch of proposed (but actually abortive) development into streets and terraces; [*top left*]: an outline of folds and older cottage properties formed by piecemeal encroachment along the edge of Woodhouse Moor.

in the North East; there were still vacant lots to be had in unfinished terrace streets begun before 1815 and none of the new terraces or streets in the North West shown on Fowler's 1831 plan was commenced before 1825.

'Row' was a term with inherited elegance, and 'Terrace' was not derogatory. A 'Street' was familiar from those in the old town centre streets begun before 1815, and none of the new terraces or streets shown on Fowler's 1831 plan was commenced before 1825.

The term 'Street' was already known in the centre and the East End but was slow to spread northwards. Templar Street (1806) was the first but it could easily have been named a Row or a Terrace since it had houses only on its north side; Hope Street was initially also only a single line of houses although they did have facing buildings in the form of the workshops and warehouses within the grounds of

Denison (Sheepshanks) House. In 1815 Nile Street (1811) and Trafalgar Street (1809) were shown on the Giles plan as no more than single rows but this was probably due to their slow progress, and they were completed as streets of facing houses. The name, although not yet frequently employed, does not seem to have had overtones of inferiority for the open ground in front of the Brunswick Place gardens (1813) was developed as Brunswick Street in 1822.

These streets lay in the North East Division: west of Long Balk Lane the only project achieved by 1815 that had a street name was the short and incomplete North Street, adjoining Queen Square, which began *c.* 1806. 'Street' had been acceptable for Albion Street at the town centre in 1792 and for Commercial Street (1803) and Bond Street (1806). After the war, the term 'Street' was happily linked to the monarchy and the victor of Waterloo in King Street, Queen Street and Wellington Street just outside the core of the Park estate.

Denison's advertisement of 1791 implied some difference between Row and Street, although there seems to have been no significant distinction between Row and that other name for a single line of buildings, Terrace. Both rows and terraces had appeared in the northern Divisions by 1815, and one – Grey's Walk – lined a footpath in the South Division behind Hunslet Lane. A more usual position for these lines of houses was at right angles to a highway, as at Brunswick Terrace and Providence Row. Despite its name, Grove Place was a short terrace on the Claypit Lane frontage: no other single-line group was built along a main highway frontage until Blenheim Terrace (1826); Sunny Bank on Cankerwell Lane seems to have been a short line of small houses – three by 1791 and eight by 1806. Blundell Place on the other side of the same lane was built as a five-house row (1825). The streets and terraces commenced between 1825 and 1831 are listed in Table 10.5.

Rows and terraces also appeared in mid-field. Grove Terrace began as a line of houses behind Grove Place, leaving the remaining two-thirds of the close open. By 1831 an independent row, confusingly also named Grove Terrace, lined the northern side of the close but leaving the remainder as open ground. Carr Place was built along a field edge with its private approach road from the end of Claypit Lane. It stood on the line of the ridge looking southwards to Little Woodhouse and northwards into the Meanwood valley past fields which were being developed with the (probably ironic) name, Little London. According to the 1817 Directory, 'Little London is an hamlet, at the bottom of Long Balk Lane, in a very pleasant situation. A few years ago the only erection here was a single garden-house. The inhabitants are principally labouring people'.[101]

Almost in Little London was Alfred Place, one of the two post-war building-club streets in the North West Division. The club, whose surviving papers were studied by Professor Rimmer, began in 1825 but was dogged by ill-fortune: its progress was interrupted by commercial crisis and put in further jeopardy by a dishonest club official.[102] Yet in 1840 it was completed, unlike Kingston Terrace on Woodhouse Lane. Fowler's plan of 1831 shows three houses in the Terrace and that was the sum of development for nearly a century since the building club which began the terrace also had a dishonest official. Like a number of these off-street groups of houses, Kingston Terrace had its ornate entrance with stone gate-posts and a gate to guard its privacy: the gate-posts and the poor quality surface of the unadopted private road still remain.[103]

Bedford Place, like the next arrival, Portland Street (*c.*1826) formed a single line, and could equally well have been called a Row or Terrace and even as late as Fowler's plan of 1831 the building-club street of St James was the only place in Woodhouse where houses were shown in facing lines although two developments in true street form had then just been initiated. Neither of these as it happened, took a 'Street' name.

These first two Woodhouse streets were longer than North Street and St James Street: when completed in 1847 Springfield Place, in grounds adjoining Springfield House, had sixty-three houses (Fig. 10.9); while Portland Place, begun *c.*1826 in the grounds adjoining Portland House, had ninety-eight. In St James Street, judging by photographs of late-surviving houses, a uniformity of architectural style had not been imposed on its members by the building club but Portland Place was uniformly built, probably under the terms of restrictive covenants accepted by the purchasers of lots.[104] A covenant for Springfield Place (1831) has survived attached to a map of the street which bears the signatures and seals of those assenting to similar restrictions. Uniformity was to be achieved by guaranteeing that when houses came to be built on the west side of the street there would 'not be any house or houses of an

[101] *1817 Directory*, p.18. For similar infill among villas see T. R. Slater, 'Family, Society and the Ornamental Villa', *Journal of Historical Geography*, IV (1978), 129–44.

[102] W. G. Rimmer, 'The Alfred Place Building Society', *PTh.S*, XLVI (1963), 303–30.

[103] LCA, ACC 1148, Emsley, no.10; LCD 9010.

[104] LCD 4092; LCA, LCEng i, no.71.

FIG. 10.9 SPRINGFIELD PLACE: THE FIRST STREET IN THE SECOND WEST END
The building plots in Springfield Place were laid out in 1830 to fill a long narrow field belonging to the villa, Springfield Lodge (Fig. 10.1), with a street made up of two identical facing terraces. All previous development of this sort had been in single terraces. By 1831 nos 2 and 4 on the east side, shown here, were occupied together with nos 6 to 12 but the street was not completed until 1839. The uniform plot size, allowing for front gardens, a feature known in a few recent terraces but not previously in any Leeds street, was set by covenants drawn up by the vendor when sales for the west side began in 1833.

inferior description to those now standing on the east side thereof'.[105]

The adjoining Hanover Street, incomplete in 1831, was adjunct to the developments in Hanover Square (above), the lodge of which formed the northernmost house in the street, but Hanover Place, complete in 1831, was one of that small number of intrusions which were now beginning to be seen within the actual grounds of a villa (cf. Carr Place and Elmwood Terrace): in this case Vauxhall

[105] Covenants of 10 Jan. 1833 with plan: LCA, North, Box 89, 'General', unsorted; LCD 8754; ULD 114.

House;[106] but in general the post-war terraces and rows were the occupants of fields which had been left intact as agricultural, horticultural or tenter ground during the period of villa building. Like the streets of the same period they were often slow to absorb so large an area as a whole close, leading to that scattered distribution of housing shown in Fig. 13.3 which is based on a series of printed town plans from 1815 to 1842.

It will be seen there that very little development took place in the westernmost parts of Little Woodhouse, furthest from town and served only by the meandering Kendal Lane. This land, part of the large Harrison (St John's) Charity Estate, was not sold for building until 1861. Thus the rear bedroom in Woodsley House which Peter Fairbairn allotted to Victoria and Albert in 1858 had a westward view up Airedale over open land, but on its way from the Town Hall the royal carriage had passed not only empty building lots on Clarendon Road – the significance of which has already been stressed – but, next to St George's church, the ends of newly-built back-to-back terraces on the Lyddon estate. The fate of the estate owned at her death in 1828 by Mrs Julia Lyddon (née Silly) epitomises the frustrated ambitions of the second West End.

THE FATE OF THE LYDDON ESTATE

Mrs Lyddon's estate in 1828 consisted partly of her inheritance from her uncle, the merchant Wade Preston, who had died in 1789, and partly of contiguous land which she had bought in 1825 when prospects for a mixture of villas and terraces were encouraging. The Preston inheritance was made up of the seven Brogden Closes, nine acres lying between Cankerwell Lane and Beech Grove House, and totally undeveloped when Mrs Lyddon began to consider opening up the area for building in the autumn of 1805.[107] She was then living in Queen Square, Bath, and on the night when Lord Nelson's death

[106] The only known view of Vauxhall House is in the background of an undated lithograph of Hanover Square chapel in Boyne's grangerised *Ducatus* (V, App., 30F). The grounds of Vauxhall House were themselves the result of the last of a series of sub-divisions of the territory of the sub-manor based on Little Woodhouse Hall (LCD 10990): first, by John Harrison's gift of the western fields to endow St John's church (DB Map 637); then the sub-division of the eastern part to create the Claremont, Vauxhall, and Denison Hall estates. This possibility was first suggested to me by Mrs Dorothy Payne.

[107] The area of Mrs Lyddon's estate lies wholly within the University campus, and except where indicated, this account of its building development is based on the accumulation of property deeds in the Bursary: especially ULD 6, 13, 81, 82, 113, 144, 160 and 170.

became known there had summoned her agent, the local architect, John Samuel Morrish, to bring her a plan of the estate, probably that made in 1739 which survives among her property deeds. It is unlikely that Mrs Lyddon was well acquainted with Little Woodhouse: although a Leeds butcher's daughter, her inheritance was enabling her to live in polite society in a fashionable Bath square, and in 1807 she was married in Bath to Captain William Lyddon; they later came to live at Boston Spa and for a time had a house in Park Square.

Morrish must have advised her that the time was not propitious for building, and he may have explained how the Brogden closes suffered from poor access, coming close to a main highway only for a few yards in their north-east corner next to Ridge House. The plan of 1739 was copied again in 1814 but nothing more was done until 1822 when a detached villa, Preston House, was erected to Morrish's design in the centre of the fields, Blundell Place commenced in Cankerwell Lane, and plots for a south-facing terrace named Preston Place were laid out along the northern side of the Brogden closes, backing on to the private road to the Beech Grove villas. 'Subsequently when certain houses and buildings were erected on part of the road leading to Little Woodhouse, Julia Lyddon née Silly called the same by the name of Preston Place after her said Uncle to perpetuate his memory'.[108]

The terrace projects did not go well: the trio of three-storey houses which now stand in front of the University Great Hall are all that were built in Preston Place by the time of Mrs Lyddon's death when there were only three of six intended houses in Blundell Place. In the heady building year of 1825 she had taken the estate across to the Moor edge and Kendal Lane by the purchase of five closes from Mary Ingledew, another 15¼ acres. A terrace, to be called Lyddon Terrace, was commenced on the western side but only two houses were built there before her death, the present nos 11 and 13, large three-storey brick houses with stables and coach houses behind, backing on to Kendal Lane. A third villa, Willow Grove, no longer standing, was completed in 1826.

Mrs Lyddon's death in 1828 set off a chain of litigation which would not have disgraced a Dickens novel. In a lengthy Chancery action, Lyddon *v.* Woolcock *et al.*, her husband claimed £1814 for bricks which he had supplied for the building of the two Lyddon Terrace houses. He died in 1843 but the action was continued by his second wife, Eliza Lyddon, and lasted, with revivors, until 1847.

[108] Affidavit of Joseph Stead of Leeds, saddler, aged 71, taken in 1847: ULD 6.

The name Lyddon did not cease to be called in the corridors of Chancery even then, for from 1852 to 1859 the second Mrs Lyddon was pursuing another action (Lyddon *v.* Moss) to challenge her solicitor's bill in the first action. Moss successfully appealed against the judgement of the Master of the Rolls but failed to get costs for the appeal.[109]

This litigation had two unintended consequences: the affidavits and interrogatories collected for it in April and May 1837 rival those from the Gott smoke case in their wealth of incidental information; while the very length of the litigation, breeding doubts about the estate's title, effectively sterilised this central area of Little Woodhouse for twenty years. By 1847 many of Mrs Lyddon's legatees were dead, and the estate had to be sold by her trustees in order to make the complex distribution.

The case turned on the contribution that Captain Lyddon had made towards the development of the estate. The main issue was the status of the brick-making plant which had been set up near Blundell Place to work the clay beneath the fields. The consensus was for the Captain: 'indeed', deposed Benjamin Clarkson, stone merchant, 'Mrs. Lyddon used frequently to joke about him being a brick-maker.' It was to William and not to Julia that Samuel Clapham's father had lent £4000 on the security of the Preston Place houses.[110]

Another issue was whether the houses in Preston Place had been fitted out at the expense of Julia or of William: no fewer than 147 promissory notes were put in as evidence: Joseph Blackburn for plastering; Samuel Atack for bricklaying; David Wilson for marble chimney pieces in Preston Place and Lyddon Terrace; John Wood for ironmongery; William Randerson for carting coal to the brick kilns; John Holmes for plumbing and glazing; Joseph Heavyside for blue slates; bricks had also been supplied to John Garland as master-builder working under the architect, John Samuel Morrish, who had come from Bath in 1821 to be Mrs Lyddon's agent in Leeds. It was he who swore an affidavit in 1847 to authenticate the 1739 plan of 'Miss Silly's Fields alias Brogden Close' which he had copied for her in Bath in 1805;[111] and it was he who designed Preston Place, Lyddon Terrace, and Blundell Place in 1821–22.

The later issue of the solicitor's costs apart, the Chancery suit was settled by 1844, and in the spring of 1845, seventeen years after her

109 I am grateful to Mr M. L. S. Passey for drawing my attention to this leading case: Lyddon *v.* Moss (*English Reports*, XLV (1859), p.41).

110 PRO, C 13/2383: interrogatories and answers, Lyddon *v.* Woolcock, April and May 1837.

111 Affidavit of J. S. Morrish, 1847: ULD 6.

death, Julia Lyddon's trustees were able to commence disposing of the estate. An auction sale was held on 17 April 1845, confined to the western part of the estate, that which had been bought from Mary Ingledew in 1825. Seven lots in Mount Preston and ten in Lyddon Terrace had been already sold privately but there remained fifty-two lots in these and other streets on which 175 houses could be built, all in terrace form. As elsewhere, this tranche of building ground was larger than the Leeds market could absorb, and most of the lots reappeared at a second sale in 1851. Meanwhile the other part of the estate was put up for sale on 4 August 1847.

> The whole of this Estate is placed on a commanding Elevation in the most healthy and respectable part of Leeds, and is admirably adapted for Building Purposes, the Estate having been laid out with considerable judgment both as regards Roads, Streets and Sewers; upon it may be erected at least 250 houses.[112]

A coloured plan published in connection with this sale shows how different was the clientèle now expected to be interested in residence in this 'healthy and respectable' part of Leeds. In the ex-Ingledew part of the estate Lyddon Terrace and Mount Preston had been laid out in 1825 with a width of 54 feet: now Caledonian Road was to be only 36 feet wide and the other streets 30 feet wide. In Mount Preston no lot was smaller than 1800 square feet and several contained 2220 square feet but only in Tonbridge Place and Willow Terrace Road did the lots of 1847 exceed 1000 square feet. The unusual superiority of the nineteen houses to be erected on the ten lots here was attested by the allowance made for their front areas between house and pavement, 24 and 33 feet respectively: in front of the Caledonian Road houses only 12 feet of area was to be allowed, reducing to 7½ feet in the other streets. The eighty-three other lots of the 1847 sale measured between 700 and 800 square feet each, and as they slowly found purchasers the character of houses built upon them fell. Preston House and Willow Grove were submerged among the terraces where back-to-back houses and tunnel courtyards began to appear.[113]

[112] Atkinson, Bolland and Atkinson, *Abstract of Title of Mrs Julia Lyddon to the Mount Preston Estate* (Leeds, 1825). Copies of the abstract, together with sale plans of 1845, 1847 and 1851 occur in most of the relevant files in ULD.

[113] The committee of the Society for Promoting Public Improvements in the Borough of Leeds, founded in 1852, had hoped that 'there would be a very great improvement to this important district' but recognised that 'the position of this estate in the Court of Chancery is an obstacle to the present accomplishment of this object': *Third Annual Report of the Society for Promoting Public Improvements in the Borough of Leeds* (Leeds, 1854), unpaginated.

By 1860, therefore, the second West End at Little Woodhouse was managing to accommodate if not all the Two Nations at least part of one and part of the other with a frontier somewhere near Springfield Place. The better tone had been established by the development of Clarendon Road and its small roadside villas, and Queen Victoria's visit to Woodsley House in 1858 must have contributed to the esteem of Clarendon Road, even against its rivals in Headingley, and building of villas was to continue there until 1890. The larger plots on the western half of Mrs Lyddon's estate had helped to keep away small houses or back-to-back pairs.

Near the Moor however there was also meaner building. Unlike Harrogate Stray or Hampstead Heath, the edge of Woodhouse Moor had not been lined with genteel villas looking into it, and until the Moor was turned into a municipal park in 1857 the view would have had little in it to attract. It was a disorganised furze, scarred with quarries for Woodhouse roofing slates and worked-out coal pits. The willingness of the lords of the manor to grant small copyright holdings to squatters had produced a fringe of small cottages on a jagged line which extended down to the larger agglomeration of poor cottage property around Woodhouse Carr (Woodhouse Street) and the mills in the Meanwood valley.

There was something of a second frontier along the ridge: to the south-west the latest of the villas with their carriage drives to Woodhouse Lane, and to the north-east the working-class streets of Little London on the sides of the Meanwood valley. When Leeds acquired three new Anglican churches in 1822, funded by the Million Act, they were designed to make provision for the infidel working class who lived remote from parish churches. It was natural to place one in the East End at St Mary's on Quarry Hill; and another among the mills of the South Division, midway between Holbeck and Hunslet at Christ Church, Meadow Lane: but it is significant that the third was placed very near the Woodhouse ridge frontier at St Mark's, Woodhouse, the only one of the three which is still standing.

How were churchgoers from the Other Nation provided for in the second West End? Until St George's was built in 1838 as part of the Atkinson development of Clarendon Road there was no church for the residents of respectable villas, rows and terraces nearer than St John's, Briggate, or the two other town-centre churches.[114]

[114] 'It was designed for the poor [in the West] but behold it emphatically the rich man's Church': pamphlet, *The Parochial System*, quoted in *LI*, 23 Feb. 1842.

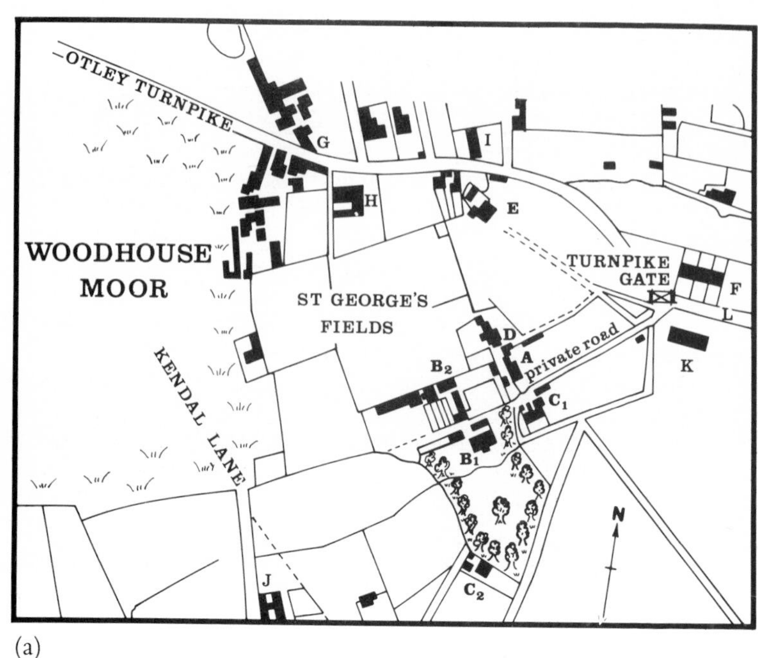
OTLEY TURNPIKE
G
I
H
E
WOODHOUSE
MOOR
TURNPIKE
GATE
F
L
ST GEORGE'S
FIELDS
D
private road
A
K
KENDAL LANE
B2
C1
B1
N
J
C2

(a)

(b)

FIG. 10.10 THE FALL OF A SECOND WEST END: A CEMETERY AND TERRACES AMONG THE VILLAS, 1833

(a) The villas were: (Great) Woodhouse Hall (H) (*see also* Fig. 10.2); Woodhouse Lodge (E); Woodhouse Grove (D); Beech Grove (A) (*see also* Fig. 10.3); Beech Grove House (B1) with workshops (B2); Hillary House (K); Virginia Cottage (C2).

Blenheim Terrace (F), with front gardens, faced Woodhouse Lane (L); Preston Place (C1, the later Beech Grove Terrace) faced a private road; the houses in Lyddon Terrace (J) had their rears on the then insignificant Kendal Lane and no front gardens. Kingston Terrace (I) was left incomplete after the collapse of a building society (Fig. 7.5) but all the terraces had prolonged interrupted development.

Villas (B1) and (C2) survive, as do the houses shown in the terraces (C1), (F), (I) and (J), together with the *Packhorse* public house (G). Villa A was purchased for the Yorkshire College and then demolished in 1884; Villas H, E and D have also been replaced by University buildings.

(b) Fields from the Great Woodhouse Hall estate (*see* Fig. 10.2) were sold to the General Cemetery Company in 1833; they had been named after the vendor's late husband, Col. St George Dalley. This panorama of the crowded private graves was taken just before the closure in 1965, authorised by an Act of Parliament. It also shows the gatehouse at the entrance and the central interdenominational chapel, designed by John Clark but never so used. The removal of most of the gravestones in 1968 created a public open space which the University re-christened St George's Fields.

The establishment of the Leeds General Cemetery in the former fields of Great Woodhouse Hall in 1832 might seem another step downward, even though it lay over the postulated frontier of gentility on the south side of Woodhouse Lane.[115] This may be a misunderstanding of the position in the 1830s when the cemetery carried something of its own seal of gentility. It was contiguous to Woodhouse Lodge, Woodhouse Grove, Beech Grove, and Beech Grove House (Fig. 10.10). It was not a public burial ground but the property of the shareholders in a joint stock company that included all the leading members of Leeds society, Anglican and nonconformist, Whig and Tory. It was a place where the middle class could rest after death beneath monuments proclaiming their fecundity, their virtues and their achievements, free from the insanitary overcrowding in the central parish graveyards which in 1842 was to drive the ratepayers into accepting the cost of a public burial ground at Burmantofts. Nor were its monuments its only architectural achievement: an open competition had been held for the design of its high walls, its gates, its gatehouse and its neo-Grecian mortuary chapel. It was won by John Clark. Here was a home for the dead: but Clark has other monuments in the second West End in those villas which he designed for the living in Clarendon Road, Hyde Terrace and Woodhouse Square.

[115] The Cemetery Company was vested in the University by The University of Leeds Act (*1965 cap. xix*), and the account here is based on R. F. Fletcher, 'The History of the Leeds General Cemetery Company, 1833–1965' (unpublished MPhil thesis, University of Leeds, 1975) which was itself based on the Company's records (LGC, 1–32) then in the Bursary, and on the company's Register of Burials.

11

Civic Pride and Civic Shame

A style of elegance to which he [Thoresby] *was a stranger.*
T. D. Whitaker, DUCATUS (1816), p.18.

A disinclination for residences in so dirty a town . . .
Surveyor's report to Earl Cowper on the prospect for developing his estate in Leeds, October 1819 (Herts. CRO, Cowper MS. T4951).

. . . Exhibiting at one View the Magnitude of its Wealth and the Importance of its Character.
Advertisement for Charles Fowler's 'Plan of the town of Leeds and the Environs' and Joseph Rhodes's 'Western Panoramic View of Leeds', LEEDS MERCURY, 25 January 1832.

THE PREHISTORY OF CIVIC PRIDE

Asa Briggs's essay on the chequered history of the project to build a Town Hall in Leeds was justifiably subtitled, 'A Study in Civic Pride': yet the civic pride of 1858 had its prehistory, not all of it expressed in public buildings.[1] Had not Thoresby's *Ducatus* resounded with civic pride? He had been able to commend recent elegance in private house-building, and in 1725 the elevations of merchants' houses in the margins of Cossins's map expressed the same satisfaction.

For a short while at the end of the eighteenth century civic pride in Leeds had a unique opportunity to show itself. Occasionally someone researching in archaeology or anthropology can make one single discovered object illumine an age: history does not proceed by such leaps but occasionally the wider significance of some small object – in this case a halfpenny piece – can be demonstrated.

The Greek city states, like imperial rulers and modern republics, used their coinage as a public gallery for the display of patriotic sentiments through symbols. In Britain the royal head and the figure

[1] A. Briggs, *Victorian Cities* (1963), pp.137–84, based on 'The Building of Leeds Town Hall', *PTh.S*, XLVI (1963), 275–302.

of Britannia served for a long time to symbolise the polity, with the aid of a few Latin words but rarely displaying any physical object beyond lions, crowns, roses, thistles and leeks; and for a maritime nation it was appropriate that the only public building ever to appear on coins issued from the Royal Mint was a lighthouse.

Very little copper coinage was issued in the reign of George III, and between 1775 and 1797 no halfpence or farthings. To meet the deficiency in small change there were large issues of private provincial currency. In 1791 Richard Paley of Leeds, soapboiler, mill owner and iron master, ordered half a million halfpenny coins in copper to be struck for him at Boulton and Watt's Soho button factory, and the lettering around their rims proclaimed that they were 'payable at the warehouse of Richard Paley' which was then at Kirk Ings next to the parish church. For symbols on the faces of his coin Paley chose the Leeds coat of arms for one side and for the other those of the legendary Bishop Blaize, patron saint of clothworkers; thus the mitred bishop held a crook, a woolcomber's card and a holy book, while in the background was a sheep; the inscription rose to the Latin tongue, *artis nostrae conditor*, words that few of those who were to handle the coins in the Leeds shops and streets could have understood. In 1793 from an unknown source the Briggate silversmith, Henry Brownbill, also issued copper halfpennies which bore the bishop's image but with an exhortation in English, 'Success to the Yorkshire Woollen Manufactory', and there was no sheep present. On the obverse side Brownbill's local pride narrowed from Yorkshire and focused on Leeds itself by picturing a public building which was serving, if not the whole county, certainly the sub-region of West Riding clothmaking: his coin showed the portico, arcades and central courtyard of the Mixed Cloth Hall, made more lively than any printed engraving by his artist achieving a three dimensional effect through an embossed image.

So, as the Leeds halfpennies circulated, the images of a bishop and the West End Cloth Hall served to display civic pride; and the long-demolished Hall still does so when it stands proudly in coin collectors' cases alongside such other images expressing a similar civic sentiment as the cathedral on Canterbury coins and the castle on halfpennies from Warwick.[2]

Art might also acknowledge the cultured status of an urban community by the portraiture of its dignitaries. The Royal Academician, John Russell, came more than once to Leeds as the guest of his

[2] R. Dalton and S. H. Hamer, *The Token Coinage of the Eighteenth Century* (1910), pp.323–25; I am grateful to Peter Mathias for drawing my attention to these coins.

patrons, the Heys, the Sheepshanks and the Wormalds: his son was bound apprentice to a Wormald and although he does not seem to have painted Leeds landscapes his sketchbooks contain Leeds views, including one of Wormald's shop (Fig. 4.6) and another of the Hey house (Fig. 6.4).

A more celebrated Royal Academician, J. M. W. Turner, was also familiar with the Leeds of this period. In 1811 he exhibited in the town at the fourth exhibition of the Northern Society for the Encouragement of Fine Art. In 1816, a year after Russell's death, he paid one of his many visits to his patron, Walter Fawkes of Farnley Hall, having been in north Yorkshire to sketch material as illustrations to T. D. Whitaker's *History of Richmondshire* which was eventually published in 1823. In 1816 Whitaker had two other volumes about to appear: the revised and enlarged edition of Thoresby's *Ducatus* and his own history of *Loidis and Elmete*, and in the latter commissioned an illustration based on a Turner watercolour of Gledhow Hall.

Whitaker had noted Thoresby's expressions of civic pride and did not draw back from following him, since 'every age applauds its own achievements'.[3] He had followed Thoresby's example by using engravings for his illustrations, commencing with a frontispiece portrait of Thoresby, while a vignette on the title page used an heraldic fancy to impale the Thoresby arms with those of the Whitakers. He also followed Thoresby by casting this larger *Ducatus* in topographical sections, with notices of the more important secular buildings added to the town since Thoresby's day.

In September 1816 J. M. W. Turner took his sketch book to the top of Beeston Hill and drew a panorama of the town extending over three pages: the roadside group of buildings known as Folly Hall is in the foreground, the Leeds Pottery and Holbeck in the mid-distance and in the far distance – beyond several smoking mills and the town's four churches – are the slopes of Woodhouse. From this sketch he then produced a larger watercolour, heightened with bodycolour over pencil, that was subsequently known as 'Leeds'.

Stephen Daniels has recently argued that *Leeds* was 'almost certainly' commissioned with the intention of using it as a frontispiece to *Loidis and Elmete*, thereby matching Thoresby's use of the Place *Prospect* in the *Ducatus*; although he adduces no documentary

[3] *Ducatus*, ed. Whitaker, p.83.

evidence.[4] The failure to use Turner's watercolour (below) is then explained as arising from Whitaker's disappointment in being offered such an industrialised vista with labouring figures prominent in its foreground. It might also be thought that Turner's artistic style, which often thrived on haze, would not in any case have lent itself to black-and-white reproduction were it not that the black-and-white reproduction, of detail from the watercolour that forms one of the illustrations to Daniel's essay, is shown as capable of doing full justice to all its smaller architectural features.

The principal argument against Whitaker having such an intention, however, must be one of date. Could he have hoped that a sketch made in September 1816 was in time for a volume already in the press? The absence of the promised Gledhow illustration from any copy of *Loidis and Elmete* bound before the appendix and a supplementary engraving were published in 1820 may also mean that the printer could not wait for the engraver.

In the event the artist whom Whitaker used to applaud the achievement of his age was the young architect, Thomas Taylor, who provided three engravings of public buildings (*see* Fig. 6.3) and there was enough interest outside Leeds for these to be taken to be sold as separate prints by booksellers.[5] Other Leeds views were being produced for reproduction and sale at this time, the most frequently found being N. Whittock's engraving of the new Court House in 1829, sold from no. 4 Warwick Square, London, while a lithograph of the Turner *Leeds* itself, made by J. D. Harding, had been available since 1823.[6] Leeds buildings began to appear at this time as marginal decorations to published town plans, beginning

[4] Stephen Daniels, 'The Implications of Industry: Turner and Leeds', *Turner Studies*, VI (1986), 10–17, with reproductions of the sketchbook pages (now in the Clore Gallery, London) and the watercolour (now in the Paul Mellon Collection at the Yale Center for British Art, New Haven). Daniels (*Ibid.*, Appendix), cites W. G. Rawlinson, *The Engraved Work of J. M. W. Turner R.A.*, vol.I (1906) where, in the preliminary listing of Harding's 1823 lithograph of the Turner *Leeds* (1823), it was stated that it was made for 'the second edition' [*sic*] of *Loidis and Elmete*. Rawlinson did not repeat the claim in his main text: perhaps because he had discovered that there was no second edition.

[5] Whitaker, *Loidis*: engravings of the Leeds Library, Holy Trinity and St Paul's churches and the Infirmary: all these provide evidence for the appearance of the streets around them; e.g., that of Holy Trinity takes in the corner of Boar Lane and Briggate.

[6] Reproduced as frontispiece to Beckwith, *Thomas Taylor*. The viewpoint, taking in Park Row, was a favourite with artists although one went a little far in civic pride by naming the Court House the 'Town Hall': E. J. Roberts (1842) as in J. Sprittles, *Links with Bygone Leeds* (*PTh.S*, LII, 1969), pl.40.

with the Court House's neighbour, the Hall of the Leeds Philosophical and Literary Society, as a decoration for Fowler's plan of 1821.[7]

When did Whitaker consider that the civic virtues which he was admiring in 1819 first began to be manifest? It was not long after 1760, he believed, when 'public spirit began to dawn in the town' with that 'rising spirit of elegance' which produced the General Infirmary and the Hunslet Lane theatre in 1771, the White Cloth Hall in 1776 and a new Assembly Room the next year.[8]

In 1819, reporting to Earl Cowper on the prospects for developing the family estates in north Leeds, his surveyors noted that 'there is an evident alteration taking place in the character of the people of Leeds. They are putting off in some degree that rudeness which is peculiar to them, enlightened pursuits are more cultivated, and the elegancies and comforts of life are more sought after'.[9] In the economic climate of 1819 the surveyors' report did not encourage the Earl to join the development of Leeds, but for novelty and numbers, as for acceleration in house-building and population, Leeds knew no years like the eighteen-twenties, especially those in the mid-decade when new churches, new commercial buildings, new institutional buildings and private housing all flourished together. On 17 February 1825 the editor of the *Mercury* wrote: 'So many projects are daily announced for improving and enlarging the town, and all so meritorious and necessary, that if we this week commend one, we apprehend that before the expiration of the next week we shall be called upon to notice some other no less meritorious'.

R. J. Morris has pointed out that the projects of these years, in contradistinction to the older Assembly Rooms and Cloth Halls, were increasingly catering for the tastes of a wider and more leisured middle class.[10] Specialist shops for middle-class goods now began to appear, and this was also the time, as S. J. Lingard has shown, when professional men such as bankers, surveyors, architects, insurance agents, attorneys and doctors began to seek specialised office accommodation divorced from the places of residence from which they had customarily operated: by 1822 ten of the town's twenty-eight attorneys had offices in either Albion Street, Bank Street or Commercial Street, and only nine in Briggate where fifty years earlier all attorneys would have been found.[11]

[7] For maps cited in the text by cartographer and date only, see Bibliography, §6, with fuller details in Bonser and Nichols.

[8] Whitaker, *Loidis*, p.83.

[9] Herts. CRO, Cowper MS. T4951.

[10] R. J. Morris, 'Middle-class Culture, 1700–1914', in Fraser ed., *History*, pp.200–21.

[11] I am indebted to Mr Lingard for these data from his unpublished researches.

Continued addition of secular public buildings, like private housing, was dependent on the continuation of commercial prosperity, and this was fickle. Civic pride might be frustrated in its expression. When John Cawood spoke at the site for a Corn Exchange at New Street in July 1827 he admitted that they were gathered to mourn as well as to rejoice, for it was 'the last foundation stone of a series of buildings having their origin during the most unexampled tide of prosperity ever remembered'.[12]

It was always necessary for promoters to kindle enthusiasm among potential subscribers, whether by press advertisements or by public oratory which it was certain would be fully reported in the *Intelligencer* and *Mercury*, thereby giving historians generous information not only on the progress of building but also on the ideology of such enterprises.

Although Leeds had no tradition of street processions on Mayor's Day, opportunities were not lost to use the central streets for exhibitions of civic display. When the new Central Market, an indoor bazaar, was opened just in time for Christmas 1824, the procession to Duncan Street was made up of a 'Band of Music, The Several Artificers with their Emblems of Trade, the Contractors, the Solicitor, the Treasurer, the Architect, the Chairman of the Committee, the Recorder, two Aldermen, the Committee abreast, and the Subscribers and Gentlemen intending to dine, also abreast'. In an editorial the *Intelligencer* commented: 'now one feeling seems to animate both Whigs and Tories, viz, an anxiety to improve the convenience and appearance of this ancient borough. We trust this spirit will remain undiminished until the town is susceptible of no further addition, either useful or ornamental'.[13]

The areas of Leeds where these lauded improvements were taking place were narrowly confined, almost all in the central streets, not extending into the West End beyond the Infirmary, and (apart from churches and chapels) totally absent from the East End. Yet it was not only public buildings which could kindle civic pride in the columns of the local newspapers. It was more than once produced by contemplating some particularly rapid increase of domestic housing, and from 1801 every census year produced admiring exclamations at the size of the town population, far from the spirit of Malthusian pessimism. For the time at least, big was beautiful.

[12] *LI*, 30 Aug. 1827.

[13] *LI*, 2 Dec. 1824. For an interpretation of the artists' views of Leeds at this time see C. Arscott and G. Pollock, 'The Partial View', in *The Culture of Capital* (Manchester, 1987).

The admiration of architectural achievement, as distinct from pride in the sheer number of new houses, was also likely to look in particular directions only: towards the villas, terraces and streets of Woodhouse and Sheepscar rather than to the East End. Even in the central streets, where public buildings could be admired, little attention was given to new private building as a contributor to an improved appearance of the town. This is not surprising since there was little new to see there at that period in the way of new houses; the rebuilding on central sites which had produced the new fashionable houses in the margins of Cossins's map of 1725 had been part of the Improvement noticed in Chapter Five but it had come to an end when houses of that class could be built in a West End. In the central streets the largest buildings, the inns, retained for the most part their traditional facades; a few houses fronts were converted to shop windows but the large retail establishments with their plate glass were yet to come.[14] A room in their house or in a yard backsides sufficed for the clients of those professional men – apothecaries, lawyers, doctors and surveyors – who had not decided to move to offices further west.

IMPROVEMENT BY DESTRUCTION

The improvement of an early nineteenth-century town was mainly a matter of novelties and additions but sometimes there had to be subtractions and destruction in the course of progress. A site for the Central Market next to Call Lane chapel was obtained only by the market company purchasing 'a spacious edifice built about a century ago for Alderman Atkinson'. This was the house applauded by Thoresby which towered over all its neighbours in the Buck *Prospect* of the town centre, although by 1820 it was reduced to housing the post office (Fig. 3.3). The ground space of the house after demolition was insufficient for the needs of the market so that the gardens behind the house also disappeared underneath the new building.[15]

As far back as 1760 the widening of Leeds Bridge was accompanied by the widening of its approaches, funded by a rate authorised by the Bridge Act 'for the purchasing of houses and buildings which straiten and obstruct the passage to the said Bridge',[16] but transport improvements did not always involve demolition. The

[14] There is an excellent description of the architecture of retail shops in Briggate at this time in unpublished notes by John Wray, 'Methodism in Leeds' (Leeds Central Reference Library MSS), vol.I, ff.163–74; see also n.5 above and 25 below.

[15] LCD 225.

[16] *Acts Local and Personal, 33 Geo.II cap. 54.*

Leeds–Liverpool canal of 1770, like the Leeds–Selby railway of 1834, terminated on the outskirts of the built-up area of its day and did not need statutory authority to demolish property; the early turnpikes likewise began where roadside houses ceased, and did not have to clear away houses to effect their routes: the destruction of the industrial complex at Drony Laith followed a private arrangement between landowners for driving an approach road through their fields to Wellington Bridge (1818) and the new western turnpike beyond.

When the promoters of the White Cloth Hall needed an avenue of access through the built-up frontages of Call Lane and Vicar Lane to the Tenter Garth where the Hall and Assembly Rooms would be built they found that an Act of Parliament was necessary, not because the frontage owners were unwilling to sell but because the land formed part of the estate held in trust for the Free School; the trustees were happy to sell since, as the Act of 1775 explained, 'the greatest part of the said Messuages or Tenements are very old and cannot be upheld nor supported without a considerable annual expense or charge'.[17]

By the eighteen-twenties only a few interior crofts at the town-centre remained undeveloped, and in every case it was necessary to demolish older frontage buildings if access to them was to be gained. For Commercial Street the buildings on a burgage plot in the west side of Briggate were sacrificed,[18] and on 19 August 1822 the readers of the *Intelligencer* learned of plans to destroy property on Park Row plots that were more newly built upon than any Briggate burgage.[19]

> Two gentlemen have recently purchased Copley's Close at the back of Park Row and a subscription has been entered into by those whose local interests are concerned for the purpose of making an opening from Commercial-Street into Park Row, by pulling down a house in the latter, and another in Albion Street – thus forming a spacious street, of which the Philosophical Hall will form a conspicuous ornament. This improvement will greatly add to the appearance of that part of the town, as well as increase the value of property there. We confess we have great pride in recording these instances of public spirit, which redound alike to the honour and to the interest of the town. It is certain that nothing can more effectually promote the latter than the improvements of all descriptions going on, for not only will they occasion a

[17] *Acts Local and Personal, 15 Geo.III cap. 90.*

[18] Most of the land concerned belonged to William Hey; see also n.24 below.

[19] The demolished property on the west side of Albion Street cannot have been more than thirty years old, and probably less: the unoccupied corner plot with Boar Lane was on the market in 1796 and 1797, and only 21 houses appeared in the 1798 *Directory*.

> considerable sum of money to be circulated amongst the labouring classes, thus adding to their comforts, but by making the town more attractive it will become a more frequent resort for strangers: and the natural consequence will result – that its trade and its importance will increase.[20]

The house that was demolished in Park Row to make this entrance into what was to be known as New Bond Street was then less than fifty years old. Elsewhere it was rare to have any need to demolish in order to have space for new building, and the first two railway stations and their goods yards (at Marsh Lane and behind Hunslet Lane) were slipped into empty fields, and lay far enough from town for their lines to proceed into the countryside without demolition.

A few derelict houses in the north-west corner of the parish churchyard were demolished in August 1780 but there were still old houses within the north-east corner as late as 1822 when that fact was adduced as evidence that the inelegance of Kirkgate made the vicarage unsuitable for the continued residence of the vicar. After the purchase of a more suitable house in the quiet of Park Place the vicarage, scarcely a century old, was sold to the Improvement Commissioners for demolition to accommodate an off-street open-air Free Market.[21]

In 1822 the traffic in Briggate, where open-air markets had been held for more than 600 years, was given priority over the stalls. On 19 August the *Intelligencer* reported:

> We are happy to state that measures are now in progress for removing the cow and pig markets into the Vicar's Croft; where also the country dealers with vegetable and fruit who supply our hucksters with these articles will have to take their carts; a portion of the Croft being appropriated for their reception. This will materially relieve the pressure in Briggate on a market day.

[20] *LM*, 1 Aug. 1780; the widening of Woodhouse Lane, North Town End, Kirkgate End and the making of Duncan Street, all within the previous forty years, were 'accomplished by our worthy magistrates': *LI*, 2 Dec. 1824; in 1805 the Corporation granted £400 towards the new Bond and Commercial Streets; street widening works in Quebec St, Mabgate, Swinegate, Vicar Lane and Water Lane were executed between 1826 and 1839 by the Improvement Commissioners. Funds from the Highways Charity could also be applied to this end; e.g. £200 towards making Bond Street in 1806; £2100 for opening up the Briggate–Kirkgate junction in 1811: LCA, DB 197/2, 10 April 1806 and 18 July 1811.

[21] Borthwick MSS, R1/40a, f.135 and LCD 21 (7 Aug. 1826).

Recalcitrant stall holders who would not transfer to the Free Market were then successfully prosecuted despite their invocation of market rights in the charter of 1207.[22]

The older streets such as Boar Lane, Vicar Lane, The Calls and Swinegate were conspiciously narrower than the newer streets but there were no schemes for widening them after the small-scale improvement of the approaches to Leeds Bridge in 1760. In the older streets the dispersed ownership of properties discouraged redevelopment that extended beyond a single frontage. Consecutive frontages under one ownership were found only on the Charities estates in Vicar Lane, Briggate, and the Upper Headrow but a mass of leases of various dates and duration inhibited the trustees from visions of redevelopment which, as the preamble to the 1775 Cloth Hall Act had argued, needed investment far beyond their current income. In 1828 the Highways Charity commissioned a survey and valuation of its estate on the Upper Headrow with the intention, unfulfilled until the building of the Lewis's store, of creating a continuous line of seven new shops.[23] Purpose-built shops were to be found at that time only in Bond and Commercial Streets.[24]

In Briggate the chronology of converting houses to shops has not yet been studied but a well known early photograph of the west side of Lower Briggate shows a characteristic mixture of houses, inns and shops with architectural styles ranging over three centuries (Figs. 4.6 and 4.7). Joseph Rhodes's earlier painting of the Moot Hall shows a similar mixture of frontage buildings in Upper Briggate where the varied heights, different building materials and different uses indicate piecemeal rebuilding with no attention either to the preservation of historic façades or to any uniformity in their replacement. The painting catches one frontage on the east side of

[22] Prosecutions, even for stalls of 24½ feet width in a street of twice that width, had failed; e.g. R. *v.* Airey, a linen draper, *LM*, 20 Oct. 1821. 'From the increased population and traffic of the Town and neighbourhood of Leeds a free open spacious and permanent Market Place for cattle and pigs, hay, fruit, vegetables and other produce has become necessary as well for the convenient sale thereof as for the personal safety of the buyers and sellers of the same': resolution of ratepayers' meeting, 5 Aug. 1824 (*LI*, 12 Aug. 1824).

[23] LCA, DB 197/2, 20 March 1828; a plan by Henry Teal and elevations of the proposed buildings by the architect, Joseph Cusworth, were lithographed for general distribution (DB 197, unsorted).

[24] The Leeds Library in Bond Street, designed by Thomas Johnson in 1808 (Beckwith, *Thomas Taylor*, pp.17–18), had shops on its ground floor; plans and elevations of four shops at the eastern end of Bond Street were prepared for William Hey by the architect, R. D. Chantrell in April 1820: LCA, DB 75.

the Shambles enveloped in scaffolding as if for demolition; beyond it the corner building at the Headrow which still stands.[25]

The public buildings of that period, especially the secular buildings, were concentrated in the town centre: it was natural that the older streets would be the preferred sites for buildings which would be used by persons coming in from all points of the compass. Across the bridge in the South Division there was a South Market in Meadow Lane and also the second of the town's cloth halls.[26] From 1771 there was a theatre but Whitaker rejoiced that it was banished over the bridge where it minimised the risk to the morals of young men who might be seduced by its charm and charmers.[27] In any event, the South Division's space was confined and, once factories had been established in it, public buildings were reluctant to follow. It is unlikely that the smoking chimneys of the Meadow Lane flax mills and the smoking engine of a Brandling railway coal train would ever have appeared in a well known engraving had they not formed the inescapable background for a prospect of Chantrell's new gothic Christ Church.[28] In the East End the only public buildings, apart from its numerous public houses, were the Lying-in Hospital for Poor Married Women (1824) and the Cholera Hospital of 1832. Both of these, significantly, were converted private houses in St Peter's Square.[29] A General Infirmary had not impugned the character of houses for the Upper Ranks residing in the Park Place but these two East End hospitals – like the gasworks in the next field[30] – were a sign that even the Middle Ranks might no longer be viewing St Peter's Square with favour.

LEEDS DISPLAYED

The production for sale of a town plan was another stage in the recognition that a town's fame was great enough to command a market for something at once ornamental and useful. In Cossins's

[25] The painting belongs to Leeds City Museum, currently (1988) on loan to the City Art Gallery where it is usually on exhibition; see also the earlier view of Briggate around the Moot Hall engraved by Charles Heath (artist not stated) in Whitaker, *Ducatus*, p.248.

[26] Grady, *Markets*, pp.165–95.

[27] Whitaker, *Loidis*, pp.86–87.

[28] Reproduced in Beresford and Jones, eds., pl. VII.

[29] K. Grady, 'The Provision of Public Buildings in the West Riding of Yorkshire, c.1660–1840' (unpublished PhD thesis, University of Leeds, 1980), Gazetteer nos 117 and 141.

[30] A. Lockwood, 'Origins of Gas in Leeds', *PTh.S*, LVI (1981), 117; Benyon had successfully opposed a site near his flax mill in Meadow Lane.

map a space on the south bank of the Aire where there were as yet no buildings had been used for a frame enclosing a eulogy of 'Leedes a Large Rich and Populous Town . . .'. Then, apart from Thomas Donald's small insert plan on the Jefferys map of the whole county (1771), no separate plan of the centre of Leeds was published until 1806 when the local bookseller, John Heaton, produced his *Plan of the Town of Leeds with its Modern Improvements*, described gently by Bonser and Nichols as 'having no attempt at accurate delineation'.

No buildings, private or public, were named on the small Donald-Jefferys plan of 1771. Tuke's map of 1781 extended to the whole borough and, although nearly four feet square, it had to take in some sixteen square miles. The town centre was accurately delineated within its small area but no individual streets could be named on that scale. A marginal table of 'Reference to all the Public Edifices of the Township of Leeds' listed ten 'Places of Worship' and nineteen 'Hospitals and Public Places'. Heaton's poor delineation of the town in 1806 was partly redeemed by having a longer list of forty-two public buildings, six fewer than those named by the Giles plan nine years later.

The first of the notable series of town plans by Charles Fowler in 1821 named fifty-four public buildings, gathered into four groups with very similar headings to those employed by the two Giles in 1815: 'churches; chapels; charitable buildings, law, commercial, and other buildings' and although the famous Leeds Pottery lay outside the area covered by the map it was introduced by an insert on the same scale. His plan of 1826 covered the same central area as in 1821 but increased the number of public buildings listed to eighty-two. A larger plan of 1831 was advertised in the very language of civic pride: 'exhibiting at One View the Magnitude of its Wealth and the Importance of its Character', [31] and at each revision the number of public buildings grew: 140 in 1831 and 205 in 1844.

In the spaces conveniently left vacant by the irregularities of the built-up area Fowler called in the graphic muse to exhibit the town: in 1821 the new Hall of the Philosophical and Literary Society and in 1826 the Commercial Buildings viewed from Mill Hill. The larger plan of 1831 displayed the borough coat of arms; an imaginary view of the town at the time of the Jefferys survey (in order to show how it had grown in the interval); and a view of 'the West Entrance to Leeds Showing the Court House, Commercial Buildings, Mixed Cloth Hall and General Infirmary Etc.', the 'Etc.' being the new houses occupying the former 'Square' north of Infirmary Street which

[31] *LM*, 25 Jan. 1832.

Fowler's artistic licence widened to seem a second Whitehall or Pall Mall although in reality no wider than 50 yards.

This unattributed view is usually ascribed to Fowler himself, but a 'Western Panoramic View' had originally been commissioned for the plan from the artist, Joseph Rhodes, and Fowler was the publisher when Rhodes's view was engraved for sale in 1832.[32] Views of the town were evidently selling well, for in 1833 the printing office for the *Leeds Times*, a new rival to the *Intelligencer* and *Mercury*, published *Mr Buttery's View of Leeds from Beeston Hill*, a large work measuring 50 in. by 36 in.

In 1834 Baines and Newsome issued with their directory a plan which was the first since Tuke's to embrace all the borough, with space left for graphics at the edge, one ancient and one modern: a view of Kirkstall Abbey alongside the prize-winning design for the gatehouse and chapel of the recently formed Leeds General Cemetery Company which, however, as we have seen, had civic shame as well as civic pride in its antecedents.

If engravings and maps were signs that a town was taking itself seriously and was expecting to be taken so seriously by others that there was a London market for views and town plans, then the publication of a town guide and then of a separate street directory were a further sign that its self-importance and self-esteem were being endorsed by the hard-headed test of the market place. In 1806 Edward Baines was the printer of an anonymous *Leeds Guide*, running to 168 pages, reprinted in 1808.

'It is not to be expected of a Guide that he should be eloquent', apologised the author,[33] but nor might it be expected that a directory should have sections that could be read as a book. Yet in the *Leeds Directory* issued from the *Mercury* printing office in 1809, Edward Baines began a tradition of informative general prefaces by prefacing the 140 pages of the directory proper with fifty pages of general information about the town, some of it grouped under headings identical with those employed by cartographers of the town: 'Charitable Institutions', 'Commercial Buildings', 'Courts of Justice' and 'Places of Worship'.[34] There was also a heading, 'History'.

He began with the comment that

[32] *Bonser and Nichols*, no.69.

[33] *Leeds Guide, 1806*, Preface.

[34] Details of the directories referred to in the text solely by date will be found in the Bibliography §5, below, p.531. The reference to an earlier directory of 1806 in Alf. Mattison's notes (LCL, SRQ 942.75 M435, folder no.1) is spurious: his notes were taken verbatim from the Baines *1809 Directory*.

> it is somewhat surprising that in a Town as extensive as Leeds, a Directory, on a scale correspondent with its commercial rank, has never yet been attempted, especially as it is obvious from the extensive circulation of these depositories of local information in Birmingham, Liverpool, Manchester and other large cities that their utility is duly appreciated by the public.[35]

There was an element of self-esteem here, as well as civic pride, for Baines's was certainly not the earliest Leeds directory. There were Leeds sections in Bailey's *Northern Directory* of 1781, *The British Directory* of 1784, and in Barfoot and Wilkes's *Universal British Directory* (1790). The first local compiler seems to have been the Charity School master, John Ryley, who was probably the 'J.R.' of the later *Leeds Guide*. Ryley contributed to a *History of the Town and Parish of Leeds* which was published in 1797 jointly with a directory, the latter being subsequently issued separately as *The Leeds Directory for the Year 1798*, 'intended to be an annual publication'. That ambition was not fulfilled but in 1800 Binns and Brown, also printers and booksellers, produced a *Directory for the Town of Leeds*, and in 1807 the Kirkgate printer, George Wilson, issued his *New and Complete Directory for the Town of Leeds . . . together with references to the Commercial Buildings, Markets, Fairs Etc.*

Thus Baines's claim to priority in 1809, repeated in 1817 in the Preface to his *Directory, General and Commercial, of the Town and Borough of Leeds* could not be justified, but since the other directories had been published by rival Leeds printers the denigration may have been deliberate, like his crass statement that 'since this period [the anti-turnpike riots of 1753] no event of sufficient importance for the notice of History has occurred in the town',[36] when the material published in the *History* of 1797 by Wright must have been known to him. This was cast in the form of letters from a Quaker in Leeds to a Quaker elsewhere, and had many interesting comments on the progress of industrialisation and urbanisation.[37] The information about the town brought together in these directories from 1790 onwards went beyond a mere alphabetical list of names, addresses and occupations, becoming true 'depositories of local information';

[35] *Directory, 1809*, 'Advertisement', unpaginated.

[36] *Directory, 1817*, p.4.

[37] Anon., *A History of the Town and Parish of Leeds [to which is] added a Leeds Directory* (Leeds, 1797). The attribution to the printer, Griffith Wright, may arise from the advertisement at p.64 for a *Catalogue* of the circulating library at the bookshop of Thomas Wright in Briggate. Griffith Wright was a staunch Tory and unlikely to write as one Quaker to another, but a Thomas Wright is credited with the anonymous *A Modern Familiar Religious Conversation* (Leeds, 1778): Leeds Central Reference Library, 821.69 W937.

even in the nine pages allocated to Leeds in the *Universal British Directory* there were brief historical notes on the town's long commercial importance which derived in part from the account in Defoe's *Tour*. In 1809 Baines's Preface had a sub-heading, 'History', enlarged in 1817 to 'History of the Borough', which was 'compiled from the most recent and respectable authorities; and it is hoped will render the work not only useful but entertaining.' Baines's authorities were actually meagre, and the local history contained in the historical sections of all these directories never formed a connected account and was tiresomely reiterated in successive volumes; in content it never strayed far from the Romans, the druids and the visit to the town of King Charles I, no doubt what Whitaker had in mind in the opening page of his *Loidis and Elmete* when he dismissed local topographical work as 'trash'.

Concluding his Preface, Baines claimed that his directory of 1817 would 'answer all the purposes of a Guide to Strangers'. In 1806, the year of the *Leeds Guide*, another anonymous topographical work was issued for the benefit of strangers by the printer and bookseller, John Hustler Leach, as *A Walk Through Leeds* (? by Francis Billam) and having the subtitle, *or, Stranger's Guide to Every Thing Worth Notice in that Ancient and Populous Town.*[38] The notion that Leeds had qualities which might attract and interest a stranger was to persist in book titles, for in 1831 an enlarged and revised edition of the *Walk* elevated the subtitle of 1806 to a main title, *The Stranger's Guide Through Leeds*. The frontispiece of this guide was S. Topham's engraving of the recently opened Commercial Buildings at the corner of Boar Lane and Park Row, viewed from the south; Fowler's map of the same year used the same buildings to close a western vista.[39]

Engravings of public buildings which were once confined to the pages of Thoresby and Whitaker were now appearing in pocket-sized guides and, from the first, the directories – with more pages than the guides but the same page size – included maps as frontispieces: that published by Wright in 1797 had a map 8¾ inches square, folded to accommodate it to the size of the book. It was *A Map of near 10 miles from Leeds* with concentric circles drawn to measure miles from the Moot Hall; no cartographer's name was given. The same map was used in 1800 for the Binns and Brown directory but with two woolpacks, symbols again of the ancient trade, added to the title drawing, and after being separately printed

[38] I have not been able to discover the origin of the attribution to Billam.

[39] See above, p. 374.

for sale in 1809 and 1812 it reappeared in 1819 as the frontispiece to Baines's directory. It was now demonstrably out of date, and for his 1821 directory Baines used a plan by Fowler of the same year, and again with revisions in 1822 and 1826.

The town was extending outwards rapidly, and the more extensive area of Fowler's new survey of that year, covering 21¾ inches by 30¾, was too large to fold into a book but the connection between Fowler's surveys and directory publishers was continued when Parson and White's directory of 1830 had as a frontispiece a small central section from Fowler's forthcoming plan. Baines turned to another source for his directory of 1834 and used a version of a plan of the borough on a small scale that had been prepared by Lieut. Robert Dawson, R.E., for the report of the Boundary Commission (1832).[40] It was revised for a directory of 1839, and for Williams's directory of 1844 Fowler himself revised the small plan of 1826: covering now six square feet, the latest in the series of his larger scale surveys was even less suited than that of 1833 for insertion in a directory, but even this plan was not on a large enough scale to be able to insert every street name, so that its usefulness for readers of directories would have been limited.

The silent indifference of directories to many aspects of industrialisation in the town may owe more to the imperceptible nature of that process than to imperceptiveness in those who compiled the descriptive material for the introductory sections. In issue after issue the transformation of the town, the process of industrialisation and urbanisation was recorded almost without comment as the list of its inhabitants spread over more and more pages; in other sections of successive directories the urban dimension could have been seen to grow with the additions to the lists of public buildings; in others by the variety of occupations named; and – most significant of all – by the lists of courts, yards, small streets and 'squares' which appear where the inhabitants were too migratory or thought to be too insignificant for inclusion in the main alphabetical sequence of names.

While the directories' successive additions to the lists of public buildings afford the local historian his only compact source of information for that aspect of urbanisation, in yet another section one turns gratefully to those depositories of local information, the miscellaneous notes on institutions which did not have their own buildings but which contributed to the quality of the town's life. A number of these, particularly the numerous friendly societies, were to be found away from the central streets.

[40] PP 1831–32, XL, plan following pp. 195–96.

The reader could also learn from the steadily lengthening introductory matter that Leeds was a town that could claim eminent persons as well as elegant buildings, and brief biographies were given of clergy, schoolmasters, booksellers, authors, physicians, painters and philanthropists who had helped to make the town distinguished. He could learn that Leeds was a town where there were private art collections such as Benjamin Gott's at his new mansion in its park at Armley, and although the town had no permanent art gallery the beginning of public art exhibitions was marked by those held by the Northern Society for the Encouragement of the Arts in 1809, 1810 and 1811. It was a town with waterworks, banks, fire engines, almshouses, markets, fairs, public gardens, and a police force with nightly watch and patrol. It had Sunday Schools and Adult Schools, billiard rooms, coffee rooms, newspaper rooms and circulating libraries, concerts and dancing masters. Country manufacturers, country carriers and country coaches could be met at its inns, other carriers at their warehouses, and water transport taken at the wharves of the canal and Navigation companies. It was a town with Bible and Missionary Societies, friendly societies galore, and charitable societies offering soup, clothing and temporary outdoor relief for those in adversity.

All these activities, and more, merited their paragraphs in Baines's directory of 1817, proving that even if the 'historical' sections of the directories consistently failed to achieve any coherent account of urbanisation and industrialisation (perhaps explaining Baines's declared belief that nothing had happened to interest History for the previous sixty-six years), yet his many pages of 'Useful and Interesting Information' provide, if not urban history, then some of its basic raw materials.

THE LARGE-SCALE SURVEYS

In 1844 Fowler produced the last and largest of the private surveys of the town in his *Plan of the Town and Environs* that extended over six square feet. By that time both national and local needs were demanding large-scale plans of the most populous towns. Locally the poor law rating officers needed up-to-date plans on a scale large enough to show every assessible building; the Improvement Commissioners had a similar interest in accurate topographical detail, as had the waterworks company and the gas companies; the reformed Corporation was intending schemes of drainage and sewerage over the whole town, and in 1844 it commissioned two excellent large-scale plans from J. F. Masser, one for Mill Hill ward and one for

Kirkgate,[41] but the commissions ceased when the intentions of the Ordnance Survey were made known. The one-inch maps of England had progressed north as far as Beeston in 1841 but it was now decided to proceed on a larger scale, the six-inch; and although not published until 1851 ('surveyed in 1847') a six-inch survey of Leeds must have been completed before October 1844 when a signed and sealed copy of the Leeds sheet was provided for the Ecclesiastical Commissioners who were needing to delineate the new parish boundaries within the borough.[42]

By 1847 the status of Leeds in the hierarchy of 'large towns and populous districts' was such as to qualify the in-township for a survey on the giant scale of sixty inches to the mile, an enduring vision of the face of Leeds at the end of the period covered by this book.[43] Yet the needs which had prompted the preparation of these large-scale plans at the public expense showed that it was now no longer at all certain that big was beautiful: it was to the 'large towns and populous districts' of England that the reformers were looking as they gathered evidence to show that there was indeed a Sanitary Question to be answered, and it was from the reports and publications of sanitary inquiries that Leeds exchanged its fame for notoriety and civic pride for civic shame.

[41] Bonser and Nichols, nos. 104–05; engraved plans, but in 1843 the Council wrote to the Board of Ordnance welcoming the news of a large-scale plan of Leeds in preparation, and asking for free copies since the Government was spending very little of taxpayers' money in towns like Leeds; they had a plan of their own just prepared on the five-foot scale, but did not wish to have it engraved if it was to be duplicated by the Ordnance map: 26 April 1843, Committee Report Book, shelf 15, Strong Room, LCH. The Royal Commission on the State of Large Towns and Populous Districts noted that the Master-general of the Ordnance Survey had agreed to proceed with large-scale plans of towns in order to aid the laying of pipes for gas, water and sewerage: PRO, MH 7/1, 25 Jan. 1844.

[42] Borthwick, CC EC 11/101.

[43] The very phrase 'large towns and populous districts' implies an association of urban growth – normally a matter for civic pride – with demographic pressures and problems which, if unsolved, might bring civic shame.

12
An East End Exposed

Until the localities of the abodes of the working classes are rendered more approachable to the higher classes of their fellow citizens by the removal of the many disgusting objects of sight and smell which abound in every quarter it is in vain to expect that any useful intercourse can be maintained.

James Smith, 'Report on the Condition of Leeds', in 2ND REPORT OF THE COMMITTEE ON THE STATE OF LARGE TOWNS AND POPULOUS DISTRICTS
(PP 1845, XVIII, 313).

REVELATIONS

Before 1832 it is rare to find published criticism of any element of urbanisation in Leeds.[1] The *Leeds Guide* of 1806 was exceptional in commenting on the undesirability of cellar dwellings, 'frequently the hotbeds of disease' but giving equal prominence to 'the danger they cause to persons walking on the foot-path'.[2] Between 1832 and 1835 Leeds, previously without separate representation, gained its two borough members of Parliament, and its unreformed Corporation was replaced by an elected town council: yet these very years, in which civic pride might seem to have been unchallenged, were darkened by the cholera and by the revelations of the sanitary consequences of urbanisation in Robert Baker's *Report to the Leeds Local Board of Health* with its accompanying 'Cholera Plan of Leeds', drawn by Charles Fowler.

Thus in 1833 (and again in 1842) the cartographic skills of Fowler, so often employed in the service of civic pride, were now brought into service to draw plans of the in-township which became nationally known as expressions of the darker side of Leeds. His 1833 plan was the first in the world to be prepared to show that the limited geographical distribution of a disease could point to a likely cause,

[1] Chapters Twelve and Thirteen are based almost exclusively on the three *Reports* of 1833, 1839 and 1842, for which see Bibliography, §2 and 4, below. Footnote references are therefore given here only for direct quotations; sources for Tables are specified separately.

[2] *Leeds Guide*, p.93.

here the quality of working-class housing.[3] In the more elaborate coloured version incorporated in a Blue Book of 1842 it achieved a more than local fame within the Sanitary Movement as a graphic criticism of the form that urbanisation was taking, and thus a critical view of Leeds came to the attention of more strangers than could ever have read about civic pride in the Guides and Directories.

A generation later, James Hole did not exaggerate when he described Baker's reports of 1833, 1839 and 1842 as 'revelations', and it will be appropriate to employ as much of their language as possible in the following pages; although the particular object will not be a reiteration of familiar material from the literature of the Sanitary Movement[4] but an examination of questions with essentially local answers: in what sense did the cholera of 1832 mark the beginning of criticism in Leeds? what were the targets for criticism? and how were they related to the separate development of an East and a West End?

The quotation from James Smith's report of 1845 at the head of this Chapter emphasised the segregation of classes within the town, and the barrier to benevolence when eye and nostril were offended by the East End; and this social segregation would have been less marked if the character of housing development described in previous Chapters had not already removed so many of the homes and workplaces of the benevolent in the 'higher classes' from proximity to the working-class streets, a segregation which by 1842 was being further marked by a third West End in the suburb of Headingley. Thus it could be called a 'revelation' to describe what lay only a few yards from Briggate in the Kirkgate courts and to describe, in print, conditions in the Marsh Lane folds which were known to every overseer of the poor, to many doctors and to most of the clergy.

In the peroration of the 1842 report Baker distinguished between two forces which had sapped 'the labouring population, the strength and glory on which the great Interests of the country have flourished'. These forces he grouped into 'local influences without . . . and within' but we shall not be concerned here with those 'within', which were the neglect of moral discipline and regulations 'which, had they been employed, would have made mills, manufactories and workshops blessings wherever they were erected'.[5] The influences 'without' were summed up as 'neglected congregations':

[3] E. W. Gilbert, 'Pioneer Maps of Health and Disease in England', *Geographical Journal*, CXXIV (1958), 172–83.

[4] J. Hole, *Homes of the Working Classes* (1866), p.123. For the Sanitary Question see the Introduction in M. W. Flinn, ed., *Report on the Sanitary Condition of the Labouring Population of Great Britain in 1842, By Edwin Chadwick* (1965).

[5] *1842 Report*, p.62.

Baker's 'congregations' were a statistical entity, the accumulation of high density housing, but the 'neglect' was a moral and social fact: a country of Two Nations, with one ignorant of the conditions in which the other laboured and lived.

Every large industrial city had its Two Nations and its East End and West End; the educated classes of Leeds were no more blind than those elsewhere. Nationwide there were deep-rooted attitudes of mind which rejected the propriety of any regulation of economic conduct which was implicit if criticism of insanitary conditions were accepted, creating a predisposition to regard the question as unimportant. The scale of remedial action also seemed forbidding when urban institutions were poorly endowed with powers of inspection and interference.[6]

Leeds was particularly ill-equipped with effective municipal institutions at the time when the insanitary conditions were being created: but it has been the repeated argument in previous Chapters that changes took place gradually, the overall and long-term consequences of which were unappreciated until they had gathered in a sorry accumulation. The cholera had stolen on Leeds overnight but the accumulation of house alongside house, of factories, dye-houses, gasworks, had been measured in years and even decades.

Serious attention to sanitary conditions was also bedevilled by their close association with the poor and the seemingly insoluble problem of poverty. A novel element in the investigations aroused by the cholera of 1832 was the shift of attention from economic impoverishment to environmental impoverishment, although Baker was well aware of the connection between disease and low or interrupted incomes. Poverty from unemployment had been particularly bad in the town since the collapse of the mid-twenties boom, and was accentuated by the displacement of domestic labour into the factories. In the July of the cholera ten thousand unemployed operatives gathered on Woodhouse Moor to demonstrate their existence, 'to show Mr. Baines', as the Tory *Intelligencer* gleefully reported.[7]

[6] B. J. Barber, 'Leeds Corporation, 1835–1905: a History of its Environmental, Social and Administrative Services' (unpublished PhD thesis, University of Leeds, 1975), Ch. 1; for the administration of public health, J. Toft, 'Public Health in Leeds in the Nineteenth Century' (unpublished MA thesis, University of Manchester, 1966).

[7] *LI*, 2 Aug. 1832; of the cholera victims, 'all the sufferers except one are in a state of comparative destitution and want': *Ibid.*, 14 June 1832; Gott's weavers had just ended an eleven month strike: *Ibid.*, 14 Jan. 1832; between December 1831 and March 1832 more than 25,000 individuals (from a population of 71,000) had received some form of poor relief, none of which was paid unless the per capita income was 2*s*. 6*d*. a week or less for those over ten and 1*s*. 6*d*. for those under ten: *Ibid.*, 14 April 1832.

Poverty in general had long been an object of enquiry both by individuals such as Sir Frederick Eden and by Parliamentary committees and commissions but hopes were current in 1832 that a reformed poor law might be devised that would alleviate poverty, similar to the hopes that Parliamentary and municipal reform would cure diseases and fevers in the body politic.

Poverty maimed, and poverty killed: the town's doctors were well aware in which of the town's streets the malignant fevers and other diseases were more likely to be encountered, but the cholera deaths were additional.[8] Charity and benevolence had been accustomed to supplement poor relief in the leanest years through soup kitchens and clothing societies, but what equivalent benevolence could effect the changes which could ward off a return of the cholera? The educated classes knew about the poor, and they paid the poor rate. They knew about criminality and immorality and idleness and irreligion: now they had to be educated into an awareness of the relation between disease and the character of the environment and to be weaned from such loose inferences as that expressed by a correspondent of the *Intelligencer* in September 1832: 'The attacks of the cholera are made principally on the careless and profligate, and few of the wealthy and respectable are subject to its influence'.[9]

The cholera, feared at first in case it was contagious, proved to be a disease which chose victims in certain parts of town and left others untouched. In the cholera months of 1832 the angel of death paid no more than the normal number of visits to the Park estate although he was often seen abroad in the fallen West End nearby; in the second West End he was a virtual stranger except in the courts behind St James Street. The cholera's distinct preference for courts and back-to-back streets considerably eased Baker's task of educating his contemporaries in the harsh facts of medical geography and their implications; and for us his necessary particularisation of good, bad and indifferent streets enables a precise reconstruction of the degree to which, by 1832, the elements of an East End had diffused to other quarters of the town.

DIRT AND DARKNESS: THE BEGINNINGS OF CRITICISM

Important as the cholera was in directing attention to a deterioration of the environment, it would not be accurate to see 1832 as the year when criticism was first heard in Leeds. Nor does criticism have to

[8] In 1816 Whitaker (*Loidis*, p.83) recalled the typhus epidemic of 1802 when 'whole streets were infected nearly house by house'.

[9] *LI*, 1 Sept. 1832.

be confined to the vocal and the explicit: the steps, identified in Chapter Ten, by which middle-class residences ceased to accumulate in the West End were as important a part of this chronology as anything written to the newspapers or said to a Parliamentary committee.

A scrutiny of Parliamentary papers yields nothing earlier than two sentences spoken in the year after the cholera: John Marshall, MP for Leeds, in his evidence to the Select Committee on Public Walks – that is, urban open spaces – said: 'It is advisable to have some improvement made in sewerage and regulation of buildings and small tenements for the health of the inhabitants, and for the comfort of the humbler classes, combined with the saving of expense in the poor's rate'.[10] Marshall's comment was undoubtedly influenced by what had already appeared in Baker's report to the Leeds Board of Health which he had undertaken to lay before the authorities in London. The other comment of that year was contained in a report from the Factory Commissioners citing James Williamson, another Leeds doctor: 'the greater part of cottage streets formed within the last fifteen years are unpaved or very partially paved and sewered'.[11]

These two comments were centred on insanitary streets and housing, brought into the centre of argument by the cholera, but the earliest record of local dissatisfaction with industrial urbanisation concerns different targets: the dirtiness of industrial smoke and the impurities of a water supply which depended on the river. The prevalence of south-westerly winds did ensure that some areas were smokier than others but the wind blew where it listed and even the best quarters sometimes lay under a pall, so that the magistrates who took action against the smoke nuisance were not speaking so much on behalf of the inarticulate as for themselves. Similarly, the search for new sources of water was of immediate interest even to those who lived in that minority of houses which were already connected to the pipes of the town waterworks, for the ultimate source of this piped water was the polluted river; while the owners of dyehouses and textile mills had their own immediate interest in seeking out sources of more abundant and less impure water.[12] It will also be recalled that criticism of cellar dwellings, found as early as 1806 in the *Leeds Guide*, was as much from the danger that their unprotected steps offered to passing townspeople as from their being hotbeds of disease for those who actually lived in them.

[10] *Report of the Select Committee on Public Walks*, PP 1833, XV, Q.620.
[11] *Second Report of the Factory Commission*, PP 1833, XXI, p.112.
[12] *LM*, 19 Aug. 1822.

Since the unreformed Corporation had no rating powers beyond those for maintaining justice and a police force it is not to be expected that concern for the environment would be shown in its records; and, as with its successor, expenditure on street improvement was acceptable only on the ground of reducing traffic congestion. Nor were the Improvement Acts of any benefit to the least improved parts of the town. The powers obtained for the Improvement Commissioners under the local acts between 1755 and 1824 were narrowly confined to the central streets in the provision that was made for paving, scavenging and a night watch.[13] Street lighting, it was reported in 1838, 'was very inefficiently done, the back streets, where there are few shops, are not lighted at all';[14] while town scavengers not only avoided the East End but took their loads eastwards to make the dirtiest areas still dirtier: 'The contractor for the street sweepings rents a plot of vacant land in the centre of the North east ward, containing the greatest number of poor, as a depot for the sweepings from the streets and markets, both vegetable and general, for the purpose of exsiccating and accumulating until they could be sold as manure and carried away'.

The scavenging of dirt from the streets was assigned by the Improvement Commissioners to the workhouse board and used to give employment as a form of poor relief.[15] There were no powers to remove offensive rubbish from private land or from private courts and backyards unless a formal complaint was made; there were few of these. No public authority had any powers to cleanse even the small length of common sewers in the town. The highway surveyors of the parish had no jurisdiction beyond the public highways and were unconcerned with the much larger number of new, unadopted private streets and courts.

With these limited powers, and haunted always by fears of any rise in the improvement rate, it is not surprising to find that matters touching on public health were not much discussed either by the

[13] The Improvement Act of 1790 had extended the lighting and paving provisions of the 1755 Act to a thousand yard radius from the bars, and that of 1809 to one mile; the 1809 Act (*Acts Local and Personal, 49 Geo.III cap. 122*) was also concerned with the new Court House and Prison; a Bill of 1823 failed through procedural error (*LI*, 8 May 1823); an identical Act of 1824 (*Acts Local and Personal, 5 Geo.IV, cap. 104*) authorised the demolition of the Middle Row in Briggate; the town's distinctive street-name signs and the compulsory black-and-white painted house numbers also originated with this Act.

[14] Council Improvement Committee, minutes (LCH, Strongroom, shelf 19), 21 Feb. 1838.

[15] *Ibid.*, 3 June 1840 and Scavenging Committee, Minutes (Shelf 85), 17 Oct. 1836 and 19 Feb. 1838.

Commissioners or by the annual meetings of ratepayers in the Vestry; nor that when concern arose it was less from compassion than from a realisation that a reduction in the most obvious causes of sickness and disease would ease the burden of the poor rate. Marshall's recommendation of legislation, cited above, had been 'for the comfort of the lower classes' but also 'combined with the saving of expense in the poor's rate'. Similarly, in 1818 the workhouse committee of the Vestry drew attention to the diseases which brought inmates to the workhouse; in the same year the vagrancy committee identified the common lodging houses as a source for spreading sickness among the poor; and between 1814 and 1829 the Vestry continued to press for the purchase of land for an extension of the overcrowded burial ground at the parish church.

Thus the characteristic criticism in the eighteen-twenties was centred on dirt: the dirtiness of mud where streets were ill-paved; the dirtiness of ineffective scavenging and street sweeping; the dirtiness of industrial and domestic effluents in the river; and the dangers to life and property from the murkiness of poorly lighted or unlighted streets. Attention was particularly concentrated on the dirtiness of smoke and the impurities of river water.

When the *Intelligencer* approvingly reported successful prosecutions of five factories for excessive smoke in August 1822 it is significant that it castigated these mill chimneys both as a physical harm, a nuisance, and a disgrace, harmful to the town's esteem: 'We are happy to see that steps are being at last taken to rid the town of the nuisance and disgrace arising from the smoke created in the different factories. And we hope that this beginning will be promptly followed up'.[16] There had been no technical improvements in methods of reducing industrial smoke since 1824, but year by year there were more smoking chimneys. In 1842 'the smoke from the low chimnies of the dyeworks and tobacco pipe furnaces is a greater nuisance in particular localities than even that of the [steam] engine chimnies, for the latter do carry the cloud above the heads of the people, but from the former dense volumes are conveyed through the streets by every breath of wind'. In the furnaces of the town's 362 steam engines it was reckoned that 200,000 tons of coal a year were then being consumed to generate some 6600 horsepower.[17]

[16] *LI*, 24 Aug. 1822; the private survey of steam engines by William Lindley in 1824 (Brotherton Library, University of Leeds, General MS. 18) may be related to this interest; the Gott smoke case of 1824 followed; and in 1825, hearing of the proposed 'New Leeds' on the Cowper estate of Chapeltown, the *Mercury* of 30 July commented that such a smokeless 'Utopia would indeed be a *new* Leeds!'

[17] *1842 Report*, pp. 59–61.

TABLE 12.1

Daily Consumption of Water Per Head for Domestic Purposes, 1790–1851

Year	Gallons
1790	2.0
1801	1.5
1811	1.2
1821	0.9
1831	0.6
1841	0.8
1851	8.1

Source: R. S. Peppard, 'The Growth and Development of Leeds Waterworks Undertakings, 1694–1852' (unpublished MPhil. thesis, University of Leeds, 1973), Table 7.

The town's water was becoming as dirty as its sky, and an additional problem was the inability to provide a volume of water to keep pace with increasing population. An Act of 1790 had established separate Improvement Commissioners to be in charge of a waterworks company, and capital was raised for a new engine and the enlargement of reservoirs but the sole source remained the Aire, and the new inlet for the supply pipes was only a furlong west of the original inlet at King's Mills, and below the discharge points from Bean Ing and the surface drainage and sewerage from the Park estate. The engines and reservoirs remained inadequate. From the data in Table 12.1 there was each year less water available, whether for drinking, cooking or washing, and a smaller proportion of houses connected to the main pipes. The engineer John Rennie made a survey of the waterworks in 1814 and recommended a new steam engine and larger pipes, but lean years intervened and nothing was then done. In 1825 another engineer, Nicholas Brown of Wakefield, was commissioned to produce a scheme to take water from Sheepscar Beck but there was strong opposition from the thirty-nine industrial establishments which already utilised that stream, and the very presence of these establishments was not a good omen for the purity of its water. It was in the deeds of one of these that the vendor reserved the right of fishing for eels at the outflow from the privies.[18] No fresh exploration of sources took place until

[18] WRRD, CN555 739; cattle were also watered in the beck: LCD 51001 (1789).

1834 and there was no augmentation of supply until the new joint-stock company established by the Act of 1837 completed the long supply lines from Eccup reservoir in 1841.[19]

These inadequacies of a pure piped supply, although it was not realised at the time, were closely related to the cholera epidemic of 1832 which spread through drinking unpiped water from wells and courtyard pumps that had been infected by contact with sewage. The report of the Leeds Board of Health after the cholera is considered in a later section of this Chapter, for it contained the first sustained criticism of a deteriorating environment, but it devoted little space to problems of water supply other than to deplore the scarcity and dearness of water as a factor in the inattention of the labouring classes to personal cleanliness: but it is our good fortune that in seeking to demonstrate why the cholera was at once so intense but so localised the Board of Health's report gave Robert Baker his apprenticeship in the collection and publication of social statistics, a skill he was to utilise again in 1839 and 1842.

THE CHOLERA AND THE SOCIAL STATISTICS OF AN EAST END, 1832–33

As Table 12.2 shows, the burials in the parish churchyard in the seven months from May to November of 1831 numbered 980: but in the same months of 1832 the cholera increased that number to 1395; additionally 1115 persons contracted the disease but recovered. In one day, 16 August, there were twenty-one deaths in the town and fifty-eight new cases reported. The alarm aroused by this sudden epidemic is sufficient to explain why the cholera months were remembered in Leeds for years to come, and why so much energy was put into the collection of data that might help to identify the causes of cholera and prevent its return.[20]

In the study of environmental deterioration the cholera epidemic of 1832 is of considerable significance, for it convinced informed medical opinion in the town that the disease was closely related to a 'defective arrangement of streets and houses', and the so-called Sanitary Question now became a central issue of public policy: thus in January 1833, after the epidemic had passed, the Leeds Board of Health was presented with a report from 'the Medical Gentlemen of

[19] These paragraphs derive from R. S. Peppard, 'The Growth and Development of Leeds Waterworks Undertakings, 1694–1852' (unpublished MPhil. thesis, University of Leeds, 1973).

[20] For the cholera generally, R. J. Morris, *Cholera* (1976).

TABLE 12.2

Burials at Parish Church, Monthly, 1829–32

	1829	1830	1831	1832*
May	101	86	127	105 + 2 cholera
June	75	83	120	111 + 37 cholera
July	80	74	148	97 + 98 cholera
August	104	122	162	119 + 257 cholera
September	106	119	172	109 + 196 cholera
October	78	95	133	110 + 54 cholera
November	110	108	118	98 + 2 cholera

* There were no cholera deaths after November 1832.

Source: *1833 Report*, p.31.

the Town' and 'a condensed report by Mr. Baker'.[21] At that time Robert Baker had been in Leeds for about seven years as 'town surgeon', an appointment made by the overseers of the poor and one which gave him daily contact with the ailments associated with poverty even before the cholera. Before the cholera reached Leeds he had gone to Newcastle upon Tyne especially to observe its effects, and there contracted a mild form of the disease.[22]

The published report, issued in the Board's name, was written in the first person, and is clearly Baker's, although unattributed. His report was both a diagnosis and a prescription for a remedy. In its conclusion he regretted that 'it is not compulsory on the proprietors of property to make good common sewerage in the commencement of new streets and dwelling houses, and that paving and draining should precede the building itself', and he recommended legislative action to these ends: 'I entertain a lively hope that some very speedy and vigorous efforts will be made to obtain a national, or, at the least, a local Act of Parliament, which shall embrace the important objects

[21] *1833 Report*, p.3.

[22] He reported to a public meeting: *LM*, 3 Dec. 1831. There is no biography of Baker (1803–80), but for his career in public health see W. R. Lee, 'Robert Baker: the first doctor in the Factory Department', *British Journal of Industrial Medicine*, XXI (1964), 85–93 and 167–79. F. Beckwith, 'Robert Baker', *University of Leeds Review*, VII (1960), 40–49, was an early appreciation of Baker's importance. Baker was awarded the CBE but fails to appear in the *DNB*; there is a full-length painting of him in the dining room of the Metropole Hotel in Leeds, and a smaller portrait in Lee, 'Robert Baker', fig.3.

now brought under consideration'.[23] John Marshall, one of the town's first two MPs, was present at the Board and promised that he would personally take a copy of the report to the Home Secretary.[24]

In his work as a pioneer social scientist Baker was applying methods similar to those already developed by his medical colleagues in Leeds in their studies of industrial disease, that is an accumulation of case histories, followed by classification and then an attempt to see what circumstances were commonly encountered in the patients' lives or environment.[25] Consequently seven pages of the report were occupied by a 'Schedule of the Streets, Lanes, Alleys and Yards in which there occurred Cases of Malignant Cholera, with the Number of Cases, Recoveries and Deaths, Male and Female'.[26] For each street the Schedule showed whether it was sewered and paved, the number of cholera deaths and recoveries, and a succinct description of the street's condition in phrases such as 'very dirty', 'generally stagnant' and 'sewer crosses into Beck'. Obviously the associations being explored here were those of insanitary surroundings and not, for example, the victims' age, sex, occupation, income, diet or moral character. To the doctors who had tended the sick or the clergy who had ministered to them, the geographical concentration of the disease had been so striking that it was reasonable to look for some peculiarity in the areas involved, and some other peculiarity in the areas that had been immune. Even though the medical investigators, in Leeds as elsewhere, failed to identify the agent that passed the cholera from victim to victim correctly as drinking water that had been polluted from infected sewage, they were at least in the right area when they drew attention to the imperfections of drainage and sewerage in the cholera streets and a widespread belief that infected air must have been the agent of transmission led them to draw attention to such other characteristics of East End housing as high densities and cellar dwellings.

Nowhere was more characteristic of the places to which the cholera was most likely to come, nor of the people who would be most vulnerable to it, than its first reported occurrence on 28 May in the Blue Bell Fold. The earlier history of this fold has already been established. It lay a little out of town on the lower slopes of the Bank behind the lane which had become dignified with the name

[23] *1833 Report*, p.19.

[24] *Ibid.*, p.3.

[25] The most active was C. T. Thackrah, author of *The Effects of Arts, Trades and Professions on Health and Longevity* (1831; republished with introduction by A. Meiklejohn (Edinburgh, 1957)) and *Cholera, Its Character and Treatment* (1832).

[26] *1833 Report*, pp.20–27.

Richmond Street, but had long since ceased to be a farmyard for folding animals. Now it was 'a small and dirty cul de sac containing about 20 houses, inhabited by poor families, many of whom are Irish'.[27] Over the four months before the cholera the average weekly income for one of these families, made up of five adults and three children, had been twelve shillings.[28]

Blue Bell Fold was a cul-de-sac because access by the former farm gate on Richmond Road had been blocked by a line of back-to-back cottages, and a small alley had been left, leading from East Street, when a four-storey carpet manufactory was built in 1793.[29] The first victim was the two-year-old son of an Irish weaver and the second, also a child, came from a back-to-back house in the nearby Cavalier Street.

The Blue Bell Fold was notable not only for an early but for an intense visitation by the cholera. Eight more inhabitants of the Fold were to die, four from one family, and fifteen others fell victims but recovered. Most of the other streets in the Schedule with a large number of cases (Table 12.3) were of some length, such as Marsh Lane, Quarry Hill and Ellerby Lane, but the Fold contained no more than thirty-three dwellings, above and below ground.

The Boot and Shoe Yard in Kirkgate was another small but crowded cul-de-sac which suffered badly from the cholera (Fig. 12.1). It had the same number of deaths as the Blue Bell Fold but became much more notorious. It was first described in the main body of the 1833 Report:

> at the bottom of the Boot and Shoe Yard a fetid water course commencing in Vicar lane receives much of the soil [sewage] from George's Street and Court and from the Yard and other places in the vicinity . . . From the privies in the Boot and Shoe Yard which did not appear to have been thoroughly cleansed for the last 30 years, 70 cart loads of manure were removed by order of the [Improvement] Commissioners.[30]

In Baker's second report of 1839[31] the removal of the excrement was again described, with the comment that 'it is reported not to have been cleaned out since;[32] and population figures were given to show

[27] *Ibid.*, p.33.
[28] *Ibid.*, and *LM*, 2 and 16 June 1832.
[29] LCD 1049: the redeveloped site is now on the corner of Richmond Hill and East Street.
[30] *1833 Report*, p.10.
[31] See below, p.397.
[32] *Ibid.*, p.11; it was also described in the report on the pilot survey made to the Council on 18 Feb. 1839 (Council Minutes, IV, ff.525–26).

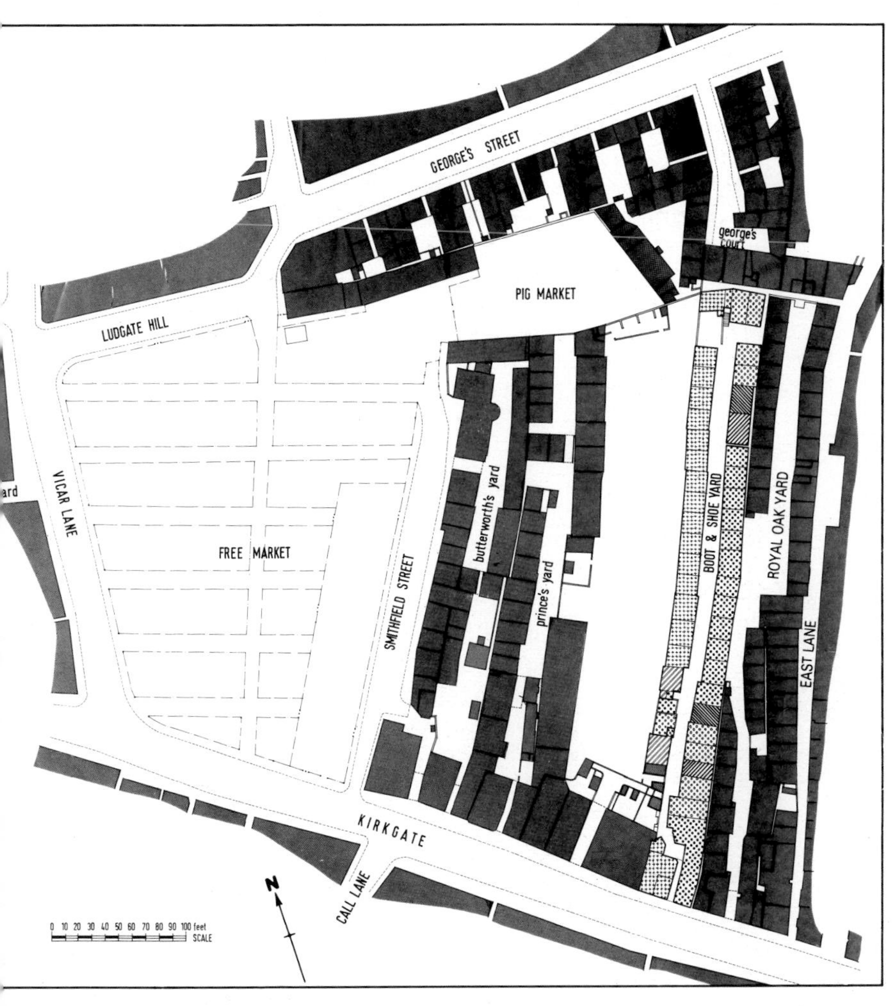

FIG. 12.1 CIVIC SHAME: THE BOOT AND SHOE YARD, KIRKGATE, 1843

The north-west end of Kirkgate before demolition of the notorious Yard and its neighbours for extension of the municipal market. Yards ('folds') behind the main Kirkgate frontages had been in-filled piecemeal with blind-back cottages, one room to a floor, set against the dividing walls between yard and yard. The houses belonging to one proprietor (John Dufton) have been shaded. Apart from its high population density, its lack of light and its absence of sanitation the Yard had the drain from the Pig Market at its northern end.

an average of six persons to a room; the landlord took £214 a year in rents. Baker twice referred to the Yard in the report he prepared for Chadwick in 1842 and it was cited again by Chadwick in the main body of his report, to be taken up by many other writers and even appear in numerous modern anthologies.[33]

Baker's account has come under attack from would-be revisionists.[34] In fact every statistic given by Baker can be confirmed from independent sources. One of these is the official survey and valuation which had to be made when the Yard was purchased by the Council under the authority of the 1842 Improvement Act, to be demolished for an extension to the public market. An accompanying large-scale plan has already been published elsewhere.[35]

When it recommended the purchase of the Yard the Council committee employed the very language of civic shame.

> The property proposed to be purchased consists of the Boot and Shoe Yard together with the Premises fronting Kirkgate . . . which is a disgrace to the town and from which locality the number of cases sent to the Infirmary, the Dispensary and specially to the House of Recovery, are of fearful extent, consequently it is and has been a heavy burthen upon all our local charities. Many of their dwellings are of the worst description.[36]

In the schedule and plan attached to the purchase deed are details of thirty-six two-roomed ('low floor and chamber') cottages rented at £3 10*s*. a year, and four with 'low floor, chamber and garret', their twelve rooms being each separately tenanted. The front premises were a butcher's shop, and there was a piggery in the yard that was rented more highly than any of the cottages. The total rent roll was near that cited in 1839.

Further confirmation of the conditions in the Yard comes from the enumerators' books for the 1841 census; there seventy families appear, totalling 321 persons, an average per house that is twice the

[33] *1842 Report*, pp. 5 and 57.

[34] Rimmer's view (*Cottages*, pp. 168 and 196) was that the 1842 Report was a 'brilliantly distorted snapshot'; and, on 'the issue whether housing got worse in a quantitative or qualitative sense between 1780 and 1840', that 'the evidence suggests that this did not happen'. His unfavourable view may rest in part on his unlucky confusion (*Ibid.*, p. 169) of this Boot and Shoe Yard with another of the same name in what became Wood Street, 'an open yard between Briggate and Vicar Lane', of which there were no complaints: but not surprisingly, since it was lined with stables and warehouses only (LCD 1091).

[35] LCA, LCEng., Box 10; Beresford, *Face of Leeds*, pl. 12.

[36] LCH, Improvement Act Committee Report Books (Leeds Civic Hall, strongroom shelf 15), 18 Jan. 1843.

TABLE 12.3

Streets with Most Cholera Cases Reported, 1832

Street*	Number of cases	Number of deaths
Marsh Lane	52	21
Quarry Hill	43	18
York St	30	8
Ellerby Lane	27	6
Richmond Rd	25	11
Blue Bell Fold	24	9
Orange St	24	8
Cavalier St	21	1
Bath St	18	8
Boot and Shoe Yard	17	9
Charles St	17	6
Cottage St	16	2
Duke St	15	5
Meadow Lane	15	6
Mill St	14	2
Providence St	14	3
Workhouse	13	8
Water Lane (Bank)	12	3
Cherry Tree Yard	12	7
St John's Place	12	6
New Lane (Meadow Lane)	12	5
Paley's Gallery	11	7
Lemon St	11	5
Goulden's Buildings	11	4
Ebenezer St	11	6
Oak St	11	6
Off St	10	3
York Road	10	2

* All places from the in-township with ten or more cases reported have been included here; it includes all places with more than five deaths except for Nelson Street which had seven deaths from nine cases reported. The out-township streets were not differentiated in the report; Holbeck had 86 deaths and Hunslet 38.

Source: *1833 Report*, Schedule, pp.21–27.

average for the town. Two-thirds of the heads of families were Irish born and almost every child enumerated was a street hawker, a 'match seller'.[37]

Table 12.3 lists the places where the cholera was most prevalent. They were predominantly in the East End, bounded by Quarry Hill, Ellerby Lane and Marsh Lane; south of the river there were black spots in Meadow Lane, and the industrial villages of Holbeck and Hunslet were badly affected. The localities of less prevalence were more widely distributed through the town, and we shall return to this topic later.[38]

Baker's argument for remedial measures rested on a demonstrated association of cholera with insanitary streets. As an alternative method of presentation to the Schedule he enlisted cartography. On a simplified map of the town prepared by Charles Fowler the 'cholera parts' were 'lined and colored [*sic*] RED' so that the significance of their close congregation in some areas and their total absence in others could be appreciated.

In the months when it was clear that the cholera would not return there seemed hope that all these 'revelations' might produce action. When the Leeds Board of Health met at the Court House for the last time on 21 January 1833 its members, which included seven physicians and thirty-nine surgeons, received the Baker report and subscribed unanimously to its diagnosis of the connection between disease and insanitation: 'We are of opinion that the streets in which the Malignant Cholera prevailed most severely were those in which the drainage was most imperfect.' They also accepted its remedy: 'the probability of a further visitation will be diminished by a general and efficient system of drainage, sewerage and paving, and enforcement of better regulations as to the cleanliness of the streets'.[39]

Yet these hopes that sanitary measures, local or national, could be achieved were to be disappointed. It is true that the Boot and Shoe Yard, 'overlooked in the later cleansing of the town' had its walls whitewashed at the public expense,[40] but this cosmetic ritual was surpassed at the Blue Bell Fold. It was simply rechristened.

The notorious name disappeared from the directories and will not be found in the street-index to the 1841 census. Its location was for a long time in doubt, but among the deeds for a group of back-to-back houses, purchased for slum clearance by Leeds Corporation earlier this century, is one with an endorsement which locates it behind

[37] PRO, HO 107/1346.
[38] See below, pp. 347–48.
[39] *1833 Report*, p.3.
[40] *LM*, 2 June 1832.

Richmond Road, and confirms what had happened to sweeten the name of the notorious fold. One deed has a contemporary endorsement, 'Tinsdill's Yard otherwise called Blue Bell Yard at the Near Bank,' and another deed has the endorsement, 'Blue Bell Fold now Richmond Court'.[41]

STATISTICS FOR OUTSIDE CONSUMPTION, 1839 AND 1842

Robert Baker's second opportunity as a social statistician came six years after the Board of Health report. The political situation in Leeds had changed meanwhile: the first election to the reformed Corporation gave a majority of Whig councillors, among them Baker, elected for the South ward. Several other councillors who were doctors had served on the Board of Health in 1832–33, and Baker had no difficulty when in May 1837 he moved a resolution for the appointment of a six-member committee 'to enquire into the best mode of obtaining statistically the condition of the borough of Leeds, and its estimated cost'.[42] By this time Baker had accumulated further experience of local social conditions: from October 1834 he was certifying surgeon to the factory inspectorate of northern England; between 1835 and 1837 he organised the assisted migration of the poor from southern England to work in Yorkshire factories; and in October 1837 produced a long memorandum on wages and prices in Leeds for the benefit of the Poor Law Commissioners.[43]

The Statistical Committee could not set to work immediately for it had to wait for the completion of a new rating valuation which was already under way but in October 1838 a questionnaire was drafted by Baker and the town clerk, Edwin Eddison. Baker himself made a tabular roll of streets in the North ward where a pilot survey was undertaken and reported to the Council in January 1839; by April the rate collectors for each ward had almost completed the collection of data 'from House to House' and a final report was made to the Council in October 1839, evoking complaints from Baker's Tory opponents that public money had been wasted on the enquiry and privacy improperly invaded. Copies of the report were then printed for Council members, and in November James Williamson, another doctor, and the mayor when the committee was set up, prepared an abstract for general publication. At this stage some errors were detected in the printed report and there were delays in publishing the

41 LCD 1325.

42 Statistical Committee, Minutes (LCH, strongroom shelf 36), 3 May 1837.

43 PRO, MH 122/15224 (3 Oct. 1837).

abstract but by February 1841 a thousand copies had been distributed. The full report was submitted to the new journal of the Statistical Society of London where it was published in January 1840.[44]

As in 1833 the report was used to urge political action: the Statistical Committee was called together again in January 1841 to draft a petition directing Parliament's attention to

> the evils of imperfect sewerage and ventilation by which the health and social well-being of their fellow citizens and fellow subjects are materially injured ... The localities in which such defective and injurious arrangements exist are almost exclusively peopled by the operative and poorer classes, the most numerous part of the Community, who individually have no control over the evils by which they are surrounded.[45]

The petition concluded with a request for a general sewerage and building act: such a bill was introduced into the Commons in May but withdrawn in 1842 in view of Chadwick's impending report to the Poor Law Commissioners *On the Sanitary Condition of the Labouring Population*.[46]

Chadwick's report incorporated a number of local reports from industrial towns. For Leeds, Chadwick first approached Williamson who had given evidence to the Select Committee on the Health of Towns in 1840 and was the abbreviator of the Statistical Committee report; Chadwick was intrigued by the cholera map in Baker's earlier report and wished to use Baker's material, but he found Baker unwilling to collaborate with Williamson. To the latter Chadwick wrote:

[44] The texts and pagination of quotations cited here are from the *Journal of the Statistical Society* [*of London*], II (1839), 397–424; no locally printed copy of the full report has survived. An abstract of the report read to the Council (16 Nov. 1839) was intended 'to be printed if necessary', but there were delays. For the Council discussions see *LM*, 2 and 30 Nov. 1839; 18 and 25 Jan. and 19 Dec. 1840.

In 1841 the Leeds printer, Pickard, issued a thousand copies of a twelve-page booklet, *Abstract of the Report of the Statistical Committee for 1838, 39 and 40 of the Town Council of the Borough of Leeds*. This contained the thirteen Tables of the report prefaced by an 'Advertisement' apologising for a delay in publication since errors of transcription had been found in the Tables. It also promised that 'Other Tables are in preparation and will be submitted to the Council at a future period' (p. 11) but the Statistical Committee Minutes (LCH, Strongroom, shelf 36) have no reference to printing after November 1839 when it was resolved to revise and print 'the Abstract prepared by Dr Williamson'. (It will be noticed that the 1841 *Abstract* dated the report 1838–40 rather than 1839.)

[45] Council Minutes, V, ff. 244–45, 1 Jan. 1841.

[46] The bill did not originate in Leeds: clause 17 banned back-to-back houses.

> Mr. Baker's peculiar means of observation in respect to the manufacturing population as superintendent of factories and in other public capacities has given him peculiar information that [the Commissioners] are desirous of obtaining. They were informed that he had declined to communicate the information to you or to any other person, and that he could only communicate it in an independent form.[47]

The copy of Chadwick's report in the set of Parliamentary papers assigns the Leeds section to no author but in a (differently paginated) reprint Baker was named as its author, and it bears his stamp throughout, although curiously the reprint omitted that map which gave such distinction to Baker's contribution, epitomising the particularisation which was at the heart of his method of enquiry and exposition.[48] The map made a strong impression on the readers of Chadwick's report, and through it the civic shame of Leeds became public property.

To Baker, particularisation was essential not only to give precision and context to the areas where conditions were at their worst, defining what was properly shameful: if Chadwick's report would bring him before a nationwide audience it was essential to particularise so that shreds of civic pride could be preserved and the town defended from the charge of being wholly deplorable. As Baker himself wrote in 1842, 'Although condemned as a town in its entire locality at the first glance [Leeds] may really have only peculiar points of local influence from whence the gross results are derived'.[49]

Baker's continuing need to convince the sceptical and the complacent among his fellow-councillors and his readers made it necessary for him to stress the difference between the good and the bad streets in the fuller 1839 report. It had to be shown that the improvement rate and the highway rate were failing to benefit the very streets that most needed improving; while the exact localisation of good and bad housing conditions was essential to his argument that the cholera was not the only distasteful product of deprivation and squalor.

The argument of the 1833 report had relied mainly on its schedule of good, bad and indifferent streets but Baker did make that attempt to enlist the aid of cartography which had impressed Chadwick. Now in 1842 the data were mapped more systematically at some risk

[47] PRO, MH 12/15225, 31 Dec. 1840.

[48] The British Library copy forms *H.L. Sessional papers 1842*, XXVI (1842), 148–209; the separate version, with the imprint of HM Stationery Office at the foot of p.62, is paginated from 1 to 62 and lacks the important map.

[49] *1842 Report*, p.23.

of over-burdening the eye with detail.[50] Fowler's 'Map exhibiting the track of fever and cholera, and the badly cleansed portions of the town of Leeds . . . engraved and printed in colours' had blue spots to designate 'localities in which Cholera prevailed' and red spots for 'localities from which Contagious diseases have been sent to the House of Recovery [Fever Hospital] from 1834 to 1839'. The association of disease and environment was presented by categorising housing into three groups, described in a key as 'Houses of the Working Classes'; 'Shops, Warehouses and Houses of Tradespeople'; and 'Houses of the First Class', although in error the non-residential and barrack-like ranges of Bean Ing Mill were depicted by the symbol appropriate to the last category. Broad washes of dark brown covered the 'least cleansed Districts' (Fig. 12.2).

The coloured spots were gathered in the areas of worst quality housing, and Baker wanted the correlation to be driven into his readers' minds. Death, disease, moral squalor, poverty, high poor relief, and high crime rates were to be found together, a 'congregation' or association of evils in industrial towns to which the term 'East End' was being increasingly applied.

Yet the Leeds thus exposed to the world here, and again in James Smith's independent *Report on the Condition of the Town of Leeds* in 1845, was certainly not that envisaged half a century earlier when Leeds first began to have an East End, and a later section of this Chapter must follow Baker's method of particularisation to identify (and to attempt to explain) what now formed a target for critics and a too long continued cause for civic shame.

The common elements in the reports of 1833, 1839 and 1842 do permit the subject matter of all three to be taken as one, and so little was done to improve conditions in the post-cholera decade that it is not improper to integrate evidence from 1833 with that from a decade later. Although the intervening decade did not have a rate of population increase as high as between 1821 and 1831, nevertheless the oppressed facilities of the in-township were further strained in those years by the addition of nearly 4000 new houses. In the

[50] The map is inserted opposite p. 160 in the British Library copy.

FIG. 12.2 CIVIC SHAME: THE WEST END IN THE SANITARY MAP OF 1842
A section of the plan prepared for Baker's contribution to Chadwick's Blue Book. A smoking chimney symbol was used for the mills — nine on the river bank and seven elsewhere in the West End; spots indicated the locality of the cholera in 1832 and contagious diseases in 1834–39; a brown wash was applied to indicate 'less cleansed districts' on West Street. The 'first-class housing' of Park Square has cross shading but in error Bean Ing mill was similarly shaded.

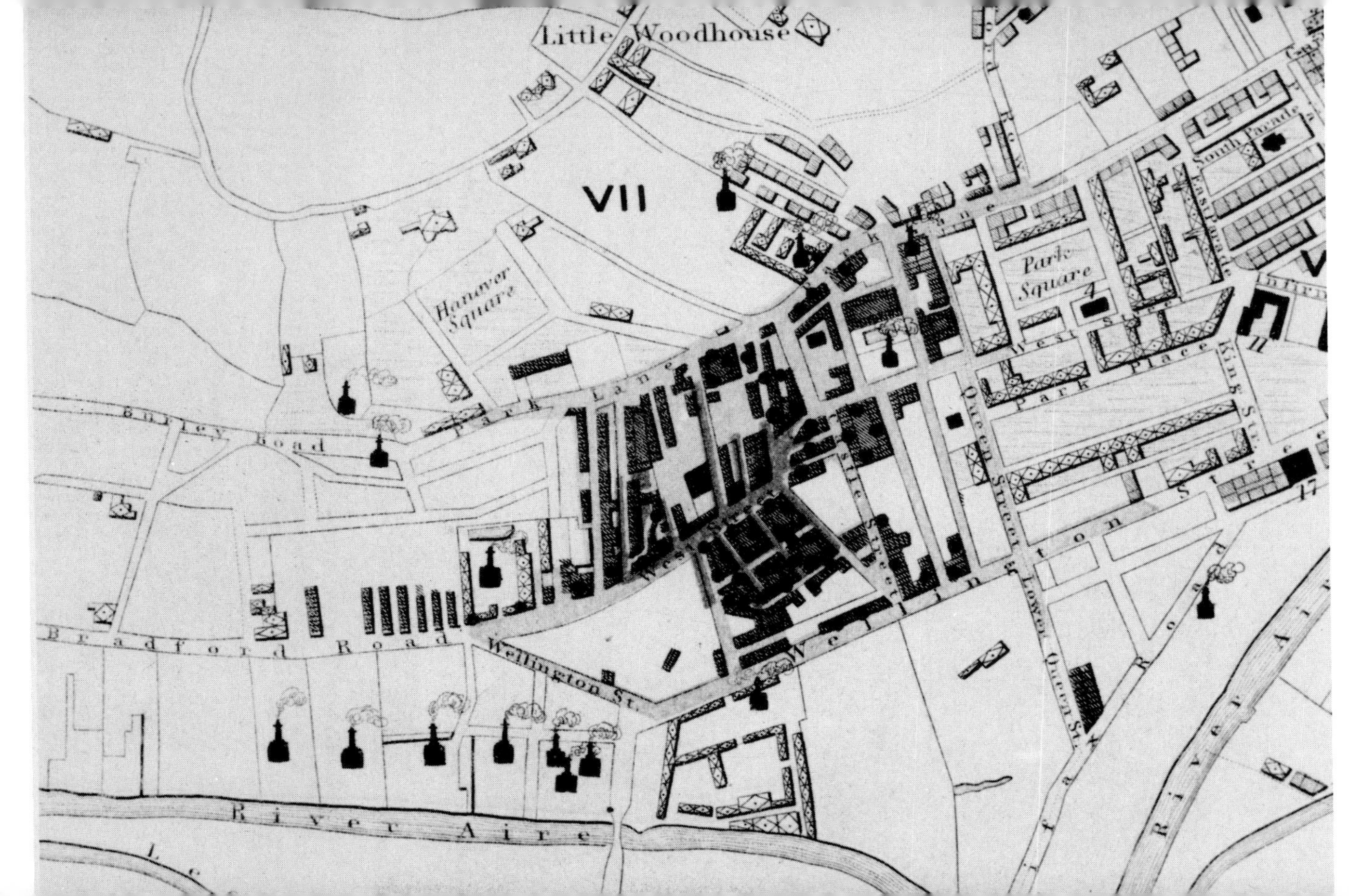

Little Woodhouse
VII
Hanover Square
Park Square
South Parade
East Parade
Park Place
West St.
King Str.
Queen Street
Lower Queen St.
Wellington St.
Castle Street
Park Lane
Burley Road
Bradford Road
Wellington Road
River Aire

circumstances more could only mean worse: not from any decline in the quality of the individual houses but from the accumulating consequences of 'congregation'.

TARGETS FOR CRITICISM

The headings of the Statistical Committee's questionnaire, as reported to the Council in January 1839, announced a formidable agenda, more ambitious than that for the national census in 1841, and not all actually achieved:

> Condition of the streets as to sewering, paving, lighting and cleansing, and the existence of public nuisances;
> Number of public houses and beer houses with their annual consumption;
> Number of schools with the kind of education taught therein, and the amount of scholars male and female;
> The numbers of Benefit and Provident Societies;
> Common lodging houses;
> Of houses generally, as to their number, with reference to the general cleanliness of their inhabitants;
> And lastly of the Inhabitants themselves, their trade and occupation, whether married or single, widows or widowers, the number of their children, how many of them work in mills or are in service, and the number of Lodgers with the accommodation for them.[51]

In 1839 the term 'statistical' was not confined, as now, to assemblies of numbers. There were numbers in abundance in the thirteen main Tables of the Statistical Committee's report but the commentary, particularly in the fuller version for the Statistical Society of London's *Journal*, took up more lines than the Tables and also introduced material which was not quantifiable.

'Statistics' had come into the English language from the French as a name for the tools of a statist, facts useful to those who exercised or studied statecraft: and while some of these facts might be quantities, such as the value of exports or the size of an army, other intelligence could take verbal form and still remain a 'statistic'.[52] It was significant that when the new town Council was setting up its

[51] Council Minutes, IV, ff.525–26 (LCH, Strongroom, shelf 17).

[52] M. J. Cullen, *The Statistical Movement in Early Victorian Britain* (New York, 1975), pp.1–16. A number of local statistical societies were founded in the eighteen-thirties including a short-lived Leeds society, founded in January 1838 (*Journal of the Statistical Society [of London]*, I (1838), 116) which Cullen (p.126) identified as an off-shoot of the Leeds Philosophical and Literary Society. The Council's Statistical Committee consulted the London and Manchester societies in the summer of 1837: Council Minutes, IV, f.398, 9 Nov. 1837.

Statistical Committee it was also proceeding to gather other facts useful for municipal government by ordering a complete revaluation of rating assessments and a large-scale cartographic survey of the town.[53]

Reform was in the air, and the Whig majority on the Leeds town Council, of whom Baker was one, shared the confidence of the Whigs at Westminster that the proper basis for reformist policies was the collection and publication of facts, whether by Select Committee or Royal Commission: the reform of the municipal corporations had followed one such inquiry, and the Poor Law Amendment Act another.

Once collected, the committee's statistics were intended to be useful; their collection was justified in the widest utilitarian terms: 'although attended with considerable expense to the council the usefulness is at once apparent not only for the Physical but the Moral Health of the People'.[54] In its prefatory 'Advertisement' or apologia for its publication of the *Abstract* of 1841 the Committee noted that the press accounts of the original report, as read to the Council in October 1839, had been reproduced in London and provincial journals, and had been quoted before Select Committees and Royal Commisions – statistics for the statists indeed.[55]

There seemed hope that more attention would now be paid to the problems of Leeds that had been aroused by the cholera report. When James Smith commented on the Leeds Improvement Act of 1842 in his report to the Commons Committee on Large Towns and Populous Districts in 1845 he looked back to the Statistical Committee report as the stimulus for that measure: 'The appalling delineation has contributed to arouse the public mind from that apathy into which it has sunk, either from ignorance or from a vague notion of the incurable nature of the evils by which the working population is surrounded.' The Leeds Improvement Act, thought Smith, had been 'drawn with a greater desire to improve the condition of the working classes and the general health and comfort of all classes, than has been seen in any other Improvement Act that has come under my notice' and the Act was firmly rooted in the recommendations made by the Statistical Committee three years earlier for 'improvements in the moral and social condition of those who, at

[53] Council Minutes, IV, f.436, 4 July 1838 (revaluation); an Improvement Commissioners map of 1824 (now lost) was ordered to be put under lock and key (*Ibid.*, f.324, 12 Feb. 1838); and a new map commissioned (f.438, 13 Aug. 1838).

[54] *1839 Report*, p.397.

[55] *1841 Abstract*, p.3.

present, from circumstances over which they have no control, are neglected and forgotten'.[56]

In this respect the Statistical Committee's report had succeeded in influencing public policy, while the Board of Health's report had become another part of that same neglect and forgetfulness.

The particular force of the three reports with which Baker was associated was their combination of vigorous prose, expressing conviction and fervour, with documentation that made their conclusions difficult to refute: judging from the almost verbatim account of the reception of the Statistical Committee report that appeared in the Leeds newspapers, no Councillor attacked it for inaccuracy.[57] The documentation was occasionally anecdotal, and in the elaboration for Chadwick some passages were cast in the first person singular. It is obvious from the description of the rear half of a back-to-back where Thomas Rooley lived with his wife and son as tenants to Benjamin Hardwick,.a coal merchant, that the writer had personal knowledge of it:

> . . . the back courtyard is covered with green water. There is a sump hole in it, a great depth, made by the landlord to take the water away but it is full of deposit. The stench is often so bad, especially after rain, that he and his wife cannot bear it. The stench comes up under the hearth in the house. The sump hole replaced a sewer which had been blocked because the owner of the next property would not allow it to be used.[58]

The core of the 1833 and 1839 reports was the massive tabulation of collected information. The 1833 report had supported its argument by its long alphabetical list of streets with a record of cholera, and sought to prove an association of disease with streets that lacked sanitation by setting in parallel columns against each street the number of cholera cases, the number of deaths and a curt verbal assessment of the sanitary condition. In 1839 the location of the cholera, now seven years past, was not set out in this way although its specificity was not ignored in the commentary: the Committee's brief was to deal with 1839 rather than with 1832.

In the 1842 report, prepared to be part of a sanitary inquiry, the location of cholera again formed part of the evidence, but it was made more intelligible than on the simple cholera map of 1833 by a much more elaborate map which had coloured dots for the places where diseases had occurred, with other symbols classifying housing

[56] *1845 Report*, p.313.

[57] The rejection of Baker in the municipal elections of 1843 seems to have been part of a general local reaction to Council expenditure rather than a criticism of his part in the statistical inquiry.

[58] *1839 Report*, p.397.

and sanitation.[59] The streets that had escaped cholera had not appeared by name in the 1833 report although a count was made of them to give emphasis to the fact that cholera was not a general contagion; and attention was then drawn to their generally good sanitary condition. On the map of 1842 they stood out boldly as white areas.

In the Statistical Committee report the argument by contrast was developed by a system of tabulation that grouped all the data by geographical areas. These were the eight wards of the in-township: as late as 1840 the Committee envisaged an extension of the inquiry to the rest of the borough but there were no meetings after August 1841.[60]

The wards were the obvious geographical units to employ: their boundaries had been drawn in 1835 for the purpose of municipal elections and were then adopted for the assessment and collection of rates, replacing the ancient Divisions. Most of the Upper Division and all Kirkgate Division were amalgamated to form a new Kirkgate ward; the North West Division was now divided by Woodhouse Lane into a West ward and a North West ward, and the large North East Division was similarly divided into a North and a North East ward. The East and South wards were identical with the Divisions of the same names.[61]

The rate-collectors for each ward were made responsible for the house to house collection of data for the Statistical Committee. The data for each separate ward might, the Committee hoped, be of particular interest to the Councillor elected for that ward: 'Your Committee hope that these facts may lead the attention of Councillors to the state of the wards which they represent, with the feeling that they are bound, by every principle of Humanity, as well as of good faith, to redeem their pledges to the electors'.[62]

The wards and the differences between them had a second and greater significance in the context of sanitary reform. The ward boundaries were similar (except at the very centre of town) to those of the old Divisions, so that there were already some ancient basic differences remaining from those discussed in Chapter One. With urbanisation and industrialisation additional differences had emerged more recently, and – as in the months of the cholera – an identification of local differences within Leeds was fundamental to the thesis which Baker wished to put forward. He found a tabulation of data by wards a very acceptable basis for his commentary, and it will be employed in the succeeding pages.

[59] See above, p.400.
[60] *LM*, 8 Jan. 1840; Statistical Committee Minutes, 16 Aug. 1841.
[61] See maps in Fraser, ed., pp.58–59.
[62] *1839 Report*, p.424.

13
A Diffused East End

The southern edge of the town is almost as disagreeable [as the eastern] *and although it has some good houses it has been said in a great measure to have the appearance of a prison.*
G. A. Cooke, TOPOGRAPHICAL AND STATISTICAL DESCRIPTION OF THE COUNTY OF YORK (1818), p. 179.

The clergy, the medical profession, the shopkeepers, the artisan and the operatives are compelled to live with their families in an impurity of atmosphere that destroys every comfort of life.
LEEDS MERCURY, 22 December 1849.

The revelations [of the Statistical Committee Report of 1839] *are astounding, and would be scarcely credible, did we not know how many of the evils depicted still remain.*
James Hole, HOMES OF THE WORKING CLASSES (1866), p. 123.

Leeds is a surprising sight, bringing to remembrance the condition of many English towns twenty years ago.
Her Majesty's Principal Medical Officer of Health, 8TH REPORT TO THE PRIVY COUNCIL, PP 1866, XXXIII, 233.

DIFFERENCES BETWEEN WARDS

Like the ancient Divisions the new ward boundaries were not drawn to equalise their areas: four of the new wards each extended over nearly one square mile while Mill Hill ward comprised 127 acres, North 92 acres, and Kirkgate only thirty-two. For many important statistical purposes, therefore, the data in the original reports must be adjusted and given in terms of densities per acre. There was also sufficient diversity within every ward, including the smallest, to call for presentation where possible by areas smaller than wards.

By 1842 bricks and mortar had overwhelmed virtually every acre of the town centre but the four large outer wards each retained much open ground, although in different proportions (Table 13.1). Three wards had more than 80 per cent of their area still unoccupied by buildings of any kind. The tithe award map of 1847 and its

TABLE 13.1

Proportion of Open Ground, by Wards, 1842

Ward	Acreage of open land	Acreage of buildings	Total acreage	Percentage of open ground
North	28	64	92	30
North East	466	75	541	86
East	517	111	628	82
South	66	57	123	54
Kirkgate	4	28	32	12
Mill Hill	26	101	127	20
West	364	176	560	69
North West	456	82	538	85
TOTAL	1947	694	2641	75

Source: *1842 Report*, p.2.

schedule enable the open and the built-up areas to be identified: the open areas comprised 403 separate fields, half of them under two acres and four-fifths under five acres (Table 13.2). As we have seen in Chapter Eight, a high price had to be offered to tempt the owners of land to turn from other uses and place it on the market, so that there was little relief from overcrowding near the town centre by overspill into the outer parts of these wards, even though there would seem to have been no problems of inaccessible remoteness. Workpeople who already walked in from Holbeck and Hunslet were accepting just as long a daily journey.

TABLE 13.2

Open Ground within the In-township, 1847

	Total number of fields	Number of fields by area: Under 2 acres	2–5 acres	6–10 acres	Over 10 acres
No. of fields	403	195	124	56	28
Percentage	–	49	31	14	7

Source: Plan of the Township of Leeds, 1847, and tithe award schedule: LCA, LPC 107/21.

TABLE 13.3

Density of Population on Built-up Land, by Wards, 1839

Ward	Population	Area of built-up land (acres)	Population per acre
North	12,506	64	195
North East	16,269	75	217
East	14,271	111	129
South	5,630	57	99
Kirkgate	3,158	28	113
Mill Hill	5,167	101	51
West	15,483	176	88
North West	9,656	82	118
TOTAL	82,120	694	1,010

Source: *1842 Report*, p.2.

For many sanitary questions it was the 'congregation' of houses and people, to use Baker's term, that was more relevant than their numbers, and the best measure of the problems of bringing in water and leading out sewage is the housing density specifically within the built-up parts of each ward.

Of all the built-up areas in the town, those in Mill Hill ward were the least densely occupied, at about half the average density for the town (Table 13.3) and the West ward included enough of the original large Park estate houses to bring its density also below average. Kirkgate ward on the other hand had a density near to average, and significantly a similar density was found in the built-up parts of the East and North West wards, showing how the back-to-back streets had reproduced their prototypes in the Kirkgate yards.[1] A density of twice the average in the built-up parts of the North East ward highlighted the grim role of the Quarry Hill courts.

Leeds was still a town of landlord and tenant, even in those streets with the most highly rated houses, for among the residences of the two West Ends, surveyed in 1839, only one in sixteen was occupied by its owner (Table 13.4). Self-help had not done much to spread property ownership among the East End streets: only one house in thirty was owner-occupied in the North and North East wards, and one in forty in the East, South and Kirkgate wards. Given the

[1] See above, p.205.

TABLE 13.4

Owner-occupation, by Wards, 1839

Ward	Dwellings owner-occupied	Dwellings tenanted	Percentage owner-occupied
North	90	2644	3.4
North East	106	3625	2.9
East	56	3190	1.8
South	21	1193	1.8
Mill Hill	54	922	5.9
Kirkgate	9	632	1.4
West	209	3043	6.9
North West	116	1929	6.0
TOTAL	661	17,178	3.8

Source: *1839 Report*, Table IV.

uniform character of housing in these streets[2] it could be expected that most of this minority of owner-occupiers were living in one half of a back-to-back pair while renting the other half to a tenant.

The majority of tenants, however, had an absentee landlord with less incentive to maintain the property. In 1842 Baker stated that a new cottage – that is, half a back-to-back – could command £12 a year in rent;[3] but the main stock of houses, being older, commanded less (Appendix XIII.1). From his rent a conscientious landlord, especially if he were one living back-to-back to his tenant, might spend from five to ten shillings a year on repairs. There was little incentive for the others.

Baker singled out Croisdale's houses at the Bank and Holdforth's in Mill Street as exceptions to a general rule of indifferent and negligent landlords: 'The tenants are not to blame, but they need protection from the cupidity of their landlords'.[4]

When Matthew Johnson, a Poor Law Guardian in Leeds, gave evidence to the Select Committee on the Rating of Tenements in 1837 he made an important statement about landlord interest in small properties: 'It is very well known that cottage property of that

[2] See below, p.427.

[3] *1842 Report*, p.13.

[4] *1839 Report*, p.399; the properties on Richmond Hill, centred on Croysdale Street, can be identified from the documents accompanying the sale of 270 houses on 24 April 1873: LCD 998, 5811, 6016 and 6055.

TABLE 13.5

Lodgers and Resident Domestic Servants, by Wards, 1839

Ward	Male lodgers	Female lodgers	Male domestic servants	Female domestic servants
North	578	309	274	391
North East	408	395	39	136
East	368	313	38	148
South	222	124	62	170
Mill Hill	166	79	247	816
Kirkgate	107	55	164	309
West	556	247	149	889
North West	205	151	49	628
TOTAL	2610	1673	1022	3487

Source: *1839 Report*, Table IV.

type [back-to-backs] realises a better rate of interest than property of a higher description. It is generally understood that cottage property in Leeds realises about 7 or 7½ per cent, and in many cases a greater percentage'.[5]

Baker in 1842 cited the most notorious yard in town in the same context: 'The Boot and Shoe Yard cottages are said to pay the best annual interest of any cottage property in the borough';[6] the value of the Yard's rent roll is known but not its capital worth so that this assertion cannot be tested but the Statistical Committee had already in an interesting aside, 'an inquiry foreign to this report', accepted and quantified that disparity of returns which favoured investors in cottage property.[7]

They estimated the purchase price of a typical working-class house, including land, to be £75. (In 1842 Baker used the higher figure of £80 for a brand new house.) From the Committee's collection of rental data for 13,603 'working-class houses' in all the wards (Appendix XIII.1) they determined an average annual rent for such a house, net of the cost of repairs, as £7: giving a 9.3 per cent yield on the investment of £80. The smaller number of superior houses, 4236, had an average value of £400 and yielded an average

[5] *Report of the Select Committee on the Rating of Tenements* (PP 1837–38, XXI, Q.2325).
[6] *1842 Report*, p.5.
[7] *1839 Report*, p.408.

TABLE 13.6

Common Lodging Houses, by Wards, 1839

Ward*	Number of common lodging houses	Number of beds
North	20	56
North East	12	70
East	6	25
Kirkgate	3	5

* No other wards than those shown in this Table had common lodging houses.

Source: *1839 Report*, Table III.

annual rent of £25: the yield on such an investment would have been 6¼ per cent. Those who were prepared to lend money at less than these market rates to the societies which were being formed to erect model dwellings for the working classes were accordingly dubbed 'five per cent philanthropists'.[8] These returns have to be compared with the return on the safest investment of the late eighteen-thirties, 3% Consols, which were then yielding about 3½ per cent.

Leeds also had its tenants who were themselves landlords, sub-letting part of their houses, even if that meant packing all the family into the remaining room. The worst complaints of overcrowding came from houses where lodgers were more numerous than the householder's family but lodgers in moderation were not contrary to respectability when wages were otherwise too low or too intermittent to sustain a family without this supplementary rent or a payment for board and lodging together. The widespread distribution of lodgers is seen in Table 13.5.

As a growing town with opportunities for unskilled and seasonal employment there was always some migrant, casual and immigrant labour seeking temporary accommodation in the town's forty-one common lodging houses (Table 13.6) which were situated predominantly in the North and North East wards, and never well regarded by sanitary reformers who were agitating for registration and inspection. A little of their crowded character can be discerned in statistics gathered for nine lodging houses from the Kirkgate yards (Table 13.7), with its evidence for multi-occupation of beds and under-enumeration in Table 13.6.

[8] J. N. Tarn, *Five Per Cent Philanthropy* (Cambridge, 1973), chapters 2 and 4.

TABLE 13.7

Accommodation in Kirkgate Yard Cottages, 1839

Yard	Day rooms	Sleeping rooms	Beds	Inmates	Inmates per bed	Cubic feet per inmate
Wellington Yard						
house A	1	3	6	13	2	100
house B	1	1	2	8	4	125
Dixon's Buildings						
house A	0	1	1	5	5	140
house B	0	1	1	6	6	100
house C	0	1	2	8	4	112
Old Post Office Yard						
house A	0	4	6	27	4½	40
house B	0	2	2	10	5	120
house C	0	12	16	39	2½	30½
Harper's Street						
house A	1	2	2	10	5	100

Source: *1839 Report*, Table II.

Among these lodgers, judging from the 1841 census, would have been men and women who were Irish-born: 'Some were fugitives from the famines of 1817–8 and 1822, some from decayed textile industries of Ireland, but others had been encouraged to leave Ireland for Leeds to work in the stuff and plaid trades of the town'.[9] On arrival in Leeds most Irish immigrants found more homely accommodation than the common lodging house with other Irish, usually from the same family or village, who had settled in Leeds earlier and were living in rented accommodation, some part of which could be used for weaving, with 'three or four looms in a bedroom and more in the cellar'. Others engaged 'in mill labour obnoxious to English constitutions, and to some unendurable' and Baker had this factory labour in mind when he wrote: 'we are indebted to the Irish peasantry for the extension of some kinds of manufacture. The flax and worsted spinning trade of Leeds and Bradford, in periods of

[9] T. Dillon, 'The Irish in Leeds', *PTh.S*, LIV (1974), 3.

TABLE 13.8

Dwellings with Irish Occupants, by Wards, 1839

Ward	Number of dwellings occupied by Irish
North	236
North East	167
East	512
South	5
Mill Hill	9
Kirkgate	11
West	48
North West	8

Source: *1839 Report*, Table IV.

great demand, have derived material assistance from immigrant labourers'.[10] The low incomes earned by this work ensured that the Irish sought accommodation with the lowest rents, in cottages at less than £5 a year or in the cheaper cellar dwellings of Table 13.15.

> A shilling a week rent of the dark and dank cellar inhabited by Irish families including pigs, with broken panes in every window frame and filth and vermin in every nook. Here, within the walls unwhitewashed for years, black with the smoke of foul chimneys, without water, with corded bedstocks for beds and sacking for bed clothing, with floors unwashed from year to year, without out-offices, and with incomes of a few shillings derived from the labour of half-starved children or the more precarious income of casual employment, are to be found within what seems to be the dregs of society but are human beings withal, existing, from hour to hour, under every form of privation and distress.[11]

The census of 1841 found 4310 Irish born in Leeds, mostly inhabiting the in-township. Two years earlier (Table 13.8) they had been found in nearly a thousand houses, half of these in a single ward, the East, and a quarter in the North ward.

There were other differences which a social statistician could observe as he passed from ward to ward. There were neither inns nor public houses (Table 13.9) in the first two West Ends but in Kirkgate, the Archbishop of York was informed, there were 'two

[10] *1842 Report*, pp.15 and 24.
[11] *Ibid.*, p.14.

TABLE 13.9

Inns and Beer Houses, by Wards, 1839

Ward	Inns	Inns which are also market houses	Inns which are also coach offices	Inns which are also waggon offices	Beer houses
North	27	19	0	2	49
North East	28	2	0	0	45
East	21	0	0	0	41
South	20	1	1	1	27
Kirkgate	45	29	5	6	11
Mill Hill	37	28	6	4	12
West	26	8	1	2	34
North West	12	0	0	0	16
TOTAL	216	87	12	14	235*

* 121 of these combined with other trades on the same premises.

Source: *Abstract* of *1839 Report*, Table XI; omitted from *1839 Report*.

Publick Houses which are a notorious Nursery of juvenile Depravity, and a public resort of Vice and Profligacy of a nature too disgraceful to mention'.[12] The reports of 1839 and 1842 also declined to be specific about certain vices which they deplored but they did not conceal the existence of brothels. These, or at least the ninety-eight admitted ones (Table 13.10) could be found in every ward but most easily in the North and North East; the area west of Park Square had a dozen brothels, and another parallel between it and the East End was the foundation of a Leeds Western Youths Guardian Society to guard the morals of youth, complementary to an existing Eastern Society. Baker took the chair at the inaugural meeting in May 1835.[13] Three 'on the town' entries in the 'occupation' columns of the 1841 census for Union Street confirm that whoredom was an admitted and presumably full-time occupation.[14]

Their poverty and their different lifestyle made the Irish immigrants stand out even among the other poor: 'that some of the persons so engaged [in factories] are more immoral than the rest, and that their habits and practices operate most unfavourably upon the

[12] Borthwick MSS, Reg. 39, f.258: 15 Aug. 1817

[13] *LM*, 25 May 1835.

[14] PRO, HO 107/1346/14, Union St.

TABLE 13.10

Houses of Ill Fame, by Wards, 1839

Ward	
North	37
North East	29
East	6
South	3
Kirkgate	4
Mill Hill	7
West	12
North West	0

Source: *Abstract* of *1839 Report*, Table XI but not included in *1839 Report*.

general character of their respective neighbourhoods is a truth that cannot be denied'.[15]

Vice was not confined to Irish cellars. If neither inns, beer houses nor brothels were permitted in the two West Ends all were to be found in other parts of the western wards. The inns which served as commercial as well as social centres were, however, confined to the town centre, three of these commercial functions – marketing, and coach and waggon terminals – appearing in Table 13.9.

The building of the three Million Act churches had attempted to remedy the shortage of Anglican churches in the new populous districts.[16] The position in 1839 is shown in Table 13.11 which takes into account the sittings in non-Anglican places of worship. However, there is bound to be a certain artificiality in relating the population of wards to the churches within them, as the statistic for the East ward shows: people were as accustomed to walk over a ward boundary on their way to church or chapel as they were on their weekday journey to work, and a similar comment could be made on Baker's tabulation of day schools by wards which is not reproduced here.

[15] *1842 Report*, p.46.

[16] The Leeds churches financed from the Million Act were St Mark's, Woodhouse; St Mary's, Quarry Hill; Christ Church, Meadow Lane: F. Beckwith, *Thomas Taylor, Regency Architect*, Thoresby Soc. Monographs, I (1949), 7–10 and 54–63.

TABLE 13.11

Religious Accommodation, by Wards, 1839

Ward	Sittings in all places of worship	Population	Ratio of population to sittings
North	3,686	12,506	1:3.4
North East	7,364	16,269	1:2.2
East	800	14,271	1:17
South	5,710	5,630	1:1
Mill Hill	5,080	5,167	1:1
Kirkgate	3,330	3,138	1:1
West	8,104	15,483	1:1.9
North West	7,377	9,656	1:1.3
TOTAL	41,451	82,120	1:2

Source: *1839 Report*, p.415.

THE QUALITY OF STREETS: PAVING AND DRAINAGE

Tabulation of social statistics had begun with the schedules at the end of the 1833 report relating the cholera to the condition of streets. In the reports of 1839 and 1842 there was no report on the condition of individual streets except when cited as instances but the condition of each must have been examined in order to compile the data of Table 13.12. The 'bad', 'middling' or 'good' condition of a street was determined by two qualities, its surface and its drains: 'by "good" is meant the state of the surface as the same term could be applied to any part of Briggate'.[17] Goodness was not easy to find: of the town's 586 streets nearly 40 per cent were classed as 'bad and very bad': the North East ward had half its streets in that category and the East ward more than half; Mill Hill ward had only 17 per cent. Yet those two wards with the worst streets contained 7274 houses, two-fifths of all those in the town.

The basis of the categorisation is set out in Table 13.13. Only seven of the 122 streets surveyed in the East ward were paved and only four of the ninety-three in the North East ward. Paving as a civilised urban amenity had been thought important enough for inclusion in the Improvement Act of 1755 but the paving rate had

[17] *1839 Report*, pp.399–400.

TABLE 13.12

Quality of Streets as Reported, by Wards, 1839

Ward	Number of streets						
	Total number of streets	Bad and very bad streets		Middling streets		Good streets	
North	80	29	(36%)	14	(17%)	37	(46%)
North East	93	47	(50%)	19	(20%)	27	(29%)
East	122	70	(57%)	17	(14%)	35	(28%)
South	23	9	(39%)	4	(17%)	10	(43%)
Mill Hill	48	8	(17%)	5	(10%)	35	(73%)
Kirkgate*	18	0	(—)	0	(—)	18	(100%)
West	125	46	(37%)	26	(21%)	53	(42%)
North West	77	22	(29%)	23	(30%)	32	(41%)
TOTAL	586	231	(39%)	108	(18%)	247	(42%)

* Kirkgate had 'two bad and very bad streets' in the draft report but 'on the whole to be in a good state' in the final report.

Sources: Leeds Civic Hall, Town Clerk's Strong Room, Council Minutes, V, p. 526; *1839 Report*, pp. 399–401.

been applied only to the central streets. The paved streets of Mill Hill and the North West wards had been laid down when their houses were first built, and not at the expense of the Improvement rate. That was the general intention for all the streets outside the central area defined in the Improvement Acts but although 'the deeds of conveyance in 99 cases out of every 100 of the small plots of town streets require the purchaser to pave and sewer and flag forthwith; yet there is no compelling power'.[18] The old Corporation had no such power; nor had the Improvement Commissioners.

The 'proverbial' condition of the North ward streets was described to the Council in the interim report of 1839: 'all more or less deficient in sewerage, unpaved, full of holes, with deep channels formed by the rain intersecting the roads and annoying the passengers'.[19] The absence of paving was certainly distasteful to passers by, forced to walk in dust or mud according to the season, but to those in adjoining houses an unpaved surface betokened more:

[18] *1842 Report*, p. 52.

[19] *1839 Report*, p. 400.

TABLE 13.13

Paving and Sewering of Streets, by Wards, 1839

Ward	Total number of streets	Condition of streets						
		Surface			Sewerage			
		good	middling	bad	wholly	partly	none	unknown*
North	80	37	14	29	10	8	11	51
North East	93	27	50	16	3	12	48	40
East	122	35	45	42	3	13	69	37
South	23	10	10	3	0	1	13	9
Kirkgate	18	15	1	2	4	5	6	3
Mill Hill	48	35	5	8	19	2	4	23
West	125	53	26	46	1	3	8	113
North West	77	32	23	22	0	3	10	64
TOTAL	586	244	109	233	38	47	159	340

* 'not ascertained because in most instances no one could inform the querist whether they had sewers or not; a presumptive proof that they had none.'

Source: *1839 Report*, Table 1.

an absence of drainage for rainwater; if there were no street drains, then probably no house drains either; and then the certain presence of rubbish, difficult to remove if there was no hard surface for the sweepers.

The disposal of rubbish from houses was a perpetual problem when there was no organised system of scavenging except in the town centre, and the street surfaces quickly accumulated domestic rubbish – 'In some cases . . . the whole of the slops and filth are thrown in front of the houses'.[20] The disposal of sewage also:

> It seems to your committee that some of the property where the working classes reside has been laid out without any reference to the erecting of out-offices [privies] . . . thus, for instance, for three streets at the Bank containing 100 dwellings and a population of 452 persons there are but two small offices, neither of which is fit for use; one street being wholly destitute of such provision . . . The streets become receptacles for ashes, filth and refuse of every description until they become far above their original level and offensive beyond measure at all times and during all seasons.[21]

[20] *Ibid.*, p.404; *1842 Report*, p.3.
[21] *1839 Report*, pp.401–02.

In these circumstances, it was reported, people preferred to use the privies at their place of work; and if any houses or groups of houses had an effective privy it was liable to be invaded by the passing public until it choked. Vertical slabs erected outside public houses as urinals for their customers quickly became places of general resort. The East End privies were not water closets and the sanitary problem of sewerage in these areas concerned the disposal of liquid domestic waste. Fewer streets had a sewer along their length than were paved (Table 13.13) and half of these lay in the Mill Hill ward, the sewers of the Park estate.

An efficient urban drainage system was particularly difficult to achieve in Leeds, as the Council found after 1842. On the south of the river the tortuous streams in the low-lying ground afforded no natural drainage and the small change in levels made it difficult to construct sewers that would discharge into the river.[22] North of the river the north–south slopes on the west of town and the east-facing slopes above the Sheepscar and Timble Becks were potentially available for a gravitational sewerage system but here a heavy price was paid for the historical accident of piecemeal development. There was no authority to oblige a builder to lay a drain and, if he did, no certainty that the line would be continued by the developer of the next plot; and development of adjacent plots, as we have seen, could be spread over many years (Fig. 13.1). Equally, undeveloped fields could block what might otherwise have been the line of a natural fall. 'Thus the sewer in Regent Street runs along its whole line parallel with the [Sheepscar] Beck, then turns up to the west at Moscow Street and part of Templar Street where it unites with the Bridge Street sewer and subsequently discharges itself into the Beck at Lady Bridge'.[23] The widespread morcellation of ownership also militated against someone laying a drain in his field for the benefit of someone else's development in another field.

The more effective the use of gravity and natural drainage the worse the fate of the river to which all streams, drains and sewers ran, the destination for any water-carried refuse from homes, markets, and the butchers' shambles. The main sewers were easily choked by the sediment from this waste and from street surfaces. In heavy rain there was back-wash into houses and cellars, made worse by the increase in the number of mill dams which raised the water

[22] These issues are treated in detail by B. J. Barber, 'Leeds Corporation, 1835–1905: a history of its environmental, social and administrative services' (unpublished PhD thesis, University of Leeds, 1975); and in J. Toft, 'Public Health in Leeds in the Nineteenth Century' (unpublished MA thesis, University of Manchester, 1966).

[23] *1839 Report*, p.403.

FIG. 13.1 AN EAST END CUL-DE-SAC AT A PROPERTY BOUNDARY: MASON'S BUILDINGS

Redrawn by John Dixon from a photograph. The short street off Orange Street, known as Mason's Buildings, built between 1821 and 1826, consisted of two facing rows, each made up of eight back-to-back pairs. The shuttered windows and architectural style resemble those of building-club houses forty years earlier (Figs 7.7 and 7.8). The wall and tall iron railing at the end marks an original field and property boundary blocking the way for interconnecting lines of drains, water and sewerage. Beyond the wall another developer (after 1847) inserted further high density housing. Whitewash on the walls remains from an earlier effort to improve insanitary streets.

level behind them and prevented the inflow from sewers. The beckside streets near Timble Bridge were afflicted more than most with these problems, compounded by the concentration of dye-houses with their smoke and effluvia.

The same beckside streets were afflicted further by their position near the town's oldest, largest but most overcrowded burial ground at the parish church: 'the habitations of the living which surround this Golgotha will be exposed to its exhalations'.[24]

[24] *1842 Report*, p.22.

In 1842, complementary to the Improvement Bill, the Council promoted a second bill to enable Leeds to have its first municipal cemetery unconnected to any churchyard.[25] When in the same year Baker and the Town Clerk appeared before the Select Committee on the Improvement of Health in Towns they were questioned about the effects of urban interment. William Beckett, the banker, and John Garland, churchwarden at the parish church, also gave evidence. There was no disagreement. In a town with a growing population, and despite some relief from the private General Cemetery at Woodhouse, churchyard burials were only possible by the excavation of bodies long before they had decayed.

Baker produced his cholera map for the Committee, explaining: 'I should mislead the committee if I said that I thought that the breaking open of coffins at the beck side was the cause of the cholera, but it is in the neighbourhood.' He was then asked: 'Is not the position of St Peter's church in the very worst part of the town?' He answered, 'It is'.[26]

CRITICS OF THE BACK-TO-BACKS

The plan which Baker produced to the Parliamentary Committee was probably that prepared for Chadwick but there was another cartographic illustration in Baker's contribution to the Chadwick report which indicates that he could not take it for granted that houses built in back-to-back terraces would be familiar to his readers in other parts of England, even those living in other industrial towns. The back-to-back houses, although not unique to Leeds were not to be found in every English industrial town. In the East End of London, for example, there were Dickensian slums of densely occupied tenements and streets of small one- and two-roomed houses: but no back-to-backs.

Baker therefore gave half a page of his report to a 'subjoined ground-plan' showing three adjacent pairs of back-to-backs in an unnamed street.[27] There was a tunnel 'entry to back property' between the first and second pairs, leading to the back yard which served all three. Since the yard behind the two right-hand pairs was seven steps lower than the end of the tunnel, the unnamed street was probably one of the many on the eastern side of town where a natural

[25] *5 & 6 Vict. cap. 103.*
[26] *Report of the Select Committee on the Health and Improvement of Towns*, PP 1842, X, Q.2554.
[27] *1842 Report*, p.7.

slope gave a difference in levels between house and house. This was the yard 'commonly covered with green water'.

A few years later, also writing with readers in mind who had no personal acquaintance with Leeds, another author had recourse to diagrams and street-plans in order to introduce this unfamiliar house form. In 1845 the twenty-four-year-old Frederick Engels published in Leipzig 'from personal, observation and authentic sources' his *Condition of the Working-Class in England*, written in Barmen after his return from a twenty-one-month stay in England. While living in Manchester he took a day excursion ticket on the railway which had then just been completed through the Pennines to connect Manchester with Rochdale, Elland, Wakefield, Normanton and Leeds. The following passage was obviously written by a man who had looked out of the carriage window to this un-German landscape of Pennine factories. 'The valleys of the Aire, along which stretches Leeds, and of the Calder, through which the Manchester to Leeds railway runs, are among the most attractive in England . . . but on coming into the towns themselves one finds little to rejoice over.' His account of Leeds rested heavily on what he had read in the Chadwick report but the next comment suggests that he may have visited Bean Ing Mill, looked over Wellington Bridge into the Aire, and then gone to the riverside mills at the East End. 'The Aire flows into the city at one end clear and transparent, and flows out at the other end thick, black and foul, smelling of all possible refuse.'[28]

In one footnote he cited the Statistical Committee report, which he had read in the *Journal* of the London Statistical Society. Cellars, he felt, must be explained to German readers in another footnote: 'They are not mere storing rooms for rubbish, but dwellings of human beings.'[29]

The present author once had the pleasure of asking a seminar at the University in Leipzig, which is named after Karl Marx, where in the collected works of Marx and Engels one could find English street plans. There was a puzzled silence among the savants. The plans he had in mind, readers will have guessed, were those needed by Engels to explain how Manchester and Leeds houses were built back-to-back with interior courts.[30]

The official approval of back-to-back housing in Leeds was exceptional among industrial towns in the years after 1845: in Manchester the Improvement [Police] Act of 1844, in Bradford a

[28] F. Engels, 'The Condition of the Working-Class in England (1845)' in *Karl Marx and Frederick Engels on Britain* (Moscow, 1953), pp.71–72.

[29] *Ibid.*, footnotes, pp.72–73.

[30] *Ibid.*, pp.89–90.

by-law of 1860, and in Liverpool an Act of 1861 prevented the further building of back-to-backs. Articles in *The Builder* in 1869, 1891 and 1897 cited Leeds as an incorrigible friend of the back-to-back, and in 1883 the author of a standard builders' textbook observed sadly: 'I understand that back-to-back houses are still being built in some northern towns';[31] and in 1888 Barry and Smith's *Joint Report on Back-to-Back Houses to the Local Government Board* found that 'In all the large manufacturing towns of Yorkshire back-to-back dwellings have been and are still being built to a considerable extent. In Lancashire, the Potteries and the Black Country it has been almost discontinued.'[32] In that year 69 per cent of new houses in the borough of Leeds were back-to-back, and in 1898 when the Corporation were planning to replace demolished houses in the York Street Insanitary Area they proposed to build back-to-backs, and sent a deputation to London to meet the Local Government Board to argue the case.[33]

Diligent reformers would wish to see the recalcitrant north. In the last year of the century two distinguished authors visited the East End of Leeds, and felt the same need as Baker and Engels to elucidate their commentary by drawing a plan of back-to-backs. According to the notes that they made at the time, Sidney and Beatrice Webb came from London and 'spent Sat. 22nd. April [1899] walking through the Insanitary Area,'[34] escorted by the Leeds councillor and solicitor, Edmund Wilson. He had been one of the founding directors of that Leeds expression of Five Per Cent Philanthropy, the Industrial Dwellings Company, which had built twenty-three four-storey houses in 1866.[35]

Wilson supplied the Webbs with a copy of a plan of King Street and Queen Street, the two streets of back-to-backs built by the Camphor Close Building Club (Fig. 13.2). This plan the Webbs fastened into their notebook, and in the middle of their note-taking they also drew a crude sketch of four pairs of back-to-backs and their yards, not dissimilar to the explanatory plan drawn by Engels half a century earlier. The plan which Wilson had supplied to them was one made for the Corporation in 1891 when the designation of Insanitary Areas had been under discussion. The Webbs noted that

31 F. Maitland, *Building Estates, a Rudimentary Treatise* (1883), p.28.

32 F. W. Barry and P. G. Smith, *Joint Report on Back-to-back Houses to the Local Government Board* (1888), p.2.

33 *The Builder*, LXXV (1898), 567 and LXXVI (1899), p.99; *LM*, 17 Dec. 1898.

34 London School of Economics, Webb Local Government Collection, vol. 265; 'Personal Investigation, 1899', ff. 1–6.

35 E. Wilson, 'The Housing of the Working Classes', *Journal of the Society of Arts*, XLVIII (1899–1900), 253–63.

> to understand this [Corporation] policy it is necessary to realise the enormity of the 'Back to Back' slums. These are abused by sanitary experts because they have no draught, the house consisting of a kitchen with a staircase out of it to an upper chamber, and finally a 'cellar' underneath. The back wall serves to partition a house opening to a parallel street . . . Not one of the owners of these cottages occupied his cottage; and so there were 20 owners to some 60 cottages.

They then let their enthusiasm for municipal socialist planning lead them into bad History: 'It was largely because the Corporation had not in the first instance exercised its power to enforce building bye laws that the Back to Back slum had arisen.'

In that 'first instance' when the Club members were building King Street and Queen Street the unreformed Corporation had had no powers to make, let alone to enforce a building by-law; nor had the reformed Corporation when the back-to-backs were first castigated; nor when Baker was calling for the regulation of building to achieve 'architectural order, size, ventilation and accommodation to the houses'.[36]

Although criticism of the back-to-backs was central to Baker's 1842 report he had not seen them as a target in 1833; on that occasion the remedy was seen to lie with improved drainage, paving, sewerage and water supply. This had also been the tenor of Williamson's evidence to the Select Committee on the Health of Towns in 1840.[37] Perhaps Baker, as a relative newcomer to the town, was not at first confident enough to attack as fatally 'confined' a form of housing that he found traditional in Leeds, prevalent in all quarters, and previously (so far as the evidence goes) criticised by no one: although John Marshall had advocated in a general way the regulation of working-class building in 1833.[38] 'Regulating the dwellings of the inhabitants', an equally vague phrase, was urged by the Statistical Committee but the report did not use the term 'back-to-back', and the only criticism of building styles in the 'Houses' section was of the size of bedrooms: 'The vitiated atmosphere of sleeping rooms of so small a size [5 yards square, and about 4 yards in

[36] *1842 Report*, p.51.
[37] *Report of the Select Committee on the Health of Towns*, PP 1840, XI, Qq. 1667–1807.
[38] *Report of the Select Committee on Public Walks*, PP 1833, XV, Qq. 599–638.

FIG. 13.2 CIVIC SHAME: SIDNEY AND BEATRICE WEBB IN THE EAST END, OCTOBER 1891

Sketch of King Street and Queen Street, 106 houses in back-to-back terraces and yards built in 1788 by thirty-two members of the Hill House Bank Building Club: supplied to the Webbs by their escort for their visit to the East End of Leeds, a local solicitor, and retained in their note book.

Private. 30.10.91.

Sketch Plan
of two Blocks of Cottages in East Street, Leeds.

EAST. STREET. MILLS

Black Lion (P.H)

1 2 3 4 5 6 7

EAST KING STREET

8 9 10 11 12 13

14 15 16 17 18 19 20

EAST QUEEN STREET

Rose & Crown (P.H.)

EAST. STREET.

No. on plan.	Name	No. on plan.	Name.
1	Timothy Taylor – Keighley	11	Kidson Swales
2	Mary Wood Bramley	12	Elizth Hogg & Emma Ackroyd
3	Jane Barker Lady Lane	13	The Lord Masham
4	Francis G. Heseldine	14	W. W. Fenn
5	Louie Courant	15	late Sarah Myers – Corporation in possession.
6	Rev J.P. Richards	16	Kidson Swales.
7	Elizth. Hartley	17	Moses Atkinson
8	J. Collier – Bldg Socy Mtgees in possession.	18	late Mary Wales
9	Mary Wood – Bramley.	19	John Rhodes, J.P.
10	John Fearnley	20	Thos. Blakey – Shadwell.

TABLE 13.14

Proportion of Working-class Inhabitants, by Wards, 1842

Ward	Total population	Working-class population	Percentage working-class population*
North	12,506	9,450	76
North East	16,269	15,399	95
East	14,271	13,261	93
South	5,630	4,243	75
Kirkgate	3,158	1,233	39
Mill Hill	5,167	1,566	30
West	15,483	9,468	61
North West	9,656	6,592	68
TOTAL	82,120	61,212	75

* 'Working-class population' as defined by Baker by assigning 4½ persons to each house with annual rental under £10; there were 13,603 such dwellings in the in-township (*see* Appendix XIII.1).

Source: *1842 Report*, p.2.

height], crammed with human beings as many of them are, both during the day and night, predisposes the system to diseases of such a character [as consumption].'[39]

The criticism, it will be noticed, was not of house size *per se* but of those houses where rooms were overcrowded because poverty denied a family the means to afford more than a share in a room. The average density per house in the eastern parts of town did not deteriorate between 1821 and 1841 so that every case of overcrowding must have been balanced by less than average occupancy in dwellings elsewhere. The 'Houses' section of the Committee's report ended tamely with no recommendations that would have made bedrooms larger, rents more affordable or occupants less numerous.

This interest in small-sized dwellings led the Committee to its elaborate attempt to determine their numbers and distribution. Although successive censuses had recorded for every Division the total number of houses, inhabited, uninhabited and in course of erection, there was no attempt to distinguish between houses of

[39] *1839 Report*, p.406.

TABLE 13.15

*Number of Cellar Dwellings, by Wards, 1839**

Ward	Number of cellar dwellings
North	100
North East	187
East	145
South	25
Mill Hill	11
Kirkgate	10
West	74
North West	3
TOTAL	555

* These dwellings are excluded from Appendix XIII.1.

Source: *1839 Report*, Table III.

various sizes; nor in 1839 was there any large-scale plan, Ordnance Survey or private, on which the separate halves of back-to-back pairs were shown, so that the absolute dominance of that size of dwelling had to be demonstrated by counting the entries in the rate books which had assessments appropriate to cottage dwellings; the rate books had the additional advantage of identifying the small separate dwellings above or below the ground floor (cellar dwellings and galleries) which no plan, however large its scale, could show.

The Committee regarded any dwelling rated at under £10 a year as 'working-class' (Table 13.14), and 13,603 such units were found, making up three-quarters of all dwellings in the town. Half of these were paying £5 or less and, like other indicators of social differentiation already encountered, these 'working-class' houses were unevenly distributed between the wards: the North and South wards had a near-average proportion but the East and North East were of a different stamp, with over 90 per cent of their houses being 'working-class'. Among the professional and shopkeeper residences of Kirkgate and Mill Hill wards the smaller dwellings in their backsides yards, although numerous, were insufficient to raise the proportion of working-class inhabitants above 40 per cent.

It was in the North East ward that the highest proportion of houses under £10 (95 per cent) was to be found (Appendix XIII.1).

TABLE 13.16

Average Rental of Houses, by Divisions, 1837

Ward	Number of houses	Average rental per house* £ p.a.
Mill Hill	994	43.11
High Town	1010	25.80
South	673	15.85
North West (lower)	2531	13.54
South West	1007	13.39
Kirkgate	1413	12.71
North West (upper)	1950	11.38
North East (upper)	1163	11.04
North	1273	10.45
South East	1771	6.30
North East	1279	5.92
East	1392	5.38
North East (lower)	2126	5.23
TOTAL	18,582	12.40

* Rental calculated from the rateable values which were ⅘ of the actual rent.

Source: *Report of the Commissioners appointed to report and advise upon the Boundaries and Wards of certain Boroughs and Corporate Towns.* PP XXVII, pt.2 of 1837, unpaginated section, headed 'Leeds'.

Cellar dwellings, with even lower rents, were excluded from this part of the tabulation but Table 13.15 shows that cellar dwellings were most numerous in the North, North East and East wards; there was one cellar dwelling to every twenty houses in the North East ward. The westward diffusion of the poorest quality housing was indicated by the presence of seventy-four cellar dwellings in the West ward. At the other social extreme Mill Hill and Kirkgate wards had over a third of their houses rented above £20.

In 1837, two years before the Statistical Committee categorised rentals in this way, the Boundary Commission had published rental data in more detail, collected firstly by Divisions and then by streets assembled into local groups. From Table 13.16, the average rental for the town appears as £12 8*s*., very near that level of rent, £12 a year or 4*s*. 6*d*. a week which Baker thought a landlord of a newly built cottage might expect from his tenant. Seven of the Divisions had

TABLE 13.17

Average Rental in Certain Streets, 1837

Street	Number of houses	Average annual rental, £
Park Pl.	23	90.32
Park Sq.	37	54.66
Blenheim Ter.	12	51.04
Brunswick Pl.	25	43
Blenheim Sq.	8	37.50
Brunswick St	20	32.25
Grove Ter.	34	27.2
Rockingham St	70	19.07
Camp Field	206	5.03
Boot and Shoe Yard	40	3.50

Source: *Report of the Commissioners appointed to report and advise upon the Boundaries and Wards of certain Boroughs and Corporate Towns*, PP XXVII, pt.2 of 1837, unpaginated section, headed 'Leeds'. Boot and Shoe Yard: LCA, LCEng. Box 10.

rents near the average; in others there were divergences. At one extreme the houses in High Town had twice the average rent for the town and those in Mill Hill nearly four times; at the other were the four sub-divisions in the east that had less than half that average.

The Commission went further and ascertained an average rental for ten single streets (Table 13.17). Since houses in terrace streets – whether back-to-back or through – were generally of similar size to their neighbours there would have been very little divergence within these streets from their average. In Park Place the fifty-year-old houses were maintaining their pre-eminence with over seven times the average rent for the town; the newer Blenheim Terrace matched the older Park Square with rentals near £50, and the genteel terraces at Blenheim and Brunswick commanded between £30 and £40.

At the very foot of this ladder were the 206 crowded dwellings in Camp Field near Marshall's mill, with rentals similar to the poorer housing of the East End, and the £3 10*s*. commanded by the forty cottages which lined the Boot and Shoe Yard (Fig. 12.1).

Despite its attention to the 'working-class' dwelling the 1839 report did not employ the term 'back-to-back' but Baker used the term in the 1842 report. He first returned to the question of house size: 'perhaps there is no question of more importance within the entire range of vital statistics than the size of the houses . . . The size of the house is 5 yards by 4 yards';[40] but although his language was rather ambiguous the reference to 'vital statistics' makes it likely that here Baker was again thinking of house size primarily in relation to those diseases which flourished with overcrowding. Overcrowding was a statistic determined by two factors, only one of which was room size; the other was the level of poverty prevailing. The rooms in the new houses were no smaller than their predecessors; nor than the general run of cottages in the countryside; and if they had occupants in separate cellars, so had the first cottages in High Street and Union Street fifty years earlier.

'Back-to-back' was certainly used by Baker in 1842 in a critical context, but a different one from house size: 'The courts and culs-de-sac exist everywhere. The building of houses back-to-back occasions this in great measure. It is in fact part of the economy of buildings that are to pay a good percentage.'[41] What was now under criticism was not the form of the back-to-backs but the economic and demographic pressures which had led to their multiplication in 'confined' groups of courts and courts within courts where light and circulating air were banished to the distance; where the provision of paving, drainage, and water supply was even more difficult and less likely than in the simple terrace streets, and where the lower levels of the yards and the cellar dwellings remained in a surround of mire, sewage and polluted wells. The cancerous affliction of the back-to-backs, originally benign cells, was that they became each year more numerous (Fig. 13.3).

An additional misery, not found widely in England although familiar in Mediterranean Europe, was the vertical stacking of back-to-backs, either in four-storey houses with an open entrance stair vanishing into a tunnel, as illustrated by surviving photographs of Millwright Street near Lady Bridge, or in the 'galleries' of which the most notorious were Paley's Galleries. These did not survive to be photographed, being demolished for the extension of Marsh Lane

[40] *1842 Report*, p. 10.
[41] *Ibid.*, p. 5.

FIG. 13.3 A DIFFUSED EAST END: THIRTY YEARS OF HIGH-DENSITY HOUSING IN PIECEMEAL STREET DEVELOPMENT, 1815–44

The houses shown are those which appear on Fowler's town plan of 1844 standing on ground unbuilt upon at the time of the Giles plan of 1815. Scattered piecemeal development within small fields produced high population densities within each individual piece of development but the many surviving fields gave a low overall figure. The piecemeal occupation was an obstacle to any co-ordinated scheme of drainage, sewerage and piped water supply that utilised the natural rise and fall of the ground.

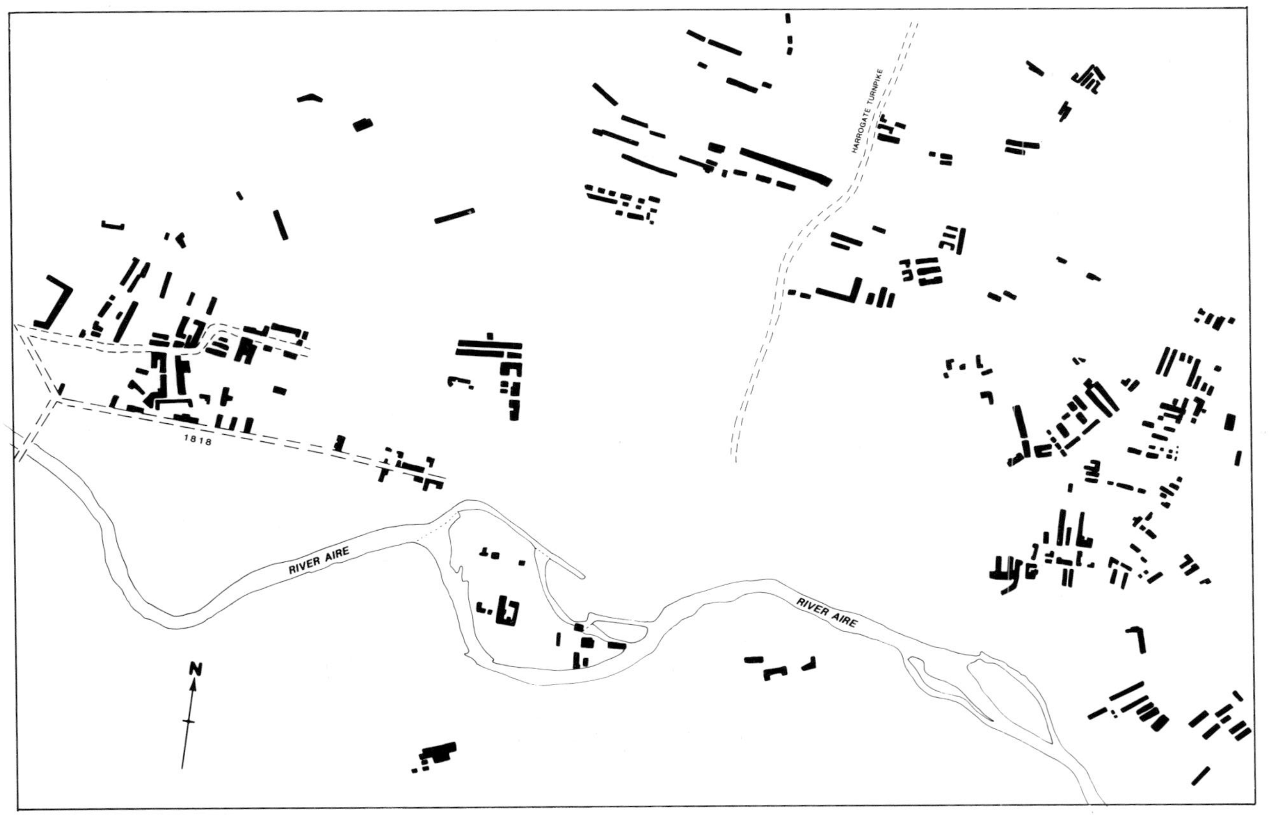
HARROGATE TURNPIKE
1818
RIVER AIRE
RIVER AIRE
N

station yard, but the galleried back-to-backs in Line Fold, boxes of single-roomed houses and cellar dwellings stacked three rows deep, can be seen in photographs, with the slope of Quarry Hill enabling one end of the gallery to be accessible at ground level.[42] Three of these properties, then in single ownership, were described in their deeds as 'six cottages and three cellar dwellings: three of the cottages entered from Line Fold, situated below three others which are entered from a gallery from Cross Billet Street'.[43] The same hill slope allowed the houses behind Charles Street to have cellar dwellings that faced an interior courtyard. There in Johnson's 'Square' a term which had first entered the Quarry Hill area in St Peter's Square might now seem to have reached its lowest debasement:[44] were it not that behind houses on the south of St Peter's Square itself was the tiny courtyard of Stainburn 'Square', separated by only five yards and a low wall from the northernmost of a line of gasometers.[45]

Baker several times used two terms which for him embodied the nature of the sanitary problem in Leeds: 'confined' and 'neglected congregations'.[46] In 'neglected congregations' Baker saw that coming together of miseries which went beyond the constricted form of houses, their high density and the additional risk of their invasion by multiple occupation. The neglect of developers and the public authority in respect of water supply, drainage, paving and sewerage was a misery quite independent of the form that houses took, but the confined space of houses, when overcrowded, was seen as contributory to immodesty and immorality. 'Those who might advocate a better state of things depart; and of those who remain, the one-half by repeated exhibition of indecency and vulgarity, and indeed by the mere fact of neighbourship, sink into the moral degradation which is natural to the other [half]: vicious habits and criminal propensities.'[47]

In his other term, 'confined', Baker summed up the miseries that arose when back-to-backs were crowded into yards and courts; and when people were crowded into back-to-backs. His introduction of back-to-backs in 1842 as a form of housing that deserved regulation probably arose from the attention which had been recently given to a proposal for a statutory ban on them. The

[42] Shown in Beresford, *Face of Leeds*, pl.27.
[43] LCD 911.
[44] Shown in Beresford, *Face of Leeds*, pls 24 and 25.
[45] LCD 8433.
[46] *1839 Report*, p.413; *1842 Report*, p.62.
[47] *1842 Report*, p.15.

opposition to this regulation centred on the impact on rents if houses were to be less densely built. Baker was of course fully aware of the level of wages which limited the ability of most people to pay higher rents, and on the other hand of the return which capital expected if it were to continue investing its savings in building ground and new houses. Many advertisements in the Leeds press were putting £5 as the expected price for that five square yards of land needed for a unit portion of a street and a single cottage, that is four shillings a square yard.

Baker related house size and form using comparable figures: 'over three to four shillings a square yard is thought too dear for cottage property ... Were the houses built upon a much larger scale, therefore and with a much larger quantity of land appropriated to them, the annual value [i.e. rent] would be beyond the income of the labourers[48] ... They are accustomed to pay from £6 to £8 for two rooms.'[49]

The Bill which might have exiled back-to-backs from Leeds was one introduced in May 1841 *For Regulating Buildings in Large Towns*; it incorporated many recommendations of the Select Committee on the Health of Towns which had reported in 1840, and at first met with little opposition.[50] It passed all its stages in the Commons and returned from the Lords in February 1842 with Clause 20 intact: 'it shall not be lawful to build any house, except corner houses, on any new foundation unless there shall be a clear space of at least Twenty Feet wide between the back wall of such house and the back wall of any opposite house',[51] the intent being made clear in a rubric which may embody the earliest use of the term 'back-to-back': 'Houses Not To Be Built Back-to-Back'.

At this late stage in the passage of the Bill the building interests seem to have become aware of its implications, and began to lobby. In 1840 the Health of Towns Committee had anticipated some criticism and tried to assuage fears that its recommendations would infringe the freedom of entrepreneurs: 'the regulations would be

[48] At this time, according to an independent report from Baker to the Poor Law Commissioners, the annual wage which could be expected by 'the most valuable class of hands to the Manufacturer' in Leeds was £52 for a 64-hour week. The handloom weavers could earn no more than £28: PRO, MH 12/15224.

[49] *1842 Report*, pp.10–11; 'to build the largest number of cottages on the smallest allowable space seems to have been the original view of the speculators': *Ibid.*, p.4; and 'it is in fact part of the economy of buildings that are to pay a good percentage': *Ibid.*, p.5.

[50] *Report of the Select Committee on the Health of Towns*, PP 1840, XI, p.xv.

[51] The Bill is bound as PP 1842, I, pp.351–67; at the Bill's introduction (PP 1840, I, pp.93–124) the clause was numbered (17).

framed so as to interfere no further with everyone's right to manage his own property than was necessary to protect the health of the community; nor would they extend beyond what that urgent duty of Government justified.'[52] The Commons now sent the Bill to a fresh Select Committee which met between March and mid-June 1842. Many witnesses were heard, from reforming interventionists to advocates of classical *laissez-faire*. The Leeds banker, Beckett, who admitted that a porter's lodge was the only house within a half-mile of his own residence at Kirkstall Grange, said that the Bill's proposals had created a very strong sensation throughout the country.[53] Eddison, the Town Clerk, also gave evidence hostile to the ban, arguing that separated houses would increase land and building costs and thus 'drive the lower classes into lodgings by putting up rents.' He reported advice given by local builders to his Council that a back yard and privy to each house, the aim of the Bill, would entail a rise of 30 per cent in the cost of a house. Eddison himself was not an opponent of sanitary reform and had subscribed as a Five Per Cent Philanthropist to one of the pioneer societies for building tenements in London. His compromise proposal to the Commons committee was that back-to-backs should be permitted but only in blocks of four pairs, with a space between each block for a yard in which privies would be sited.

The opposition in the Select Committee to Clause 20 was now so strong that it was deleted, and at the end of June the whole Bill was dropped, ostensibly to await the Chadwick report. The Public Health Act of 1848 contained no reference to back-to-backs, and so any regulation was left to municipal action. The Leeds Improvement Act of 1842, by its Clause 190, did give the Council power to compel a privy for each newly erected house but the clause became a dead letter, as Hole complained in 1866: 'if the cottage speculator chooses to disregard such regulations, he may do so with impunity. The back-to-back system of house-building has rendered this [clause] all but impracticable.'[54]

However, a by-law of 1866, which had building inspectors and a Council Building Plans committee to enforce it, took up the proposal which Eddison had made to the Select Committee in 1842: 'In no case shall dwelling houses be erected in blocks so that any block contain more than eight dwelling houses'. Three years later

[52] *Report of the Select Committee on the Health of Towns*, PP 1840, XI, p.xv.

[53] *Report of the Select Committee on Buildings Regulation Bill and Improvement of Boroughs Bill*, PP 1842, X, pp.143–49, 160–61 and 306.

[54] James Hole, 'The Working Class of Leeds', prize essay of Jan. 1865, reprinted as appendix to his *Homes of the Working Classes* (1866), p.125.

the number of one-room houses, *blind-backs*, that could be built contiguously was limited to four.[55] The by-law of 1866, together with the earlier clause on privies, created the blocks of back-to-backs in eightsomes with intervening yards that survive in many parts of Leeds; as far as is known, no back-to-backs earlier than 1866 can now be seen in the city.

THE TWAIN SHALL MEET

The tabulation of differences between wards served Baker by indicating the agenda for Improvement if the Two Nations were to be brought more closely together. The gap between them was most glaring when the statistics for the East, North, and North East wards were set against those for others, particularly the West. If these were the sole data available, then the contrast between the West and a disadvantaged East End could be set out as below (Table 13.18). It should be borne in mind that these statistics, collected by wards, inevitably understate the difference between 'East' and the real West End, since the diffusion of East End characteristics (below) had already begun.

It is instructive to identify the transmission to other parts of town of those 'neglected and confined congregations' that were originally exclusive to an East End. The first East End had lain east of the town, and its characteristics were to be found in hardly any other quarter; and nowhere in such concentration. The first West End, with its very different characteristics, also had narrow limits and a style of housing not exactly replicated elsewhere in the town, and the second West End of villas and terraces was also innovative in its styles.

On the other hand the new streets which began to occupy the western fields that were left void after the fall of the first West End were in most respects a simple replication of streets that the building clubs and the speculators had already built in the East End. Surviving photographs testify to the similarities of their architectural style, while the large-scale Ordnance Survey plans show their houses to have been of the same size, and arranged similarly in back-to-back terraces with tunnels to interior courtyards. Table 13.15 has shown that by 1839 there were more cellar dwellings in the West ward than in the North West or South wards.

The principal difference between the original East End and its westward diffusion was one of date: and it was of little significance.

[55] By-laws enrolled in LCA, QS Minute Books, November 1866 and April 1869; no printed copy has been found.

TABLE 13.18

Some Contrasts between 'East' and 'West', 1839–42

	West	East
Streets with most cholera cases	nil	24
Population per acre on built up land	88	172
Proportion of township population	19	52
Percentage of houses rented under £10 p.a.	61	88
Percentage of houses rented under £5 p.a.	10	39
Number of cellar dwellings	74	432
Average rental (£ p.a.)	14	5
Percentage of owner-occupied houses	7	3
Common lodging houses	nil	38
Dwellings with Irish heads of households	48	915
Houses of ill fame	12	72
Inns	26	76
Beer houses	34	135
Population per sitting in churches and chapels	2	4
Percentage of 'good' streets	53	34

Source: Tables in Chapters 12 and 13.

This may be surprising to some readers. Proponents of slum clearance in the present century saw such an association between aged housing and unacceptable living conditions that it is important to distinguish the attitude of the sanitary reformers of the eighteen-forties. At no time did Baker and his contemporaries criticise the housing of Leeds on account of its age or its dilapidation. If structures were criticised, it was on other grounds.

Table 13.19 regroups some of the evidence from the Schedule of the 1833 report in order to show that no street was immune from the cholera because it was new. This is most strikingly shown in western Leeds where the diseased inhabitants of uncleansed streets were living in houses that were absurdly young. Not a single one had been standing fifteen years before the cholera; very few were more than ten years old in 1832; and many of the streets in the west which were castigated by critics had vacant plots in 1842 still waiting for occupants.

The lesson from the West End is that if the social and economic forces continued to create 'confined and neglected congregations' then all the miseries of the East End would be transferred westward, independent of the age of the houses, and despite some respects in which the new western streets were better placed. In the East the passage of time had seen conditions worsen as successive additions made housing more continuous, green fields and fresh air more distant, and the overall population density greater. Yet in the western fields the belt of housing was still narrow in 1842 and overall density low: but without preventing the same impact of cholera and fever that afflicted the East End.

The West, as we have seen, proved attractive to factories. In the 1842 cholera map the area south and west of the Park estate had just as many of the smoking chimney symbols which denoted 'Woollen, Worsted, Cotton, Silk or Flax Mills' as the East End. Its factories included many that were the newest, and therefore the biggest, in Leeds, but it could be argued that cottages in the western streets were in some respects better placed than those in the east: they were near to factory smoke but much of it was quickly swept eastwards by the prevailing south-west wind and, unlike the East End, there was no invasion of smoke from further west. The western streets were also more elevated on the hillside and did not extend down to the Aire for there, right up to the end of the nineteenth century, the riverside meadows, with an attractive location next to a turnpike and with access to water, were exclusively occupied by mills and factories. Their elevated position also ensured that these cottage streets would not suffer one affliction that beset the many waterside streets near the Timble Beck in the east: 'The [Bridge Street and Regent Street] sewers discharge into the Beck at Lady Bridge. It was thus in the spring of 1839 during some days of uninterrupted wet weather that this sewer was engorged and emptied itself into the cellar dwellings of that densely populated neighbourhood, producing all the results of malaria.'[56]

The western streets also knew nothing of another kind of nuisance. In 1845 James Smith reported that 'the lower classes . . . inhabit the less comfortable and less healthy localities, along both sides of the [Timble] Beck, and a great number of dyehouses are erected on the margin and intersperse with them'.[57] Yet in the West, Drony Laith, once the town's largest dyeworks, had been demolished to make way for building ground, and the hillside brooks of the west, mere drains and rivulets, were too small to attract new dyehouses.

[56] *1839 Report*, pp.403–04.

[57] *Second Report of the Royal Commission for Inquiring into the State of Large Towns and Populous Districts* (PP 1845, XVIII, p.313).

TABLE 13.19

Cholera in Streets of Different Origin, 1832

Location*	Cases	Deaths	Condition of street
A. *Older streets and yards:*			
Boar Lane	0	0	
Briggate	12	4	clean
Boot and Shoe Yard	17	9	wretchedly filthy
Cherry Tree Yard	12	7	open privies, very bad
Kirkgate	7	1	often dirty
Lower Headrow	4	1	many yards
Meadow Lane	15	6	always dirty
Marsh Lane	52	21	very dirty, confined
Swinegate	8	5	dirty, confined
Vicar Lane	2	0	scavenged
Wade Lane	1	1	clean street
Wellington Yard	13	8	drained but very dirty
Woodhouse Lane	1	0	clean street
B. *Building club streets*			
Back George St	6	2	dirty, confined
Back Nelson St	1	0	confined, dirty
Ebenezer St	11	6	very dirty
George St	10	6	beck at bottom
High St	7	3	generally dirty
King St	4	2	dirty, confined
Nelson St	9	7	very confined
Queen St	2	0	confined
St James St	9	3	some dirty yards
St Peter's Square	7	2	clean but confined
Union Row	6	1	'in Quarry Hill'
Union St	8	2	many dirty yards
C. *Speculative builders' streets before 1815*			
Brass St	3	2	dirty, stagnant
Camp Field	10	1	always stagnant
Goulden's Buildings	11	4	very dirty, confined
Grove Ter.	1	1	drained into pond
Kendal Row	9	5	most deplorable
Off St	10	3	confined, always stagnant

TABLE 13.19 (*continued*)

Location*	Cases	Deaths	Condition of street
Paley's Gallery	11	7	very very dirty
Riley's Court	7	2	confined, dirty, many inhabitants
Skinner Lane	1	0	a dirty lane
York St	30	8	very dirty
D. *Streets built after 1815*			
Brunswick St	1	0	moderately clean
Cambridge St	3	3	very dirty, morassy
Cato St	4	1	very dirty; by a beck
Castle St	5	2	very dirty
Hanover St	2	1	drained at top
Hope St	2	1	most dirty
Lemon St	11	5	a foot deep usually
Madras St	12	3	opposite morassy land
Nile St	1	1	clean, respectable
Orange St	24	8	most wretchedly bad
Portland St	1	0	cleanish
Savile St	9	2	very dirty
Trafalgar St	3	1	clean
Vincent St	5	2	very dirty
Vienna St	3	2	very dirty
West St	7	3	near morassy land

* None of the Park estate streets were included in Baker's schedule except Back Park Street which had 3 cases and 2 deaths, being 'in a most stagnant state'; there was one death at Preston Cottage on the Lyddon estate.

Source: *1833 Report*, Schedule, pp.21–27.

Despite these advantages the 'parts lined and colored RED' in the first cholera map included streets west of Park Place and north of Wellington Street; while in 1842 blue and red spots, locating the victims of cholera and contagious fevers, appeared in the western streets, including some that had been built since 1832. Between Wellington Street and West Street the cartographer employed the same wash of brown colour that denoted the 'less cleansed Streets' east of Kirkgate.

Though less extensive, there were other concentrations of red, blue and brown away from the first East End. In the North West ward Little London was an enclave of houses totally surrounded by

TABLE 13.20

Back-to-back Streets most frequently Castigated, 1830–45

	Number of back-to-back pairs	Description and notes
Brighton Court	8	open court
Camp Field	92	four rows with interior courts and row of one-room cottages
Cavalier St	31	second of initial cholera deaths here, 1832
Clarkson's Yard	8	entered by tunnel and narrow alley
Dufton's Yard	12	two alley entrances
Ebenezer St	38	
George St	18	
Goulden's Buildings	24	interior court, adjoining graveyard
Mill St	31	
Nelson St	41	
Noah's Ark, Meadow Lane	10	totally enclosed
Off St	53	
Orange St	40	
Phillip's Yard	11	tunnel entrance
Quarry Hill	26	long frontages of mixed character
Somerset St	29	adjoining Sheepscar Beck
Spring St	23	
Sykes Yard	14	alley and tunnel entrance
Templar St	49	
Union St	53	
Walker's Yard	18	open entrance shared with mill
Wellington Place	12	

Source: Beresford, *Back-to-Back House*, Appendix I, p.127.

fields, yet much afflicted by cholera, as was the isolated concentration at Camp Field in the South ward, where the yards between Meadow Lane and the flax manufactories had proved as liable to cholera and fever as the older yards of Kirkgate.

Finally, from a variety of sources named, Table 13.20 lists those streets which were most frequently deplored by contemporaries, indicating the number of back-to-back pairs in each. Blue Bell Fold and the Boot and Shoe Yard are omitted as over-familiar examples.

For death, disease and dirtiness these areas were castigated as one. The most numerous were in the East End narrowly defined, that is the Kirkgate yards, Quarry Hill and the Bank, but – like the blue and red spots on Baker's map – they were drawn from all the wards, and from houses of all periods. The names will be only too familiar from previous pages. In the list are three of the first Club streets; four streets from speculative builders of that period, including Richard Paley; backsides yards; courts behind back-to-back streets; roadside folds from the slopes of the Bank; and one from the western fields: a grim review of developments that have occupied earlier Chapters.

The distribution of blue and red spots on the cholera map, a different badge of shame, also brings us back to a familiar theme. Continuous in some parts of the East, North and North East wards, elsewhere they formed isolated exceptions, such as St James Street in Woodhouse Lane, Camp Field in the South ward and Little London in the North West: each created out of place, as it were, by one of those historical accidents of personality and place which, for better or worse, imposed such a piecemeal character on so much of the development which has been traced in the pages of this book, the trademark of an earthquake architect.

14
Epilogue: Two Aspects of 1842

We left Leeds on 7 January 1831. In 1841 from May 28 to January 5, at first moved almost to tears, I revisited Leeds with a deeply felt pleasure, which did not prevent me from finding it [since 1831] *now abominably smoky and evil smelling.*

Alphonse Dousseau, artist, [translated] manuscript note, written *c.*1869, accompanying a copy of his painting, *Leeds drawn from the hill called Rope-hill to the south of Leeds* (1827–1831). Thoresby Society, MS.39B32.

Cudgel thy brains no more about it . . . and when you are asked this question next, say 'a grave maker'. The houses he makes last till doomsday.

HAMLET, V, 1, 57–59.

BROWN'S SQUARE

Chadwick's report with Baker's appendix was published in July 1842. While it was being printed and its coloured cholera map engraved a Leeds solicitor was preparing a conveyance in relation to the sale of two adjacent houses in Brown's Square. Although then almost brand-new, they offended every sanitary ethic but still survived in occupation until 1951 when the *Leeds Skinner Lane No. 2 Housing Confirmation Order* authorised the Corporation to purchase them compulsorily from their owners, J. W. Pickles and C. R. Brooke, trustees of the late Henry Bingley.

They were erected sometime between August 1834 and September 1838 by a master bricklayer, George Brown of Nile Street, and located out of sight from any thoroughfare, between Skinner Lane, which Richard Paley had created in 1793 within White Cross Close, and an undeveloped field belonging to the Whitelocks of Sheepscar mill.[1] Before his bankruptcy Paley had built two large semi-detached houses on the Skinner Lane frontage with impressive bay windows and a range of workshops rising to three storeys at the rear (Fig. 8.5(a) and (b)). Known as Sheepscar Place, Paley's two houses

[1] Plan and elevation in Beresford, *Paley*, pp.302–05.

stood a little back from Skinner Lane, with small front gardens; each had a larger garden and orchard at its side, with a well and a pump.[2] By the time of the bankruptcy in 1803 there had also been some development on the Harrogate turnpike frontage which formed the western boundary of the close, and a row of blind-back houses, South Row (renamed later as Brown's Yard) had been built along half the northern side. As in the East End, the assignees in Paley's bankruptcy found purchasers for the vacant parts of the close only slowly, and those who purchased plots were slow to develop them. The orchard to the east of Sheepscar Place remained intact until at least 1850 but that to the west was supplanted by what came to be called Brown's Square.

Brown's Square was one of those squares (like Johnson's Square on Quarry Hill) the audacity of whose naming strains belief. The 'square' consisted of the side yard to Paley's workshops in Sheepscar Place and a further inner courtyard approached only through a tunnel (Figs. 14.1(a) and (b)). Its genesis can be traced from the conveyance of 30 May 1842 when the legatees in Brown's will were selling the houses that he had recently built. Brown had purchased 426 square yards of land in August 1834 from the Headrow bootmaker, Robert Hopps, paying him a penny over that five shillings a square yard which Baker regarded as the limit for land designed for cottage building: but even with the interest to pay on a mortgage of £150, it was no bad bargain since Brown was intending to achieve a density higher than that of the standard back-to-backs.[3]

In the conveyance the premises were imprecisely described as 'several messuages, cottages and other buildings' but on the back of the document a large-scale plan by the surveyor, John Crookes, made the nature of the structures explicit: beside a crude, ladder-like representation of the tunnel and steps that divided the two houses Crookes wrote: 'Two Cellar Dwellings & 4 Upper Dwellings Over': that is, each house was made up of three dwellings arranged vertically; and since the houses were blind back to Brown's Yard each dwelling consisted of one room with a single window facing into the square; half the window of each cellar dwelling lay below the level of the unpaved surface of the square.

Too mean for the attention of the compilers of the street directories, the square's first occupants were enumerated for the census of 1841:[4]

[2] Fig. 14.1.
[3] LCD 8879.
[4] PRO, HO 107/1346/7 and 2320/3 (Brown's Square).

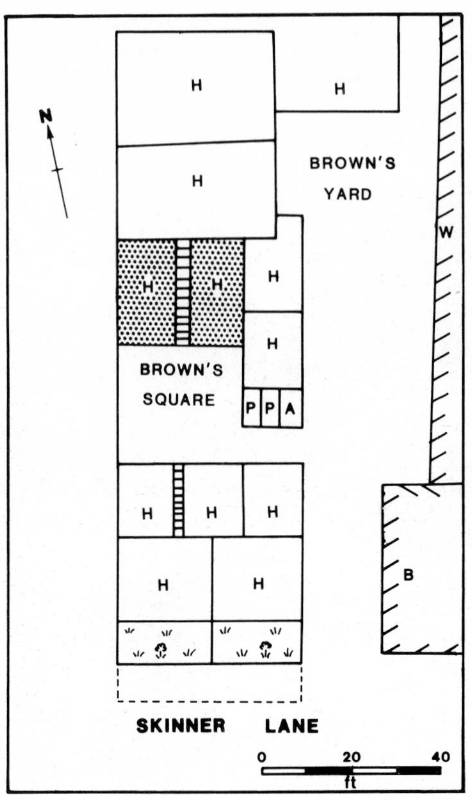

FIG. 14.1(a) A SQUARE OF HIGH-DENSITY HOUSING, 1842

From a plan accompanying a conveyance: the three-storey bay-windowed merchant's house (B) was one of a pair built by Paley in 1792 (Fig. 8.5); it was integral with six bays of workshops (W) making up Brown's Yard; houses (H) accumulated between 1831 and 1842 in the former garden to the west, completed by Brown's Square, 162 square feet in area and approached through an archway from Brown's Yard. The two pairs of buildings facing the interior of the square were probably identical: a photograph exists for the pair (H, dotted) on the north. Each building of a pair comprised a one-room cellar dwelling, a one-room dwelling on the ground floor, and a third one-room dwelling above it which was reached by a stair rising within a narrow tunnel dividing the two buildings, drawn as a ladder on the plan. P: privy; A: ashpit.

FIG. 14.1(b) BROWN'S YARD AND BROWN'S SQUARE, 1951

The photograph, taken at the time of the Compulsory Purchase Order, looks northwards from Skinner Lane into Brown's Yard from the same angle as the plan in Fig. 14.1(a). Despite the name plate, Brown's Square is invisible behind the houses on the left: the tunnel entrance can be seen at the break in the pavement just beyond the line of washing, itself evidence that the houses were still occupied. On the right is the west side of the house and workshops erected in 1792 (Fig. 8.5) and in 1951 empty and awaiting demolition.

No. 6	No. 7
Thomas Long age 39 tailor Martha Long age 17 dressmaker George Long age 13 Alfred Sutcliffe age 11 errand boy Mary Esther Long age 5 Sarah Jane Long age 6 months	John Rollston age 45* watch-maker Ann Rollston age 35* dressmaker John Rollston age 15* apprentice saddler Ann Rollston age 15* William Rollston age 12 Henry Rollston age 5 (* = Irish born)
No. 5	No. 8
John Thackray age 36 cloth dresser Mary Thackray age 35 housewife Frederic Thackray age 15 William Thackray age 14 Alice Thackray age 11 Wallace Thackray age 7 Thomas Thackray age 5 Charles Thackray age 1 day	John Turner age 29 cloth dresser Sarah Elizabeth Turner age 27 milliner Sarah Ann Turner age 77 Mary Ann Turner age 5 Samuel Joseph Turner age 3 Pamela Mary Turner age 10 months
No. 4 (cellar)	No. 9 (cellar)
Sarah Aram age 68 washerwoman	Jonathon Shore age 59 blacksmith

A century later in May 1951 the condition of the houses on the north side of the Square was described in the compulsory purchase and clearance orders, and a record photograph taken from which their structure can be confirmed. Henry Bingley's 'dwelling-house no. 6, Brown's Square' lay 'over Reference No. 9', that is, the 'dwelling-house no. 5, Brown's Square'; similarly no. 7 was over no. 8. These two upper dwellings were entered by steps ascending a tunnel between the front doors of the lower houses. Additionally, but disused in 1951, each house had a semi-submerged cellar dwelling, entered down steps which were protected by a wooden railing.

The houses in Brown's Yard were occupied for some 113 years, and would have been for longer had their owner's objections to compulsory purchase been sustained. They were left empty for several years after the compulsory purchase, and then demolished (Fig. 14.1(b)). Larger buildings from the period of Brown's Yard, warehouses and through houses in terraces, do survive elsewhere in Leeds. How long Brown anticipated that his investment would survive we cannot tell. He would have known that property could be demolished for development long before it became derelict: but only in central streets, and mostly for street widening or to make space for public buildings. No frontage on Boar Lane had then been disturbed and in Briggate there were frontage houses whose appearance betrayed their sixteenth-century date: and more backsides.

THE DOOMSDAY HOUSES

Elsewhere in Leeds in 1842 there were preparations to build for eternity. Immediately before giving the royal assent on 16 July 1842 to 5–6 Victoria cap. 104, *An Act for better lighting, cleansing, sewering and improving the Borough of Leeds in the County of York*, the Queen assented to cap. 103, *An Act for Additional Burial Grounds in Leeds*. The pressure on the ancient burial ground at the parish church and on the limited auxiliary grounds at other churches and chapels had been an acknowledged part of the insanitary state of the East End, hardly relieved by the joint stock company's General Cemetery at Woodhouse. Largely from the diplomacy of Dean Hook, vicar of Leeds since 1837, it had been possible to resolve conflicting sectarian interests and for all parties to support the Bill for a municipal cemetery.[5]

Ground had already been allotted on the outskirts of town in a new street laid out across land north of Burmantofts belonging to the banker, William Beckett, and named after him. Ten-and-a-half acres are marked on Fowler's town plan of 1884 as 'New Burial Ground'; by the time of the Tithe Award plan in 1847 the ground was walled and trees were planted on the Beckett Street frontage opposite the Industrial School (later St James's Hospital). The plan showed two detached buildings already erected within the walls but no graves.[6] A little later that year the Ordnance Survey had progressed far enough out of town to reach the cemetery. The five-foot plan[7] shows an ornamental lodge for the sexton's residence completed, and identifies the southern of the two buildings within the walls as a 'Chapel for performing the Rites according to the Church of England'; and, had the sheet extended further, the other would have been credited with the rites appropriate for the nonconformist dead. Thus the concordat achieved by Hook, and thus the architectural expression of the deep divisions between the Anglican and the nonconformist Nations in early Victorian England.

5 D. Fraser, 'The Leeds Churchwardens, 1828–1850', *PTh.S*, LIII (1971), 16–17.

6 LCA, LPC 107/21.

7 Sheet 8.

FIG. 14.2 THE TWO NATIONS AT REST

The town's first municipal cemetery, authorised by Act of Parliament in 1842, was located on the then edge of town in Beckett Street, opposite the new workhouse. It had separate sections (and chapels) for Anglicans and Nonconformists: in each section there was a further division, illustrated here, between those who could afford a separate family plot and a gravestone (as in the background) and those (as in the foreground) whose grave and plain stone was shared with nine strangers. The four collective stones shown here date from the spring of 1891.

The cemetery is now (1988) full and its future in debate. The two chapels have been demolished but in its internal topography the Beckett Street cemetery bears the authentic stamp of 1842. The carriage drive from the lodge gates divides the area: on the right hand side are buried the Anglicans and on the left the remainder.

Within each half of the cemetery a further subdivision marks a segregation for the dead that was more defined and unchallenged than any achieved in the history of the two West Ends and a diffused East End. Trees and shrubs have lodged everywhere in the abandoned walks, with ivy and creeping plants in abundance. But not everywhere equally: in each half, Anglican or nonconformist, there is a quarter with elaborate and ambitious monumental sculptures where climbing plants can grow to six or seven feet and obscure the carved biblical texts and the encomia for families buried in each vault (Fig. 14.2).

There is also in each half a quarter where stonework, two or three feet high, hardly protrudes from the enveloping shroud of rank grass. Here lichen has brought its own form of concealment to many of the names carved on these smaller and totally plain gravestones but it cannot conceal that the names are very numerous, often ten or fifteen to a stone, and that the plainness of the stone is matched by the brevity of the lettering: a name and a date.

These are the dead of a Second Nation. Some died in the workhouse hospital nearby but most lived and died in the terraced streets of back-to-backs which spread in the eighteen-fifties from the York Road up across the slopes of the North and North East wards. At the same time on the other side of York Road the back-to-backs of the first East End – thought incapable of structural modification and abandoned by all who could afford to flee their streets – were abandoned to those with the lowest incomes and the lowest expectations from their environment, and were well on their way to becoming the classic slum.

In both the East and West Ends of Leeds earthly mansions have been demolished and their sites taken up by motorways, superstores, a university, a hospital, a polytechnic and by grass and high-rise flats, but so long as Beckett Street cemetery survives so long will its gravestones mark out the lasting frontiers between an East End and a West End.

Appendices

All which will require Briarius his hundred hands, Argus his hundred eyes, and Nestor's centuries of years to marshall them into distinct files and make exact Alphabetical Tables of the several Things, Names, Places, comprised in them.

William Prynne, BREVIA PARLIAMENTARIA (1661), p. 2.

Earliest Fire Insurances, 1716–24

Date of policy	Name	Location	Value of house	Reference	Notes
5 Nov. 1716	William Cookson, merchant	Kirkgate*	not stated	Sun OS 6 7533	
14 March 1717	Alderman Atkinson	Call Lane*	not stated	Sun OS 6 8424	
Jan. 1718	William Totty, linen draper	Briggate, Shambles	not stated	Sun OS 7 10215	
12 March 1718	Robert Denison, merchant	Town's End*	not stated	Sun OS 7 10572	
April 1718	John Wynne	Briggate	not stated	Sun OS 8 10783	
June 1718	Abigail Askwith, widow	Kirkgate	not stated	Sun OS 8 11189	
May 1719	Samuel Powell, mercer	Shambles, Briggate	not stated	Sun OS 9 14016	address from WRRD, L343/452
June 1719	Rachel Dixon, widow	Briggate	not stated	Sun OS 9 14397	
Jan. 1720	John Harrison, ironmonger	Briggate	not stated	Sun OS 10 16455	
April 1720	Edward Tildesley, grocer	Kirkgate	not stated	Sun OS 11 17569	
Oct. 1721	Joshua Rider, merchant	'of Leeds'	£200 + 150 + 100 + 110	Sun OS 13 24032	includes shop and warehouse
Oct. 1721	Thomas Fenton	Hunslet	£300	Sun OS 13 23906	
March 1722	John Dixon, merchant	Briggate	£100	Sun OS 13 24457	Warehouse 'adjoining his house'; goods only insured Dec. 1721
March 1722	Samuel Killingbeck, linen draper	Shambles, Briggate	not stated	Sun OS 14 25844	
Aug. 1722	James Pinckney, watchmaker	Briggate	Ten @ £50 each	Sun OS 14 26089	
Aug. 1722	James Pinckney	Briggate	Ten others @ £50	Sun OS 14 26090	
July 1724	Thomas Lee	Briggate*	£300 + 200	Sun OS 15 21899	
July 1724	Thomas Lee	Briggate	Five others @ £100	Sun OS 15 21900	

* House depicted on Cossins's map, 1725.

Source: Guildhall Library, London, Sun Insurance Co., Policy Registers, vols 6–21; there were some other policies insuring goods only.

APPENDIX IV.1

(pp. 454–58)

The Divisions of Leeds and the Rateable Assessments

Leeds, like Yorkshire itself, may once have had its three Ridings or *thirdings*, the name surviving in the 'Mainridding' or Manor Riding: no other name compounded with *-riding* has survived, but the two other subdivisions are known to have been 'Kirkgate Riding' and a 'Town Riding'.[1] The boundaries of the Ridings overrode that between manor and borough (Fig. 1.4) and may therefore have been more ancient. Medieval boroughs were usually assessed separately from adjoining manors when national taxes were levied, and at higher rates: but the petty seigneurial borough created within the manor of Leeds in 1207 (Fig. 1.4) was never taxed separately from the manor, and the first subdivisions encountered in the Exchequer records are not between manor and borough but Mainriding and High Town.

Although the amounts paid from Leeds for such taxes as the hearth tax or the excise duties depended on the number of hearths or the quantity of goods traded, for others, even the poll taxes of 1692, the Exchequer was content to receive fixed proportions from each place in the county, leaving the localities to distribute the burden to individuals; when a West Riding county rate developed, the same principle was followed, and traditional proportions were paid to the county treasurer from each parish, fossilising some long-forgotten assessment. Within each locality, especially in large parishes like Leeds, a similar principle was used to determine the different contribution of each township. In Leeds the proportions traditional for national taxes seem to have been adopted for the local rates collected to relieve the poor and maintain the highways.

So long as changes in the number and values of properties followed a similar course in each of the sub-areas the traditional proportions were acceptable to all parties. For example, in 1703 the in-township contributed just under a half and the thirteen out-townships together just over a half of the total for the borough (which at that time lay within the same boundary as the parish). To the out-townships' total, five – Hunslet, Holbeck, Armley, Headingley and Chapel Allerton – contributed at double the rate of their fellows.[2]

Yet the tradition was not to survive for ever: in so large a parish as Leeds it would have been truly remarkable if in periods of substantial economic

[1] A. H. Smith, *The Place-names of the West Riding of Yorkshire, Part Four* (English Place-Name Society, XXXIII, 1961), p.129: in his treatment of Mainrid(d)ing Smith did not see the possibility of a *-riding* element, being diverted to *rydding*, 'clearing'.

[2] Thoresby Society, MS.D VIII, ff.57 and 65–67.

change each locality increased its wealth at the same rate, so that dissension and sometimes litigation could result. The latest record of the traditional contributions is dated 1703, and the first surviving rate book for the in-township, dating from 1713, may indicate a decision that year to abandon tradition and begin regular reassessments.

The annual rate levied in Leeds was originally one penny in the pound of a single month's rent in respect of a building, and three halfpence from rents for land: for buildings an allowance of 10 per cent of this gross rental was made, presumably for repairs, maintenance and other expenses: an allowance was made in respect of rents from land but not in any uniform way. On these bases the 'month's rate', as it was called, yielded £55 11*s*. in 1713, £79 15*s*. in 1741 and £95 16*s*. in 1754, almost all the increment coming from the erection of new buildings. As necessary expenditure grew, more than one 'month's rate' was levied in a year: thus there were seven such levies in 1743, five in 1744, six in 1745 and eight in 1746:

Navigation Rated	£	*Waterworks Engine Rated*	£
1741–51	500	1741	–
1752–74	600	1751	30
1790	1000	1752	15
1795	3000	1754	30
1800	3000	1765–74	120
1805	3000	1790	65

Tithe Rated (£)

	East	North East	North West
1741–47	24.10*s*. 0*d*.	6	12
1748–50	Nil	6	12
1751–52	10	2	12
1754	3.10*s*.0*d*.	2	12

Tolls Rated (£)

	N.W. Bar	Bridge End	Fruit and Roots	Corn
1741–44	21	30	6	51
1745–50	21	15	6	50
1751–52	16	15	6	?
1754	13	–	6	60
1765–74	–	–	–	60

The rate assessments had some further components: tithe income and the tolls at the North, West and Bridge End Bars, together with the tolls of the markets for fruit and roots, were subject to a conventionalised rate but only between 1741 and 1754; the corn tolls seem to have been always rated.

Tenter frames were rated at 25*s*. per dozen, and until 1754 the wealthier inhabitants were additionally rated on their personalty or 'stock'; from 1713 to 1726 these were intermingled with the assessments on land and buildings but from 1741 to 1754 the names were set out separately: their number varied between 345 and 429, their contribution made up 9 per cent of the township rate in 1742 and 8 in 1754. The water mills were assessed at round sums, as was the engine of the town waterworks. The largest toll was that levied on the proprietors of the Aire and Calder Navigation who were rated to the relief of the poor both at Leeds and Wakefield: unsuccessful attempts to determine these contributions by Act of Parliament, to the proprietors' advantage, were made in 1743 and 1759.

The assessments in the first surviving poor rate book (1713) were set out under seven 'Divisions' but another term, 'Part', lingered in the eighth rubric, 'South Part'.[3] (Did not the ancient county of Lincoln have both Ridings and Parts?) In 1725 the jurors of the borough Quarter Sessions were listed under three 'Divisions' (Kirkgate, High Town and Middle) and the remainder under three 'Parts' – North, South and East.[4]

Boundaries between taxation units had always been important and sensitive matters, witnessed by ceremonies associated with Rogationtide and the beating of bounds. The boundaries between the in- and out-townships of Leeds were well known, and Thoresby took his readers carefully along their ancient course,[5] but there is no corresponding record of the boundaries of the Divisions until they came to be marked (for the central part of the in-township) on the Giles town plan of 1815 and then, for the whole in-township, on Fowler's more extensive plan of 1831. Yet knowledge of them must have been commonplace since they were needed to determine the basis of levies for the parish poor rate, and then for the rates levied by the successive Improvement Acts. The private census of 1775 was collected by Divisions,[6] as were the Land Tax[7] and the first national census.[8]

The rate books did not proceed further and locate each property in its street but it is possible to assign streets to their Divisions since in 1740 the

[3] LCA, LORB 1.
[4] LCA, LQS 3, f.21.
[5] *Ducatus*, pp.83–85 and 95–97; for 1612 see Kirby, *Manor*, pp.72–75.
[6] British Library, Add MS.33770, ff.56–57: but by division of labour the voluntary census-takers ended up with nineteen units.
[7] LCA, DB 227.
[8] LCA, LPC 104.

APPENDIX IV.1 LEEDS RATING DIVISIONS TO 1835

Employed for many rating and taxation purposes in the late seventeenth century, these Divisions are of unknown antiquity but they clearly took some account of the intrusion of the borough into the extended village (cf. Fig. 1.4).

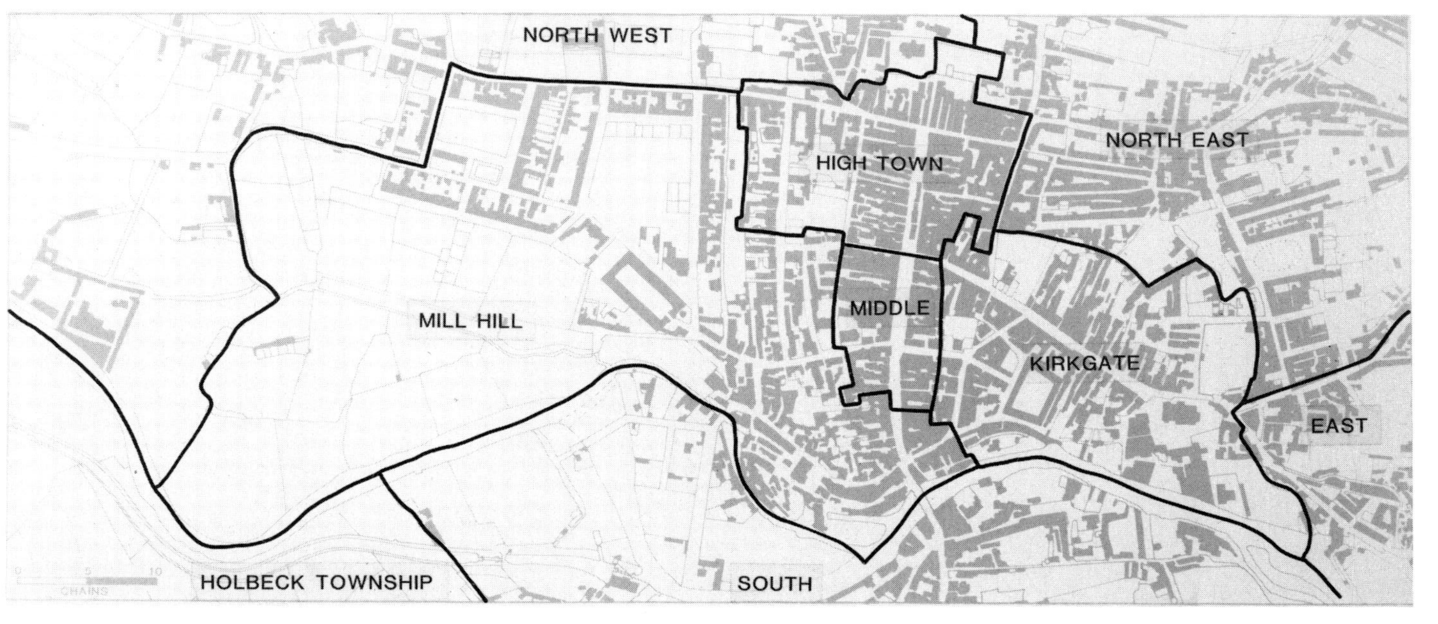
NORTH WEST
NORTH EAST
HIGH TOWN
MIDDLE
KIRKGATE
EAST
MILL HILL
SOUTH
HOLBECK TOWNSHIP
0 5 10
CHAINS

Charity School master, Thomas Wilson, made a copy of the assessments into his commonplace book but added street names as additional rubrics.[9]

Between the last surviving rate book (1805) and the Giles plan of 1815 each of the large North West and North East Divisions was further divided into an Upper and a Lower: the North West by resolution of the overseers of the poor on 27 October 1809 and the North East at an unknown date.

After 1835 the Divisions were superseded by Wards, employed for electoral purposes, and by Enumeration Districts for taking the census. A convenient map of the township and Division bounds will be found in Fraser, *History of Modern Leeds*, Figs 1 and 9.

The structure of the original eight Divisions was as follows:

1. *Kirkgate*

In 1740: Kirkgate, Call Lane east side, The Calls and Upper Tenters.

Basically the original village street and the church with the gardens and folds on either side. The eastern limit was defined by the Timble Beck and the bridge-stones at the East Bar. Much of the Division lay in the manorial jurisdiction of Leeds Kirkgate-cum-Holbeck, a survival of a separate church manor.[10]

2. *High Town*

In 1740: Burley Bar Without, Upper and Lower Headrow, High Causeway, Vicar Lane west side, Kirkgate End, Upper Briggate, Shambles and Lower Briggate west side.

This was the area of the medieval borough, hence the inclusion of Kirkgate End with the borough prison where Kirkgate entered Briggate through a gap between two burgages. The corn toll and North West Bar tolls were rated in this Division. The east side of Vicar Lane, unbuilt upon north of the vicarage, fell into the rural North East Division, below.

3. *Mill Hill*

1740: Boar Lane, Cripplegate, the Parks, Mill Hill, Swinegate, Lower Tenters, part of Lower Briggate, lower part of Call Lane.

Probably the two remaining parts of the village after the borough had been laid out west of Kirkgate. It contained the manor house, its park and the manorial mills to the west but extended eastwards past the bridge to the waterworks and the Navigation warehouse. Its older name was 'Leeds Main [or Manor] Riding' (i.e. the 'Manor-third' of the town: cf. the three Ridings of the county), the other two *thirdings* being probably Kirkgate and the borough. Entries for the eastern parts of this Division always appear near the end of the assessments but without a rubric.

[9] LCA, DB 204/3, ff.153–211.

[10] For its bounds see LCA, DB 213/97.

4. *South*

1740: Meadow Lane and part of Hunslet Lane.

The least complex boundary, following streams and fields against Holbeck and Hunslet with the Aire as its longest boundary.

5. *East*

1740: Timble Bridge, Hillhouse Banks, Cross Green, Knowestrop, Black Bank, Marsh Lane south-east side.

In the 1726 rate book it was named 'Knowsthorp'.

An extensive rural area reaching as far as Osmondthorpe township but encroached upon by ribbon development in Marsh Lane and at the hamlet on the (Hillhouse) bank. It included the Nether Mills.

6. *North East*

1740: Marsh Lane north side, Quarry Hill, Mabgate, Burmantofts, North Hall (Lady) bridge, Lady Lane, Vicar Lane east side, New Chapel Lane and Sheepscar.

Also a rural area on either side of Timble (Sheepscar) Beck extending towards Potter Newton township with Long Balk Lane, formerly an important lane into the open fields, as its western boundary. The sub-manor of North Hall lay just north of the Kirkgate garths near Lady bridge. This division contained all the water mills on the Beck except the Nether Mills.

7. *North West*

1740: Lidgate, Wade Lane, Jacob's Well, Claypit House, Buslingthorpe, Wood[house] Carr, Ridge, Nether Green, Great and Little Woodhouse, Park Lane, North Hall, Spring Garden, Drony Laith.

In the 1726 rate book its name was 'Great Woodhouse'.

The most extensive and populated of the rural Divisions, extending to the town moor at Woodhouse and the Headingley-cum-Burley boundary. Its North Hall should not be confused with North Hall manor, above (6).

8. *Middle*

1740: Part of Lower Briggate, Call Lane west side (but Call Lane entries actually in Kirkgate, (1) above, and boundary on 1815 Giles plan excludes Call Lane).

Probably a later sub-division, taking in part of High Town and Kirkgate Divisions. Its entries both for personalty and property were reckoned a separate Division in the rate books of 1713–26 and from 1747, but were sometimes placed under sub-headings within High Town and Kirkgate; where the sub-headings were omitted the same sequence of entries occurred, usually after a few blank lines. In 1740 there were 68 properties in the Middle section of Kirkgate, and 103 in High Town Middle.

The tolls of the fruit and vegetable market were included in this Division.

APPENDIX IV.2

Landownership: Rateable Value of Holdings, by Divisions, 1740

	up to £10	11–20	21–30	31–40	41–50	51–60	61–70	71–80	81–90	91–100	ove £10
Town Centre											
High Town	3	0	0	0	0	0	0	0	0	0	0
Middle	0	0	0	0	0	0	0	0	0	0	0
Kirkgate	2	1	0	0	0	0	0	0	0	0	0
Periphery											
South	1	1	0	0	1	0	1	0	0	0	0
East	10	5	1	1	1	1	0	0	0	0	3
North East	18	6	1	2	2	1	3	0	1	1	1
North West	22	10	2	1	1	0	1	1	2	1	1
Mill Hill	0	2	0	0	0	0	0	0	0	0	1
Whole Town: 113 holdings	56	25	4	4	5	2	5	1	3	2	6

Source: LCA, DB 204/3.

APPENDIX IV.3

Number of Properties Rated £25 and over, by Divisions, 1740

	Owner-occupied	Tenanted
Town Centre		
High Town	1	9
High Town Middle	0	1
Kirkgate Middle	1	6
Kirkgate	3	2
Periphery		
South	4	3
East	0	1
North East	0	0
North West	0	2
Mill Hill	3	6
TOTAL	12	30

Source: LCA, DB 204/3.

APPENDIX IV.4

Inhabitants Assessed to 'Personalty' or 'Stock', 1741–54

	1741	1742	1744	1745	1752	1754
High Town	56	66	57	57	63	65
High Town Middle	30	20	35	20	45	41
Kirkgate Middle	18	20	19	20	28	24
Kirkgate	51	49	48	55	52	50
South	50	48	51	54	52	55
East	20	25	22	23	35	26
North East	35	37	35	36	39	35
North West	43	42	45	44	53	38
Mill Hill	42	41	41	45	62	58
TOTAL	345	348	353	354	429	392

Source: LCA, LORB 10–31.

APPENDIX V.1

Development of Rateable Values on Twenty Frontage Properties in Briggate (High Town Middle Division), 1741–74

	A	B	C	D	E	F	G	H	I	J	K	L	M	N	O	P	Q	R	S	T
1741	13	23	15	15	12	15	18	18	11	19	18	11	30	18	13	16	10	18	10	16
1742	18	15	e	15	12	15	18	18	11	19	18	11	30	18	13	16	10	18	10	16
1744	18	22	e	15	12	15	18	18	11	18	18	11	30	18	13	16	11	11	12	16
1752	14	22	14	14	14	14	15	15	15	15	15	?	30	20	16	16	16	16	?	16
1754	20	22	16	16	10	15	18	18	16	20	20	14	30	20	16	16	11	14	?	16
1765	13	24	21	16	15	23	18	22	20	15	15	14	30	20	16	20	15	11	10	24
1774	13	45	23	24	15	23	20	22	18	25	25	14	30	25	16	?	15	19	19	24

Source: LCA, LORB 10–32; 'e' = empty.

APPENDIX V.2

(pp. 463–64)

Development of Frontage Houses and Yards: Free School Estate, Vicar Lane, 1727, 1754 and 1793

Length of street frontage in feet and inches	13′ 3″		15′ 3″		27′ 0″	17′ 9″	12′ 0″	16′ 3″	19′ 3″	3′ 0″ tunnel
Tenant in 1728	Baynes	Baynes	Baynes	Baynes	Thoresby	Hargrave		Horn		—
Rent in 1727	5s 0d				8s 9d	3s 0d		14s 6d		—
Ground floor	lr	lr + p	lr	lr	library	lr	lr	r + pn	lr + pn + cl	—
Upper floor	ch	ch	ch	ch	2 ch + g	ch	ch	2ch	ch	—
Buildings in yard	—	—	—	—	3 (r + ch) 2 stables + chambers over	—	—	3 (r + ch)	r + ch + g	—
Additions, 1728–54	—	—	—	—	—	k + 2 lr	—	—	—	—
Additions, 1754–93	*united*		*united*		—	—	—	—	—	—
Tenant in 1793	Dixon		Derwent		Crocker*	Broadley snr	Boshall	Broadley jnr	How†	—

Length of street frontage	9′ 0″	9′ 6″	5′ 0″ passage	18′ 8″	3′ 0″ tunnel	20′ 3″	10′ 6″	10′ 6″	3′ 0″ tunnel
Tenant in 1728	Whalley		—	Smith	—	Pye's heirs		Elston	—
Rent in 1727	6s 0d		—	4s 0d	—	6s 0d		3s 0d	—
Ground floor	2r	r	—	r + sp + ch	—	lr	lr	lr	—
Upper floor	2ch	ch	—	ch	2ch	ch	ch	ch	—
Buildings in yard	—	—	—	—	—	4 r	4 r	—	—
Additions, 1728–54	lr	lr + ch	—	—	—	—	—	—	—
Additions, 1754–93	2 (r + ch)		—	—	—	—	—	2 lr	—
	3 (r + ch + cl)		—	—	—	—	—	2 (r + ch + g)	—
Tenant in 1793	Smith	Turner	—	Firth†	—	—	Sutcliffe†	Lightfoot‡	—

Key: ch: chamber; cl: cellar; g: garret; k: kitchen; lr: low room; p: parlour; pn: pantry; r: room; sp: small parlour; st: stable.
* By 1793 ground floor, a shop, warehouse, parlour and back kitchen.
† 'Necessary house' (i.e. privy) in yard.
‡ Five coal houses in yard.

Note: In 1794 all the properties were declared 'ruinous and unwholesome for Habitation' and then demolished (LCA, DB 197/2, 18 Dec. 1794). The House of Recovery (or fever hospital) was built on part of the site in 1804. It is now bounded by Kirkgate and Fish Street.

Sources: 1727 rental: LCA, LPC 72/4; 1728 and 1754 surveys with plan of the ex-Thoresby houses in 1754: LCA, DB 197, unlisted; 1793 survey and plan: DB 204/8.

APPENDIX V.3

Houses and Shops on Highways Charity Estate, Upper Headrow, 1754 and 1793

1754 survey		1793 survey and plan	
House	o/o	Shop	o/o
+ shop at rear	ten.		
House	o/o	House	o/o
Shop	o/o	Shop (saddler)	o/o
House	o/o	Wheatsheaf p.h.	o/o
House	o/o	Shop	o/o
Shop	o/o	Shop	o/o
Shop	o/o	Shop	o/o
House/brewhouse	o/o	Anchor p.h. (vacant)	
Shop	ten.	Nag's Head Inn	o/o
House	ten.	Shop	o/o
Shop	ten.	Shop (grocer)	o/o
House	o/o	Shop	ten./o
House	ten.	House	o/o
House	ten.	Shop	ten./o

Key
o/o = own occupation
p.h. = public house
ten. = as tenant
ten./o = as tenant with owner living adjacent

Note: When the site was given to endow a fund for highway repair in February 1530 (Wade's Charity) it had only three cottages.

Sources: 1530: LCA, DB 204/3; 1754: DB 197, unlisted; 1793: DB 204/8.

APPENDIX VI.1

Park Estate: Accumulation, 1667–1780

Date	Property and Location	Vendor	Price £ where known
23 Dec 1667	Mansion – Mill Hill Three houses – Mill Hill Seven Park Closes incl. Gowland Close Park Butts, South	Dawson (to Sykes: Elizabeth Sykes married Thomas Wilson; their son was Richard (1678–1761)).	
4 Sept 1683	Great Monkpits (5¼ ac.)	Benson and Poole	150
3 Nov 1701	Three Park Closes (10 ac.)	Rayner	373
5 Feb 1717	Pease Close, Squire Close, Tenant Close, Holme Close, Parkinson Close, Ogle Close, Forest Close (part of the ancient park)	Hough	200
10 Feb 1718	Park Hill Close or Far Park Hill	Kirshaw and Mitchell	100
12 Nov 1724	House on Mill Hill (near almshouses)	Sykes	
23 Aug 1725 (first moiety: second on 10 Dec 1728)	St Peter's Well Close, Clausewell Close, Middle Close, Half Close, Well Close, Well House (in two moieties)	Mitchell and Douglas	
7 Nov 1726	Several cottages, Mill Hill, 'by goit of old corn mill'	Netherwood	
4 Aug 1727	Applegarth Close, Woodhouse Lane	Mitchell and Douglas	
17 May 1728	Two Cloudesley Closes	Hough	950
3 July 1728	Four houses, Mill Hill	Helm	
27 March 1729	Moiety of Park Butts (7¾ ac.)	Sager	450
19 Aug 1731	House, Mill Hill	Senior	
30 Dec 1733	Near Park Hill Close (2 ac.)	Hunter	150
7 April 1735	House, Cripplegate and Mill Hill		
20 Jan 1743	Sparrow Hall Close Two Monkpitt Closes Three houses and closes in Boar Lane (one, the Rooke Mansion – sold 5 Oct 1747)	Rooke	700

APPENDIX VI.1 (*continued*)

Date	Property and Location	Vendor	Price £ where known
3 Feb 1748	Other Moiety of Park Butts	Sager	450
15 Aug 1775	Tenter Garth (2½ ac.)	Stanley	840
12 Feb 1777	Drony Laith Farm and Dye House, Great and Little Giant Hill Closes, Great Pasture Close, Upper Garden Close, Upper and Lower Meadow, Long Balk, Arthington Close, Mackerell Close (44 acres)	Dixon	5500
31 July 1777	Margaret Holme Close	Kenion	700
12 Sept 1780	Three Upper Monkpitt Closes	Kirshaw	611

Sources: LCA, DB 5/8; 32/7 and 27; 32/15: 'Schedule of Mr. Christopher Wilson's Title Deeds, Box 1'; this box now forms DB 239/1–3, with some losses; WRRD, M 19/26, O 541/822, Z 604/807, Z 605/809, UU 490/660 and XX 178/210.

APPENDIX VI.2

(*pp. 467–68*)

Park Row, 1767–76

Development unit, from north to south	House frontage in feet	House no.	Date of first lease; ground rent (£.*s*.*d*.)	Leaseholder	Builder
A	45	23	1 Jan 1768 2.5.0	Ikin, gentleman	Thomas
B	26	22	30 Dec 1771 2.12.4	Ibbetson, woolstapler	Adamson
B	26	21	30 Dec 1771 included above	Ibbetson	Adamson
C	52	20	30 Dec 1771 2.12.4	Thompson, merchant	Adamson
D	37	19	30 Dec 1771 1.17.0	Dunderdale, linen merchant	Adamson
E	37	18	30 Dec 1771 1.17.0	Armistead, gentleman	Adamson
F	21	17	30 Dec 1771 1.1.0	Armistead	Adamson
G	22	16	30 Dec 1771 1.2.0	Armistead	Adamson

APPENDIX VI.2 (*continued*)

Development unit, from north to south	House frontage in feet	House no.	Date of first lease; ground rent (£.*s.d.*)	Leaseholder	Builder
H	41	15	30 Dec 1771 2.1.0	Armistead	Adamson
I	37½	14	4 Sept 1776 1.12.6	Markham, merchant	–
I	37½	13	4 Sept 1776 1.12.6	Markham	–
I	37½	12	4 Sept 1776 1.12.0	Markham	–
I	37½	11	4 Sept 1776 1.12.0	Markham	–
J	40	10	29 Sept 1773 2.0.0	King	William Smith, bricklayer
K	44	9	17 May 1775	Scott, widow	Smith
L	44	8	20 Jan 1775	Lister, merchant	Smith
M	42	7	20 Aug 1772 2.2.0	Ibbetson, gentleman	Smith
N	30	6	20 Aug 1772 1.10.0	Oates, spinster	–
O	49	5	10 Sept 1771 2.9.0	William Hargrave, carpenter	Hargrave
P	45	4	1 May 1769	Rayner, spinster	–
Q	35	3	1 Jan 1769 1.15.0	Walker, salter	–
R	57	2	15 Sept 1767 2.13.0	Barstow, gentleman	–
S	42	1	1 Jan 1768 2.2.0	Trustees of Mill Hill chapel	–
Mill Hill Chapel and Graveyard					

Source: LCA, DB 32/19 and 58/34.

South Parade, 1776–80

Development unit, from west to east	House frontage in feet	House no.	Date of first lease; ground rent (£.*s*.*d*.)	Leaseholder	Builder	Insured values and dates: House & contents £	Insured values and dates: Other buildings & contents £	Rateable values and dates	Insurance references	Sale value of house and date £	Notes
A	45	22*	13 Jan 1780 3.7.6	Cookson, gentleman	William Smith						
B	78	7	3 Jan 1777 5.17.9	Smith, bricklayer	Smith	1800 (1802)	1250 (1802)	23 (1805)	Sun CS 49 739169		
B		6		Smith	Smith	incl. above	incl. above	10 (1790)			
C	60	5	1 Jan 1778 4.10.0	Lloyd, merchant and wool-stapler	Smith	1500 + 600 (1794)	200 + 200 (1794)	20 (1795)	Sun CS 8 636170	460 from builder (1778)	
D	60	4	31 Dec 1776 4.10.0	Cattaneo, merchant and wool-stapler	–	1250 (1782)	40 + 6000 (1782)	18 (1795)	Sun OS 303 461806–7		Insurance calls it 'Park Row'.†
E	100	3	24 April 1776 7.10.0	Lloyd, merchant	Smith						
F	65	2		Lloyd, merchant	–	1000 + 500 (1790)	100 (1790)	20 (1790)	Sun OS 366 569216		*LM*, 19 March 1776‡

* Numbered in East Parade.
† The interior 'Square' is 'Cattaneo's Garden' in deeds of nos 16–19 East Parade, 1779.
‡ Industrial buildings erected 'and the Front of the same length not builded upon, and which will pay no more Ground Rent unless Houses are erected'.

Source (where not cited in Appendix): LCA DB 32/20.

APPENDIX VI.4

(*pp.* 470–71)

East Parade, 1779–88

Development unit, from south to north	House frontage in feet	House no.	Date of first lease; ground rent (£.*s.d.*)	Leaseholder	Builder	Insured values and dates: House & contents £	Insured values and dates: Other buildings & contents £	Rateable values and dates	Insurance references	Sale value of house and date £	Notes
O	50	1	1 May 1785 4.10.0	Davison, doctor	–	–	–	–	–	–	–
N	45	2	3 April 1788 4.17.6	Beaumont, merchant	–	750 + 250 (1794)	–	16 (1795)	Sun CS 3 629213	–	–
M	21½	3	1 Jan 1787 2.6.6	Eastland, spinster	John Kendall, cabinet maker	–	–	–	–	500 (1789)	Sept. 1787 unfinished: OS 346 534665
L	21½	4	1 Jan 1787 2.6.6	Lee	Kendall	400 (1789)	–	–	Sun OS 359 555877	–	–
K	21½	5	1 Jan 1787 2.5.10	Webster, surgeon	Kendall	350 + 250 (1798)	–	–	Sun CS 25 683645	500 (1788)	–
J	21½	6	1 Jan 1787 2.6.6	Barnard, widow	Kendall	300 (1791)	–	9 (1790)	Sun OS 374 579972	520 (1788)	3 storeys
I	28	7	7 July 1786 3.1.0	John Smith, gentleman	William Smith, brick-layer	300 unfinished (1786)	–	16 (1795)	Sun OS 341 524349	–	3 storeys
H	62	8	1 Dec 1787 6.14.4	Sheepshanks, merchant				13.10.0 (1790)	–		3 storeys, built with no. 9
		9	1 Dec 1787 included	Sheepshanks	Smith	–	–	13.10.0 (1790)	–	–	–

Development unit, from south to north	House frontage in feet	House no.	Date of first lease; ground rent (£.*s*.*d*.)	Leaseholder	Builder	Insured values and dates: House & contents £	Insured values and dates: Other buildings & contents £	Rateable values and dates	Insurance references	Sale value of house and date £	Notes
G	23	10	1 June 1786 2.10.0	Jowett, spinster	–	–	–	–	–	–	–
F	22	11	21 May 1786 1.7.8	Atkinson, gentleman	–	200 (1781)	–	7.10.0 (1790)	Sun OS 343 527497	–	Plots A to F had 'Cattaneo's Garden' in South Parade as their boundary.
E	23	12	20 May 1786 2.9.10	Shepherd, gentleman	Smith	250 (1781)	–	7.10.0 (1790)	Sun OS 343 527496	–	–
D	30	13	1 Nov 1785 3.5.0	Barwick, surgeon	–	300 + 300 (1788)	–	10 (1790)	Sun OS 351 541136	–	–
C	37½	14	31 Dec 1785 3.15.0	Jameson, gentleman	–	–	–	–	–	–	LCA, DB 13/32/20
B	27	15	4 August 1784 2.14.0	Gatliff, spinster	Smith	800 + 200 (1785)	–	–	RE 33 156394 and Sun OS 333 511842	–	In early deeds reckoned part of South Parade
A	–	16	21 Dec 1779 9.0.0	Barnard, gentleman	–	400 (1780)	–	–	Sun OS 185 431614	–	The only premises on Tuke's map, 1781.
A	167	17	21 Dec 1779 incl. above	as above	–	500 (1796)	100 (1796)	–	RE 31 154023	–	3 storeys.
A	–	18	21 Dec 1779 incl. above	as above	Smith	–	–	–	–	–	–
A	–	19	21 Dec 1779 incl. above	as above	Smith	–	–	–	–	–	–

Source (where not cited in Appendix): LCA, DB 32/21.

APPENDIX VI.5

Park Place, 1778–94

Development unit, from west to east	House frontage in feet	House no.	Date of first lease; ground rent (£.*s*.*d*.)	Leaseholder	Builder
A	44	22	(1790) 5.7.3	Rhodes, merchant	William and Richard Hargrave
B	48	21	11 Sept 1794 5.4.0	William and Richard Hargrave, carpenters	as above
C	46	20	21 Sept 1789 4.19.8	Plowes, merchant	
D	25	19	20 Oct 1791 2.14.2	Vincent	as above
E	45	18	1 Aug 1788 4.17.6	Cotton, gentleman	as above
F	25	17	1 April 1788 2.14.2	Hargrave	as above
G	48	16	1 May 1788 5.4.0	Ridsdale, merchant	as above
H	44	15	1 Jan 1788 4.16.5	Coulman, gentleman	as above
I	25	14	1 Jan 1788 2.14.2		as above
J	26	13	1 Jan 1788 2.16.4	Vincent, gentleman	as above
K	83 (K–M)	12	1 Jan 1786 7.7.4	Hargrave	as above
L		11	1 Jan 1786 included above	as above	as above
M		10	1 Jan 1786 included above	as above	as above
N	44	9	7 Dec 1785 4.15.4	Reade	as above
O	41	8	1 April 1785 4.8.10	Pearson, gentleman	as above

APPENDIX VI. 5 (*continued*)

Develop-ment unit, from west to east	House frontage in feet	House no.	Date of first lease; ground rent (£.*s*.*d*.)	Leaseholder	Builder
P	104 (nos. 5–7)	7	1 Jan 1778 11.0.0	Arthington, gentleman	
P		6	included above	as above	
P		5	included above		
Q	50	4	1 May 1778 5.8.0	Lodge, widow	
R	50	3	1 May 1778 5.8.0	Wilson, spinster	
S	65½ (nos. 1–2)	2	24 May 1778 7.10.0	Walker, wine and spirit merchant	
S		1	included above	as above	

Source: LCA, DB 32/24.

APPENDIX VI.6

Park Square, 1788–1810

Develop-ment unit	House frontage in feet	House no.	Date of first lease; ground rent (£.s.d.)	Leaseholder	Builder
N.W. corner west side					
A	120	corner: 4 houses in Park Lane	1 Jan 1791 10.10.0	Benjamin Wilson, brickmaker	Wilson
B	24	33	1 Jan 1793 9.12.0	Parker, merchant	–
B	24	32	1 Jan 1793 included above	–	–
B	24	31	1 Jan 1793 included above	–	–
B	24	30	1 Jan 1793 included above	–	–
C	23½	29	8 Aug 1796 5.1.0	Griffin, Revd	–
C	23½	28	8 Aug 1796 included above	Griffin, Revd	–
D	23	27	1 Jan 1797 2.9.10	John Cordingley, carpenter	Cordingley
E	23	26	1 Jan 1797 2.9.10	Cordingley	Cordingley
F	37	25a	–	? Cordingley	–
F	37	25	–	? Cordingley	–
F	36	24	–	? Cordingley	–
G	110	23	1 Jan 1793 11.0.0	William Hargrave, carpenter	? Hargrave 1806–09
end of west side					
S.W. corner south side					
H	24	22	1 Nov 1797 12.15.0	William Lawrance, carpenter, joiner, architect	Lawrance
H	24	21	included above	as above	Lawrance
H	24	20	included above	as above	Lawrance
H	24	19	included above	as above	Lawrance

APPENDIX VI.6 (*continued*)

Development unit	House frontage in feet	House no.	Date of first lease; ground rent (£.s.d.)	Leaseholder	Builder
H	24	18	included above	as above	Lawrance
H	24	17	included above	as above	Lawrance
H	24	16	included above	as above	Lawrance
H	24	15	included above	as above	Lawrance
I	210	St Paul's church	Foundation stone, 4 Oct 1791; consecrated 16 Sept. 1793; first service, 13 May 1794.		
end of south side					
S.E. corner east side					
J	48½	14	13 March 1790 10.12.2	Plowes, merchant	–
J	48½	13	included above	as above	–
K	34	12	1 Jan 1790 7.7.4	Lawrance	Lawrance
K	34	11	1 Jan 1790 included above	as above	Lawrance
L	65	10	1 Jan 1790 7.0.10	as above	Lawrance
M	41	9	1 March 1789 4.8.10	Atkinson, Revd	–
N	46	8	1 May 1788 4.19.8	Wilson, gentleman	–
O	40	7	19 July 1794 4.0.0	Winter	Hargrave
P	40	6	1 Jan 1790 4.0.0	Vincent, merchant	Hargrave
Q	40	5	19 July 1794 4.0.0	Hargrave, carpenter	Hargrave
R	21	4	1 Jan 1790 3.3.0	as above	Hargrave
R	20	3	1 Jan 1790 included above	as above	? Hargrave
R	20	2	1 Jan 1790 included above	as above	? Hargrave
S	40	1			? Hargrave
end of east side					

Source: LCA, DB 32/22 and 58/48.

APPENDIX VII.1

Insurances of Multiple Cottage Property in the East End, 1784–1806

Date	Location	Owner	Number of houses	Insurance references
Jan. 1784	Quarry Hill	Fearne	8	Sun OS 326 501078
April 1785	Various	Wood	44	Sun OS 328 503985
June 1785	Meadow Lane	Greaves	13	Sun OS 320 505595
July 1787	Meadow Lane	Shepherd	18	Sun OS 346 532508
April 1788	Swinegate	Coates	10	Sun OS 353 542509
Nov. 1788	Low Fold	Newsom	12	Sun OS 357 530899
Dec. 1789	Bank	Musgrave	35	Sun OS 365 563517
May 1791	Marsh Lane	Ripley	15	Sun OS 377 583492
Oct. 1791	Hill House Bank	Proctor	6	Sun OS 381 589410
Oct. 1792	Marsh Lane	Watkinson	16	RE 22 130329
Dec. 1792	Skinner Lane	Paley	8	Sun OS 391 608040
Dec. 1793	Hill House Bank	Scott	9	RE 25 136877
April 1794	Bank	Upton	10	RE 26 139455
May 1794	Bowman Lane	Kendall	20	Sun CS 2 627688
June 1794	Hill House Bank	Stocks	13	Sun CS 4 629384
June 1795	Hill House Bank	Pickering	26	Sun CS 9 641292
May 1797	Marsh Lane	Goulden	12	Sun CS 18 667012
March 1798	Simpson's Fold	Wainwright	13	Sun CS 20 676678
July 1799	Quarry Hill	Johnson	48	Sun CS 28 691793
Feb. 1801	York Street	Dixon	10	Sun CS 39 716371
Dec. 1801	Quarry Hill	Baxter	18	Sun CS 43 726300
June 1803	*Nr* St Peter's Sq.	Scott	19	Sun CS 56 749111
July 1803	Marsh Lane	Simpson	14	Sun CS 55 749624
Oct. 1804	Providence Row	Wigglesworth	12	Sun CS 64 774803
Aug. 1806	Hill House Bank	Kendall	40	Sun CS 72 793666

APPENDIX VII.2(a)

(pp. 477–78)

Union Row Building Club: Members, 1789

Key to members*	Number in ballot	Name and occupation	Other information
West end			
A	1	Joseph Longbotham, inn-keeper	back-to-back pair
B	2	William Crann, dyer	back-to-back pair
C	3	Mary Musgrave, widow	back-to-back pair
D	4	Jacob Ellis, mason	back-to-back pair
E	5	Thomas Brumfitt, carpet-maker	back-to-back pair
F	6	Leonard Newsom, roper	back-to-back pair
G	7 8	James Gledhill, presser	back-to-back pair back-to-back pair
H	9 10	Isaac Fletcher, stuff-weaver	back-to-back pair back-to-back pair insured May 1790
I	11	Henry Wright, plumber and glazier	cottage
J	12	Leonard Atkinson, stuff-weaver	back-to-back pair
K	13	Sarah Massey, spinster	back-to-back pair
L	14	William Robinson, clothier	back-to-back pair
M	15 16	David Midgley, stuff-maker	back-to-back pair
N	17	Samuel Thornton, weaver	back-to-back pair
O	18	John Dickinson, stuff-presser	cottage
P	19 20	Joseph Wood, victualler	cottages, built by William Brown
Q	21	James Jubb, yeoman	cottages, built by William Brown

APPENDIX VII.2(a) (*continued*)

Key to members*	Number in ballot	Name and occupation	Other information
R	22	Richard Jubb, packer	cottages, built by William Brown
East end	not allocated	Later site of *Reindeer*	

Total number of members: 18; houses: 32.

* Where a Club member acquired adjacent lots they are indicated in Appendix VII.2(a)–(f) by a bracket: thus in Union Row (as in Appendix 2(a) and diagram below) Lots 7 and 8 were assigned to one member (G); 9 and 10 to another (H); and 15 and 16 to another (M).

The key letters assigned in the Appendix to members in each Club allow multiple holdings to be identified even when non-adjacent lots were acquired: thus in Appendix VII.2(d) (St James Street) Richard Kendall (W) had Lots 46–50, 53–6, 59–64 and 72–3: and each of these groups of lots has *W* in the left-hand column of that Table.

Schematic Diagram of Lots and Owners in Union Row (West end)

Key letter assigned to member:	A	B	C	D	E	F	G	G	H	H	I	J	K	L	M	M
Lot numbers:	1	2	3	4	5	6	7	8	9	10	11	12	13	14	15	16

Sources: The data in Appendix VII.2(a)–(f) derive from property deeds in WRRD, LCD and LCA.

APPENDIX VII.2(b)

(*pp. 478–80*)

Boggart Close Greater Building Society (St Peter's Square): Members, 1789

Key to members*	Number in ballot	Name and occupation, where known	Other information
A	1	Ralph Sampson	Large house with Peter's Yard behind
B	2	John Hanworth, merchant	large house
C	3	Robert Randall, grocer	two houses
	4		two houses
	5		later *King's Arms*

APPENDIX VII.2(b) (*continued*)

Key to members*	Number in ballot	Name and occupation, where known	Other information
D	6	Henry Shute, cabinet maker	two houses
E	7 }	George Smith, gentleman	two houses
	8 }		large house
F	9 }	Thomas Barnes, nursery and seedsman	two houses at SW corner with four others on St Peter's St
	10 }		two houses in yard behind
G	11	Charles Boynton, cardmaker	two houses with half of Lawrence Court behind
H	12	Jonathon Lawrence, carpenter	two houses with other half of Court
I	13	William Lindley, whitesmith	large house with half of Lawrence Yard behind
J	14	William Lawrence, joiner	two houses with other half of Yard
K	15	William Barwick, whitesmith	large house
F	16	Thomas Barnes (above)	two large houses at SE corner
L	17	Henry Wright, plumber and glazier	two houses
M	18	Samuel Stephenson, merchant	two houses
C	19	Robert Randall (above)	two houses
N	20 }	Tobias Appleyard, common brewer	two houses
	21 }		small house
O	22	William Wright, cloth-dresser	large corner house and yard, later *Falstaff Inn*
P	23	Joshua Jefferson, gentleman	two houses
Q	24	Abraham Croft, joiner	two houses
R	25	John Shaw, ironmonger	one house

APPENDIX VII.2(b) (*continued*)

Key to members*	Number in ballot	Name and occupation, where known	Other information
S	26	John Browne, book-keeper	two houses
C	27	Robert Randall (above)	two houses
T	28	William Westerman, stuff-maker	two houses
U	29	Henry Cooper, pawnbroker, and Matthew Cooper	large house
F	30	Thomas Barnes (above)	large house at NW corner, with two houses facing St Peter's St

Total number of members: 21; houses: 83

* See Appendix VII.2(a), note

Sources: See Appendix VII.2(a).

APPENDIX VII.2(c)

(*pp. 480–83*)

Boggart Close Lesser Building Society (High Street): Members, 1789

Key to members*	Number in ballot	Name and occupation	Other information
north side corner of St Peter's Street			
A	1	John Palister, joiner	back-to-back pair and yard cottage
B	2	John Coultate, cord-wainer	back-to-back pair and yard cottage
C	3	Thomas Barker, clothworker	back-to-back pair and yard cottage via tunnel
D	4	William Barwick, whitesmith	through house and yard cottage via tunnel
E	5	John Hirst, cloth-worker	through house and yard cottage via tunnel

APPENDIX VII.2(c) *(continued)*

Key to members*	Number in ballot	Name and occupation	Other information
F	6	Lucas Nicholson, attorney	through house and yard cottage via tunnel
	7		back-to-back pair and yard cottage via tunnel
G	8	Thomas Glover, whitesmith	back-to-back pair and yard cottage via tunnel
H	9	John Hodgson, tailor	back-to-back pair and yard cottage via tunnel
I	10	William Watkinson, joiner	back-to-back pair and yard cottage via tunnel
J	11	John Groundwell, mason	back-to-back pair and yard cottage via tunnel
K	12	William Moore, cloth-dresser	back-to-back pair and yard cottage via tunnel
	13		back-to-back pair and yard cottage via tunnel
L	14	Thomas Robinson, cloth-dresser	back-to-back pair and yard cottage
	15		back-to-back pair and yard cottage
M	16	Anthony Mires, clothworker	back-to-back pair and yard cottage
N	17	John Howgate, millwright	back-to-back pair and yard cottage
O	18	Marmaduke Bullogh, whitesmith	back-to-back pair and yard cottage
P	19	Ebenezer Webster, book-keeper	back-to-back pair
	20		back-to-back pair
Q	21	John Whittaker, joiner	back-to-back pair and yard cottage via tunnel
R	22	William Denison, book-keeper	back-to-back pair and yard cottage via tunnel
Q	23	John Whittaker, joiner	back-to-back pair and yard cottage via tunnel

APPENDIX VII.2(c) (*continued*)

Key to members*	Number in ballot	Name and occupation	Other information
S	24	Joseph Dixon, bricklayer	back-to-back pair and yard cottage via tunnel
	25		back-to-back pair and yard cottage via tunnel
T	26	Henry Woodhead, joiner	back-to-back pair and yard cottage via tunnel
U	27	William Lindley, whitesmith	back-to-back pair and yard cottage
	28		back-to-back pair
	29		back-to-back pair
south side			
V	30	William Wright, cloth-dresser	back-to-back pair
W	31	Edward Beaumont, bricklayer	back-to-back pair
X	32	Abraham Croft, joiner	through house
	33		back-to-back pair and yard cottage
Y	34	William Conyers, cordwainer	back-to-back pair and yard cottage
Z	35	Joseph Briggs, plumber and glazier	back-to-back pair
I	36	William Watkinson, joiner	back-to-back pair and yard cottage via tunnel
AA	37	John Hargrave, cabinet-maker and builder	back-to-back pair and yard cottage via tunnel
BB	38	William Copperthwaite, butcher	back-to-back pair
CC	39	James Toulson, cord-wainer	back-to-back pair and yard cottage via tunnel
DD	40	William Golding, bricklayer	back-to-back pair and yard cottage via tunnel
EE	41	William Ripley, stuff-maker	back-to-back pair and yard cottage via tunnel
	42		
FF	43	Benjamin Carr, joiner	through house
GG	44	Christopher Lawson, miner	through house

APPENDIX VII.2(c) (*continued*)

Key to members*	Number in ballot	Name and occupation	Other information
HH	45	William Rathmell, painter	back-to-back pair and yard cottage
II	46	Thomas Blakey, tailor	back-to-back pair and yard cottage
	47		
JJ	48	James Fletcher, joiner	through house and yard cottage via tunnel
KK	49	Solomon Colbourn, joiner	back-to-back pair and yard cottage via tunnel
LL	50	William Fletcher, clothworker	back-to-back pair and yard cottage via tunnel
MM	51	John Cordingley, joiner	back-to-back pair and yard cottage via tunnel
NN	52	Thomas Barnes, nurseryman and seedsman	back-to-back pair and yard cottage via tunnel
	53		back-to-back pair and yard cottage via tunnel
	54		back-to-back pair and yard cottage via tunnel
			back-to-back pair and yard cottage via tunnel
	55		
In St Peter's Street	56	Mrs Sarah Wilson, widow	large front house and cottage in yard via tunnel
OO	57		large front house and cottage in yard via tunnel
PP	58	John Beecroft, mason	back-to-back pair and yard cottage via tunnel
	59		through house and yard cottage via tunnel
QQ	60	Richard Woodhead, joiner	through house
RR	61	William Gillyard, dyer	through house, 30-foot frontage

Total number of members: 44; houses: 152

* See Appendix VII.2(a), note.

Sources: See Appendix VII.2(a).

APPENDIX VII.2(d)

(pp. 484–87)

St James Street Building Club: Members, 1788–95

Key to members*	Number in ballot	Name and occupation, where known	Other information
NE End, south side			
A	1	John Cryer, joiner	through house on Woodhouse Lane
B	2	John Beanland, farmer	through house
C	3 }	Joshua Ingle, shoemaker	through house
	4 }		back-to-back pair
D	5 }	George Roper, merchant	back-to-back pair
	6 }		back-to-back pair
	7 }		back-to-back pair
	8 }		back-to-back pair
E	9 }	Thomas Thompson, yeoman	back-to-back pair
	10 }		back-to-back pair
F	11	Catherine Radford, widow	back-to-back pair
G	12	Joshua Mawson, joiner	back-to-back pair
H	13	Christopher Heaps, plumber and glazier	back-to-back pair
I	14	Rose Rushworth, widow	back-to-back pair
J	15	Thomas Glover, cloth-dresser	back-to-back pair
K	16	Joseph Bowling, book-keeper	back-to-back pair
L	17 }	Jonathan Hopkinson, clockmaker	back-to-back pair
	18 }		back-to-back pair
M	19 }	James Thomas, yeoman	large house set back in garden
	20 }		
	21 }		
	22 }		

APPENDIX VII.2(d) (*continued*)

Key to members*	Number in ballot	Name and occupation, where known	Other information
N	23	Richard Threlfall, yeoman	'dry house and buildings'
	24		
	25		
	26		
	27		
	28		
O	29	David Joy, apothecary (president of club)	unbuilt 1815
	30		unbuilt 1815
	31		unbuilt 1815
	32		unbuilt 1815
	33		through house
—	34	'extinguished'	agreed by members to use as common entry
P	35	Anthony Knowles, dealer in glass and china	
Q	36	Thomas Barnes, nurseryman and seedsman (committee)	
	37		
	38		
R	39	Thomas Firbank, staymaker	
S	40	?	(unbuilt 1815)
T	41	?	(unbuilt 1815)
U	42	?	(unbuilt 1815)
V	43	Leonard Newsom, roper	
	44	William Mann, gentleman (committee)	foot path at end of close to St James Place
north side	45	Leonard Newsom (above)	
W	46	Richard Kendall, cordwainer and pocket bookmaker	
	47		
	48		
	49		
	50		

APPENDIX VII.2(d) (*continued*)

Key to members*	Number in ballot	Name and occupation, where known	Other information
V	51, 52	Leonard Newsom (above)	large house
W	53	Richard Kendall (above)	house
	54		house
	55		house and offices
	56		house and offices
X	57, 58	Robert Oastler, merchant	back-to-back pair house
W	59	Richard Kendall (above)	unbuilt 1815
	60		unbuilt 1815
	61		through and back-to-back pair
	62		through and back-to-back pair
	63		through and back-to-back pair
	64		through back-to-back pair
Y	65, 66	James Thomas, yeoman	large through house
Z	67	Edward Braithwaite, gentleman	through house
K	68	Joseph Bowling, book-keeper	back-to-back pair
BB	69	James Grey, glazier (committee)	10 cottages in yard
CC	70	Robert Weare, joiner (ex-president of club)	workshop
DD	71	Mark Reader (committee), bricklayer	workshop
W	72	Richard Kendall (above)	back-to-back pair
	73		back-to-back pair
EE	74	John Beverley, pawnbroker	through houses

APPENDIX VII.2(d) (*continued*)

Key to members*	Number in ballot	Name and occupation, where known	Other information
FF	75	James Nixon, attorney	back-to-back pair
GG	76	Matthew Balmforth, farmer	large through house
HH	77	Christopher Johnstone, gentleman	through house
II	78 }	John Ingle, mason	back-to-back pair
	79 }		back-to-back pair
HH	80	Christopher Johnstone (above)	back-to-back pair and tunnel to Johnson's [*sic*] Court
JJ	81	John Plowes, merchant	through house
KK	82	Joseph Heath, innkeeper	through house
LL	83	William Bowling, clockmaker	through house
MM	84 }	John Leigh, whitesmith (committee)	back-to-back pair
	85 }		back-to-back pair
NN	86	William Walker, clothdrawer	corner house and offices

Number of members: 37–40; houses: 94

* See Appendix VII.2(a), note.

Sources: See Appendix VII.2(a).

APPENDIX VII.2(e)

(pp. 488–90)

Hill House (Camphor Close) Building Club (East King Street and Queen Street): Members, 1788

Key to members*	Number in ballot	Name and occupation	Other information
King Street *north side* A	1	Arthur Cryer, victualler, and Henry Brownbill, watchmaker	back-to-back pair and yard cottage via tunnel (later *Black Lion*)
B	2	William Hodgson, corn-miller	back-to-back pair and yard cottage via tunnel
	3		back-to-back pair and yard cottage via tunnel
C	4	Miles Procter, shopkeeper, and John Procter	back-to-back pair
D	5	Richard Selby, yeoman, and Thomas Selby, watchmaker	back-to-back pair and yard cottage via tunnel
E	6	William Gowthorp, stuff-weaver, and	back-to-back pair
	7	William Stoyle, tailor	back-to-back pair
F	8	Roger Briggs, joiner, and Thomas Lee, gentleman	back-to-back pair
	9		back-to-back pair and yard cottage via tunnel
G	10	George and Joseph Haigh, stuff-makers	back-to-back pair
H	11	Thomas Rushworth, dyer, and William Hodgson, miller	back-to-back pair and yard cottage via tunnel
I *south side*	12	John Canny, tailor, and John Baxter, translator	back-to-back pair and yard cottage via tunnel
J	13	Richard Constantine, shopkeeper	back-to-back pair
K	14	Thomas Wadsworth, shopkeeper	back-to-back pair

APPENDIX VII.2(e) (*continued*)

Key to members*	Number in ballot	Name and occupation	Other information
L	15	Charles Boynton, cardmaker, and Rachael Boynton, spinster	back-to-back pair
M	16	William Blackburn, bricklayer, and Thomas Rushworth, dyer	back-to-back pair
N	17	Thomas Inkersley, hairdresser & hatter, and William Shepherd, roper	back-to-back pair
	18		back-to-back pair
O	19	John & Martha Wheelhouse, gentleman and spinster	back-to-back pair and yard cottage via tunnel
J	20	Richard Constantine, shopkeeper	back-to-back pair and yard cottage via tunnel
	21		back-to-back pair and yard cottage via tunnel
K	22	James Whitaker, cloth miller, and George Whitaker, stuff-weaver	back-to-back pair and yard cottage via tunnel
L	23	Richard King, yeoman, and William King, labourer	back-to-back pair and yard cottage via tunnel
Queen Street *north side* M	24	Samuel Appleyard, victualler	back-to-back pair and yard cottage via tunnel
N	25	Jacob Watson, stuff-maker and (?) Jepson, woolcomber	back-to-back pair
O	26	Joseph Inglestone, stuff-maker and James Smithies, brickmaker	back-to-back pair
P	27	John Ward, dyer, and Joseph Thorp, cloth-dresser	back-to-back pair and yard cottage via tunnel
	28		back-to-back pair and yard cottage via tunnel

APPENDIX VII.2(e) (*continued*)

Key to members*	Number in ballot	Name and occupation	Other information
P	29	John Etherington, shoemaker, and John Pyemont, tanner	back-to-back pair
R	30	John Cookson, merchant, and Joseph Fawcett, merchant	back-to-back pair and yard cottage via tunnel
	31		back-to-back pair
S	32	John Scott, presser, and Thomas Wadsworth, shopkeeper	two back-to-back pairs with yard cottage via tunnel
south side			
T	33	William Randell, cheesemonger, and William Randell, Jnr	back-to-back pair and yard cottage via tunnel
	34		back-to-back pair and yard cottage via tunnel
	35		back-to-back pair
U	36	Tobias Appleyard, common brewer, and John Taylor, book-keeper	two back-to-back pairs
	37		two back-to-back pairs
	38		back-to-back pair
V	39	William Stirk, woolstapler, and Thomas Parkinson, surgeon	two back-to-back pairs
	40		back-to-back pair
facing East Street			
W	41	Samuel and Theophilus Stead, stone masons	back-to-back pair
X	42	James Hartley, stuff-maker, and Nathaniel Hartley, woolstapler	back-to-back pair

Total number of members: 24; houses: 106

* See Appendix VII.2(a), note.

Sources: See Appendix VII.2(a).

APPENDIX VII.2(f)

(pp. 491–92)

Crackenthorpe Garden Building Club (Union Street): Members, 1788

Key to members*	Number in ballot	Name and occupation	Other information
A *in Harwood Street*	1	John Kendall, Jnr, joiner	two through houses
	2		three cottages
B *Union Street south side*	3	George Pattison, labourer and yeoman [*sic*]	back-to-back pair
	4		back-to-back pair
C	5	Thomas Boddy, stonemason of Ripley	back-to-back pair
	6		cottage
	7		cottage and yard cottage
D	8	John Mires, painter	back-to-back pair and
	9		cottage in Union Court
	10		back-to-back pair
	11		back-to-back pair
	12		back-to-back pair
E	13	Edward Headley, joiner	back-to-back pair
F	14	Mark Pallister, joiner	back-to-back pair
	15		back-to-back pair
G	16	Christopher Heaps, plumber and glazier	back-to-back pair
	17		back-to-back pair
H	18	Thomas Hinde, cordwainer	back-to-back pair
I	19	Benjamin Tebbs, gardener	back-to-back pair
J	20	Edward and John Atkinson, joiners	back-to-back pair
	21		back-to-back pair
	22		back-to-back pair
K	23	John Sewell, joiner	back-to-back pair
	24		back-to-back pair
L	25	John Umpleby, joiner	back-to-back pair
M	26	Henry Chambers, joiner	back-to-back pair
	27		back-to-back pair
N *north side*	28	John Taylor, bricklayer	back-to-back pair
	29		back-to-back pair

APPENDIX VII.2(f) (*continued*)

Key to members*	Number in ballot	Name and occupation	Other information
O	30	Tobias Appleyard, common brewer	back-to-back pair
	31		back-to-back pair
P	32	Joseph, William, Henry and Richard Woodhead, joiners	back-to-back pair
	33		back-to-back pair
	34		back-to-back pair
Q	35	James Nelson, tailor	back-to-back pair
	36		back-to-back pair
R	37	John Burton, saddler	back-to-back pair
S	38	William and Isaac Whitelock, merchants	back-to-back pair
	39		back-to-back pair
	40		back-to-back pair
	41		through house
T	42	Francis Shield, painter	through house
U	43	Joshua Eastburn, schoolmaster	back-to-back pair
	44		back-to-back pair
	45		back-to-back pair
	46		back-to-back pair
V	47	Joseph Dixon, bricklayer	back-to-back pair
	2/3 48		back-to-back pair
W	1/3 48	John Kendall, Jnr, joiner	back-to-back pair
	49		back-to-back pair
	50		back-to-back pair
	51		back-to-back pair
	52		back-to-back pair

Total number of members: 23; houses: 108

* See Appendix VII.2(a), note.

Sources: See Appendix VII.2(a).

APPENDIX VII.3

(*pp. 493–97*)

The Chronology of the East End, 1785–91

		Boggart Close			Hill House Bank, King St and Queen St	Crackenthorpe Garden			
Number of Lots	Union Row 22	St Peter's Square 30	High St 61	St James St 86	42	Union St (Club) 52	Non-club –	Other Developers –	Sources
1785									
1 Feb.	–	–	–	–	–	–	–	Purchase by Croft for Nelson St.	LCD 3359 and 3644
1786									
21 July	Purchase of site	–	–	–	–	–	–	–	LCD 1602B
15 Sept.	–	Advertisement for building workers		–	–	–	–	–	*LI*, 19 Sept. 1786
6 Oct.	–	Purchase of site		–	–	–	–	–	LCD 8433
16 Oct.	–	–	–	–	–	–	–	Paley agrees to purchase Coneyshaws, Marsh Lane	LCA, DB 233: Elsworth
13 Dec.	–	–	–	Articles and rules	–	–	–	–	LCD 4027
1787									
29 Jan.	–	Advertise-ment for brick-layers	–	–	–	–	–	–	*LI*, 29 Jan 1787

APPENDIX VII. 3 (*continued*)

Number of Lots	Union Row 22	Boggart Close: St Peter's Square 30	Boggart Close: High St 61	St James St 86	Hill House Bank, King St and Queen St 42	Crackenthorpe Garden: Union St (Club) 52	Crackenthorpe Garden: Non-club –	Other Developers –	Sources
2 Feb.	–	–	–	–	Advertisement for tenders for 42 club houses	–	–	–	*LI* 2 Feb 1787
6 Feb.	–	–	–	Purchase of site	–	–	–	–	LCD 10837
Feb.	–	–	–	–	–	–	–	Paley purchases Forster's Close and another Marsh Lane close	WRRD, CT 417/546
6 June	–	–	–	–	Agreement to purchase	–	–	–	WRRD, DF 374/452
7 June	–	Insurance of 9 houses 'unfinished'	–	–	–	–	–	–	RE 13 102207
7 June	–	–	Insurance of 9 houses 'unfinished'	–	–	–	–	–	RE 13 102208
2 Aug.	–	–	–	–	–	–	–	Paley purchases McAndrews Garden	LCA, YM/D/NOR
3 Aug.	–	–	–	–	–	Purchase of site	–	–	LCD 435; LCA, DB 233

		Boggart Close			Hill House Bank, King St and Queen St	Crackenthorpe Garden			
Number of Lots	Union Row 22	St Peter's Square 30	High St 61	St James St 86	42	Union St (Club) 52	Non-club –	Other Developers –	Sources
1 Sept.	–	–	–	–	–	–	Site sold for Ebenezer chapel	–	LCD 2116
1788 Jan.	–	–	–	–	–	–	–	Paley sells 238 sq. yds. from McAndrews Garden	–
29 Feb.	–	–	–	–	Mortgage of 19 houses	–	–	–	WRRD, DF 327/450
11 June	–	–	–	–	–	Convey-ances to members	–	–	LCD 1263
13 June	–	–	–	–	–	–	Purchases by Turner, Heaps and Glover	–	WRRD, CX 744/995–7
26 June	–	–	–	Convey-ances to members begin	–	–	–	–	LCD 10837
8 July	–	Houses vacant lots advertised	–	–	–	–	–	–	*LI*, 8 July 1788

APPENDIX VII.3 (*continued*)

		Boggart Close			Hill House Bank, King St and Queen St	Crackenthorpe Garden			
Number of Lots	Union Row 22	St Peter's Square 30	High St 61	St James St 86	42	Union St (Club) 52	Non-club –	Other Developers –	Sources
Nov.	–	–	–	–	–	Insurance of 4 houses	–	–	Sun OS 357 550198
31 Dec.	–	Insurance of 2 houses	–	–	–	–	–	–	Sun OS 357 550878
1789									
20 Jan.	–	–	–	–	Insurance of 23 houses	–	–	–	Sun OS 359 553499
10 Feb.	–	–	–	Houses advertised	–	–	–	–	*LI*, 10 Feb. 1789
April	–	Society rules printed	–	Society rules printed	–	–	–	–	–
4 May	Conveyances to members	–	–	–	–	–	–	–	LCD 404
4 May	–	Further houses advertised	–	–	–	–	–	–	*LI*, 4 May 1789
July	–	–	–	–	–	–	Insurance of 6 houses in Ebenezer St	–	Sun OS 361 559345
9 Dec.	–	–	Insurance of 4 houses	–	–	–	–	–	RE 17 114241

APPENDIX VII. 3 (*continued*)

		Boggart Close				Crackenthorpe Garden			
Number of Lots	Union Row 22	St Peter's Square 30	High St 61	St James St 86	Hill House Bank, King St and Queen St 42	Union St (Club) 52	Non-club –	Other Developers –	Sources
9 Dec.	–	–	–	Insurance of 4 houses	–	–	–	–	RE 17 114236
1790 May	Insurance of 6 houses	–	–	–	–	–	–	–	Sun OS 369 570099
May	–	Houses rated on 11 lots	Houses rated on 8 lots	Houses rated on 30 lots	Houses rated on 31 lots	Houses rated on 33 lots	–	Paley rated on 30 houses	LCA, LORB 34
1791 29 Mar.	–	–	–	–	Conveyances to members of 32 of the 42 lots	–	–	–	WRRD, DF 372 to 395

APPENDIX VII.4

Turner's Sales Identified in Crackenthorpe Garden, 1788–96

Date	Area of plots sq. yds	Sale price per sq. yd (*s.*)
11 June 1788	700	3.0
27 April 1791	242	3.47
16 September 1790	224	3.5
20 May 1789	192	3.56
9 May 1789	143	4.03
3 June 1789	627	4.2
18 July 1796	460	4.8
23 December 1789	2508	4.9
10 April 1794	95	6.0
25 December 1796	340	6.0

Note: This land had been purchased at 1*s.* 8*d.* per sq. yd.

Sources: LCD 341, 360, 398, 401, 404, 423, 440, 447, 780, 788, 1824, 2116 and 4387.

APPENDIX VIII.1

(*pp. 499–502*)

North East Division: Streets, Terraces and Courts Commenced by 1815

			State of Street Development, 1815 Giles Map						
			Complete			Incomplete			
Locations*	Date	Landowner	Houses	Back-to-back pairs	One-room cottages	Houses	Back-to-Back pairs	One-room cottages	Notes and sources
Bramley's Row (later Little Templar St, south side)	after 1798	Bramley	–	–	14	–	–	–	LCD 1887
Bridge St	by 1801	Rhodes	–	–	–	–	15	17	LCD 2234
Brunswick Place	1813	Bischoff	–	–	–	3	–	–	LCD 20952
Camp Place (Long Balk Lane)	1808	Hirst	–	–	–	–	–	–	Unbuilt, 1815 Giles map
Clarkson's Yard(north side Quarry Hill)	by 1804		–	9	–	–	–	–	LCD 1802; Clarkson rated in 1805 here
Club Court (York Road)	1812	Building club	–	–	–	–	–	–	1812 from LCD 4643 but not on 1815 Giles map: 8 houses in 1816: LCD 4556
Coach Lane (later Charles St)	by 1805		–	–	–	–	31	–	WRRD, ES 698/830
Copenhagen St	1809	Bischoff	–	–	–	–	–	–	accommodation lane only

APPENDIX VIII.1 (*continued*)

			State of Street Development, 1815 Giles Map						
			Complete			Incomplete			
Locations*	Date	Landowner	Houses	Back-to-back pairs	One-room cottages	Houses	Back-to-Back pairs	One-room cottages	Notes and sources
Edward St	by 1798	Rhodes	–	–	–	3	–	–	LCD 1691
Far Fold (later Ward's Fold, east side Mabgate)	1793–1803	Molyneux	–	–	15	–	–	–	LCD 5100
High St extension	? after 1806		–	–	–	–	19	–	LCD 1542
Hope St	1809	Bischoff	–	17	18	–	–	–	LCD 2376
Johnson's Square (north side Charles St)	*c.*1806		–	14	–	–	–	–	stacked vertically
Line St			–	–	–	–	19	–	
Linsley's Fold (east side Mabgate)	by 1793		–	–	–	–	8	–	Linsley purchased it in 1793 when already 7 houses
Lovell St	1792	Cadman and others	–	–	–	–	–	–	accommodation road only
Lydia St (south side)	1800	Rhodes	–	–	–	–	–	6	
Middle Fold (east side Mabgate)	before 1802	Lupton	–	7	62	–	–	–	LUL, Lupton deeds: map
Near Fold (later New Church Place, east side Mabgate)			–	–	–	–	–	16	

APPENDIX VIII.1 (*continued*)

Locations*	Date	Landowner	State of Street Development, 1815 Giles Map						Notes and sources
			Complete			Incomplete			
			Houses	Back-to-back pairs	One-room cottages	Houses	Back-to-Back pairs	One-room cottages	
New Row (later Brown's Yard, Skinner Lane)	1796	Paley	–	–	–	–	–	15	
Nile St	1809	Bischoff	–	–	–	13	14	–	the larger houses cost £123–£170; LCD 2376
Skelton's Yard (north side Charles St)	1790		–	–	–	–	8	–	LCD 1705
Skinner Lane	1793	Paley	–	–	–	9	–	–	aborted by bankruptcy, 1803
St John's Square (north side Lady Lane)	? 1808		–	–	–	–	3	–	
St Mary's Lane			–	–	–	–	11	–	
St Peter's Court (east side St Peter's St)	by 1811		–	9	–	–	–	–	
Templar Lane	by 1798	Rhodes	–	–	–	–	3	–	LCD 1691
Templar St (north side)	1805	Rhodes	–	–	–	5	9	–	LCD 1861; insured in 1805: Sun CS 54 218733
Trafalgar St	1809	Bischoff	–	–	–	7	–	–	LCD 2376
Tunstall's Fold (east side Mabgate)	by 1805		–	–	–	–	–	6	LCD 646 and 1972

APPENDIX VIII.1 (*continued*)

Locations*	Date	Landowner	State of Street Development, 1815 Giles Map						Notes and sources
			Complete			Incomplete			
			Houses	Back-to-back pairs	One-room cottages	Houses	Back-to-Back pairs	One-room cottages	
Union Place (later Waterloo St, east side Burmantofts St)	by 1809	Armitage, ? Building Club	–	11	–	–	–	–	LCD 6306: but no other evidence
Waterloo Court (Quarry Hill)	by 1806	Richardson	–	–	–	–	18	–	Waterloo name presumably later
TOTALS OF HOUSES			–	134	109	40	316	60	
			659						

* This Appendix excludes the club developments at High St, St Peter's Sq., Union Row together with the streets initiated by Paley (Table 7.7) at York St, Off St, Birch St and Duke St.

† Intercensal increase, 1801–11, was 641.

APPENDIX VIII.2

(*pp. 503–04*)

East Division: Streets, Terraces and Courts Commenced by 1815

			State of Street Development, 1815 Giles Map						
			Complete			Incomplete			
Locations*	Date	Landowner	Houses	Back-to-back pairs	One-room cottages	Houses	Back-to-back pairs	One-room cottages	References
Bow St	by 1793	Smithies	–	–	–	–	8	–	LCD 1052
Cavalier St	1793	Upton	–	–	–	–	23	–	
Club Court†	1812		–	–	–	–	4	–	
Cotton St	1814	Holdforth	–	–	–	–	–	–	
Garden St	by 1807		–	–	–	3	–	–	3 houses in 1809 Directory
King St			–	23	12	–	–	–	
New Row, Mill St	1789–96	Paley	–	–	8	–	–	–	LCD 4982 and 5031; adjoins Bank Low Mill
Queen St			–	19	7	–	–	–	
Steander Row	1813	Upton	–	9	–	–	–	–	LCD 2171; *LI*, 18 Oct. 1813
Well House Place (later Richmond Rd)	1788	Paley	–	7	–	–	–	–	
Well Houses (later Richmond Rd)	1792	Paley	–	–	–	–	2	11	

APPENDIX VIII. 2 (*continued*)

Locations*	Date	Landowner	State of Street Development, 1815 Giles Map					References
			Complete			Incomplete		
			Houses	Back-to-back pairs	One-room cottages	Houses	Back-to-back pairs	One-room cottages	References
Worsted St	1814	Holdforth	–	–	–	–	–	–	LCD 12646; but unbuilt, 1815 Giles map
Zion St	1792	Cookson and Fawcett	–	–	–	–	3	–	
TOTALS OF HOUSES			–	116	27	3	80	11	
						237			

* Excluding the scattered houses on the Bank (cf. Table 7.1)
† Club Court had ten pairs when completed in 1831 by Club Yard: LCD 4643; WRRD, HL 128/124.

Sources: Apart from specific references in the right-hand column this and other street chronologies derive from an examination of maps, directories and deeds in many collections, principally WRRD, LCA and LCD.

APPENDIX IX.1

Park Estate: Fines on Renewal of Leases, 1807–10

Date	Name of leaseholder	Street	Fine £	Annual ground rent £ s. d.
23 Jan. 1807	York	?	100	6.14. 0
1 Oct. 1807	Benson	Park Row	80	2.13. 0
12 Oct. 1807	Scaley	Park Row	50	2. 1. 0
6 Feb. 1808	Ibbetson	Park Row	105	?
2 March 1808	Shepherd	Park Place	60	2.14. 2
16 April 1808	Pullan	Park Square	70	4.15. 8
2 June 1808	Hague	?	42	2. 6. 6
11 March 1809	Atkinson	Park Square	55	4. 8.10
5 July 1809	Beckett	Park Square	120	6.15. 2
6 July 1809	Elam	Park Square	111	4. 8.10
11 July 1809	Rayner	Park Row	55	2. 5. 0
4 Sept. 1810	Miss Elam	Park Square	56	4. 0. 0

Source: Day Book, LCA, DB 32/8.

APPENDIX IX.2

Park Estate: Leaseholds Enfranchised 1808–24

Date	Name of leasehold	Street	Sum £ *s*. *d*.	Annual ground rent redeemed £ *s*. *d*.
1808	Joshua Turner	Park Row	not known	
1808	Dr Davison	East Parade	not known	
1811	Samuel Hague	East Parade	not known	
1811	Samuel Hague	Park Row	not known	
1814	Edward Armitage	East Parade	not known	
1815	Edward Armitage	South Parade	not known	
1815	Croft	Park Square	328.15.0	7. 3. 0
1816	Gatliff	Park Place	156. 0.0	2.12. 6
1817	Crossley	?	113. 0.0	2. 9.10
1817	Holdforth	Eye Bright Pl.	170. 0.0	4. 4. 0
1817	Miss Lodge	Park Place	not known	
1817	Mrs Ridsdale	Park Row	not known	
1817	Infirmary	West St	not known	
1818	T. Wright	Park Row	not known	
1824	Lee	Park Row	207.10.0	2. 4. 0

Sources: Notes in Wilson Ledger, LCA, DB 32/7; DB 239B

APPENDIX IX.3

(pp. 507–10)

New Streets on the Wilson Estate, 1817–31

Name	First recorded date	House types: One-room ground plan	Back-to-back pairs	Larger through	Other buildings	Sources
Abbey St	after 1826	–	6	–	–	
Airedale Place	1826	–	9	–	–	
Algiers St (later Caroline St)	–	–	–	–	–	
Bean St	after 1826	–	3	–	–	
Beverley St	after 1826	–	2	–	–	
Blucher St (later Castle St)	–	–	–	–	–	
Bramma St	–	10	–	–	saw mill	
Britannia St (later New Park St)	–	–	–	–	–	
Brunswick St (later Grace St)	–	–	–	–	–	
Calder St	1826	6	–	2	–	
Caroline St	1821	–	11	–	Wesleyan Methodist chapel	–
Castle St	–	9	24	–	–	
Chatham St	1822	4	10	–	–	

APPENDIX IX.3 (*continued*)

Name	First recorded date	House types: One-room ground plan	Back-to-back pairs	Larger through	Other buildings	Sources
Croppergate	1826	6	25	–	–	
Cross Park St (including 3 courts)	1821	22	9	–	–	
Darlington St	after 1826	–	–	–	–	
Durham St	after 1826	–	–	–	–	
Fartham St	after 1826		–	3	public house	
Fountain St (including 3 courts)	1817	13	25	–	–	Directory
Grace St	1821	–	–	–	cloth mill	
Grove St	–	–	11	3	cloth-dressing mill	
Harcourt Place	1831	–	5	–	woollen mill	
Harrison Row	–	21	–	–	–	
Infirmary St	1817	–	–	4	–	LCA Oates, C.1
King St	1817	–	–	–	–	DB 32/5
Lisbon St	1817	1	23	–	–	LCA, DB 32/5
Little Queen St (earlier Victoria St; including 2 courts)	–	–	–	–	–	

APPENDIX IX. 3 (*continued*)

Name	First recorded date	House types: One-room ground plan	House types: Back-to-back pairs	House types: Larger through	Other buildings	Sources
Low Lane (later Fountain St)	–	–	–	–	–	
Marlborough St (including 1 court)	1821	15	23	2	–	
Newcastle St	–	–	–	6	–	
New Park St	1822	–	20	–	oil gas works	
Parliament St	–	–	3	–	–	
Princes St	1822	–	8	–	–	
Queen St	1817	–	–	7	Methodist chapel	LCA, DB 32/5
Russell St	1819	–	–	4	–	LCA, Oates, C.1
Savile St (including 4 courts)	1822	–	18	–	flax mill	
School St	1826	5	14	–	warehouse or mill; Wesleyan school	
Skinner St	1822	9	12	–	cloth-dressing mill; tavern	
Somers St (including 3 courts)	1822	–	13	–	cloth mill; timber yard; printing office	
Spark St	–	–	3	1	–	

APPENDIX IX.3 (*continued*)

Name	First recorded date	House types: One-room ground plan	Back-to-back pairs	Larger through	Other buildings	Sources
Wardle St	–	11	–	–	–	
Waterloo St (later Savile St)	–	–	–	–	–	
Well St	1822	14	16	1	–	
Wellington Lane (including 1 court)	–	–	6	–	–	
Wellington Road (later Wellington St)	–	–	–	–	–	
Wellington St	1818	–	5	13	warehouses; cloth mill; baths; foundry	DB 58/33; turnpike, 42 Geo. III cap 51
Wellington Terrace		–	6	–	–	
West St	1794	5	2	3	militia store; cloth-dressing mill	DB 58/33; turnpike, 34 Geo. III cap. 134
Westminster Place	–	2	6	–	–	
Wortley St	–	–	6	–	–	
TOTALS	–	154	324	49	–	
TOTAL DWELLINGS (excluding cellars)			851			

Sources: Apart from specific references in the right-hand column this and other street chronologies derive from an examination of maps, directories and deeds in many collections, principally WRRD, LCA and LCD.

APPENDIX IX.4

(*pp.* 511–12)

Continuity of Residence, Park Place, 1798–1849

No.	1798	1800	1809	1816	1822	1826	1830	1834	1839	1842	1849
1			Pease (merchant)	S*	S	S					
2				Fawcett (merchant)	S	S	S				
3	Benyon (flax manufacturer)	S	S	S	*to Headingley*						
4											
5											
6				Knubley (gentleman)	S	widow *to* *Portland St*	Vicarage	S	S	S	S
7				Hardwick (mercer)	S	S	S				
8											
9	Reade (merchant)	S	S	Willans (stuff merchant)	S	S	S	S	S	S	S
10											
11											

APPENDIX IX.4 (*continued*)

No.	1798	1800	1809	1816	1822	1826	1830	1834	1839	1842	1849
12	Gatliff (stuff merchant)	S	S	S	S	S	S	S	S	S	S
13											
14	Lapage (dry salter)	S	S	S	S	S	S	*to Mount Preston*			
15	Mrs Kershaw	S	S	S	S	S	S	S			
16			Brown (merchant)	S	S	S	S	S	S	S	S
17											
18			Bellhouse (corn merchant)	S	S	S	S	S			
19											
20	Mrs Blackburn	S	S	S	S	S	S	S	S	S	
21	Ard Walker (wine and spirit merchant)	S	S	S	S	S	S	S	S	S	
22	Peter Rhodes (merchant)	S	S	S	S	S	S	S	S	S	

* S indicates the same occupant or one of the same surname; only the longer continuities are shown here.

Sources: Directories and LCA, DB 32/6A.

North-West Division: Streets and Terraces Commenced by 1815

Locations*	Date	Landowner	State of Street Development, 1815 Giles Map: Complete			Incomplete			Sources
			Houses	Back-to-back pairs	One-room cottages	Houses	Back-to-back pairs	One-room cottages	
Carr Place	1807	Dowgill	–	–	–	10	–	–	*LM*, 6 April 1807; June 1807 'staked out': WRRD, FA 234/300
Coburg Street	by 1815	Strother	–	–	–	12	2	4	
Grove Place	1802–6	Bramley	–	–	–	6	–	–	Insured 1789: Sun OS 365 563803; LCD 16800
Grove Terrace	1812–13	Crossley	–	–	–	4	–	–	LCD 16777 with plan
North St (later Cato St)	by 1806		–	–	–	–	–	–	*Leeds Guide*, 1806, p.82
Providence Row	1789	Nelson	12	–	–	–	–	–	Insured 1796: Sun CS 11 649821; 1798 Directory
Queen Square	1803	Bischoff	–	–	–	12	–	–	*LM*, 21 Jan. 1803; LCD 3398
Reuben St	1808	Hirst	–	22	–	–	–	–	LCD 16477 with plan of 1809 has all plots sold
Wellington St (late Oxford St)	by 1815	?	–	–	–	–	–	–	unbuilt, 1815 Giles map
		Total of houses		56			52		
					108				

Note: 351 houses were built in the Division between the censuses of 1801 and 1811. The hamlets of Great Woodhouse and Buslingthorpe lay within this Division but beyond the area of the 1815 Giles map. The first map to include them (Fowler, 1831) shows only extensive scattered encroachments on the commons except three back-to-back streets at New Huddersfield, north of St Mark's Church and probably later than 1821.

Sources: Apart from specific references in the right-hand column this and other street chronologies derive from an examination of maps, directories and deeds in many collections, principally WRRD, LCA and LCD.

APPENDIX XIII.1

Rental Value of Houses, by Wards, 1839

Ward	Number of dwellings*	Number rented at			
		£5 and under	above £5, under £10	£10 to £20	above £20
North	2734	540 (20%)	1560 (57%)	524 (19%)	110 (4%)
North East	3731	1546 (41%)	1876 (50%)	264 (6%)	45 (1%)
East	3246	1662 (51%)	1285 (40%)	226 (7%)	73 (2%)
South	1214	300 (25%)	643 (53%)	194 (16%)	77 (6%)
Mill Hill	976	102 (10%)	246 (25%)	184 (19%)	444 (45%)
Kirkgate	641	82 (13%)	192 (30%)	130 (20%)	237 (37%)
West	3252	340 (10%)	1764 (54%)	778 (24%)	370 (11%)
North West	2045	700 (34%)	765 (37%)	340 (17%)	240 (12%)
TOTAL	17,839	5272	8331	2640	1596
		(30%)	(47%)	(15%)	(12%)

* 555 cellar dwellings excluded; see Table 13.15

Source: *1839 Report*, Table III.

Manuscript Sources and Select Bibliography

All books and articles cited in footnotes have full bibliographical references there, except for those listed in *Abbreviations and Short Titles* (p. xxix). In the Bibliography only the more important titles have been included, together with a complete list of Private Acts of Parliament, Parliamentary Papers, Directories, Printed Maps, Topographical Views and unpublished works that have been consulted.

1. *Manuscript Sources*

Beverley, Humberside Record Office

DD HV 60 Deeds of Wilson (Pawson), North Hall estate

Hertford, County Record Office

D/EP/T	Earl Cowper's estate:
4695	Schedule of deeds
4945	Agent's letters, 1793–97
4948	Field book, 1789–97
4949	Survey, 1808
4950–1	Agent's reports, 1819
4962	Agent's letters, 1839–46
4967	Plan of Great Woodhouse estate, 1819
4968	Plan of New Leeds, 1828
4968A	Plan of Great Woodhouse estate, 1830

Leeds, Civic Hall, strongrooms (LCH)

(A) Deeds (LCD):

This archive consists of many thousand boxes of documents relating to properties owned by the Corporation, and is still growing. The contents of each box are unlisted but the exact area concerned was plotted on to large-scale maps to form a terrier; after local government reorganisation (1974) the terriers were redrawn for current use on more modern base maps and the former terriers are now available at the WYJAS Leeds Office where some boxes of deeds concerned with the property of obsolete authorities have been transferred.

(B) Minute Books:

This archive consists mainly of the minute books of the reformed Corporation from 1835 together with committees and sub-committees.

Shelf 15:	Leeds Improvement Act Report Book, vol. 1, 1842
	Municipal Report Book, vol. 1, 1842
Shelf 17:	Council Minutes, vols. I–VI, 1835–42 with index
Shelf 19:	Leeds Improvement Act, Proceedings of Commissioners, 1835–42
	Council Minutes: Improvement Act, vol. 1, 1842
Shelf 36:	Statistical Committeee of the Council, minutes 1839–42

Shelf 82:	Improvement Bill Committee, minutes 1841–42
Shelf 83:	Improvement Act Scavenging and Nuisances [incl. smoke] Committee, minutes, 1833–42

Leeds, Leeds General Infirmary, Secretary's Office

Deeds and plans relating to the site.

Leeds, The Leeds Library, Commercial Street

Thomas Wilson's notes in margins of Thoresby's *Ducatus*

Leeds, Thoresby Society

Box B46	Views of old Leeds
Box II.9	William Wheater's scrapbooks and notes
	Printed particulars of Richard Lee's estate, Sept. 1809 (see also Hobson in §8 below)

Leeds, Leeds University [Brotherton] Library (LUL)

Gott MS. Box VII	Documents relating to smoke prosecution, with printed *Report of the Trial and Indictment . . . against B. Gott and Sons* (Leeds, 1824).
LUL, MS. 18	William Lindley's census of steam engines in Leeds, 1824
Lupton MS. 113	'Number of pieces milled at the Several Mills . . .', 1805–21
Lupton MS. 124	Mabgate estate deeds
Lupton MS. 126	Valuation of whole estate, 1811
Lupton MS. 127	Merrion Street deeds and plan
Lupton MS. 128	Mabgate deeds

Leeds, University of Leeds, Bursary (ULD)

Deeds of properties purchased by the former Yorkshire College and the University. These are arranged by chronological order of purchase in numbered parcels, with a typescript street and house index.

Leeds, West Yorkshire Joint Archive Service, Leeds District Office, Sheepscar (LCA)

ACC 1148/7	Kingston Terrace
ACC 1250	Leeds Estate Co. (Briggate), Makins (Park Row, Bond St., Russell St.)
AM	Shambles (Briggate), 1739–1836
DB 5	Atkinson (Claremont and Little Woodhouse Hall)
DB 6	Chorley (Little Woodhouse and Mabgate)
DB 23	Ard Walker (Briggate, St Peter's Hill, Mill Hill and Hunslet)

DB 24 Mixed (Coloured) Cloth Hall
DB 27 Holroyd (Mabgate)
DB 32 Wilson (Park Estate – whole unless indicated):
1. Survey, 1776
3. Plan by J. Teal, April 1806
3A. Plan by H. Teal, Feb. 1809
3B. Plan, Aug. 1793 by J. Teal
5. Survey and plan of Mill Hill properties by H. Teal, Dec. 1816
6A and B. Plan and valuation by H. Teal, 1816
7. Ledger (vol.2), 1791–1829 with index and 'arrears from the old book [vol.1, lost]'.
8. Day book, 1803–23
9. Day book, 1824–42
10. Accounts of R. F. Wilson, 1824–56
11. Accounts of R. F. Wilson, 1824–39
13. Will of Christopher Wilson (d. 1842)
15. 'Schedule of Mr Christopher Wilson's deeds Box 1'
16. Mill Hill deeds
17. Mill Hill deeds
18. Leeds General Infirmary deeds
19. Park Row deeds
20. South Parade deeds
21. East Parade deeds
22. Park Square deeds
23. Park Lane deeds
24. Park Place deeds
25. Quebec deeds
26. Park Butts deeds
27. Valuation of Drony Laith, 1774
28. Properties near Leeds Bridge, deeds
31. Green Hill deeds
32. Eye Bright Close deeds
DB 36 Denison (Great Woodhouse)
DB 39 Armitage and Rhodes (Leylands, Byron St and Cannon St)
DB 41 Philemon Land (Woodhouse Lane)
DB 42 Atkinson (Little Woodhouse Hall)
DB 43 Hebblethwaite (Ridge House, Hillary Place, Woodhouse Lane) with some Lyddon deeds
DB 44 Beckett (North Hall, Burley Road and Red Bear estate, Quarry Hill and Burmantofts)
DB 58 Wilson (Park) estate:
1. Wilson family wills and settlements

31j. Correspondence with Lincoln's Inn
33. Particulars for sale, conveyances of properties sold, 1804–21
34. Park Hill Close deeds
42. Particulars for sale, conveyances of properties sold, 1818–50
43. Plan of Butts Lane, *c.* 1800
45. Rental, 1811
46. Plan of estate by J. Teal, 1817
48. Valuation of Park Square, south side, 1838

DB 64 Calverley (Blayds)
1. Claypit House, Woodhouse Lane and Sunny Bank
2. Plan of estate by H. Teal, 1836 and Park Lane deeds
3. Portland Street deeds

DB 68 Fearne and Bolland deeds, Nether Mills with plans by J. Teal, 1824 and 1825

DB 69 Bolland, Mabgate, Great Woodhouse and 39 Park Square

DB 75 Hey estate
5. Albion Place deeds
9. Plans of Bond (Commercial) Street shops by R. D. Chantrell, 1820
19. Accounts for building shops in Bond St, 1823–24

DB 78 Plan of Park (Bean Ing) Mills, 1814

DB 97 Wild (Skinner Lane)

DB 116 R. *v.* Gott (smoke case), 1823–24

DB 126 Robert Denison, Town's End, 1786–92

DB 129 Denison (Great Woodhouse)

DB 147 Leeds Kirkgate manor:
2. rentals, 1774–1802

DB 149 Manor of Leeds:
11 and 11a. Survey of encroachments on Woodhouse Moor and Carr, 1825
13(a–g). Rentals 1709–85
13(h). Draft survey, *c.* 1800, including burgages
31. Woodhouse Moor
32. Identification of Briggate burgages, 1833.

DB 179 Calverley (Blayds), schedule of deeds, survey and map by J. Teal, 1809

DB 180 Rawson (Hanover Square)

DB 196 Charity School:
1. Subscription List, 1705
129. Schedule of deeds and accounts, 1711–1815

DB 197 Pious Uses [Town charities] Committee:
1. Minute Book, 1664–1788
2. Minute Book, 1788–1844
Unlisted:
Survey of Free School lands, June 1728
Survey of Free School lands, Dec. 1754
Minute Books, 1788–1815, with list of leases, 1776–1810

DB 204 [Various]
1–5. Thomas Wilson's antiquarian note books
8. Survey of Pious Uses estates, 1792–94, with plans

DB 211 Holy Trinity deeds, 1721–27

DB 213 Leeds Kirkgate manor:
60/12. Survey of fields for hay modus, 1676
97. Boundaries of manor, 1731

DB 233 Paley bankruptcy papers, unlisted

DB 239 Wilson (Park estate) deeds and map, 1779, unlisted

DB Maps All the plans in this collection, numbering more than 700, have been examined but only the most important are listed here:
14. Quebec, 1825
55. Hey, Albion St, 1825
119. Paley's estate, 1809
215. Lee, Briggate, 1809
233. Paley's estate, 1807
288. Cowper, Woodhouse Lodge, n.d.
331. Brown, Wellington St, 1832
334. Green, Richmond Hill, 1823
356. Lyddon, 1825
357. Rawson, Hanover Square, 1824
364. Capper, Buslingthorpe, 1830
365. Lupton, Merrion St, 1830
366. Lupton, Nippet Lane and Dolly Lane, 1823–24
372. Unpublished (printed) O.S. map of Leeds (6 in. = 1 mile), 1844
373. Vicar Lane, 1784
389. Mrs Dalley, Great Woodhouse Hall, 1796
391. Leylands, 1793
394. Green Row, Quarry Hill, 1837
396. Lee, Woodhouse Lane, 1825
398. School Close, 1832
399. St Peter's Hill, Park Lane [n.d.]
406. Sheepscar, 1833
407. Little Woodhouse, 1836

408. Quebec, 1829
411. Camp Road and Claypit Lane, 1825
418. Elmwood Street, 1828
419. Paley's estate, 1810
420. The Hotel, Lower Briggate, 1825
422. Ellerby Lane, 1825
423. Milner, Great Woodhouse, 1776
427. St Peter's Hill, 1831
437. Upper Headrow, 1811
445. 'The Square', 1819
447. Holdforth, Well Houses and Mill St, 1815
525. Flay Crow Mills, 1831
637. St John's church estate, Little Woodhouse, 1806
663. Philemon Land, Woodhouse Lane, 1843
671. Leeds General Cemetery, 1833
701. Woodhouse Square, 1835–39 and Hyde Terrace
704. Little Woodhouse, 1847

FW 206 Briggate, Wood St

FW 212 Briggate and St Peter's Square

FW 215 Whitelock, Burmantofts

FW 222 Rhodes, Sheepscar and Woodhouse Carrs

LCEng Building Inspectors' plans:
1/35 Chadwick, Crown Point, 1840
1/40 Cowper, New Town, 1828–1862
1/60 Hewitt, Linsley's Fold, 1825
1/81 Blenheim Square, 1822
2/1 Garden St, 1825

LCM Corporation Minute Books:
2. 1705–72
3. 1773–1835

LORB Poor rate books:
1. May 1713
9. Aug. 1726
10. Dec. 1741
11. May 1742
29. Jan. 1752
31A. Highway rate book, 1765
32. May 1774
34. May 1790
35. May 1795
36. November 1800
37. May 1805

LPC 30/2 Vicarage and vicarage lands, 1764–1817
71/1 Highways estate, account book, 1680–1826
72/4 Free School lands, account book, 1692–1826
72/7 Poor estate, account book, 1797–1826
104 Census enumeration, 1801: original returns, by Divisions
107/21 Tithe award

NORTH'S General Box 89: map of Springfield Place, 1833

O Oates estate:
C. 'The Square', 1819–23

TN/M Leeds Kirkgate manor:
12/17–8 Court call books, 1772–80
14/22 Poor rate book, Leeds Kirkgate Division, 1748
15/7 List of householders, *c.* 1750

Leeds, Yorkshire Archaeological Society

MS.543 Subscribers to Mill Hill chapel, 1779–99

London, British Library, Department of Manuscripts

Add. MS.33770 Glebe terrier, Leeds, 1764 and Census of Leeds, 1775
42232 Forrest's tour of England, 1773 (Leeds, ff.32–37)

London, Guildhall Library

MS.7252–3 Royal Exchange fire insurance policy registers
MS.11935 Sun Fire Insurance Company, committee minutes, including record of provincial agents' remittances.
MS.11936 Sun policy registers, Old Series (OS)
MS.11937 Sun policy registers, County or Country Series (CS)

London, House of Lords Record Office

Minutes of Evidence on private bills:
Evidence (1842), vol.7: Leeds Improvement Bill (30 May–3 June)

London, Public Record Office

B3/3975/3417/954 Coupland bankruptcy
C13/2383 Lyddon *v.* Woolcock, depositions
C104/85 Strother estate, Woodhouse Lane and Dolly Lane, plans, 1805
E179/262/9 Hearth tax, 1663
E179/210/421 Hearth tax, 1666
E179/210/417 Hearth tax, 1672
E179/218/219–10 Poll tax, 1692

HO 107	Census enumerators' original returns, 1841
MH7/1	Royal Commission on the State of Large Towns, manuscript minutes
MH12/15224–5	Poor Law Commission files, Leeds, 1834–42
MPC 109	Plan of Leeds, 1560
MR 986/5	Plans of Cowper estate, 1797–1808
RG4/3432	Ebenezer Street chapel registers
T47/2	Tax on owners of coaches, 1754–56
T47/5	Tax on owners of gold and silver plate, 1757–62
T47/8	Tax on servants, 1780

Nottingham, County Record Office

DDH 162 Hodgkinson MS: Wormald and Gott, Headrow estate

Nottingham, University Library Department of Manuscripts

De H	Denison MSS
H1b	Kirk Ings deeds and plans, 1819
H19 and 21	Plans of Kirkgate estate
H20	Plans of Leeds estates
H23	Crown Point, 1805
H27	Denison estate, Leeds, survey book, 1825–32
H30	Survey of Woodhouse estate, 1826
H41	Plans of Woodhouse estate

Wakefield, West Yorkshire Joint Archive Service, Headquarters

West Riding Registry of Deeds:

Enrolled deeds (WRRD): the volumes follow an alphabetical sequence from A to Z and then from AA to ZZ. There are place- and personal-name indexes. The earliest registration of a property in Leeds is A 20/34, a deed of 10 Jan. 1704, enrolled on 9 Feb., concerning a cottage on Mill Hill.

York, Borthwick Institute of Historical Research

CC EC	Ecclesiastical Commission
	11/101 Unpublished (printed) Ordnance Survey plan, Leeds, 1844
Fac.	Faculty papers
	Leeds, Holy Trinity; St John's; St Paul's; St Peter's
Fac. Bk.	Faculty Books
Reg. 39	Archbishop Vernon's register, 1808–23
Reg. 40a	Archbishop Vernon's register, 1823–30
Reg. 40b,	Archbishop Vernon's register, 1830–41
f.403	Plan of St Mark's church district, 1833
Ter.	Glebe terriers, Leeds

York, Dean and Chapter Library

Hailstone MS.2/21/2 Harrison estate, Little Woodhouse, deeds

2. *Books and Articles*

(Place of publication, unless otherwise stated, is London.)

Aikin, J. *A Description of the Country from thirty to forty Miles around Manchester* (1795).

Anon. *The Stranger's Guide through Leeds and its Environs* (H. Cullingworth, publr., 1831 and 1842).

Anon. *Walks Through Leeds* (J. Heaton, publr., 1835).

Anon. See also Billam, Ryley and Wright, below.

Arscott, C. and Pollock, G. 'The Partial View: the visual representation of the early nineteenth-century city', in J. Wolff and J. Seed, eds, *The Culture of Capital: art, power and the nineteenth-century middle class* (Manchester, 1987).

Atkinson, D. H. *Ralph Thoresby the Topographer; His Town and Times* (2 vols, Leeds, 1885–7).

Barry, F. W. and Smith, P. G. *Joint Report on Back-to-back Housing to the Local Government Board* (1888).

Beckwith, F. *Thomas Taylor Regency Architect* (Thoresby Soc. Monographs, I (1949)).

'The Population of Leeds during the Industrial Revolution', *PTh.S*, XLI(1945), 118–96.

Beresford, M. W. 'The Back-to-Back House in Leeds, 1787–1937', in *The History of Working-class Housing: a Symposium*, ed. S. D. Chapman (Newton Abbot, 1971), pp.93–132.

'The Face of Leeds, 1780–1914', in Fraser, ed. (below), pp.72–112.

'Leeds in 1628: a Ridinge Observation from the City of London', *Northern History*, X(1975), 135–40.

'The Making of a Townscape: Richard Paley in the East End of Leeds, 1771–1803', in *Rural Change and Urban Growth, 1500–1800*, ed., C. W. Chalklin and M. A. Havinden (1974), pp.281–320.

'Prometheus Insured: the Sun Fire Insurance Agency in Leeds during urbanization, 1726–1826', *Economic History Review*, 2nd. ser. XXXV(1983), 373–89.

Beresford, M. W. 'Prosperity Street and Other Streets' in *Beresford and Jones*, eds (below).
'Red Brick and Portland Stone', in P. H. J. H. Gosden and A. J. Taylor, eds, *Studies in the History of a University* (Leeds, 1975), pp.133–80.

Beresford, M. W. and Jones, G. R. J., eds. *Leeds and Its Region* (Leeds, 1967).

Billam, F. T. [attr.] *A Walk Through Leeds, or, a Stranger's Guide* (Leeds, 1806).

Bonser, K. J. and Nichols, H. *Printed Maps and Plans of Leeds, 1711–1900 (PTh.S*, XLVII, 1960).

Briggs, A. *Victorian Cities* (1963).

Burt, S., ed. *Lantern slide Leeds* (Leeds, n.d. [1983]).

Caffyn, L. *Workers' Housing in West Yorkshire, 1750–1920* (Royal Commission on Historical Monuments, Supplementary Ser., IX, 1986).

Chalklin, C. W. *Provincial Towns of Georgian England: a study of the building process, 1740–1820* (1974).

Chapman, S. D. and Bartlett, J. N. 'The Contribution of Building Clubs and Freehold Land Societies to Working-class Housing in Birmingham', in *The History of Working-class Housing: a Symposium*, ed. S. D. Chapman (Newton Abbot, 1971).

Crump, W. B., ed. *The Leeds Woollen Industry, 1780–1820* (*PTh.S*, XXXII, 1931).

Daniels, S. 'The Implications of Industry: Turner and Leeds', *Turner Studies*, VI(1986), 10–17.

Dillon, T. 'The Irish in Leeds, 1851–61', *PTh.S*, LIV(1974), 1–28.

Eden, F. M. *The State of the Poor* (2 vols, 1797).

Engels, F. 'The Condition of the Working-Class in England [1845]', in *Karl Marx and Frederick Engels on Britain* (Moscow, 1953), pp.1–338.

Flinn, M. W., ed. *Report on the Sanitary Condition of the Labouring Population of Great Britain in 1842. By Edwin Chadwick* (1965).

Fraser, D., ed. *A History of Modern Leeds* (Manchester, 1980).

Fraser, D. 'The Leeds Churchwardens, 1828–1850', *PTh.S*, LIII (1971), 1–22.

Gilbert, E. W. 'Pioneer Maps of Health and Disease in England', *Geographical Journal*, CXXIV(1958), 172–83.

Grady, K.	'Profit, Property Interests and Public Spirit: the provision of markets in Leeds, 1822–29', *PTh.S*, LIV(1977), 165–95.
Hall, I., ed.	*Samuel Buck's Yorkshire Sketchbook* (Wakefield, 1979).
Hole, J.	*Homes of the Working Classes* (1866).
Jenkins, D. T.	'The Cotton Industry in Yorkshire, 1780–1900', *Textile History*, X(1979), 75–95.
	The West Riding Wool Textile Industry, 1770–1835 (Edington, 1975).
Kirby, J. W., ed.	*The Manor and Borough of Leeds, 1425–1662: an edition of documents* (*PTh.S*, LVII, 1983).
Kirby, J. W.	'Restoration Leeds and the Aldermen of the Corporation, 1661–1700', *Northern History*, XXII(1986), 123–74.
Le Patourel, J., ed.	*Documents relating to the Manor and Borough of Leeds, 1066–1400* (*PTh.S*, XLV, 1956).
Lee, W. R.	'Robert Baker, the first doctor in the Factory Department', *British Journal of Industrial Medicine*, XXI(1964), 85–93 and 167–79.
Leeds Board of Health	*Report of the Leeds Board of Health* (Leeds, 1833).
Leeds Council, Statistical Committee	'Report upon the Condition of the Town of Leeds', *Journal of the [Royal] Statistical Society*, II(1840), 397–422.
	Abstract of the Report of the Statistical Committee for 1838, 39 and 40 (Leeds, 1841).
Linstrum, D.	*Historic Architecture of Leeds* (Newcastle upon Tyne, 1965).
	West Yorkshire Architects and Architecture (1978).
Lumb, G. D.	'Burials at St Paul's Church', *PTh.S*, XV(1905), 56–70.
	'Leeds Manor House and Park', *PTh.S*, XXIV(1917), 399–400.
Lupton, F. M.	*Housing Improvement, a Summary of Ten Years' Work in Leeds* (Leeds, 1906).
Morris, R. J.	*Cholera* (1976).
	'Middle-class Culture, 1700–1914', in Fraser, ed. (above).
Muthesius, S.	*The English Terraced House* (Yale, 1982).
Price, S. J.	*Building Societies, their Origin and History* (1958).
Ryley, J.	[attr.] *The Leeds Guide* (Leeds, 1806).
Rimmer, W. G.	'Alfred Place Terminating Building Society, 1825–43', *PTh.S*, XLVI(1963), 303–30.

Rimmer, W. G. *Marshall's of Leeds* (Cambridge, 1960).
'Middleton Colliery near Leeds (1770–1830)', *Yorkshire Bulletin*, VII(1955), 41–57
'Working Men's Cottages in Leeds, 1770–1840', *PTh.S*, XLVI(1963), 165–99.

Sprittles, J. *Links with Bygone Leeds* (*PTh.S*, LII, 1969).

Tarn, J. N. *Five Per Cent Philanthropy* (Cambridge, 1973).

Taylor, R. V. *The Biographia Leodiensis* (1865).

Thoresby, R. *Ducatus Leodiensis* (1715).
Vicaria Leodiensis (1725).

Treen, C. 'The Process of Suburban Development in North Leeds, 1870–1914', in *The Rise of Suburbia*, ed. F. M. L. Thompson (Leicester, 1982), pp. 158–209.

Unwin, R. W. 'Leeds becomes a Transport Centre', in Fraser, ed. (above), pp. 113–41.

Whitaker, T. D., ed. *Ralph Thoresby, Ducatus Leodiensis* (1816).

Whitaker, T. D. *The History of Loidis and Elmete* (1816).

Wilson, E. 'The Housing of the Working Classes', *Journal of the Society of Arts*, XLVIII(1899–1900), 153–63.
'Two Old Plans of Leeds', *PTh.S*, IX(1899), 196–204.

Wilson, R. G. *Gentlemen Merchants* (Manchester, 1971).
'Transport dues as indices of Economic Growth', *Economic History Review*, 2nd ser., XIX(1966), 110–23.

Woledge, G. 'The Medieval Borough of Leeds', *PTh.S*, XXXVII (1945), 288–309.

Wright, G. [attr.] *A History of the Town and Parish of Leeds* (Leeds, 1797).

Yasumoto, M. 'Urbanization and Population in an English Town: Leeds during the Industrial Revolution', *Keio Economic Studies*, X(1973), 61–94.

3. *Acts of Parliament*

Acts Local and Personal relating to Leeds topography

10 & 11	Wm. III	cap. 19	Aire and Calder Navigation
2	Geo. II	cap. 16	Holy Trinity church
28	Geo. II	cap. 10	Ibbetson estates
28	Geo. II	cap. 41	Improvement (lighting and paving)
31	Geo. II	cap. 22	Middleton railway
33	Geo. II	cap. 54	Leeds bridge
5	Geo. III	cap. 25	Ann (Pawson) Wilson estates
15	Geo. III	cap. 90	Grammar School lands (Cloth Hall)
30	Geo. III	cap. 49	Wilson estates
32	Geo. III	cap. 89	St Paul's church
34	Geo. III	cap. 14	Harrison estates
34	Geo. III	cap. 32	Wilson, Wormald and Gott agreement
41	Geo. III	cap. 64	St James church
43	Geo. III	cap. 30	Wilson estates
49	Geo. III	cap. 122	Improvement (court house and prison)
55	Geo. III	cap. 42	Improvement (police and watch)
56	Geo. III	cap. 13	Wilson estates
4 & 5	Wm. IV	cap. 32	Wellington bridge
5	Geo. IV	cap. 124	Improvement
6	Geo. IV	cap. 97	Monk bridge
9	Geo. IV	cap. 87	Accommodation Road bridge
7	Wm. IV	cap. 83	Waterworks
2 & 3	Vic.	cap. 17	Mill soke
3 & 4	Vic.	cap. 26	Crown Point bridge
5 & 6	Vic.	cap. 103	Burial grounds
5 & 6	Vic.	cap. 104	Improvement

4. *Parliamentary Papers*

1806	*Report of the Committee on the State of the Woollen Manufactures of England*, PP 1806, III.
1831–32	*Reports from Commissioners on proposed Division of Counties, and Boundaries of Boroughs, with plans: report on the borough of Leeds* (1831). PP 1831–32, XL, 195–96.
1833	*Report of the Select Committee on Public Walks*. PP 1833, XV.
1833	*Second Report of the Factory Commission*. PP 1833, XXI.
1834	*Supplementary Report of the Factory Commission, Pt 2*, PP 1834, XX.
1835	*Report of the Royal Commission on Municipal Corporations*. PP 1835, XXV (Leeds: pp. 1617–24).
1837	*Report of the Commission appointed to report and advise upon the Boundaries and Wards of Certain Boroughs and Corporate Towns*. PP 1837, XXVII part 2 ('township of Leeds', unpaginated).
1837–38	*Report of the Select Committee on the Rating of Tenements*. PP 1837–38, XXI.
1840	*Report of the Select Committee on the Health of Towns*. PP 1840, XI.
1842	*Report of the Select Committee on the Building Regulations Bill and Improvement of Boroughs Bill*. PP 1842, X.
1842	*Report of the Select Committee on the Improvement of the Health of Towns: effect of interment of bodies in towns*. PP 1842, X.
1842	*Report to the Poor Law Commissioners on the Sanitary Condition of the Labouring Population. By E. Chadwick*. PP 1842 (Lords), XXVI; *England and Wales, local reports. Ibid.*, XXVII.
1844	*First Report of the Royal Commission on the State of Large Towns and Populous Districts*. PP 1844, XVII.
1845	*Second Report of the Royal Commission on the State of Large Towns and Populous Districts*. PP 1845, XVIII.
1845	*Report of the Select Committee on Smoke Abatement*. PP 1845, XIII.
1860	*Second Report of the Medical Officer of the Privy Council for 1859*. PP 1860, XXIX.
1884–85	*First Report of the Royal Commission on the Housing of the Working Classes: minutes of evidence*. PP C.4402–I.
1910	*Dr L. W. Darra Moir's Report on Back-to-back Houses*. PP 1910, XXXVIII; also Cd.5314.

5. *Directories*

(Place of publication, unless otherwise stated, is Leeds.)

1781 William Bailey, *Bailey's Northern Directory* (Leeds section, pp.221–25) (Warrington).

1784 William Bailey, *Bailey's British Directory* (Leeds section, pp.560–64) (London).

1793 Peter Barfoot and John Wilkes, *Universal British Directory* (Leeds section, pp.532–541) (London).

1797 [attr.] Griffith Wright, . . . *A Leeds Directory* (with corrected re-issue, 1798).

1800 Binns and Brown, *A Directory for Leeds.*

1807 George Wilson, *A New and Complete Directory for Leeds.*

1809 Edward Baines, *The Leeds Directory for 1809.*

1817 Edward Baines, *Directory, general and commercial . . . of Leeds.*

1822 Edward Baines, *History, Directory and Gazetteer of the County of York*, vol. 1, *West Riding.*

1826 William Parson, *General and Commercial Directory of . . . Leeds.*

1830 William Parson and William White, *Directory of the Borough of Leeds.*

1834 Baines and Newsome, *General and Commercial Directory . . . of Leeds.*

1837 William White, *History, Gazetteer and Directory of the West Riding* (Sheffield).

1839 Baines and Newsome. *General and Commercial Directory of the Borough of Leeds.*

1842 William White, *Directory and Topography of the Borough of Leeds.*

6. *Printed Maps*

(For fuller descriptions see Bonser and Nichols.)

1712 Sutton Nicholls (?Shelton), '. . . *map of 20 miles round Leedes*' (in R. Thoresby, *Ducatus* (1715)).

*c.*1725 John Cossins, *A new and exact plan of the town of Leedes.*

1768–70 Thomas Donald, *A plan of Leeds* (insert on plate XVII of Thomas Jefferys, *The County of York*) (1772).

1781 John Tuke, *A map of the Parish or Borough of Leeds.*

1806 John Heaton, *Plan of the town of Leeds with its modern improvements.*

1815 Netlam and Francis Giles, *Plan of the town of Leeds and its environs.*

1821 Charles Fowler, *Plan of the town of Leeds with the recent improvements.*

1821 Joshua Thorp, *Map of the town of Leeds and neighbourhood.*

1826 Charles Fowler, *Plan of the town of Leeds, with the recent improvements.*

1831 Charles Fowler, *Plan of the town of Leeds and its Environs.*

1833 Robert Baker, *Cholera plan of Leeds* (in *Report of the Leeds Board of Health*).

1842 Robert Baker, *Sanitary map of the town of Leeds* (in PP 1842 (Lords), XXVII).

1844 Ordnance Survey, *Six inches to one mile* (dated copy (seven years before publication in 1851: Borthwick MS. CC EC 11/101).

1844 Charles Fowler, *Plan of the town and environs of Leeds.*

1844 J. F. Masser, *Plan of the Kirkgate Ward.*

1844 J. F. Masser, *Plan of the Mill Hill Ward.*

1847 Ordnance Survey, *Five-foot Plan of Leeds* (25 sheets, 1850).

7. *Topographical Views*

Drawings, paintings and other works of art with details of streets and buildings erected by 1842.

I Reproductions

(Place of publication, unless otherwise stated, is Leeds.)

1684–89 William Lodge, . . . *Leeds as it appears from Holbeck Road* (in *Ducatus* (1715)).

1715 Francis Place, *The Prospect of Leeds from the Knostrop Road (Ibid.).*
The Prospect of Leeds from the Knostrop Road (in Whitaker, *Ducatus*).
The South Prospect of St Peter's church at Leeds (Ibid.).
The South Prospect of St John's church at Leeds (Ibid.).

1720 Samuel Buck, *East prospect of the town of Leedes . . . from Chaveler Hill* (London, 1722) (Thoresby Society and Society of Antiquaries of London).

1728 Anon., *A View of Leeds* (title page, *LM*, 6 Aug. 1728 to 5 Oct. 1731).

1745 Samuel and Nathaniel Buck, *The South-East prospect of Leeds* (London).

1771 J. Butterworth, *A View of the General Infirmary at Leeds*

before 1787 W. Livesey, *William Shent's shop, Briggate* (inserted in John Wray's 'Notes on Leeds Methodism' (Leeds Reference Library, Local History Collection), I, f. 162).

1793 Anon., *Leeds Cloth Hall* (engraving on copper halfpenny, Henry Brownbill, Briggate, in author's collection).

1816 T. Taylor, *The Parish Church of Leeds* (in Whitaker, *Ducatus*).
The Leeds Library; Holy Trinity church; St Paul's church (with Park Square); The Leeds Infirmary (with St Paul's and East Parade) (in Whitaker, *Loidis*).

1816	Anon., *St John's church* (Whitaker, *Ducatus*).
1816	[attr.] Taylor, *The Moot Hall* (in Whitaker, *Ducatus*, 1816).
1821	R. D. Chantrell, *View of Philosophical and Literary Society's Hall* (inset on Fowler's printed plan of Leeds, q.v.).
1821	Anon., *The Philosophical Hall* (Sprittles, *Links with Bygone Leeds*, Plate 42).
1823	J. M. W. Turner, *Leeds* (see 1816 in §7(II), below).
1825	Charles Fowler, *Wellington Bridge and Toll Bar* (inset on his plan of an estate in Wortley (Bonser and Nichols no. 52)).
1826	Charles Fowler, *Commercial Buildings, Boar Lane* (inset on his printed plan of Leeds, q.v.).
*c.*1822–26	Charles Cope, *View of Leeds.*
1827–31	Alphonse Dousseau, *Leeds from Rope Hill* (*c.*1869: Bonser and Nichols, no. 90).
1828	N. Whittock, *Trinity Church* (London).
1828	N. Whittock, *Central Market, Leeds* (London).
1829	N. Whittock, *Corn Exchange, Leeds* (London).
1829	N. Whittock, *Commercial Buildings, Leeds* (London).
1829	N. Whittock, *Court House, Leeds* (London).
1829	N. Whittock, *Central Market, Leeds* (London).
1829	N. Whittock, *Christ Church and Coal Staith* (London).
1829	N. Whittock, *The Aire & Calder at Leeds* (London).
1831	N. Whittock, All the Whittock views reprinted in T. Allen, *A new and concise History of the county of York . . . illustrated by a series of views* (London, 1831: vol. 3 of large paper edn; vol. 4 of small paper edn.
1831	Charles Fowler, *Western Entrance to Leeds* (inset on his printed plan of Leeds, q.v.).
1832	Joseph Rhodes, *Western-Panoramic-View-of-Leeds.*
1833	Robert Buttery, *Leeds taken from Beeston Hill.*
1835	J. N. Rhodes, *The Central Market &c. Leeds, from the end of Cloth Hall Street*, in J. Heaton, *Walks Through Leeds.*
1842	E. J. Roberts, *Commercial Buildings and Yorkshire District Bank* (London, 1842).
1842	W. Nelson, *Town Hall* [sic] *and Commercial Buildings, Leeds* (London); also in *The Stranger's Guide* (Leeds, 1842, frontispiece).
1846	Henry Burn, *View of Leeds from near the Halifax New Road.*

n.d. Anon., *Mill Hill chapel* (Thoresby Society; Sprittles, *Links with Bygone Leeds*, Plate 17).

n.d. Pulleyn and Hunt, *Hanover Place Wesleyan Chapel* (Leeds).

II Original works

1719 Samuel Buck, Sketchbook (prospects and views: see Hall, *I* in *Bibliography*, §2, above) (British Library, Lansdowne MS.914).

*c.*1790 John Russell, Sketchbooks (various scenes) (City of Birmingham Art Gallery).

1816 J. M. W. Turner, *Leeds* (Paul Mellon Collection, Center for British Art, Yale, New Haven; published as a lithograph by J. D. Harding, 1823: Bonser and Nichols, no.48).

1816 J. M. W. Turner, *Sketch of the Town of Leeds*: Sketchbook CXXXIV, ff.38, 45 and 79–80 (Clore Gallery for the Turner Bequest, London); G. Wilkinson, *The Sketches of Turner, R.A.: 1802–20: genius of the Romantic* (1974), pp.144–5.

1821 R. D. Chantrell, *The Philosophical Hall, Leeds* (Park Row and environs) (Leeds City Museum).

*c.*1825 Joseph Rhodes, *The Old Moot Hall* (Leeds City Museum, on loan to City Art Gallery).

*c.*1820–25 Joseph Rhodes, *Leeds from the Meadows* (Leeds City Art Gallery).

1844 Thomas Burras, *View of Leeds* [from Armley Old Hall] (Thoresby Society).

1851 J. Greig, *Upper Part of Briggate, formerly called Cross Parish* (in vol.iv of W. Boyne's grangerised edn. of *Ducatus*, Leeds City Reference Library).

1852 John O'Rourke, *Leeds Old Workhouse* (North Street) (Leeds City Museum).

n.d. Joseph Rhodes, *Old Shambles, Middle Row* (in vol. I of Boyne's grangerised *Ducatus*).

III Vases

*c.*1830 *Leeds Methodist Chapels* [St Peter's St, Albion St and Meadow Lane], (Swansea, on porcelain). Leeds City Museum.

8. Unpublished Works

Barber, B. J. 'Leeds Corporation, 1835–1905: a history of its environmental, social and administrative services' (unpublished PhD thesis, University of Leeds, 1975).

Connell, E. J. 'Industrial Development in South Leeds, 1790–1914' (unpublished PhD thesis, University of Leeds, 1975).

Fletcher, R. F. 'The History of the Leeds General Cemetery Company, 1833–1965' (unpublished MPhil thesis, University of Leeds, 1975).

Grady, K. 'The Provision of Public Buildings in the West Riding of Yorkshire, *c.*1660–1840' (unpublished PhD thesis, University of Leeds, 1980).

Hobson, J. 'Leeds Directory of 1725', note book by Job Hobson (1924): Thoresby Society MSS, Box V.10.

Peppard, R. S. 'The Growth and Development of Leeds Waterworks Undertakings, 1694–1852' (unpublished MPhil thesis, University of Leeds, 1973).

Treen, C. 'Building and Estate Development in the Northern Out-townships of Leeds, 1781–1914' (unpublished PhD thesis, University of Leeds, 1977).

Toft, J. 'Public Health in Leeds in the Nineteenth Century' (unpublished MA thesis, University of Manchester, 1966).

Ward, M. F. 'Industrial Development and Location in Leeds north of the River Aire' (unpublished PhD thesis, University of Leeds, 1972).

Wheater, W. 'A List of the Freeholders of Leeds, 1741', compiled *c.*1885 by William Wheater: Leeds Reference Library, Local History Collection.

Wray, J. 'Methodism in Leeds', manuscript notes by John Wray, eleven vols (1835–45): Leeds Reference Library, Local History Collection.

See also §7 (II), above.

Sources and Acknowledgements for Figures

1.1, 7.1 and 8.6	From Giles map, 1815, in the Thoresby Society Library
1.2	Based on LCA, DB 32/3 and 5; LCD 1123
1.3	Tracing of plan then in the offices of British Waterways, Leeds, by Michael Ward
1.4	Based on Cossins map, *c.*1725
1.5	Based on Giles map, 1815
1.6	Based on Thomas Donald, inset to Jefferys map, 1768–70
2.1	Reproduced from the copy of the *Ducatus* in the Thoresby Society Library
2.2 and 3.5	By courtesy of the Library of the Society of Antiquaries of London
3.1	By courtesy of Leeds City Museum
3.2	After Cossins map, *c.*1725
3.3, 6.4 and 10.2	After John Russell's sketchbooks, by courtesy of Birmingham Museums and Art Gallery
3.4	Thoresby Society Library, 'Views of Old Leeds', file B2
4.1	LCA, DB 5/18
4.2	LCA, DB 196/1, f.84
4.3 and 4.4	From data supplied by the author
4.5	Drawn by R. Stuart Fell
4.6	As Fig. 3.3 with additional data from LCA, DB Map 215
4.7	After Thoresby Society Library, 'Views of Old Leeds', file A2
6.1	Based on LCA, DB 32/1 and 3; survey by John Crookes (1779) in DB 239 Box 1; and deeds in DB 32, 58 and 239
6.2	Based on LCA, DB 32/38
6.3	Reproduced from the copy of *Loidis and Elmete* in the Thoresby Society Library
6.5, 6.6 and 6.7	By courtesy of Royal Commission on Historical Monuments, England (National Monuments Record)
7.1	Thoresby Society Library, photographic collection
7.2, 7.7, 7.11, 7.13, 7.14, 8.1, 8.3, 9.2, 10.5, 10.6 and 13.1	By courtesy of Leeds City Libraries (Local History Collection)

7.3, 7.10 and 8.2	After sixty-inch O.S. map, 1847
7.4	LCA, DB Map 373
7.5, 10.4, 10.7 and 10.9	Photographs by author
7.6	After LCD 1767
7.8	Author's collection, gift of E. A. Kirkby
7.9	After F. M. Lupton, *Housing Improvement* (Leeds, 1906), plan 4
7.12	After LCA, DB Maps 119 (1809) and 233 (1807): by R. Stuart Fell
8.4	As Fig. 7.9, plan 6
8.5	(a) After LCD 8899 and 12939; (b) author's collection
9.1	After LCA, DB 179
9.3	After LCA, DB 32/3 (1806); 3A (1809); and 5 (1816)
9.4	From original in Thoresby Society Library
9.5 and 9.6	After plans in LCA, DB Box 78 (unlisted)
10.1	After plans in ULD files
10.3	LCA, Town deposit, by courtesy of Mr John Town, Follifoot
10.5	Simon Pentelow and Barry Watson, University of Leeds Audio-Visual Service, General Photography Section
10.8	After Nottingham University Library, Dept. of MSS, DeH 20 and 38
10.10	After University of York, Borthwick Institute, Reg. 40(ii), f.403
12.1	After LCA, LCEng Box 10: by R. Stuart Fell
12.2	*1842 Report*, p. 160
13.2	By courtesy of London School of Economics (Webb Local Government Collection, vol. 265, insert)
13.3	Based on Giles map, 1815, and Fowler maps, 1821, 1826, 1831 and 1844
14.1	(a) After LCD 8879; (b) Author's collection, gift of Joseph Buckman
14.2	By courtesy of Mrs Sylvia M. Barnard and the Friends of Beckett Street Cemetery
Appendix IV.1, p.457	Based on bounds shown in the 1815 Giles map
Front Endpaper	From copy in Thoresby Society Library
Back Endpaper	By courtesy of the Trustees of the British Museum (Dept. of Prints and Drawings, Eng. Topog. Yorks, 1981, U2659)

Cover — By courtesy of Yale Center for British Art, Paul Mellon Collection, New Haven, Conn., U.S.A.

Material with the reference DB is used by courtesy of Dibb Lupton, solicitors, Leeds; that with the references LCA and WRRD by courtesy of West Yorkshire (Joint) Archive Committee; that with the reference ULD by courtesy of the Bursar, University of Leeds; that with the reference LCD by courtesy of the Town Clerk of the former Corporation of Leeds.

Figs 1.2–6, 3.2, 4.3–4, 6.1–2, 7.3, 7.6, 7.9–10, 8.5, 9.1, 9.3, 9.5–6, 10.1, 10.8, 10.10, 13.3, 14.1 and the Fig. in Appendix IV are redrawn from original sources by Tim Hadwin, Department of Geography, University of Leeds.

Figs 3.3, 4.6–7, 6.4, 10.2 and 13.1 are redrawn by John Dixon, Department of Geography, University of Leeds, from original photographs and drawings.

Central Leeds in 1815

Key to numbers (1–26 Briggate and eastward; 27–43 westward)

1 New Street
2 Free (Grammar) School
3 Templar Street
4 Workhouse
5 Leylands
6 Bridge Street
7 Mabgate
8 Lady Bridge, Lady Lane
9 George Street
10 Charles Street
11 York Street
12 The Square, Kirkgate
13 Vicar's Croft
14 Boot and Shoe Yard, Kirkgate
15 Forster's Close (burial ground)
16 Timble Bridge
17 Off Street
18 Marsh Lane
19 Crown Point
20 Cooper's Court, Bowman Lane
21 Bowman Lane
22 Waterloo Street, Hunslet Lane
23 Hunslet Lane
24 Leeds Bridge
25 Moot Hall and Shambles, Briggate
26 Market Cross (Cross Parish)
27 Woodhouse Lane
28 Lydgate
29 Park Square
30 South Parade
31 East Parade
32 Park Row
33 Albion Street
34 Bond Street (Commercial Street)
35 Court House and Prison
36 General Infirmary
37 Park Place
38 Eye Bright, Quebec
39 Mill Hill
40 Swinegate
41 Water Lodge
42 Canal warehouse
43 Meadow Lane

Albion Street 33
Bond Street 34
Boot and Shoe Yard, Kirkgate 14
Bowman Lane 21
Bridge Street 6
Briggate 25
Canal warehouse 42
Charles Street 10
Commercial Street 34
Cooper's Court 20
Court House and Prison 35
Cross Parish 26
Crown Point 19
East Parade 31
Eye Bright 38
Forster's Close 15
Free (Grammar) School 2
General Infirmary 36
George Street 9
Hunslet Lane 23
Kirkgate 12
Lady Bridge, Lady Lane 8
Leeds Bridge 24
Leylands 5
Lydgate 28
Mabgate 7
Market Cross 26
Marsh Lane 18
Meadow Lane 43
Mill Hill 39
Moot Hall, Briggate 25
New Street 1
Off Street 17
Park Place 37
Park Row 32
Park Square 29
Quebec 38
South Parade 30
Square, The (Kirkgate) 12
Swinegate 40
Templar Street 3
Timble Bridge 16
Vicar's Croft 13
Water Lodge 41
Waterloo Street, Hunslet Lane 22
Woodhouse Lane 27
Workhouse 4
York Street 11

INDEXES

I Index of Subjects

(Numbers in italic indicate illustrations.)

II Index of Persons

(Some persons remain unidentified except by surname; in these cases forenames have been replaced by 'Mr', 'Mrs'. Partners in industrial, business and property-owning enterprises appear under the name of the partnership, with cross-references to and from the individual partners where these have been identified.)

III Index of Places and Buildings

(*Numbers in italic indicate Illustrations*)

THE THORESBY SOCIETY

CLAREMONT, 23 CLARENDON ROAD, LEEDS LS2 9NZ

Patron
PROFESSOR M. W. BERESFORD, F.B.A.

President
E. A. ELTON, M.A.

Vice-Presidents

G. BLACK, M.B., B.S., F.R.C.S.

S. H. BURTON, M.A.
MRS DERWAS CHITTY, M.A., F.S.A.
G. C. F. FORSTER, B.A., F.S.A., F.R.HIST.S.
MRS G. C. F. FORSTER, M.A.
MISS A. G. FOSTER, B.A.
MRS R. S. MORTIMER
G. WOLEDGE, B.A.

Council

P. C. D. BREARS, DIP.A.D., F.M.A., F.S.A.
S. BURT, B.ED.
J. M. COLLINSON, M.A.
D. COX. B.A., A.L.A.
E. L. EMPSALL
D. B. FEATHER, CH.M., F.R.C.S.
K. GRADY, B.A., PH.D.
C. M. G. OCKELTON, M.A.
A. R. STEVENS, B.ED.
MRS B. K. STRONG, B.A.
C. TREEN, B.A., PH.D.

Hon. Editors
MRS P. S. KIRBY, B.A., M.PHIL.
MRS W. B. STEPHENS, B.A.

Hon. Librarian
MRS G. C. F. FORSTER, M.A.

Hon. Treasurer
G. A. ASCOUGH, F.C.A., Claremont, 23 Clarendon Road, Leeds LS2 9NZ

Hon. Secretary
D. M. WATSON, M.A., Claremont, 23 Clarendon Road, Leeds LS2 9NZ

Hon. Assistant Secretary
MRS A. M. WARBURTON

Hon. Excursions Secretary
MRS A. M. WARBURTON

Hon. Lectures Secretary
P. S. MORRISH, M.A., A.K.C., A.L.A.

Hon. Distribution Secretary (Publication)
MRS J. A. CREBBIN

P. 293
263
190
176

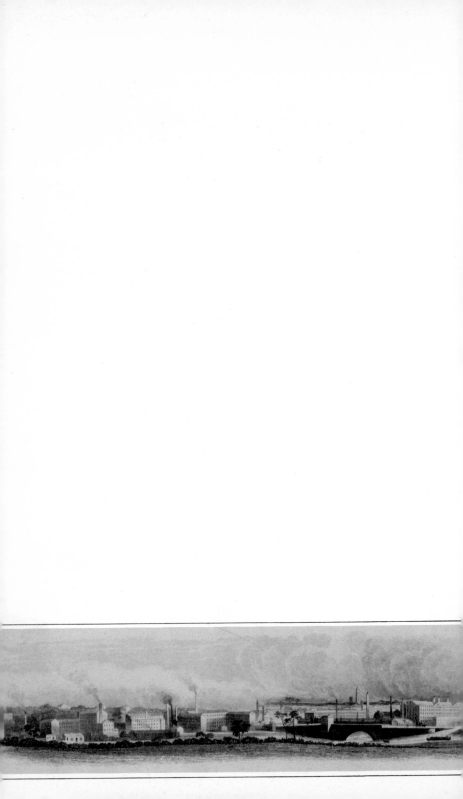